Praise for the sixth edition

"…*The Psychology of Criminal Conduct* is the most important book ever written in criminology. A scientific *tour de force*, it outlines the evidence-based RNR paradigm for understanding why people break the law and how to affect their rehabilitation. This paradigm has been used across and beyond North America to save countless offenders from a life in crime and thus countless citizens from victimization. To be literate in criminology and in correctional treatment, all scholars, students, and practitioners should read this book—and then, as I do, keep it close by and consult it often."

> – **Francis T. Cullen**, *Distinguished Research Professor Emeritus, Criminal Justice, University of Cincinnati, Recipient of the 2022 Stockholm Prize in Criminology*

"No other single book has so transformed the field of correctional intervention. For more than 20 years this volume has been essential reading for everyone: from students of criminal psychology to correctional professionals, including prison officers, probation officers, case managers, and experienced psychologists."

> – **Devon Polaschek**, *PhD DipClinPsyc, Professor, Criminal Psychology, Victoria University of Wellington*

"The book shows how to explain, predict, and treat sexual, violent, acquisitive, and other offending and puts the findings in a convincing theoretical and practice-oriented framework. It is essential reading not only for students in the fields of criminology, psychology and law, forensic psychology and psychiatry, sociology, social work and other crime-related disciplines, but also for researchers, practitioners, and policy makers in these areas."

> – **Friedrich Lösel**, *Professor and Director Emeritus, Institute of Criminology, Cambridge University (UK), and Institute of Psychology, University of Erlangen-Nuremberg*

THE PSYCHOLOGY OF CRIMINAL CONDUCT

The Psychology of Criminal Conduct, Seventh Edition, provides a psychological and evidence-informed perspective of criminal behavior that sets it apart from many criminological and mental health explanations of criminal behavior. Drawing upon the General Personality and Cognitive Social Learning theory, James Bonta and Donald Andrews provide an overview of the theoretical context and major knowledge base of the psychology of criminal conduct, discuss the eight major risk/need factors of criminal conduct, examine the prediction and classification of criminal behavior along with prevention and rehabilitation, and summarize the major issues in understanding criminal conduct. This book also offers the Risk-Need-Responsivity (RNR) model of assessment and treatment that has guided developments in the subject throughout the world.

Bonta carefully maintains the book's original contributions while presenting core concepts succinctly, clearly, and elegantly. Appropriate for advanced undergraduates and graduate students as well as for scholars, researchers, and practitioners, *The Psychology of Criminal Conduct*, Seventh Edition, further extends and refines the authors' body of work.

James Bonta served as Director of Corrections Research at Public Safety Canada from 1990 until 2015. He received his PhD in Clinical Psychology from the University of Ottawa in 1979. Bonta was a psychologist, and later Chief Psychologist, at the Ottawa-Carleton Detention Centre, a maximum-security remand facility for adults and young offenders. Throughout his career, Bonta has held various academic appointments and professional posts. He is a Fellow of the Canadian Psychological Association, a recipient of the Association's Criminal Justice Section's Career Contribution Award for 2009, the Queen Elizabeth II Diamond Jubilee Medal, 2012, the Maud Booth Correctional Services Award, 2015, and the 2015 Community Corrections Award from the International Corrections and Prisons Association.

The late **D. A. Andrews** was a noted psychologist affiliated with Carleton University throughout his academic career. His work on the psychology of criminal conduct produced what became known as the "theory of correctional intervention," which set the standard for successful intervention practices throughout the field of corrections worldwide. He was a founding member of Carleton's Criminology and Criminal Justice Program and a Fellow of the Canadian Psychological Association.

The Psychology of Criminal Conduct

This book provides a psychological and evidence-informed perspective of criminal behavior. It gives an overview of the theoretical context and major knowledge base of the psychology of criminal conduct, and offers the Risk/Need/Responsivity (RNR) model of offender assessment and treatment that has guided developments in the subject throughout the world.

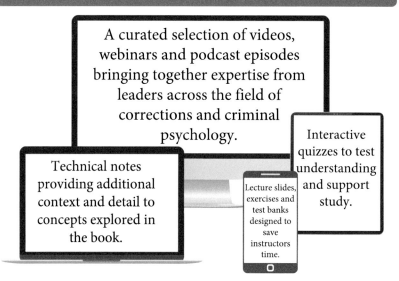

A curated selection of videos, webinars and podcast episodes bringing together expertise from leaders across the field of corrections and criminal psychology.

Technical notes providing additional context and detail to concepts explored in the book.

Lecture slides, exercises and test banks designed to save instructors time.

Interactive quizzes to test understanding and support study.

Go online to access these resources and more at:

FREE

INSTRUCTOR & STUDENT RESOURCES

psychologycriminalconduct.routledge.com

Routledge
Taylor & Francis Group

THE PSYCHOLOGY OF CRIMINAL CONDUCT

SEVENTH EDITION

JAMES BONTA
and
D. A. ANDREWS

Routledge
Taylor & Francis Group

NEW YORK AND LONDON

Designed cover image: ©Getty Images

Seventh edition published 2024
by Routledge
605 Third Avenue, New York, NY 10158

and by Routledge
4 Park Square, Milton Park, Abingdon, Oxon, OX14 4RN

Routledge is an imprint of the Taylor & Francis Group, an informa business

First edition published by Anderson Publishing 1994
Sixth edition published by Routledge 2016

ISBN: 978-1-032-27283-2 (hbk)
ISBN: 978-1-032-27285-6 (pbk)
ISBN: 978-1-003-29212-8 (ebk)

DOI: 10.4324/9781003292128

Typeset in ITC Garamond Std
by Newgen Publishing UK

Access the Instructor & Student Resources: psychologycriminalconduct.routledge.com

CONTENTS

PREFACE

I find it remarkable that I am now writing a preface for the seventh edition of *The Psychology of Criminal Conduct* (*PCC*). I thank the readers of the sixth edition for this opportunity. The last edition underwent significant changes in structure and "readability" and, according to feedback from readers, the changes were well-received. Therefore, the new edition continues in the structure and spirit of the sixth edition.

In writing the present edition I was struck by some of the remarkable changes in the field since 2016. First of all, meta-analytic reviews have exploded. There is hardly a topic in the field of criminal behavior that does not have a meta-analysis. The importance of meta-analysis in our empirical understanding of criminal conduct is highlighted in Chapter 2. In this edition, references to meta-analyses will be the major source for the research supporting the perspective presented in PCC.

Second, the importance of trauma and adverse childhood experiences (ACEs) on behavior has reached widespread recognition. I tried to weave the research on trauma and ACE at a number of points in the text, such as family (Chapter 7), assessment (Chapter 10), and treatment (Chapter 12). Third, the reader will note that the language around the criterion of interest has changed. In keeping with a core principle in the risk-need-responsivity model (Chapter 9), "respect for the person," the label "offender" has been replaced, as much as possible, by person-first language (e.g., "justice-involved persons"). A number of professional associations now have written statements encouraging non-pejorative, inclusive language.

There is also a new feature that accompanies this text that professors, students, and readers will enjoy. We have on the website a number of audio and video resources to bring to life some of the material in the book. Experts will discuss a range of topics that I hope will enrich the experience of those who read this seventh edition.

This book has a hopeful agenda. Yes, there are some criticisms of the viewpoints and research that do not inform theory, policy, and practice in helpful terms. However, my main message is that the people who come into conflict with the law are real people like anyone else and they deserve *help* and not just punishment. Importantly, we now have the means to provide assistance that is humane, decent, and effective (see Part 3). I hope that the reader will also feel this way after reading the book.

Many people from Routledge were indispensable in the preparation of this edition and I truly owe them my thanks. Pam Chester, who is now happily retired, initiated negotiations and discussions almost two years ago. The torch was then ably carried by my editor of 30 years, Ellen Boyne. She has been amazing. New to the editorial team is Kate Taylor, our editorial assistant.

I appreciate all her efforts in helping with various stages of production. As I mentioned earlier, this edition now has considerable web resources with a number of my colleagues sharing their knowledge. Our digital resources lead is Leah Burton. Thanks to all the experts who contributed to the web resources and thank you Routledge!

Finally, I cannot express enough my deepest appreciation to my wife Christine for supporting me not only in this seventh edition but also the previous six editions starting in 1993. My forever thanks.

James Bonta

PART 1 The Theoretical Context and Knowledge Base to the Psychology of Criminal Conduct

CHAPTER 1 An Overview of the Psychology of Criminal Conduct

Almost everyone knows someone who has committed a criminal act or has been affected by crime. People will often ask, why does a person engage in such harmful behavior? The psychology of criminal conduct (PCC) outlined in this book seeks to answer this question. PCC describes and accounts for the fact that not all human beings are involved in crime and those that are engaged in crime vary in the number, type, and variety of antisocial acts. They also differ in when and under what circumstances they act in harmful ways, and they differ in when and under what conditions they reduce and may even cease their criminal activity. In brief, this psychology seeks to account for variation in the criminal behavior of individuals.

If PCC has something of value to offer, it should be able to assist in predicting who will or will not commit crimes in the future and suggest deliberate interventions that will reduce future crime. As will be seen, we will ask PCC to not only assist in predicting and influencing criminal activity but also to explain its occurrence in theoretical terms. That is, how do we explain the facts that some people are more into criminal behavior than others, that some leave it behind and others do not, that some start early and may or may not continue, and that some start late and may or may not continue?

Do we need different explanations for different types of offenses (e.g., violent and nonviolent) and for different types of people (e.g., boys and girls, men and women, white and nonwhite) in different socioeconomic circumstances (e.g., rich and poor)? In this book a *general* theoretical explanation is presented arguing, for the most part, that there is little need to have a specific theory for sexual offenders, white-collar criminals, women in conflict with the law, and so on. Granted, aspects of the theory will need to be tweaked or adjusted, but the grand factors remain stable across offenders and their situations.

As much as PCC values a general understanding of wide applicability, special interests are going to press for an appreciation of their concerns in particular circumstances. Such pressure is totally understandable, greatly appreciated, and likely to ultimately enhance the overall levels of understanding achieved. A dramatic example currently is in the domain of feminist criminology, wherein frequent references to "unique gendered contexts" and to the limits of

DOI: 10.4324/9781003292128-2

male-centric theory are employed to challenge general understandings. When accompanied by systematic empirical research, explorations of unique contexts can only strengthen understandings, be they general or specific.

Definition of the Psychology of Criminal Conduct

The following constitutes a working definition of a psychology of criminal conduct:

> As a science, the psychology of criminal conduct is an approach to understanding the criminal behavior of individuals through: (1) the ethical and humane application of systematic empirical methods of investigation, and (2) the construction of rational explanatory systems.

> For professionals working with those in conflict with the law, a psychology of criminal conduct involves the ethical application of psychological knowledge and methods to the practical tasks of predicting the likelihood of criminal behavior. It also involves, perhaps most importantly, influencing the likelihood of criminal behavior in order to reduce human and social costs associated with crime and criminal justice processing.

This general description makes two points. First, PCC does not encompass the wide variety of interests that psychologists have in the area of criminology. Nor does it cover the many roles that psychologists play in criminal justice. Many psychologists are interested in the behavior of victims, legislators, voters, and the public in general. Similarly, many psychologists are interested in the behavior of police, judges, jurists, prison guards, probation officers, and practitioners in forensic mental health. Moreover, many psychologists in correctional practice probably spend more time dealing with the mental health needs of offenders than with criminality issues. All of these matters are interesting and important, but they are of concern in this text only insofar as they contribute to an understanding of individual criminal conduct.

Second, grounds have been established for making a distinction between psychology and the other disciplines and professions that share an interest in crime. Our focus is the criminal behavior of individuals. That focus is different from studies of bodily systems (biology), studies of variations in aggregate measures of crime rates and the structure of groups (sociology), and studies of the history and political economy of law and criminal justice. As important as these interests are for a general understanding of crime and criminal justice, they are outside the main focus of this text.

At the same time, many biologists, sociologists, social workers, political scientists, and economists share an interest in the psychology of criminal behavior. Their contributions to the psychology of criminal behavior are significant and will be represented throughout this text. Indeed, in the areas of the measurement of criminal behavior and in studies of the correlates of criminal behavior, many of the most important contributions of the last 30 years have been made by sociologists who conducted studies of the social psychological variety.

Values at the Base of PCC

Before describing the objectives of PCC, some statements of values are required. The psychology of criminal behavior outlined in this book has certain values at its base. First, and foremost, is respect for the person. Each individual has a unique history and story to tell and all deserve respect. We may not like the behavior but the person can be accepted and treated with dignity (parents will often admonish a child for undesirable behavior but the child is still accepted). For this reason, the book will adopt, as much as possible, a less biased language to promote respect for the person without stigmatizing the individual (American Psychological Association, 2020). Early language guidelines focused on broader issues such as gender, racial, and ethnic identity. However, they have now been extended to those in conflict with the law (American Psychological Association, 2021; Willis, 2018a). People vary tremendously and placing them into homogenous groups with labels that are sometimes inaccurate and evaluative is a disservice to them.

In past editions of this book the term "offender" was often used (and it is still common today, with many correctional agencies having the word in the title). Although the word is simple and brief, it does convey a sense that the person has an inherent tendency to engage in criminal behavior (Willis, 2018b). This view of criminal behavior as a trait of the person is unsupported by the evidence. The present guidelines encourage researchers and practitioners to be specific and to use "person-first language" separating the individual from the behavior. For example, instead of the term "addict," which conjures up many condescending attitudes, the American Psychological Association recommends "a person with a substance use disorder" (American Psychological Association, 2021). As much as possible, this "person-first language" will be applied to the subject matter of this book: the person in conflict with the law. As the reader will also discover while reading this text, I am a strong advocate for rehabilitation and believe that corrections should provide assistance to those convicted of a criminal offense. For these reasons the reader will also see the term "client" along with other person-first language.

The second important value is a respect for human diversity and the complexity of human behavior. Respect for human diversity entails a respect for the differences between people that extend well beyond the socially or biologically defined categories of ethnicity, race, gender, social class of origin, or any other broad or narrow definitions of social arrangements. Individual differences are apparent in biology, personality, cognition, behavioral history, and social relationships in the domains of home, school, work, leisure, and community. Are all women the same or are all men the same? Of course not! Likewise, the poor are not all the same. They will differ in their biological makeup, aspirations, personality, and social relationships. These differences are clearly recognized and valued in PCC. Thus, PCC is very suspicious of any account of human behavior that claims that individual differences in behavior may be attributed to any single type of variable, be it biological (e.g., a crime gene), psychological (e.g., poor self-control), or political-economic (e.g., poverty).

PCC is holistic and interdisciplinary at its core. PCC is open to the contributions of any discipline that assists in accounting for individual differences in the criminal behavior of individuals. It is also built to serve the interests of all who are interested in the criminal behavior of individuals, be they criminologists, sociologists, social workers, or practitioners in justice, corrections, youth services, or any other sector of society. It should be expected to serve the public as a whole (public well-being), individual members of the public, and any subgroup defined in psychological, socioeconomic, and/or political-economic terms.

PCC values personal autonomy as a key aspect of ethical practice and rehabilitation efforts. The person is responsible and in control of his or her behavior. This point cannot be overemphasized. The recent contributions in clinical/forensic psychology demonstrate the value of collaborative relationships between the professionals and their clients and respect for the personal autonomy of the individual.

This psychology of criminal conduct welcomes unsparing criticism of theoretical assertions and research findings. Unsparing criticism is a major source of advancement. At the same time, all criticism, including criticism of theoretical and research-based assertions, is best combined with respect for evidence. Additionally, a reduction of the costs of both crime and criminal justice processing for those who violate the law, victims, and the general public is viewed as highly desirable.

There exists a general personality and cognitive social learning perspective within PCC that has conceptual, empirical, and practical value within and across social arrangements, clinical categories, and various personal and justice contexts. PCC seeks a rational and empirical understanding of variation in the occurrence of criminal acts and individual differences in criminal activity.

Objectives of PCC

The objective of PCC is to understand *variation* in the *criminal behavior* of individuals. In order to understand this objective, we need to dissect what we mean by criminal behavior and variation.

Definitions of Criminal Behavior

"Criminal behavior" suggests a large number and variety of acts. Specific meanings vary according to the concerns of users of the phrase as well as historical and social contexts (Mannheim, 1965). This text draws upon four definitions of criminal behavior and will be most concerned with those acts that fit within the domains of all four definitions. These four definitions are as follows:

1. *Legal*: Criminal behavior refers to actions that are prohibited by the state and punishable under the law.

2. *Moral*: Criminal behavior refers to actions that violate the norms of religion and morality and are believed to be punishable by supreme spiritual beings.

3. *Social*: Criminal behavior refers to actions that violate the norms of custom and tradition and are punishable by the community.

4. *Psychological*: Criminal behavior refers to actions that may be rewarding to the actor but inflict pain or loss on others. That is, criminal behavior is antisocial behavior.

Criminal acts, no matter which of the four above-noted definitions are employed, are part of a more general class of behavior that social psychologists have been calling "problem behavior" or "deviant behavior" since the 1970s (e.g., Jessor & Jessor, 1977; Ullmann & Krasner, 1976). The essence of deviant acts is that their occurrence places the actor at risk of being targeted for interventions by figures of authority, control, regulation, and assistance. Problematic acts may occasion the intervention of parents, teachers, religious leaders, and neighbors. They may place the actor at risk of being attended to by mental health professionals, or by an army of regulators of business, labor, professional practice, government, and civil and human rights.

The psychological definition of crime as antisocial behavior is best combined with the broader definition of "problem behavior." If not so combined, some of the non-deviant practices of dentists, surgeons, and teachers would surely be judged criminal. No definition of criminal behavior is totally satisfactory. Over the years, criminologists have proposed definitions of criminal behavior that were culturally and morally dependent (e.g., homosexuality was a crime in many countries until recently and remains a crime today in some countries). It was also argued that, since most people have broken the law or hurt someone at some point in their lives, criminal behavior was normative. However, with thanks to Ullmann and Krasner (1976), our working definition of criminal behavior is as follows:

> Criminal behavior refers to antisocial acts that place the actor at risk of becoming a focus of the attention of criminal justice professionals within the juvenile and/or adult justice systems.

An important positive function of this psychological definition (i.e., criminal behavior as antisocial behavior) is to prevent us from losing touch with characteristics of justice-involved persons and the pain of victims.

Variation in Criminal Conduct

As defined earlier, criminal behavior refers to acts that are injurious and prohibited under the law, and render the actor subject to intervention by justice professionals. The specific acts included are many and they may change over time and from culture to culture. However, the acts of theft, robbery, and physical assault appear to be consistently denounced and punished across time and culture. Variation in the occurrence of acts injurious to others is the primary focus of the psychology of crime, even though antisocial acts may not always be prohibited under the law and, under some temporal and cultural circumstances, may even be prescribed (for example, killing the enemy under conditions of war). With a general perspective, it makes sense to explore the idea that variation in both types of injurious behavior may be predicted, influenced, and explained by the same general psychology that explains all human behavior. That is, the mechanisms and factors that explain, for example, depressive behaviors will be similar to criminal behavior.

The differences in the occurrence of criminal behavior are truly amazing. Criminal behavior is not black and white; that is, committing a criminal or antisocial act does not define a person or his or her destiny. Just because someone commits an assault does not mean he or she is a dangerous or violent person that will never change. PCC wants to understand the variability in criminal acts. Variation in the occurrence of antisocial behavior at the individual level is of two types. First, people differ in the number, type, and variety of criminal acts in which they engage. This variation is typically referred to as *inter-individual* differences or the differences between people. Simply reflecting upon your own social circle, you may find examples of inter-individual differences. Some may have a criminal record and others do not, and there may be people that you know who use illicit drugs or are abusive to their partners.

In addition, variation is found over time and across situations for particular individuals. This variation is called *intra-individual* variation and refers to differences within the person either over time or in different situations. Once again, simple self-observation may demonstrate this variation. For example, you may note that when you were a teenager you engaged in some criminal activity or that you are more likely to lose your temper when intoxicated than when sober.

Systematic observation (i.e., empirical research) yields more detailed information on the variation of criminal conduct of individuals. To illustrate, we examine an important longitudinal study of crime from the United Kingdom. The Cambridge Study in Delinquent Development (CSDD) was initiated by Donald West and has continued under the leadership of David Farrington (Farrington, 2019; Farrington, Jolliffe, & Coid, 2021). The CSDD began with a sample of 411 mostly white boys about the age of eight drawn from a working-class district in south London, England (West & Farrington, 1977). From 1961 to 1962, the boys, their parents, and their teachers were interviewed, and official records of convictions were collected. This sample has been followed through the years with interviews and checks for criminal convictions. Most recently, interview data is available on 365 men at age 48 (loss in number due to deaths, refusals, and unable to locate) and criminal record data up to the age of 61. Here are some results from the CSDD demonstrating the variability in criminal conduct:

- Overall, 44 percent of the sample had a criminal conviction by age 61.

- 26 percent of convicted males had a criminal career that lasted over 20 years.

- 7 percent of the sample had 10 or more convictions, and this group of "chronic offenders" accounted for 52 percent of the total number of convictions.

- 5 percent of the boys were first convicted of an offense at age 14; 31.9 percent between the ages of 10 and 20; 8.7 percent between the ages of 21 and 40; and 1.5 percent over the age of 40.

- 93 percent of the men reported criminal behavior more than three times that of officially documented convictions (29 percent).

Surveys of the findings of many research studies similar to the one just described have established a few basic facts regarding the criminal behavior of those officially convicted—facts that have been established in many areas of the world. Individual differences in criminal behavior are substantial:

1. Individual differences in criminal activity are apparent in many ways. They may be inferred from knowledge of aggregated crime rates based on both official records of crime and surveys of victims. They are discovered more directly by systematic surveys of criminal histories (officially defined or self-reported) and by systematic studies of criminal futures (officially defined or self-reported).

2. Individual differences in criminal activity are apparent within samples of people differentiated by country of origin, gender, age, race, social class, and any other means of differentiating subgroups of humanity.

3. While victim- and self-reported crime rates are much higher than rates based on official records, the demographic correlates (e.g., being young, male, nonwhite, poor) of criminal activity remain very similar for different measures of criminal activity.

4. Official recidivism rates vary with the specific measure of official processing employed (for example, arrested versus convicted versus incarcerated) and with length of the follow-up period.

5. Those with repeat convictions, a small subset of all who come into conflict with the law, account for a disproportionate amount of total criminal activity. Careful study of criminal careers over the life span reveals,

however, that early, frequent, serious, and violent offending represents a small number of cases.

PCC has much to understand and explain given the facts of the differences in the criminal behavior of individuals.

A Look Ahead

Part 1 of the text includes three chapters that summarize the empirical base and theoretical context of PCC. Part 2 surveys the major risk/need factors, including the risk/need factors referred to as the "Central Eight." Part 3 gives a detailed review of applications of PCC in the areas of prediction and effective intervention along with an exploration of how PCC can be applied to some specific criminal subpopulations. Part 4 presents the summary and conclusions.

Part 1

Following the introductory material of Chapter 1, Chapter 2 lays out how we examine research findings and understand the empirical basis to PCC. For many students, Chapter 2 will serve as a primer on research designs and statistics. The word "primer" is emphasized. This chapter is not meant to be a comprehensive summary of research methodology but will provide sufficient detail to give the reader an appreciation of the science in support of PCC. The value of PCC does not simply reside in theoretical satisfaction (Part 2) but also in the empirical support for PCC and, as described in Part 3, its applications.

Chapter 3 summarizes the dominant theoretical perspectives of criminal conduct. A variety of perspectives from the criminological and psychological traditions are reviewed and compared with a General Personality and Cognitive Social Learning (GPCSL) perspective. The GPCSL perspective outlines how key personal and social relationship variables interact with the environment to shape criminal behavior.

Part 2

Chapters 4 through 8 explore potential sources of variability in criminal behavior that in total have been major preoccupations for years within mainstream criminology. These chapters also summarize much of the research around what GPCSL calls the "Central Eight" risk/need factors. In Chapter 4, biological factors are reviewed along with genetics and the mediating variable of temperament (or personality as it emerges through the interaction of biology and the environment). Although genetics and personality are well-established risk factors for criminal activity, only temperament/personality will enter our Central Eight set of major risk/need factors (Chapter 5).

Chapter 6 explores procriminal associates and attitudes. Chapter 7 extends the discussion of the person in a variety of social contexts, including family of origin, marriage and romantic attachments, school/work, leisure/recreation, and neighborhoods. The focus of Chapter 8 is on substance misuse and crime.

Part 3

Chapters 9 through 14 are concerned with applications of PCC (e.g., practical prediction and treatment). Chapter 9 describes the relationship between GPCSL theory with the Risk-Need-Responsivity (RNR) model of assessment and rehabilitation, which has become the premier model to guide applications in corrections and criminal justice.

Chapter 10 describes how the RNR model has influenced the development of offender risk/need instruments. The interrelationship between the RNR model and assessment is illustrated by the development and application of the Level of Service instruments. A history of rehabilitation and present status is discussed in Chapter 11. A careful examination of the evidence shows that rehabilitation can be effective in reducing criminal behavior, and dramatically so, if the rehabilitation programs follow the principles of the RNR model. Chapter 12 outlines a major challenge in applications of PCC knowledge. Tightly controlled programming in the context of short-term demonstration projects reveals positive effects that greatly exceed those found in "real-world" programs. Real-world programs take what is shown to be effective in a small demonstration and then try to apply it on a large scale. Moving from the small, controlled study to the real world is fraught with challenges and "technology transfer" has become a most exciting emerging field of study.

Although a strong case is made for rehabilitation, deterrence is immensely popular. Getting tough and punishing more swiftly and with more force is thought to deter criminal activity. Drawing upon the evidence and the psychology of punishment, Chapter 13 will demonstrate that deterrence does not work in reducing crime. In fact, a policy of deterrence has only resulted in increased financial costs to taxpayers and misery for countless justice-involved persons, their victims, and members of the community at large.

Chapter 14 extends applications of PCC with special groups and explores our understanding of violence in its many forms (e.g., intimate partner violence and sexual violence).

Part 4

Chapter 15 assesses the extent to which PCC achieves the objectives that were outlined in Chapter 1.

Worth Remembering

1. Definitions of criminal behavior draw upon legal, moral, social, and psychological factors. In PCC, criminal behavior is behavior that requires attention and intervention from the criminal justice system.

2. The objective of PCC is to understand variation in the criminal behavior of individuals. This variation can occur between people (inter-individual): Why does Joey commit crimes but not Sally? Variation can also occur within the individual (intra-individual): Why does Joey behave badly in one situation but not in another, and why was Sally always in trouble as a youth but not as an adult? These are the questions PCC seeks to answer.

 Visit the Instructor and Student Resource to access additional exercises, videos and study materials to support this chapter: psychologycriminalconduct.routledge.com

CHAPTER 2 The Empirical Basis to the Psychology of Criminal Conduct

The understanding of criminal behavior sought by the psychology of criminal conduct (PCC) is empirical, theoretical, and practical. In brief, this means that psychology seeks explanations of criminal conduct that are consistent with the findings of systematic observation (empirical), rationally organized (theoretical), and useful to people with interests in criminal behavior (practical). These three interrelated aspects of understanding criminal conduct are stressed throughout the text.

Empirically, PCC seeks knowledge not only of the observable facts regarding the nature and extent of individual variation in criminal conduct, but also knowledge of the biological, personal, interpersonal, situational, and social variables associated with or correlated with criminal behavior. These are termed *covariates* and include the correlates of individual differences in a criminal history and the predictors of the criminal futures of individuals. The predictors are called risk factors and there are two types. Static risk factors are historical and do not change. If a 30-year-old had a conviction for a criminal offense at the age of 18 then this fact cannot be undone. Dynamic risk factors (or criminogenic needs) are subject to change. For example, a person can develop an alcohol misuse problem but that person can also follow a life of sobriety. Perhaps most importantly, PCC seeks knowledge of the *causes* of criminal conduct. Causal covariates offer the potential to influence the likelihood of a criminal act through deliberate intervention. These three types of covariates—correlates, predictors, and causal variables—may, once again, be found in biology, personality, attitudes and cognitions, aptitudes and skills, learning history, family, peer relationships, broader social arrangements, and the immediate situation of action.

Although the aforementioned appears straightforward, distractions from our quest for an empirical understanding are many. The snake oil salesman is alive and well in the criminal justice system (Gendreau, Smith, & Thériault, 2009). Latessa, Cullen, and Gendreau (2002) described a number of theories and interventions that have little basis in evidence and yet are accepted almost

DOI: 10.4324/9781003292128-3

without question. They called this "correctional quackery" and gave such examples as acupuncture, pet therapy, and drama therapy. Another entertaining example of quackery is the viral video of Filipino inmates doing the zombie dance with Michael Jackson's "Thriller" playing in the background (simply enter "thriller in Filipino prison" in a Google search). Dance as therapy may help people feel happy and alive and, despite declarations from some inmates that dancing to pop music is rehabilitative, there is no convincing evidence that it reduces reoffending. The reader will find other examples of quackery sprinkled throughout this text and we will wonder about their enduring appeal.

How do we differentiate quackery and snake oil from true evidence? In part, the answer lies in a solid understanding of the scientific method, including the application of statistics to the research findings. This chapter is not meant to provide a comprehensive summary of research design and statistics. It is intended to give the necessary foundation to make decisions about whether the results from studies are worth considering or should be thrown into the garbage bin. Therefore, this chapter presents a primer on research designs and the statistics used in much of the research of interest to PCC.

The Importance of Research Designs and Methods

One focus of this chapter is to understand the importance of research designs in the establishment of the type of covariation. The chapter does not include a comprehensive review of the many potential sources of error in measurement, operationalization, and conceptualization. However, potential errors of measurement and conceptualization may inflate estimates of covariation, deflate estimates of covariation, or have no effect on level of covariation, depending upon the specifics of the threats.

The research approaches reviewed here are in the systematic quantitative tradition. The emphasis on quantitative methods does not deny the contribution of qualitative approaches to research. Sometimes quantitative methodologies are presented as superior to qualitative investigations because they are more numerically precise. Presenting quantitative and qualitative approaches as a dichotomous, either/or choice for researchers is misleading (Madill, 2015). Many, if not most, scientific advances have used a mix of the two approaches (Sechrest & Sidani, 1995). Simply consider Darwin's observations on the Galapagos islands or Freud's rich description of a *Case of Hysteria*. Where would evolutionary theory and psychoanalysis be today without qualitative investigation?

A qualitative approach also plays important roles in PCC, such as building tentative models (initial conceptualization of variables and the relationships among variables). Many examples of a nonquantitative approach (and more often a mixed approach) will be described in this book. The reader will learn how Hervey Cleckley's (1941) clinical experiences with 15 patients led to an understanding of psychopathy, Shadd Maruna's (2001) interviews of inmates released from prison informed an understanding of desistance from crime, and the feminist scholars (e.g., Daly, 1992; Van Voorhis, Wright, Salisbury, & Bauman, 2010) remind us how women come to the attention of the criminal justice system in ways different from men. However, the hypothesis forwarded from qualitative research then should be applied and tested through quantitative research. Researchers may then return to a qualitative study in order to explore whether the model possesses the "ring of truth" and, thus, knowledge progresses.

A case study is often fascinating to read and inspires a feeling that we really understand the phenomenon of interest. Case studies have been used in criminology for some time (Shaw, 1930/1966) and still garner attention (Maruna & Liem, 2021). The problem arises when case studies are used as "proof" for favored theoretical positions. Their methodological shortcomings are many, including selection bias (why was *this* person chosen by the investigator?), the lack of a comparison (how do we know that this person's experiences are somehow special from others?), and the absence of objective observations made earlier in time (just because the person says s/he assaults others because of earlier child abuse doesn't make it so). The list goes on. The limitations of a case study are so severe that some consider it unethical to use case studies to formulate cause and validate theories (Campbell & Stanley, 1966). Fortunately, most qualitative researchers are well aware of the problems with a case study and have taken steps to mitigate these shortcomings. When a case study is provided in this text, it is meant only to illustrate a finding already established by systematic research, not to serve as the research evidence itself.

Table 2.1 summarizes the relationships among the type of covariate (e.g., is it a simple correlate of criminal behavior or is it a cause of behavior?), how the covariate is applied in practice, and the research design required to establish the type of covariate. Note that the single case study is not included in the table for the reasons cited earlier. Also note that the cross-sectional research design speaks only to past criminal behavior, whereas the other research designs address criminal futures. Finally, the covariate type is purposively ranked from the least informative at the top row (i.e., a correlate) to the most informative at the bottom (i.e., causal).

The Correlates of Crime and the Cross-Sectional Research Design

Knowledge of correlates comes from cross-sectional observations of individuals known to differ in their criminal history. Cross-sectional studies tend to be of two types: *extreme groups* and *surveys*. In the extreme groups approach, individuals are selected for observation precisely because they are known in advance to differ in their criminal histories. For example, a sample of high school students may be compared with a sample of juvenile probationers, or a group of first-time convicted persons may be compared with a group

TABLE 2.1 Type of Covariate, Type of Application, Research Design, and Criterion Variable

Covariate type	Application type	Research design	Criterion
Correlate	Potential Risk/Need Factor	Cross-Sectional	Criminal Past
Predictor	Risk Factor	Longitudinal	Criminal Future
	Strength Factor	Longitudinal	Criminal Future
Dynamic Predictor	Need Factor	Multi-Wave Longitudinal	Criminal Future
	Stable Need	Multi-Wave Longitudinal	Criminal Future
	Acute Need	Multi-Wave Longitudinal	Criminal Future
Causal	Intervention	Randomized Experimental	Criminal Future

of persons with lengthy criminal histories. The empirical issue here is to discover which of the potential covariates studied do, in fact, distinguish between those who commit crimes and those who do not. Alternatively, in the survey approach, a representative sample of individuals from some specified population is selected for systematic observation. One of the variables studied is the level and/or type of criminal activity in which the individuals have engaged. Other variables assessed are the potential covariates of that criminal history. Here, too, the task is to identify the variables that correlate with a criminal past. In brief, correlates are covariates of a criminal past.

Cross-sectional designs are frequently used in the analysis of criminal behavior. They tend to be less expensive to implement, and they provide information much more quickly than alternative approaches. Two of the most important and most cited studies in the whole of PCC and criminology are those of Sheldon Glueck and Eleanor Glueck (1950) and Travis Hirschi (1969). The studies differed in many ways, yet their findings were remarkably similar and have been supported in many subsequent studies. Glueck and Glueck used an extreme groups design. They compared 500 boys from a juvenile delinquency facility with 500 nondelinquents selected from schools in the Boston area matched on age (average age of 14). They then conducted social history interviews with the boys, their relatives, and others (such as social workers and teachers). Social welfare, court and correctional records, and school files were reviewed. Information from these sources was further enriched with medical examinations, psychiatric interviews, psychological tests, anthropometric analyses of photographs of the boys, and teacher-completed checklists.

Hirschi used a survey design. He selected a representative sample of delinquents and nondelinquents in high schools from the San Francisco area. School records and police records were consulted, but the most important source of data was a questionnaire survey asking the more than 4,000 students

TABLE 2.2 **Correlates and Potential Risk/Need Factors from Two Cross-Sectional Studies**

Potential risk/need factor	Cross-sectional classics	
	Glueck & Glueck (1950) (Extreme groups)	Hirschi (1969) (Survey)
Energetic and easily bored	✓	✓
Lacking in self-control	✓	✓
Multiple rule violations	✓	✓
Procriminal attitudes	✓	✓
Delinquent associates	✓	✓
Dislike for school	✓	✓
Poor family relations	✓	✓
Poor parental supervision	✓	✓

about school, family, and work. Most of Hirschi's delinquents, however, were not persistent and serious official offenders, unlike the delinquents in the Glueck and Glueck sample. A comparison of the findings displayed in Table 2.2 shows the similarities in covariates despite the differences in methods of inquiry.

The results from these two studies highlight a few observations. First, the common findings identify certain risk/need factors that come up again and again in the study of criminal behavior—that is, personality (energetic, poor self-control), criminal history, attitudes, associates, school, and family. As we will soon see in the next chapter, the risk/need factors described by Glueck and Glueck and by Hirschi are part of the Central Eight risk/need factors that are so important in PCC. Second, despite Hirschi titling his book *Causes of Delinquency*, there is no way that the cross-sectional design permits a conclusion about cause.

In order to conclude a causal relationship, it must be demonstrated that the causal variable came *before* the criminal behavior. Thus, if we take the example of "poor parental supervision," does poor monitoring and supervision by the parents free the child to spend more time in delinquent activities, or does the child's delinquency frustrate the parents and they give up trying to supervise the child? In cross-sectional designs, the information is collected simultaneously and, therefore, does not meet the time criteria for establishing cause. In fact, because we cannot establish what came first, we cannot even call the risk/need factor a predictor, and for this reason in Table 2.2 it is labelled a *potential* risk/need factor. Finally, although the table indicates the presence of a risk/need correlate, it says nothing of the magnitude of the relationship between the risk/need factor and criminal behavior. Are the eight variables in Table 2.2 equally important, or do any of them take prominence? To explore the magnitude of the relationship, we need to apply statistics, which will be described shortly.

Predictor Variables and the Longitudinal Design

Knowledge of predictors of criminal behavior comes from observations conducted within a longitudinal study. In a longitudinal study, hypothesized predictor variables are examined in relation to subsequent or future criminal activity. Relative to cross-sectional studies, longitudinal research has the advantage of ensuring that the covariation established is truly prospective. That is, we may feel reasonably confident that the criminal behavior was not responsible for the association because the assessment of criminal behavior was based on events that *followed* the assessment of predictor variables. In cross-sectional designs, when we observe an association between two variables, we can never be sure what came first (e.g., does a muscular body type lead to criminal behavior, or does criminal activity produce a muscular figure?).

For purposes of illustrating the practicality of longitudinal designs, a concrete example of the ability to forecast future crime follows. Yessine and Bonta (2008) applied a simple, eight-item risk scale to a large sample of delinquent girls and boys whose criminal convictions were measured five years later. These predictors (or risk/need factors) included two static criminal history items and dynamic items measuring employment, delinquent associates, alcohol/drug problems, psychological distress, procriminal attitudes, and poor parental relationship. Each youth was assigned a score of "1" for each risk factor that was present. Thus, the risk scale could take values from "0" (no risk factors present) to "8" (all factors present). Observe in Table 2.3

TABLE 2.3 Reconviction Rates at Five Years by Risk Score

Risk score	Reconviction rate
8	90.9%
7	89.3%
6	85.6%
5	82.2%
4	76.9%
3	69.1%
2	52.3%
1	39.3%
0	19.4%
Total sample	71.6%

Source: Yessine & Bonta, 2008

that at the five-year mark official reconvictions increased with scores on the risk scale.

Dynamic Predictors and the Multi-Wave Longitudinal Design

Definitive knowledge of dynamic predictors comes from multi-wave longitudinal studies. Observations are made on *at least* three occasions in a multi-wave longitudinal study. The first occasion involves the initial assessment of potential predictors and the second involves a reassessment of these potential predictors. For purposes of establishing dynamic predictors, changes observed between the initial assessment and the reassessment are examined in relation to the third assessment, namely that of criminal conduct, which follows at some later date.

Dynamic predictors (dynamic risk factors) are ones in which assessed change is associated with subsequent criminal behavior. Some dynamic risk factors are relatively stable in that change occurs over a matter of weeks, months, or even years. Examples of dynamic risk factors are enhanced interpersonal relationships at home, school, or work, and reductions or increases in association with criminal others. Some dynamic risk factors are much less stable and some may change almost instantaneously. These relatively fast-changing dynamic risk factors are often called *acute* dynamic risk factors and typically reflect immediate situations or immediate circumstances (such as hanging out with a drug user tonight) and/or immediate emotional states such as anger, emotional collapse, or desire for revenge (Brown, St. Amand, & Zamble, 2009; Hanson, 2009; Vasiljevic, Öjehagen, & Andersson, 2020). We begin with the more stable dynamic risk factors.

As an illustration of dynamic predictors, Peter Raynor (2007) found that intake assessments of more than 2,000 British probationers on a risk/need instrument called the Level of Service Inventory-Revised (LSI-R; Andrews & Bonta, 1995) predicted criminal recidivism one year later. That is, as LSI-R scores increased, then so did the recidivism rate. If this was all that Raynor did, then we would have a standard longitudinal design establishing the LSI-R as a predictor of criminal behavior.

With dynamic predictors, we are interested in the *changes* in scores between the first and second assessments and future recidivism. Raynor (2007) displays the results for a small subset of 203 probationers from the island of Jersey in the United Kingdom who were administered the LSI-R near the beginning of probation and again approximately six months later. He found that probationers who scored low risk at the first assessment and remained low risk had a recidivism rate of 29 percent. However, those low-risk offenders who *increased* their risk score and now scored high risk upon reassessment had a recidivism rate of 59 percent. Correspondingly, high-risk probationers who remained high risk had a recidivism rate of 76 percent, whereas those high-risk offenders who scored low risk upon reassessment had a recidivism rate of 54 percent (we do not know why some offenders changed in their risk scores). The important points are that the changes from intake to retest were linked with criminal outcomes and that measurement occurred at three points in time. A multi-wave study, however, is not limited to three measurement points; for example, reassessments can be conducted every six months over a two-year period and then linked to changes in recidivism five years later.

The identification of simple predictors in single-wave longitudinal studies shows that individuals may be reliably assigned to groups with different levels of risk for future criminal activity. The discovery of *dynamic* predictors confirms: (1) that risk levels are subject to change (someone assessed as high or low risk at Time A does not necessarily remain high or low risk at Time B), and (2) that these dynamic predictors may serve as treatment goals. For example, in many probation agencies, a primary objective is to provide treatment services and supervision to probationers in such a way that the lower-risk cases remain low risk and that the higher-risk cases become lower-risk ones. In the case of the LSI-R, the instrument measures various dynamic risk factors such as employment, companions, and substance misuse. Therefore, a probation officer is able to identify which of these factors are salient for the client and target them in treatment. Thus, knowledge of dynamic predictors focuses a probation officer's efforts in bringing about change in his/her client.

An understanding of dynamic predictors is very important within PCC, because a psychology of criminal behavior rejects outright an exclusive focus on the more static aspects of individuals and their situations. Indeed, when PCC practitioners and researchers uncover highly stable predictors, they immediately begin to think in terms of what may be the dynamic correlates of that stable predictor. For example, past criminal behavior is a major predictor of future antisocial behavior, but it is a static risk factor that cannot be reduced. However, dynamic predictors of criminal conduct or *criminogenic need* factors have great practical relevance because they inform interventions that reduce criminal behavior by identifying the targets of treatment.

Reassessments over a period much shorter than six months or more (e.g., monthly, weekly, or even daily) may lead to the discovery of acute dynamic risk/need factors that will predict criminal occurrences over the very short term. If a parolee begins to talk with considerable resentment and anger over how things are going (at home or on the job), risk of recidivism may be considered to have increased at least for the short term. In the past, there has been little research on acute risk/need factors. However, this situation is changing.

Just as knowledge of predictor variables leads us closer to knowledge of causes than do simple correlates, so does knowledge of dynamic predictors yield a still higher level of empirical understanding. PCC, however, seeks more than knowledge of dynamic predictors. PCC seeks an understanding that offers the potential not to simply forecast criminal events but to influence the chances of criminal acts occurring through deliberate intervention.

Causal Variables and the Randomized Experimental Design

The causes of crime are most convincingly established not through the determination of correlates and predictors, but through demonstrations of the effects of deliberate interventions. As the conditions of intervention approximate experimental ideals, confidence in the causal status of any particular variable increases. The randomized experimental design is the main research design that permits the conclusion that *x* caused *y* (there is also the A-B-A type design, but it is rarely employed in the study of criminal behavior and will not be discussed).

Before describing the features of the randomized experiment, it is instructive to examine the *quasi*-experimental design. Quasi-experimental research designs are relatively common and do tell us a great deal about what may be causal. However, quasi-experiments still leave uncertainty as to whether the variable of interest is truly causal or whether there is some other explanation for the results. Other explanations are referred to as "threats to validity," and we want to minimize these threats if we are to draw conclusions about cause. For example, earlier we noted that with cross-sectional designs we do not know what variable came first, and this is a threat to the validity of a causal effect.

A quasi-experimental design has most of the features of a randomized experiment. There are a minimum of two groups, an experimental and a control group, although there can be more than two groups (e.g., two different treatment programs being compared to an untreated control group). There is also an assessment of criminal behavior for both groups at the same point in time after the intervention. However, there is no randomized assignment of the research participants to the experimental and control groups. The importance of random assignment will soon become apparent.

In order to illustrate the features of a quasi-experimental design, we take a fictitious evaluation of an electronic monitoring (EM) program. A correctional agency wants to know if placing electronic bracelets on clients to track their whereabouts in the community will make it less likely that they will commit new crimes. That is, does EM *cause* a change in the likelihood of criminal behavior? A quasi-experimental design is chosen where one group of clients in by far the largest city in the state, Gotham, will all be placed on EM for a year (the experimental group), and police records will be checked in three years to examine this group's crime rate (post-assessment). The experimental group's recidivism rate will then be compared to the three-year recidivism rate of a matched group of state offenders outside of Gotham who are supervised in the usual way (i.e., without EM; control group). The EM program goes on for a year, and three years later we find the recidivism rate is 40 percent for the experimental group and 50 percent for the control group.

Given the results from the evaluation of the EM program, can we conclude that EM reduced or caused a reduction in recidivism? Let's start dissecting the methodology to see if the design eliminates alternative explanations for the findings (i.e., threats to validity). The first thing we note is that we are comparing the recidivism rate of those from Gotham to the rate outside of the megacity. Perhaps the difference in recidivism rates is due to an overstretched police force in Gotham that cannot keep up with crime in the city, while the police in the smaller and more rural centers have the time to track down the law-violators and make arrests. Or, maybe the Gotham police force has more lax arrest policies. Thus, the reduction in recidivism seen among the experimental group may have nothing to do with being electronically monitored but rather more to do with local police practices.

The biggest and most glaring alternative explanation to EM as a causal factor is the comparability of the controls to the experimentals. The participants in the two groups were matched on variables that the researchers thought were related to recidivism. Typically, groups are matched on variables such as age, gender, and criminal history, to name a few. Being young, being a male, and having a criminal history are all related to criminal behavior. Therefore, the researchers made sure that there were equal numbers of young persons, males, and persons with a prior record in both the experimental and control groups. Otherwise, one may conclude that the recidivism differences between the two groups may be due, for example, to one group having more women or older offenders.

The first problem with matching is that it is impossible to match on every single factor related to criminal conduct because one would need to begin with an extremely large control population to draw a sample that matches the experimental group on the variables selected. As an example, if we have one individual who is male, under the age of 21, and has a prior criminal record, then we need to find from the non-Gotham population another male under the age of 21 with a prior record to be assigned to the control group. The more variables, the more difficult it becomes to find an exact match. Researchers sometimes try to get around this by using statistical techniques to do the matching, but you still need large numbers.

The second problem with matching is that you can never be sure that you matched on all the relevant variables. Even if you check that the experimental and control participants are similar on the variables chosen at the beginning of the study, there remains the possibility that some very important variables are missing and that these variables explain the differences in the findings. For these aforementioned reasons, the classic experimental design, with random assignment, is the "gold standard" of research deigns and leaves one the most confident with making statements regarding cause (Farrington, 2013).

Now with an appreciation of the need to eliminate alternative explanations before we can safely say that x caused y, the key features of the randomized experimental design are as follows:

1. A minimum of two groups: an experimental group exposed to the hypothesized causal variable and a control group not subjected to the hypothesized causal variable.

2. Random assignment of subjects to groups. Random assignment ensures that the typical person in the experimental group will be similar in their characteristics, whether measured or not, to the typical person in the control group. As a consequence, differences in outcomes for the two groups are due to the intervention and not participant characteristics.

3. Post-testing on the criterion variable (i.e., criminal behavior) of both groups at the same point in time.

A randomized experimental design controls for bias from subject-selection factors through random assignment. Furthermore, post-testing both the experimental and control groups during the same time period addresses other threats to validity. It controls for maturation (i.e., growing older) and history factors (i.e., naturally occurring experiences between the time of the intervention and the time of the post-tests), because these factors would be expected to influence the control subjects in the same manner as the experimental subjects. There are a number of other important considerations (e.g., using objective measurement, controlling for experimenter bias through double-blind procedures, testing the results for statistical significance), but the three features listed are the essential features of a randomized experimental design, and it is only this design, aside from the A-B-A design previously mentioned, that allows us to make causal statements.

Approximations of the ideals of true experimentation are difficult to achieve even under highly controlled laboratory conditions with nonhuman animals. The difficulties are compounded when attempts are made to study human behavior that is as socially significant as criminal behavior. Some social agencies, however, are formally called upon to intervene in the lives of individuals with the expressed and socially approved purpose of controlling their criminal conduct. These agencies are also expected to perform their duties in effective, efficient, fair, and just ways. However, there continues to be significant resistance against the use of experimental designs (Dezember, Stoltz, et al., 2021; Weisburd, 2010). One of the arguments against random assignment, especially in a treatment study, is that effective treatment is being denied to the control group. However, how can we know if the treatment really *causes* a beneficial result if we do not use random assignment? Randomized experimentation is a requirement for evaluating medical interventions. Why do we demand less with interventions in the criminal justice system? Is it unethical to deny active experimentation when it is feasible to do so?

In summary, much of our understanding of the covariates of criminal behavior is dependent upon the research methodology used in studies. This methodology informs our level of understanding and reminds us of the importance of empirical research to building knowledge. For all of this, literature reviews suggest that the findings of cross-sectional studies and the findings of longitudinal studies have been highly compatible. The validity of potential risk factors identified in cross-sectional studies has tended to be confirmed in longitudinal studies of risk factors.

The number of multi-wave longitudinal studies of potential criminogenic need factors has been low, but in recent years it has grown to place us in a position to assert with high degrees of confidence the nature of some of the major dynamic risk factors. We are now at the point of conducting the ultimate tests of criminogenic needs within the structure of the experimental design. For the strict determination of criminogenic need, what we need to show is that: (1) deliberate interventions produce changes in the potential criminogenic need, and (2) changes in the potential need lead to changes in criminal conduct.

Some Commonly Used Statistics

Having established that the covariates of criminal conduct may be of several types, depending upon the research design used, we turn to the questions of: (1) are the results from the study significant or due to chance? and (2) what is the magnitude of the covariation? A discussion of both questions follows.

Statistical Significance: $p < 0.05$ and Confidence Intervals

Until recently the social sciences have relied on statistical significance testing to evaluate their findings. The researcher assumes that there is no relationship between the covariates studied (called the null hypothesis with a p or probability value equal to 0). When a relationship is found, then a p value is calculated to help decide whether the observation is real or due to chance. As an example, a researcher may want to know if teaching yoga to inmates decreases prison assaults. An experiment is set up: 50 prisoners are randomly assigned to yoga training or a control group (no yoga), and the number of assaults committed by the research participants are counted six months later. The researcher finds that the average number of assaults committed by the inmates in the experimental group is 2.1 and for the control group it is 2.7.

Like most researchers trained in the null hypothesis tradition, the researcher begins with the assumption that yoga will not make a difference on assault rates (the null hypothesis). However, a difference is found and the question becomes, can we reject the null hypothesis? The researcher applies a t-test (a statistic for calculating differences in averages) and finds a $p < 0.05$. This is called Null Hypothesis Significant Testing (NHST). The p is interpreted to mean that there is a less than 5 percent chance that the differences are a matter of luck (sometimes research reports may use more stringent criteria such as $p < 0.01$ or $p < 0.001$).

Problems with NHST have been noted for years, with calls for the abandonment of NHST (Cohen, 1994; Rozeboom, 1960; Schmidt, 1996), and they continue to this day (Hanson, 2022; Hubbard, 2019; Trafimow & Marks, 2015). Problems with NHST include dichotomous thinking (the findings are or are not significant) and selecting an arbitrary p value to define significance (why

$p < 0.05$; why not $p < 0.10$?). Perhaps most problematic is the possibility that NHST is likely to miss a real effect that could have important clinical and cost implications (Cumming, 2014; Hunt, 1997; Schmidt, 1996). This is called a Type II error (i.e., concluding there is no relationship when there actually is a relationship). If other researchers replicated our hypothetical yoga experiment using the same procedures and measures with a new sample, it is exceedingly unlikely that they would find a similar difference score. Indeed, some researchers may find "no statistically significant" difference, others even a much larger difference, and a few would report the control group doing better! What then is our conclusion? Does yoga training work or not?

Despite the significant problems with NHST, the general research community continues to defend the NHST tradition. The reader is invited to peruse Table 1 of Gendreau and Smith (2007), which outlines 25 suspect justifications to continue with significance testing. However, there has been a growing trend to move away from reporting p values. The alternative to p is to report the confidence interval (CI).

Gendreau and Smith (2007) provide an example of using the CI in making a decision to choose between two offender risk instruments. The two instruments in their example were the Level of Service Inventory-Revised (LSI-R) and the Psychopathy Checklist-Revised (PCL-R). They summarized the literature on these two instruments and found that the correlation (r) between LSI-R scores and recidivism was 0.37 with a 95 percent CI ranging from 0.33 to 0.41 (more will be said about r shortly). For the PCL-R, $r = 0.23$, and the CI ranged from 0.17 to 0.28. The CI provides a range of plausible values within a lower and upper limit. The two correlation coefficients are called point estimates. The CI is an interval estimate and selecting a 95 percent confidence level gives us a margin of error and tells us something about how precise our point estimates are. It does not tell us that there is a 95 percent chance that, if the study was repeated, the point estimates would fall within the range of the specified CI. It tells us that, on replication, there is a 95 percent chance that the new confidence intervals will fall in the specified range. Observe that the width of the CI for both instruments is between 8 and 11 points and is viewed as a satisfactory precision estimate. Note also that the two CIs do not overlap. This suggests that the LSI-R may predict better than the PCL-R.

The reader may think that the use of CIs has some of the same problems as NHST (Cumming, 2014). Instead of assuming the null hypothesis, we are assuming that a difference exists, and we want to know if the difference is real. Thus, the American Statistical Association has called for a ban on NHST (Wasserstein, Schirm, & Lazar, 2019) and the journal *Basic and Applied Social Psychology* (Trafimow & Marks, 2015) has gone so far as to also ban CIs, calling for the reporting of results (e.g., percentages, r, and other descriptive statistics) without trying to test for statistical significance. This then leaves us with a quandary. Is there any value in reporting CIs? The answer is yes and will be presented in the section on meta-analysis. One important outcome of the debate over NHST and CIs is that it asks researchers to think more about the magnitude of the effect than the presence or absence of an effect and the precision of the estimate. Therefore, we look at some of the statistics that are used in this book that measure magnitude before describing the value of meta-analysis.

Statistical Measures of the Magnitude of Covariation

One of the most widely and best understood measures of the magnitude of covariation is the Pearson Product Moment Correlation Coefficient, also known as *r* (Gendreau & Smith, 2007). For this reason, it will be the preferred measure used in this text. Taking values between −1.00 and +1.00, *r* expresses the magnitude of a linear relationship between two variables (see Figure 2.1). A linear relationship is one that may be described by a straight line (there are also non-linear relationships requiring statistical measures other than *r*). As the observed level of one variable increases, so does the observed level of the other (e.g., as risk scores increase so does the recidivism rate). The correlation coefficient will take a negative value if there is an inverse relationship. That is, as the observed level of one variable decreases, the observed level of the other variable increases (e.g., as IQ decreases, crime increases).

The *r* statistic takes a value of 1.00 when the level of association is perfect, or 100 percent. For example, if all men (100 percent) had a criminal record and no women (0 percent) had a record, the correlation between gender and a criminal history would be 1.00. On the other hand, if the percentage of men and women with criminal records were equal (for example: 20 percent and 20 percent, 50 percent and 50 percent, or 70 percent and 70 percent), the *r* would be 0.00. Generally, the magnitude of the *r* reflects the difference in percentage criminal for one group relative to another. For example, if the recidivism rate for a treatment group is 15 percent and the rate for the control group is 40 percent (a difference of 15 percentage points), then the *r* would be 0.15. Another reason why being able to measure the magnitude of a relationship is important is that it rank orders risk factors, allowing us to make statements as to their relative importance.

Thanks to the Binomial Effect Size Display (BESD; Rosenthal, 1984), we can go in the other direction and estimate the proportion for two groups with

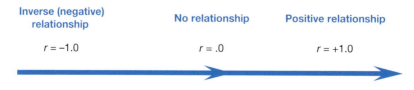

Figure 2.1

Pearson Product Moment Correlation (*r*)

knowledge of only r. Later in this text, evidence is presented that with the right type of treatment a reduction in recidivism is found with an average effect size of $r = 0.30$ (approximately). Now, let's take an example of a study where 100 individuals receive appropriate treatment and another 100 are assigned to a control group. Furthermore, we find a treatment effect of $r = 0.30$ for this specific study. The formula for BESD would go like this. The proportion of treated individuals who are successful (i.e., do not recidivate) would be 0.50 *minus r* divided by two (0.15) or 0.35. The proportion untreated who are unsuccessful (i.e., recidivate) is 0.50 *plus r* divided by two (0.15) or 0.65. Thus, out of the 100 treated individuals, 35 would recidivate (65 do not recidivate) and in the control group 65 would recidivate (35 do not).

A note about r^2 or "the variance accounted" needs mention. Sometimes the effects from a study are criticized because the r^2 is too small to be meaningful (Rosenthal & Rubin, 1979). In the previous example, if the effect size is squared then $r^2 = 0.09$. Does this mean that the variance in outcome accounted for by treatment is insignificant? Not at all—in our example treated clients had a recidivism rate of 35 percent and the untreated had a rate of 65 percent, almost half!

The correlation coefficient may be used to describe the findings of many types of studies. Sometimes, the results will be reported in terms of the percentage of one group who reoffend relative to the percentage of another group who reoffend. Sometimes research results will be reported in terms of the association of a multilevel variable (such as verbal intelligence) and a multilevel measure of criminality (such as number of new offenses). At other times, research may be reporting how a two-level variable such as gender (men/women) is associated with a multilevel variable such as the average number of offenses. The findings of all of these examples of research may be defined in terms of r.

One more statistic merits discussion, as it is used widely in studies of the predictive validity of risk instruments. It is called the Area Under the Curve (AUC). The importance of AUC, unlike r, is that it is unaffected by extreme base rates and selection ratios. A selection ratio can be illustrated by considering the Level of Service/Case Management Inventory (LS/CMI), a risk scale that will be presented in more detail later in the book. The LS/CMI produces scores from 0 to 43. Thus, low risk can be defined as "0 to 7" or "0 to 14" or "0 to 30." Changing the "cutoff" score, or the selection ratio, will affect how many offenders are defined as low risk or high risk and, therefore, will influence the number of correctly identified recidivists and nonrecidivists. For example, if you used a cutoff score of 30 and under to define a low-risk case, you will surely capture most of the nonrecidivists, but you will also capture a great many who will recidivate (certainly running counter to the notion of "low risk").

A base rate is the typical or expected occurrence of behavior. When the base rate for criminal behavior is either very low or very high, not only does *r* provide an inaccurate estimate of predictive validity, but it also creates a situation in which prediction is no problem at all. Take, for example, a situation in which the base rate of a certain type of criminal behavior, such as a sadistic sexual murder, is close to zero (e.g., 5 percent). Prediction is easy, and risk assessments are not needed because the best strategy is to predict that no one will recidivate; in this case you will be correct 95 percent of the time. Likewise, when the base rate is close to 100 percent (e.g., 96 percent), if you predict that everyone will recidivate, you will be correct 96 percent of the time. Thankfully, the base rates for most criminal behavior (e.g., property offenses, assaults, drug violations) fall in the 20 to 80 percent range, making prediction a worthwhile pursuit.

The analysis often used in evaluating offender risk scales is called the Receiver Operating Characteristic (ROC). A more detailed description of the ROC is given in Technical Note 2.1 on the textbook website at psychologycriminalconduct.routledge.com. However, for now the key point to remember is that ROC analysis yields the AUC measure. If a risk instrument has an AUC of 1.0, then we have a perfect prediction, and if the AUC equals 0.50, then the instrument performs no better than chance. The AUC also gives the probability of a score drawn at random from one sample being higher than a score drawn at random from another sample. For example, let us suppose that we have a risk scale with an AUC of 0.75, and we have two groups. One group consists of recidivists and another consists of nonrecidivists. If we randomly selected an individual from the recidivist group, there is a 75 percent chance that this person will have a higher score than that of a randomly selected nonrecidivist. By examining the AUCs, we can compare the predictive accuracies of different risk scales after taking into account base rates and selection rates. Sometimes, AUCs are presented in a graphical form (see Figure 2.2).

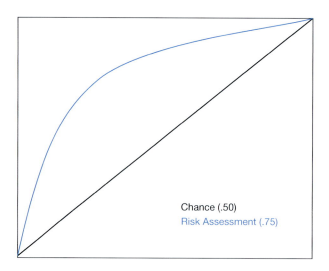

Figure 2.2

Area Under the Curve (AUC)

TABLE 2.4 **Conversion Chart for Interpreting Predictive Validities of Risk Instruments**

r	AUC
.00	.50
.05	.53
.10	.56
.15	.59
.20	.61
.25	.64
.30	.67
.35	.70
.40	.73
.45	.79

Source: Adapted from Rice & Harris, 2005

Although reporting AUCs is now almost standard, that was not always the case. Prior to 2000, most evaluations reported the accuracy of risk scales in terms of r or some other statistical index. Fortunately, Rice and Harris (2005) have provided a handy conversion table that allows one to convert various statistics to describe predictive accuracy to an AUC. A modified chart is provided in Table 2.4 to allow the reader to interpret r values commonly reported as AUCs.

Note that the values in the chart are approximations, as certain assumptions were made in the construction of the conversion chart (e.g., it assumes a 50 percent base rate). Formulas are provided by Rice and Harris (2005) to deal with different base rates, and the reader should consult these formulas for precise conversions.

Meta-Analyses

Almost every student and practitioner, and certainly every professor, is familiar with literature reviews. Scholarly journals are devoted to articles that review areas of interest, and every dissertation and research report begins with a review of the literature. The traditional literature review has been narrative in nature, and the qualities of the reviews depend very much upon the expertise and thoroughness of the author(s). The reviewer is relatively free to select studies and to attend to those results viewed as relevant. Thus, it is not uncommon for two independent reviews of a particular literature to reach very different conclusions.

The replication of findings is a convincing feature of science. Recently, some scholars have become alarmed that this failure to reproduce some findings has led to a "crisis of confidence" in psychology (Pashler & Wagenmaker, 2012) and the issue has also been raised in criminology (Farrington, Lösel, et al., 2019). To be clear, not everyone agrees that there is a "crisis" (Lösel, 2018; Stroebe & Strack, 2014). Moreover, the solution to dealing with reviewer bias and replication is meta-analysis (Edlund, Cuccolo, Irgens, Wagge, & Zlokovich, 2022; Stanley, Carter, & Doucouliagos, 2018).

Meta-analytic reviews permit a more unbiased analysis of the literature, and they also provide a *quantitative* estimate of the importance of the results. Many now regard meta-analysis as the standard approach for reviewing the literature. In essence, the results from individual studies are converted into a common metric or statistic referred to as the *effect size*. The effect size allows more direct comparisons of the results from various studies and the averaging of effect sizes across studies.

As an illustration, let us examine the relationship between intelligence and crime. Our fictional study is presented in Figure 2.3. Study A reports the results using a *t*-test (a statistic measuring the difference in the means of two groups). An average IQ score is 100, and in Study A, the first individual has an IQ of 90 and has a criminal record, the next individual has an IQ of 110 with no criminal record, and so on. In Study B, the statistic used is chi square (x^2), which is a measure that tests how well the observed findings fit with the expected findings. In this case, study participants are divided by low or high IQ and whether or not they have a criminal record. Finally, in Study C, the percentage of individuals in a *group* is linked to the percentage with a criminal record (note that Study C speaks of a group and not individuals as in Study A and B).

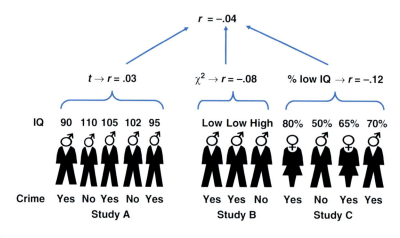

Figure 2.3

Meta-Analysis

With all of these different statistical measures, how can we best compare the results? In the traditional, narrative literature review, reviewers must make a judgment of the relative importance of the three studies. Reviewer A may emphasize the results from Study B and discount the results from the other two studies. Reviewer B may prefer the results based upon the t-test and minimize the other statistics. We can see how this approach may lead to different conclusions.

In a meta-analysis, the results from the three studies would all be converted into the same statistic or effect size (e.g., r or other common statistics such as Cohen's d or the odds ratio). In this text, the effect size that will most often be used is the Pearson correlation coefficient, or r, since the reader has already been introduced to this easily understood measure (meta-analyses that use other effect sizes are converted to r for consistency). In the example illustrated in Figure 2.3, the t score and x^2 would be converted to r, as would the percentage differences (recall how easily percentage differences can be transformed using Rosenthal's Binomial Effect Size Display). Consequently, we can compare the effect sizes from the three studies, and by averaging them, we can more accurately estimate the "true" relationship between intelligence and crime. Because many studies are conducted in various locations with different samples and time periods, the generalizability of the results from meta-analyses is enhanced.

Typically, researchers will also calculate the CI for the effect size providing an estimated range where the true value lies. In the previous example of the relationship between intelligence and crime, there were only three studies. If we did calculate the CI, it would likely be very wide. However, as more and more primary studies are added to the meta-analysis, regardless of how small the effect size is for the individual study, the CI would narrow. As it narrows, our effect size would become more precise. Two other symbols need to be introduced that will often appear in the results from meta-analyses. First, there is N, which represents the number of people in the study. Second, there is k, which stands for the number of comparisons and, therefore, the values a study may yield. A study may yield more than one comparison or value. For example, a treatment study may have three groups (the treatment of interest, an alternative treatment, and a no-treatment control). We can compare the treatment of interest to the alternative treatment, and we can also compare it to the control group. Thus, even though there is only one study, $k = 2$.

At a number of points in the text, we will refer to the results from different meta-analyses. For the reasons outlined, we place more confidence in the results from a meta-analysis than from the traditional literature review. Indeed, we are interested in the results of individual "primary studies" (the separate studies that compose the collection of studies reviewed). Yet we would not put all of our faith in a single study. We look for the overall effect evident from analyses of many primary studies (usually displayed as N, although it may also refer to the number of participants in a study; in the text I will note what N refers to).

Moderator Variables

Moderator variables are variables that interact with covariates on criminal behavior. For example, "Social Support for Drug Use" may interact with "Attitudes Favorable to Drug Use" in such a way that attitudes are strongly associated with drug use when social support for use is high but only weakly linked when social support for use is low. Moderator variables are a formal way of recognizing the complexity of human behavior—often, the correlates of criminal behavior "depend" upon other variables and/or the social context. One may also search for moderators of the mean effect size from a meta-analysis. As an example, the results from cross-sectional studies may (or may not) differ from the results of longitudinal studies (i.e., study design is a moderator). Similarly, the findings may vary depending upon whether the measure of criminal behavior is based on scores from a self-reported paper-and-pencil questionnaire or measures of official processing such as arrests or convictions (i.e., the measure of criminal behavior is a moderator).

It is important to note that PCC readily recognizes the complexity of human behavior and demands that the general validity of conclusions be explored under a variety of conditions. Most obviously these days, it is important to be able to demonstrate whether a conclusion from research is valid for people who may vary in age, gender, race, and socioeconomic class. Similarly, it is important to show whether methodological issues such as randomization, sample size, and deviations from the ideals of research design are associated with increases, decreases, or null effects on effect size estimates. Any variable is a potential moderator. Yet the actual moderator variables are those that do influence how one variable correlates with criminal behavior. Many tests of moderator variables follow in this text. For example, the effects of correctional treatment programs depend upon what the targets of change are and what behavior change techniques are used.

A Comment on Aggregated Crime Rates

Within PCC a major distinction is drawn between studies of *aggregated* crime rates and variation in the criminal behavior of *individuals*. Crime rates are an aggregation or clustering of many things: the behavior of individual offenders, police arrest policies, court proceedings, etc. Correlates of aggregated crime rates are not the same as the correlates of the criminal conduct of individuals. Technical Note 2.2 explores the problem in more detail (psychologycriminalconduct.routledge.com.). The basic message is straightforward: if you want to understand variation in the criminal behavior of individuals, study individuals and do so with a full range of potential factors from the biological, personal, interpersonal, community, and sociological-cultural arenas.

Worth Remembering

1. PCC seeks to understand the personal, interpersonal, social, and situational variables associated with criminal conduct. There are different types of covariates: simple correlates, predictors, dynamic risk factors (criminogenic needs), and causal variables.

2. Different research designs yield different types of covariates. Cross-sectional research designs identify correlates; longitudinal designs yield information on predictors; multi-wave longitudinal designs identify dynamic risk factors; and randomized experiments provide the highest level of knowledge: causal variables. Knowledge of the causes of criminal behavior has the potential to develop interventions that may reduce criminal conduct.

3. Testing the null hypothesis through statistical significance is falling out of favor.

4. A very handy and powerful way of describing the strength of the covariates of criminal behavior is the Pearson Product Moment Coefficient, or r. The r may be also interpreted through the Binomial Effect Size Display (BESD). BESD is the difference in the percentage of cases criminal in one condition (e.g., high risk) compared to the percentage criminal in another condition (e.g., low risk).

5. The Pearson Product Moment Coefficient (r) is not without limitations, especially when base rates and selection ratios are at the extremes. Therefore, the Area Under the Curve (AUC) measure is often used in studies of risk scales because it is unaffected by base rates and selection ratios.

6. A meta-analysis is a quantitative review of the literature. The results from primary studies are converted into a common metric or effect size and averaged. With the addition of the confidence interval (CI), we come closer to estimating the "true" relationship.

7. The covariates of criminal behavior, regardless of their type (e.g., predictors, causal variables), will often depend on other variables. These are called moderator variables.

8. There is a direct connection between individual differences in criminal behavior and aggregated crime rates, but one must be cautious when interpreting findings at the aggregate level with reference to individual differences.

Recommended Readings

Perhaps the most straightforward and understandable introduction to experimental design is the classic book by Donald Campbell and Julian Stanley, *Experimental and Quasi-Experimental Designs for Research*. Although it is long out of print (published in 1966), a PDF version is available online at: (http://moodle.technion.ac.il/pluginfile.php/367640/mod_resource/content/1/Donald_T._(Donald_T._Campbell)_Campbell,_Julian_Stanley-Experimental_and_Quasi-Experimental_Designs_for_Research-Wadsworth_Publishing(1963)%20(1).pdf).

For introductions to the significance testing debate the reader is directed to two articles. The first by Charles Lambdin (2012) gives a sharp and acerbic critique of 70 years of psychological and statistical research that has promoted significance testing. The second article by Paul Gendreau and Paula Smith (2007) is also written in a similar vein but focuses on the importance of meta-analysis to influence correctional policy and practice.

Finally, for the reader interested in a more comprehensive presentation of statistics used in prediction (e.g., AUC, Cohen's d, and meta-analysis), Karl Hanson's *Prediction Statistics for Psychological Assessment* (2022) is highly recommended.

 Visit the Instructor and Student Resource to access additional exercises, videos and study materials to support this chapter: psychologycriminalconduct.routledge.com

CHAPTER 3 From Criminology Theories to a Psychological Perspective of Criminal Conduct

The search for theoretical understanding is a search for general, rational, simple, and empirically accurate explanations of variation in criminal behavior. General explanations are ones that apply to a number of specific observations. For example, a general theory of criminal conduct will account for variation in both violent and nonviolent offenses, and will do so for men and women of different ages, races, nationalities, and socioeconomic origins.

Rational explanations are ones that withstand logical analyses, and are internally and externally consistent. *Internal consistency* refers to how well the assumptions and explanatory variables fit together within a theory. *External consistency* refers to how well a theory fits with other scientific theories. For example, a theory of criminal behavior may make internally consistent use of certain biological assumptions, but it would be less than satisfactory if those assumptions were at odds with reasonably well-established theory in the broader biological sciences. Simple explanations are ones that make relatively few assumptions.

The most important aspect of theoretical understanding, however, has to do with the empirical support for the theory. Here, we are especially interested in cause. Theories try to explain the relationships among the variables of interest and, as Hunter and Schmidt (1996) point out, these explanations are always causal. In PCC, a practical goal is the rehabilitation of justice-involved persons, and you can only treat effectively by knowing the mechanisms of behavior. By focusing on the causal variables suggested by theory, we have the potential to influence criminal activity through deliberate interventions. For example, does the delivery of intervention programs aimed at improving family relationships actually reduce criminal futures?

Before outlining the General Personality and Cognitive Social Learning (GPCSL) theory, the psychological perspective of criminal conduct used in this text, a brief overview of some of the important criminological theories that influenced GPCSL is in order. Many of the criminological perspectives,

DOI: 10.4324/9781003292128-4

in their original formulations, situated the root cause of crime in one's disadvantageous position in society. That is, crime is a product of poverty, social class, race, or some other indicator of social location. Societal imbalance and injustice are seen as the cause of crime. The criminological theories have much to say about criminal conduct, but they do not give a complete and empirically satisfying explanation. There are also psychopathological theories that view criminal behavior as inherent to the person and see the cause of crime as a psychological disturbance. However, a fuller discussion of psychopathological theories is reserved for Chapter 5. We begin with the criminological theories.

Criminological Theories

From the 1930s to the 1980s, the dominant criminological theories took on a class-based sociological perspective of delinquency. Noteworthy are strain theory, subcultural theory, labeling, and Marxist/conflict theory. These theories hypothesized that social class of origin is a major source of variation in illegal conduct at the individual level. However, as the evidence grew showing that social class was a relatively minor correlate of criminal behavior (see Resource Note 3.1), some of the theories evolved to include social-psychological factors. Other criminological theories—control theory and differential association—did not locate the cause of crime in social class but in the failure by the immediate community to ensure conformity to prosocial norms.

RESOURCE NOTE 3.1

Social Class and Crime

Perhaps no single variable has been more important in criminological theorizing than social class. Many of the major sociological theories of crime and delinquency were theories of crime in the lower social classes. The origins of crime were to be found in being lower class, disadvantaged, poor, and frustrated in trying to acquire what the middle and upper classes have.

Tittle, Villimez, and Smith (1978) were the first to question the strength of the class–crime link through a meta-analysis of 35 studies that examined the class–crime link at the *individual* level, thus avoiding the ecological fallacy (Technical Note 2.2 on the textbook website at psychologycriminalconduct.routledge.com). Studies that characterized individuals in traditional measures (personal or familial, occupational, educational, and income) of socioeconomic status (SES), as well as the class structure of their areas of residence, were included. The important question is whether decreases in SES are associated with increases in the proportion of criminals.

continued

The 35 studies yielded 363 effect size estimates for various combinations of sex, race, and other factors. Tittle et al. used the gamma coefficient to calculate their effect size, but one can interpret it similarly to an r. The average effect size was −0.09, a relatively modest relationship between class and crime. In addition, the mean effect sizes were in the same range for men (−0.08) and women (−0.11), and for whites (−0.07) and nonwhites (−0.01). Tittle and his associates recognized that some of the individual effect sizes were strong and negative, even though the average effect size was weak. Similarly, some effect size estimates were actually positive in sign, suggesting that, under some circumstances, increases in SES were associated with higher, rather than lower, levels of criminality (a finding opposite to that predicted by class-based theories).

Further analyses found that the class–crime relationship did not depend on the type of offense (e.g., violent, nonviolent). However, the magnitude of the association did vary with how criminality was measured (self-report versus official records) and with the decade in which the study was completed. The mean effect size from the self-report studies was small (−0.06) but larger (−0.25) for studies of official records. The relatively large effect size for official records was traced to studies conducted prior to the 1970s. Before 1950, the mean effect size was a whopping −0.73 but then diminished. After 1970, the effect size dropped to +0.004. On the other hand, the effect sizes based on self-reported criminality were relatively constant over time and small in magnitude (ranging from −0.03 to −0.11). This was interpreted to mean that in the 1970s there was essentially no relationship between class and criminality as evidenced by the marginal effect size estimates for both self-reported and official measures of crime. One may have existed prior to 1950, but that may have reflected criminal justice processing effects rather than criminality (thus explaining the large effect size in the early studies when official measures of crime were used).

Tittle et al.'s (1978) general findings have been replicated by a number of reviews of the literature post 1978 (Gendreau, Little, & Goggin, 1996; Katsiyannis, Whitford, Zhang, & Gage, 2018; Tittle & Meier, 1991) and by more direct tests of the class–crime link (Dunaway, Cullen, Burton, & Evans, 2000; Savage, Ellis, & Wozniak, 2019). However, recognizing a weak class–crime link does not dismiss the real problems of the poor, nor does it deny the existence of high-crime neighborhoods. What the recognition of a weak class–crime link does is to remind students, scholars, and policymakers that the socioeconomic context makes a minor contribution to variation in crime, relative to a host of other personal, interpersonal, familial, and structural/cultural variables, including the immediate situation of action.

There are other approaches to understanding the relationship between crime and class. One approach is to specify the possible conditions under which a relationship may exist by focusing upon the levels of disposable income available to individuals at particular periods of time. What are the implications of having some loose change in your pocket or purse? Some American (e.g., Wright, Cullen, & Williams, 2002) and British (e.g., West & Farrington, 1977) studies suggest that relative wealth in the immediate sense is a correlate of juvenile delinquency. However, it is the delinquent who tends to have more money than the nondelinquent.

Strain Theory

One of the earliest examples of strain theory is Robert Merton's (1938, 1957) theory of limited opportunity. Merton hypothesized that social structures exert a strain upon certain persons to engage in deviant behavior. Deviant behavior is said to occur because the lower social class has limited opportunities to achieve the goals of society. In America, the dominant aspiration to which all people are socialized (or which people come to share) was said to be "success" (money, property, and prestige). Anyone can grow up to be president, and the legitimate route to success is working hard in school and on the job. The power of this aspect of the theory is clear because it is nothing less than the collective myth of the "American dream" (Lamont, 2019). Counter to the dream, however, is the fact that access to the best schools and well-paying jobs are unavailable for many members of the lower class. Thus, criminal behavior was conceptualized as an innovative route to the same rewards that conventional employment would bring if only legitimate channels were available. Instead of labeling those in conflict with the law as deviant, Merton called them "innovators."

Innovation (i.e., crime) was not the only way to adapt to limited opportunities. The other adaptations were retreatism (mental disorder and substance misuse among the real "down and out" of society), rebellion (attempts to create a new social order on the part of the more able and intellectual within the lower class), and ritualism (the mindless grinding away of the working poor who have transferred the dream to that of their children "making it").

The notions of anomie and strain enter as mediating variables between the disjunction of legitimate means and the pursuit of illegitimate means. For traditional strain theorists, the psychological mediator is anomie. That is, feelings of alienation arise from limited opportunities and become the motivation for crime. For these theorists, criminal behavior reflects awareness of limited opportunity and feelings of alienation, isolation, powerlessness, normlessness, and personal distress.

In 1992, Robert Agnew (1992) de-emphasized the role of social class in the path to deviance with a more psychological explanation. Frustrations and difficulties at home (e.g., abusive parental discipline), school (e.g., conflictual relationships with teachers), and work (e.g., frequent unemployment) are the indicators of a strain–crime link. Agnew calls his perspective *general strain theory* (GST), and the sources of negative affect (that is, anger rather than alienation) extend well beyond an aspiration–achievement discrepancy in the arena of conventional success. GST has taken on a more psychological explanation of crime with a particular interest in negative emotionality and personality characteristics such as low self-control (Agnew, 2012; Agnew & Brezina, 2019).

Subcultural Perspectives

Subcultural theorists spoke primarily of young, lower-class men who conformed to the lower-class subculture in which they were located. As in limited opportunity theory, persons in the lower class are excluded from the mainstream culture, and as a reaction, a subculture is formed. This culture devalued conventional routes to success and valued hedonism and destruction. While Merton's people were allowed to "innovate," within subcultural theory, criminal behavior is conformity. Stealing was conforming to the criminal subculture, using drugs was conforming to the retreatist subculture, and fighting was conforming to the conflict subculture.

Cohen (1955) examined the content of the values and norms said to be dominant in deviant subcultures. He suggested that criminal subcultures shared procriminal attitudes and values in direct opposition to such middle-class values as delayed gratification and respect for property. That is, the major values were immediate gratification and short-term hedonism, hostility, and aggression. Furthermore, dropping out of school and not working were seen as acts of defiance toward middle-class values. Miller (1958) was still more informative in his specification of the content of procriminal sentiments. He viewed the following "focal concerns" as peculiar to the lower classes: trouble (generalized difficulty), toughness (physical prowess, "masculinity," daring), smartness (outsmarting others), autonomy (independence, not being bossed), fatalism (luck), and excitement (thrills, danger). One can see that having such values and attitudes can lead to conflict with the rules of mainstream society.

Just as Agnew distanced strain theories from social class, Matza (1964) became concerned that the class–subculture link was an inadequate explanation of crime. It appeared to overpredict delinquency among the young lower-class males and it did not account for the delinquency of occupants of higher social positions. The solution to this problem was to give credit to psychological factors. Matza referred to an "impetus" that realizes the criminal act. This impetus comes from being pushed around, which then leads to a mood of fatalism and a feeling of desperation. Not everyone is exposed to and affected by this impetus, but for those affected, engaging in delinquent behavior serves to overcome these feelings and provide a sense of control and power.

Sykes and Matza (1957) were less inclined than subcultural theorists to accept the image of the delinquent as one committed to criminal values. They suggested that delinquents know that certain acts, if detected, will be punished. However, they are enabled to act antisocially by engaging a set of verbalizations that function to say that, in particular situations, it is "OK" to violate the law (referred to as "techniques of neutralization"). Note that these verbalizations may be used prior to action and may be considered causal. Their use is not limited to deflecting blame or controlling guilt after an offense has occurred.

Labeling and Marxist/Conflict Theories

Labeling theory and the Marxist/conflict theories see crime as a result of the powerful in society selecting the less powerful (the poor and minorities) for official criminal justice processing (i.e., being arrested, appearing in court, going to prison). It is the upper classes that make the rules of society, and everyone breaks these rules, but not everyone is subjected to criminal justice processing (Becker, 1963; Schur, 1973). It is the disadvantaged in society who are targeted by the criminal justice system. In labeling theory, once processing begins, the offender develops a self-image of being a criminal (called "secondary deviance"). If one believes he/she is a criminal, then he/she begins to act like a criminal and a self-fulfilling prophecy is launched. Note that labeling theory begins with class location but quickly turns into a psychological, cognitive process. The best way to manage crime, according to labeling theorists, is to do less. Later in the book, we will see that minimizing contact with the criminal justice system can be the right thing to do, but not for all who come into contact with the justice system.

Control Theories

In the control theories, the crucial explanatory issue is "why *don't* we violate the law?" rather than "why *do* we violate the law?" In brief, it is conformity rather than deviance that must be explained.

Walter Reckless (1967) suggested that there were both outer and inner sources of control. The external controls were social pressures to conform, and the strength of these controls would increase with a sense of belonging to prosocial groups. These groups include the family, social clubs, schools, and religious organizations. "Inner containment" is Reckless' term for what psychologists call self-control, and he listed five indicators of inner control:

1. Positive self-concept that involves not only self-esteem but also seeing one-self as conventional as opposed to criminal.

2. A commitment to long-range, legitimate goals.

3. Setting realistic objectives.

4. High tolerance for frustration.

5. Identification with lawfulness and respect for the law.

From the perspective of sociological theorizing, the major theoretical significance of Reckless' theory was that the social networks of young people constituted something more than socioeconomic status and subcultural membership. He also gave ascendancy to psychological mechanisms related to internal control and to the recognition of individual differences in socialization.

Travis Hirschi's *Causes of Delinquency* (1969), a classic cross-sectional study (recall Chapter 2), assumed that there are individual differences in morality. For Hirschi, the moral ties consist of attachment, commitment, involvement, and belief in the validity of the law:

1. Attachment to (or caring about) the opinions of family, teachers, and peers.

2. Commitment to conventional pursuits involves increasing the risk of losing one's investment should deviance be detected.

3. Involvement in conventional pursuits reduces delinquency simply by the limited time available for deviant pursuits.

4. Belief in validity of the law refers to individual differences in the extent to which people believe they should obey the rules.

Noteworthy is that Hirschi's ideas involve rejection of the causal significance of social class. Able to draw upon the post-1950s research evidence, Hirschi acknowledged that class was at best a weak correlate of delinquency. Surprisingly, Hirschi downplayed the role of delinquent associates, which is the empirically weakest of his theoretical positions. In his own survey, the students were asked, "Have any of your close friends ever been picked up by the police?" Of those who answered that they had no friends picked up by the police, only 7 percent were delinquents. However, for those who answered that they had four or more friends known to the police, 45 percent were delinquents. Hirschi's four-factor theory places an overemphasis on ties to convention, underemphasizes ties to crime (only procriminal attitudes are included and procriminal associates are excluded), and relegates the temperamental/personality variables such as self-control, taste for adventure, and hostility to background factors with unspecified linkages to either crime or convention.

In 1990, in collaboration with Michael Gottfredson (Gottfredson & Hirschi, 1990), Travis Hirschi further modified his views. Ties to convention and procriminal attitudes (belief in the illegitimacy of the law) were minimized, and self-control was emphasized. Gottfredson and Hirschi's (1990) "general theory of crime" suggests that *one* construct, low self-control, accounts for stable individual differences in criminal behavior.

Hirschi's control theory has continued to evolve (Gottfredson & Hirschi, 2020; Hirschi, 2004). In the early 1990s self-control was "the tendency to avoid acts whose long-term costs exceed their monetary advantages" (Hirschi, 2004: p. 542). Apparently, every day people calculate the long-term costs in advance of the moment of behavioral action (in some ways, an economics rational man type of theory). However, in 2004 Hirschi refined self-control as "the tendency to consider the full range of potential costs of a particular act" (p. 543). Now cause (low self-control) and effect (criminal activity) are at least contemporaneous. This is to be preferred over an effect that precedes the cause. In addition, by considering the "full range of potential acts," social bonds return to control theory (e.g., the costs of losing friendships). More will be said on self-control in Chapter 5 (Antisocial Personality Pattern).

Differential Association Theory

There is much of immediate value within differential association theory (Sutherland, 1939; Sutherland & Cressey, 1970). Simply stated, a person becomes delinquent because of an excess of "definitions" favorable to violation of law over "definitions" unfavorable to violations of law. Furthermore, the importance of procriminal associates resides in a fundamental theoretical principle: criminal behavior is learned by associations with criminal and prosocial others, and the principal part of that learning occurs in interaction with other persons in a process of intimate communication (Sutherland, 1947). Thus, the causal chain in classical differential association theory is from procriminal associates to the acquisition of procriminal attitudes to criminal behavior in particular situations (Cullen, Wright, Gendreau, & Andrews, 2003; Salisbury, 2013).

When a theory identifies powerful correlates of criminal conduct that are readily validated empirically, it deserves serious attention. Interest increases further when the theory has obvious practical value for purposes of prediction and prevention. An attractive aspect of differential association theory is the inclusion of two well-validated correlates of criminal conduct: procriminal attitudes and procriminal associates. This evidence is highly relevant to differential association because a central causal assumption of differential association is that criminal acts reflect cognitions favorable to criminal activity. Every perspective on crime reviewed gives causal status to procriminal attitudes. Even Merton's original statements regarding structurally induced anomie were qualified by a footnote to the effect that alienation would not lead to criminal acts if there were internalized prohibitions against law violation.

Summary of Criminological Theories

Social location was, for many criminological theories (e.g., limited opportunity, subcultural, labeling/Marxist/conflict), at the root of crime. The strain and frustration of not being able to achieve success through legitimate means pushed some to pursue illegitimate ways to obtain success, to create subcultures where the behavioral expectations could be more easily achieved, or to accept and act upon the label of criminal. From a practical perspective, the major risk factor was socioeconomic status (as indicated by income, race, age, and gender), and the prevention of crime was the redistribution of wealth and equality, especially in access to work and education.

For the control theorists and the later strain theorists, social class is a minor consideration. Crime is a failure to develop control over behavior, and the control comes from oneself and our social network (e.g., parents, teachers, employers). Here the major risk factors are poor self-control, disturbed interpersonal relationships with family and friends, and poor educational and work success. With these theories, compared to the social location theories, there is a wider range of possibilities for assessment and intervention. And finally, we have differential association theory. In differential association theory, those with whom we associate and what we think are key to understanding criminal behavior. The major risk factors are procriminal associates and procriminal thinking, and if we are to intervene, then we must target these two risk factors. Reducing interactions with delinquents and increasing interactions with pro-social individuals is the goal of treatment, but on exactly how to do this, differential association theory is silent. The "how" of change is left to the principles of learning in a social learning psychology of criminal conduct.

Toward a General Theory in PCC: Social Learning Theory and Criminal Behavior

Social learning theory advances the "how" of change in accordance with well-established principles of learning. These principles will be described shortly in the section entitled *The Principles of Learning and Criminal Behavior*. In addition, most of behavior is learned within a social context. One of the earliest examples of the application of a social learning perspective is the reformulation of Freud's frustration–aggression hypothesis by Dollard and his colleagues (Dollard, Miller, Doob, Mowrer, & Sears, 1939). Instead of aggression being an unlearned response to frustration (Freud's view), Dollard and his colleagues argued that aggression is a response to frustration *if* aggression was rewarded in the past. Furthermore, as a result of consequences to behavior, other responses to frustration may occur (e.g., one works harder to deal with the frustration, asks for help).

Albert Bandura, more than any other psychologist, established social learning theory as the dominant perspective in psychology to explain the acquisition and maintenance of behavior (Bandura, 1969, 1989). He rejected attempts to marry psychoanalytic theory with a learning approach and criticized learning theories for minimizing the importance of observational learning (Bandura & Walters, 1963). This latter idea of watching a model performing a task and what happens as a consequence is extremely important. Learning through observation requires internal cognitions and information processing in order to anticipate the consequences for behavior. Thus, Bandura rejected the radical behaviorism of Skinner. With the introduction of his concept of self-efficacy (i.e., beliefs in one's abilities; Bandura, 1977), the transformation to a social-cognitive theory was complete (Bandura, 1986).

In criminology, Sutherland clearly saw the value of social-cognitive learning (i.e., learning of "definitions" in social groups). However, he was unable to articulate the mechanisms of learning. Unfortunately, Sutherland promoted criminology as a sub-discipline of sociology and he not only minimized the contributions of psychology but was also quite hostile toward biosocial explanations of criminal behavior (Laub & Sampson, 1991; Wright & Miller, 1998). Burgess and Akers (1966), however, addressed the weakness in Sutherland's theory and at the same time revitalized a social-psychological perspective within criminology by arguing that differential reinforcement is the learning mechanism for criminal behavior. That is, criminal groups that model and reward procriminal attitudes and behaviors outweigh reinforcements for prosocial behaviors. Akers later introduced macrosocial factors such as social disorganization that have their own influence in the micro differential reinforcement mechanisms. His social structure social learning theory became very influential within criminology (Akers & Jennings, 2016).

A General Personality and Cognitive Social Learning Theory of Criminal Conduct

General Personality and Cognitive Social Learning (GPCSL) has many similarities to the social learning perspectives just described. GPCSL also assumes that criminal behavior is a learned behavior, it is learned within a social context, and the learning follows established principles. It is different from Akers' theory in that temperamental and personality factors play a larger role. Thus, GPCSL is more in the tradition of Bandura's theorizing.

We begin our presentation of the GPCSL theory by directing the reader's attention to Figure 3.1. In this figure, the major psycho-social-biological factors that influence and maintain criminal behavior are schematically summarized. The model recognizes that there are multiple routes to involvement in illegal conduct. Just because the model identifies personality/temperament and family relationships as correlates of criminal behavior, it does not assume, for example, that all young offenders are restless or aggressive, or that all young offenders are weakly tied to their parents.

GPCSL theory gives salience to what is called the Central Eight risk/need factors. They are (1) criminal history, (2) procriminal attitudes, (3) procriminal

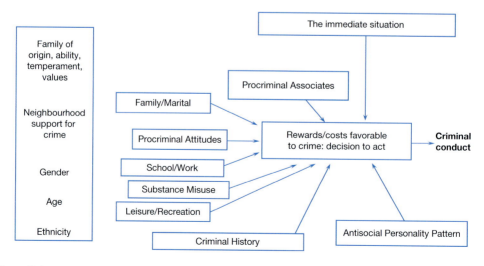

Figure 3.1

A General Personality and Cognitive Social Learning Perspective

associates, (4) antisocial personality pattern, (5) family/marital, (6) school/work, (7) substance misuse, and (8) leisure/recreation. This is a far cry from Hirschi's single factor theory of poor self-control or any other theory that attempts to explain criminal behavior by one or two constructs. The Central Eight risk/need factors are described more fully in Table 3.1, but it is important to note

---

TABLE 3.1 The Central Eight Risk/Need Factors

1. **Criminal History**. This includes early involvement in a number and variety of criminal activities across a range of settings, such as in the home and outside of the home. Major indicators include being arrested at a young age, a large number of prior offenses, and rule violations while on conditional release.
   Strength: Criminal behavior is absent or so rare that criminal acts contribute minimally to procriminal attitudes.
   Dynamic need and promising intermediate targets of change: A history cannot be changed, but appropriate intermediate targets of change include building up new noncriminal behaviors in high-risk situations and building self-efficacy beliefs supporting rehabilitation.

2. **Procriminal Attitudes**. This set of variables includes attitudes, values, beliefs, rationalizations, and thoughts that are favorable to crime. The cognitive-emotional states associated with crime are anger and feeling irritated, resentful, and/or defiant. Specific indicators would include identification with criminals, negative attitudes toward the law and justice system, a belief that crime will yield rewards, and rationalizations that specify a broad range of conditions under which crime is justified (e.g., the victim deserved it, the victim is worthless).
   Strength: Rejects procriminal sentiments; personal identity is explicitly prosocial.
   Dynamic need and promising intermediate targets of change: The procriminal attitudes and cognitions are subject to change through reduction of procriminal thinking and through building and practicing prosocial thoughts.

3. **Procriminal Associates**. This risk/need factor includes both association with procriminal others and relative isolation from prosocial others.
   Strength: Close and frequent association with prosocial others; no association with criminal others.
   Dynamic need and promising intermediate targets of change: This factor is dynamic, and the appropriate intermediate targets are reduce association with procriminal others and enhance association with prosocial others.

4. **Antisocial Personality Pattern**. In everyday language: impulsive, adventurous, pleasure-seeking, generalized trouble (multiple victims, multiple settings), restlessly aggressive, callous disregard for others.
   Strength: High self-control and good problem-solving skills.
   Dynamic need and promising intermediate targets of change: Increase self-management skills, build empathy, anger management and improve problem-solving skills.

5. **Family/Marital**. The key to assessing both family of origin for young people and marital circumstances for older people is the quality of the interpersonal relationships within the unit (parent–child or partner–partner) and the behavioral expectations and rules in regard to criminal behavior, including monitoring, supervision, and disciplinary approaches.
   Strength: Strong nurturance and caring in combination with strong monitoring and supervision.
   Dynamic need and promising intermediate targets of change: Reduce conflict, build positive relationships, enhance monitoring and supervision.

continued

TABLE 3.1 *(Continued)*

6. **School/Work**. Emphasis is on the quality of the interpersonal relationships within the settings of school and/or work. Generally, the risk/need factors are low levels of performance and rewarding involvement and satisfactions.

 Strength: Strong attachments to fellow students/colleagues along with authority figures in combination with high levels of performance and satisfaction at school/work.

 Dynamic need and promising intermediate targets of change: Enhance performance, involvement, and rewards and satisfactions.

7. **Substance Misuse**. Problems with alcohol and/or other drugs (tobacco excluded). *Current* problems with substances indicate higher risk than a prior history of abuse.

 Strengths: No evidence of risky substance misuse, and sentiments tend to be negative toward substance use.

 Dynamic need and promising intermediate targets of change: Reduce substance misuse, reduce the personal and interpersonal supports for substance-oriented behavior, enhance alternatives to substance misuse.

8. **Leisure/Recreation**. Low levels of involvement and satisfactions in prosocial leisure pursuits.

 Strength: High levels of involvement in and satisfactions in prosocial leisure pursuits.

 Dynamic need and promising intermediate targets of change: Enhance involvement and rewards and satisfactions.

Note that Table 3.1 includes seven *dynamic* risk factors (that is, criminogenic need factors). This is important for two reasons: 1) assessing dynamic risk factors with multi-wave assessments over time permits the monitoring of changes in risk and need, and 2) these criminogenic needs serve as appropriate intermediate targets of change when an ultimate interest is reducing future offending (i.e., potential causal factors). The positive extremes of risk are listed as strengths.

that all of these factors influence the decision to behave criminally. In the first five editions of *The Psychology of Criminal Conduct*, a distinction was made between the first four risk/need factors, called the "Big Four," and the remaining "Moderate Four." This was based on findings from prediction studies, mostly with general offenders, where the first four factors displayed higher effect sizes than the other four factors. However, research from the past decade with adults (Goodley, Pearson, & Morris, 2022; Katsyiannis, Whitford, Zhang, & Gage, 2018; Olver, Stockdale, & Wormith, 2014), youth (Grieger & Hosser, 2014; Scott & Brown, 2018), the mentally disordered (Bonta, Blais, & Wilson, 2014; Eisenberg, Van Horn, et al., 2019), racial minorities (Gutierrez, Wilson, Rugge, & Bonta, 2013), illicit drug users (Wooditch, Tang, & Taxman, 2014), and a combination of the aforementioned (Pratt, Cullen, et al., 2010) have not found this demarcation between the Big Four and Moderate Four. Nevertheless, the Central Eight risk/need factors are consistently observed across the meta-analytic reviews. Therefore, in the sixth edition presentation of the Big Four was replaced with the Central Eight and remains so in the present edition.

The specification of a history of criminal behavior notes the importance of not equating risk of offending with seriousness of the current offense. The indicators of risk are early involvement, an extensive history, a variety of antisocial activities (nonviolent plus violent offenses), and rule violations while under supervision (e.g., parole violations). A major error in assessment is to score seriousness of the current offense as a risk factor. It is not a major risk factor in and of itself. A serious and violent offense becomes an important risk factor when it is combined with a history of violence. The seriousness of the current offense, however, is an aggravating factor in sentencing (in the sense that the more serious the injury imposed by an offense, the more severe the penalty). Just punishment and risk of reoffending reflect different concerns.

The description of Antisocial Personality Pattern (APP) uses everyday language (a more precise language will be described in subsequent chapters). APP in regard to risk/need typically involves at least two relatively independent dimensions. One is weak self-control and a lack of planning. The second is negative emotionality (in the sense of irritability, feeling mistreated, and being antagonistic). It is important to note that the trait measures of APP assess these predispositions as relatively stable, enduring factors. However, self-control and negative emotionality may also be assessed as acute dynamic factors. Acute changes, such as an angry outburst, are highly important in a GPCSL understanding of variation in criminal activity.

Finally, the personality research is very helpful in identifying factors that have very little to offer in understanding individual differences in criminal activity. Considering so many misunderstandings of crime and criminals that are widely and actively promoted, it is quite helpful to attend to those aspects of personality that are *not* associated with criminal activity in a major way. These weak noncriminogenic factors include happiness, self-esteem, sociability, feelings of anxiety and worry, and psychopathology. We will be returning to these issues throughout the text because misunderstandings of those involved in the criminal justice system are so common. It appears that some happy people break the law, but many do not; some sad people commit crimes, but many sad people do not; and so on.

Reflecting on Figure 3.1 and considering the Central Eight risk/need factors the reader will observe that the chances of illegal conduct for an individual increase dramatically as the number of the Central Eight factors increase. GPCSL also suggests that procriminal attitudes and associates may be particularly important risk factors as reflected in the proximity of these two variables in the decision to act criminally. A meta-analysis focusing on core variables within social learning theory did find large effect sizes for attitudes and procriminal associations (Pratt, Cullen, et al., 2010). It is premature to speak of a "Big Two" without confirmatory evidence. However, when we turn to our discussion of rehabilitation in later chapters, an argument can be made that these two risk/need factors may indeed have added practical relevance over the other Central Eight factors.

Immediate causal significance is assigned to the cognitive decision to commit a criminal act. Some theorists speak of "definitions favorable to law violation" (Sutherland, 1947), others of "self-efficacy beliefs" (Bandura, 1989), "behavioral intentions" (Ajzen, 2020; Ajzen & Fishbein, 1980), and "the balance of rewards and costs" (Andrews & Bonta, 2010a). It remains to be seen whether operational distinctions among assessments of these variables may be differentiated in construct validity studies. The main problem for the field may be to settle on a common vocabulary. So far, assessments of behavioral intentions and self-efficacy beliefs have impressive predictive validities in many different situations (Ajzen, 2011; Ajzen & Cote, 2008; Bandura, Caprara, Barbaranelli, Regalia, & Scabini, 2011; De Buck & Pauwels, 2019; Johnston, Brezina, & Crank, 2019; Walters, 2018a, 2022).

The major sources of variation in judgments of appropriateness and the decision to act are a combination of the immediate environment and many of the Central Eight risk/need factors. The immediate environment consists of facilitators and obstacles to criminal conduct. For example, a person is less likely to steal a car if it is locked rather than unlocked. The person scans the environment as part of judging whether or not a certain behavior will be rewarded. Of course, if the attitudes and cognitions held by the person are supportive of criminal behavior, there is social support for the behavior (either perceived and/or direct assistance), there is a history of having engaged in criminal behavior, and the person has relatively stable personality characteristics conducive to antisocial conduct (e.g., anger and poor self-control), then the decision to act criminally becomes very likely.

Where do social class, social structure, and culture fit into this general personality and cognitive social learning of crime? Because they are constants, they are distal background contextual conditions that cannot account for variation in individual conduct within particular social arrangements such as social class. Not everyone in the lower social class is a criminal. What explains the variability in criminal conduct is the distribution of the Central Eight risk/need factors in interaction with the reward–cost contingencies that are in effect within each particular social arrangement. An understanding of how rewards and costs modify and maintain behavior follows.

The Principles of Learning and Criminal Behavior

GPCSL assumes with other varieties of social learning theories that all behavior, including criminal behavior, is learned. Having identified the major social and interpersonal sources of criminal conduct (i.e., the Central Eight), the question then becomes, how is criminal behavior learned within these settings? The answer lies in the principles of learning, and here the concepts of rewards and costs are fundamental. A reward is any stimulus that increases the probability of behavior, and a cost decreases the likelihood of behavior. Note that the word "cost" is used rather than "punishment" in order to avoid unnecessary negative emotions associated with the word. We usually think of rewards and costs *following* a behavior (referred to as operant conditioning by psychologists). For example, an employer may give a financial bonus to an employee for working particularly hard, or a parent may scold a child for not sharing a toy. However, our cognitive ability to anticipate an outcome brings the control of a reward or cost *before* the behavior, influencing the likelihood of the behavior occurring. This type of learning is usually the result of experiences that associate a behavior with rewards or costs (Pavlovian or classical conditioning). We call these *signaled* rewards and costs and they reflect the internal, cognitive control of behavior. We may turn off our cell phone when entering a theater because in the past others in the audience shouted at us when our phone rang. Entering the theater signals that turning off the cell phone will avoid a potential cost.

Models also serve as signaled rewards and costs. For example, we are more likely to jaywalk after watching another do it if that model is expensively dressed as opposed to being shabbily dressed. All behavior, criminal or not, is under the control of rewards and costs that come either prior to the behavior or after it. In any situation, the contingencies of rewards and costs are responsible for the acquisition, maintenance, and modification of human behavior. It is also important to note the important role that internal thinking processes play in learning. For signaled rewards and costs to control behavior the formation of memories is necessary. Memories store information (rewards and costs associated with behavior) for later use. Most psychologists and cognitive scientists follow an information processing model of memory that follows three basic steps. First, to form memories one must attend to the behavior and the outcomes. Second, the information must be retained, usually through rehearsal and practice. Finally, the information is retrieved when needed. As this discussion highlights, humans think, and that is why "cognitive" is in GPCSL theory.

The antecedents and consequences are of two major types: additive events (rewards/costs are introduced, extended, or augmented) and subtractive events (rewards/costs are withdrawn, postponed, or diminished). Additive rewards are consequences that add something pleasing to the environment (e.g., delivering praise to a child for a valued act). Subtractive rewards are consequences that remove something unpleasant (e.g., the chances of an assault recurring will increase if the assault was successful in stopping someone from behaving undesirably). Additive costs augment or add something unpleasant (e.g., a slap on the face for an unwanted kiss). Subtractive costs remove pleasantness (e.g., feeling sick after drinking excessively). The point to remember is that a reward leads to an increased likelihood of the behavior reoccurring while a cost decreases the chances. Resource Note 3.2 provides an example of additive and subtractive rewards in operation.

RESOURCE NOTE 3.2

Case Study: The Simultaneous Operation of Additive and Subtractive Rewards

Julia was sentenced to 30 days in jail for prostitution and possession of drugs. She was 19 years old, and this was her first time in jail. Upon entry to jail, Julia was processed like all the other admissions: fingerprints were taken, a medical checkup completed, and a brief social history recorded. Nothing out of the ordinary was noted.

continued

On the first check of the nightly rounds, a correctional officer found Julia semi-conscious and bleeding from the forearms. Earlier that day she had asked for a razor to shave her legs. The razor had not been collected, and she used it that night to cut her forearms. Julia was given prompt medical attention. Except for a few stitches, the physical harm Julia inflicted upon herself was minor.

The next day Julia was interviewed by the psychologist for a suicidal assessment. Julia was somewhat surprised that the staff thought she was suicidal and denied any intention of killing herself. "It was just one of those things," she said. That night, once again, she was found bleeding, having cut her arm with her eyeglasses (she took the glass out of the rim). Even though the cuts were superficial, staff members were alarmed. She was placed in the hospital ward under 24-hour nursing care.

Frequently, behavior such as Julia's is seen as a "call for help" or a "search for attention." Suicidal gestures often bring a great deal of attention from others and, for someone who is terribly lonely, the reinforcing properties can be powerful. When Julia was seen again by the psychologist, the working hypothesis was that the slashes to the forearm produced "interpersonal additive rewards" (i.e., attention from others).

What was surprising was that the behavior also brought subtractive rewards (i.e., the removal of unpleasant stimuli). On the second interview, Julia was more relaxed and open. She revealed a life of physical and sexual abuse, extreme poverty, and addiction to cocaine. She also reported that she had, in the past, cut her forearms when feeling particularly anxious. As painful as this was, it created a distraction from her problems. While watching the blood ooze out of her cut, for the moment her mind was not dwelling on her horrendous life. As the blood continued to flow, she felt a sense of relaxation and peacefulness (no doubt brought on by the gradual loss of blood). Finally, she could drift off to a sleep that would re-energize her to face a new day when she awoke.

There are no universal rewards and costs that work for everyone in all situations. What may be a reward for one person may be a cost for the next person. What may be a powerful reward for one individual may mean little for another. A masochist may enjoy physical pain but not a non-masochist. A hundred dollars may be very motivating to a person with no money but not for the millionaire. What acts as a reward or cost depends on a range of factors. They include genetic disposition and capability (e.g., the rewarding power of cocaine may be dependent on the presence of certain neuro-receptors), cognitive functioning (e.g., a cost occurring days later requires the ability to think in the long term), human development (e.g., a cookie is more effective than a dollar for a one-year-old), and state conditions (e.g., scolding is less effective when the person is intoxicated than when the individual is sober). There are many physical and cognitive characteristics of the person that influence the capability to respond and learn. Sometimes these person factors are permanent (e.g., brain damage), sometimes they are transitory (e.g., developmental and maturational changes), and sometimes they are acute (e.g., intoxication; feeling mistreated in a particular moment in a particular situation).

B. F. Skinner recognized that rewards and costs may operate on different "schedules." A reward or cost may follow every occurrence of the behavior (e.g., pain every time you touch a hot stove), at fixed intervals (e.g., paycheck every two weeks), or seemingly on a random basis (e.g., the jackpot from the slot machine). When and how often the rewards and costs occur can have a tremendous effect on behavior. In GPCSL, this is called the *density* of rewards and costs.

Also important is that, when we choose to act in a certain manner, we are forgoing other alternative behaviors. When prosocial alternative behaviors are highly rewarded, the motivation for some forms of deviance may be reduced. The potential for reduced criminal behavior resides not so much in reduced motivation for crime but in the potential for dramatic increases in the subtractive costs of crime. As the rewards for "noncrime" increase, the individual has more to lose. For example, when we choose to get up in the morning to go to work, we also forgo the pleasure of sleeping in. Why do we go to work? It is because the density of rewards for going to work (money, interacting with coworkers, receiving praise from the employer) outweighs the costs of sleeping in (losing our job, not having money to pay for food, housing, and recreational pleasures, and enjoying the company of fellow workers and employers).

With respect to crime, variations in the probability of occurrence of criminal behavior are a positive function of the signaled density of the rewards for criminal behavior and a negative function of the signaled density of the costs for crime. The probability of criminal behavior is also a positive function of the signaled density of the rewards for prosocial behavior and a negative function of the signaled density of the costs for prosocial behavior. If the rewards for criminal behavior are perceived to outweigh the rewards for prosocial behavior and there are few costs for criminal behavior, then criminal conduct is the likely result. The impact of altering the density of rewards and costs is greatest at the intermediate levels and less so at the extremes of very low or very high densities (adding one more reward or cost to a behavior that already has many rewards or costs will not make much of a difference).

Antecedents and consequences arise from three major sources: (1) the actor (personally mediated events), (2) other persons (interpersonally mediated events), and (3) the act itself (nonmediated or automatic and habitual events). The strength of personally mediated influence is maximized when the person has high self-control skills and when personal cognitions, attitudes, and self-efficacy beliefs are either supportive of criminal behavior (likelihood of criminal behavior) or supportive of prosocial behavior (likelihood of prosocial behavior). Personally mediated control is weakened when cognitions are neutral.

The strength of interpersonally mediated influence increases with adherence to the *relationship* and *structuring* principles. The relationship principle states that if the other is respected, valued, and liked, the effect of interpersonal

TABLE 3.2 **Types and Sources of Control**

Source	Reward		Cost	
	Additive (add "pleasant")	Subtractive (remove "unpleasant")	Additive (add "unpleasant")	Subtractive (remove "pleasant")
Interpersonal	Praise, hug from a friend, pay increase, cookie	Help from a friend, parent comforts a child, dentist says there is no cavity	Judge imposes a prison sentence, loved one yells, parent spanks a child	Loved one ignores you, child is sent to room ("time out"), denied entry to a club
Personal	"I feel great for what I did"; "I am proud"	"What a relief"; "I am not a coward"	"That was stupid of me"; "I really messed up"	"I am not a good person"; "I have lost their respect"
Nonmediated	Rush from a drug, relaxation from alcohol	Taking a pain reliever, removing stone from sock	Touching a hot stove, falling off a bike	Reading glasses break, power outage while watching TV

influence is enhanced. The structuring principle states that the direction of the influence is determined by the procriminal versus prosocial nature of the other's cognitions, expectations, and behavior. As an illustration of the interaction between the relationship and structuring principles, think of two children both living in a warm and loving family. The children both have a positive relationship with their parent(s). However, one child has parent(s) in conflict with the law who encourage and model antisocial acts, while the other child has parent(s) who have never been involved in crime. You can see how the former child has a higher likelihood of engaging in delinquency.

Nonmediated influences are relatively automatic. They come from the act itself and primarily reflect a history of reinforcement for the target behavior. Through repeated and heavily rehearsed associations of other stimulus events with reinforced behavior, the stimuli may also come to exert automatic control (i.e., a habit). Thus, as examples, simply thinking of a significant other may influence the occurrence of behaviors preferred by the other or the very act of ingesting a drug produces sensory change. Table 3.2 summarizes the key types and sources of control.

Up to this point, the importance of rewards and costs in the immediate situation has been stressed. However, rewards and costs are also dependent upon historical, geographic, and political-economic factors (recall Akers' macrosocial factors). The availability of rewards and costs and the rules for delivering them vary from society to society and according to the economic-social-political conditions inherent in a particular society or culture. To illustrate, a society with high unemployment cannot provide sufficient rewards for prosocial behavior through jobs, thereby making alternative antisocial behaviors as a means to earn money more attractive. From a normative perspective, cultures will vary on what they expect from their members and what will be rewarded. Consider the behavior of drinking alcohol. The "rules" under which alcohol consumption is sanctioned can vary across cultures, from drinking only under strict, ceremonial conditions to displays of public drunkenness. Our social settings, our communities, and our culture significantly influence what is rewarded and what is punished.

A Glimpse at the Evidence Supporting GPCSL and the Central Eight

Theorizing is of little value if it is not supported by empirical evidence. In GPCSL, the Central Eight are highly relevant while some other sociological and psychopathological factors are less relevant. Throughout the text a range of evidence in support of GPCSL will be provided. For now, one meta-analysis in support of GPCSL in Resource Note 3.3 is presented.

RESOURCE NOTE 3.3

The University of New Brunswick/Carleton University Predictors of Criminal Behavior: Highlights of Findings

Gendreau, Little, and Goggin (1996) from the University of New Brunswick originally reviewed 372 studies of the correlates of crime published in the English language between 1970 and 1990. These studies yielded more than 1,770 Pearson correlation coefficients with some measure of criminal behavior. Subsequently, additional results from the University of New Brunswick and Carleton University (Ottawa, Ontario) were added and are presented here.

Reflecting the GPCSL perspective underlying this text, particular risk/need factors were assigned to six categories. These categories were: (1) lower-class origins as assessed by parental educational and occupational indices and neighborhood characteristics, (2) personal distress indicators, including "psychological" measures of anxiety, depression, and low self-esteem as well as more "sociological" assessments of anomie and alienation, (3) school/work, (4) family/marital (i.e., family cohesiveness and parenting practices), (5) antisocial personality pattern (APP; antisocial temperament, personality, and behavioral history), and (6) procriminal attitudes and procriminal associates (unfortunately the two constructs were combined).

The mean correlation coefficients for each of the six categories are displayed in the top row of Table 3.1.1. The research findings also reveal that lower-class origins and personal distress are *minor* risk factors for criminality relative to indicators of four of

continued

TABLE 3.1.1 Mean *r* by Type of Risk/Need and Various Control Variables Risk/Need Factor

Control Variable	Lower Class	Personal Distress	School/ Work	Family/ Marital	APP	Attitudes/ Associates
Overall						
Gender	.06	.08	.12	.18	.21	.22
Male	.04	.09	.11	.16	.18	.21
Female	.03	.08	.13	.16	.23	.23
Age						
Juvenile	.03	.09	.10	.18	.22	.23
Adult	.05	.09	.12	.11	.18	.19
Race						
White	.05	.09	.10	.20	.19	.24
Black	.07	.05	.17	.12	.22	.29
Crime measure						
Self-reported	.00	.08	.10	.14	.20	.25
Official	.06	.10	,12	.18	19	.19
Design						
Longitudinal	.11	.08	.14	.17	.21	.20
Cross-sectional	.03	.08	.08	.19	19	.27

the Central Eight. This rank ordering of the six sets of risk/need factors displayed in Table 3.1.1 was very robust across various types of subjects (differentiated according to gender, age, and race) and across methodological variables (crime measures and research designs).

Summary

In the context of GPCSL, crime cannot be understood without understanding whether the personal, interpersonal, and community supports for human behavior are favorable or unfavorable to crime. It is not sufficient to highlight the accumulation of rewards and satisfactions (strain theory and subcultural theory) and the imbalance of social power (labeling and conflict/Marxist theories). It is also not sufficient to highlight the external and internal controls on criminal behavior. Both motivation and control must be considered within the context of person factors in order to understand criminal behavior.

Worth Remembering

1. Historically, sociological criminology has been a dominant force in theories of criminal behavior. Some of the theories placed the individual's location in the social hierarchy as the cause of crime. However, the evidence shows that social class is a minor correlate of criminal conduct.

2. Other criminological theories have taken on a more social-psychological approach. Self-control, procriminal associates, and procriminal attitudes were seen as more important than social location.

3. A General Personality and Cognitive Social Learning (GPCSL) theory postulates eight major risk/need factors called the Central Eight. They are: (1) criminal history, (2) procriminal attitudes, (3) procriminal associates, (4) antisocial personality pattern, (5) family/marital, (6) school/work, (7) substance misuse, and (8) leisure/recreation. The effect size for the Central Eight risk/need factors is larger than for social class and personal distress.

4. GPCSL assumes that criminal behavior is learned in accordance with the principles of learning and behavior is under antecedent and consequent control.

5. Variation in criminal behavior is a reflection of the density of signaled rewards and costs for criminal and noncriminal alternative behaviors.

6. The sources of signaled rewards are personal, interpersonal, and nonmediated. Cognitions play an important role in the control of behavior.

7. A major feature of GPCSL is the strength of its implications for the design of prevention and rehabilitation programs.

Recommended Readings

Criminology has a rich theoretical tradition. In this chapter only a handful of perspectives that bear more directly on GPCSL were summarized. Francis Cullen and Pamela Wilcox's edited book, *The Oxford Handbook of Criminological Theory* (2013), is certainly the go-to volume for a reader's introduction to theories that shaped criminological thinking in 2013 and today.

A major part of this chapter was the "how" of learning and we only scratched the surface of what we know about human learning. For those interested in a more in-depth analysis of conditioning theories, Michael Domjan's *The Essentials of Conditioning and Learning* (2018) will not disappoint. For an easy-to-read summary, Clive Hollin's chapter (2017) in *The Routledge Companion to Criminological Theory and Concepts* is suggested.

 Visit the Instructor and Student Resource to access additional exercises, videos and study materials to support this chapter: psychologycriminalconduct.routledge.com

PART 2 The Major Risk/Need Factors of Criminal Conduct

CHAPTER 4 The Biological Basis of Criminal Behavior

An important point made in Chapter 3 is that the influence of rewards and costs depends upon person factors. Two sets of person factors are cognitive and personality based. Another set is biological factors. In general, biological factors have received little attention within criminology (Wright & Cullen, 2012). Note the almost complete absence of biological factors in theories of anomie and strain, differential association, and Hirschi and Gottfredson's self-control theory. However, that has changed rapidly in recent years (Walsh, 2019; Wells & Walsh, 2019). This chapter examines how what we are born with interacts with the environment to shape behavior. Interactions also explain why some person factors are risk/need factors and others may be strengths. For example, opportunistic rewards for criminal behavior (e.g., an unattended car) may be more appealing to the individual with low self-control (risk/need factor), whereas high self-control serves as a strength or protective factor against the very same opportunistic rewards for crime. Biological factors lie at the base of criminal behavior. It is the foundation not only for personality development but also cognitive development.

Children begin life with certain inherent biological capabilities and predispositions that interact with specific familial, social, and cultural circumstances. Personal capabilities and predispositions affect how the environment influences the shaping of behavior and, reciprocally, how the behavior can modify biological tendencies. For example, a child may be born with average intelligence, but a stimulating and enriching environment can lead to achievements beyond those possible in a deprived environment. Importantly, environmental events may nourish further biological growth (e.g., an enriching family environment increasing nerve connections and cognitive growth) and can also cause harm to biological growth (e.g., maternal substance misuse during pregnancy can impair the child's cognitive functioning; Miguel, Pereira, Silveira, & Meaney, 2019).

An exciting area that emerged in the 1990s is developmental criminology. Developmental criminology tries to understand how children and youths grow in and out of crime (Farrington & Loeber, 2013; McGee & Farrington, 2019), and it does so by following cohorts of infants/children into adulthood.

DOI: 10.4324/9781003292128-6

An example is the Cambridge Study in Delinquent Development (CSDD) described in Chapter 1, where eight-year-old children have now been followed into adulthood (age 61). A consistent finding from developmental criminology is that most youths, especially males, engage in various antisocial acts as they grow into adulthood, but these youths follow different trajectories or criminal pathways. There is no consensus as to how many trajectories exist and estimates have ranged from three to seven (Van Hazebroek, Blokland, et al., 2019), but it is safe to describe two general trajectories common across gender (Ahonen, Jennings, Loeber, & Farrington, 2016) and race (Baglivio, Wolff, Piquero, & Epps, 2015; Yessine & Bonta, 2009).

Using Terri Moffit's taxonomy (1993, 2018), the first trajectory is the *adolescent-limited*, which represents the majority of youths who will engage in delinquent activities at some point during adolescence but desist in early adulthood. The second trajectory is called the *life-course-persistent*. These are the children, usually males, who start behaving antisocially early and continue through to adulthood, often escalating in the seriousness of their acts. The life-course-persistent represent the minority of delinquents (5–10 percent) but commit over half of the crimes (MacLeod, Grove, & Farrington, 2012; Rivenbark, Odgers, et al., 2018). For example, selecting all children born in Sweden between 1958 and 1980 (over 2 million individuals), Falk, Wallinius, et al. (2014) identified 24,342 medium-to-high persistent violent offenders (defined as having committed three or more violent offenses). This 1 percent of offenders committed 63 percent of all violent offenses. Most studies of life-course-persistent individuals go into young adulthood, with a few extending in age to the 50s, 60s, and even 70s (Farrington, 2019; Laub & Sampson, 2011; Silvertsson & Carlsson, 2015). These life-course-persistent offenders certainly have many childhood risk factors (e.g., poor parental supervision, school difficulties), but they may also be particularly influenced by biological factors.

Heredity and Crime

Most everyone agrees that both nature and nurture are important. However, how much one or the other contributes to behavior has been the subject of debate that is not only scientific but also cultural and political (e.g., promoting an immigration policy that denies citizenship to those with low intelligence; Babcock, 2015). PCC's emphasis is on nurture because the environment, including internal psychological processes, is the *immediate* source of control over behavior. Nevertheless, we need to examine the more distal factors that contribute to the development of criminal behavior for a fuller understanding of criminal conduct. We start with the search for a single gene to explain crime, then we move to a general understanding of the influence of heredity, provide summaries of some specific biological risk/need factors, and end with a few thoughts on evolutionary criminology. By the end of this chapter, it is hoped that the reader will recognize the importance of biological variables for understanding criminal behavior but also appreciate the limits to biological determinism.

The Search for a Crime Gene

Heredity is the transmission of genetic information from one generation to the next. Genes are the basic units of heredity that dictate the production of proteins and enzymes that, in turn, influence how we look and how we act (see Technical Note 4.1 on the textbook website at psychologycriminalconduct. routledge.com). In 2003, the Human Genome Project identified the complete sequence of human DNA, the programming code for each individual gene. In medicine there are some diseases (e.g., Huntington's disease, cystic fibrosis, muscular dystrophy) that are caused by abnormalities or mutations of a single gene. Such findings offer the promise of developing new medical treatments that alter the way our genes govern the biochemical processes and functions that lie at the heart of being human. Wouldn't it be nice if there was a single gene for crime for which we could develop treatments that would diminish or even "turn off" criminal behavior?

The XYY chromosome abnormality is the story of the search for a crime gene. Chromosomes are made up of DNA (the genetic programs), and humans have 46 chromosomes. Sometimes chromosomes can become damaged or fail to combine properly. Chromosomal alternations of the genetic sequence (mutations) can happen through unexplainable spontaneous means or through accidents (e.g., X-ray exposure). These mutations may affect the location of the gene in the chromosome, result in the complete absence of a chromosome, or result in an extra chromosome. For example, Down syndrome is caused by the presence of an extra chromosome.

For those interested in criminal behavior, the XYY chromosomal aberration has attracted the most attention. The Y chromosome carries the genes that determine male sexual features (e.g., genital development, hair distribution). Most who are assigned male at birth will have an XY chromosome and those assigned female at birth will have a XX chromosome. In 1961, Sandberg, Koepf, Ishihara, and Hauschka described an individual with an extra Y chromosome. Although this individual was by no means a "super male" (he had no criminal record and had average intelligence), a subsequent study by Jacobs, Brunton, Melville, Brittain, and McClemont (1965) suggested a link between an extra Y chromosome and violent behavior. Enthusiasm over these findings spawned not only the expected court defense of the "gene made me do it" (e.g., Richard Speck, who strangled eight student nurses, tried unsuccessfully to use this defense) but also some drastic measures such as screening infants and high school students for the extra Y chromosome (Navon & Thomas, 2021). However, the early studies involved biased samples of institutionalized, often intellectually handicapped males (Jarvik, Klodin, & Matsuyama, 1973).

The initial excitement quickly wore off when well-designed epidemiological studies found that having an extra Y chromosome was largely irrelevant.

First of all, the incidence of XYY is extremely small. Witkin, Mednick, et al. (1976) found only 12 XYY in a sample of 4,558 Danish men (0.002 percent). In a larger Danish sample, Stochholm, Bojesen, et al. (2012) found 161 of 105,280 (again, 0.002 percent) with the XYY aberration. Götz, Johnstone, and Ratcliffe (1999) found 17 among a sample of 17,522 Scottish men (0.001 percent). Upon follow-up, all three studies found that XYY men had slightly more criminal convictions than XY men. However, an extension of the Danish study also found a higher incidence of medical and psychiatric disorders (Berglund, Stochholm, & Gravholt, 2020). Second, in order to ascertain that it was the extra Y chromosome and not just simply having any extra chromosome that accounted for differences in criminal conduct, the researchers compared the XYY men to men who had an additional X chromosome (a condition known as Klinefelter's syndrome, which is characterized by male genitals but often with sterility, breast enlargement, and intellectual delay). Again, the incidence of XXY is very low, less than 1 percent. There were no differences in criminal offending between the men with an extra Y chromosome and the men with an extra X chromosome.

In the only longitudinal study of XYY children (Geerts, Steyaert, & Fryns, 2003), half of the 38 boys in the study evidenced psychosocial problems, but childhood autism was a more likely outcome than conduct disorder. Both Ike's (2000) and Re and Birkhoff's (2015) reviews of the XYY literature found that most XYY carriers showed few behavioral problems, and the reports of antisocial behaviors may be the result of selective screening of individuals with the XYY syndrome. To conclude, the XYY abnormality, although an interesting story, falls into the trap of oversimplification and genetic determinism. Granted there are examples of one gene = one disorder, but the more common scenario is that there are many genes operating on the expression of behavior, and this is in interaction with the environment.

Intergenerational Crime

The idea that crime runs in families has been a high-consensus inference of casual observers for years. Almost anyone who has worked in a criminal justice setting can provide vivid examples of intergenerational criminality. A famous, early study of the heritability of criminal traits is Richard Dugdale's (1877/1970) analysis of the Juke family. Beginning with the children of Max Juke (circa 1750), Dugdale traced the Juke lineage to 1870. Of the 709 descendants, nearly 20 percent were criminals, and slightly more than 40 percent were dependent upon the state for financial support. Dugdale concluded that the high rate of criminality and "pauperism" was evidence for the heritability of criminality and poor social adjustment.

Today, there is a large body of evidence for intergenerational crime (Besemer, Ahmad, Hinshaw, & Farrington, 2017; Eichelsheim & van de Weijer, 2018; Wildeman, 2020). A meta-analysis by Besemer and his colleagues (2017) is quite telling. They found that children of criminal parents were almost two and a half times more likely to engage in criminal behavior than children without criminal parents. This intergenerational transmission of crime applies equally to boys and girls (Van de Rakt, Nieuwbeerta, & De Graaf, 2008); it has been found across three generations (Dubow, Huesmann, Boxer, Smith, & Sedlar, 2018; Farrington, Ttofi, Crago, & Coid, 2015), with a Dutch study planning to follow five generations (van de Weijer & Bijlevid, 2018). This line of research has even been extended to organized crime (think of *The Godfather* trilogy; e.g., van Dijk, Eichelsheim, Kleemans, Souddijn, & van de Weijer, 2022).

These and other findings on intergenerational crime do not necessarily mean that there is solely *genetic* transmission of criminality. A number of environmental mechanisms have been forwarded to account for the intergenerational transmission. They include inadequate parental monitoring and disciplining practices, having a father with an unstable work record, living in poor housing (Besemer, Farrington, & Bijleveld, 2013; Besemer et al., 2017), and parents who themselves suffered maltreatment as children (Craig, Malvaso, & Farrington, 2021). The complexity of the relationship between nature and intergenerational criminality also varies by gender and how crime is measured. For example, Auty, Farrington, and Coid's (2017) analysis of data from the CSDD found that a criminal father's drug misuse mediated the male child's future convictions but not the female offspring's criminal activity. In addition, the criminal mother's harsh disciplining practices was a significant mediator of the daughter's criminal activity but not the son's antisocial behavior. Besemer and his colleagues (2013) found that having a criminal father was the best predictor of the son's involvement in delinquency, but other indicators of social difficulties (e.g., low family income) also predicted delinquency. However, these social indicators predicted better for *officially* recorded delinquency than for self-reported delinquency.

Another explanatory factor is "assortative mating." Assortative mating occurs when individuals mate with similar individuals (Boutwell, Beaver, & Barnes, 2012; Krueger, Moffitt, Caspi, Bleske, & Silva, 1998; Rhule-Louie & McMahon, 2007). The findings are remarkable. In the CSDD, 83 percent of the boys in the study grew up and married women who also had criminal records (Farrington, Barnes, & Lambert, 1996). Indeed, Farrington (2007) found that family criminality was the best predictor of antisocial behavior for any family member. A Dutch study of 1,681 families found that when the mother was arrested, the chance of the father having been arrested was five times more likely (Junger, Greene, et al., 2013). Furthermore, life-course-persistent offenders tend to partner with the same kind (van de Weijer & Boutwell, 2022). The likelihood that antisocial individuals tend to cohabit with procriminal partners or that delinquent children tend to be raised in dysfunctional, strife-ridden families all point to the influence of the social learning environments within these families. In order to better separate the influences of heredity and the environment, investigators have turned to the study of twins and adopted children.

What Twin and Adoption Studies Tell Us about Nature and Nurture

Twin Studies. Twin studies compare monozygotic (MZ) twins and dizygotic (DZ) twins. Monozygotic twins, or "identical" twins, originate from one egg fertilized by one sperm. After fertilization, the egg splits into two, eventually producing two fetuses with identical genetic makeups. Dizygotic twins (DZ), or fraternal twins, originate from two separate fertilized eggs (see Figure 4.1). Although the fetuses share the same placenta and are often born within minutes of each other, they are as genetically different as any brother and sister, or same-sex siblings, born years apart. Identical twins are always of the same sex and are indistinguishable in appearance, while fraternal twins can be different genders, and even if they are the same gender, you can tell them apart. Now, if heredity has an influence, then the behaviors (and not just the physical appearance) of MZ twins should show more similarity or "concordance" than that found in the behaviors of DZ twins.

In the first study of twins and criminality, Lange (1929) identified 13 pairs of monozygotic (MZ) twins and 17 pairs of dizygotic (DZ) twins from birth registries in Germany. Criminality was defined as a history of imprisonment. Lange found that the similarity/concordance rate for MZ twins with respect to criminality was 77 percent and only 12 percent for DZ twins. That is, for 10 of the 13 pairs of MZ twins, both siblings had histories of incarceration, whereas only two pairs of the 17 pairs of DZ twins had joint histories of incarceration.

While the magnitude of the effect was impressive, Lange's study and those by others conducted during the same period were suspect for a number of reasons. For one thing, social scientists in Britain and North America were not about to be impressed by a report originating from Germany during the rise of Nazism (for a review of criminology in Nazi Germany and Fascist Italy, see Rafter, 2008). The early studies were also plagued by serious methodological problems. For example, Lange grouped the twins into MZ and DZ categories by

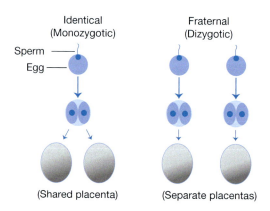

Figure 4.1

Identical and Fraternal Twins

looking at their pictures, knowing beforehand who had the history of imprisonment. This methodology makes it very tempting for an experimenter with a certain set of beliefs and expectations to place one set of twins that did not look quite identical into the MZ group.

Studies that were methodologically more refined emerged in the 1970s. For example, Christiansen (1977) drew upon the Copenhagen birth registry to locate a large sample of twins (3,586) that could be reliably identified as MZ or DZ. Criminal activity was defined according to official records. For MZ twins, the concordance rate was 35 percent; it was 12 percent for DZ twins. As twin studies became methodologically more sophisticated, the concordance rate for MZ twins decreased from the 77 percent reported by Lange to as low as 26 percent (Dalgaard & Kringlen, 1976). Except for a few exceptions that may be explained by methodological and sampling factors, general reviews and meta-analytic summaries of the twin literature find a moderate relationship between heredity and antisocial behavior (Carey & Goldman, 1997; Frisell, Pawitan, Långström, & Lichtenstein, 2012; Rhee & Waldman, 2002, 2007). Although the heritability of antisocial personality was not reported, the largest ever review of twin studies estimated that on average 49 percent of nearly 18,000 traits measured were inheritable (Polderman, Benyamin, et al., 2015). There is little reason why this estimate would also not apply to antisocial traits.

An important assumption in twin research is that the greater concordance found among MZ twins compared to DZ twins is due to the influence of genetics since the environments of twins are more or less the same (e.g., same parents, shared friends, same teachers). This is called the "equal environments assumption." However, Burt and Simons (2014) argued that this assumption is a fatal flaw in twin research and called for an end to studies of heritability. Yet an empirical analysis of 61 studies found 48 studies (78.6 percent) *supporting* the equal environment assumption (Barnes, Wright, et al., 2014; Wright, Tibbets, & Daigle, 2014).

A more informative type of twin study involves MZ twins separated at birth and raised in different environments. Although such studies date back to at least the 1930s (Newman, Freeman, & Holzinger, 1937), their sample sizes have been relatively small. The largest study, The Minnesota Study of Twins Reared Apart, gathered more than 100 sets of twins (including a few triplets; Bouchard, Lykken, McGue, Segal, & Tellegen, 1990). With respect to the subject matter of this book, a large study of MZ twins reared apart was conducted by William Grove and his colleagues (Grove, Eckert, et al., 1990). Thirty-two pairs of MZ twins who were separated before the age of five (one-half were separated within the first few months of birth) were followed into adulthood (median age of 43). The concordance rate for antisocial personality disorder was 29 percent, about the range found by most twin studies on crime.

Recently, there has been a new twin approach to understanding the role of heredity and the environment: the discordant MZ-twin method. The discordant MZ-twin method begins with the assumption that MZ twins raised together do not share *exactly* the same environments. For example, one twin may suffer an accident or illness while the other does not. In other words, the twins are discordant on environmental experience. Therefore, twin MZ research can tell you a great deal about potential specific *environmental* causes since genetics and, to some extent, general environmental experiences (i.e., the equal environments assumption) are held constant. Researchers have called this the counterfactual model of causality since instead of using twins to understand the effects of heredity, we are trying to understand the effects of the environment (Johansson, Rötkönen, & Jern, 2021; McGue, Osler, & Christensen, 2010).

The application of the discordant MZ-twin method to our understanding of criminal conduct has been infrequent but holds great promise. For example, there is a strong correlation between hostile, cold mothers and aggressive behavior in the children. The question in a twin study is: do the mothers genetically transmit hostility to the children, explaining the aggressive behavior, or does the aggressive behavior of the child produce a hostile reaction from the mother, thus ruling out heredity?

Caspi and his colleagues (Caspi, Moffitt, et al., 2004) tried to answer the preceding question by studying 565 MZ pairs of twins born in England and Wales between 1994 and 1995. When the twins reached age five, the mothers of the twins were asked to describe their children for five minutes, and their responses were audio recorded. The recordings were then coded with respect to positive and negative comments made about the child. Rather than asking the mothers for a rating of their child's aggressiveness, which could introduce bias (e.g., a hostile mother may be more likely to rate her child higher in aggression), the *teachers* were asked to rate the child's aggressiveness. Approximately 18 months later, the researchers interviewed the mothers and teachers once more. The first important finding was that the mothers did not treat each twin similarly. Many times, one twin would be described positively and the other negatively. Second, negative emotions expressed by the mother predicted aggression in their child. Thus, the researchers concluded that it was the mother's treatment and not heredity that explained the child's aggressiveness. Another more detailed example of the discordant MZ method is provided in Resource Note 4.1.

RESOURCE NOTE 4.1

Does Having Sex Earlier than Your Peers Increase the Risk of Delinquency? A Genetic Perspective

A consistent finding from cross-sectional research is that engaging in adult-like behaviors at an early age is associated with delinquency. Hirschi (1969) observed that 78 percent of youths who reported smoking, drinking, and dating were also engaged in delinquent behavior, whereas only 25 percent of the youths who reported no engagement in these activities were delinquent. Glueck and Glueck (1950) found delinquents to be more likely

continued

to smoke (90 percent vs. 22.8 percent) and drink (29.2 percent vs. 0.4 percent) at an early age than nondelinquents. They also found that 19.4 percent of the delinquents had sex compared to only 1.8 percent of the nondelinquents. More recently, Armour and Haynie (2007) analyzed data from more than 7,000 adolescents participating in a longitudinal study in the United States. The results showed that youths who made their sexual "debut" earlier than their peers were at a 20 percent increased risk of delinquency (measured by self-report).

As pointed out in Chapter 2, neither cross-sectional nor longitudinal studies can conclude a causal relationship. Does early sexual behavior really cause delinquent behavior, or is there an alternative explanation? Perhaps poor parental monitoring of the teenager's behavior is the real cause. Perhaps genetics are in play. For example, evolutionary theory would say that early (and frequent) sex is in the best interest of the gene. One approach to gain a better understanding of the relationship between sexual debut and delinquency is to examine twins.

Harden and her colleagues (Harden, Mendle, Hill, Turkheimer, & Emery, 2008) studied 534 same-sex twins who were assessed in 1994–95, one year later, and then again four years later. By the third assessment, the average age of the participants was 22 years. There were 289 MZ twins and 245 DZ twins. Using same-sex twins also controlled for potential differences in how boys and girls are treated by the family environment (e.g., girls may be more closely monitored by the parents). Studying twins has two important advantages. First, if one twin has sex at an earlier time than the other, then you can eliminate genetic influence. Second, you can also discount but not eliminate the effects of the twins sharing a similar environment (i.e., family factors). Thus, one comes closer to making a causal conclusion.

Controlling for genetic and shared environmental influences, Harden et al. also introduced statistical controls for non-shared environmental influence (e.g., one twin may associate with delinquent peers, but the other sibling has prosocial friends). The surprising result was that early sexual debut was associated with *lower* delinquency involvement. This finding certainly sheds a different light on the findings from cross-sectional and longitudinal studies. Harden and her colleagues (2008; Harden, 2014) have hypothesized a number of possible explanations including a healthier sense of self-worth in romantic relationships and that it may even be normative within a *consensual* relationship. It appears that much remains to be learned about such a seemingly simple covariate of antisocial behavior.

Adoption Studies. Most adoption studies use a method called the cross-fostering design. This design analyzes the behavior of children who are separated soon after birth from their biological parents and raised, or fostered, by nonrelatives. In adoption studies, the criminal futures of adopted children are analyzed in relation to: (1) criminal history of the biological parents, (2) criminal history of adoptive parents, and (3) particular combinations of criminality in the biological and adoptive parents. The assumption is that if the rate of criminality among adopted children is higher for those who

TABLE 4.1 **Cross-Fostering Analysis of Criminality in Male Adoptees by Criminality of Biological and Adoptive Parents**

Criminal adoptive parents?	Criminal biological parents?	
	Yes	**No**
Yes	24.5% (of 143)	14.7% (of 204)
No	20.0% (of 1,226)	13.5% (of 2,492)

Source: Adapted from Mednick et al., 1984

have a biological parent with a criminal record than for the adoptees with a noncriminal biological parent, then heredity has an effect.

The classic cross-fostering study on criminal behavior is by Mednick, Gabrielli, and Hutchings (1984). They drew upon a databank that included social history information on more than 14,000 children who were adopted in Denmark between 1924 and 1947. The researchers tabulated the conviction rate of male adoptees in relation to the criminal convictions of their biological and adoptive parents. Inspection of Table 4.1 finds a very small genetic effect ($r = 0.03$). Note in the bottom row of the table that adoptees raised by noncriminal parents but who had criminal biological parents were at a higher risk of being convicted than adoptees from noncriminal biological parents and raised by noncriminal foster parents (20 percent vs. 13.5 percent).

In a follow-up investigation, Mednick, Gabrielli, and Hutchings (1987) focused on what they called chronic (i.e., life-course-persistent) youths. Chronic youths were defined as having at least three prior convictions. They represented 4 percent of the sample but were responsible for 69 percent of all the crimes. The biological parents were also categorized according to their convictions (from 0 to 3 or more). As the number of convictions for the biological parents increased, so did the number for the adoptees. These results, however, held for property offenses only and not for violent offenses. Parental criminality by itself appeared insufficient to explain violent crime in the offspring.

Another adoption approach to investigating the role of heredity in behavior, not yet applied to criminal behavior, is the study of virtual twins. Virtual twins are children of the same age who are unrelated but raised together. This is very rare but it does happen. For example, a family may want to have a child but are having difficulty conceiving. The family then adopts an infant and soon after conceives a child as a result of successful reproductive technology. The Fullerton Virtual Twin Study began in 1991 in California and had 169 virtual twin pairs in 2019 (Segal & Niculae, 2019). Additional criteria for being considered a virtual twin are that the adoption must occur prior to age one and the difference in age between siblings is less than nine months. Thus, the siblings are like twins but without any genetic link. Like the discordant MZ method, this provides another approach to studying environmental influences on behavior. At the last report in 2019 the average age of the siblings was 8.7 years and the research has focused on intelligence, physical traits, and other non-problematic characteristics. Hopefully, as these children grow older, researchers will study childhood aggression and, eventually, delinquency.

Earlier we noted Burt and Simons' (2014) call for ending heredity research. On one hand, one may agree with them, as it is now well-established that almost all personality traits are influenced by genetics (Sanchez-Roige, Gray, MacKillop, Chen, & Palmer, 2018). However, agreeing still means that we can use twin and adoption studies to explore possible environmental influences on criminal behavior. The discussion of discordant MZ-twins and adoption studies, hopefully, has persuaded the reader of the usefulness of such studies. Rather than studies of heredity in the classical sense, Burt and Simons (2014) saw epigenetic research as the future. "Epi" comes from the Greek meaning "on" or "addition to," and so epigenetics involves changing the way genes work without altering the DNA. Consequently, it becomes difficult for the DNA code to be read for the production of proteins (Feinberg, 2018; Walsh & Yun, 2014). The DNA in our genes is the blueprint for growth and how we look but environmental mechanisms can regulate genetic expression (i.e., turn on or off a gene). For example, smoking cigarettes leads to a decrease in DNA methylation (methyl molecules added to the DNA), which inhibits gene expression. This in turn can increase the risk for cancer and inflammatory illnesses. Quitting smoking can increase DNA methylation. Epigenetic research has led to many important discoveries and treatments for physical diseases (e.g., cancer, kidney disease) and some psychological disorders (e.g., childhood stress alters brain functioning, leading to adult depression).

In recent years there has been increasing interest in the role of epigenetics and aggression/criminal behavior. There are two general interrelated areas of research. The first is the examination of stressful events at critical points in human development and their impact on brain maturation and aggressive behavior (Walton, 2021). For example, stress during pregnancy and adverse childhood experiences are known to alter neural connections. More will be said about this in the next section. The second newly emerging area of research has to do with the relationship between stressful criminogenic *neighborhoods* (termed "hot spots" in the criminological literature) and brain development that is related to aggression (Leshem & Weisburd, 2019). Note that both lines of research are interested in how the environment influences neurobiological factors; one is at the more proximal level (e.g., alcohol consumption during pregnancy and fetal alcohol syndrome) and the other more distal (e.g., a chaotic neighborhood).

Assembling the findings from studies of twins and adoptees, it is hard to ignore genetic factors in behavior. Carey and Goldman (1997) found that all six of the adoption studies in their review showed a genetic effect. In the meta-analyses by Walters (1992) and Rhee and Waldman (2002), the concordance rate for the adoption studies decreased significantly from the rate found in the twin studies, but it was not zero. Barnes, Boutwell, Beaver, Gibson, and Wright (2014) estimated the correlation between genetic and criminological variables to range from 0.30 to 0.60.

One important observation is that the severity of the problem behavior may have a higher heritability component. John Malouff, Sally Rooke, and Nicola Schutte (2008) examined eight meta-analyses of twin and adoption studies investigating a range of problems (e.g., intelligence, language ability, major depression, antisocial behavior). They found higher heritability was associated with the severity of the problem. Furthermore, being female or having a diagnosis of a conduct disorder (a feature of the life-course-persistent offender) had higher heritability than being male or the absence of a conduct disorder. Similarly, Barnes, Beaver, and Boutwell (2011) found in an analysis of 2,284 sibling pairs that up to 70 percent of the variance among life-course-persistent offenders was due to genetic factors, whereas 35 percent of the variance was explained by genetics for adolescence-limited delinquents. In other words, the more infrequent/severe type of offender (i.e., the female justice-involved person and the career criminal), the stronger the genetic influence (Moffitt, Ross, & Raine, 2011).

The Nature–Nurture Interaction

Our earlier discussion of epigenetics naturally transitions us to a conversation on the interaction between biological predispositions and the environment (Gard, Dotterer, & Hyde, 2019; McAllister, Mechanic, et al., 2017). That is, under what environmental conditions do biological factors play a lesser or greater role? What other biological factors depend upon the environment for their behavioral expression? A study by Barnes, Liu, et al. (2019) illustrates the conditional nature of an interaction. A sample of American adults over the age of 50 ($N = 6,716$) have been followed since 1992 and assessed every two years. DNA samples and sociodemographic and life event data were gathered. Of specific interest to us was the assessment of aggressive behavior (by paper-and-pencil test) and a history of incarceration (5 percent reported being incarcerated). The researchers found that a genetic predisposition to aggression (e.g., serotonin and dopamine receptor activity) predicted lifetime incarceration especially for the men; no surprise there. However, the incarceration rate depended on the level of education of a parent. For males with at least one parent who completed high school the relationship between genetic predisposition to aggression and incarceration was nonsignificant. That is, the effect of genetics conducive to aggression on incarceration depended upon the environment.

Exploring the nature–nurture interaction can proceed on two levels. There is the molecular genetic level and then there is a higher level of the behavioral markers representing the biological systems that underlie criminal conduct. For example, negative emotionality reflects underlying biochemical processes that can be linked back to the operation of genes.

With technical advances, interactions at the molecular genetic level are being more frequently reported (Byrd & Manuk, 2014; Liu, Li, & Guo, 2015; McAllister, Mechanic, et al., 2017). In one study, Guo, Roettger, and Cai (2008) demonstrated that such simple routine activities as eating meals with parents mitigated the effects of the DRD2 gene (a dopamine receptor) on delinquency. They went further and showed that school attachment and repeating a grade, both risk factors for delinquency, interacted with the MAOA gene. The MAOA gene is widely regarded to influence aggression via serotonin and dopamine neurotransmission (Byrd & Manuk, 2014; Moffitt, Arsenault, et al., 2011). This research at the genetic molecular level reinforces the view that the influence of heredity depends on the presence of certain environmental risk factors that, in a sense, release the power of the gene. For example, family dysfunction (Button, Scourfield, Martin, Purcell, & McGuffin, 2005) and low socioeconomic status (Tuvblad, Grann, & Lichtenstein, 2006) have been shown to increase the heritability of antisocial behavior.

Moffitt (2005: p. 548) has listed a number of behavioral markers indicative of biological system processes that may interact with environmental factors. They include: sensation-seeking, high energy, low self-control, emotionality, and callousness. Depending upon the environment, children with such characteristics differ in their antisocial outcomes. The general message is that the expression of genetic and biological factors is often dependent upon the right environmental conditions.

Neurophysiological Factors and Crime

The brain as the center of thinking, emotion, and motivation is as undisputable as the fact that it is also the most complex of all human organs. How the processes in the brain influence antisocial and violent behavior is a subject of great interest (Loeber, Byrd, & Farrington, 2015; Raine, 2013; Walsh, 2019).

The complexity of the influence of neuropsychological variables is reflected in the search for the localization of aggression in the brain. The search started off simply enough but ended with a much more elaborate understanding of brain function and aggressivity. In 1970, Vernon Mark and Frank Ervin described a patient who would assault his wife and children during fits of uncontrollable rage. By surgically removing part of the brain (the right amygdala, to be precise), they were able to halt the violence. What is so special about the amygdala, and is this tiny structure the possible center of all that is evil and bad?

The amygdala is an almond-shaped structure found buried within the temporal lobe of the brain. Together with other nearby structures it forms the limbic system. The limbic system is commonly referred to as the "old brain" because it looks like that found in lower-level animals and it had developed early in human evolution. In fact, in the human fetus, the limbic system develops first, and then the cerebral cortex (the soft convoluted tissue) grows over the area.

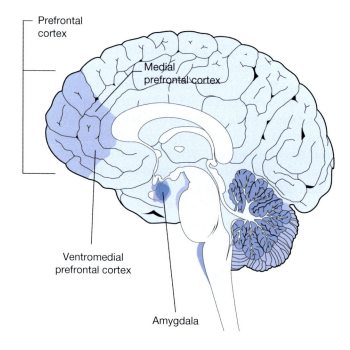

Figure 4.2

The Brain

It is the cortex that mediates higher levels of thinking. Figure 4.2 presents the basic structures of the brain along with the amygdala.

The old brain (limbic system), having developed earlier, is thought to control the basic emotions (anger, fear) and motivations (hunger, thirst, sex). Thus, it became the natural target for localizing anger and aggression in the brain. Early studies would stimulate or remove parts of the limbic system, especially the amygdala, in order to observe the expression of anger and aggression, but these often came with serious side effects. Today, non-invasive brain stimulation techniques across the prefrontal cortex, rather than one particular area, are used in an effort to reduce aggression. However, the methodological weaknesses associated with the techniques prevent any unequivocal conclusions (Romero-Martinez, Bressanutti, & Moya-Albiol, 2020). These studies also showed that the amygdala is not totally responsible for aggressivity and that other structures in the limbic system (e.g., hippocampus, thalamus, etc.) were also involved.

By the 1990s, it was clear that aggression does not depend upon what happens only in the limbic system (Golden, Jackson, Peterson-Rohne, & Gontkovsky, 1996). The brain is a network of interconnecting neurons that number in the billions. When some neurons do not function well, it is common to see other adjoining neurons assume the function of the damaged areas. This is referred to as "plasticity," and the human brain is much more plastic in youth than in adulthood. For example, a cerebral stroke may damage a portion of the brain affecting behavior, but the effect may be transitory as neighboring neurons take over the function of damaged neurons. This explains the difficulty in proving that one area of the brain, and one area only, mediates behaviors (this is a general statement and there are areas in the brain that have a very specific function and if damaged are irreparable).

Violent behavior appears to depend on a combination of processes within the limbic system and the prefrontal cortex (Ling, Umbach, & Raine, 2019; Romero-Martinez, González, et al., 2019). The frontal areas of the brain are associated with attention, planning, and the inhibition of behavior or, generally speaking, executive function. In a review of 126 studies, criminal behavior displayed a fairly large relationship with measures of executive function ($r = 0.31$; Ogilvie, Stewart, Chan, & Shum, 2011). Also, there is some evidence that white-collar criminals have more gray matter thickness in their frontal lobes than the average criminal (Ling, Raine, Yang, et al., 2019), and with it, higher executive function (Alalehto, 2018). Although damage to the frontal lobes and the limbic system may result in violent behavior, there are not enough people with brain damage to these areas to explain the relatively high prevalence of violent behavior. Instead, it is likely that diffuse cerebral dysfunction affecting multiple sites of the brain plays the predominant role in aggressive behavior. Diffuse neurological dysfunction may have its onset early in development, perhaps neonatally, and long before the occurrence of a direct physical injury and trauma (Eme, 2020; Moffitt, 1990). However, such a dysfunction often does not become apparent until later, when tests are able to measure verbal and memory deficits and intelligence.

The frontal lobes develop throughout adolescence, and the myelin, or the insulating sheath around the nerves that facilitates electrical conduction, continues to develop into adulthood (Fields, 2005). Consequently, the frontal lobes are not fully developed until the age of 25, at best (Prior, Farrow, et al., 2011). This delayed development may partially explain the impulsivity and poor attention span of young children and the age–crime curve (Loeber, Menting, et al., 2012). The age–crime curve describes the prevalence of antisocial behavior increasing with age, peaking in late adolescence, and then beginning a decline around the age of 20 (i.e., the adolescent-limited; Loeber & Farrington, 2014). However, this age–crime curve may vary slightly by gender and the type of crime (Matthews & Minton, 2018). In addition, delays in neurophysiological development affect attention skills, verbal language development, and intelligence in general. Moffitt (2003, 2018) has argued that adolescence-limited delinquents may suffer from a "maturity gap" created by delayed neurophysiological development and the adolescent's desire to be treated like an adult.

For the life-course-persistent individual, it may be more than delayed neurological maturation but actual impairment to the frontal lobe and limbic systems (Eme, 2020; Raine, Moffitt, et al., 2005). These findings have huge implications for the application of law with justice-involved youth. If brain capacity and function is still developing, with the frontal lobes developing last, or if there is mild neurological impairment, can we hold adolescents responsible for uninhibited, antisocial behavior (Scott & Steinberg, 2008)? Considering this evidence, the U.S. Supreme Court banned the death penalty for youths under the age of 18 (*Roper v. Simmons*, 543 U.S. 551, 2005). However, and somewhat antithetically, many states and countries still permit the transfer of youths (ages 12 to 21 depending on the jurisdiction) to adult court for trial (Abrams, Jordon, & Montero, 2018).

What are the implications of transferring youth to adult court? Setting aside the issue of immature brain development and the concomitant problem of being held fully accountable for one's criminal actions, there is an additional important factor to consider. And that is, most youth courts emphasize rehabilitation rather than deterrence as in adult courts. The question arises, are youth who are tried in youth court better off compared to those being before adult court? One way of answering the question is to examine the presumed specific deterrent effect of transferring youth to adult court for trial. Zane, Welsh, and Mears (2016) conducted a meta-analytic review of nine studies where transferred juveniles were compared with juveniles who were tried in youth court. No statistically significant effect on recidivism was found for those transferred to adult court. However, there was considerable heterogeneity in the findings across studies.

Another approach is to evaluate the rehabilitative effect of being tried in youth court. Fowler and Kurlychek (2018) took advantage of a policy change in the state of Connecticut. In 2010 the state expanded juvenile court proceeding to the age of 17 from age 16. This change allowed the researchers to compare the recidivism outcome of youth tried in adult court (16-year-old youth in 2009) to the 16-year-old youth who appeared in juvenile court in 2010. The re-arrest rate for the young persons who were tried in youth court was almost half of that for youth adjudicated in adult court. It is clear that understanding brain development has far-reaching consequences for justice-involved youth.

In the Dunedin Multidisciplinary Health and Development Study (New Zealand), approximately 1,000 children born between 1972 and 1973 were tested on a range of factors every two years (Moffitt, Lynam, & Silva, 1994). At age 13, they were administered neuropsychological and IQ tests; at age 18, delinquency was assessed. Terri Moffitt and her colleagues found that many of the neuropsychological tests predicted delinquency at age 18. Tests that measured verbal abilities, as opposed to tests measuring visual-motor abilities, showed the highest correlations with future delinquency. The researchers found that poor performance on these tests was associated only with the life-course-persistent male delinquents. This was a very small group (12 percent of the sample), but its members accounted for 59 percent of all convictions. For those whose delinquency was adolescent-limited, neuropsychological test performance was not predictive of outcome. These results have now been extended to age 38 for both the men and women in the Dunedin sample (Poulton, Moffitt, & Silva, 2015).

The findings described speak to one of the major questions asked by developmental criminology: What are the factors that lead youths into chronic criminality? Moffitt and her colleagues (Moffitt, 2003, 2018; Moffitt et al., 1994) have proposed a biosocial model of life-course-persistent offending that identifies neuropsychological factors, temperament (discussed in the next section), and socialization experiences. Thus, biological factors are one piece of the formula for the development of persistent, and often violent, criminal behavior. For many persisters, neurological variables such as lower average cortical thickness in the temporal lobes appear to increase the risk of offending (Carlisi, Moffitt, et al., 2020; Eme, 2020). The addition of psychosocial risk factors (recall the interaction effect) makes matters worse (Moffitt, Caspi, & Rutter, 2012).

The relationship between biology and crime is not direct and simple. The consistent findings are poor verbal/language skills, impulsiveness, and poor attention and planning abilities. Whether these deficits have direct effects or are mediated by other environmental factors (as they likely are) remains an unresolved question. Generally, it appears that genetic and neurophysiological contributions to criminal conduct will be greatest when the social environment is least supportive of crime in general and serious crimes in particular (Malouff, Rooke, & Schutte, 2008; Meier, Slutske, Arndt, & Cadoret, 2008; Scarpa & Raine, 2007; van Hazebroek, Wermink, et al., 2019). Although a comprehensive theory of criminal behavior must include biological and genetic factors, it is important to remember that the environment explains a great deal.

The Difficult, Impulsive, Sensation-Seeking Temperament

Temperament refers to inherent and stable characteristic tendencies of responding to the environment (Else-Quest, Hyde, Hill, Goldsmith, & Van Hulle, 2006). Temperament is usually thought to comprise a few dimensions of behavior describing how individuals react to the environment. For example, some babies always seem content, and as they grow, they continue to adapt well to whatever challenges life presents. Other babies are quite fussy, and as they grow, they may be described as "high-strung." Certainly, learning experiences can have a large effect on how individuals behave in different situations, but underlying an individual's response is a general predisposition that is evident at birth. Temperament is the biological precursor to personality and explains the heritability of personality (Saudino & Ganiban, 2020; Vukasović & Bratko, 2015). In general, personality refers to typical patterns of thinking, feeling, and acting. We will see that temperamental characteristics are evident soon after birth and remain relatively stable throughout life.

The origin for today's research on temperament can be traced to the work of Alexander Thomas and his spouse, Stella Chess, and their colleagues. In the original New York Longitudinal Study (Thomas, Chess, Birch, Hertzig, & Korn, 1963), 133 newborn infants were assessed along nine characteristics that described how they typically responded to their environments. For example, a newborn's activity level can be categorized as low (lies still when being changed) or high (fidgets while being changed), the quality of mood as negative (fusses after nursing) or positive (quiet after nursing), and distractibility as low (stops fussing when given a pacifier) or high (continues fussing when given a pacifier). The categories were further clustered into three types: "easy," "slow to warm," and "difficult." It is common for personality theorists to reduce specific descriptors to a few general, temperamental traits. We will use their terminology of "facets" and "traits." Traits are the big-picture descriptors of temperament (e.g., difficult temperament), and facets are more specific descriptors that make up a trait (e.g., activity level, negative mood, etc.).

Our interest is in what Chess and Thomas (1984) called the "difficult" child, a category that comprised 10 percent of the 133 children. The difficult child demonstrated the following facets:

1. Intense reactions to stimuli.

2. A generally negative mood.

3. A slowness to adapt to change.

4. Irregularity in sleep, hunger, and other bodily functions.

Chess and Thomas (1984, 1990) followed their difficult children into early (ages 18–24) and young (ages 25–30) adulthood and found significant stability. For example, in early adulthood, 10 of 12 cases diagnosed with a behavior disorder were temperamentally difficult children. Research over the past decade confirms a moderate level of stability for many temperamental traits (Bornstein, Hahn, Putnick, & Pearson, 2019; Kopala-Sibley, Olino, Durbin, Dyson, & Klein, 2018).

Today, researchers have identified a number of temperamental traits, many of which are important to an understanding of delinquency, especially the life-course-persistent youth. Two interrelated temperamental traits are especially important (DeLisi & Vaughn, 2014). The first is high stimulation-seeking combined with low self-control. It is one thing to have a high activity level with an interest in experiencing life to its fullest (a characteristic of many successful individuals), but if this energy level is not controlled, then it can lead to problems (Fosco, Hawk, Colder, Meisel, & Lengua, 2019; Loeber, Byrd, & Farrington, 2015; Morizot, 2015).

The second major temperamental characteristic is along a social-emotional dimension. A term that Moffitt uses is *negative emotionality*. The facets of negative emotionality are aggression (causes discomfort for others), alienation (feels mistreated), and stress reaction (anger and irritability). Life-course-persistent offenders score higher on measures of negative emotionality than adolescent-limited offenders. Furthermore, a subset of life-course-persistent offenders (psychopaths) also show a *callous-unemotional* quality to their social interactions (Thornton, Frick, et al., 2019). This temperamental characteristic is biologically based (Viding, Jones, Frick, Moffitt, & Plomin, 2008), and it is as relevant to girls as it is to boys (Hipwell, Pardini, et al., 2007).

Regardless of the terminology used by researchers, some form of a "difficult" temperament is common to almost all classification schemes (Eme, 2020; Walters, 2011a). We will continue to use the term "difficult" because it conveys well the potential problems these children can create. A difficult temperament, as characterized by impulsive sensation-seeking and negative emotionality, would certainly tax many a parent and school teacher. Although all children begin life with no self-control skills, most gradually do learn to control their impulses. Where self-control matters the most is in the inhibition of aggressive behavior, and learning to inhibit aggressive behavior takes time. It is expected that children with difficult temperaments would have a more arduous time learning these skills.

A difficult temperament in infancy or early childhood has predicted aggressive behavior, adolescent delinquency, and psychopathy. Schwartz, Snidman, and Kagan (1996) followed young children assessed before the age of 31 months until the age of 13 years. Difficult ("uninhibited") temperament predicted delinquency and aggressiveness as reported by the parents. Terri Moffitt and her colleagues found a difficult ("lack of control") temperament as early as age three to be predictive of maladaptive behaviors ranging from depression to criminal convictions at age 32 (Moffitt, Arsenault, et al., 2011), whereas Glenn et al. (Glenn, Raine, Venables, & Mednick, 2007) found uninhibited sensation-seeking at age three to predict psychopathy at age 28.

If a child is born with a difficult temperament, how does this temperament promote the development of criminal behavior? As suggested earlier, parenting and teaching such a child is demanding. A positive outcome for the child could result if the child has the "right" parent(s) and "right" teachers (caring, patient, and flexible in adapting to the child's behavioral pattern). However, if there is a "poorness of fit" (Chess & Thomas, 1990) between parenting and teaching styles and the child's temperament, then there could be trouble.

There is good evidence that parent(s) who find it difficult to cope may distance themselves emotionally from the child (Laukkanen, Ojansuu, Tolvanen, Alatupa, & Aunola, 2014; Walters, 2014a) or may resort to inflexible and inappropriate disciplinary techniques (Armour, Joussemet, et al., 2018). For example, Gerald Patterson and his colleagues (Patterson, 2016; Smith, Dishion, et al., 2014) hypothesized that hyperactivity is the first stage on the road to chronic delinquency. The child's hyperactivity interferes with effective discipline and consequently contributes to an early onset of delinquency. Matching a child with a difficult temperament with impatient, impulsive, and hostile parents (a likely scenario considering the intergenerational data) makes for unfortunate consequences. Poorness of fit between the child and teacher has also been observed in school settings (DeLisi & Vaughn, 2014).

In Moffitt's (2003) model, the major environmental risk factors are inappropriate parenting and poor parent–child relationships. Thus, the combination of a difficult temperament and the associated disruptive behavior of a child, along with a high-risk family environment, produce the perfect recipe for the creation of the life-course-persistent offender. In PCC, temperament is an ever-present characteristic of the individual. For the development of criminal behavior, a temperament characterized by poor self-control, high activity levels, and negative emotionality is very important.

The concept of the energetic, impulsive, sensation-seeking temperament describes behavior. What causes this behavior? One suspect factor is neurophysiological arousal (Cornet, de Koegel, Nijman, Raine, & van der Laan, 2014a; Moore, Hubbard, et al., 2018). People differ in their general state of neurophysiological arousal or excitability. Some of these processes are obvious, such as heart and breathing rates, eye pupil dilation, and sweating, while others require special instruments to detect neurophysiological processes (e.g., the electrical activity of the brain). Some theories place neurophysiological *underarousal* as central to a predisposition to criminal behavior. Eysenck (1977), Eysenck and Gudjonsson (1989), and Quay (1965) postulated that criminals are neurophysiologically hypoaroused. Think of all those neurons in your body operating like they were half asleep. In order to "wake up" and bring some balance to the neurophysiological system, you need to seek out stimulation and excitement. Pair this state of underarousal with poor self-control, and there is little wonder that some find themselves in conflict with the law.

Another aspect of neurophysiological underarousal is how it affects learning self-control. In Sarnoff Mednick's (1977) biosocial theory, self-control is learned through a combination of instructions, modeling, and the reinforcement of prosocial behaviors and the punishment of inappropriate behaviors. Normally, punishment elicits fear, which is a physiologically based emotion as indicated by increased heart rate, blood pressure, and sweating (these indicators can also describe excitement and anger—it all depends on how you cognitively label these feelings). Inhibiting the inappropriate behavior (i.e., self-control) avoids the unpleasant fear reaction.

Thus, critical inhibitory learning requires that: (1) antisocial behavior is punished, and (2) the child has the capacity to learn to inhibit antisocial behavior. The antisocial behavior of some people may be traced to the fact that they did not receive the appropriate socialization training. That is, they have normal neurophysiological arousal patterns, but either their parent(s) did not monitor their behavior closely enough or the parent(s) did not properly identify the antisocial behavior and consequently failed to punish that behavior. The antisocial behavior of others may be traced to a breakdown in the biological ability to effectively learn self-control (Beaver, Shutt, et al., 2009; Meldrum, Trucco, Cope, Zucker, & Heitzeg, 2018). There is also evidence linking adverse childhood events to poor neurocognitive functioning that interferes with passive avoidance learning (Yazgan, Hanson, et al., 2021).

Learning self-control to avoid punishment involves "fear reduction"; it is called *passive avoidance learning*. Passive avoidance learning proceeds in this manner:

1. The child contemplates an aggressive act.

2. Previous punishment produces fear in the child (increased heart rate, blood pressure, sweating).

3. Fear, an unpleasant emotion, causes the child to inhibit the aggressive response in order to escape from feelings of fear.

4. The child no longer entertains the aggressive impulse, and the fear dissipates.

5. The immediate reduction of fear reinforces the inhibition of the anti-social act.

In addition to requiring a socialization agent to deliver the original lessons through punishment, the process requires the ability to acquire the fear response, and a rapid dissipation of fear in order to receive the natural subtractive reward for inhibition (that sense of relief of avoiding punishment). Several studies have found that individuals with antisocial personalities show diminished fear responses to aversive stimuli, and once fear is aroused, the biological markers of fear (i.e., increased heart rate, high blood pressure, sweating) are slow to dissipate (Pemment, 2013; Raine, 2018).

The extent to which neurophysiological underarousal is prevalent among justice-involved samples and children with difficult temperaments needs further exploration. The hypotheses and few studies that relate underarousal to impulsivity and poor self-control skills are enticing. A deficit in passive avoidance learning may, however, be caused by factors other than a fear deficit. For example, some psychopaths may have the potential to feel fear but simply do not attend to the stimuli that provoke fear (Hiatt & Newman, 2006). However, the response to fear may differ based on the subtype of psychopathy (more will be said on psychopathy subtypes in the next chapter). A common taxonomy is to distinguish between primary (the type most people think of) and secondary (neurotic and anxious) psychopaths (Fanti, Kyranides, Petridou, Demetriou, & Georgiou, 2018). In a recent review of 17 studies Hofmann, Schneider, and Mokros (2021) found primary psychopaths showed more fearlessness than secondary psychopaths, although caution was advised due to the poor methodology in many of the studies.

Within the context of PCC, neurophysiological underarousal and the need for stimulation highlight the automatic, nonmediated reward potential of criminal behavior described in Chapter 3. That is, some individuals may engage in criminal acts not so much because of peer approval or some type of self-reinforcement strategy but because the act itself feels good (here we are referring to nonsexual offenses). Compared to nonoffenders, criminals tend to score higher on measures of sensation-seeking (Harden, Quinn, & Trucker-Drob, 2012; Thornton, Frick, et al., 2019) and will readily report a feeling of a "high or rush" when committing crimes (Wood, Gove, Wilson, & Cochran, 1997). In addition, a meta-analysis by Glenn Walters (2022) found sensation-seeking to be predictive of future offending ($r = 0.28$, $k = 18$). All in all, the neurophysiological arousal hypothesis provides a plausible explanation for criminal behavior in the absence of interpersonal or personally mediated controls.

Difficulties in self-control and disturbances in neurophysiological arousal do not mean that hope is lost for the chronic offender. A meta-analysis of self-control training programs for children under the age of 10 found improvements in self-control and reductions in delinquency (Piquero, Jennings, & Farrington, 2010). Furthermore, there is some evidence that participation in cognitive-behavioral treatment programs is associated with changes in neurobiological functioning (Cornet, de Koegel, Nijman, Raine, & van der Laan, 2014b; Vaske, Galyean, & Cullen, 2011). If environmental interventions change the likelihood of criminal behavior by changing brain function, then direct biological interventions may change antisocial behavior.

Two randomized, double-blind experiments have been reported by Adrian Raine and his colleagues on the relationship between poor nutrition and aggressive behavior mediated through brain development. In the first study (Raine, Portnoy, Liu, Mahoomed, & Hibbeln, 2015), 200 children (aged eight to 16 years) were randomly assigned to receive an omega-3 supplement in their fruit drink or to receive only the fruit drink. Neither the study participants nor the researchers knew who was administered the placebo or omega-3 supplement. After six months, the children who received the omega-3 supplement showed reductions in aggressive behavior. The parents of the children who had the omega-3 supplement also showed reductions in aggressiveness toward their children (presumably because the children were more compliant).

In the second experiment (Raine, Leung, Singh, & Kaur, 2020), 145 Singaporean youths (mean age 19 years) were assigned to: (1) omega-3 supplements, (2) no supplements, or (3) treatment-as-usual (e.g., educational programming, family counselling). The researchers found reductions in self-reported antisocial behavior for the group receiving the supplement, particularly for impulsive aggression, but not in officially measured institutional misconducts. Although the overall effect of omega-3 supplements on antisocial behavior is relatively small ($r = 0.10$; Choy & Raine, 2018), there remain many unanswered questions as to why it works and the dosage needed for maximum benefit.

We now leave the review of the proximal biological covariates of crime and turn to more distal biological factors, namely, evolution.

Crime: A Failure or Success of Evolution?

Darwin's theory of evolution by natural selection proposed that, through gradual adaptations to the environment, a species would evolve into a new species quite different from its ancestor. The modifications made to a species' physical appearance and physiology are adaptive, and they are adaptive because they allow the organism to survive and reproduce (e.g., a swallow uses its wings to fly and catch aerial insects, while a penguin cannot fly but uses its wings to swim after fish; in both cases the wings assist the bird with obtaining food). The two major tenets of Darwin's theory are (1) today's species evolved from ancestral species, and (2) organisms that adapt to their environment are more likely to reproduce, thereby ensuring the continued viability of the species (organisms that fail to adapt are less likely to reproduce; these lineages die off, thus the "survival of the fittest").

At the time, Darwin did not understand how certain adaptations are passed from one generation to the next. As we have seen, it is the gene that holds the programs that influence biological, physiological, and (some argue) psychological processes and transmit adaptations from one generation to the next. Congruent with the Darwinian perspective, genes are seen as trying to maximize their present and continued survival. The title of Richard Dawkins' (1989) book, *The Selfish Gene*, says it all. The sole purpose of genes is to "replicate" (using Dawkins' word), and genes use the body of the organism to succeed in a very competitive world (remember, there are other organisms with their own genes wanting the same thing).

A Failure in Evolution: The Caveman Awakened

Cesare Lombroso (1835–1909) is considered to be one of the founders of modern criminology. Trained as a physician with an interest in psychiatry (a "professor of mental disease"), he was particularly taken by the physical features of criminals. Lombroso measured and tabulated the size of the head, ears, and arms, and also noted unusual physical features such as eye defects and oddly shaped noses. Why this interest in physical characteristics, and what does it all mean?

A "revelation" came to Lombroso while conducting an autopsy on a prison convict (Lombroso, 1895/2004: pp. 65–66). He observed that the occipital part of the brain located at the back of the brain and responsible for vision looked like the brain of a rodent. Therefore, three conclusions were made. First, biologically the criminal has similarities more in common with lower-order animals than the rest of the human race. Second, because of this biological backwardness, the individual is likely to behave like an animal with few inhibitions. More to the point, the criminal is a biological throwback to an earlier evolutionary stage (Lombroso's theory of "atavism" means a reversion to the characteristics of some remote ancestor). Finally, *some* criminals are simply "born bad."

For Lombroso, not all criminals are born bad and not all are "atavistic." Most criminals were the result of adverse environments and experiences. However, the minority of the really unpleasant sorts (chronic, career criminals) suffered from a woefully inadequate biological makeup that prohibited successful coping in the modern world. If we review the physical characteristics of Lombroso's atavistic criminal (i.e., long arms, large jaw, ears standing out like a chimpanzee), then we get the picture of a Neanderthal who we can imagine having great difficulties in the modern world.

Criminal man was seen as a failure of successful adaptation and evolution to a higher level. The atavistic criminal had some success in reproducing

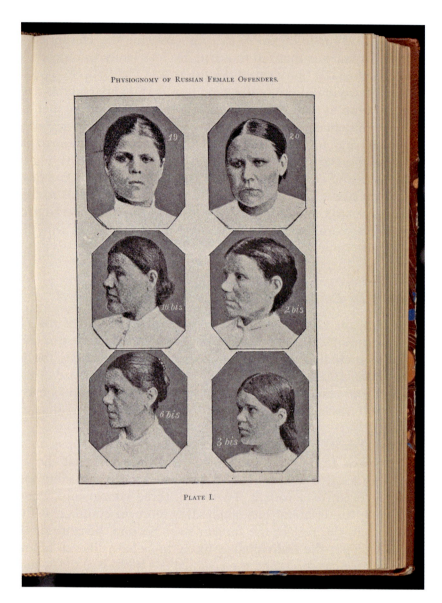

Figure 4.3

Physiognomy of "Fallen Women" (Lombroso & Ferrero, 1895)

Source: Wikimedia Commons

because of aggressive sexual behavior (rape) and copulating with those who were similarly malformed (i.e., assortative mating). Lombroso did not limit his studies to males but also gathered morphological (physical) data on women (Lombroso & Ferrero, 1895/1980). Compared to a sample of female "peasants," criminal women (which included prostitutes) had shorter arms, smaller head size, and darker hair and eyes. Figure 4.3 displays a page from Lombroso and Ferrero's *The Female Offender* (1895/1980).

Lombroso's theory of the atavistic criminal and emphasis on biology were reflective of the times. The validity of the theory depended partly on the demonstration that criminals do indeed show more physical anomalies than noncriminals. Lombroso's own work on this was limited to rather small samples (383 male criminals and 80 female criminals) with dubious comparison groups. Subsequent studies with much larger samples found mixed results, with many plagued by poor methodologies. Charles Goring's (1913) investigation of 3,000 English convicts who were compared on 37 physical characteristics to university students, hospital patients, and soldiers found no differences. In the United States, Hooten (1939) compared 14,000 inmates with 3,000 noncriminals and found differences on 19 of the 33 physical characteristics, with criminals featuring low foreheads and protruding ears and being generally physically inferior to noncriminals.

The efforts to identify a "born criminal" who is biologically weak and evolutionarily stunted led some to consider eugenics. Eugenics is the study of altering human reproduction in order to increase *desirable* heritable traits. Unfortunately, this also involves eliminating *undesirable* traits within the human population. For example, Hooten believed that the way to deal with criminals was to make sure that they did not reproduce. The New York State reformer Josephine Shaw Lowell established an "asylum" in Newark in 1885 for "feeble-minded" women in order to prevent them from producing criminal children (for a summary of early criminologists' views on eugenics, see Rafter, 2009). After the horrifying revelations from Nazi Germany, eugenics in the extreme may have diminished (although genocide still occurs) but other interventions intended to control reproduction among selected groups have continued. Forced sterilization of female inmates continued in California until 2014 (Kruttschnitt, 2016), sexual offenders were castrated for non-therapeutic reasons (Voultsos, 2020; Wessel, 2015), and some have argued that the high incarceration rates of Blacks in America serve to limit their reproduction (Oleson, 2016).

Finally, we have Glueck and Glueck's (1950) classic comparison of delinquents and nondelinquents using William Sheldon's (1942) three body types of ectomorph (thin), endomorph (overweight), and mesomorph (muscular). Each body type was associated with different temperaments. For example, the mesomorph had a high activity level and was more aggressive. Of course, many individuals cannot be definitively classified into any one body type. To deal with this problem, Sheldon developed a rating scheme by which points were assigned for each body type (there was an atlas of more than 1,000 male college students, with 46,000 photographs to help assign ratings). The Gluecks found that the delinquents were more likely to fall in the mesomorph category. Although this body type pattern has been repeatedly found to be associated with criminal behavior (Ellis, 2000), we cannot conclude that this body type was predetermined by genes. The mesomorphic body type could just as well have been the result of a physical, adventuresome lifestyle.

Lombrosian-like explanations of criminal conduct have continued into the present century. The most well-known and controversial views are those of

Phillipe Rushton. Rushton, along with Arthur Jensen, proposed that there are racial differences in intelligence, temperament, social organization (e.g., respect for the law, marital stability), and sexual restraint (Rushton, 1988; Rushton & Jensen, 2005, 2006, 2008). More to the point, they argued that Asians are the most advanced, followed by Caucasians, and then Blacks. Furthermore, these differences are explained by genetics and, by association, evolution. Thus, the higher crime rates observed among Blacks may be traced to their lower intelligence, poorer sexual restraints, and social disorganization.

Rushton and Jensen draw on many different types of evidence, but in order to link our discussion of Lombroso and Hooten we point to their use of cranial measurement and brain weight as proxies for intelligence. The claim is that the differences in cranial capacities and brain weight, with Asians showing the largest values and Blacks the smallest values, reflect the corresponding differences found in IQ scores (Rushton & Jensen, 2005, 2006, 2008; Templer & Rushton, 2011). To be clear, however, Rushton's interpretation of morphological differences among races was widely criticized on methodological and theoretical grounds (Cofnas, 2016; Sternberg, 2005; Winston, 2020) as well as his links to the white supremacist-leaning Pioneer Fund (he was actually a president of the organization until his death in 2012). This brief discussion of Rushton and Jensen's views is included only to show that Lombroso's work has had a long legacy.

Criminal Behavior as an Evolutionary Adaptation

In the previous section, Lombroso's theory of atavism was described as a backdrop to modern evolutionary explanations of crime. Contrary to the opinion of many of today's evolutionary theorists, Lombroso took the position that criminal man and woman were defects of evolution—not at all a positive step in evolutionary development. However, modern evolutionary theorists stress the *successful* adaption to the environment (there are exceptions; for example, the HIV virus *kills* the infected person, thereby killing itself).

Evolutionary criminologists and psychologists have proposed that some forms of criminal behavior can be understood as a product of successful evolution. When evolutionary theory is applied to criminal behavior, attention is given to temperaments, personality traits, and behaviors that maximize reproduction. Thus, risk-taking, aggression, and dishonesty may lead to consensual sex without birth control, nonconsensual sex (rape), and multiple sexual partners, thereby increasing the likelihood of offspring (Beaver, Wright, & Walsh, 2008; Buss, 2009; Ellis & Walsh, 1997; Walsh & Jorgensen, 2018). Particularly attractive is Ellis and Walsh's characterizations of *cads and dads*.

Cads are men who reproduce with women in sneaky, aggressive, or cheating ways and then leave the women while they go looking for another reproducing partner. Dads, on the other hand, remain monogamous and participate in the raising of the young. It is easy to use evolutionary theory to explain the origins of criminal behavior. Simply think of the early sexual behavior of delinquents (Glueck & Glueck, 1950), the promiscuity and parasitic life-style of psychopaths (Hare, 1996), and the general dishonesty of criminals (Quinsey, Skilling, Lalumière, & Craig, 2004). There are also a number of areas where the application of evolutionary theory is quite problematic because it suggests an excuse for truly abhorrent behaviors and minimizes other plausible causal mechanisms (Buss & Schmitt, 2019). Evolutionary theory has been used to explain the behavior of the rapist (Lalumière, Harris, Quinsey, & Rice, 2005; Thornhill & Palmer, 2000), intimate partner violence (the male controlling the woman's chances of bearing someone else's child; Archer, 2013; Peters, Shackelford, & Buss, 2002), and child abuse (nonrelated parents are more likely to abuse the child because there is no genetic investment; Hilton, Harris, & Rice, 2015).

Quinsey and his colleagues (Quinsey, 2002; Quinsey et al., 2004) have suggested that there are actually two types of life-course-persistent offenders. The first is that described by Moffitt (1993) as the child with neuropsychological problems, a difficult temperament, and poor socialization experiences. The second is the psychopaths, who follow an evolutionary adaptive, "life history" strategy (Harris, Rice, Quinsey, & Cormier, 2015: p. 275). These individuals demonstrate relatively few neuropsychological deficits (although they do have some) and their behavior reflects a genetically determined strategy to maximize mating success.

Although we have been discussing the selfish behavior of the male, a woman's behavior with respect to reproduction also has adaptive significance. Women, according to evolutionary theory, would seek the "dad" who would commit to raising the child and ensure the continuity of the genetic pool. Childrearing by a single parent runs the risk of the offspring not reaching maturity and reproducing. Therefore, it is in the mother's (gene's) best interest to choose a partner that helps her raise the children.

Ellis (2005) and Buss (2009) argue that mothers are also predisposed to pick "status-striving males," which puts evolutionary pressure on males to be highly competitive (and in the process of being competitive, people are also victimized in order to get ahead). Another important feature of a "dad" is that of nurturance (i.e., caring for children). Of course, the male is not entirely ignorant of the female's preferences and men try to make themselves attractive and worth keeping (in many bird species, males have evolved colorful plumage; in humans, men buy fancy suits but they tend to be "cads"; Kruger & Fisher, 2005). Alas, choosing a father that will remain loyal, considerate, and have the resources to care for the offspring is not easy. The high sexual and physical victimization rates of children attest to that.

Looking closely at the mating behaviors of justice-involved people, it is difficult to see that these behaviors are adaptive in the long run. Yes, delinquents and criminals do begin sexual intercourse earlier than noncriminals (although this may have nothing to do with delinquency; Resource Note 4.1), have children earlier, and have more sexual partners. However, they tend to mate with partners who have similar temperaments, personalities, and social backgrounds (i.e., assortative mating), with the result that they actually have higher levels of failed intimate partnerships, poorer health, and higher mortality (Jaffe, Belsky, Harrington, Caspi, & Moffitt, 2006; Laub & Vaillant, 2000; Moffitt, 2018; Piquero, Farrington, Shepherd, & Auty, 2014; Piquero, Farrington, Nagin, & Moffitt, 2010; Zane, Welsh, & Zimmerman, 2019). In addition, the products of these unions tend to be children with a low birth weight, a difficult temperament, and neurological problems. Certainly not in the best interest of the gene.

Evolutionary theory is changing. At times it appears that evolutionary theorists adhere to genetic determinism (Lickliter & Honeycutt, 2003) or a gene-based evolutionary theory that assumes that all changes are adaptive (Beaver, Wright, & Walsh, 2008). However, this is not true (e.g., eye color has no adaptive function; Daly, 1996). Many of the arguments for evolution are based on studies of lower species and then extrapolated to human behavior. Yes, humans are not guppies but why would we be the sole animal species to escape the laws of evolution (Walsh & Jorgensen, 2018)? The more complex the organism, the greater the influence of extra-genetic factors. Even in lower-level species, environmental factors can profoundly alter genetic programs (e.g., the sex of turtles depends on the incubation temperature of the eggs). Evolutionary theory is morphing into a developmental biology-informed theory of evolution. For example, the life-course-persistent and their early sexual experiences and multiple partners reflect accelerated reproductive strategies (Boutwell, Barnes, et al., 2015; Kavish & Boutwell, 2018). However, the bottom line is that environmental influences are given equal billing to genetic influences.

Three Closing Comments

Before closing this chapter a few comments relevant to a PCC are in order. First, biological factors contribute to criminal behavior. It is not that biology determines crime but that the biological processes behind a temperament exemplified by low self-control, negative emotionality, and other antisocial personality traits increase the probability of antisocial behavior under the right environmental conditions. The precise measurement of the underlying biological processes is rapidly progressing, but we are already there with reliably differentiating individuals on the behaviors described.

Second, assessment and treatment interventions need to include biological considerations (Loeber, Byrd, & Farrington, 2015). Neurobiological factors can predict treatment outcome (Bootsman, 2019; Cornet, de Koegel, Nijman, Raine, & van der Laan, 2014b). However, these factors need to be integrated into structured offender risk instruments. For example, Cheng, O'Connell, and Wormith (2019) have suggested adding behavioral indicators (e.g., attention, emotional control) of executive functioning (i.e., frontal lobes) to assessment batteries. We also know that biological factors can change as a result of treatment interventions (Cornet et al., 2014a; Vaske, Galyean, & Cullen, 2011), and more research is needed to help us understand this nature–nurture interaction.

Third, biological factors appear to play a greater role with the life-course-persistent offender. Although it is tempting to explain their behavior as a product of disadvantaged social environments, the evidence simply does not allow us to say this. Many children grow up in poverty and in homes with dysfunctional parenting, but not all of them follow a path of chronic and violent criminality. Why some children in these environments follow this path and others a less antisocial trajectory appears to reside in biological differences.

Worth Remembering

1. The environment influences how biological predispositions are expressed in behavior.

    There are many aspects to individuals that are biologically based—age, gender, race, and temperament. However, just because certain factors have a biological basis does not mean that behavior is predetermined. The path to crime, or to good citizenship, depends more on what happens as the individual grows up than on what capabilities the individual was born with.

2. A minority of youths account for most crimes. The majority of youthful males will engage in crime during adolescence but then stop in early adulthood. Developmental criminologists refer to this trajectory as adolescence-limited. However, a small minority of youths will continue their criminal activity into adulthood. This trajectory is called life-course-persistent.

3. There is a hereditary component in criminal behavior that interacts with the social environment. The findings from family lineage, twin, and adoption studies point to a genetic component to criminal conduct. It is not criminal behavior per se that is inherited but temperamental characteristics such as low self-control, sensation-seeking, and a negative emotionality. A "difficult" temperament may predispose some to an increased risk of crime, but the environment influences whether the predisposition translates into criminal behavior. Genes determine biochemical reactions; the environment determines what you think and how you behave.

4. Other biological factors can play a role with some individuals, some of the time. A variety of biological factors (e.g., neurophysiological underarousal) have been documented as risk factors in some individuals. These neurophysiological factors may be especially important with life-course-persistent and violent offenders.

5. Evolutionary explanations of criminal behavior have interesting implications, but the field remains highly controversial. The idea that criminal behavior has an adaptive function underlies evolutionary perspectives of crime. That is, the aggression and dishonesty of criminals have payoffs beyond immediate gratification. The early perspective that genes are all-important has diminished with a reminder of the tremendous importance of the environment.

Recommended Readings

For the reader interested in the work on developmental trajectories and the life-course-persistent offender, Robert Eme's (2020) 25-year summary of Terri Moffitt's ground-breaking work from the Dunedin longitudinal study along with David Farrington's (2021) eight-page summary of the CSDD are recommended. If one is interested in delving deeper into the major theoretical approaches to developmental criminology, the "go-to" source is Farrington, Kazemian, and Piquero's (2019) *The Oxford Handbook of Developmental and Life-Course Criminology*. Finally, to give a face to life-course-persistent offenders, Georgia Zara and David Farrington (2016: Chapter 3) provide eight fascinating case studies from their CSDD files. They demonstrate that research does not have to be only numbers and statistics.

The relevance of genetics is nicely presented in Robert Plomin and his colleagues' (Plomin, DeFries, Knopik, & Neiderhiser, 2016) "top ten" behavioral genetic findings. Along with this article, a companion reading is a primer of epigenetics by Jamie Walton (2021). Some readers will also be interested in the legal implications of genetic findings as they relate to crime. These readers are referred to the edited collection by Jeffrey Botkins and his colleagues, *Genetics and Criminality: The Potential Misuse of Scientific Information in Court* (Botkins, McMahon, & Francis, 1999).

Adrian Raine's (2013) text, *The Anatomy of Violence: The Biological Roots of Crime*, is a must read for those interested in the neurophysiological correlates of violent behavior. His review of the literature is comprehensive and written in an understandable manner. For a novel perspective on the role of temperament in criminological theory, Matt DeLisi and Michael Vaughn's (2014) article is suggested. It not only provides a succinct review of the literature but also raises issues of how the criminal justice system interacts, poorly, with those of difficult temperament. Finally, for those with an interest in evolutionary theory and crime the reader is directed to the chapter by Anthony Walsh and Cody Jorgensen (2018).

 Visit the Instructor and Student Resource to access additional exercises, videos and study materials to support this chapter: psychologycriminalconduct.routledge.com

CHAPTER 5 Antisocial Personality Pattern

Antisocial Personality Pattern. In everyday language: impulsive, adventurous, pleasure-seeking, generalized trouble (multiple victims, multiple settings), restlessly aggressive, callous disregard for others.

From Chapter 3

First described in Chapter 3, Antisocial Personality Pattern (APP) is one of the best predictors of criminal behavior and forms one of the Central Eight risk/need factors. The origins of APP were seen in what is called a difficult temperament (described in Chapter 4), and this personality constellation of poor self-control and negative emotionality appears central in the makeup of life-course-persistent justice-involved. Moreover, these personality characteristics predispose the person to problematic social relationships in a variety of settings. This chapter explores the notion of APP in more depth, with discussions of different perspectives of antisocial personality.

First, current knowledge of personality in general is outlined. The study of personality is a branch of psychology and should inform our understanding of criminal conduct. Next, criminology's position on personality and its transition to greater acceptance for personality constructs are reviewed. A third section examines forensic/clinical psychology and psychiatry's preoccupation with mental disorder through the study of antisocial personality disorder and psychopathy. Finally, the chapter ends with a critique of forensic/mental health conceptualizations of antisocial personality and a call for a more general perspective.

Psychology's View of Personality

Almost everyone has asked, at one time or another, "Who am I?" Usually, the answer to the question involves evaluations of the self ("I am a good person"), motivations ("I am lazy"), intelligence ("I am smart"), emotionality ("I am nervous"), and relationships to others ("I am kind"). The answers to the question also imply relative stability. That is, if we say we are nervous or

DOI: 10.4324/9781003292128-7

kind to others, then we act this way most of the time and with most people. Personality reflects typical patterns of thinking, feeling, and acting.

Traits describe our general pattern of responding to different situations. Some examples of traits associated with criminal behavior are aggressivity, impulsiveness, sensation-seeking, risk-taking, dishonesty, and emotional negativity. Sometimes when we look at the research on personality traits, we are left feeling that it is overly complex—there are so many different traits measured in so many different ways according to so many different theoretical perspectives. However, personality researchers and theorists have brought organization to the study of traits by developing descriptive systems of a few basic personality dimensions that encompass the multitude of traits.

The Super Trait Perspective of Personality

Most personality traits can be described by five general dimensions, referred to as the Five-Factor Model (FFM; Digman, 1990). Not everyone agrees on the precise labels for the five super traits, but we will use the labels proposed by Paul Costa and Robert McCrae (1992, 2010). The five factors are composed of subtraits or "facets." Here are the "Big Five," along with examples of their corresponding facets:

1. *Neuroticism*—anxious, angry hostility, impulsive.

2. *Extraversion*—positive emotions, excitement-seeking.

3. *Openness to Experience*—creative, open-minded, intelligent.

4. *Agreeableness*—trustworthy, altruistic, compliant.

5. *Conscientiousness*—competent, orderly, self-disciplined.

Research on the Five-Factor Model suggests that these personality dimensions are found across gender and culture and that there is a heritability component (Costa, McCrae, & Löckenhoff, 2019; Kajonius & Johnson, 2018; Nikolaševic, Dinić, et al., 2021). Although FFM is a major influence in personality theory, it does not have a monopoly on the field. Some psychologists (e.g., Mayer, 2005) feel that the Big Five model fails to adequately capture some commonly studied traits such as locus of control and masculinity–femininity. Others have argued that we need to consider more or different factors, especially if we are to describe psychopathologies. For example, Christine Durrett and Timothy Trull (2005) add two dimensions, *Positive Valence* (e.g., "I am superior" vs. "I am ordinary") and *Negative Valence* (e.g., "I am a bad person" vs. "I am a decent person"), creating a Big Seven model. However, Widiger and colleagues (Miller & Widiger, 2020; Widiger & Costa, 2013) have presented convincing arguments that FFM applies to psychopathologies and, indeed, the Big Five has been studied among an array of personality disorders and pathologies.

Although the majority of the research on FFM has been conducted on non-justice-involved samples, there is considerable interest in translating psychopathy into FFM terminology (Derefinko & Lynam, 2013). Part of the reason for considering FFM in understanding psychopathy is the growing consensus that psychopathy represents the extreme end of normal personality traits (i.e., as described by FFM). Most studies have used a cross-sectional methodology, often with extreme groups (e.g., college students vs. prisoners) or survey methodologies (e.g., scoring high or low on paper-and-pencil measures), thereby maximizing the chances of finding differences. What these studies find is that Agreeableness and Conscientiousness almost always differentiate antisocial individuals from prosocial individuals (Dam, Hjordt, et al., 2018; Falkenbach, Reinhard, & Zappala, 2021). Most studies also find Neuroticism and Extraversion to be important. Neuroticism and Extraversion have long been recognized as important personality variables playing central roles in Hans Eysenck's (1964) model of criminal behavior. Note the consistency in the findings compared to what was described in the biological chapter (Chapter 4) and our definition of APP.

Caspi, Moffitt, et al. (1994) found Constraint and Negative Emotionality linked to crime across countries, gender, race, and methods. The facets of Constraint are traditionalism (endorses high moral standards), harm avoidance (avoids excitement and danger), and control (is reflective, planful). Offenders scored lower on Constraint than did nonoffenders. The facets of Negative Emotionality are aggression (causes discomfort for others), alienation (feels mistreated), and stress reaction (expresses anger and irritability). Justice-involved persons scored higher on Negative Emotionality than non-involved persons. The two groups did not differ on measures of Positive Emotionality (e.g., feelings of well-being and sociability).

Related to the above are the findings reported in a meta-analysis of the three-factor models of Eysenck (1977). In Cale's (2006) review, the best correlate of antisocial behavior was Impulsivity ($r = 0.37$, $k = 96$), followed by Neuroticism ($r = 0.18$, $k = 90$). Extraversion evidenced the smallest effect size ($r = 0.10$, $k = 94$).

There is one important conclusion to be drawn from models of personality that use the Big Five or some variation of it. That is, the super traits are *normal* aspects of personality. They can describe all of us to some degree, and we all have more or less of these general dimensions of personality. We can use the super trait models to describe justice-involved persons without the need to invoke pathology and disease to explain their behavior, the usual approach taken by forensic psychiatry and psychology. Those in conflict with the law fall on the wrong end of constraint (self-control, impulsive, low conscientiousness) and emotionality (hostile, aggressive, callous disregard for others). This APP reflects a constellation of personality dimensions that we all share, but one's position on these dimensions accounts for the differences between the antisocial and the prosocial.

Is Personality Just a Matter of Traits?

Up to this point the discussion has been on personality from a trait per-spective. The trait perspective emphasizes the stable, enduring features of per-sonality. Certainly, there is some evidence of the stability of traits; however, we sometimes act differently in certain situations. When faced with a crisis, the cautious individual may muster the courage to rise to the challenge, or the shy person will speak out when a loved one is criticized. So then, just how stable and consistent are personality traits?

Walter Mischel (1968) reviewed the stability of various personality traits and found that the average correlation between a particular trait and the expression of that trait in various situations was about 0.30. Mischel suggested that viewing personality traits as highly stable across situations is a mistake. He went on to say that more attention to how people *interpret* situations is needed. As a consequence of Mischel's (1968) review, the study of traits fell into disfavor until its re-emergence with the development of FFM. The study of psychological processes that tried to make sense of the immediate situation grew in favor. The goal was to specify under what situational conditions a trait was expressed, and it was necessary to: (1) be very specific in describing the situation, and (2) understand how the individual personally interprets or encodes the situation. The encoding of information depended upon cognitive processes. Thus, if you wanted to predict whether an individual would behave aggressively, then you needed to know the specific situation (e.g., is a police officer present?) and how the individual interprets the situation (e.g., "the police officer may put me in jail" or "I hate cops").

Although the situation/psychological processing approach did yield improvements in the prediction of behavior, one could not escape the fact that, in general, people do have characteristic ways of responding to the envir-onment. For 20 years following Mischel's (1968) seminal work, personality research consisted of two solitudes—a trait perspective and a situational/psychological-processing perspective. However, personality researchers have been trying to integrate the two perspectives, and some of this work is led by no other than Mischel (Mischel & Shoda, 2010; Shoda & Mischel, 2006).

Mischel and Shoda (2010; Shoda & Mischel, 2006) describe their integra-tive theory as the Cognitive-Affective Personality System. Cognitive-affective processing (i.e., encodings, affect, expectancies, self-regulatory plans) can be relatively stable mediators between personality traits and the situation. For example, the general belief that people are out to get you leads to many social situations being interpreted the same way, resulting in similar behav-ioral responses. The direction of today's personality theories is toward greater integrations of various psychological subsystems. Personality is no longer just the study of stable personality traits but also the study of the dynamic psy-chological processes that are the mediators between traits and the situation of action.

Criminology's View of Personality

There has been a remarkable shift in mainstream criminology's view of personality and crime. From the 1930s to about 1990, the importance of personality had been largely ignored. Early reviews tried hard to discredit the evidence on personality in order to maintain a central role for social class in criminological theory. Today, personality is seen as pivotal in many criminological theories. Here follows the story of this remarkable transition.

Then …

The first substantive review of the personality–crime link was by Schuessler and Cressey (1950). They reviewed 113 studies and found that 42 percent of those studies reported a difference in the personalities of justice-involved and non-involved persons. Next, we have Waldo and Dinitz (1967) who reviewed 94 studies published after the Schuessler and Cressey (1950) review (i.e., 1950–1965). This review was more important than the previous one because the tests used to measure personality were more sophisticated and the studies better designed. A personality–crime association was found in 81 percent of the studies. Jumping to 1977, Tennenbaum located 44 studies of personality and crime published between 1966 and 1975. He noted that the methodological quality of the studies had improved and that a wider range of personality tests was being explored than in the earlier years. Eighty percent of the 44 studies reported a personality–crime association.

One of the major findings in Tennenbaum's review, as well as the other two preceding reviews, was that assessments of antisocial personality consistently differentiated between justice-involved and non-involved samples. Two of the most widely used measures of antisocial personality were the Socialization (So) scale from the California Personality Inventory and the Psychopathic Deviate (Pd) scale, as it was then called, from the Minnesota Multiphasic Personality Inventory (MMPI). These inventories are well-validated self-report, paper-and-pencil questionnaires. Scores on So and Pd are known to correlate with familial and biological variables, measures of self-management skills and impulsivity, and measures of deviance that extend well beyond the issue of the legality of conduct. In addition to their known correlations with theoretically relevant constructs, the scale items were deliberately selected to distinguish between justice-involved and non-involved samples.

Despite finding a relationship between personality and crime in 42 to 81 percent of studies found by all three reviews, the reviewers concluded that personality is irrelevant to the study of crime. How is this possible? The answer is in the knowledge destruction techniques used by the reviewers to minimize the value of the evidence. Tennenbaum's (1977) paper serves to illustrate knowledge destruction in action. The process was as follows:

1. Tennenbaum noted that he found it "disconcerting" that personality tests are no better predictors of criminality now than they were 10 years ago.

   Comment. He is concerned, but about what? The interstudy hit rate was 42 percent in 1950, 81 percent in 1967, and 80 percent in his own review of 1977. Does he think an interstudy hit rate of 100 percent is required?

   Knowledge Destruction Technique #1. Plant a vague suspicion or sense of uneasiness in the minds of the readers.

2. Tennenbaum accepted the fact that assessments of antisocial personality have consistently demonstrated concurrent validity. However, this achievement was then described as "surface validity." In Chapter 2 we discussed empirical understandings (e.g., causal validity, predictive validity). However, what is "surface validity"?

   Comment. Again, the reader is being emotionally prepared for an exercise in knowledge destruction. Initially alerted to a vague sense of negative concern, uneasy feelings have been reinforced by the term "surface validity."

   Knowledge Destruction Technique #2. Raise suspicion by inventing scientific-sounding words. The term "validity" tends to work well.

3. Because the So and Pd were constructed so that they might successfully distinguish between justice-involved and non-involved samples, their success in actually doing so in one study after another is a hollow achievement. More specifically, Tennenbaum (p. 288) states that the measures of antisocial personality provide "no information not obtainable simply by procuring a list of offenders."

   Comment. What is meant by this last statement? Yes, a few of the items from the Pd and So scales are direct indicators of criminal behavior. For example, the Pd scale has "I have never been in trouble with the law" and the So scale has "A lot of times it's fun to be in jail." Tennenbaum capitalized on this feature of the scales to conclude that there is no value added by the scales to a simple list of names of justice-involved persons. However, *most* of the items in the scales are not obvious measures of criminal conduct (e.g., "I am neither gaining or [sic] losing weight," from the Pd scale) and yet these items contribute to the differentiation of those who violate the law and those who do not. Moreover, the scales have predicted future recidivism in samples in which everyone had a criminal record.

   Knowledge Destruction Technique #3. Minimize the importance of new knowledge by questioning the value added.

Some of the knowledge destruction techniques used by Tennenbaum were outlined here to alert the reader that sometimes ideological beliefs get in the way of empirical understanding.

And Now ...

The days of ignoring the evidence on personality are now gone. Today's criminology theories have incorporated personality as an important theoretical construct. There is considerable consensus regarding the aspects of personality that are most strongly associated with criminality. Most notably, assessments of APP consistently differentiate between justice-involved and non-involved samples and predict criminal behavior.

Gottfredson and Hirschi's (1990) *A General Theory of Crime* was one of the most influential works to turn mainstream criminology to the study of personality. In their work, self-control is the cause of crime. However, they (1990: p. 49) rejected the position that their notion of self-control is a personality trait, blaming "the logic of psychological positivism" for a misunderstanding of their theory (knowledge destruction again). For them, poor self-control is evident in the behavior itself, and there is no need to hypothesize a predisposition to crime. For example, reckless criminal behavior is an indicator of poor self-control, and poor self-control causes criminal behavior. As Ronald Akers points out in the following statement, Hirschi and Gottfredson's explanation is circular and not helpful at all:

> It would appear to be tautological to explain the propensity to commit crime by low self-control. They are one and the same... the assertion means that low self-control causes low self-control. Similarly, since no operational definition is given, we cannot know that a person has low self-control (stable propensity to commit crime) unless he or she commits crime... the statement that low self-control is a cause of crime, then, is also tautological.
>
> (Akers, 1991: p. 204)

Putting aside Hirschi and Gottfredson's own views of self-control, their book did reintroduce personality to criminology. Furthermore, although the meta-analytic evidence between self-control and deviance is strong ($r = 0.42$ for cross-sectional studies and $r = 0.35$ for longitudinal; Vazsonyi, Mikuša, & Kelley, 2017), self-control theory continues to generate research and debate (Burt, 2020; Pratt, Cullen, et al., 2010; Vaughan, Ward, Bouffard, & Piquero, 2019).

From another perspective, the work of Terri Moffitt and her colleagues, along with other developmental criminologists and psychologists such as David Farrington, Rolph Loeber, Richard Tremblay, and Terence Thornberry, highlighted the importance of temperament, especially in the development of life-course-persistent offenders. A landmark study by Caspi and his colleagues (Caspi et al., 1994) firmly affirmed the study of personality in criminology. Drawing on their own Dunedin, New Zealand data and the Pittsburgh Youth Study, they convincingly showed that the personality characteristics of Negative Emotionality and poor Constraint (low self-control) were related to delinquency across culture, gender, and race. Miller and Lynam (2001) went further to show, through a meta-analytic review, how the Five-Factor Model (Agreeableness and Conscientiousness) was related to antisocial behavior. The study of personality and crime was no longer limited to psychological and psychiatric journals.

One of the spin-offs from criminology's newfound interest in personality was a rediscovery of the importance of general psychology. Suddenly, we began to see articles in criminological journals that could have just as easily been published in psychological journals (we do recognize the heroic efforts of a few—e.g., Ronald Akers, Paul Gendreau—to make a dent in the criminological literature). For example, Peter Wood et al. (Wood, Gove, Wilson, & Cochran, 1997) wrote about how crime can be maintained by the act itself through nonmediated reinforcement (i.e., doing crime for the thrill of it). Personality has also found its way into mainstream criminological theories. We have seen it in Chapter 3 with Hirschi and Gottfredson's extension of control theory via low self-control and in Agnew's strain theory where coping with stress and having a difficult temperament increases the chances of crime.

Antisocial Personality as Pathology

There are different meanings that can be assigned to the term "antisocial personality." The first meaning is simply the extremes of normal dimensions of personality described by FFM. The second meaning is rooted in psychopathology. A psychopathological perspective considers antisocial personality as a mental disorder, sees it as unhealthy and abnormal, as a disease. In medicine it is relatively easy to identify what is unhealthy and abnormal, but it is not so easy when it comes to psychological processes. How much hand washing is needed to cross the line between cleanliness and compulsiveness? How much lying and dishonesty is needed to call someone a psychopath? Much of psychiatry and clinical psychology deals with individuals who are seen as "crossing the line" into behavioral and thinking patterns that are considered abnormal, that is, considered to be a mental illness. Some of these mental illnesses show well-defined patterns that allow for reliable diagnosis and classification (e.g., schizophrenia, manic depression). Other "mental illnesses" are not so clearly defined. Antisocial personality is one of them.

Psychiatry and Antisocial Personality Disorder

Psychiatry is the branch of medicine that studies mental disorders. In general, psychiatry views most psychological problems as having a biomedical basis and practitioners will often prescribe medications, in addition to counseling, to treat individuals. Clinical psychologists, in most states and countries, do not have prescription privileges. They specialize in psychological assessment and counseling services. What many in both professions have in common is a belief that psychological abnormalities can be classified into distinct groupings with their own etiologies, developmental course, treatment, and prognosis. Physical illnesses are diagnosed or categorized (e.g., a common cold) with a cause (e.g., viral infection), a natural course for the illness (e.g., develop a sore throat and runny nose), a treatment (e.g., drink your mother's chicken soup), and a prognosis (e.g., don't worry, you will be just fine in about 10 days). Mental illnesses can also be classified into diagnostic categories with an etiology, course of development, and so on.

The two most influential taxonomies or classification systems for mental disorder are the American Psychiatric Association's *Diagnostic and Statistical Manual of Mental Disorders* (DSM) and the World Health Organization's (WHO) International Classification of Diseases and Related Health Problems (ICD). The fifth edition of DSM was published in 2013 nearly 20 years after the fourth version (DSM-5; American Psychiatric Association, 2013), and ICD-11 was released for use by the member countries in February 2022 (approximately 15 years after ICD-10). The United States is a signatory to the ICD-11 but implementation is not expected for another five years or so (it will take insurance providers some time to shift their third-party billing from DSM-5 to ICD-11). Therefore, because of the widespread use of DSM-5 (e.g., US, Canada, Australia, and other countries), and recognizing some of the weaknesses found in DSM-5 (e.g., poor retest reliability for some diagnoses, criteria that permit almost any level of human misery to be labelled a mental disease), the DSM-5 will serve the discussion on antisocial personality disorder.

DSM-5 describes behavioral patterns and psychological characteristics, which are clustered into diagnostic categories. For example, someone with auditory hallucinations, bizarre delusions (e.g., a pet dog controlling the behavior of the person), and a history of these delusions and hallucinations lasting more than six months is likely to be diagnosed as schizophrenic. One general area covered by DSM-5 comprises personality disorders. The personality disorders include, for example, obsessive-compulsive personality, paranoid personality, narcissistic personality, and, of course, antisocial personality disorder (APD). Most of the personality disorders have an early onset, and APD is differentiated from the other personality disorders by a "pervasive pattern of disregard for, and violation of, the rights of others" (American Psychiatric Association, 2013: p. 659). In children, the corresponding mental disorder is called *conduct disorder*. A summary of the diagnostic criteria for APD and conduct disorder (the childhood precursor to APD) is given in Table 5.1.

APD is estimated to affect approximately 3 to 4 percent of the population, with men approximately four times more likely to meet the diagnostic criteria (Volkert, Gablonski, & Rabung, 2018; Werner, Few, & Buchotz, 2015).

TABLE 5.1 Psychiatric Disorders of Relevance to Antisocial Behavior

DSM-5 Criteria for Antisocial Personality Disorder (Adults)

I.   Disregard for the rights of others. At least three of the following:
   a) behaves in a way that is grounds for arrest
   b) deceitful and manipulative
   c) impulsive
   d) aggressive
   e) irresponsible
   f) lack of remorse
II.   Age 18 or more
III. A history of childhood conduct disorder
IV.   Antisocial behavior not a product of a schizophrenic/manic episode

DSM-5 Criteria for Conduct Disorder (Children)

I.   Disregard for the rights of others or violation of age-appropriate social norms. At least three of the following:
   a) bullies, threatens, or intimidates others
   b) initiates physical fights
   c) has used a weapon
   d) physically cruel to people
   e) physically cruel to animals
   f) has stolen while confronting a victim
   g) forced someone into sexual activity
   h) fire setting
   i) destroyed property
   j) broken into a house, building, or car
   k) lies to obtain goods or favors
   l) steals
   m) stays out at night despite parental prohibitions beginning before age 13
   n) has run away from home at least twice
   o) truancy beginning before age 13

Source: American Psychiatric Association, 2013

In prison populations, the prevalence of APD exceeds 40 percent (Fazel & Danesh, 2002); however, the disorder is also relatively common among individuals who have broken no laws (e.g., alcoholics, compulsive gamblers). The disorder is seen as difficult to treat, and considerable research has focused on identifying the childhood predictors of APD in the hope that early intervention may be more successful (DeLisi, Drury, & Elbert, 2019; Rhee, Woodward, et al., 2021).

There are two points to be made about APD before moving on to a discussion of psychopathy. First, the assessment of APD is usually conducted by an unstructured clinical interview. More will be said about unstructured clinical assessment in Chapter 10, but for now the point is that the diagnosis of APD in the real-world clinical practice tends to be quite unreliable. Researchers studying APD may use structured assessment tools, but they are not used often enough in daily clinical-forensic practice (Vrieze & Grove, 2009). Second, the criteria for APD in DSM-5 stress behavioral characteristics. As we will see shortly, the public and some researchers also view certain emotional and personality characteristics as unique to some justice-involved persons. Think of the "cold-blooded killer." The DSM-5 criteria capture the aggressiveness and unremorsefulness but none of the emotional coldness of this individual.

We now turn to the personality construct of psychopathy that: (1) is assessed in a highly structured manner, (2) captures not only behavioral but also personality characteristics, and (3) is strongly linked to criminal conduct.

Psychopathy

The term *psychopathy* is widely used by both professionals and the general public; it is firmly entrenched within our culture (see Resource Note 5.1 for a clinical illustration). The public's image of the psychopath is the smooth charmer who is also capable of violent and sadistic behavior. Variations of the concept have been within the professional domain for more than a century, from Pinel's "mania without frenzy" to Prichard's 1835 description of "moral insanity" (Pichot, 1978) to Freud's underdeveloped superego. However, it was Hervey Cleckley (1941, 1982) who presented the contemporary clinical description of the psychopath.

RESOURCE NOTE 5.1

A Case Study of a Psychopath

Everybody called him "Red." He was 30 years old, tall and good looking, with red hair and a neatly trimmed red beard. Red came from a middle-class background. His father was a government civil servant, and his mother was a journalist for the city newspaper. When Red was four years old, his parents divorced and he went to live with his father until he was six years old. From age six on, he was sent to boarding school.

Boarding school was difficult for Red. He hated the school ("It was like the army"), the work, and the teachers. He ran away many times and, finally, at age 17, it was for good. Red ran to Florida, where he found his older sister. He told her that things were going so well in school and he was so advanced that the teachers said he could take a holiday and visit his sister. At his sister's house Red began to drink by sneaking liquor from the cabinet and replacing it with colored water. Three weeks later a telegram came to his sister.

continued

As she was not home, he opened the telegram and learned that their father died suddenly in a car accident.

Red returned to his home in New York state to claim his inheritance. He told authorities that his sister had committed suicide six months ago; he showed forged documents to support his claim. Red inherited everything. He lived in his father's house and began to party. Red's friends drank and took other drugs. Most had been in juvenile detention homes at some time in their lives or in jail. Red enjoyed his life: no school, no work, and lots of excitement.

The party ended quickly. One night he was drunk and assaulted his "best friend" with a baseball bat. Although the friend suffered a broken wrist, he refused to press charges. The police came, but there were no formal charges. For the next five years Red had numerous skirmishes with the law, was married one time, and became addicted to drugs.

At age 21 all the inheritance was spent. Red began moving from city to city. In each city he met a woman who worked at a low-paying job, and he moved in with her. Each woman learned after a few months that he brought trouble along with him. He continued to drink, injected cocaine, and committed "break and enters" and thefts to support his drug habit. Jail sentences rarely exceeded 60 days.

Then, at age 30, Red violently assaulted the woman with whom he was living. This time the judge gave him two years. The day after he was brought into custody, Red began phoning his common-law wife, pleading forgiveness. At first, she would hang up, but this did not discourage Red. Within two weeks she was accepting his calls. Within the month, she was visiting him in jail; she continued to do so until his release. While Red was receiving visits from his common-law wife and accepting the money she brought, he was also busy with other plans. He was not only lining himself up with women introduced by his fellow inmates, but he was also phoning the "companions" advertisements in the newspaper.

At the time of his release, Red had offers from three women for a place to live. Tests completed in prison showed the following results:

Level of Service Inventory-Revised (LSI-R):	48 (maximum possible 54)
Psychopathy Checklist-Revised (PCL-R):	36 (maximum 40)
Identification with Criminal Others:	92 percentile
Anxiety Scale:	4 (maximum is 10)
Self-Esteem Scale:	81 percentile

The test results from the PCL-R indicated that Red met the diagnosis of psychopathy (a score of 30 or more is needed). Red is also at a high risk to reoffend, as measured by the LSI-R. Finally, we can say that Red is relatively free from debilitating anxiety (a score of 4 on the Anxiety scale indicates a moderately low level of anxiety) and feels pretty good about himself as a criminal (a high score on the Self-Esteem measure and on the Identification with Criminal Others scale).

Drawing upon his many years of experience as a psychiatrist, Cleckley noted three characteristic patterns shown by some of his patients. First, psychopaths have all the outward appearances of normality. They do not hallucinate or have delusions, and they do not appear particularly encumbered by debilitating anxiety or guilt (Cleckley titled his book *The Mask of Sanity*). Second, psychopaths appear unresponsive to social control. For example, they continue to get into trouble despite punishment from society and those around them. Third, criminal behavior was not a necessary requirement for the diagnosis of psychopathy. In fact, Cleckley presented many examples of patients with no (known) criminal record.

This last point is particularly important. If we accept the assumption that a psychopath is not necessarily a criminal, then a number of important corollaries follow:

1. Not all criminals are psychopathic.

2. An explanation of crime may not serve as an explanation of psychopathy, and vice versa.

3. Following from Corollary 2, assessment and treatment methods for psychopaths and criminals should be substantially different.

The Assessment of Psychopathy: Hare's Psychopathy Checklist (PCL-R)

Robert Hare (2003) has taken the diagnostic criteria proposed by Cleckley and developed it into an objective assessment instrument called the Psychopathy Checklist-Revised or PCL-R, first published in 1991 and revised in 2003 (see Table 5.2). Each item is scored on a three-point scale: "0" (zero) for

---

TABLE 5.2 The Psychopathy Checklist-Revised™ 2nd Edition (PCL-R™ 2nd Ed.): A Sample of the Items

Pathological lying
Conning/manipulative
Callous/lack of empathy
Impulsivity
Juvenile delinquency

not applicable, "1" for uncertain, and "2" for definitely present. The higher the score, the more likely the individual is a psychopath.

What is the difference between APD, as defined in DSM-5, and psychopathy as measured by the PCL-R? When DSM-5 was being developed, consideration was given to integrate the affective and interpersonal aspects of psychopathy (e.g., empathy, arrogant self-appraisal) into the diagnostic category but it was eventually rejected (Widiger & Costa, 2013). As a result, the essential difference between DSM-5 APD and the PCL-R's psychopathy is on the emotional-interpersonal dimension.

This difference has a number of implications. First, DSM-5's APD is not the same as psychopathy; two separate sets of criteria are used in making the diagnosis, although some see psychopathy as a subtype of APD (Coid & Ullrich, 2010). Second, the DSM-5 diagnosis, relying on behavioral antisocial history, may measure persistent criminality more than a personality characteristic. This limits the usefulness of the APD diagnosis in forensic and correctional settings. For example, in a survey of 12 countries and nearly 23,000 prisoners, 47 percent of male prisoners and 21 percent of females were diagnosed with APD (Fazel & Danesh, 2002). It is estimated that 25 percent of male prisoners can be diagnosed as psychopaths (De Brito, Forth, et al., 2021). In some correctional agencies, the rates of APD are higher, falling in the 50 to 80 percent range (Ogloff, 2006). It is not surprising to find such a high base rate given the diagnostic criteria of age 18 and failure to conform to social norms with respect to lawful behavior. However, such high base rates are not very helpful in making decisions around treatment, security, and release. These rates also give an indication of the enormous monetary costs associated with psychopaths. Dylan Gatner and his colleagues (Gatner, Douglas, Almond, Hart, & Kropp, 2022) have estimated that psychopaths cost the criminal justice system and victims at least $12 billion in Canada and $245 billion in the United States.

Scholars have long debated how many subtypes of psychopathy there are and what to call them. Most popular is the notion of primary and secondary psychopaths (recall Chapter 4). The primary psychopath is the fearless, callous, impulsive person and the secondary psychopath is the neurotic, anxious, moody individual (Poythress & Skeem, 2006; Sellbom & Drislane, 2021). Others, however, have proposed three (Magyar, Edens, Lilienfeld, Douglas, & Poythress, 2011), four (Swogger & Kosson, 2007), and even 10 subtypes (e.g., "malignant psychopath", "abrasive psychopath"; Millon & Davis, 1998).

What characteristics make up a "psychopath"? Much of the answer is found in factor analytic studies of psychopathy assessment instruments. Factor analysis is a statistical technique that identifies test items that are intercorrelated or "hang together." So, with the 20 items of the PCL-R one can examine which items correlate with each other and reduce the PCL-R into "factors" (think of the facets in FFM). In early research, Hare and his colleagues reported that the PCL-R consisted of two factors; the first factor is interpersonal/affective (e.g., callousness) and the second is lifestyle/antisocial (Hare, Harpur, Hakstian, Forth, & Hart, 1990; Harpur, Hare, & Hakstian, 1989). Later, Hare adopted a four-factor model (Hare & Neumann, 2006), although he views the original two factors as "higher order" (Hare, 2016). The four factors are:

Factor 1: Interpersonal, tapping items such as glibness and conning.

Factor 2: Affective, focused on emotions (e.g., lack of remorse, callous).

Factor 3: Lifestyle (e.g., need for stimulation, impulsivity).

Factor 4: Antisocial (e.g., juvenile delinquency, criminal versatility).

The four-factor model has held up remarkably well in American and Canadian studies (Mokros, Hare, et al., 2015), across gender (Guay, Knight, Ruscio, & Hare, 2018), ethnic groups (Olver, Neumann, Wong, & Hare, 2013), and internationally (Neumann, Schmitt, Carter, Embley, & Hare, 2012). We will return to this more recent development in the PCL-R at the end of this chapter, but for now note how psychopathy is being conceptualized into more discrete domains. One important conceptualization is the triarchic model (Patrick, Fowles, & Krueger, 2009). The model describes three general traits of disinhibition (similar to Factor 3 of the PCL-R), meanness (Factor 2), and boldness (Factor 1 of the PCL-R). A recent meta-analysis of 84 studies by Sleep, Weiss, Lynam, and Miller (2019) found disinhibition ($r = 0.44$) and meanness ($r = 0.38$) robustly related to poor outcomes (e.g., aggression, antisocial behavior) but not boldness ($r = 0.10$). What is important in the factor analytic work and the triarchic model is that they identify personal traits that could possibly serve as treatment targets (e.g., treatment to improve empathy, learn self-control).

An important question is whether psychopathy Is a discrete personality construct (i.e., a taxon) or is dimensional, a matter of degree? Certainly, Cleckley took the position that psychopathy is a distinct personality construct with a constellation of affective, cognitive, interpersonal, and behavioral characteristics not shared by other disorders. However, most studies have found little support for a taxon among men (Edens, Marcus, Lilienfeld, & Poythress, 2006; Guay, Ruscio, & Knight, 2007; Poythress & Skeem, 2006), women (Guay et al., 2018), and youth (Edens, Marcus, & Vaughn, 2011). Earlier, Hare had taken the position of an "underlying dimensionality" of psychopathy (Hare & Neumann, 2006: p. 73), but more recently he appears to have slightly shifted his views, writing that at the extremes of the four dimensions (factors) the psychopath is qualitatively different and may well be "a good candidate for arguing in favour of taxonicity" (Hare, 2016: p. 28).

The PCL-R has always presented a bit of a confusing picture regarding the question of psychopathy as a taxon or a personality dimension. Scores on the PCL-R can fall between 0 and 40 and, therefore, one can ask if there is a certain score where one *becomes* a psychopath (i.e., a taxon). For example, Hare (1991, 2003) recommends a cutoff score of 30, but researchers have used scores varying from 25 (Harris, Rice, & Cormier, 1989) to 32 (Serin, Peters, & Barbaree, 1990). Nevertheless, the PCL-R appears to largely follow a dimensional model of psychopathy, reflecting a general trend to move away from considering personality disorders as diagnostic categories to dimensional classifications.

PCL-R and the Prediction of Criminal Behavior. The PCL-R does a very good job of predicting both general and violent recidivism. A number of meta-analytic reviews on the topic have found almost identical average correlations between PCL-R scores and future general recidivism ($r = 0.27$, Salekin, Rogers, & Sewell, 1996; $r = 0.28$, Gendreau, Little, & Goggin, 1996). Using a broad definition of recidivism that included new charges and "institutional maladjustment," Leistico, Salekin, DeCoster, and Rogers (2008) found $r = 0.27$. Three meta-analyses of the PCL-R with violent recidivism also reported nearly identical rs of 0.27–0.28 (Campbell, French, & Gendreau, 2009; Hemphill, Hare, & Wong, 1998; Yang, Wong, & Coid, 2010), whereas Salekin et al. (1996) found a slightly higher r of 0.32. When compared to other risk instruments, the PCL-R predicted general and violent recidivism as well as (and sometimes better than) the other scales.

Earlier it was noted that the PCL-R consists of a number of factors. Two dealt with personality and the other two with antisocial lifestyle (e.g., early behavior problems, impulsiveness, thrill-seeking). Four meta-analyses have examined the relative contribution of the factors (Hemphill et al., 1998; Kennealy, Skeem, Walters, & Camp, 2010; Leistico et al., 2008; Yang et al., 2010). All reviews found the antisocial lifestyle factors were better predictors of recidivism than the personality factors (Factors 1 and 2 combined). These findings suggest that the personality features of psychopathy, as measured by the PCL-R, may play a lesser role in predicting criminal behavior, but recent studies and literature reviews have delved deeper by examining each factor separately. A number of reports have found Factor 2 (Affective, e.g., lack of remorse, callous) a robust predictor of *violent* recidivism (O'Connell & Marcus, 2019; Porter, Woodworth, & Black, 2018; Sohn, Raine, & Lee, 2020; Walters, Wilson, & Glover, 2011).

The predictive validity of the PCL-R is impressive, and its core findings have been replicated across settings (prisons, psychiatric hospitals), gender, and race (Douglas, Vincent, & Edens, 2018; Olver, Neumann, et al., 2018). Although the PCL-R predicts recidivism among different samples, it appears to predict significantly better with certain groups. Leistico and her colleagues (2008) found that the PCL-R had higher predictive validities among Caucasians, females, and psychiatric patients than with minority ethnic groups, males, and inmates. The PCL-R still predicted recidivism for the latter groups but not as well as the former groups and, therefore, care was advised when applying the PCL-R for ethnic minorities, males, and prisoners.

There is an additional caution to give. In medico-legal-forensic settings, psychopathy is often equated with dangerousness and may provide grounds to subject psychopathic offenders to severe measures. In a meta-analysis of 10 jury simulation studies, psychopaths were seen as more dangerous than non-psychopaths ($r = 0.31$) and deserving of longer sentences ($r = 0.27$; Kelley, Edens, Mowle, Penson, & Rulseh, 2019). In another meta-analysis, Berryessa and Wohlstetter (2019) summarized 22 studies that examined how the label "psychopathy" influenced perceptions of dangerousness, the legal sanction, and treatment amenability. The studies were not real-world investigations but used vignettes rated by university students, judges, probation officers, and the general public. Two comparisons were made: (1) an accused with a psychopathic label vs. no mental health diagnosis, and (2) an accused with a psychopathic label vs. another psychiatric diagnosis (e.g., conduct disorder, antisocial personality disorder).

In the first comparison (label vs. no label), those labelled as psychopathic were viewed as more dangerous ($r = 0.28$), deserving of a more severe sanction ($r = 0.08$) and not very amenable to treatment ($r = 0.15$). However, when the comparison was to another psychiatric disorder the psychopath label was no worse. In other words, punishment outcomes were due more to having any mental disorder diagnosis and not limited to the diagnosis of psychopathy. In addition to the diagnosis of psychopathy, DeMatteo, Hart, et al. (2020) have gone so far as to conclude that the PCL-R assessment instrument "*cannot and should not*" (p. 134) be allowed in capital-sentencing cases. The claim by DeMatteo and his colleagues that the PCL-R fails the standards for use in court has been hotly contested (Hare, Olver, et al., 2020).

The popular media certainly paints such a picture, and it is hardly disputed by clinical professionals (Larsen, Jalava, & Griffiths, 2020; see Figure 5.1). However, there is evidence that not all psychopaths are violent (more on this in the next section), nor are all who committed violent crimes psychopaths (Harris, Rice, & Quinsey, 1993). In a study of 2,603 individuals convicted of homicide, the mean score on the PCL-R was 21.2, far below the cutoff score of 30 to be diagnosed a psychopath (Fox & DeLisi, 2019). In another study of those declared by Canadian courts as "dangerous offenders," only 39.6 percent were assessed as psychopaths by the PCL-R (Bonta, Harris, Zinger, & Carriere, 1998).

Are There Noncriminal Psychopaths?

Are there individuals with the characteristics of psychopathy whose behavior does *not* bring them into conflict with the law? Cleckley certainly thought so. Cathy Widom (1977) reasoned that it is possible that criminal psychopaths, the ones on which most of the research is based, represent only the unsuccessful psychopaths (the ones that get caught). Skeem and Cooke (2010) argued that criminality is central to psychopathy, while Hare and Neumann (2010) responded that criminality is not the important feature but rather antisociality or problematic behavior. Perhaps there are "successful" psychopaths who, though engaging in questionable behavior, elude the criminal justice system. The questions arise: How do you identify these successful psychopaths and how do they differ from criminal psychopaths?

Widom developed a procedure of recruiting psychopaths from the general population by placing advertisements in the newspaper searching for

Figure 5.1

Psychopathy

Source: Shutterstock

people who were "charming, aggressive, carefree people who are impulsively irresponsible but are good at handling people and at looking after number one" (Widom, 1977: p. 675). In her first study (Widom, 1977), the majority reported having been arrested as an adult (64.3 percent), but only 17.9 percent of the sample ($n = 28$) had a conviction, suggesting an element of success at having avoided a more severe sanction. Similarly, in a second study (Widom & Newman, 1985), 41 percent were arrested but only 5.1 percent ($N = 40$) reported a history of incarceration.

Since Widom's groundbreaking research, there have been sufficient studies using various community samples and more structured assessments of psychopathy including the PCL-R to allow Ana Sanz-Garcia and her colleagues (Sanz-Garcia, Gesteira, Sanz, & Garcia-Vera, 2021) to provide reasonable estimates of the prevalence of psychopathy in the general population. They reviewed 15 studies with a total of 11,497 individuals drawn from the community (curiously, Widom's research was not included). It was estimated that the overall prevalence rate of psychopathy was 4.5 percent. Six studies reported on gender and in this case the rate of psychopathy was higher for males (7.9 percent) than females (2.9 percent). However, when the PCL-R was used to identify psychopaths, a rigorous measure as we have seen, the rate dropped to 1.2 percent. Unfortunately, none of the reviewed studies reported what percentage of the psychopaths from the general population had involvement with the criminal justice system.

The general value of this research is establishing that there are some people who have psychopathic characteristics and who have seemingly avoided criminal justice intervention. When speaking of the successful psychopath, political or business leaders quickly come to mind. These "psychopaths" are cunning, manipulative, and ruthless in their relationships with people—interested only in pursuing what is best for themselves. And they are seen as "successful" in professional life, although these same characteristics plus others (e.g., impulsiveness) can cause significant problems in their personal life as they climb to the top (Benning, Venables, & Hall, 2018). However, a recent study of psychopaths from the CSDD study who obtained white-collar jobs found that few of them made it to a managerial position and they also demonstrated other problems (e.g., alcohol and drug misuse; Piquero, Piquero, Narvey, Boutwell, & Farrington, 2021).

Lilienfeld, Watts, and Smith (2015) have reviewed three different perspectives of the successful psychopath. The differential-severity model views the successful psychopath as less severe than the full-blown version. Then, there is the moderated expression model where certain protective factors such as good executive functioning (i.e., self-control) moderate some of the nasty qualities of psychopathy. Finally, there is the differential-configuration model that adds on to the basic psychopathy characteristics the traits of conscientiousness and boldness. After reviewing the evidence, no one model clearly explained the successful psychopath. Rather, it appears to be a mix of the moderated-expression and differential-configuration models creating "a subspecies of psychopathy" (p. 302).

In 2018, Boccio and Beaver raised the interesting proposition that if there can be successful psychopaths that avoid the criminal justice system, is it possible to have successful *criminal* psychopaths? That is, they may be apprehended by authorities but not easily. Boccio and Beaver (2018) selected participants from the fourth wave of the National Longitudinal Study of Adolescent to Adult Health (ages 24–32), who were administered a measure of psychopathy created from the FFM ($N = 14,857$). They found that high scorers showed no particular skill in avoiding arrests although the women in the sample had a greater likelihood of avoiding arrest. This latter finding may have more to do with the fact that women who do become involved in crime tend to commit less serious crimes (e.g., violent acts) and avoid detection. In addition, higher scorers on the psychopathy measure are more likely to have *more* arrests than low scorers.

The Etiology of Psychopathy

One of the lessons of Chapter 4 is that early negative family experiences interact with neurobiological deficits to produce life-course-persistent justice-involved persons. The factors that lead to this trajectory are much the same factors that contribute to the development of APD and psychopathy (Piquero, Farrington, et al., 2012). For example, environmental risk factors include early onset of antisocial behaviors (DeLisi, Neppi, Lohman, Vaughn, & Shook, 2013), unstable parent(s) (Auty, Farrington, & Coid, 2015), and childhood maltreatment (DeLisi, Drury, & Elbert, 2019). However, the bulk of the research has been devoted to neurobiological factors.

Although psychopaths and those diagnosed with APD have similar neurobiological factors, there are also some differences. Brain imaging studies suggest, especially with violent psychopaths, that the prefrontal (executive function) areas of the cortex are less developed (Ling & Raine, 2018; de Brito, Forth, et al., 2021; Patrick, Perkins, & Joyner, 2019). In a meta-analysis of 43 studies, Yang and Raine (2009) found a negative correlation ($r \sim -.30$) between prefrontal lobe structure/function and psychopathy. However, this meta-analysis had only 789 antisocial subjects, with nine of the 43 studies examining psychopaths (the number of individuals was not specified).

There is also evidence for a genetic component to psychopathy (Mariz, Cruz, & Moreira, 2022). Two twin studies have estimated that between 58 percent (Lewis, Connolly, Boisvert, & Boutwell, 2019) and 69 percent of the variance in psychopathy was explained by genetics (Tuvblad, Bezdjam, Raine, & Baker, 2014). A number of heritable mechanisms have been suggested ranging from callous-unemotional traits (Moore, Blair, Hettema, & Roberson-Nay, 2019) to an inability to learn from punishment (Jean-Richard-dit-Bressel, Killcross, & McNally, 2018). The identification of neurophysiological deficits through brain-imaging studies has led some scholars to question whether criminal (unsuccessful) psychopaths can be held legally accountable for their actions (Anderson & Kiehl, 2012; Umbach, Berryessa, & Raine, 2015). However, a successful defense depending on a diagnosis of psychopathy is unlikely. As already noted, most studies show that such a diagnosis actually leads to a harsher response from the courts.

The Treatment of Psychopaths

Clinicians, in general, have viewed psychopaths as difficult to treat if not incurable (Larsen, Jalava, & Griffiths, 2020). Certainly, this has been Cleckley's view. Their intractability has been attributed to a biological deficit and/or early childhood experiences so severe that they are beyond hope. The notion that some psychopaths do not feel guilt and remorse (i.e., lack a conscience) hits at the core of treatability. Those with a capacity for emotionality and a "conscience" are more amenable to treatment (Blackburn, 1993; Eysenck, 1998). In addition, psychopathic and antisocial personality features are associated with treatment attrition (Olver, Stockdale, & Wormith, 2011). Treatment methods supposedly tailored for psychopaths, such as therapeutic communities (Blackburn, 1993; Hobson, Shine, & Roberts, 2000), have failed to show positive results and have actually shown increases in recidivism for psychopaths (Harris & Rice, 2006).

Clinical anecdotes and a few published studies may fuel the belief that psychopaths are untreatable, but this may not be an accurate picture. Reviews of the treatment literature have all come to the same conclusion: there is insufficient evidence to say whether treatment does or does not make a difference (Hecht, Latzman, & Lilienfeld, 2018; Polaschek & Skeem, 2018; Polaschek & Wong, 2020). Part of the problem is that almost all the treatment programs have been poorly conceived interventions. Later in the book evidence will be reviewed showing that treatment can be effective if certain principles are followed. Treatment will be more effective if: (1) intensive services are delivered to higher-risk cases (risk principle), (2) treatment targets criminogenic needs (need principle), and (3) cognitive-behavioral interventions are used (responsivity principle). These principles have yet to be widely applied to psychopaths and experimentally evaluated. There is hope on the horizon. Treatment programs for psychopaths that are influenced by these principles have been developed in Canada and New Zealand with promising results but much more is needed (for a summary see Polaschek & Wong, 2020).

Can Children Be Psychopaths?

Psychopathy is seen as a stable personality pattern that changes little from year to year. Although the criminal activity of psychopaths decreases with age (Vachon, Lynam, et al., 2013), it is unclear whether the reduction is due to avoiding apprehension or a real change in behavior. The stability of the psychopathic construct also suggests that the personality and behavioral traits must have started early in life. In Chapter 4, we saw that the origins of APP characterized by impulsiveness, sensation-seeking, restlessness, and a callous unemotionality could easily be identified in early childhood. Some researchers have taken a special interest in exploring the possibility of extending the notion of psychopathy to children or at least identifying the childhood precursors of adult psychopathy.

Adelle Forth and her colleagues (Forth, Hart, & Hare, 1990; Forth, Kosson, & Hare, 2003) modified the PCL-R for use with adolescents (age 13 and up). The modifications involved deleting some items (e.g., "many short-term marital relationships") and altering the scoring criteria for some of the other items (e.g., "criminal versatility"). Most of the research has demonstrated that the PCL: YV (Psychopathy Checklist: Youth Version) has good reliability, appears to measure what it is supposed to measure (i.e., construct validity), and produces scores that are correlated with general criminal behavior (Brazil & Forth, 2016; Stockdale, Olver, & Wong, 2010) and institutional misconduct (Edens & Campbell, 2007). However, the findings with respect to violent recidivism have been mixed (Debowska, Boduszek, & Woodfield, 2018).

Researchers such as Paul Frick (Frick, Barry, & Bodin, 2000; Frick, O'Brien, Wootton, & McBurnett, 1994) and David Lynam (1997) have gone one step further and modified the PCL-R and the key diagnostic features of psychopathy for use with children as young as six years old. Some of the more widely researched instruments are the Antisocial Process Screening Device (Frick & Hare, 2001), the Childhood Psychopathy Scale (Lynam, 1997), and the Inventory of Callous and Unemotional Traits (Roose, Bijttebier, Decoene, Claes, & Frick, 2010). Typically, items are scored based on information provided by parents and teachers, although self-report versions are available for adolescents. Much of the research with the scales has been limited to reliability and normative data (Cardinale & Marsh, 2020; Colins, Bijttebier, Broekaert, & Andershed, 2014). However, predictive validity with respect to delinquent behavior has been mixed (Ansel, Barry, Gillen, & Herrington, 2015; Ray & Frick, 2020).

Regardless of what the research will uncover in the coming years, the utility of applying the construct of psychopathy to children and adolescents has yet to be resolved (da Silva, Rijo, & Salekin, 2020). Basically, does it make sense to extend a personality construct that has always been limited to adults to children? Recall that a diagnostic criterion for APD requires a minimum age of 18.

A number of researchers have raised concerns about the idea of "juvenile psychopathy" (da Silva et al., 2020; Viding & McCrory, 2018). Some of the concerns include the following. First, as already noted, the research on youth measures of psychopathy, particularly with younger children, has been mixed in regard to predictive validity. Second, at times, the research has had serious methodological weaknesses, ranging from small samples to difficulties in translating adult-like items to child-friendly items. Third, some of the items in the various youth versions may be normative or related to their development. What adult has not chuckled at the adolescent's "grandiose sense of self-worth" or "failure to accept responsibility"? Is impulsiveness, the need for stimulation, and lack of realistic, long-term goals reflective of normal adolescence? Items such as these may overestimate psychopathic features in adolescence. Finally, there is the danger that a diagnosis of childhood psychopathy may overestimate risk and apply a stigmatizing label.

A General Personality and Cognitive Social Learning Perspective: APP

The DSM-5, the PCL-R, and other clinical classification systems operate on the assumption that certain behavioral patterns "hang together" to create categories that can be reliably differentiated from other classifications and have their own etiologies and course of development. For example, someone who is diagnosed as schizophrenic has characteristics different from a manic depressive, with a unique etiology and prognosis. The same may be said for APD and psychopathy. One of the problems with APD and psychopathy is that there is little consensus as to their specific etiology and prognosis.

PCC's definition of Antisocial Personality Pattern (APP) encompasses behavioral *and* personality characteristics that are relevant to the assessment and treatment of criminal behavior. The word "pattern" is underscored because it includes personality facets (i.e., impulsiveness, sensation-seeking, fearlessness, egocentrism, hostile emotions, and attitudes) and a pattern of law-violating and problematic behaviors, often evidenced early in life. Note that there is no need to hypothesize the constructs of APD or psychopathy. This more comprehensive definition adds significantly to our understanding of high-risk, high-need justice-involved persons. Furthermore, assessing APP can be conducted by any reasonably trained correctional and forensic staff without the need for specialized credentials and training as with the PCL-R and DSM-5.

Poor Self-Control: A Facet of Antisocial Personality

Gottfredson and Hirschi (1990) argued that low self-control is sufficient to explain criminal conduct. The GPCSL perspective argues for many more variables to explain the frequency, severity, and variety of criminal acts. Criminal history, procriminal attitudes and peers, and an antisocial personality that includes poor self-control, egocentrism, and sensation-seeking are some of the other major explanatory factors (i.e., the Central Eight; Chapter 3). There are also family/marital, school/work, leisure/recreation, and substance misuse factors. Mindful of the preceding comments, a few words on the psychology of self-control are warranted.

Self-control is a process through which an individual directs his or her behavior in the service of achieving a long-term goal. This process typically requires delaying immediate gratification. When we consider criminal behavior, it is often a choice between vice and the more long-term benefits of adherence to the social norms. Poor self-control is an overreliance on the present at the expense of long-term consequences. Those in conflict with the law, in this light, are too much focused on the concrete here-and-now and have difficulty with the more abstract future. The predominant model of self-control is the strength model first proposed by Baumeister and his colleagues (Baumeister, Heatherton, & Tice, 1994).

The strength model views self-control as a limited energy resource and analogous to a muscle (Alquist & Baumeister, 2012; Baumeister, Tice, & Vohs, 2018). Like a muscle, self-control can be exercised to become stronger and more efficient, but it can also fatigue and not work as well. Baumeister and his colleagues referred to this fatigue as ego depletion, although the construct's value has been questioned (Freise, Loschelder, Giesler, Frankenbach, & Inzlicht, 2019). Laboratory studies show that when participants are first required to exercise self-control in a task (e.g., resist cheating on a task for a longer-term monetary benefit), they then do more poorly in the next self-control task (Mead, Baumeister, Gino, Schweitzer, & Ariely, 2009). It is as though the energy required to exercise self-control in the second task was sapped by the first task.

This model has some interesting implications for our understanding of self-control among justice-involved persons. Perhaps some, on average, begin with lower levels of self-control (low constraint in Moffitt's model) and this baseline predisposes them to choosing the quick and easy over the slow and difficult. Furthermore, when they do exercise some self-control, their energy depletes more quickly, raising their vulnerability to giving in to crime. However, self-control can be purposively improved. A recent meta-analysis of 33 studies found a small but significant overall effect of training on self-control (Friese, Frankenbach, Job, & Loschelder, 2017). An interesting variable with the potential to influence strength is prosocial attitudes. Kivetz and Zheng (2006) found that an attitude of entitlement can disengage self-control processes in favor of choosing immediate gratification (i.e., "I have worked hard and held off long enough that I deserve it"). Undoubtedly, self-control needs to be considered as part of a complex and interdependent variety of psychological processes.

Antisocial Personality Pattern: Risk and Treatment

By focusing on the characteristics that describe antisocial personality, we can avoid the pessimistic attitude that APD or psychopathy is untreatable. In some jurisdictions, such a diagnosis and the associated "unable to learn from experience" is used to justify criminal justice sanctions (Blais, 2015). However, there is little evidence that psychopaths and APD individuals *cannot* learn new behaviors.

Psychopathy and APD are viewed as stable personality traits that change little with time. From a prediction perspective, they are static risk factors. However, viewing psychopathy/APD as a constellation of static risk factors may be unhelpful. Examination of the items of the PCL-R finds that up to 14 of the 20 items are dynamic. There is no a priori reason to assume that the administration of the PCL-R following appropriate treatment would not show changes in scores.

Alternatively, Bergstrøm, Larmour, and Farrington (2018) have argued that a better measure of the dynamic features of psychopathy is the Comprehensive Assessment of Psychopathic Personality (CAPP) scale developed by Cooke and his colleagues (Cooke, Hart, Logan, & Michie, 2004). CAPP consists of six domains with four to seven behavioral indicators for each domain. The domains reflect traits important in the assessment of psychopathy (e.g., the emotional domain has the item "lacks remorse"). These dynamic features of CAPP are thought to better detect changes that may occur during treatment (Cooke, Hart, Logan, & Michie, 2012). However promising the CAPP may be as an alternative to the PCL-R, its dynamic validity has yet to be demonstrated.

TABLE 5.3 **The PCL-R as Seen from a Psychology of Criminal Conduct**

Static Criminal History
  Short-term romantic relationships
  Childhood behavior problems
  Early delinquency and past failure on parole
  Varied criminal history

Dynamic Criminogenic Needs
  Lying and manipulative, indiscriminative sexual relationships
  Shows little guilt, denies responsibility
  Poor self-control, unrealistic goals

Responsivity
  Overly charming, shallow
  Narcissistic
  Sensation seeker

Gradually, the PCL-R (and the concept of psychopathy) is being considered in ways that are not bound to the psychopathological tradition. For example, researchers have "translated" the DSM-5 and PCL-R into the language of the Five Factor Model (Lynam & Derefinko, 2006; Trull & Widiger, 2013), and Hare has also broken down the PCL-R into finer parts (from two to four factors, three of which are dynamic). Taking some liberty in categorizing the risk/need factors measured by the PCL-R, Table 5.3 reconfigures them in accordance with PCC. The PCL-R and the construct of psychopathy fit very nicely into the principles of risk, need, and responsivity. By conceptualizing psychopathy as a broad APP within PCC, a more positive, proactive agenda for treatment is offered.

Such an application of PCC to the PCL-R has been described by David Simourd and Robert Hoge (2000). The LSI-R, a general risk/need assessment instrument, and PCL-R were administered to 321 inmates in a Canadian penitentiary. Approximately 11 percent scored 30 or above on the PCL-R. Comparing the psychopaths to the non-psychopaths, the psychopaths scored higher on the LSI-R and on all of the dynamic subcomponents except for "financial." In other words, psychopaths are at high risk to reoffend, and their risk is partly accounted for by higher levels of criminogenic needs.

Perhaps psychopathic offenders are nothing more than high-risk, high-need offenders, and if researchers selected the top 10th percentile of LSI-R scores or any other general risk/need scale, all the experiments conducted with the PCL-R would be replicated. At the risk of sounding like Tennenbaum, what is the added value of having a construct such as psychopathy or APD? With respect to the prediction of criminal behavior, probably little. However, the constructs may be relevant in *how* we approach psychopaths and persons with APD in treatment and case management. For example, a psychopathic cocaine addict may be placed into a treatment program targeting substance misuse, but we would want to be careful of the client's efforts to manipulate other group participants.

Worth Remembering

1. General personality theory describes five basic personality dimensions. The FFM model of personality reduces all the personality traits to five general dimensions. These personality dimensions are common to all and are seen as normal features of personality. Two of these "super traits," Weak Constraint and Negative Emotionality, are particularly relevant factors in our concept of APP.

2. Personality encompasses traits and psychological processes that make sense of the situation of action. The expression of personal traits depends on the situations in which we find ourselves and the way we interpret or encode meaning from these situations. To understand behavior we need knowledge of the individual's personality traits, the situation, and the individual's characteristic way of encoding the situation.

3. Criminology has rediscovered the importance of personality in crime. For much of the twentieth century, mainstream criminology ignored the evidence linking personality, especially antisocial personality, with crime. Criminology's favorite explanatory variable, social class, has now been replaced by more psychological explanations of crime.

4. Antisocial personality disorder (APD) and psychopathy view some criminals as psychopathological.
   Many forensic mental health specialists see APD and psychopathy as extremely difficult to treat, although the evidence for this conclusion is very weak.

5. APD may be more relevant than psychopathological models of antisocial personality.
   A major advantage of a GPCSL perspective of antisocial personality over psychopathological models is that the door to treatment is opened wider. The dynamic needs of highly antisocial personalities can serve as targets for planned interventions.

Recommended Readings

The Five Factor Model (FFM) has become very influential in personality theory, especially during the past decade. A comprehensive summary of the contributions of FFM can be found in Costa, McCrae, & Löckenhoff (2019).

Readers interested in the concept of psychopathy are invited to read Hervey Cleckley's *Mask of Sanity*, which is now freely available at: https://gwern. net/doc/psychology/personality/psychopathy/1941-cleckley-maskofsanity.pdf. In addition to this primary resource, the contributions of Cleckley are summarized by Lilienfeld, Watts, Smith, Patrick, & Hare (2018). Christopher Patrick's second edition *Handbook of Psychopathy* (2018) is an excellent source of everything you want to know about psychopathy.

 Visit the Instructor and Student Resource to access additional exercises, videos and study materials to support this chapter: psychologycriminalconduct.routledge.com

CHAPTER 6 The Role of Procriminal Associates and Attitudes in Criminal Conduct

Figure 6.1 is a simplified version of Figure 3.1, modified to reflect the content of this chapter. In the GPCSL model, cognition (i.e., the decision to act in a specific way) plays a central role. Ultimately, the cause of behavior resides in the cognitions of the individual. People make a choice, and they are responsible for their choices. Sometimes we may not be fully aware of our decision to act because of the automatic nature of some behaviors, or impulsive-emotional reactions, or the disruption of thinking processes due to alcohol or other drugs. However, even in these situations, we can trace back in the chain of behavioral events to a point where an active choice was made that accounts for the present behavior. For example, an angry individual may choose to go to the bar and get drunk before ending up in a fight, or the drug addict chooses to leave his house to buy some drugs. Self-agency is a powerful construct.

The decision to act is influenced by a number of personal-social factors and the immediate situation. The presence of a police officer, a weapon, a car with the key in it, and so on are powerful inhibitors or facilitators of criminal conduct. Criminal history reflects a history of rewards for criminal behavior and the longer and more varied the history, the more "automatic" the behavior. At a certain point, there is almost a sense of criminal expertise that makes crime quick and efficient. A criminal history is also an indicator of a history of decision-making supportive of crime. An APP (Chapter 5) of impulsivity, emotional callousness, sensation-seeking, and negative emotions also favors a decision to act in an antisocial manner. Finally, we have procriminal associates and attitudes contributing to our list of the major determinants of criminal behavior and also the foci of this chapter.

A discussion of procriminal associates continues from the developmental perspective in Chapter 4. We examine how, specifically, associates may facilitate criminal acts before turning to procriminal attitudes. As Sutherland pointed out in 1939, many procriminal attitudes are learned and maintained in association with criminal others and exert a direct control over the decision to

DOI: 10.4324/9781003292128-8

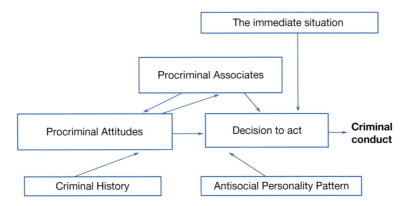

Figure 6.1

Proximal Factors Affecting the Decision to Act

engage in antisocial conduct. Together, procriminal associates and attitudes are commanding determinants and targets of change for criminal behavior.

Procriminal Associates

When Parents Lose Control: The Path to Delinquent Associates

Adolescence is a period of profound biological, cognitive, and emotional maturation and a period when youths begin to define themselves as separate and independent from their parents. One potential path toward autonomy, suggested by Granic and Patterson (2006), is to engage in delinquent behavior. Delinquent behaviors represent more "adult-like behaviors" (at least in the mind of the youth), challenge the authority of the parents, and attract the attention of peers. Glueck and Glueck (1950) noted more than 70 years ago that adult-like behaviors (e.g., smoking, drinking, early sexual activity) differentiated delinquents from nondelinquents. However, there is more to delinquent behavior than a need for autonomy. As seen in the previous chapters, temperamental and personality factors play a role. For example, the desire for excitement and thrills among some youths can be fulfilled by engaging in behaviors frowned upon by many adults, and impulsiveness leads to the instant gratification afforded by some delinquent activities.

Inappropriate parenting also has a profound impact on the development of criminal behavior. A fuller discussion on family factors related to crime will be presented in the next chapter but, for now, there are four important points to make. First, parents may actually model and reinforce antisocial behavior while discouraging prosocial behaviors and attitudes (Newcomb & Loeb, 1999). Recall in Chapter 4 our discussion of intergenerational crime and heredity. From Dugdale to the CSDD, we see that crime runs in families

TABLE 6.1 **Parents as Socialization Agents for Criminal Behavior**

Parenting characteristic	Delinquent	Nondelinquent
Criminal father	66.2	32.0
Criminal mother	44.8	15.0
Poor working habit (father)	25.7	5.7
Conduct standards poor (family)	90.4	54.0
Supervision by mother (unsuitable)	63.8	13.0
Hostile/indifferent affection by father	59.8	19.9
Mother discipline (lax/erratic)	91.4	32.8
Physical punishment (father)	55.6	34.6

Source: Adapted from Glueck & Glueck, 1950

and it is not entirely due to heredity. To illustrate the point of how parents can encourage (perhaps inadvertently) the wrong behaviors, the findings from the classic study by Glueck and Glueck are presented in Table 6.1. Notice that for the delinquents, the parents were more likely to be criminals themselves, fail to model prosocial behaviors (work), and supervise and discipline inappropriately.

The second point is that in families with poor relationships and inadequate monitoring and disciplining, aggressive and other antisocial behaviors become established very early. This severely limits the type of peer social network that the child develops (Lacourse, Nagin, et al., 2006). Well-socialized children (and their parents) will not accept the friendship of antisocial children, and these children become socially excluded from their normative peers, putting them at risk to gravitate toward similarly deviant peers.

Third, poor emotional attachments with the parent(s) may leave the child emotionally underdeveloped and lacking in self-esteem. The relationship between self-esteem and antisocial behavior, however, is complex. Some (e.g., Bushman, Baumeister, et al., 2009) have argued that it is people with *high* self-esteem (mainly narcissists) who are aggressive while others think it is low self-esteem that is the culprit (Donnellan, Trzesniewski, Robins, Moffitt, & Caspi, 2005). Carrie Mier and Roshni Ladny (2018) conducted a comprehensive meta-analysis on the relationship between self-esteem and criminal behavior. Forty-two studies met the selection criteria and the overall effect size was $r = -0.10$. Although the effect size was small, it was significant (the 95 percent confidence interval did not include 0).

Finally, as the child becomes older and spends more time outside of the home, opportunities to develop delinquent friends increase. If the caregiver does not know or does not care with whom the child associates, then involvement in "unsupervised routine actives" with delinquents and even joining a youth gang becomes more likely (Ahmadi, Sangdeh, Aminimanesh, Mollazamani, & Khanzade, 2013; Walters, 2018b, 2020a). This differential association may be heightened among children with some of the risk markers for a life-course-persistent trajectory (e.g., callous-unemotional traits; Ray, Frick, et al., 2017). Some scholars have remarked that parental monitoring may actually be a protective factor to crime (Merrin, Davis, Berry, & Espeiage, 2018; Walters, 2020a). In a study of 10- to 12-year-old "early starters" from 673 African American families, Simons and his colleagues (Simons, Simons, Chen, Brody, & Lin, 2007) found poor parental monitoring and discipline and parental hostility the best predictors of delinquent peer affiliation ($r = 0.12$ and $r = 0.19$, respectively).

Psychological Perspectives on Delinquent Associates

From the perspective of psychology, research on social exclusion can inform our understanding as to why delinquents seek out each other's company. Criminal behavior is non-normative behavior that is widely disapproved of. Consequently, those who engage in crime will be excluded from the mainstream (the subcultural criminological theories also saw exclusion as a problem but exclusion was made on the basis of class and not crime). Developmental psychologists are well aware that exclusion of young children from peers leads to a host of problems.

Mark Leary and his colleagues have studied self-esteem for 40 years and have developed what they call sociometer theory (Leary, 2005, 2021). Essentially, people are always (or most of the time) monitoring how they respond to rejection from their peer group. The more one feels rejected, the lower the self-esteem and, on the other hand, the more one feels included, the higher their self-esteem. Self-esteem is basically an internal measure of how socially appealing one is to his or her peers. It seems that decreases in self-esteem alert one to being potentially excluded from social groups and may motivate the individual to engage in efforts to increase social inclusion. For the youth, joining criminal groups promotes social inclusion and may increase self-esteem (à la Cohen, 1955). Of course, involvement in such groups also distances the offender from the influence of prosocial others.

Social exclusion has also been linked to aggressive behavior (Leary, Twenge, & Quinlivan, 2006) and one related area of interest is bullying (Swearer & Hymel, 2015). In a meta-analysis of 28 studies, school bullies were over twice as likely to commit crimes 11 years later than non-bullies (Ttofi, Farrington, Lösel, & Loeber, 2011). The risk factors for bullying are much the same as for delinquent and adult criminal behavior, including peer rejection, impulsiveness, attitudes supportive of bullying, inappropriate parental monitoring, and stressful life events (Swearer & Hymel, 2015; Walters & Espelage, 2019). There are a couple of features to bullying that stand out. First, there is a high correlation ($r = 0.40$) between being victimized and being the perpetrator (Walters, 2021). That is, a victim can become a bully and vice versa. Going from a victim to becoming a bully appears to be mediated by hostility and delinquent peer attachments (Walters, 2020b; Walters & Espelage, 2018a).

Second, there appear to be significant differences between direct, confrontational bullying and cyberbullying. Glenn Walters and Dorothy Espelage (2020) analyzed data from the Illinois Study of Bullying and Sexual Violence, a longitudinal study of over 2,000 high school students. Two hypotheses were tested: the stepping stone hypothesis of youth starting with cyberbullying because their identity is hidden and then moving up to face-to-face bullying, and the displacement hypothesis of youth who were victimized in-person and then turn to cyberbullying to fight back. The findings supported the displacement hypothesis. Also noteworthy is that the extent of involvement in cyberbullying may vary according to gender. For example, although bullying and cyberbullying overlap considerably, Baldry, Farrington, and Sorrentino (2017) found girls who limited their bullying to the school yard did not engage in cyberbullying to any significant extent but the boys did.

Delinquent Associates: Training in Criminal Behavior

One of the consequences of associating with delinquents is the increased opportunity to learn a variety of criminal behaviors, particularly covert antisocial behaviors. Patterson and his colleagues (Granic & Patterson, 2006; Patterson & Yoerger, 1999) speak of "phase transitions" in describing the development of chronic offending as progressing from the overt, aggressive behavior evident at a young age to covert antisocial behaviors such as stealing and drug use in adolescence. Furthermore, delinquent peer groups contribute to this transition. Thus, the chronic delinquent becomes quite versatile, demonstrating both aggressive and nonaggressive antisocial behaviors. Although there is evidence that some forms of criminal behavior (i.e., physical aggression) vary by gender and age (Krahé, 2021; Marsee et al., 2014), it appears that even the girls who follow a life-course-persistent trajectory show a versatility and level of aggressiveness similar to boys (Farrington & Loeber, 2013; Fontaine, Charbonneau, et al., 2008).

Reviews of the literature consistently rank procriminal associates as one of the strongest correlates of criminal behavior (Gendreau, Little, & Goggin, 1996; Goodley, Pearson, & Morris, 2022; Gutierrez, Wilson, Rugge, & Bonta, 2013; Wilson & Gutierrez, 2014). As expected, the influence of delinquent peers increases with age (van der Put, Stams, et al., 2012). In the meta-analysis by Lipsey and Derzon (1998), the average effect size for procriminal associates was 0.12 for children aged six to 11 years and 0.43 for children aged 12 to 14. The question that researchers have been grappling with is the interpretation of the relationship. Two hypotheses have been presented. The first, originally proposed by Glueck and Glueck (1950), is that the youths have already established procriminal behaviors and attitudes before joining delinquent social networks ("birds of a feather flock together" hypothesis). Similarly, Gottfredson and Hirschi's (1990) self-control theory also hypothesized that low self-control individuals, already predisposed to delinquency, self-select others with low self-control (similar to the assortative mating discussed in Chapter 4). Thus, associating with other delinquents does not really increase the chances of criminal behavior; the youths would engage in crime regardless of with whom they associate.

The second hypothesis is that delinquent youths may be attracted to each other for the reasons noted above, but once they form association and friendship bonds, the interpersonal reinforcements for delinquent behavior would augment the risk for criminal behavior. That is, procriminal friends directly model and reward antisocial behavior and discourage prosocial behavior, thereby increasing the risk of criminal behavior (Matseuda & Anderson, 1998). Furthermore, the stronger the friendship bond, the more likely the youth will follow the lead of delinquent friends (Payne & Cornwell, 2007). Both randomized experiments with undergraduate students (Gallupe, Nguyen, et al., 2016; Mercer, Crocetti, Meeus, & Branje, 2018) and studies of the social interactions among delinquents and nondelinquents clearly show that peers can encourage procriminal attitudes and behaviors and punish prosocial behavior (Buehler, Patterson, & Furniss, 1966; Paternoster, McGloin, Nguyen, & Thomas, 2013; Shortt, Capaldi, Dishion, Bank, & Owen, 2003).

The GPCSL perspective would suggest that there is truth to both hypotheses. An APP characterized by poor self-control, callousness, hostile emotions, and egocentrism predisposes one to criminal behavior regardless of procriminal peer networks. However, such a personality pattern increases the likelihood of joining deviant peer groups. An APP would make it difficult to form relationships with well-controlled, emotionally stable individuals and to achieve success in school and work. Spending less time in school frees up time to spend with procriminal associates in aimless and deviant activity. A recent meta-analysis provides empirical support to both hypotheses. Gwenn Gallupe, John McLevey, and Sarah Brown (2019) reviewed 24 studies investigating selection ("birds-of-a-feather") and peer influence (social learning). They found a moderately large effect size with antisocial behavior for peer influence ($r = 0.32$, $k = 21$) and a smaller but still significant effect size for peer selection ($r = 0.08$, $k = 28$).

Youth Gangs. In keeping with the theme of this chapter, we turn to youth gangs. Youth gangs operate at the street and prison levels, and many are extremely violent and sometimes well organized (Decker, 2007; DeLisi, Spruill, Vaughn, & Trulson, 2014). Criminologists have a long history of trying to understand the formation and maintenance of criminal groups (e.g., Cloward & Ohlin, 1960; Cohen, 1955), and this interest continues to flourish.

The first challenge faced by researchers studying gangs is to answer the question: What makes a gang? Do two delinquents regularly hanging around with each other count as a criminal gang, or do you need more than two? Do members have to commit all their crimes together, or can they go off by themselves to commit crimes? Is actual participation in criminal activity required,

Figure 6.2

Gang with Colors

Source: Getty Images

or is simple association sufficient (the "gang wannabes")? Must there be some concrete symbol such as a colored kerchief or hand sign indicating their affiliation (Figure 6.2)? Is it necessary to have a high level of organization with leadership? The issue of definition is complex but the U.S. National Gang Center has adopted the following features defining a youth gang: (1) three or members between 14 and 24 years, (2) members see themselves as part of a gang, (3) others recognize the group as a gang, (4) there is a shared identity defined by name or symbols, (5) there is a permanence and organization to the group, and (6) there is an increased level of criminal activity.

It is estimated that in 2012 there were more than 30,700 youth gangs in the United States, with 850,000 gang members (Egley, Howell, & Harris, 2014; 2012 was the last reported year by the U.S. National Gang Center). It is also important to note that gangs are not limited to the United States: it is an international problem (Tasgin & Aksu, 2015). The question most often asked is whether gang membership increases the likelihood of criminal activity. In general, the answer appears to be yes. In a meta-analysis of 179 studies, Pyrooz, Turanovic, Decker, and Wu (2016) found a mean r of 0.22 between gang membership and criminal behavior. The association is weaker in longitudinal studies but it is still there (Gordon, Rowe, et al., 2014; Melde & Esbensen, 2013). Walters (2019) has argued that the reason for increased criminal activity is because criminal thinking is reinforced by gang members (i.e., a social learning perspective).

In the Pittsburgh Youth Study (Gordon et al., 2014) more than 600 boys were followed over a 10-year period as they joined and left gangs (approximately 25 percent had been or were still involved in a gang). The Rochester Youth Study (Thornberry, Krohn, Lizotte, Smith, & Tobin, 2003) was based on 1,000 boys and girls and the study by Melde and Esbensen (2013) sampled 3,700 youths from seven cities (approximately 5 percent were gang members at one time or another). All three studies found increases in general criminal activity with gang membership and violent crimes specifically. Although gang members were already quite delinquent before joining, their delinquent activity increased more than expected when they joined a gang. For example, delinquents in the Rochester Youth Study who belonged to a gang represented one-third of the sample but accounted for two-thirds of the crimes.

The longitudinal studies are also instructive in that membership in a gang is fluid. Gordon and colleagues (Gordon et al., 2014) found that 85 percent of the boys who joined gangs had left the gangs within four years. In the Rochester sample, almost 93 percent of the boys and all of the girls had left the gangs (Thornberry et al., 2003). In general, it is estimated that the average length of time spent in a gang is one year (Mora & Decker, 2019). In addition, commitment to the gang varies widely. Some just like to "hang out" with the gang rather than directly engage in crime. Esbensen and colleagues (Esbensen, Winfree, He, & Taylor, 2001) describe "core members," and the data from longitudinal studies suggest that these core members represent no more than 15 percent of gang members. However, there has been the suggestion that there may be a rise in these core members, at least in the United States, as a result of incarceration. In prisons, gangs are more organized and this may continue upon release to the community, creating a more stable "adult" group of gang members (Shelden, Tracy, & Brown, 2012).

There are remarkable similarities between delinquents who fully participate in gang activity and those who play a minimal role. The differences that do exist appear to be a matter of degree. For example, parental attachment, supervision, and monitoring are important for both groups but, in a study of 940 gang members, the core members had much lower levels of parental monitoring than delinquents who were more casual in their commitment to the gang (Esbensen et al., 2001). On the whole, the risk factors for gang membership are similar to the risk factors for life-course-persistent delinquency (Higginson, Benier, et al., 2018). Coming from a disadvantaged neighborhood and being raised in a dysfunctional family (Decker, Melde, & Pyrooz, 2013; De La Rue & Espelage, 2014) as well as having procriminal attitudes and elements of APP have all been related to gang membership (Walters, 2019; Wood, 2014). Moreover, the risk factors for girls appear to be no different than for boys (De La Rue & Espelage, 2014; Gomez Auyong, Smith, & Ferguson, 2018).

Although APP is indicative of gang membership, psychopathy per se does not appear to be a major element among gang members (despite mass media portrayals). This may be somewhat surprising considering that many psychopathic traits (e.g., callousness, hostility) would fit well in a gang environment.

However, Avelardo Valdez, Charles Kaplan, and Edward Codina (2000) administered the screening version of the PCL-R to 50 gang members and a matched sample of 25 non-gang members. They found that only 4 percent of gang members could be classified as psychopaths (24 percent of the non-gang members were diagnosed with psychopathy). In a larger study of more than 1,000 Singaporean adolescents, psychopathy was unrelated to gang membership (Ang, Huan, Chan, Cheong, & Leaw, 2015).

The lower prevalence of psychopathy among gang members may indicate that these individuals have such low affectional bonds to others that they prefer to operate on their own rather than with others (or regular criminals with any amount of common sense want nothing to do with them). However, Joseph and Rembert (2022) found similar but significant correlations between the PCL-YV scores (Chapter 5) and gang membership for females ($r = 0.36$) and males ($r = 0.25$). The differences between the correlation coefficients for the females and males were not statistically significant. The mixed findings and the fact that most studies of the psychopathy–gang link use cross-sectional designs leaves us with no definitive conclusions (Tostlebe & Pyrooz, 2022).

Intervention efforts have focused on "get tough" approaches such as increased police patrols and aggressive prosecution, which have not demonstrated much success (Decker, 2007). Two widely used interventions are to prevent youths from joining gangs in the first place and help youths leave gangs. With respect to the former, the best-known program is Gang Resistance Education and Training (GREAT). GREAT is a school-based prevention program that is used throughout the United States and internationally (Esbensen, 2004). Uniformed police officers speak to seventh-grade students about the negative aspects of gang membership and drugs, and teach conflict resolution techniques. The goal is to give youths the skills to resist peer pressure and the temptation to join a gang.

In a large-scale evaluation of the program, Esbensen and Osgood (1999) compared 2,629 students who completed the program to 3,207 students who did not complete it. GREAT completers reported lower rates of drug use, fewer delinquent friends, and more negative attitudes toward gangs. The researchers concluded that GREAT produced "modest short-term benefits," but the results were based on self-reports, and the participants were too young to allow researchers to conduct a follow-up about actual entry into gangs. The caution was well deserved as a two-year follow-up of the children found no effect.

The disappointing results led to something all too infrequent in the offender treatment literature—a revised program. Usually, programs that fail to demonstrate effectiveness are abandoned wholesale or continue in the line of correctional quackery. The revised GREAT program became more structured, taught self-management skills, and focused more on the risk factors for gang involvement, qualities associated with effective offender rehabilitation programs (Esbensen, Peterson, et al., 2011). The revised program involved a process evaluation to ensure that the program was delivered as intended (Esbensen, Matsuda, Taylor, & Peterson, 2011). More importantly, the evaluation employed a randomized experimental evaluation (Esbensen, Osgood, Peterson, Taylor, & Carson, 2013). Nearly 4,000 students were randomly assigned to GREAT or to school as usual and followed up four years later. The findings were much more positive than the original GREAT evaluation. The GREAT students had lower odds of joining a gang and more negative attitudes to gang membership at one year (Esbensen, Peterson, Taylor, & Osgood, 2012) and at four years (Esbensen et al., 2013).

A meta-analysis of six gang prevention programs with outcome data by Jennifer Wong and her colleagues (Wong, Gravel, Bouchard, Descormiers, & Morselli, 2016) found an average effect size of 0.06 (converted from the log odds ratio reported in the review). Although this is a very small but significant effect size, it was mainly accounted for by the large evaluation of GREAT (Esbensen et al., 2013). When this evaluation was removed from the analysis, the findings from the prevention programs were nonsignificant. Thus, we cannot draw any firm conclusions on gang prevention programs other than the GREAT model holds promise.

Evaluations of rehabilitation interventions intended to help gang members leave gangs and reduce their antisocial behavior are few and far between. Therefore, meta-analytic reviews assessing rehabilitative efforts per se are absent from the literature. The most relevant review available is by Huey, Lewine, & Rubenson (2016). Their meta-analysis included 26 studies but it was a mix of prevention, criminal justice sanction, and treatment. Overall, a reduction in gang involvement was found but there was no significant reduction in antisocial behavior. Unfortunately, Huey and his colleagues did not break down the results by intervention type.

Other treatment interventions that are promising include Functional Family Therapy (FFT) and Multisystemic Therapy (MST) and both are discussed in the next chapter. The research has focused more on youth *at risk* for gang involvement rather than established gang members. For example, an experimental evaluation of FFT by Denise Gottfredson and her colleagues (Gottfredson, Kearly, et al., 2018) found a reduction in criminal recidivism 18 months later and substantial cost saving compared to the control group. However, an evaluation of MST with gang-involved youth showed no differences in re-arrest rates with non-gang members (Boxer, Docherty, Ostermann, Kubik, & Veysey, 2017). This is surprising given that MST, in general, has been quite effective with serious justice-involved youth (next chapter). Boxer et al. (2017) called for caution in dismissing the value of FFT as their evaluation was non-experimental, preventing a conclusion on cause and effect.

Although rehabilitation is viewed in a very positive light throughout the text, treatment programs do not always provide benefit. Sometimes, interventions can make matters worse. More will be said about this later in the book, but there is a literature on the harmful effects of some gang intervention programs. This literature is summarized by Rubenson, Galbraith, and Huey (2020) and they note, for example, that police presence in the program and boot camps *increased* recidivism.

To date, there is only one treatment study that has applied the principles of effective rehabilitation (i.e., risk, need, and responsivity) to gang members (Di Placido, Simon, Witte, Gu, & Wong, 2006). A high-intensity cognitive behavioral treatment program was delivered to 40 gang members in a maximum-security forensic facility in central Canada. Most of the gang members came from Aboriginal gangs (61 percent), and the remainder came from various other gangs (e.g., Hell's Angels, Bloods, Crips). Upon follow-up (average of 13.7 months post-release), 20 percent of the treated gang members recidivated violently compared to 35 percent for the untreated gang members.

Summary. One consequence of being in a family in which there are poor emotional bonds, monitoring, and disciplining practices is that the child is free to associate with other delinquent children. Social support for crime is theoretically and empirically one of the most important correlates of criminal behavior. From a prevention perspective, effectively intervening at the family level would not only benefit families directly but also impact on the associational patterns that the child develops. Another consequence of being raised within a dysfunctional family environment is the learning of procriminal attitudes.

Cognitions Supportive of Crime: Procriminal Attitudes

Attitudes are evaluative cognitions toward a person, thing, or action that organize the person's decision to act (recall Figure 6.1). One may view a teacher as knowledgeable, cars as polluters, and jogging as boring. These attitudes toward the teacher, cars, and jogging also imply a behavioral action. The teacher will be listened to attentively, a bus is taken rather than a car, and watching television becomes a major recreational activity. We do not really see "attitudes," but we infer them from the behavior of individuals. For many social psychologists, the study of attitudes forms a major aspect of their work.

Generally speaking, procriminal attitudes are thoughts, feelings, and beliefs that are supportive of criminal conduct. If you think that there is nothing wrong with cheating on your income tax, or that a person deserves to be hit for insulting you, or because the person is simply making you angry, then guess what is likely to happen? Notice the importance of making a favorable or unfavorable evaluation, considered by Ajzen and Fishbein (1980) to be a fundamental component of an attitude. Procriminal attitudes are all about when it is acceptable to break the law.

Development of Procriminal Attitudes

There are two ways we can look at the origins of attitudes relevant to criminal behavior. First, there are the perspectives that emphasize a *failure* in the development of a conscience or in moral reasoning. Second, there are the perspectives that highlight the social environment in shaping attitudes irrespective of a failure to understand what is right and what is wrong.

Freud's concept of lack of superego (or conscience) is an example of the first perspective. As the child matures, the id (basic impulses) comes under the control of the ego (reality constraining id impulses) and eventually the superego (impulses under self-control). The development of the superego is dependent upon identification with the parent(s) and the internalization of parental norms and values. Identification with a parental figure requires some affectional bond to the parent(s). Thus, disruptions in caregiver attachment may interfere with the development of a conscience.

Another example is Kohlberg's theory of moral development (Kohlberg, 1958; Kohlberg & Candee, 1984). Kohlberg's three-level/six-stage model of moral reasoning is summarized in Table 6.2. Progress through the stages is orderly and dependent upon maturation and age (i.e., biologically based). You cannot skip Stage 2 and go directly to Stage 3, although you can speed it up with some treatments (e.g., Moral Reconation Therapy; Ferguson & Wormith, 2012). In general, meta-analytic findings show that most offenders are morally delayed (van Vugt, Gibbs, Stams, Bijleveld, Hendriks, & Van der Laan, 2011).

The second perspective on the origins of procriminal attitudes stresses the role of the social environment in shaping attitudes. Sociologists see the broad social groups that vary along race, culture, religion, etc. as shapers of attitudes. The attitudes of interest are generally attitudes held by the group rather than individual specific attitudes. For example, Americans may have different attitudes toward work compared to Italians, attitudes regarding church attendance are different for Roman Catholics and Buddhists, and attitudes toward courtship are different for those from India and those from the United Kingdom.

In sociological criminology, smaller fragments of broader society (i.e., criminal subcultures) have their own normative attitudes, which are reinforced for

TABLE 6.2 Kohlberg's Theory of Moral Development

Level	Stage	Description
I Preconventional	1. Punishment and obedience	Egocentric
	2. Instrumental hedonism	(Obey the rules because it is a rule; What happens to me?)
II Conventional	3. Approval of others	Social expectations
	4. Authority maintaining morality	(What do others expect of me?)
III Principled law	5. Democratically accepted (What is best for all?)	Universality
	6. Principles of conscience	

their individual members. Thus, the lower classes may have a general set of attitudes specific to that class. This is Miller's (1958) idea of "focal concerns." The upper classes do not share these focal concerns of toughness, fate, and so on—only the lower classes do so. Most people within the lower classes are thought to have these attitudes, and individuals are socialized into these beliefs. The same theme of adhering to shared group attitudes can be observed in the various subcultural theories.

GPCSL also places the learning of procriminal attitudes within a social context but at the more immediate social contexts of family, associates, school, and work. However, there are two advantages to GPCSL. First, it specifies the mechanisms of learning (modeling and conditioning). This is important because it informs treatments designed to change procriminal attitudes. Second, it allows for inquiries into understanding *individual* attitudes rather than group-held attitudes. That is, people may hold attitudes very different from the larger group, and it is the understanding of attitudes at the individual level that helps in prediction and treatment.

The Attitude–Behavior Link

Studying procriminal attitudes is deemed important because it is assumed that there is a large correlation between attitudes and behavior. However, as Walter Mischel (1968) showed with personality and behavior (Chapter 5), the relationship between attitudes and behavior is far from perfect. Individual studies on the relationship between attitudes and general behavior have ranged from the negative to the positive, with an average r of 0.40 (Kraus, 1995). What has become the focus of the psychological study of attitudes is to understand the conditions under which the degree of consistency between the attitudes and the behavior increases.

There are many factors that influence the attitude–behavior association (for a review see Ajzen, 2020). Three important conditions have been subjected to meta-analysis. First, there is the issue of social pressure to behave in accordance with an attitude. Obviously, this is highly relevant to individuals operating within a procriminal group such as a youth gang. In a review of nearly 800 studies on attitudes, Wallace, Paulson, Lord, & Bond (2005) found peer pressure to have an unexpected effect on behavior. The highest degree of consistency between attitudes and behavior was under *moderate* levels of peer pressure. Under high levels of peer pressure, the average correlation dropped from 0.41 to 0.30. Apparently, when the immediate situation requires a high degree of conformity to group norms, individually held attitudes have less of an influence. It is important to note, however, that the review did not include procriminal attitudes (examples of attitudes included were those toward smoking, donating blood, and drinking soft drinks). Studies specific to procriminal attitudes and peer affiliation are needed to expand upon the peer-pressure hypothesis.

A second general condition is the "accessibility" of the attitude. "Accessibility" means repetitive, easy to remember, and relevant to behavioral decisions. In other words, it is the saliency and personal meaningfulness of the attitude to the individual that increases behavioral adherence. A review of 41 studies found an overall r of 0.50 under conditions of high accessibility, with some correlations from individual studies reaching the range of 0.70 (Glasman & Albarracín, 2006). Once again, the meta-analysis did not include procriminal attitudes, but the results suggest that accessibility would play a factor in interactions between the individual's procriminal attitudes and involvement in procriminal peer groups.

A third condition, yet to be subjected to meta-analysis, is the specificity of the attitude and the behavior. For example, pro-bullying attitudes have been linked to bullying (Walters & Espelage, 2018b) and violent attitudes are distinctly associated with violent behavior (Nunes, Hermann, Maimone, & Woods, 2015). Throughout this book the reader will find many other examples.

Classifying Procriminal Attitudes

There are many attitudes that support criminal behavior. Although there is no complete consensus on grouping these attitudes, it is helpful to have such a classification (acknowledging that a person is not limited to just one category). Partly based on theory and partly on research, the following is proposed:

1. Techniques of Neutralization

2. Identification with Criminal Others

3. Rejection of Convention

With regard to the first categorization, *Techniques of Neutralization*, the label comes directly from Sykes and Matza (1957). Sykes and Matza argued that most justice-involved persons have some belief in conventional values, and they *know* the difference between right and wrong. That is, they do not all have a deficit in conscience. Therefore, the important question to ask is: "Why do they continue to break the law when they know that it is 'wrong' and frowned upon by most people?"

For Sykes and Matza, the answer to the question is that offenders "neutralize" the potential punishment associated with criminal behavior. They proposed five techniques of neutralization summarized in Table 6.3. Variations on the theme of neutralization can also be found in the work of Hartung ("vocabulary of motives"; Hartung, 1965) and Bandura's "moral disengagement" (Bandura, 2002, 2015; Bandura, Barbaranelli, Caprara, & Pastorelli, 1996). These techniques and mechanisms to avoid guilt and punishment have robust relationships with delinquency and adult crime ($r = 0.34$; Walters, 2022), externalizing behaviors ($r = 0.35$; Helmond, Overbeek, Brugman, & Gibbs,

TABLE 6.3 **Techniques of Neutralization**

Technique	Examples	Comments
Denial of responsibility	"I couldn't help it," "The devil made me do it," "It's not my fault," "It was an accident"	If delinquent acts are due to factors beyond the control of the individual, then the individual is guilt-free
Denial of injury	"I didn't hurt anyone," "I borrowed the laptop," "We just took the car for a ride"	The delinquent admits responsibility for the act but not for any serious injury
Denial of the victim	"He had it coming to him," "She deserved what she got"	In situations where responsibility and injury are difficult to deny, one denies a victim by reversing the perpetrator and victim roles
Condemnation of the condemners	"Lawyers are no good," "Courts can be fixed," "The police are brutal"	Those who would disapprove are defined as immoral, hypocritical, or criminal themselves
Appeal to higher loyalties	"I didn't do it for myself," "I had to steal to feed my family"	The demands of the larger society were sacrificed for the demands of more immediate loyalties

Source: Adapted from Sykes & Matza, 1957

2015), and aggressive behaviors ($r = 0.28$; Gini, Pozzoli, & Hymel, 2014). These techniques not only minimize punishment from interpersonal sources but also from personal sources. By providing a rationale for bad behavior, one minimizes negative repercussions from others *and* alleviates negative feelings and self-evaluations.

Neutralizations, rationalizations, and excuses are but one general set of prosocial attitudes that essentially deal with how to avoid society's and the self's recriminations. In a sense, they allow the person to act outside of mainstream norms without giving up some belief in these norms. Another set of prosocial attitudes are cognitions that reflect *Identification with Criminal Others*. These attitudes assign favorable evaluations to criminal behavior and criminal others. That is, it does not matter that general society does not like the behavior; it is the approval of the self and procriminal associates that is important. Tony Soprano may have expressed many techniques of neutralization over the course of the popular television series *The Sopranos*, but he was also, quite literally, proud and satisfied with his criminal behavior. It was "the Family" and his own view as a competent criminal that was important to Tony, and he accepted no other normative value.

Once again, we find variations on the theme of criminal identity in criminology. William Miller (1958) described the focal concerns of the lower classes, but one does not need to view these attitudes as tied only to the lower classes.

Attitudes such as "I am tough," "I'm trouble," and "stuff happens" clearly signal an increased likelihood of law-breaking. The focal concern of a belief that what occurs in life depends more on fate than personal responsibility ("stuff happens") may justify disengaging personal self-control (Kivetz & Zheng, 2006). Albert Cohen (1955) described youths adopting a subcultural value system that rejected middle-class values (e.g., "spontaneous" vs. "rational"), and Daniel Glaser (1956) wrote of identification with a criminal reference group. Even a casual observation of organized crime syndicates and gangs quickly reveals patterns of thinking and values that are sources of pride in a violent image such as a belief in the "code of the street" (e.g., toughness, no one can disrespect me) and not efforts to make excuses and avoid negative consequences. In Glenn Walters' (2022) meta-analysis, criminal identity demonstrated an effect size of $r = 0.24$ ($k = 11$). Another meta-analytic review specifically examining the relationship between belief in the "code of the street" and criminal behavior yielded $r = 0.11$ ($k = 38$; Moule & Fox, 2021).

The third general set of procriminal attitudes, *Rejection of Convention*, devalues the social institutions of work and education, and the institutions of law and order (e.g., police, the courts). Admittedly, negative attitudes toward work and school are not necessarily procriminal, but by minimizing their importance, crime becomes a more favorable alternative to prosocial behavior—if you do not have a job or you do not like school, you have less to lose by adopting a criminal lifestyle.

To summarize, procriminal attitudes are central to most theories of criminal behavior and there has been considerable progress in describing the various types of procriminal attitudes. Some (Maruna & Copes, 2005; Ward, 2000) have complained that too much effort has been spent on developing lists of criminal attitudes and not enough on integrating them into more general theories of criminal behavior. We agree and see procriminal attitudes as integral to the GPCSL model of criminal conduct, representing one of the major correlates of criminal conduct. Much more research is required to flesh out how procriminal attitudes specifically influence criminal behavior, its limits, and most importantly how they can be changed.

Assessment of Procriminal Attitudes

Procriminal attitudes are important predictors of criminal behavior. In the meta-analytic reviews, the studies varied with regard to how procriminal attitudes were measured. Some studies used qualitative assessments (e.g., interviews to assess "thinking errors"; Samenow, 2014), and others used structured paper-and-pencil measures that were empirically validated. Here, a few of the more structured assessment instruments are described.

One of the earliest measures of neutralization is Ball's (1973) neutralization scale. The scale consisted of four scenarios (two assaults, an armed robbery, and shoplifting), followed by 10 neutralization statements for each scenario. Subjects are asked to rate each neutralization on a five-point scale from "strongly agree" to "strongly disagree." As noted in the previous section neutralizations demonstrate relatively robust correlations with problematic behaviors (Gini, Pozzoli, & Hymel, 2014; Walters, 2022).

A good example of a measure of Identification with Criminal Others (IWCO) is the Pride in Delinquency Scale (Shields & Simourd, 1991). This is a very simple scale that lists 10 criminal behaviors, and each behavior is rated using a 20-point scale ranging from −10 (very ashamed) to +10 (very proud). Two examples of items that are rated on this 20-point scale are "Carrying a concealed weapon, like a pistol, without a licence" and "Selling cocaine." Three studies yielded acceptable predictive validities ranging from $r = 0.23$ to as high as $r = 0.42$ (O'Hagan, Brown, Jones, & Skilling, 2019; Simourd & Van De Ven, 1999; Skilling & Sorge, 2014).

One widely researched measure of prosocial attitudes is the Criminal Sentiments Scale (CSS; Andrews & Wormith, 1984). What is interesting about the CSS is that it taps into the three general categories of procriminal attitudes: Techniques of Neutralization, IWCO, and Rejection of Convention. Table 6.4 provides a few examples of the items, along with the categories they measure. There are a total of 41 items that are rated on a five-point scale, from "strongly agree" to "strongly disagree." Walters (2016a) conducted a meta-analysis of the CSS and its subscales across 10 longitudinal studies. The total score was significantly related to recidivism ($r = 0.17$, $k = 13$). The subscale scores had slightly smaller correlations ranging from 0.09 to 0.15 but all were significant.

Of course, there are many other measures of procriminal attitudes in addition to the ones described. Notable measures include the subscales from Glenn Walters' (1996) Psychological Inventory of Criminal Thinking Styles (PICTS; for a meta-analytic review of the evidence, see Walters, 2012) and Measures of Criminal Attitudes and Associates (Mills, Kroner, & Hemmati, 2005). In terms of structured interview-based assessments of antisocial attitudes, the most widely used is the Attitude/Orientation subcomponent of the Level of Service offender risk/need instruments (discussed in Chapter 10). For now, the basic message is that

TABLE 6.4 The Criminal Sentiments Scale

Item	Antisocial subcomponent
A hungry person has a right to steal.	Neutralization
Most successful people used illegal means to become successful.	Neutralization
People who have been in trouble with the law have the same sort of ideas about life that I have.	IWCO
Police rarely try to help people.	Rejection of Convention
Laws are usually bad.	Rejection of Convention

IWCO = Identification with Criminal Others

procriminal attitudes are important theoretically, they can be reliably measured, and they are predictive of criminal behavior. The next question is: Does replacing procriminal attitudes with prosocial attitudes reduce criminal behavior?

Targeting Procriminal Attitudes in Treatment

Procriminal attitudes are a *dynamic* risk factor for criminal behavior. That is, changes in procriminal attitudes are associated with changes in criminal behavior. For example, Walters and Cohen (2016) administered the General Criminal Thinking subscale of PICTS to over 40,000 men and women under community supervision separated by one year. Increases in scores on the subscale were associated with increases in arrests one year after the second scale administration for both the men and women even after controlling for various risk factors. Facilitating changes in procriminal attitudes can be as simple as altering the associational patterns of participants or it can be more complicated with specific training (see Resource Note 6.1).

The research *specifically on changing procriminal attitudes* among offenders is promising, but unsettled. Today, many cognitive-behavioral interventions include a component to address procriminal attitudes (e.g., Bonta, Bourgon, Rugge, Pedneault, & Lee, 2021). Although there are interventions that have demonstrated changes in attitudes (see the review by Banse, Koppehel-Gossel, Kistmaker, Werner, & Schmidt, 2013), linking the changes in attitudes to recidivism is mixed. In the review by Banse et al. (2013), the effect size was estimated to be small ($r = 0.20$) and many of the studies were methodologically weak. More recent research has found either no relationship between attitudinal changes during treatment and recidivism (Howard & van Doorn, 2018) or reductions in recidivism depending on the measure used (Juarez & Howard, 2022; Kingston & Olver, 2018; Simourd, Olver, & Brandenburg, 2016).

RESOURCE NOTE 6.1

Changing Miniature Social Systems to Change Procriminal Attitudes

Rideau Correctional Center was a medium-security prison housing adults outside the city of Ottawa, Canada. It was also a placement setting for criminology and psychology students from Carleton University and for citizen volunteers who participated in various research studies. A series of studies was conducted to try and change procriminal thinking among the inmates.

The community volunteers visited the prison one evening a week and met with inmates in groups to discuss current affairs or whatever consensus suggested as the topic of the night. The discussion groups were composed of eight to 14 participants that met once a week for eight weeks. The leaders of the groups initially were clinical staff of the prison and then other staff such as shop instructors and ultimately university graduates

continued

of earlier groups. The leaders encouraged open, warm, honest, and enthusiastic talk, and structured that talk around issues of rules, rationalizations for law violations, and self-management processes.

Study One: The effects of participation in "community groups" and "recreation groups."
Prisoner volunteers and citizen volunteers were assigned randomly to community groups, recreation groups, or to a waiting list. The recreation groups did not involve structured opportunities for exposure to the prosocial patterns of community volunteers. Rather, volunteers and prisoners played cards or other board games. The Criminal Sentiments Scale was administered prior to group involvement and at the end of eight weeks. At pre-test, the prisoners presented with more negative attitudes toward the law, courts, and police, with higher levels of identification with criminal others, and with greater acceptance of rationalizations for law violations. At post-test, prisoner participants showed *reduced* procriminal thinking compared to prisoner non-participants. Notably, the participating community volunteers showed *increased* procriminal thinking.

The study demonstrated that simply changing the social composition brought about changes in the procriminal attitudes of both the inmates and the citizen volunteers. The inmates had increased exposure to prosocial attitudes resulting in positive changes but the community volunteers were exposed to procriminal attitudes and demonstrated an unwanted change in attitudes. Therefore, it was important to enhance training of the community volunteers to protect them from assimilating procriminal attitudes in their interactions with the inmates.

Study Two: Training community volunteers.
Stephen Wormith (1984) randomly assigned inmates to one of five community groups. Group 1 was facilitated by volunteers trained to lead the group in a prosocial manner, and the inmates also received self-control training; Group 2 was trained volunteers with recreation; Group 3, untrained volunteers with recreation; Group 4, untrained volunteers with self-control training; and Group 5, a waitlist control. He found that training the volunteers to address the procriminal attitudes of the inmates appropriately led to decreases in procriminal attitudes. Moreover, with self-control training, the changes were also associated with reductions in institutional misconducts and recidivism.

The program Counter-Point is presented to illustrate an intervention program that focuses on procriminal attitudes. Over the course of 25 sessions offenders learn to identify their procriminal attitudes and replace them with prosocial attitudes. The treatment is delivered in a group format. In an evaluation of the program (Kroner & Yessine, 2013), parolees who attended Counter-Point ($N = 331$) were compared to a group of 331 parolees matched on risk level who received routine community supervision. Program participants were administered the measures of procriminal attitudes described earlier (i.e., CSS, Pride in Delinquency). For the program participants, not only were there reductions in scores on the attitudinal measures but also reductions in recidivism. The recidivism rate for the program participants, as measured by new offenses, was 37 percent; it was 60 percent for the comparison group.

Summary. GPCSL identifies attitudes as one of the Central Eight risk/need factors. With respect to prediction, procriminal attitudes perform on a par with the other Central Eight factors. However, with respect to theory and treatment, they appear to be especially important. Theoretically, cognitions associated with attitudes are: (1) under the control of the person, and (2) closest to the action. With respect to rehabilitation, attitudes and cognitions are highly susceptible to change with the promise of achieving reductions in criminal conduct.

Worth Remembering

1. Two factors that have a very strong influence on the decision to engage in criminal behavior are procriminal associates and attitudes. Procriminal associates provide opportunities to learn procriminal attitudes and the techniques of crime.

2. Inappropriate parenting can lead the youth to procriminal associations and the learning of procriminal attitudes.
   Lack of parental monitoring and discipline frees the youth to associate with procriminal others without fear of censure from the parent(s). Poor emotional ties to the parents may further exacerbate the situation. Antisocial parent(s) may also model and reinforce criminal behavior.

3. Gang membership enhances criminal behavior.
   Most individuals who join gangs already have a well-entrenched criminal propensity. However, belonging to a gang appears to increase criminal behavior beyond what is expected from the individual.

4. Procriminal attitudes can be reliably measured and changed.
   Assessments of antisocial attitudes fall into three general categories: (1) Techniques of Neutralization, (2) Identification with Criminal Others, and (3) Rejection of Convention. A number of treatment programs have demonstrated that procriminal attitudes can be reduced. Changes in attitudes may lead to reduced recidivism.

Recommended Readings

Any of the classic writings on delinquent gangs is highly recommended. Sutherland (1939) may have been the first to highlight the importance of delinquent associations, but it was Cohen (1955) and Cloward and Ohlin (1960) who gave a face to it. Either book is easy to read—maybe short on empirical research but rich in narrative. For an empirical review of gang prevention programs, the reader is asked to consult Wong, Gravel, Bouchard, Descormiers, & Morselli (2016).

Shadd Maruna and Heith Copes' (2005) chapter in the *Crime and Justice* series gives a detailed and comprehensive review of Sykes and Matza's neutralization theory. They review the criminological roots of the theory and its present-day connection to cognitive psychology. Together with the meta-analysis by Walters (2022), excellent summaries of the research on attitudes and the issues that still need to be addressed are provided.

 Visit the Instructor and Student Resource to access additional exercises, videos and study materials to support this chapter: psychologycriminalconduct.routledge.com

CHAPTER 7 The Person in Social Context: Family, Marital, School, Work, Leisure/Recreation, and Neighborhood

Procriminal attitudes, values, and beliefs suggest the standards that may be applied in personally mediated control. In assessing one's own behavior, the standards may be favorable to crime or unfavorable to crime. Procriminal cognitions also include the negative cognitive-emotional states of resentment and feeling mistreated. These too may result in self-management that is favorable to crime. When cognitions are highly favorable to crime, their influence on behavior may even become relatively automatic and not require effortful self-regulation. Procriminal associates suggest whether the reactions of others will tend to support noncriminal alternative behavior or support criminal actions. Just thinking of the attitudinal position or even the person of another may initiate mental processes supportive or not supportive of crime.

A history of criminal behavior significantly increases the chances that self-efficacy beliefs will be highly favorable to crime and is a direct indicator of the habitual (automatic) strength of the criminal response. APP suggests a range of supports for criminal activity, including weak self-control and a tendency to feel mistreated by others. These traits may result in problematic circumstances in a variety of settings (e.g., home, school, work). Problematic circumstances in such settings may substantially reduce the socialization value of those settings as well as the punishment of crime. If one is not in receipt of a high density of rewards for prosocial behavior then the power of subtractive costs for criminal behavior is greatly reduced.

The reward and cost contingencies in effect for criminal and noncriminal behavior in the major behavioral settings impact our attitudes, friends, personality, and behavioral habits. In this chapter the Central Eight risk/need factors of family/marital, school/work, and leisure/recreation are explored. The chapter closes with a general commentary on the effects of neighborhoods on the development and maintenance of criminal behavior.

DOI: 10.4324/9781003292128-9

The Family of Origin

Chapter 4 described how biologically based factors may predispose one toward criminal behavior. Some people may be born with temperamental characteristics (e.g., impulsiveness, sensation-seeking, and negative emotionality) or neurological impairments that increase the risk for criminal behavior. This does not mean that these people are simply born bad. Perhaps the most important lesson from Chapter 4 is that the social environment can have an enormous effect on how our predispositions are expressed in behavior. The current chapter continues this lesson by exploring how the early socializing environment—the family of origin—influences the development of criminal behavior.

The discussion opens with a review of social attachments, a concept that finds its beginnings in the caregiver–child relationship. There will be the suggestion that the caregiver–child relationship may influence the quality of attachments formed in other social settings.

Next is a description of how family dynamics can impact the criminal trajectory of children. Parents can model and reinforce antisocial behaviors, sometimes inadvertently, and they can also model and reinforce prosocial behaviors. Parental affection, or the lack of it, can determine the child's motivation to please his or her parent(s). In more extreme situations, the physical and emotional harms or Adverse Childhood Experiences (ACEs) can have profound effects on the futures of children. Finally, some of the more effective family interventions are described.

This section ends with a review of marital and romantic attachments and their role in criminal conduct. Does marriage lead to a decrease in crime? How do procriminal romantic relationships influence criminal behavior? Does family therapy work? These are the major questions asked.

Learning to Care: The Parent–Child Relationship and the Development of Social Bonds

In Chapter 3 the point was made that the probability of a behavior depends upon the number, variety, quality, and immediacy of rewards and costs for that behavior. Now the focus is on the *quality* aspect of rewards and costs within the social context. That is, why are the rewards and costs delivered by some individuals so important to us? Why do we do things for only a smile or a word of praise? On the other hand, why do we inhibit some behavior in order to avoid a frown or a cold shoulder? The people around us can strongly influence our behavior, but it is clear that not everyone has the same level of influence over what we say and what we do.

The degree of interpersonal influence depends on the quality of the relationship between the giver and the receiver of rewards and costs. Travis Hirschi (1969) recognized the importance of this statement in his control theory (relationship bonds to the parents are central to his thesis). When the source of rewards and costs is a person who is highly valued, loved, and respected, then we attend to that person and care about that person's reactions to our behavior. Individuals who are poorly valued, unloved, and disrespected have little influence on our behavior. After all, why change for someone whom you do not like?

We all know adults who show great difficulty in establishing warm, friendly, enduring interpersonal relationships. They somehow lack the ability to form social attachments and are egocentric and uncaring individuals. Certainly, some temperamental qualities (e.g., introversion, extreme cautiousness) may contribute to difficulties in forming positive social relationships, but social conditioning factors are important. Most theorists and researchers look to the family context and attachment to parental figures as the prototype for all future social relationships.

Attachment theory has its roots in the work of John Bowlby (1971, 1988). Most children, beginning around 10 months of age and extending to 18 months or so, become emotionally distressed when separated from the parent. Bowlby saw this "separation anxiety" as an indication that the child had established an attachment to the parent. Originally, Bowlby thought that it was an attachment to the mother that was critical, but later (1988) he modified his view to include any consistent caregiver. In Bowlby's view, the function of attachment was that it provided the infant the security needed to explore the environment and develop independence. The mother/caregiver was the safe haven to return to when the world became frightening. Ideally, a healthy caregiver–child attachment needed to be established within the first two years of life in order to serve as a positive template for future social attachments.

With the parent–child bond as the building block for future interpersonal relationships, disruption of the bond was thought to herald difficulties in attachment to other adults, peers, and symbols of authority (e.g., teachers, employers). Bowlby (1971) contended that lengthy and frequent disruptions would lead to a situation in which children "stop altogether attaching (themselves) to anyone" and develop a "superficial sociability" (p. 50). One way of examining the effects of disruptions of the parent–child bond is to study the impact of divorce on children. Studies of disrupted bonds due to divorce show a small but significant relationship with future delinquency in the range of $r = 0.09$ to 0.11 (Petrosino, Derzon, & Lavenberg, 2009) and it appears that the effect endures into adulthood although diminished (Boccio & Beaver, 2019; Sillekens & Notten, 2020).

The variability in the effect sizes suggests two possible mediating mechanisms. First, there may be differences in the children's behavior depending on whether there were "messy divorces" or "amicable separations." The available evidence suggests that the difficulties experienced by the children are more the result of the emotional conflicts within separating families than separation from a parent per se. Jacobsen and Zaatut (2022) used data ($N = 4,626$) from the National Longitudinal Study of Adolescents and family structure was categorized as follows: (1) both biological parents present (56 percent of the sample), (2) single biological parent (33 percent), and (3) biological parent and stepparent (10 percent). The adolescents (average age of 15 years) were also asked six questions on their relationship with the caregiver(s).

Jacobsen and Zaatut found that family structure was unrelated to delinquency. In fact, the youth in single family homes were *less* likely to engage in delinquency. It was parental relationships that were important. A positive relationship with a parent was associated with lower youth delinquency (a strength or protective factor) and a poor parental relationship with higher self-reported delinquency (a risk factor). This finding is consistent with GPCSL theory. Close parental attachments mean that engaging in behavior frowned upon by the parent leads to the risk of losing parental affection (subtractive cost; Chapter 3). Similarly, a poor relationship means there is less to lose, "freeing" the youth to engage in delinquent acts.

In Chapter 2 the point was made that drawing conclusions based on the results from a single study requires caution. Jacobsen and Zaatut's study (2022) is informative empirically and theoretically and should be duly noted. However, a review by Kroese, Bernasco, Liefbroer, and Rouwendal (2021) reveals that the results from parental separation and divorce may not be so straightforward. The focus of their report was on single-parent families and the delinquent outcomes of youths. This was not a true meta-analysis with the calculation of effect sizes but more of a vote count summary (i.e., counting how many studies found a relationship between single parenting and delinquency and how many did not). Forty-eight studies, a mix of cross-sectional and longitudinal designs, published between 1939 and 2014, were reviewed. The majority of studies (70.8 percent) found a relationship between living in a single-parent household and youth involvement in the criminal justice system.

A second explanation of the possible impact of family disruption is found in the nature of the relationship with the parent *following* divorce. Whiteside and Becker's (2000) early review of 12 studies on the effects of divorce for children under the age of five found that children who continued to have a positive relationship with their father were less likely to have "externalizing symptoms." A more recent meta-analysis by van Dijk et al. (van Dijk, van der Valk, Deković, & Branje, 2020) also examined the parent–child relationship *post*-divorce and child adjustment. A number of child adjustment behaviors were measured and our interest here is externalizing behaviors which included delinquency, aggression, and substance misuse. The meta-analysis was based on 115 studies of families where the parents had been separated or divorced an average of four years (the average age of the children was 12 years). Parental conflict was moderately associated with externalizing behaviors ($r = 0.25$).

The importance of *when* the bond is disrupted was raised by Bowlby, who predicted that disruption of the parent–child bond at an early age would be more detrimental than at a later age. The evidence on this issue is mixed. Hirschi (1969) found that age at separation (before or after the age of five) was unrelated to delinquency. Mark Lipsey and James Derzon (1998) could not locate enough studies of children prior to age six to which they could apply meta-analytic techniques. They were able to compare studies of "broken homes" experienced between the ages of six and 11 to those of separations between the ages of 12 and 14. At the younger age, the average effect size for violent behavior was $r = 0.06$; it was $r = 0.10$ for the older children (the differences were not significant). However, based on longitudinal data from the National Youth Survey ($N = 1,725$ adolescents), Rebellon (2002) found that earlier parental divorce/separation was related to both violent and non-violent delinquency. This data set also included a variety of measures on peer associations and conventional beliefs. His analyses suggested that early family disruption may provide earlier opportunities for the youth to associate with delinquent peers and learn procriminal attitudes.

Another potentially relevant variable is the *frequency* of disruptions. Even a casual reading of crime stories in the local newspaper will reveal descriptions of law violators who went from foster home to foster home and institution to institution as they were growing up. Frequent disruptions can occur with re-marriages and multiple romantic adult relationships and these too can increase the risk for delinquency (Goodnight, D'Onofrio, et al., 2013). However, multiple placements in foster care provide a salient picture of how frequent disruptions can increase antisocial behavior. Although caregiver maltreatment often triggers the involvement of child welfare authorities, multiple foster care placements also occur due to the aggressive and problematic behavior of the child. For example, in an analysis of 8,853 youth under state care, as the presence of youth aggressive and emotional dysregulation increased, so did the number of foster placements (Vreeland, Ebert, et al., 2020).

Drawing upon data from three longitudinal studies, Thornberry, Smith, Rivera, Huizinga, & Stouthamer-Loeber (1999) found that 90 percent of youths who endured five or more disruptions were at an increased risk for criminal behavior. Rolf Loeber and his colleagues (Loeber, Pardini, et al., 2005) followed more than 1,500 boys from childhood into adulthood (30 years of age). Children who experienced two or more caregivers before the age of 10 were almost twice more likely to commit a violent offense than children without this experience. In an incarcerated sample, youths with a history of foster care were four times more likely to follow a life-course-persistent trajectory than youths without a history of foster care (Alltucker, Bullis, Close, & Yovanoff, 2006). Interestingly, Ryan and Testa (2005) found in their sample of children removed from homes because of maltreatment that the frequency of disruptions was a risk factor for boys but not for girls. Boys with four or more home placements had a delinquency rate of 21 percent, compared to 12 percent for those with no change in placement. The comparable rates for girls were 7 percent and 6 percent.

A final comment concerns the association between parent–child attachment and later peer attachment. Recall that Bowlby saw the parent–child attachment as the prototype for future attachments with non-caregivers. In other words, if there are poor attachments with the parent(s) then there will be problems with friends. Indeed, there is some evidence that successful peer relations are related to positive attachments to the parent. For example, a meta-analysis of 63 studies found an average effect size of $r = 0.20$ between attachment to mother and successful peer relations (Schneider, Atkinson, & Tardif, 2001). Fonagy and colleagues (Fonagy, Target, et al., 1997) hypothesized that adolescence is a particularly important time, as there is a fundamental shift from the importance of the parent–child bond to more general adult and social bonds. There is a "moment of detachment when neither old [nor] new (attachment) patterns are fully active" (p. 241). This "moment of detachment" is a normal process, but it also represents a point when parental controls are loosened, possibly giving rise to adolescence-limited delinquency. Building social relationships and really caring about others may find its origins in the attachment patterns within the caregiver–child relationship, but the parents' role in delinquency goes beyond providing emotional warmth and security. It also includes parenting practices.

Adverse Childhood Experiences (ACEs)

The disruption of caregiver–child bonds is one consequence of Adverse Childhood Experiences (ACEs). Traumatic experiences can also affect adults (e.g., criminal victimization) and this will be a topic for discussion when we turn to rehabilitation (Chapter 11). Presently, however, the focus is on ACEs. In general, there are 10 ACEs subsumed under three categories (Folk, Kemp, Yurasek, Barr-Walker, & Tolou-Shams, 2021). The categories are:

1) Abuse: physical, sexual, and emotional.

2) Neglect: emotional and physical.

3) Household dysfunction: caregiver substance misuse, mental illness, intimate partner violence, and parental separation.

ACEs can result in a variety of negative outcomes such as depression, heart disease, and substance misuse. One can have only one ACE or many. In the general population, the prevalence of ACEs among children is estimated to range from 6 percent (four or more ACEs) to 52 percent, or higher, when only one ACE is reported (Crouch, Probst, Radcliff, Bennett, & Hunt McKinney, 2019; Felitti, Anda, et al., 1998). Some of the very high rates reported reflect geography and a lack of uniformity in defining ACEs. For example, some studies may include exposure to war, as in South Africa (93 percent), and extreme poverty (100 percent) in Zambia (Carlson, Yohannan, et al., 2020). ACEs also vary by gender. In a study of 16 countries, the rate of childhood sexual abuse among women was 24 percent (Pan, Lin, et al., 2021). For males, another world review found that the rates for men suffering sexual abuse as children fall into the 5–10 percent range (Stoltenborgh, van Ijzendoorn, Euser, & Bakermans-Kranenburg, 2011). Among justice-involved samples, histories of

ACEs are in the order of 50 percent (Bodkin, Pivnik, et al., 2019). Experiencing ACEs is predictive of a range of undesirable health, psychological, and behavioral outcomes (Felitti, Anda, et al., 1998). They are also predictive of delinquency and adult criminality.

A 2020 meta-analysis by Lucy Fitton, Rongqin Yu, and Seena Fazel examined the relationship between childhood abuse and violent behavior. Eighteen prospective studies were identified and they found a substantial effect size of $r = 0.44$. Other reviews of the literature on ACEs and criminal outcomes have reported similar results (Daisklev, Cunningham, Dempster, & Hanna, 2021; Herrenkohl, Fedina, et al., 2022).

It also appears that the more serious and frequent the ACEs, the more detrimental and long-lasting the outcomes. Two studies have found that as the number of ACEs increased the risk of becoming a life-course-persistent justice-involved youth increased by up to fourfold (Fox, Perez, Cass, Baglivio, & Epps, 2015; Baglivio, Wolff, Piquero, & Epps, 2015). ACEs, especially child abuse, also have shown strong associations with antisocial personality disorder (Schorr, Tietbohl-Santos, et al., 2020), psychopathy (Moreira, Moreira, et al., 2020), and intimate personal violence (Craig & Zettler, 2021). Finally, childhood sexual abuse predicts adult sexual offending and the earlier the sexual abuse occurred the higher future offending (Drury, Elbert, & DeLisi, 2019).

In summary, ACEs are predictive of criminal conduct and, therefore, a risk factor. However, the reader will note that ACEs are not part of the Central Eight. ACEs play a different and important role within the Psychology of Criminal Conduct (i.e., a responsivity factor) and this will be presented in Chapter 11 of Part 3.

Parenting Practices and Delinquency

As with any interpersonal source of influence, parental influence operates along a relationship and a structuring dimension. As described previously, poor parent–child relationships lead to antisocial behavior. The parent(s) also have to teach and instill prosocial norms, values, and beliefs, as well as the skills to succeed in society. Failure to model prosocial behavior, poor monitoring, and inconsistent discipline are critical in this regard.

The relationship and structuring dimensions are often difficult to separate in a particular study, which prevents us from assessing the relative importance of each. Nevertheless, the working hypotheses are that families that promote prosocial norms and are characterized by warm emotional attachments would have the lowest rates of delinquency and families that fail to provide training in social conventions and are characterized by weak affective bonds would have the highest rates of delinquency. Finally, families may show other combinations of the structuring and affective dimensions (e.g., high prosocial norms and low attachment), with delinquency outcomes in the middle range.

Family Interventions and the Reduction of Delinquent Behavior

Every single longitudinal study of delinquency has found poor emotional relationships within the family and inconsistent monitoring and disciplining predictive of antisocial behavior. Knowing the importance of family factors as predictors of delinquent behavior, our focus turns to intervention. There are two general categories of family interventions: primary and secondary prevention.

Primary Prevention. Primary prevention programs target very young children and their families. The children have not yet been identified by the criminal justice system but have the risk factors for delinquency. An example is the Oregon Social Learning Center Program developed by Gerald Patterson and his colleagues. The clientele of the program are conduct-disordered and hyperactive children and their families. In their theoretical model, coercive family processes are central (Granic & Patterson, 2006; Patterson, 1982, 2016). Children learn at a very young age that behaving in an aversive and annoying manner results in reinforcement—for example, when the parent gives in to the child's temper tantrum (Smith, Dishion, et al., 2014). The parent not only rewards bad behavior but by doing so ensures that next time the inappropriate behavior will escalate. Thus, their treatment centers on disrupting the coercive cycle by teaching parents to reinforce positive behavior and to ignore negative behavior. Evaluations of the Oregon treatment program have demonstrated success in changing family interactions and parental disciplining practices (Forgatch & Rodriguez, 2016).

In general, primary intervention programs have proven to be quite effective in reducing the problematic behaviors of children and their parents. Piquero and his colleagues updated an earlier 2009 meta-analysis expanding the number of early interventions targeting children less than five years old (Piquero, Jennings, et al., 2016). The majority of the studies were from the United States, but there were also studies from Europe, Australia, New Zealand, Canada, and even one from China. The average effective size was $r = 0.18$. Not only were the programs effective in reducing antisocial behavior but there was also evidence that these programs are very cost-effective. For example, Farrington and Koegl (2015) found that a prevention program designed for boys aged six to 11 saved up to $37 in criminal justice costs for every $1 spent on the program.

Secondary Prevention. Secondary programs target criminal justice-involved adolescents. Two well-researched programs are Functional Family Therapy (FFT; Barton & Alexander, 1980) and Multisystemic Therapy (MST; Henggeler, Schoenwald, Bourduin, Rowland, & Cunningham, 2009). FFT's main goal is to improve family relationships by changing family communication patterns. Delinquent families show a lot of "defensive communication" (harsh and angry communications, being highly critical) and little "supportive communications" (being empathic, providing helpful information, not interrupting while the other person is talking). In FFT family members are taught to use less defensive communication and more reciprocal supportive communication.

In the first outcome study, families were randomly assigned to one of four groups (Alexander & Barton, 1976; Alexander & Parsons, 1973). All of the families had a child, ranging in age from 13 to 16 years, who was involved in relatively minor delinquent activity (e.g., runaway, truant, "ungovernable"). In addition to the FFT group, there were two other treatment groups (client-centered family therapy and psychodynamic-oriented family therapy) and a no-treatment control group. The client-centered program was nondirective and focused on family feelings. In psychodynamic family therapy, the goal of treatment was described as providing "insight."

By the end of treatment, the FFT group showed more supportive communications and less defensive communications. Parents also learned better behavioral techniques of reinforcing their child's behavior. As Table 7.1 shows, these intermediate targets translated to decreases in delinquent behavior. A second FFT group was later added, replicating the initial results. The FFT group showed a recidivism rate that was one-half the rate for those receiving no treatment. The client-centered treatment had no impact on future delinquent behavior, and the psychodynamic insight approach actually increased the recidivism rate (73 percent).

FFT adheres to a family systems model. As a system, whatever happens to one family member also has an effect on other family members. Herein is the strength of a systems model of intervention. Changes in behavior can be seen not only in the child that first brought the family to the attention of the therapist but also in the siblings of the target children. Nanci Klein, James Alexander, and Bruce Parsons (1977) searched juvenile court records and found that for the no-treatment control group, 40 percent of the siblings had official court records. The recidivism rate for the siblings in the client-centered group was 59 percent; for the psychodynamic group it was 63 percent. The rate for the FFT group was 20 percent.

Most of the early FFT evaluations were limited to the state of Utah but they have since expanded to other jurisdictions in the United States and internationally. A meta-analysis of 14 studies by Hartnett, Carr, Hamilton, and

TABLE 7.1 Family Intervention and Recidivism

Group	N	% Recidivated
FFT: 1st group	46	26
2nd group	45	27
Client-centered	19	47
Psychodynamic	11	73
No treatment	46	48

Source: Adapted from Alexander & Barton, 1976; Alexander & Parsons, 1973

O'Reilly (2017) found effect sizes ranging from $r = 0.10$ (randomized with a treatment-as-usual comparison) to $r = 0.45$ (nonrandom with a control group not receiving any treatment). Furthermore, it costs approximately $2,380 to deliver the program for each client but saves the taxpayer $49,776 over the course of the youth's career (Drake, Aos, & Miller, 2009).

Multisystemic Therapy (MST) was originally designed to deal with the more serious delinquent. At its core is a family therapy component ("family preservation") that teaches parents the skills needed to deal with adolescent problems (normative) and to reduce conflict within the family (relationship). MST also enlists the school, peers, and other key community agents in order to maintain the benefits of treatment (see Resource Note 7.1). MST essentially broadens the intervention beyond the nuclear family.

RESOURCE NOTE 7.1

Multisystemic Therapy: Theory and Practice

Multisystemic therapy (MST) has been widely disseminated and studied as an intervention for high-risk delinquents. Much of the success of MST in changing the behavior of difficult youths may be due to the comprehensive nature of the intervention. MST draws heavily on family systems and social ecological theories. The individual is part of a broad social context that includes family, peers, school, and community. That is, high-risk individuals with many needs require multiple interventions that change the reward–cost contingencies associated with antisocial behavior.

MST attempts to promote positive changes in the family both through direct intervention and arranging community supports that help families maintain the benefits of family therapy. Youths are given assistance with school performance and social adjustment, including the development of prosocial friends. Finally, individual counseling is provided to meet the unique needs presented by the delinquent. All of these services are given in a highly professional context with extraordinary efforts to maintain treatment integrity.

Therapists work directly with families, observing their interactions. Strengths are noted and serve as building blocks to more effective family functioning. The family is viewed as a social system in which changes in one family member can alter the behavior of the other members. Family members are asked to monitor their own behaviors and the behaviors of other family members. After the initial assessment stage, parents are taught to change their discipline strategies and use rewards and costs more effectively. MST therapists are also attentive to the personal problems that the parent(s) may have. If a psychiatric disorder is evident, for example, then the appropriate community treatment is secured. If the parent needs help in monitoring a child, then a neighbor may be enlisted to help. The value of community resources in helping families is taken very seriously by MST.

As the therapist works with the family, efforts are made to diminish associations with deviant peers. Therapists try to understand issues of prosocial peer rejection and teach parent(s) to monitor their children's social interactions. Parent(s) are taught to

continued

communicate more effectively to their children the harm that results from procriminal peer associations (e.g., they should not berate the child's delinquent peers, as it may only harden the youth's resolve to associate with them). During individual counseling, discussion of peers and the teaching of interpersonal skills are common.

The school is an important part of the social ecology of the high-risk delinquent. The youth is given assistance with academics, parents are supported in monitoring their children's school activities, and teachers are enlisted as agents of change. MST leaves no stone unturned in identifying the immediate social and community supports that can increase the rewards for prosocial behavior and interfere with the social forces that support antisocial activity.

MST has been subjected to multiple controlled evaluations and to a variety of problems (e.g., adolescent sex offenders; Borduin & Dopp, 2015). The early evaluations were quite promising but more recent reviews have been mixed. In probably the most comprehensive review of MST undertaken to date the general conclusion was "the effects are inconsistent across studies" (Littel, Pigott, Nielsen, Green, & Montgomery, 2021: p. 3). Littel and her colleagues examined 23 randomized experiments of MST with two outcomes: out-of-home placements and criminal behavior. Overall, there was little impact on the outcomes measured. However, and this is important, there were significant differences between the evaluations conducted in the US and those conducted outside of the US. Out-of-home placements were reduced in the US studies ($r = 0.14$) but not in other countries (confidence interval included 0). There were no overall significant reductions in arrest rates measured at 2.5 years in the US although there was wide variability in the findings. Surprisingly, outside the US arrest rates *increased* ($r = 0.33$).

The authors of the meta-analysis did identify some methodological weaknesses in the studies reviewed. For example, the US studies tended to have control groups that received no or little treatment whereas outside of the US control groups consisted of other forms of treatment interventions. A major source of criticism was bias. Most of the US experiments were conducted by the developers of MST and this may introduce a potential conflict of interest. Developers may select control groups to increase the chances of finding significant differences or selectively report results. Although this is a possibility and should be addressed by program evaluators, there is also the possibility that the developers of a program may be in a better position to ensure that the program is implemented as intended. We will return to the issue of program integrity and the role of developers in Chapters 10 and 12. For now, MST and other family-based interventions cannot be dismissed as having no value. Family-based treatments include other important outcomes such as peer relationships and emotional problems and these are very meaningful to troubled families (Carr, 2019; Dopp, Borduin, White, & Kuppens, 2017).

Summary of Family Treatment. There are three important conclusions that we can draw from the family intervention studies. First, both the structuring and relationship dimensions are important.

Second, behavioral treatment approaches can change family interactions along the structuring and relationship dimensions, and these changes are associated with decreases in delinquent behavior. Improved family functioning and relationships have also demonstrated decreased delinquent peer associations.

Finally, the reasons for the success of family programs go beyond attention to the relationship and structuring dimensions of interpersonal influence. They each involve detailed attention to program integrity. The most effective programs have smaller samples where the intervention can be more easily implemented and monitored. Program effectiveness depends upon appropriate and intensive strategies being carried out with integrity.

Marital and Romantic Relationships

Combined with family, marital factors represent one of the Central Eight risk/need factors. Referring to the meta-analysis of the predictive validity of the LS assessment instruments, to be reviewed in Chapter 10 (Olver, Stockdale, & Wormith, 2014), the subcomponent family/marital yielded mean effect sizes of 0.14 and 0.11 for general and violent recidivism, respectively. A recent study of nearly 16,000 inmates by Giguère, Brouillette-Alarie, and Bourassa (2023) found an average $r = 0.67$ (two-year follow-up) for the family/marital subcomponent of the LS/CMI, much higher than that reported by Olver et al. (2014). However, Giguère et al. also provided the results for the four items in the Family/Marital subcomponent and found the following predictive validity estimates:

Dissatisfaction with partner relationship: $r = 0.57$

Dissatisfaction with parental relationship: $r = 0.56$

Dissatisfaction with relatives: $r = 0.60$

Criminal family/partner: $r = 0.56$

In desistance theory, to be described in the last chapter, there are a number of "turning points" at which life events such as new employment or a residential change may facilitate the turning away from crime. Another turning point is marriage. Using a subsample ($N = 52$) drawn from the original 500 boys in the Glueck and Glueck study, Sampson, Laub, and Wimer (2006) examined the effects of marriage on criminal behavior. They found a 35 percent reduction in the odds of criminal behavior associated with being married. Further analysis indicated that being in a stable relationship, although infrequent for this group (recall the assortative mating discussion from Chapter 4), contributed to reduced crime after controlling for marriage. Similar findings have been reported in the United States and internationally although there have been exceptions (Bersani & Doherty, 2018). Stable cohabitation also appears to reduce offending but not to the same extent as marriage (Gottlieb & Sugle, 2019). The interesting question then becomes, "How does marriage work to reduce recidivism"?

In an analysis of longitudinal data from the United States, Warr (1998) found that after marriage the amount of time spent with peers, prosocial or antisocial, decreased significantly. That is, marriage may have its effect through altering the reward/cost distribution associated with procriminal supports for crime. Marriage may also lead to higher job stability, particularly for those who have had histories of erratic employment (Berg & Huebner, 2011; Skardhamar & Savolainen, 2014), once again affecting the reward/cost contingencies. Finally, for women it may be motherhood rather than marriage per se that is the turning point (Kreager, Matseuda, & Erosheva, 2010).

The effects of marriage are not always positive. In a New Zealand study of self-reported criminal activity at age 21, it was found that, relative to single peers, those romantically involved with a *deviant* partner were at higher risk of offending (Woodward, Fergusson, & Horwood, 2002). Those involved with a non-deviant partner were at lower risk of offending. Jennifer Cobbina and her colleagues (Cobbina, Huebner, & Berg, 2012) found marriage had a positive effect on women but not for men unless they were low-risk males. Apparently low-risk males are less likely to cohabit with criminal women. That is, examination of the criminal versus noncriminal partners is important to explore because generally there is a tendency for mating to occur among persons with similar backgrounds. Although adult bonds tend to succeed because of shared attitudes and values, it is not beneficial when it comes to outlaws.

School

Relatively low levels of academic achievement are risk factors for criminal behavior, and their predictive validity persists into adulthood. But the predictive validity of indices of achievement pale in comparison to the predictive levels achieved by assessments of misconduct problems in school. The latter, for the most part, reflect the predispositions suggested by an early history of antisocial behavior, by APP, and most likely by procriminal attitudes among older students. Indeed, a major predictor of poor academic and vocational achievement into late adolescence and adulthood is an early history of anti-social behavior. In an analysis of more than 8,000 youths, dropping out of school had no effect on delinquency after controlling for antisocial behavior and trouble in school (Sweeten, Bushway, & Paternoster, 2009). In brief, early-onset antisocial behavior comes before poor academic performance.

Robert Agnew (2001: pp. 158–161) provided a particularly valuable list of the characteristics of schools that link with the delinquency of their students.

What are the correlates of school differences in delinquency? Rates of delinquency are higher in schools with higher percentages of students who are poor, male, and members of minority groups. Most interestingly, Agnew summarizes the school differences by reference to the relationship and structuring principles:

> The schools with the lowest rates of delinquency are firm on the one hand: they have clear rules that are uniformly enforced and they are academically demanding. On the other hand, they are "warm"; they treat students in a fair manner, teachers are interested in students, provide opportunities for success, and praise student accomplishments; and school staff attempt to create a pleasant environment for the students.
>
> (Agnew, 2001: p. 161)

Can changes in school performance (academic achievement) and changes in attachment to school (to conventional activities and conventional others such as fellow students and teachers) influence criminal activity? The theoretical answer is yes, if the school-based change actually produces changes in the actual density of rewards and costs relevant to criminal behavior.

Within juvenile and adult corrections, the evidence is promising regarding the value of educational programming (see Figure 7.1). Mark Lipsey (1999)

Figure 7.1

Correctional Education for Adults

Source: Getty Images

described the effects of academic programs on young people as generally positive but small ($r = 0.05$). A more recent meta-analysis of educational interventions for *incarcerated* youth by Steele, Bozik, and Davis (2016) found a larger effect ($r = 0.18$, $k = 8$). The higher effect size reported by Steele and her colleagues may reflect the fact that the programs targeted higher-risk (incarcerated) youth who may benefit more from intervention. Lipsey's review included youth with a wide range of risk levels exposed to a range of interventions (e.g., counseling, family therapy). Although he found that interventions were more effective with higher-risk youth in general, Lipsey did not report specifically on educational interventions.

With respect to educational programs for *adult* offenders, a meta-analysis of 57 studies conducted between 1980 and 2017 found a mean effect size of $r = 0.18$ ($k = 81$; Bozick, Steele, Davis, & Turner, 2018). If only the methodologically better studies are considered, participants in correctional education programs were 28 percent less likely to recidivate than those who did not participate ($r = 0.16$, $k = 16$). What remains unclear is that the positive effect might well be based on lower-risk cases choosing to participate in advanced education programs.

School-based programs have focused on problematic/antisocial behavior in an effort to maintain youth involvement in academics and their attachment to school by avoiding expulsions. It is anticipated that success in maintaining problematic youth in the schools will lower the risk of delinquent behavior. From a GPCSL perspective the goal is to maximize the rewards for prosocial behavior within the school setting and avoid opportunities to be rewarded for delinquent behavior in an unstructured setting. The interventions usually focused on assisting students and their families to control aggressive and disruptive behaviors, academic tutoring, and mentoring. The programs are typically delivered by specially trained teachers, psychologists, and even police.

Sandra Jo Wilson and Mark Lipsey (2007) reviewed 249 experimentally and quasi-experimentally evaluated school-based interventions and their impact on aggressive and problematic behaviors. Interventions aimed at reducing problem behaviors such as fighting and rebelliousness were effective in reducing these outcomes ($r = 0.21$), and, consistent with the risk principle of effective treatment, more effective for higher-risk students. In addition, behavioral strategies were also more effective than other treatment modalities (e.g., social problem-solving, counseling).

Since Wilson and Lipsey's (2007) meta-analysis, there have been four recent and important reviews. First, there is the work of Healy, Valente, Caetano, Martins, and Sanchez (2020). They summarized 15 high-quality school-based prevention programs for aggressive children between the ages of six and 11 years. Fourteen of the studies found reductions in aggressive behaviors. Moderator analysis also showed that the programs were particularly effective for higher-risk children (i.e., children with more problematic behaviors and low self-control). In a broader review of the literature, James McGuire, Emily Evans, and Eddie Kane (2021) reviewed 165 reports targeting a range of problem behaviors (e.g., aggression, bullying, substance misuse). They found that police-delivered programs did not work. However, non-punishment interventions within schools that had a positive social climate were reasonably successful in reducing problem behavior among students.

The next two reviews were meta-analytic and investigated more serious outcomes. Valdebenito and her colleagues (Valdebenito, Eisner, Farrington, Ttofi, & Sutherland, 2019) analyzed 37 randomized experiments intended to reduce school expulsions. The interventions consisted mostly of skills training for teachers and students. They found a reduction in expulsions at six months ($r = 0.15$), but after a year the effect was nonsignificant. As we saw with our review of MST, the strongest effects for the school-based interventions were observed in studies where the evaluator was involved ($r = 0.23$).

Finally, Monica Mielke and David Farrington (2021) reviewed 14 randomized experiments with a minimum of 100 students receiving the intervention. Two outcomes were measured: school suspension ($k = 12$) and arrest ($k = 6$). There were no significant overall reductions in the two outcomes. By now, it should be no surprise to the reader, well-implemented programs showed a small but significant effect in reducing suspensions ($r = 0.05$). There were too few studies to evaluate the effect of program fidelity on arrest.

As a closing comment, certain social facts must be noted. In the United States, 4.8 percent of students failed to complete high school in 2016 (McFarland, Cui, Rathbun, & Holmes, 2018). Although the percentage may be small, in absolute numbers it represents over half a million individuals. There were no differences in the drop-out rates between Whites and Blacks but the rate was higher for Hispanics (approximately 8 percent). Now contrast this finding to that found among justice-involved persons and the results are both sad and extraordinary. In US prisons, approximately 36 percent of adults had not completed high school (Davis, Bahr, & Ward, 2013). When broken down by race it is 27 percent for Whites, 44 percent for Blacks, and 53 percent for Hispanics. Furthermore, in a follow-up of released inmates from Indiana ($N = 6,561$) where nearly two-thirds of the African Americans had less than high school, educational attainment was one of the best predictors of reincarceration (Lockwood, Nally, Ho, & Knutson, 2012). As one-half part of the Central Eight risk/need factors, the other being employment, attention to education by policymakers and practitioners bears top consideration.

Employment

Employment is part of being an adult for many people. Seeking work is also a reality for many unemployed adults. Not surprisingly most of this section deals with adults. However, work is also an issue for a large number of young people. National data show that between 30 percent (UK) and 60 percent (US and Canada) of high school students have a part-time job. Robert Agnew (2001) suggested that, although there may be benefits to working during high school, the research evidence reveals a small criminogenic effect of work on the part of young people. The money and time away from home and the schoolyard are thought to support additional drug use and minor delinquency. The finding recalls that of Cullen and colleagues (Wright, Cullen, & Williams, 1997), who found that more money in the pocket was associated with delinquency. The relationship, however, is complicated. Robert Apel and his colleagues found that the more hours worked, the greater the likelihood of dropping out of school, but delinquency was lower (Apel, Bushway, Paternoster, Brame, & Sweeten, 2008). They argued that it is important to understand the reason *why* the youth leaves school. Leaving for economic reasons to support a young family is far different than leaving because of a dislike of school. Further research in this area would explain some of the discrepancy in this literature.

Level of education, level of employment, and money earned are all risk factors for criminal behavior. Mark Olver, Karen Stockdale, and Stephen Wormith (2014) reviewed 128 studies of the Level of Service (LS) offender risk–need assessment instruments. One of the subscales of the LS instrument measures problems in the domains of education and employment, and the meta-analysis yielded 55 effect size estimates of predictive validity in this regard. The average r for general recidivism was 0.24, and it was 0.20 for violent recidivism.

Vocational training and correctional industries are classic elements of correctional programming. In Byrne's (2020) review of programs across US prisons, working in a prison industry or participating in vocational training were both associated with reductions in recidivism. Vocational training and working in a prison industry likely provide skills to facilitate the transition to release and finding and holding employment. In the Steele, Bozik, and David (2016) meta-analysis, attending vocational training while in prison was significantly related to reduced recidivism ($r = 0.18$, $k = 42$) and, as hypothesized, also related to obtaining employment ($r = 0.32$, $k = 10$).

Moreover, investments in prison-based training programs, such as prison work release, can save money in the long run. Grant Duwe (2015) compared inmates from the state of Minnesota who completed a prison work release program to a matched group of inmates who did not participate in work release. The inmates were released during the day to work or attend vocational training and then returned to prison at the end of the day. The program participants had a slightly lower reconviction rate than the comparison group but were much more likely to be employed upon full release, with net cost benefit of nearly $700 per person. This may not seem like much but considering there were 1,785 men and women participating in the program the savings amounted to one and a quarter million dollars.

A discussion of employment cannot end without reference to the influential work of Robert Sampson and John Laub (1993). Following up on the youth in the classic Glueck and Glueck (1950) study, these researchers produced quantitative and qualitative evidence for the importance of obtaining meaningful long-term employment as "turning points" for frequent and serious criminals. They argued against the position that early entry into criminal activity seals one's fate. They suggested that, as unusual and unlikely it is that high-risk criminals would achieve a good job, it does happen, sometimes. And such unlikely events (as a result of chance or deliberate action) can result in cessation of criminal activity, over and above any of the standard stable predictors of crime. The advantage to employment is that it can greatly redistribute the reward–cost contingencies in effect for criminal and noncriminal behavior.

The redistribution of rewards and costs associated with stable employment is illustrated in John Wright and Francis Cullen's (2004) analysis of the longitudinal National Youth Survey (NYS). The NYS study began in 1976 with interviews of a nationally representative sample of youths between the ages of 11 and 17. These youths have been reinterviewed at set time periods since 1976. Analyzing data from Waves 5 and 6, when the youths were between the ages of 15 and 24, they found that the number of hours worked per week and contact with prosocial coworkers were associated with reduced drug use and criminal offending. Additional analyses showed that contact with prosocial coworkers decreased associations with delinquents. That is, the influence of prosocial work colleagues on criminal behavior mitigates the effects of prosocial supports for crime.

Not the least of the potential effects is to enhance the rewards and satisfactions for noncriminal behavior so that the potential subtractive costs of crime increase. The opportunity for a major shift in personally and interpersonally mediated influence may also be expected through reductions in procriminal associates and attitudes. Shadd Maruna (2001) has suggested that turning away from a life of crime is dependent upon creating a new identity of being a law-abiding citizen. The construct of identity change carries with it the notion of major cognitive change.

Leisure/Recreation

In PCC leisure/recreation describes the person's free choice to engage in prosocial activities outside of work, school, and family. Failure to do so increases the risk for crime, presumably by increased opportunities to interact with delinquents and engage in risky behaviors (Hoeben & Weerman, 2016). Structured activities such as volunteer work and scouting enhance exposure to adults supporting moral cognitions and behavior (Walters, 2018b). The Olver et al. (2014) review of the LS instruments discussed earlier also yields information on the predictive validity of leisure/recreation. They found a mean r of 0.16 in the prediction of general recidivism and an $r = 0.12$ for violent recidivism. That is, leisure/recreation appears to be a moderate risk/need factor.

Reviews of the literature have been of the narrative type and focused on the relationship between youths' unstructured time and delinquency. Hoeben, Meldrum, Walker, and Young (2016) reviewed a large number of studies (the authors did not specify the exact number) and found "clear evidence that peer delinquency and unstructured socializing play important roles in understanding the etiology of delinquency and substance use" (p. 118). Similarly, Trinidad, Vozmediano, and San-Juan's (2018) review of 88 studies concluded that "evidence of unstructured activities increasing the risk of antisocial behaviour is strong" (p. 61). We will have to wait for a quantitative meta-analysis to permit further specification.

Although the evidence is robust that unstructured leisure activities are related to a heightened risk for antisocial behavior, it may not mean that increasing structured prosocial leisure activities is protective of crime. As examples, prosocial leisure activity reduced the risk of delinquency for boys but not girls (Kang, Tanner, & Wortley, 2018), and in an evaluation of a physical activity recreational program, delinquency *increased* for Latino males (Roman, Stodolska, Yahner, & Shinew, 2013). A case in point is organized sports for youth. Many young persons are involved in sports. There are many health benefits to engaging in sports, but what about its relationship to delinquency? Anouk Spruit and her collaborators (Spruit, van Vught, van der Put, van der Stouwe, & Stams, 2016) reviewed 51 studies with over 130,000 participants. They found no overall relationship between sport participation and delinquency ($r = 0.005$, $k = 431$). However, delinquency was less when it was a team sport occurring in school, rather than outside of school.

An important factor not measured in the meta-analysis is risk. Many children and youth who participate in organized sport come from families that can afford the costs associated with the sport. At-risk youths often do not have this benefit and, even if the school provides the activity, such youth may show little interest in what the school offers. Another study by Spruit (Spruit, Hoffenaar, van der Put, van Vught, & Stams, 2018) evaluated a sports-based program for youth at risk for delinquency in the Netherlands. They found a small but significant decrease in police contact ($r = 0.17$). From our own data set of treatment programs, the mean effect size was a modest 0.09 (CI = 0.02 to 0.15).

After-school recreational programs in disadvantaged neighborhoods are hypothesized to decrease delinquency by providing supervision to youths who are free to get into trouble between the end of school and before the parent(s) come home from work. However, a meta-analysis by Sema Taheri and Brandon Walsh (2016) found little support for these programs in reducing delinquency. Structured programs occurring after the end of the school day were reviewed and all of the evaluations required experimental or quasi-experimental designs. Seventeen studies were identified and the effect size was an insignificant $r = 0.03$ ($k = 12$), with two studies demonstrating *increased* delinquency. All of the after-school programs had two or more components (e.g., skill training plus group recreation). None of the programs had an influence on delinquency.

The meta-analysis is noteworthy in that it assessed risk (two levels: high or mixed). In the six studies for which youth risk data was available, again after-school programming had no effect by risk level. In an early study of five after-school programs by Cross, Gottfredson, Wilson, Gaskin, and Connell (2009) that found no overall effect, further analysis showed that: (1) not all youths regularly attended the programs, and (2) the at-risk youths were the most likely not to attend. That is, the program did not reach those who could potentially benefit the most.

Many comprehensive community and school-based interventions involve citizen and student volunteers spending time mentoring and often engaging in recreational activities. As described in Resource Note 6.1, recreational interactions with citizen volunteers had little impact on the procriminal attitudes of prisoners until the interactions were structured to deliberately increase prosocial modeling and reinforce prosocial behavior. That is, there is little reason to expect reduced criminal behavior unless the learning opportunities are structured into the program.

Neighborhood

In addition to some of the Central Eight risk/need factors discussed in this chapter, the neighborhood social context can influence criminal behavior. Neighborhoods where families live can affect the behavior of parents and children. High-crime, disadvantaged neighborhoods can impact a variety of outcomes ranging from mental health (Baranyi, Di Marco, Russ, Dibben, & Pearce, 2021) to physical illnesses and mortality (Gaskin, Roberts, et al., 2019). These neighborhoods can also interfere with good parenting practices, stress parent–child bonds, expose youths to other criminals, and provide opportunities for crime. This appears to be especially true for boys (Walters, 2016b). The relationship between neighborhood context and crime is complex. However, the research suggests that neighborhood is rather minimal compared to the more immediate personal, interpersonal, and familial risk/need factors (McGee, Wickes, Corcoran, Bor, & Najman, 2011).

Some studies find that those most at risk for delinquency do worse in highly disadvantaged neighborhoods. For example, Wolff and his colleagues (Wolff, Baglivio, Piquero, Vaughn, & DeLisi, 2016) found that juveniles under community supervision with low self-control and negative emotionality reoffended more quickly when they lived in a disadvantaged neighborhood, what the authors called "the triple crown." Patrycja Piotrowska and her colleagues (Piotrowska, Stride, Croft, & Rowe, 2015) conducted a meta-analysis of 133 studies on the relationship between socioeconomic status (a proxy for disadvantaged neighborhood) and the antisocial behavior of children and youths up to the age of 18. The overall effect size was a small $r = 0.10$. The impact of low socioeconomic status was moderated by a number of factors (e.g., geographical location, age of the child/youth), but the largest factor was callous-unemotional traits ($r = 0.24$). That is, being socially disadvantaged had a larger effect on a certain subtype of youth. Unfortunately, this finding was based on only five effect sizes out of a possible 139, so the results should be viewed with caution.

Knowing that high-risk families may be worse off in poor neighborhoods has led to a few experiments in which families are moved into middle-class neighborhoods. These studies have shown to decrease delinquency, but the effects were small. The typical ways of dealing with crime in disadvantaged neighborhoods are by police crackdowns on minor crimes and trying to make neighborhoods more visually appealing. However, improving the look of the neighborhood and increasing police presence is not enough. Furthermore, relying on policing to manage neighborhood crime is also fraught with discriminatory practices (Braga, Brunson, & Drakulich, 2019). What appears to be much more important is enhancing social control (Sampson & Raudenbush, 2001), which from a GPCSL perspective means getting down to the major personal and interpersonal factors as risk/need and/or as strengths.

Many disadvantaged neighborhoods have characteristics (e.g., high concentrations of justice-involved persons) that increase the risk for crime, but within these neighborhoods there are some protective factors. There are residents with strong attachments to their neighborhood who respect the police (Hostinar & Miller, 2019), show confidence in their local schools (Eamon & Mulder, 2005), and demonstrate positive parenting practices (Sharma, Mustanski, Dick, Bolland, & Kertes, 2019; Walters, 2016c). Family and social support may be particularly important protective factors. In a longitudinal study of more than 2,000 twins, antisocial behavior among twins at age five worsened as the children grew older (Odgers, Caspi, et al., 2012). By age 12 the correlation between disadvantaged neighborhood and antisocial behavior was a sizeable $r = 0.25$. However, the researchers also found that positive parental relation and monitoring protected against the criminogenic effect of the neighborhood.

Readers are reminded that the major characteristics of any setting (home, school, work, neighborhood) are membership composition (criminal versus noncriminal others), quality of the interpersonal relationships, and the criminal versus anticriminal nature of the cognitive and behavioral patterns modeled, reinforced, and punished. The work of Stouthamer-Loeber, Loeber, Wei, Farrington, and Wikström (2002) is highly relevant here. They carefully documented the nature of disadvantaged neighborhoods as well as the contributions of disadvantaged neighborhoods to persistent and serious delinquency. A basic finding is that a disadvantaged environment has no impact on frequent and serious delinquency for high-risk young people. Rather, they report that it is the low-risk young people who are influenced by "bad" neighborhoods.

Two findings are worth repeating. First, one of the major characteristics of disadvantaged areas is a population of individuals and families characterized by high risk/need scores for offending and low strength scores. That is, there is a membership composition effect. Second, the correlation between assessments of risk, need, and strength with criminal behavior is large, while the correlation between the socially defined disadvantaged area and criminal conduct is real but relatively small in magnitude.

Summary of the Person in Social Context

This chapter has illustrated how the contributions of the social context and neighborhood setting may be approached from a GPCSL perspective. From a membership composition perspective on social structure, we want a handle on the proportion of criminals found in the settings of home, school, work, and leisure. We seek an understanding of the rewards and satisfaction evident within the setting. We need to know where significant others such as parent(s) and partners stand on the relationship and structuring dimensions of interaction.

There are certainly differences in the state of knowledge. In the domain of family of origin, the ability to predict and influence youthful offending is truly impressive. It is approaching causal significance. Dramatic gains in the achievement of reduced reoffending are seen when elements of parent–child relations and supervision are targeted. The level of knowledge in the domains of marital attachments and leisure/recreation is weaker when it comes to controlled efforts at influencing criminal activity.

The studies of school and work are at the intermediate level of knowledge development. The predictive validity of relevant assessments is reasonably well established in both domains. To date, however, the value of academic and vocational programming awaits further research before coming to firm conclusions.

Worth Remembering

1. Forming social attachments is the basis to healthy relationships that could protect a child from a criminal trajectory. Children who become attached to a caregiver develop fewer psychological difficulties than young children who do not, and they grow up with healthier relationships with peers and adults. Problematic attachment patterns do not result simply from disruptions in the parent–child bond due to divorce. It is the nature and frequency of the disruption that is important. High-conflict families, parents who emotionally neglect their children or treat them harshly, and moving from one foster care home to another produce the most harm.

2. Families operate along two dimensions: relationship and structuring.
   Children who are raised in families in which there are poor relationships and the parent(s) exercise poor parenting techniques are most at risk for delinquency. Furthermore, children in such families are more likely to associate with procriminal peers.

3. At the extremes of the relationship and structuring dimensions children may be exposed to Adverse Childhood Experiences (ACEs).

    ACEs predict future criminal conduct and multiple traumatic experiences place youth on a life-course-persistent trajectory.

4. Family interventions can reduce delinquency.

    Treatment programs that address the relationship and normative dimensions of family functioning have demonstrated less delinquency in the problem child and even among siblings of the child.

5. Marital and romantic relationships are important covariates of criminal behavior. Assessments of marital relationships predict future criminality. In addition, research suggests a stable marital/romantic relationship can be a "turning point" in the life of a criminally involved person, *if* the partner is prosocial.

6. School/employment is a Central Eight risk/need factor.

    Participation in school and work settings increases opportunities to receive rewards for prosocial behavior and increases the costs for criminal behavior. There are many programs that succeed in increasing ties to school (for youths) and employment (for adults).

7. The impact of leisure/recreation programs has not been sufficiently explored.

    Although leisure/recreation shows moderate predictive validity there have been few controlled studies of systematically altering the leisure activities and observing its impact on criminal behavior. However, the research that does exist is promising.

8. Disadvantaged neighborhoods can affect the criminal actions of individuals.

    Deprived neighborhoods can impact physical and mental health and crime within the setting. These neighborhoods operate by altering the membership composition to favor criminal behavior. Buffering the impact can be achieved by deliberately increasing prosocial orientation among the community members.

Recommended Readings

The late Gerald Patterson's work on the development of Coercion Theory has been highly influential to those responsible for delivering interventions to families with difficult to manage children. A clear and recent summary of the theory is the chapter written by Patterson in Thomas Dishion and James Snyder's 2016 edited book, *The Oxford Handbook of Coercive Relationship Dynamics*. The book also features the application of Coercion Theory to a range of topics, from genetics to intimate personal relationships, and it is not limited to children and their families.

Robert Sampson and John Laub's (1993) *Crime in the Making: Pathways and Turning Points Through Life*, a follow-up of Glueck and Glueck's (1950) study of 500 delinquents, makes for fascinating reading. It is one of the few studies that provides evidence for the importance of major adult life events (employment and marriage) on criminal conduct.

 Visit the Instructor and Student Resource to access additional exercises, videos and study materials to support this chapter: psychologycriminalconduct.routledge.com

CHAPTER 8 Substance Misuse

Rounding off the last of the criminogenic needs of the Central Eight is substance misuse. Like the preceding criminogenic needs described in Chapters 4 through 7, substance misuse is predictive of antisocial behavior and it is dynamic or changeable. Subsumed under substance misuse are problematic alcohol use and the use of illegal drugs. The purpose of separating alcohol use from drug use is twofold. First, the relationship between alcohol misuse and crime is generally weaker than the relationship between illegal drug use and crime. Second, the criminal justice system is far less tolerant of drug use than alcohol misuse. For adults, purchasing alcohol is legal, and consuming alcohol is punished only in specified situations (e.g., driving under the influence). The possession and use of illegal drugs, even small amounts, can result in severe criminal justice penalties.

Alcohol Misuse

Definition and Prevalence

The first task is to define what we mean by "alcohol misuse." At what point does drinking legally available alcohol become problematic? Is it a matter of quantity, and if so, how much? Is it a matter of age, and again, at what age? How about the situational context—driving a car, intoxication in a public place? Finally, what about the interpersonal and personal context—partner breakups, feelings of guilt and worthlessness, etc.? Generally, alcohol misuse is defined as the consumption of alcohol in situations that are hazardous and that leads to physical, social, work, or psychological problems.

In the 2020 National Household Survey on Drug Use and Health, more than 67,500 Americans over the age of 12 were asked about their alcohol use during the previous year (Substance Abuse and Mental Health Services Administration, 2021). The prevalence rate for alcohol misuse (binge and heavy drinking in the past 30 days) was 22.4 percent. The US prevalence rate for alcohol misuse is higher than that found in other countries, but this may be due as much to differences in methodology as to culture (Somers, Goldner,

DOI: 10.4324/9781003292128-10

Waraich, & Hsu, 2004). Turning to criminal justice populations, Fazel, Yoon, and Hayes (2017) undertook a comprehensive review of 24 studies reporting the prevalence rates of substance use disorders among prisoners from 10 countries. The average prevalence of alcohol use disorder was 24 percent (26 percent for men and 20 percent for women). Although the rates do not seem much higher than in the US general population, the reader should keep in mind that Fazel et al. reviewed *psychiatrically* diagnosed alcohol use disorder, a much higher standard than the self-reports often used in prevalence studies.

Another way of approaching the definition of alcohol misuse and its prevalence among justice-involved populations is to use the results from risk/need assessment instruments. Risk/need instruments, to be discussed in more detail in Chapter 10, sample a variety of criminogenic needs, including substance misuse. Although the criteria for assessments of substance problems in these risk/need scales are not as stringent as with some other specialized assessment instruments, they have a number of advantages. First, risk/need instruments are routinely administered by correctional staff and thereby provide regular prevalence data without the need for expensive, specialized surveys. Second, the assessment of criminogenic needs by these instruments drives the delivery of treatment services within a criminal justice system. Finally, we can investigate the predictive validity of the various criminogenic needs.

One family of risk/need instruments that assesses alcohol misuse is the Level of Service (LS) instruments. One of the areas covered is called Alcohol/Drug Problem. Table 8.1 shows a part of this section. If there is a current problem with either alcohol or other drugs, then the assessor explores further the nature of the problem. For example, does the person steal to buy drugs, or does drinking excessively cause arguments in the home or at work?

Table 8.2 presents some prevalence data based on assessments using an LS instrument. One advantage of this data is that it permits us to separate alcohol misuse from problematic drug use. Most general risk/needs assessment

---

TABLE 8.1 Alcohol/Drug Problem and the Level of Service: Example Items

Item	Problem Examples
1. Alcohol problem, current	Any of 3 to 5
2. Drug problem, currently	Any of 3 to 5
3. Law violations	Stealing to buy drugs; impaired driving
4. Marital/Family	Arguments over substance use
5. School/Work	Difficulties maintaining employment; asked to leave school due to intoxication

Source: Andrews, Bonta, & Wormith, 2004. Reproduced with permission of Multi-Health Systems, Inc., P.O. Box 950. North Tonawanda, NY 14120-0950 (800/456-3003)

TABLE 8.2 Alcohol Misuse: Prevalence (%) with Drug Misuse and Alone

Sample (N)	Country	Co-misuse	Alcohol only
Male			
Prison (956)	Canada	47.2	42.3 (634)
Law violations		98.4	
Marital/family		48.8	
School/work		45.7	
Prison (16,635)	US	29.2	13.3 (9,344)
Law violations		90.4	
Marital/family		74.3	
School/work		61.6	
Community (664)	UK	30.9	27.6 (504)
Law violations		89.2	
Marital/family		70.4	
School/work		39.9	
Community (46,417)	US	35.5	19.9 (9,344)
Law violations		88.3	
Marital/family		73.5	
School/work		60.6	
Community (464)	Canada	15.3	13.3 (428)
Law violations		78.9	
Marital/family		46.5	
School/work		42.3	
Female			
Prison (647)	Canada	41.0	38.8 (312)
Law violations		92.8	
Marital/family		71.3	
School/work		47.5	

continued

TABLE 8.2 *(Continued)*

Sample (*N*)	Country	Co-misuse	Alcohol only
Prison (1,657)	US	31.1	11.1 (614)
Law violations		65.7	
Marital/family		61.0	
School/work		52.3	
Community (2,193)	Canada	24.0	21.1 (1,783)
Law violations		88.0	
Marital/family		63.1	
School/work		29.8	
Community (10,970)	US	29.1	16.3 (4,471)
Law violations		87.7	
Marital/family		80.3	
School/work		65.0	

Source: Author's Level of Service database

instruments combine the two into a general substance misuse category. Among criminal justice clients, alcohol and drug use often co-occur but not always. Some people misuse alcohol and avoid drugs and vice versa. As shown in Table 8.2, co-abuse is more frequent than alcohol use only. The LS permits further exploration into how drug and alcohol misuse cause problems in the domains of law, family/marital, and school/work. For example, substance use and conflict with the law (e.g., stealing to buy drugs) is by far the most prevalent problem for both men and women.

Alcohol Misuse and Crime

The prevalence of problematic drinking among criminal justice samples is quite high, certainly much higher than that found in the general population. Justice-involved persons also report a high incidence of drinking at the time of the offense (Felson, Burchfield, & Teasdale, 2007; Felson & Staff, 2010). This is especially true in cases of violence and homicide. Aaron Duke and his colleagues (Duke, Smith, Oberleiter, Westphal, & McKee, 2018) conducted a most extraordinary review of the literature: a *meta*-meta-analysis. They collated the results from 32 meta-analyses that reported on the relationship between substance misuse and violence. The mean effect size for alcohol use and violence was $r = 0.19$ ($k = 18$). For males $r = 0.23$ ($k = 8$) and for females the effect size nearly halved ($r = 0.11$, $k = 3$). Turning to homicide, a review of 23 studies from nine different countries found 37 percent of homicide offenders were intoxicated at the time of the offense (Kuhns, Exum, Clodfelter, & Bottia, 2014).

Lipsey and his colleagues (Lipsey, Wilson, Cohen, & Derzon, 1997), in addition to their meta-analysis of correlational studies, also reviewed *experimental* studies of the potential causal role of alcohol use to violence. In these experiments, alcohol was given to participants, and their aggressive behavior, usually electric shocks administered to another subject, was compared to that by participants in a no-alcohol condition. In these studies, the independent variable (alcohol) is manipulated by the experimenter, thus permitting evaluations of the effects of alcohol on aggressive behavior.

In comparing the alcohol versus the no-alcohol conditions in the laboratory experiments, the overall mean effect size was a large $r = 0.54$ ($k = 42$). This finding was identical to an earlier meta-analysis of 49 experimental studies of alcohol consumption and aggression in *laboratory* settings (Ito, Miller, & Pollock, 1996). However, both quantitative reviews found important variability in the findings, depending on experimental procedures and individual characteristics of the participants. Mary McMurran's (2012) review suggested a number of individual-level factors that could mediate the role between alcohol and violence and can be used as treatment targets. Some examples that she described are perceived provocation and the person's evaluation that aggression has personal benefits. As Lipsey et al. (1997: p. 278) concluded: "While a causal influence of alcohol consumption on violence cannot be ruled out.... it seems apparent that there is no broad, reliable, 'main effect' of alcohol on violence."

Treating Alcohol Misuse

Treatments for alcohol misuse include a variety of interventions. Not all of them will be reviewed here, only a select few that are widespread—pharmacological treatment and Alcoholics Anonymous. More will be said on cognitive-behavioral techniques when we discuss the treatment of drug use later in this chapter and more generally in the rehabilitation chapters (11 and 12).

Pharmacological treatments include two classes of drugs: disulfiram (Antabuse), which has been used for nearly 80 years, and a newer class of drugs (naltrexone, acamprosate). The mechanism of action for Antabuse is that, when disulfiram interacts with alcohol (ethanol), it triggers a violent physiological reaction. The person becomes sick to the stomach, vomits, develops headaches, and feels highly anxious. It is presumed that this aversive conditioning to alcohol will deter the person from further drinking. The challenge with disulfiram, not surprisingly, is getting the individual to comply with taking the medication. Naltrexone (also used to treat opioid addiction) and acamprosate block the pleasurable effects of alcohol and stop the "cravings." Given that these drugs have fewer of the ethical problems associated with disulfiram (i.e., purposely inducing harm) and higher compliance rates, they are presently the pharmacological treatment of choice.

With respect to treatment efficacy (usually measured by drinking frequency or abstinence), these medications have shown small to moderate effects. In a meta-analysis of 64 studies comparing the two drugs, the average effect size for abstinence was $r \sim 0.18$ for acamprosate and $r \sim 0.06$ for naltrexone (Maisel, Blodgett, Wilbourne, Humphreys, & Finney, 2013). There were only 14 studies of post-treatment outcome, with acamprosate maintaining its advantage over naltrexone.

A recent systematic review of 14 studies with correctional populations found naltrexone to be more effective in reducing alcohol consumption than disulfiram (Slavin-Stewart, Minhas, et al., 2022). Of the 10 studies examining the effectiveness of naltrexone, all found reductions in alcohol use. Two of the four disulfiram studies found a decrease in alcohol-related outcomes. Reductions in recidivism were mixed. From a GPCSL perspective this is anticipated. Controlling cravings for alcohol and reducing alcohol consumption is certainly welcomed, but many high-risk criminal justice-involved clients also have other criminogenic needs intertwined in substance misuse. Changing attitudes, securing stable employment, and altering procriminal social networks cannot be achieved by medication alone, even when coupled with alcohol misuse counselling. A variety of, and more intensive, services are needed to help clients transition to a prosocial lifestyle.

Alcoholics Anonymous (AA) is a social support group for clients trying to quit drinking. Founded in 1935, AA has grown into an international organization operating in more than 40 countries. Participants must admit that they cannot stop drinking on their own and submit to a "higher power" (interpreted individually to mean a sponsor, or the group, or God). A sponsor, who has been abstinent for at least one year, acts as a 24-hour support and teacher for the newly initiated. Meetings are held regularly during which other members offer support as they follow the 12 steps to recovery (the 12th step is a "spiritual awakening").

Evaluations of AA using stringent controls (e.g., random assignment) are difficult to conduct for a number of reasons. For example, records of membership are not kept, and not all AA meetings operate in the same manner (Williams & Mee-Lee, 2019). However, there are a sufficient number of well-designed evaluations of AA to conduct a meta-analysis. Kelly, Abry, Ferri, and Humphreys (2020) reviewed 27 studies that included randomized and nonrandomized methodologies. They found that AA performed as well as other treatments and, compared to traditional health care treatments, was more cost-effective. This most recent meta-analysis is in sharp contrast to an earlier review of eight randomized experiments that found no effect (Ferri, Amato, & Davoli, 2009). Unfortunately, the authors reported their results as risk ratios, preventing the conversion to r. Kelly and his colleagues also noted that higher participation rates led to better outcomes, a finding noted more than 25 years ago. A meta-analysis of 74 studies (Tonigan, Toscova, & Miller, 1996) found a mean r of 0.08 for the variable *affiliation* with AA (i.e., attending meetings), rising to 0.22 under conditions of AA *involvement* (e.g., leading a meeting, sharing at meetings, etc.).

If AA does have an effect, then why would AA work? There are a number of plausible reasons for the efficacy of AA in reducing alcohol use (note that the outcome is not criminal recidivism). First, AA shares some of the therapeutic ingredients found in models of cognitive-behavioral therapy (Kelly et al., 2020). For example, the sponsor functions like a therapist who has been trained in the AA model and instructs the newcomer in the approach. The sponsor models abstinence and reinforces it during interactions with the new member. Another important factor is the power of the group. The group not only motivates the individual to maintain abstinence but also provides rewarding alternative activities to drinking and teaches coping skills to deal with the urge to drink. A review of 24 studies concluded that AA's greatest impact is on altering the social network of the recovering alcoholic (Groh, Jason, & Keys, 2008).

Self-help groups provide a variety of supports to the individual. The group may support, for example, general feelings of self-worth, or it can be specific to alcohol abstinence such as a sense of hope in overcoming a dependency. There are groups that are highly structured and follow behavioral principles without reliance on AA. Perhaps the earliest and best-known example is Hunt and Azrin's (1973) Community Reinforcement approach (Resource Note 8.1). Reviews of the literature have repeatedly shown that AA helps the alcoholic to leave behind drinking friendships and establish new social networks that value abstinence (Groh et al., 2008; Kelly, Magill, & Stout, 2009; Vigdal, Moltu, Bjornestad, & Selseng, 2022). For example, the Network Support Project actively encourages the client to attend AA meetings while giving up social interactions with drinking friends (Litt, Kadden, Kabela-Cormier, & Petry, 2007). A two-year follow-up found that the alcohol-dependent participants assigned to the network support condition had 20 percent more days of abstinence than those in the alternative treatment conditions (Litt, Kadden, Kabela-Cormier, & Petry, 2009).

RESOURCE NOTE 8.1

The Community Reinforcement Approach to Alcohol Misuse

In 1973, George Hunt and Nathan Azrin introduced an operant conditioning approach to the treatment of alcoholism. Eight men with serious alcohol problems from a state hospital were selected to participate in a Community-Reinforcement (CR) program. The CR program enlisted the help of family, friends, and community groups to deliver rewards for nondrinking behaviors. The goal was to make life without alcohol more enjoyable and fulfilling. If more social reinforcement was provided for nondrinking behaviors, then reverting to drinking would result in a loss or time out from these reinforcements (i.e., a subtractive cost). The general approach involved rearranging the density of rewards and costs associated with drinking behavior.

continued

Involving the family, usually the spouse of the alcohol user, is a major component of the program (Meyers, Roozen, & Smith, 2011). Beginning in the hospital, the couple meet and agree on a list of activities that would be mutually satisfying. In general, they would agree to make each other happy by addressing problem areas (e.g., finances, child responsibilities) and spending more time together in rewarding activities. For the user without a family, a "synthetic family" was created from relatives, an employer, or a church minister. The synthetic family would invite the person into their home for regular visits and meals. If the client was unemployed, they would join a "Job Club" that helped the person search for a satisfying job and prepare for a job interview. Because most alcoholics spend their time with other alcoholics, it was important to change the person's social network. One way that Hunt and Azrin achieved this change was to convert a former tavern into a social club that showed movies, held dances, and ran bingo games. Carefully and systematically the alcoholic's social environment was changed to redistribute rewards from drinking to nondrinking behaviors.

In the first evaluation of CR, eight men were matched to eight others on age, employment history, marital status, and education. The control group went through the standard hospital program of 25 hours of didactic teaching on the effects of alcohol. A six-month follow-up showed dramatic improvements for the CR group. Not only did the CR group show a large decrease in the amount of time spent drinking (14 percent for the CR group and 79 percent for the control group), but the group was also less likely to be unemployed (5 percent vs. 62 percent). In terms of family life, prior to the program all five married men in the CR group were contemplating divorce. At follow-up, the five men remained married while two of the four couples in the control group had separated.

Since the 1973 demonstration study, the CR approach to alcohol abuse treatment has evolved. Today, it is called Community Reinforcement and Family Training (CRAFT) and it is used in community settings with adults and adolescents. CRAFT also has been delivered to clients who misuse drugs and who have gambling problems. Marc Archer and his colleagues (Archer, Harwood, Stevelink, Rafferty, & Greenberg, 2020) conducted a systematic review of 14 studies that compared CRAFT to various comparison groups (e.g., treatment-as-usual, AA). Overall, CRAFT interventions were twice as effective than the compared treatment, as reported by the significant other. The one area of exception was in the treatment of a gambling disorder, where no significant treatment effects were noted.

Drug Misuse

Prevalence

In 2020, the percentage of Americans over the age of 12 who reported the use of illicit drugs in the past year was 21.4 percent (Substance Abuse and Mental Health Services Administration, 2021). Marijuana was by far the most used substance, accounting for nearly half of drug use. Although the drugs commonly associated with criminal behavior (cocaine, methamphetamine, and heroin) accounted for less than 4 percent, the absolute number is approximately nine million. Returning to Fazel et al.'s (2017) international review, the prevalence rate of drug use disorder among prisoners was 30 percent. Half of the women prisoners met the criteria for a substance abuse disorder (51 percent). In the author's data sets, the prevalence rates for illegal drug use, without alcohol misuse comorbidity, range from a low of 5.6 percent to a high of 56.1 percent (Table 8.3).

TABLE 8.3 Illegal Drug Abuse: Prevalence (%) with Alcohol Misuse and Drug Only

Sample (*N*)	Country	Co-abuse	Drug only
Male			
Prison (956)	Canada	33.7	27.4 (504)
Law violations		64.4	
Marital/family		29.1	
School/work		28.0	
Prison (16,643)	US	43.8	31.1 (11,773)
Law violations		49.6	
Marital/family		38.7	
School/work		32.8	
Community (663)	UK	24.0	20.5 (459)
Law violations		51.7	
Marital/family		19.9	
School/work		39.9	
Community (29,779)	US	52.9	41.6 (18,147)
Law violations		60.6	
Marital/family		48.2	
School/work		40.4	
Community (464)	Canada	7.8	5.6 (393)
Law violations		61.1	
Marital/family		33.3	
School/work		33.3	
Female			
Prison (647)	Canada	51.8	50.0 (382)
Law violations		89.9	

continued

TABLE 8.3 *(Continued)*

Sample (N)	Country	Co-abuse	Drug only
Marital/family		72.8	
School/work		56.1	
Prison (216)	Canada	52.3	56.6 (143)
Law violations		65.3	
Marital/family		55.6	
School/work		12.5	
Prison (1,658)	US	62.9	52.3 (1,659)
Law violations		65.7	
Marital/family		61.0	
School/work		52.3	
Community (2,182)	Canada	18.3	15.3 (1,659)
Law violations		78.7	
Marital/family		57.1	
School/work		39.3	
Community (263)	Canada	19.0	17.8 (208)
Law violations		30.4	
Marital/family		25.9	
School/work		27.2	
Community (9,317)	US	58.5	51.8 (6,628)
Law violations		60.9	
Marital/family		52.5	
School/work		41.2	

Source: Author's Level of Service database

Unlike alcohol, drug misuse has a closer relationship to crime because of its illicit status. An addiction to an illegal drug puts one directly into contact with other criminals and, in many cases, may exert pressure to engage in other illegal activity in order to buy drugs. Substance use, undifferentiated from alcohol misuse, is a commonly found risk factor for crime among adults (Gendreau, Little, & Goggin, 1996), young offenders (Viljoen, Shaffer, Gray, & Douglas, 2017), and forensic outpatients (Eisenberg, Van Horn, et al., 2019). There have been a number of meta-analyses that have reported specifically on the relationship between illicit drug use and recidivism.

Craig Dowden and Shelley Brown (2002) reviewed 45 studies, yielding 116 effect size estimates, where substance use was measured prior to the recidivistic event. Thirty-three estimates were solely on illegal drug use (the others included alcohol misuse). The average effect size between drug use and recidivism was $r = 0.13$. Trevor Bennett and his colleagues (Bennett, Holloway, & Farrington, 2008) analyzed 30 studies that investigated the link between drug misuse and crime. On average, the odds of criminal behavior were 2.79 times greater for drug users than for non-drug users. For crack users, the odds of crime were six times greater.

Two more recent meta-analyses confirm the earlier findings on the predictive validity of illicit drug use. The first meta-analysis by Gary Goodley, Dominic Pearson, and Paul Morris (2022) focused on adult inmates being released from prison. Sixty-seven studies from five countries measuring possible predictors of recidivism met the inclusion criteria. For illicit drug use they found a moderate effect size of $r = 0.34$ ($k = 14$). Interestingly, a history of alcohol misuse was unrelated to recidivism. The second meta-analysis centered on clients under community supervision (Yukhnenko, Blackwood, & Fazel, 2019). The correlation between illicit drug use and recidivism was $r = 0.42$ ($k = 5$). This review did find a significant relationship between alcohol use and recidivism but it barely reached significance, with the confidence interval bordering on zero ($r = 0.29$, $k = 3$).

Finally, in Table 8.4, the predictive validity of illegal drug use in our data sets, without the presence of alcohol misuse, is displayed. The most striking result is that drug misuse was more highly correlated with recidivism in all five female samples compared to the male samples.

TABLE 8.4 Drug Abuse Only (without Alcohol): Predictive Validity with Recidivism (1 year)

Sample (N)	Country	r
Male		
Prison (504)	Canada	.08
Community (393)	Canada	.03
Community (459)	UK	.17
Female		
Prison (382)	Canada	.19
Prison (208)	Canada	.26
Community (1,659)	Canada	.20
Community (143)	Canada	.42
Community (107)	UK	.24

Source: Author's Level of Service database

In 1971, then US President Richard Nixon announced his "war on drugs." Under Nixon federal money was allocated to prevention and rehabilitation, but over the ensuing years law enforcement took the lion's share of resources. For the first 40 to 50 years the "war" was fought in the US and internationally (Rosen, 2021), but, as we know today, it has not produced the desired effect. The war has failed to reduce crime and resulted in increased police powers that threatened personal rights, clogged courts, and created overcrowded prisons (Cooper, 2015; Saadatmand, Toma, & Choquette, 2012). Some have questioned whether the increased emphasis on punishment and control was merely a disguised effort to control racialized minorities (Earp, Lewis, & Hart, 2021; Farahmand, Arshed, & Bradley, 2020).

The general failure of the "war on drugs" has brought renewed efforts to treat rather than punish. This shift can be seen in response to the fentanyl/opioid crisis, with the growth of harm reduction programs and the legalization of marijuana in many US states and countries. The reasons for the failure of deterrence-based programs will be discussed in detail in Chapter 13 but, for now, we turn to a more optimistic topic: rehabilitation.

Treating Drug Misuse in the Criminal Justice System

Evaluations of drug treatment programs within prison and community settings generally indicate positive effects (Doyle, Shakeshaft, Guthrie, Snijder, & Butler, 2019; Koehler, Humphreys, Akoensi, Sánchez de Ribera, & Lösel, 2014) and a high level of cost-effectiveness (Washington State Institute for Public Policy, 2019). An important meta-analysis explored the effectiveness of treatment by testing some of the principles of drug addiction treatment (Pearson, Prendergast, et al., 2012). In 1998 the U.S. National Institute of Drug Abuse gathered experts in substance misuse treatment to formulate a set of treatment principles based on the evidence. Thirteen principles were generated. The meta-analysis by Frank Pearson and his colleagues tested the validity of seven of the 13 principles. Studies published between 1965 and 2006 were reviewed (232 studies yielding 243 effect size estimates). Empirical support was found for five of the seven principles tested (Table 8.5). The one surprise was that duration of treatment had no effect, but the authors of the report think that the measure used in the studies ("percentage of clients who complete treatment;" Pearson et al., 2012: p. 10) is inadequate. It is also possible that duration of treatment is important for only the higher-risk client (Walters, 2016e).

One promising treatment for drug misuse is therapeutic communities (TC). Therapeutic communities are usually operated within prison settings where the inmates live together in segregated units helping each other toward abstinence and prosocial lifestyle change. TC has been in operation in California prisons, on and off, for over 60 years (Mullen, Arbiter, Plepler, & Bond, 2019). Although many studies have been criticized because of poor methodology (e.g., participant selection bias, vague program description and implementation), the interventions do appear to reduce recidivism (Aslan, 2018; Beaudry,

TABLE 8.5 **A Meta-Analytic Test of Seven of the National Institute of Drug Abuse's Principles of Effective Drug Treatment**

Principle	r
Match to client's needs	.12
Target multiple needs	.16
Provide counseling	.10
Contingency management	.10
Cognitive-behavioral treatment	.05
Therapeutic community	.18
Reassess of treatment plan	.12
Provide counseling to reduce HIV risk	.09
Ensure treatment is sufficiently long	No effect
Do drug testing	No effect

Source: Adapted from Pearson et al., 2012

Yu, Perry, & Fazel, 2021; Doyle et al., 2019; Pearson et al., 2012). Why they work remains unclear, with some researchers pointing to the aftercare component of TC, others claiming it is a sense of belongingness and well-being (Pearce & Pickard, 2012), and some arguing it is because of peer influence (Kreager, Schaefer, et al., 2019).

Relapse Prevention

Most treatment programs for substance misuse hold the belief that many, if not most, clients will relapse at some point. Thus, rehabilitation interventions have the goal of avoiding a relapse into substance use. However, there is one treatment model that integrates the process of relapse with evidence-based treatment.

In 1980, Alan Marlatt and Judith Gordon noted that behavior therapy was effective in producing change in behavior, but the maintenance of change was problematic. Reviewing the results of interventions with a variety of addictions (alcohol, cigarettes, and heroin), they observed that within a matter of months after completing treatment, most participants relapsed. Marlatt and Gordon reasoned that the avoidance of relapse was not to be found in "bigger and better treatment packages" but rather in providing clients direct training in recognizing the situations that trigger relapse and teaching them how to cope with these situations.

Cognitive-behavioral treatments for substance use disorders have been shown effective in reducing both alcohol and drug consumption (Magill, Ray, et al., 2019). Relapse prevention (RP) is a cognitive-behavioral intervention that promotes self-management skills in high-risk situations. It has been applied to a variety of addictions (Hsu & Marlatt, 2011), general justice-involved persons (Dowden & Andrews, 2007), and even the treatment of sexual offenders with cognitive disabilities (Frize, Griffith, Durham, & Ranson, 2020). The first step is to recognize situations that elicit substance misuse. This may be done by a detailed review of situations in which the client misused a substance or with the aid of objective assessment measures. The second step is to teach the client alternative responses to high-risk situations (e.g., refusing a drink, planning a different activity for Saturday night).

The RP model has considerable intuitive appeal, research on its effectiveness has been widespread, and the findings from meta-analytic reviews have been remarkably consistent. For example, a meta-analysis of 26 studies ($n = 9,504$) found RP generally effective for smoking, drug, and alcohol problems ($r = 0.14$; Irvin, Bowers, Dunn & Wang, 1999). Another analysis of four different interventions for drug misusers that included RP found an effect size for RP of $r = 0.14$ ($k = 5$; Dutra, Stathopoulou, et al., 2008). Moreover, RP interventions were equally effective compared with other interventions (i.e., cognitive behavior therapy, contingency management).

Mindfulness practices have become ubiquitous in psychotherapy and applied to a wide range of human problems. Mindfulness has its origin in Buddhist philosophy and it involves focused attention, in the here and now, to one's thoughts and emotions in a non-judgmental manner. Cravings are a characteristic of substance addiction and mindfulness-based interventions may be a suitable addition to more conventional treatments. Today, RP has also evolved to include mindfulness training (Bowen, Witkiewitz, et al., 2014). A direct comparison of RP to mindfulness RP found similar effectiveness (Bowen et al., 2014).

There have been a number of reviews of mindfulness-based treatments for substance misuse. As expected, reductions in cravings were quite substantial. The meta-analysis by Cavicchioli, Movalli, and Maffei (2018) found an average effect size of $r = 0.41$ ($k = 7$). However, the effect size was considerably smaller when abstinence was the measured outcome ($r = 0.19$, $k = 21$). Another meta-analysis by Sean Grant and his colleagues (Grant, Colaiaco, et al., 2017) calculated a small but significant effect size for cravings ($r = 0.06$) and no relationship between mindfulness-based treatment and relapse. However, the latter review focused on randomized evaluations with psychiatrically diagnosed substance-disordered clients. Systematic reviews of the literature (i.e., non-meta-analytical) have also found this pattern of reductions in cravings but small or no reductions in abstinence (Korecki, Schwebel, Votaw, & Witkiewitz, 2020; Sancho, De Gracia et al., 2018). Although cravings as a causal factor in substance misuse makes intuitive sense, it appears to be insufficient to promote abstinence.

Summary. Our discussion of the addiction treatment field suggests that the effective ingredients are similar to those found in the general treatment of justice-involved persons. Programs that promote a positive therapist–client relationship but follow a structured format are associated with decreased relapse rates. Moreover, cognitive-behavioral styles of interventions and intensive services appear to be more effective with higher-risk substance-using clients. Community support and specific training on relapse prevention techniques may also enhance the long-term success of treatment.

From a theoretical perspective, offsetting the rewards associated with substance misuse involves altering many reinforcement contingencies. Shifting the reward balance to favor nonuse requires changes in the individual's attitudes, social community, and feelings of competency and self-control. Family members, employers, and friends can systematically learn to reinforce abstinence and express disapproval for drug use. Individuals can learn cognitive skills to cope with high-risk situations and stop themselves when they begin to rationalize their drug use or think in a way that supports substance use. The importance of involving the family, especially with adolescents, is highlighted in a meta-analysis by Tanner-Smith, Wilson, & Lipsey (2013a). Reviewing 73 evaluations of treatments for adolescents with substance use disorders, family therapy demonstrated the greatest improvements in outcomes ($r = 0.13$, $k = 25$). However, behavioral changes do not come easily.

Dealing with Resistance to Treatment

For many who misuse substances, the behavior is frequent (often daily) and has a long history. The automatic, habitual nature of substance use presents a serious challenge. Treatment programs for those in conflict with the law are faced with getting clients into treatment and keeping them there. However, as the evidence suggests, there are interventions that can overcome these obstacles.

High attrition rates from treatment are not only common for substance-using clients but they are also a problem for justice-involved clients in other types of treatment (e.g., anger management). Attrition is particularly high among those who need treatment the most (Olver, Stockdale, & Wormith, 2011). A recent review by Lappan, Brown, and Hendricks (2020) found almost one in three persons (30.4 percent, $k = 299$) starting substance use treatment failed to complete the program. The drop-out rate increased dramatically the more severe the problem (e.g., 66.7 percent of heavy cocaine users failed to complete treatment). Furthermore, those who need treatment the most often have numerous problems (e.g., multiple drug dependencies, mental health problems).

Two general approaches have been used to direct and maintain clients in treatment. One approach relies upon psychological techniques to engage the client in treatment, while the other uses the threat of negative consequences.

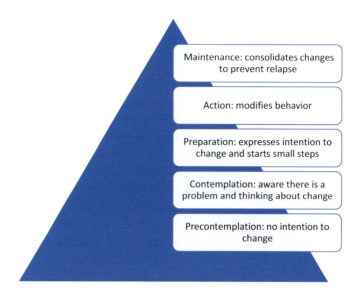

Figure 8.1

Stages of Change

Motivational Interviewing

Motivational interviewing (MI) originated out of the need to deal with the client who, by denying that there is an addiction, is unmotivated to attend treatment. James Prochaska and Carlo DiClemente (1982) formulated a model that describes clients as being at different stages in their readiness to change. These stages range from just thinking about the possibility of having a problem to actually doing something about it. At the precontemplation and contemplation stages, the client does not see that there is a problem that requires a change. Behavior is rationalized or denied, or the client is "thinking about it." Gradually the client progresses to actually changing and maintaining the new behavior (Figure 8.1). In a meta-analysis conducted by Krebs, Norcross, Nicholson, and Prochaska (2018), the relationship between stage of change, or treatment readiness, and success in drug treatment was $r = 0.15$ ($k = 22$). As Prochaska and DiClemente's model would predict, operating at a higher stage is associated with positive outcomes. The task is: How do you help the resistant client progress through the stages?

William Miller and Stephen Rollnick (2002) developed motivational interviewing as a technique to move the client from "I am thinking about it" to "I am going to do something about it." Essentially, the therapist engages the client in a nonthreatening relationship, builds rapport, and gently and cautiously nudges the client in the direction of accepting that there is a problem that must be faced.

MI is often a preparatory step to more formal, structured treatment and relapse prevention training (Marlatt & Witkiewitz, 2010). This technique recognizes that not all people referred to treatment are equally motivated (i.e., they are at a different stage of change). Considering that many justice-involved persons come to treatment because of external motives (e.g., mandated by court, applying for parole), MI provides a way of enhancing motivation from within.

Early meta-analytic reviews of the MI literature targeting addictions found the average effect size falling between $r = 0.13$ and $r = 0.25$, depending upon the length of follow-up (Hettema, Steele, & Miller, 2005; Vasilaki, Hosier, & Cox, 2006). However, two recent reviews paint a different picture. Pederson, Curly, and Collins (2021) located five high-quality randomized experiments targeting adult justice-involved substance users. None of the studies found differences between the treatment and control group. The second report (Frost, Campbell, et al., 2018) summarized 104 previous reviews and meta-analyses of MI across a range of problems (e.g., weight loss, diabetes management). Thirty-one of the reviews dealt with substance misuse (13 focused solely on alcohol use). There were two important findings. First, when the reviews were analyzed for methodological quality, 82.6 percent were judged very low or low. Second, analyses of the addiction area found "statistically significant small beneficial effects" of MI (p. 1).

Given the recalcitrant nature of most of those caught up in the justice system, and despite the equivocal results from the MI literature, many correctional agencies are training their staff in MI techniques (Blasko, Viglione, Toronjo, & Taxman, 2019; Bogue, Pampel, & Pasini-Hill, 2013). One benefit to MI training is that it helps to replace the more typical authoritarian and confrontational approach used by staff with a collaborative and relationship-building tactic (Tafrate, Hogan, & Mitchell, 2019). An important point is that MI as a sole technique of intervention is unlikely to have an impact on criminal recidivism. MI basically increases motivation to attend and adhere to treatment (McMurran, 2009). In Chapter 5 under the discussion of families, two general dimensions of interpersonal influence were described: a relationship dimension and a structuring dimension. In treatment the client must like/respect the therapist (relationship) and then it is up to the therapist to teach and facilitate the learning of prosocial behavior (structuring). Thus, MI does the first part very well but the second part less well.

Mandated Treatment and Drug Courts

Not surprisingly, the criminal justice system is an area in which coercion is fairly commonplace. For example, courts routinely add treatment conditions to probation orders, and parole boards "expect" inmates to have taken advantage of prison treatment programs. Klag, O'Callaghan, and Creed (2005) view coercion as a complex construct and not a simple dichotomy of forced versus voluntary treatment. Within the criminal justice system, coercion is very much a continuous variable ranging from the compulsory to subtle pressures to participate in treatment. Recognizing the dimensional nature of coercion leads to a fuller understanding of ethical and motivational issues (e.g., if coercion to participate in treatment comes from family members rather than the courts, is it more ethically acceptable? Will the client be more motivated in treatment?).

There have been a number of narrative reviews of the coercion literature concluding that justice-involved persons subjected to mandatory treatment do just as well as those who volunteer for treatment (Prendergast, Farabee, Cartier, & Henkin, 2006; Stevens, Berto, et al., 2005). However, a meta-analysis found that mandatory or coerced treatment was not as effective as voluntary treatment. Karen Parhar and her colleagues (Parhar, Wormith, Derkzen, & Beauregard, 2008) reviewed 129 studies of mandated and non-mandated treatment programs. Parhar et al. coded treatment along a three-point scale from mandated (legal consequences for not participating in treatment), coerced (minor consequences for not attending treatment), and freely voluntary. Across all studies, treatment had a small effect on recidivism ($r = 0.06$, $k = 129$). However, when the results were broken down according to the three-point scale, an important difference emerged. Voluntary treatment displayed a larger effect ($r = 0.17$) than mandatory treatment ($r = 0.08$) but no difference when compared to coercive treatment ($r = 0.16$). A review of nine clearly mandatory drug treatment programs found only two studies reporting less drug use and decreased recidivism (Werb, Kamarulzaman, et al., 2016). None of the studies used MI techniques to entice clients to maintain program participation. We now turn our attention to drug courts as an illustration of a widely used mandated treatment for substance users in the criminal justice system.

Drug courts began in the United States in 1989. By 2021, there were more than 3,500 drug courts in all 50 states (U.S. Department of Justice, 2022). The popularity of drug courts, strongly supported by public opinion (Thielo, Cullen, Burton, Moon, & Burton, 2019), has spread beyond the American border, and they operate in North and South America, Australia, New Zealand, and parts of Europe. Drug courts have been extended to juveniles and "specialty courts" have been created to deal with other groups (e.g., mental illness, justice-involved veterans, intimate partner violence). The way they all operate is that prior to sentencing and with the support of the court, the convicted person is placed into community treatment with regular drug screening (for the drug user), and the court monitors the person's progress. Successful completion of treatment is usually rewarded by avoidance of a custodial sentence.

Do drug treatment courts help to reduce incarceration, substance use, and recidivism? Answering this question is difficult because many evaluations have been plagued by methodological problems. Leticia Gutierrez and Guy Bourgon (2012) rated 78 of 96 drug treatment courts as having "little confidence" in their methodology. Leslie Blair and her colleagues applied an objective scale and only three of 18 drug courts reviewed were rated as "effective" (Blair, Sullivan, Lux, Thielo, & Gormsen, 2016). However, there are some well-designed evaluations. Sevigny, Fuleihan, and Ferdik (2013) reviewed 19 studies (more than half were experimental or strong quasi-experimental designs) and calculated an effect size of $r = 0.18$ for reduced incarceration. Now, this appears as a favorable outcome with respect to reducing the use of custody. However, the researchers also found that the aggregate amount of time served was no different for the drug court clients than the comparison clients. Sevigny et al. hypothesized that the closer monitoring of clients may lead to detection of drug use and with noncompliance comes a more severe prison sentence.

Turning now to recidivism outcomes, Logan and Link (2019) summarized the results from seven meta-analyses with adults and found an average reduction in recidivism in the order of 12 percent. However, there was considerable variability in the results, ranging from 8 percent to a high of 26 percent. Some individual evaluations of drug courts have even found *increases* in recidivism. A meta-analysis of 31 juvenile drug courts by Stein, Homan, and DeBerard (2015) arrived at similar results, with an 8 percent reduction in recidivism. However, Tanner-Smith, Lipsey, and Wilson's (2016) meta-analysis with youth found no difference between drug court clients and control clients in drug use or recidivism (46 studies). The heterogeneity in the findings point to a need to understand who drug courts target and what is meant by "treatment."

As noted earlier, there has been a proliferation of specialty courts serving a wide range of clients. Evaluations of these courts also yield similar effects to those found with drug courts. For example, the average effect size was $r = 0.10$ from a meta-analysis of mental health courts (Lowder, Rade, & Desmarais, 2018). Travis Pratt and Jillian Turanovic (2019) recently challenged a fundamental assumption of these courts: that the clients are specialists themselves.

Pratt and Turanovic's review indicated that, on average, justice-involved persons are more generalist, especially among the higher risk. In other words, a person who is a high risk to reoffend is likely to engage in a variety of crimes and have many criminogenic needs. A second important issue is whether drug courts adequately target those most in need. An evaluation of data from 8,000-plus US cities and counties found a 15.6 percent increase in arrests (Lilley, 2017). A follow-up analysis focusing on 372 of the largest US cities and this time controlling for client risk observed that drug courts were associated with a 17 percent increase in arrests, mostly for minor drug crimes (Lilley, Stewart, & Tucker-Gail, 2020). It seems that, as Sevigny et al. (2013) have suggested, close monitoring by the courts has some drawbacks. Drug courts can also have a net-widening effect.

A second issue is to specify the treatment offered to drug court clients. In a 2011 review of 76 drug courts, Deborah Koetzle Schaffer found that 70 percent of the drug courts required attendance at AA or Narcotics Anonymous; only 32 percent reported that they provided evidence-based treatment ("evidence-based" was not defined). Furthermore, other than substance use, half of the programs did not target other criminogenic needs. Gutierrez and Bourgon (2012) reported similar results. Out of the 25 methodologically acceptable studies, 11 did not adhere to *any* of the principles of effective rehabilitation (the principles are described in detail in the next chapter). These findings also extend to juvenile drug courts, where attention to the wide range of needs presented by youths and their families are often lacking (Wilson, Olaghere, & Kimbrell, 2019).

Drug courts and other specialty courts operating within a therapeutic juris-prudence model (providing treatment within the context of law) are laudable. However, some of the treatments offered may be questionable. It is important to recognize that the person who misuses substance *and* is in conflict with the law treatment is qualitatively different than the law-abiding substance user. The treatment providers in these courts sometimes rely on methods that may work with non-justice-involved clients and pay little attention to the research from the correctional rehabilitation field. The silos need to come together in order to maximize the benefits to the client and the community.

A Few Comments on Substance Misuse

Alcohol misuse by itself has been inconsistently associated with criminal behavior; illicit drug use has been more clearly linked to recidivism (Goodley et al., 2022). However, many justice-involved persons misuse both. When we consider those who use alcohol *and* other drugs, then the association crystallizes. Returning to the data presented by Olver and his colleagues (2014), scores on the Alcohol/Drug subcomponent of the LS instruments demonstrate moderate to high predictive validities depending on the outcome measure. For general recidivism, $r = 0.20$ and for violent recidivism, $r = 0.13$.

In the last paragraph of the previous section the point was made that the substance-using person may be qualitatively different than the law violator who does not use drugs. Glenn Walters (2014b, 2015a) has developed this view further by suggesting that criminal behavior, together with substance misuse, is a more potent mix for criminal conduct than criminal behavior or substance misuse alone. His "worst of both worlds" hypothesis was originally based on findings from a longitudinal study of youths who were convicted of an offense between the ages of 14 to 18. At ages 16 to 21, those who self-reported crim-inal behavior *and* problematic substance use in the past six months were the most likely to have an APP (callous-unemotional, impulsiveness), procriminal attitudes, and higher reoffending and drug use rates (two-year follow-up and self-reported) than those with: (1) no criminal activity, (2) criminal activity, and (3) substance misuse only.

Walters continued this line of research and has replicated the findings in two more longitudinal studies. In the Study of Adolescent Health, Walters (2015b) found that procriminal thinking was important in maintaining the relationship between the "worst of both worlds" and future offending and sub-stance misuse. Another important factor related to the hypothesis, early age onset, was identified in a UK study of 2,539 children (Walters, 2016c, 2016d). Furthermore, Walters (2017) has demonstrated that as the person transitions from early adolescence, when the worst of both worlds is just developing, the effects of substance use and criminal offending become cumulative in early adulthood. Finally, the "worst of both worlds" hypothesis has been extended to male and female inmates (Walters & Magaletta, 2015), and in both cases, misuse was shown to increase the risk of reoffending beyond consideration of criminal history alone.

GPCSL theory outlines the learning of behaviors within social contexts. Substance misuse draws one to the social context of substance misusers and procriminal others who model and differentially reinforce the problematic behavior. In turn there is the learning of attitudes supportive of substance use and procriminal attitudes. An early meta-analysis by Pratt, Cullen, et al. (2010) and a more recent one by Kruis, Seo, and Kim (2020) found modeling, differential association, differential reinforcement, and attitudes predictive of substance use. The effect sizes ranged from a modest $r = 0.10$ (differential reinforcement) to a more substantial $r = 0.39$ (attitudes).

It is also important to keep in mind that problematic substance use is interrelated with other criminogenic needs. Chronic substance use interferes with stable marital and family relationships, hampers success at employment and school, and may lead to financial hardship. Too much of criminal justice policy has emphasized substance misuse as the root of crime and, thereby, required a war on drugs. A more balanced approach that includes attention to the numerous needs presented by justice-involved persons offers a more evidence-based approach to the problem.

Worth Remembering

1. Alcohol and other drug use are quite prevalent among criminal justice populations, but their relationship to crime is moderate.

   Meta-analytic findings of correlational studies of alcohol/drug use and crime show average effect sizes (r) in the range of 0.10 to 0.20. There is no conclusive evidence that alcohol use actually causes crime, although there is a more direct link with illicit drug use.

2. Treating those who misuse substances has been more effective than the "war on drugs."

   Punishing drug users through the increased use of imprisonment has not reduced reoffending rates. Treatment programs appear to be a more effective way of dealing with the substance misuser.

3. Drug courts hold promise but they can be much more effective if the treatments offered are more in line with the latest evidence from the correctional rehabilitation literature.

Recommended Readings

There are two very easy-to-read, nontechnical books that will give the reader a broader context to this chapter. The first is Lance Dodes and Zachary Dodes' *The Sober Truth* (2014). The book begins with a history and critical review of Alcoholics Anonymous but ends with a summary of what works in addictions treatment. Elliott Currie's *Reckoning: Drugs, the Cities, and the American Future* (1993) is a terrific overview of the challenges brought on by the war on drugs. The book may seem dated but it remains relevant today.

For an introduction to the treatment of substance misuse, *Rethinking Substance Abuse*, by William Miller and Kathleen Carroll (2006) is recommended. In this text, Miller and Carroll provide a comprehensive, nonquantitative review of the science of treatment. A recent summary of the Community Reinforcement approach to alcohol misuse (Resource Note 8.1) is provided in the open access article by Archer, Harwood, Stevelink, Rafferty, and Greenberg (2020) in *Addiction, 115*, 1024–1037.

 Visit the Instructor and Student Resource to access additional exercises, videos and study materials to support this chapter: psychologycriminalconduct.routledge.com

PART 3 Applications

CHAPTER 9 The Risk-Need-Responsivity Model of Assessment and Treatment

The General Personality Cognitive Social Learning (GPCSL) perspective of criminal behavior presented in Chapter 3 has very practical implications. As seen in that chapter, GPCSL identifies the Central Eight risk/need factors that are at the core of many of today's assessment instruments in the criminal justice system (Chapter 10). GPCSL also informs effective treatment programs (Chapters 11 and 12). GPCSL does this through the Risk-Need-Responsivity (RNR) model, which has become a major paradigm for assessment and treatment across many criminal justice jurisdictions throughout the world (Newsome & Cullen, 2017; Polaschek, 2012; Taxman & Smith, 2021; Wormith & Zidenberg, 2018). In this chapter the full RNR model is presented, with the supporting evidence in the following chapters.

By the late 1980s it was becoming clear that treatment could be effective in reducing recidivism, but it was unclear why some rehabilitation programs were more effective than others. When reviewing the rehabilitation literature, D. A. Andrews, myself, and Robert Hoge (1990) observed certain patterns associated with the more effective treatment programs. Together we formulated three general principles for purposes of effective classification and correctional treatment: the (1) risk, (2) need, and (3) responsivity principles. A fourth principle, professional override, was also described but it was the first three that garnered all of the attention. Since then, as Table 9.1 demonstrates, others have been added but the name RNR remains since they are the core principles.

The Overarching Principles

In Chapter 1, a definition of a psychology of criminal conduct was presented. This definition included a respect for the individual and "the ethical and humane application of systematic empirical methods of investigation." The RNR model codifies this theme in Principles 1 to 3.

DOI: 10.4324/9781003292128-12

TABLE 9.1 The Risk-Need-Responsivity (RNR) Model of Assessment and Treatment

The Overarching Principles

1. **Respect for the Person and the Normative Context:** Services are delivered with respect for the person, including respect for personal autonomy, being humane, ethical, just, legal, and being otherwise normative. Some norms may vary with the agencies or the particular settings within which services are delivered. For example, agencies working with youth may be expected to show exceptional attention to education issues, Adverse Childhood Experiences, and to child protection. Mental health agencies may attend to issues of personal well-being. Some agencies working with women may place a premium on attending to trauma and/or to parenting concerns.

2. **Psychological Theory:** Base programs on an empirically solid psychological theory (e.g., General Personality and Cognitive Social Learning).

3. **General Enhancement of Crime Prevention Services:** The reduction of criminal victimization may be viewed as a legitimate objective of service agencies, including agencies within and outside of justice and corrections.

The Core RNR Principles and Key Clinical Issues

4. **Introduce Human Service:** Introduce human service into the justice context. Do not rely on the sanction to bring about reduced offending. Do not rely on deterrence, restoration, or other principles of justice.

5. **Risk:** Match intensity of service with risk level of cases. Work with moderate- and higher-risk cases. Generally, avoid creating interactions of low-risk cases with higher-risk cases.

6. **Need:** Target predominately criminogenic needs. Move criminogenic needs in the direction of becoming strengths (e.g., from currently unemployed to fully employed).

7. **General Responsivity:** Employ behavioral, social learning, and cognitive-behavioral influence and skill-building strategies.

8. **Specific Responsivity:** Adapt the style and mode of service according to the setting of service and to relevant characteristics of individual offenders, such as their strengths, motivations, preferences, personality, age, gender, ethnicity, cultural identifications, and other factors. The evidence in regard to specific responsivity is generally favorable but very scattered, and it has yet to be subjected to a comprehensive meta-analysis. Some examples of specific responsivity considerations follow:

a) When working with the weakly motivated:
   - build on strengths;
   - reduce personal and situational barriers to full participation in treatment;
   - establish high-quality relationships; and
   - deliver early and often on matters of personal interest.
b) Attend to the evidence in regard to age, gender, and culturally responsive services.
c) Attend to the evidence in regard to differential treatment according to interpersonal maturity, interpersonal anxiety, cognitive skill level, and the responsivity aspects of psychopathy.

continued

TABLE 9.1 *(Continued)*

---

    d) Consider the targeting of noncriminogenic needs for purposes of enhancing motivation, the reduction of distracting factors, and for reasons having to do with humanitarian and entitlement issues.

9.   **Breadth (or Multimodal):** Target a number of criminogenic needs relative to noncriminogenic needs.

10. **Strength:** Assess strengths to enhance prediction and specific responsivity effects.

11. **Structured Assessment:**

    a) Assessment of Strengths and Risk-Need-Specific Responsivity Factors: employ structured and validated assessment instruments.

    b) Integrated Assessment and Intervention: every intervention and contact should be informed by the assessment.

12. **Professional Discretion:** Deviate from recommendations only for very specific reasons. For example, functional analysis may suggest that emotional distress is a risk/need factor for *this* person.

Organizational Principles: Setting, Staffing, and Management

---

13. **Community-based:** Community-based services are preferred but the principles of RNR also apply within residential and institutional settings.

14. **GPCSL-based Staff Practices:** Effectiveness of interventions is enhanced when delivered by therapists and staff with *high-quality relationship skills* in combination with *high-quality structuring skills*. Quality relationships are characterized as respectful, caring, enthusiastic, collaborative, valuing personal autonomy, and using motivational interviewing to engage the client in treatment. Structuring practices include prosocial modeling, effective reinforcement and disapproval, skill building, cognitive restructuring, problem-solving, effective use of authority, and advocacy/brokerage.

15. **Management:** Promote the selection, training, and clinical supervision of staff according to RNR and introduce monitoring, feedback, and adjustment systems. Build systems and cultures supportive of effective practice and continuity of care. Some additional specific indicators of integrity include having program manuals available, monitoring of service process and intermediate changes, adequate dosage, and involving researchers in the design and delivery of service.

Source: Andrews, Bonta, & Hoge, 1990; Andrews & Bonta, 2010a; Bonta & Andrews, 2007

Principle 1

(Respect for the Person and the Normative Context) is overarching because any intervention is expected to respect the norms of the social community of which it is a part. Ethicality, legality, and cost-efficiency are widely appreciated standards of conduct and all forms of human, social, and clinical services are subject to these standards. It is equally true, as indicated in Principle 1, that there is some setting-specificity in the normative context. For example, it is perhaps fair to say that an ethic of caring is more readily evident in some forensic mental health settings than in some prison settings.

Norms are not to be confused with the active "ingredients" of service. The active ingredients for reduced offending are adherence with the core principles of human service (principles of risk, need, and responsivity). Under certain conditions, adherence with relevant norms will have a positive impact on treatment outcome. For example, addressing noncriminogenic needs may well enhance motivation for participation in treatment and/or enhance a person's ability to participate more fully in treatment.

Principle 2

(Psychological Theory) recommends that psychological understandings of crime be drawn upon. If you are interested in the criminal behavior of individuals, be sure to work from theoretical perspectives on the criminal behavior of individuals. In particular, GPCSL theory is recommended. The power of GPCSL resides in: (1) the specification of major risk, need, and responsivity factors in the analysis and prediction of criminal behavior, (2) the identification of effective treatment strategies of wide applicability, (3) a ready integration with biological/neuropsychological perspectives as well as broader social structural and cultural perspectives, and (4) the flexibility to incorporate new conceptions and strategies (such as motivational interviewing).

Principle 3

(General Enhancement of Crime Prevention Services) extends the RNR model to health and other agencies outside of justice and corrections that deal with criminal justice clientele. For example, substance misuse providers are encouraged to adopt RNR services when dealing specifically with those in conflict with the law.

The Core RNR Principles and Key Clinical Issues

The core RNR principles were first described in 1990. Principle 4 was never stated as a principle in 1990 but was presumed. Here, the principle of human service is formally described. More detail on the core principles is provided because they are at the heart of clinical interventions and have been the most widely researched.

Principle 4

(Introduce Human Service). The typical legal and judicial principles of deterrence, restoration, just desert, and due process have little to do with the major risk/need factors. It is through human, clinical, and social services that the major causes of crime may be addressed.

Principle 5

(Risk). There are two aspects to the risk principle. The first is that criminal behavior can be predicted. The second aspect involves the idea of *matching level of treatment services to the risk level of the client*. This matching of service to risk is the essence of the risk principle and it is the bridge between assessment and effective treatment. More precisely, higher-risk clients need more intensive and breadth of services if we are to hope for a significant reduction in recidivism. For the low-risk individual, minimal or even no intervention is sufficient.

Although the risk principle appears to make a great deal of common sense, sometimes theory and practice do not always agree. Some human service workers prefer to work with the motivated, lower-risk clients rather than with the high-risk, resistant clients. After all, it is personally reinforcing to work with someone who listens and is willing to follow advice.

The largest known test of the risk principle was conducted by Christopher Lowenkamp and his colleagues (Lowenkamp, Latessa, & Holsinger, 2006). Ninety-seven residential and nonresidential programs in the state of Ohio were reviewed as to how well they adhered to the risk principle. Information was collected on the length of time in a program, whether more services were offered to higher-risk clients, and the delivery of cognitive-behavioral programs to offenders. Providing intensive services to higher-risk clients was associated with an 18 percent reduction of recidivism for those in *residential* programs and a 9 percent reduction for justice-involved persons in nonresidential programs (usually, the effects are greater in community-based programs).

Table 9.2 provides some further examples of what happens when treatment is—or is not—matched to the risk level of the client. In each of the studies, reductions in recidivism for high-risk clients were found only when intensive levels of services were provided. However, when intensive services were provided to low-risk cases, they had a negative effect. This detrimental effect is not found in all studies. In general, there is a very small positive treatment effect for low-risk offenders ($r = 0.03$; Andrews & Dowden, 2006).

The risk principle is interrelated with other principles. Noteworthy is Principle 11 (Structured Assessment). In order to properly apply the risk principle, one must reliably differentiate client risk. Chapter 10 will provide the evidence that the best way of achieving useful risk assessment is through validated structured assessments. The two other principles that touch upon the importance of conducting a comprehensive assessment are Principle 9 (Breadth or Multimodal) and Principle 10 (Strength).

TABLE 9.2 **Risk Level and Treatment (% Recidivism)**			
Study	**Risk level**	**Level of treatment**	
		Minimal	**Intensive**
Hanley (2006)	Low	19	25
	High	47	33
Lovins et al. (2009)	Low	26	12
	High	49	43
Andrews & Kiessling (1980)	Low	12	17
	High	58	31
Bonta et al. (2000)	Low	15	32
	High	51	32
Lovins et al. (2007)	Low	12	26
	High	49	43

Principle 6

(Need). Many justice-involved persons, especially high-risk clients, have multiple needs. They "need" a place to live and work and/or they "need" to stop taking drugs. Some have poor self-esteem, chronic headaches, or cavities in their teeth. These are all needs or problematic circumstances. The *need principle* makes a distinction between criminogenic and noncriminogenic needs, a point introduced when discussing dynamic risk factors in Chapter 2. Criminogenic needs are a subset of a client's risk level. They are dynamic risk factors that, when changed, are associated with changes in the probability of recidivism. Noncriminogenic needs are also dynamic and changeable, but they are weakly associated with recidivism.

The argument is that if treatment services are offered with the intention of reducing recidivism, changes must occur on criminogenic need factors. Persons involved in the criminal justice system also have a right to the highest-quality service for other needs, but that is not the primary focus of *correctional* rehabilitation. Addressing noncriminogenic needs is unlikely to alter future recidivism significantly unless doing so indirectly impacts on criminogenic needs. Typically, noncriminogenic needs may be targeted for motivational purposes or on humanitarian grounds.

The reader will note that criminogenic needs are actually represented by seven of the Central Eight risk/need factors outlined in Chapter 3. The major criminogenic needs and some noncriminogenic needs are described in Table 9.3. As an illustration of the link between criminogenic needs and criminal behavior, we select the criminogenic need of procriminal attitudes. Most

TABLE 9.3 **The Seven Major Risk/Need Factors and Some Noncriminogenic Needs**

Major risk/need factor	Indicators	Intervention goals
Antisocial Personality Pattern	Impulsive, adventurous, pleasure seeking, aggressive, irritable	Build self-management skills, teach anger management
Procriminal Attitudes	Rationalizations for crime, negative attitudes to the law	Counter rationalizations with prosocial attitudes, build up a prosocial identity
Procriminal Associates	Criminal friends, isolation from prosocial others	Replace procriminal friends and associates with prosocial friends and associates
Substance Misuse	Misuse of alcohol and/or drugs	Reduce substance use, enhance alternatives to substance use
Family/Marital	Poor parental monitoring and disciplining, poor family relationships	Teach parenting skills, enhance warmth and caring
School/Work	Poor performance, low levels of satisfaction	Enhance work/study skills, nurture interpersonal relationships within the context of work and school
Leisure/Recreation	Lack of involvement in prosocial recreational/ leisure activities	Encourage participation in prosocial recreational activities, teach prosocial hobbies and sports

Noncriminogenic, minor needs	Indicators	
Self-esteem	Poor feelings of self-esteem, self-worth	
Feelings of personal distress	Anxious, sad	
Major mental disorder	Schizophrenia, manic depression	
Physical health	Physical handicap, nutrient deficiency	

criminological theories (e.g., control theory, differential association) assign a major role to procriminal attitudes and assessments of procriminal attitudes are predictive of criminal behavior (recall Chapter 6). There is also evidence for the *dynamic* validity of procriminal attitudes. Increases in procriminal attitudes are associated with increased recidivism, and recidivism decreases when the individual holds fewer procriminal beliefs and attitudes. In contrast, traditional clinical treatment targets, such as anxiety and emotional empathy, fail to demonstrate dynamic predictive validity. Continued research and development into the assessment of criminogenic needs will have an enormous impact on the rehabilitation of justice-involved clients and the development of our conceptual understanding of criminal behavior.

Principle 7

(General Responsivity). The responsivity principle refers to delivering treatment programs in a style and mode that is consistent with the ability and learning style of the client. The *general responsivity principle* is quite straightforward: those in conflict with the law are human beings, and the most powerful influence strategies available are cognitive-behavioral and cognitive social learning strategies. It matters little whether the problem is antisocial behavior, depression, smoking, overeating, or poor study habits—cognitive-behavioral treatments are often more effective than other forms of intervention. These powerful influence strategies include modeling, reinforcement, role playing, skill building, cognitive restructuring, and practicing new, low-risk alternative behaviors repeatedly in a variety of high-risk situations.

Principle 8

(Specific Responsivity). Generally speaking, specific responsivity calls for the matching of services at the individual level. In PCC, individual differences are highly valued and in the ideal world each individual would have a tailored intervention to suit that person. This is an impossible task but we can, and should, consider some key characteristics of the client that would maximize the benefits of treatment. For example, an insight-oriented therapy delivered in a group format may not "connect" very well for a neurotic, anxious individual with limited intelligence. Characteristics such as interpersonal sensitivity, anxiety, verbal intelligence, and cognitive maturity speak to the appropriateness of different modes and styles of treatment service. It is under the specific responsivity principle that many of the psychological approaches to offender assessment may have their value. By identifying personality and cognitive styles, treatment can be better matched to the client.

There have been a number of personality-based systems developed to guide the treatment of justice-involved adults and youths. For example, the Conceptual Level system (Hunt & Hardt, 1965) was developed for use with juvenile delinquents and describes four stages of cognitive development (from egocentric thinking to an ability to think of problems from many different perspectives). Youth are assessed and categorized into one of the four conceptual level stages and then matched to different degrees of structured treatment. What is important in the Conceptual Level system and other similar systems is the idea of differential treatment. That is, a certain treatment strategy and/or therapist are matched to the characteristics of the client.

Another important psychological factor under specific responsivity is motivation for treatment. Motivation for treatment is an important area of research and was touched upon in the last chapter, whereas, in the area of substance misuse, some of the principles of "motivational interviewing" have relevance to general and sexual offenders. Increasing motivation may be particularly important with high-risk clients who tend to drop out of treatment. If we are to adhere to the risk principle, then we must ensure that the high-risk remain in treatment.

Principle 9

(Breadth or Multimodal) highlights the importance of targeting multiple criminogenic needs when working with high-risk cases. The higher the risk, the more criminogenic needs become evident. Thus, addressing only one or two criminogenic needs among high-risk clients does not go as far as targeting the multiple criminogenic needs of these individuals.

Principle 10

(Strength) has implications for both the accurate prediction of recidivism through structured assessment (Principle 11) and for specific responsivity. To date, however, there are few examples in the practical world of risk assessment that actually demonstrate improved accuracy when considerations of strengths and risk are combined. However, when it comes to treatment, building upon strengths (even the high-risk will have a strength) can be an effective counterbalance to the criminogenic needs presented by the client. The RNR model is not simply about risk.

Principle 11

(Structured Assessment) underscores the evidence that the validity of structured assessments exceeds that of unstructured professional judgment. To follow the risk principle, one must reliably differentiate low-risk cases from higher-risk cases, and structured risk assessments do a better job at this than unstructured judgments of risk.

Principle 12

(Professional Discretion) recognizes that professional judgment on rare occasions may override structured decision-making. This principle was present in the original 1990 formulation of RNR as the "override principle." However, this principle also stresses that the use of professional discretion must be clearly documented and empirically defensible.

Organizational Principles: Setting, Staffing, and Management

Principles 13 through 15 stress the importance for management to support the integrity of RNR programming. Staff cannot deliver programs and services in adherence to RNR without the support of their own organization and those of other agencies (mental health, social services, etc.) that can support rehabilitation efforts. Note that the relationship and structuring skills inherent in staff practice draw directly upon GPCSL-based interpersonal influence strategies and behavior change approaches.

Principle 13

(Community-based) highlights the enhanced effectiveness of RNR-based programming in community settings. When interventions are delivered in the community one can capitalize on the prosocial supports that are more readily available compared to the supports available within custodial settings. There is also less of an influence from procriminal others in community settings. This does not deny the importance of RNR interventions in closed settings. Within custodial environments RNR treatments do work but not to the same extent as when the interventions are delivered in the community.

Principle 14

(GPCSL-based Staff Practices) require organizations to train staff in relationship and structuring practices. Principle 14 is quite specific on the relationship and structuring skills needed to perform optimally. Furthermore, the mental health and substance use treatment agencies that provide services to justice-involved clients have an obligation to support these skills.

Principle 15

(Management) puts into real-world practice Principle 14. Attending to the details of implementing RNR practice is the responsibility of policymakers, senior managers, and front-line supervisors. Management must also monitor the implementation, sometimes with the help of researchers, and be prepared to make adjustments to the organization when needed.

Summary

The GPCSL approach to building a predictive understanding of criminal conduct has made considerable progress. In order to move into the realm of demonstrated causal significance, PCC needs an approach that is linked with a general psychology of human behavior that has demonstrated functional value. Criminal behavior reflects not just particular motivations or particular constraints but also the density of signaled rewards and costs.

In the context of GPCSL, crime cannot be understood without understanding whether the personal, interpersonal, and community supports for behavior are favorable or unfavorable to crime. When the contingencies of human action are ignored, actions based on official punishment, fundamental human needs, and positive goals can be criminogenic. It is not sufficient to highlight personal well-being or to highlight the accumulation of rewards and satisfactions. It must be made explicit that the contingencies should be supportive of noncriminal alternative routes to rewards. That is what adherence with the principles of RNR is designed to support.

Worth Remembering

1. The applied face of the GPCSL perspective is the RNR model.
    There are two general applications of the RNR model. The first is the area of assessment, and the second area is treatment.

2. There are a number of principles that are core to effective treatment programs.
    First of all, providing direct human service is preferable to punishment when the goal is recidivism reduction. Human service should follow the risk principle (match treatment intensity to risk level); the need principle (target the seven dynamic risk/need factors in the Central Eight); and the general responsivity principle (use cognitive-behavioral intervention techniques). Other core clinical principles are specific responsivity, breadth, strength, structured assessment, and professional discretion.

3. Following the core clinical principles is enhanced when there is quality organizational support for these principles.
    The organizational principle, community-based, states that providing treatment in the community is preferable over custodial settings, although this is not to say that treatment in prisons does not work. The remaining two organizational principles speak to the importance of GPCSL-based staff skills along the relationship and structuring dimensions and management support for RNR practice.

Recommended Readings

Two readings are suggested. The first reading is by Bonta and Andrews (2007), where the expanded RNR model described in this chapter was first presented. The reader is encouraged to read *The Risk-Need-Responsivity Model of Offender Assessment and Rehabilitation* available at: www.publicsafety. gc.ca/cnt/rsrcs/pblctns/rsk-nd-rspnsvty/rsk-nd-rspnsvty-eng.pdf

The second recommendation is the book chapter by Wormith and Zidenberg (2018). This chapter traces the history of the RNR model, its influence on assessment and treatment, and future directions.

 Visit the Instructor and Student Resource to access additional exercises, videos and study materials to support this chapter: psychologycriminalconduct.routledge.com

CHAPTER 10 Prediction and Classification of Criminal Behavior

Having described the RNR model in the last chapter, we transition to the prediction and classification of risk and needs. The following three questions are asked: (1) How well can criminal behavior be predicted? (2) What can we do with that knowledge in order to reduce the chances of criminal acts occurring? and (3) To what extent do the Central Eight risk/need factors apply to age, gender, and race?

The prediction of criminal behavior is perhaps one of the most central activities of the criminal justice system. Predicting who will reoffend guides police officers, judges, corrections officials, and parole boards in their decision-making. Knowing that poor parenting practices lead to future delinquency directs community agencies in providing parenting prevention programs to families. As the risk principle advises, treatment programs may be most effective with moderate- to high-risk clients. Ethically, being able or unable to predict an individual's future criminal behavior may weigh heavily upon the use of dispositions such as imprisonment and parole.

In prison, probation, and parole systems, one of the major purposes of risk assessment is the classification of individuals into similar subgroups in order to assign them to certain restrictions and interventions. For example, the risk for violence or escape forms part of the decision to classify inmates to maximum-security prisons or the risk of reoffending is critical in assigning the frequency of contact in parole supervision. Just how correctional systems reliably separate justice-involved individuals into risk groupings is part of the focus of this chapter.

The various issues raised by prediction are relevant to the concerns of citizens as a whole because the human, social, and economic costs of prevention are not trivial, and because the power that criminal justice professionals have over people who are arrested, detained, convicted, probated, or incarcerated is extraordinary. The issues are of immediate interest to those who become entrapped in the process of criminal justice by way of being a victim, an offender, or a criminal justice professional. Whatever our current role might be—concerned citizen, perpetrator, victim, or involved professional—we all

DOI: 10.4324/9781003292128-13

share an interest in prediction. Thus, we all have a right to insist upon knowledge of the following aspects of prediction:

1. Demonstrations of the extent to which criminal behavior is predictable (the issue of predictive accuracy).

2. Clear, transparent statements regarding how the predictions are made so that the information used in making predictions may be evaluated on ethical, legal, economic, and humanitarian criteria.

3. Demonstrations of the extent to which the ways of making predictions actually facilitate criminal justice objectives and practice.

4. That predictions and the actions based on them are recorded, monitored, and explored empirically in a way that increases our understanding of crime and criminal justice.

We begin with a general discussion of what is meant by predictive accuracy and some of the challenges in its measurement. Although the focus is on the technical aspects of prediction, it is necessary because the discussion provides the backdrop for the topics that follow. Following the issue of predictive accuracy is a brief overview of how theory can inform the practice of risk prediction and the relevance of the principles of risk, need, and responsivity to the assessment of those involved in the criminal justice systems. Showcased will be "fourth-generation" assessments that integrate the assessment of risk, need, and responsivity with planned intervention and its wide applicability across age, race, and gender. Finally, the chapter ends with a look into the future and a summary of the obstacles to implementing the knowledge reviewed.

Assessing Predictive Accuracy

Correlation coefficients and similar statistical measures of association are valuable for research and theory. However, when it comes to everyday, practical situations, more meaningful measures of predictive accuracy are needed. Take, for example, the problem faced by a parole board that must decide whether or not to release an inmate. Many factors weigh on the minds of board members. Foremost is making a correct decision that encompasses both a safe release and the denial of parole for a highly dangerous individual. In addition, there is consideration of the costs of making a mistake, either by releasing someone who commits another crime or denying parole to someone who is unlikely to commit another crime. Prediction is never perfect, and the parole board members in the example must decide based on a reasonable balance between a correct choice and a mistake. To add to the difficulty in decision-making, the value placed on correct decisions and mistakes is usually socially defined. For example, for some, releasing someone who commits another crime is more serious than denying parole to an inmate who does not reoffend.

This very practical problem is illustrated by what researchers call the two-by-two (2 × 2) prediction accuracy table (see Part A of Table 10.1). Inserted in each cell is the language of prediction. There are four possible outcomes: (a) *True Positive* —"I am positive he will reoffend and it turns out to be true"; (b) *False Positive* —"I am positive he will reoffend but he doesn't" (prediction was false); (c) *False Negative* —"He will not reoffend, but he does" (prediction was false); and (d) *True Negative* —"He will not reoffend and he does not." Note that cells (a) and (d) are correct predictions and Cells (b) and (c) are errors. Obviously, we want to maximize the numbers in (a) and (d) and minimize the numbers in (b) and (c).

In addition to the four outcomes that are generated from the 2 × 2 table, we can calculate the following indices of predictive accuracy:

1. The overall proportion of correct predictions (true positives plus true negatives divided by the total number of predictions): (a + d)/(a + b + c + d).

2. The proportion of cases judged to be at risk that did recidivate: a/(a + b).

3. The proportion of cases judged not to be at risk and that did not recidivate: d/(c + d).

4. The proportion of recidivists correctly identified: a/(a + c).

5. The proportion of nonrecidivists correctly identified: d/(b + d).

Part B of Table 10.1 presents real data from our research files. The risk factor was being male, and the outcome measure was officially recorded reconvictions over a two-year period. The *r* is a moderate 0.15. What can be said about predictive accuracy in this case depends, in part, upon how we choose to report on the findings:

1. The recidivism rate of males (the "high-risk" cases) was five times that of females (24 percent vs. 4.8 percent).

2. Classifying males as high risk identified 97.3 percent of the recidivists (109/112). A total of 112 offenders were reconvicted; of these, 109 were males predicted to recidivate.

3. The true negative rate was 95.2 percent (59/62), in that 59 of the 62 cases that we predicted would not recidivate did not recidivate (and thus the false negative rate was only 4.8 percent (3/62).

4. However, the overall rate of correct predictions was only 32.6 percent: (109 + 59)/516.

5. The true positive rate was only 24 percent (109/454), and thus the false positive rate was 76 percent (345/454).

TABLE 10.1 **Two-by-Two Prediction Accuracy Tables**

A: Two-by-two prediction accuracy table

Predict recidivism?		Actually recidivated?	
		Yes	No
Yes:	High Risk	(a) True Positive	(b) False Positive
No:	Low Risk	(c) False Negative	(d) True Negative

B: Two-by-two prediction accuracy table ($r = 0.15$)

		Predict recidivism?	Actually recidivated?		
		Yes	No	N	Rate
Yes:	High Risk (male)	109	345	454	24.0%
No:	Low Risk (female)	3	59	62	4.8%
	N	112	404	516	21.7%

For assessing predictive accuracy, the lesson to be learned is that more information is required than any one of the above statements provides on its own. Imagine a parole board making decisions based on gender. In our example, many inmates would remain incarcerated unnecessarily and at great financial costs. For a more complete appreciation of predictive accuracy, one needs to be able to recreate the full 2 × 2 prediction table.

In Part B of Table 10.1, the outstanding accuracy achieved in capturing recidivists (97.3 percent) was due in large part to the fact that our risk assessment (gender) assigned a very large proportion of the cases to the category predicted to reoffend. That is, 88 percent of the cases were male (454/ 516). The proportion of cases assigned to the high-risk group (or to the category of people we predict will reoffend) is called the *selection ratio*. Because the selection ratio was high (88 percent), our hit rate for recidivists was high, but our hit rate for nonrecidivists was low (14.6 percent or 59/404). When the selection ratio is high, the false positive rate will also tend to be high— particularly when relatively few people actually do recidivate. The number of cases that do recidivate is called the *base rate*, which in the example was a fairly low 21.7 percent (112/516).

The rates of false positives, false negatives, true positives, and true negatives, as well as the magnitude of the association between the risk predictor and criminal behavior, are all influenced by base rates and selection ratios. In assessing the predictive accuracy of different approaches to risk assessment, examining the 2 × 2 tables they generate is the ideal. In practice, however, the risk assessment approach that yields the greatest number of overall correct predictions may not always be chosen. For example, one may be willing to tolerate a few more false positives in order to maximize the number of recidivists correctly identified; or there may be a situation in which it is judged more important to minimize false positives.

How many false positives and false negatives there are depends on: (1) the accuracy of the risk measure itself, (2) the selection ratio, and (3) the base rate. The importance of considering the 2 × 2 tables for evaluating predictive accuracy has been emphasized but we also know that base rates and selection ratios can influence predictive accuracy as measured by r. Most of this chapter deals with the accuracy of risk measures, and in Chapter 2, the Area Under the Curve (AUC) was described as a measure that is little affected by base rates and selection ratios. Therefore, as much as possible the AUC will be used in this chapter as the measure of risk accuracy.

PCC and Prediction

As described in Chapter 3 there are many theories or explanations of criminal conduct. In PCC, the GPCSL perspective is championed. GPCSL posits the Central Eight risk/need factors (criminal history, procriminal attitudes, procriminal associates, antisocial personality pattern, family/marital, school/work, substance misuse, and leisure/recreation) as more important than risk factors suggested by sociological criminology (e.g., social status) and forensic/psychopathological criminology (e.g., anxiety, poor self-esteem). The Central Eight are the best predictors of criminal behavior.

As signified in the "SL" of GPCSL, criminal behavior is learned in accordance with the principles of learning. Learning is dependent upon the signaled rewards and costs for a particular behavior, and the strength of the behavior is dependent on the density of rewards and costs. Therefore, GPCSL offers the following lessons for assessment:

1. Sample multiple domains of criminal conduct

Do not restrict assessments to only a few domains. GPCSL posits that criminal behavior is a function of the number and variety of rewards and costs for both criminal and noncriminal behavior. These rewards and costs arise from multiple sources and social contexts, some of which are described by the Central Eight (family/marital, procriminal associates, school/work, and leisure/recreation). At a minimum, assess the Central Eight risk/need factors.

2. Assess the dynamic as well as the static covariates of criminal conduct

It is noteworthy that many of the predictors are dynamic or changeable. Social supports for crime, procriminal attitudes, substance misuse, etc. are predictive of recidivism and amenable to change. Static factors such as a prior criminal record may predict but, once convicted, the record is a mark that stays. Dynamic predictors have the advantage of offering an idea of what needs to be changed in order to reduce the person's risk to reoffend. For example, poor use of leisure time is a predictor of recidivism. It is also dynamic and subject to change (therefore, possibly causal). An individual with productive leisure pursuits receives rewards for prosocial behavior (from others or from the activity itself). An individual without hobbies or involvement in organized prosocial activities may want to consider what can be done to promote prosocial leisure activities.

3. Assessment can guide the intensity of treatment

Dynamic risk factors are the potential targets for intervention. However, the RNR model, derived from GPCSL, also says that risk is directly proportional to the number of different risk factors present. That is, a high-risk person will have more risk factors (e.g., criminal friends, procriminal attitudes, substance use problems, unstable employment) than a low-risk person who simply has problems in one or two risk domains. In addition, the number and variety of risk factors reflect the density of rewards and costs for behavior. Consequently, knowledge of an individual's risk level tells us something about how much treatment is needed to reduce one's risk.

4. Assessment can guide how we provide treatment

An individual's ability to learn from the environment is dependent upon a number of personal-cognitive-emotional factors. For example, a person's responsiveness to advice from a therapist, correctional worker, or family member is dependent upon cognitive ability. If the individual is of low intelligence, then providing the advice in a complex, abstract manner will be less effective than if the advice is given in a simple, concrete manner. Thus, one may choose to assess characteristics that may not be predictors of criminal behavior but are still relevant for the delivery of services.

Assessment and the Principles of Risk, Need, and Responsivity

An assessment does not need to be limited to making judgments of the risk to reoffend. This is certainly important, but assessment can also be useful for guiding treatment. In Chapter 9, the expanded RNR model was presented. Here three principles that are fundamental to risk assessment—the principles of risk, need, and responsivity—are revisited.

Risk Principle: Match the Level of Service to the Level of Risk

The principle tells us *who* to treat (i.e., the higher-risk offender). In Andrews and Dowden's (2006) meta-analysis, appropriate treatment delivered to higher-risk cases showed a modest correlation ($r = 0.17$) with reduced recidivism. Treatment delivered to low-risk cases had hardly any effect ($r = 0.03$). Therefore, if we are going to treat effectively, then we must have a reliable way of assessing risk so that we can make sure it is the higher-risk rather than the lower-risk who receive most of the treatment services.

Need Principle: Target Criminogenic Needs

This principle makes a distinction between criminogenic needs (dynamic risk factors) and noncriminogenic needs (dynamic *non-risk* factors). The need principle tells us *what* to treat. Thus, risk instruments should include assessments of criminogenic needs, and the Central Eight reflect seven of the most relevant criminogenic needs (one of the Central Eight is criminal history, a static factor). From this point, the terms "risk/needs" will be used to describe the assessment process.

Responsivity Principle: Use Cognitive-Behavioral Interventions with Attention to Personal Learning Styles

The responsivity principle tells us *how* to treat. General responsivity demands the use of cognitive-behavioral techniques to influence change because they are the most effective interventions to help people learn new attitudes and behaviors. Specific responsivity calls for adapting our general cognitive-behavioral techniques to specific person characteristics. These characteristics range from the biological (e.g., gender) to the social (e.g., culture), and to the psychological (personality, emotions, and cognitive ability).

It is under specific responsivity that issues concerning assessment arise. Traditional forensic assessment instruments that attend to cognitive and personality characteristics become important for identifying the factors that may serve as obstacles for addressing criminogenic needs. One cannot successfully deal with a substance addiction if the client is psychotic; one cannot deal with employment problems if the person is suicidal. The biological-social constructs of gender and race present their own unique considerations for assessment and treatment. In order to successfully address the criminogenic needs of women, for example, parenting, victimization experiences, and issues of financial dependence on a partner may need to be integrated into assessment and treatment.

Approaches to the Risk/Needs Assessment

The assessment of offenders is not just a question of risk to reoffend but also of treatment. Here the story continues of how the assessment of justice-involved persons has changed over the past 40 years. In 1996, Bonta reviewed the correctional assessment literature and described "three generations" of risk assessment. In the first decade of the twenty-first century there are four generations (Bonta, 2019a; Andrews, Bonta, & Wormith, 2006).

First-Generation Assessment: Professional Judgment

Here is what typically happens in a first-generation assessment. A professional, trained in the social sciences, conducts an interview in a relatively unstructured manner. The clinician may ask some basic questions of all interviewees, but for the most part there is considerable flexibility in the questions asked. Sometimes psychological tests may be given; which ones are administered varies from one test administrator to another. Files may be reviewed, but what is attended to in these files is also at the discretion of the professional. At the end of the process of information gathering, the assessor makes a judgment regarding the person's risk to the community and his or her treatment needs. The key feature of the clinical approach is that the reasons for the decision are subjective, sometimes intuitive, and at times guided by "gut feelings"—they are not empirically validated.

Professional judgments of risk by highly trained clinicians are not very accurate. The reasons for such poor performance are twofold. First, there is the problem of using informal, unobservable criteria for making decisions. Second, there is the problem of attending to characteristics of the person that may not be empirically related to criminal behavior.

Second-Generation Assessment: Actuarial, Static Risk Scales

Such agreement does not happen often, but there is consensus on this point—actuarial assessments outperform clinical judgment in general cases of prediction (Ægisdóttir, White, et al., 2006; Grove & Vrieze, 2013) and in the prediction of criminal behavior (Andrews, Bonta, & Wormith, 2006; Goel, Shroff, Skeem, & Slobogin, 2021; Hanson, 2009; Harris, Rice, Quinsey, & Cormier, 2015; Viljoen, Vargen, et al., 2021). One of the earliest examples of the actuarial method comes from Burgess (1928). Burgess examined more than 3,000 parolees and found 21 factors that differentiated parole successes from parole failures. Burgess then gave to every parolee one point for each factor that was present. For the parolees scoring the maximum points, the recidivism rate was 76 percent; for those with the least points, the rate was 1.5 percent. The actuarial approach of summating items, perhaps because of its simplicity, has been the preferred choice in risk assessment methodology. Sophisticated techniques (e.g., multiple regression, iterative classification) have been applied to the prediction problem, but these newer techniques have shown little improvement in predictive power (Grann & Långström, 2007; Silver, Smith, & Banks, 2000).

Second-generation assessment instruments are evidence-based, but they have two major limitations. Nearly all second-generation assessments have no theoretical basis, and they consist almost entirely of static, historical items. In Table 10.2 are three examples of second-generation assessment instruments—the Salient Factor Score (SFS), which was widely used in the United States in the 1980s and 1990s (Hoffman, 1994), the Statistical Information on Recidivism (SIR) scale, which is still used in Canada (Nuffield, 1982), and the Offender Group Reconviction Scale (OGRS) used in the United Kingdom (Copas & Marshall, 1998). All three instruments have demonstrated satisfactory predictive accuracies, with AUCs ranging from 0.64 to 0.76 (Hoffman, 1994; Coid, Yang, et al., 2007; Nafekh & Motiuk, 2002).

TABLE 10.2 Examples of Second-Generation Risk Scales and Their Ites

Item	SFS (US)	SIR (Canada)	OGRS (UK)
Static:			
Type of offense	✓	✓	✓
Prior criminal history	✓ (2 items)	✓ (5 items)	✓ (3 items)
Age	✓	✓ (2 items)	✓
Prior parole failure	✓	✓	-
Gender	-	-	✓
Security classification	-	✓	-
Sentence length	-	✓	-
Risk interval	✓	✓	-
Drug abuse history	✓	-	-
Dynamic:			
Unemployed	-	✓	-
Marital status	-	✓	-
Number of dependents	-	✓	-
Total items	6	15	6

Apparent in the scales are the neglect of many factors theoretically relevant to criminal conduct (e.g., procriminal associates and attitudes) and the predominance of items that are static or unchangeable. On this last point, look at the SFS scale where all the items are static. Someone who was imprisoned at the age of 16 for an auto theft while high on heroin will fall into the "poor" category even if this occurred 20 years ago and s/he has been crime-free ever since. These scales give little credit to the individual who changes for the better. Nor do they inform the practitioner or supervising staff as to what needs to be done to reduce the person's level of risk.

Improvements to assessment can be made with a more comprehensive assessment of the factors—both static and dynamic—that are associated theoretically and empirically with criminal behavior. The single-minded focus on static variables and attempts to reduce more comprehensive assessment instruments to a few static items for the sake of efficiency (Caudy, Durso, & Taxman, 2013; Zhang, Roberts, & Farabee, 2014) place limits on the utility of the assessment. The second-generation scales are useful for release decisions and security and supervision classification, but the criminal justice system is also charged with minimizing the person's risk to the community and with reintegrating inmates into society. To reach these goals, dynamic factors that are theoretically informed should be applied to assessment technology.

Third-Generation Assessment: Risk/Needs Scales

Third-generation assessments distinguish themselves from second-generation assessments in that they measure criminogenic needs. Examples of risk/needs instruments are the Level of Service Inventory-Revised (LSI-R; Andrews & Bonta, 1995), and more recently the Post Conviction Risk Assessment (PCRA) developed for U.S. Federal Probation (Lowenkamp, Holsinger, & Cohen, 2015) and the Ohio Risk Assessment System (Latessa, Smith, Lemke, Makarios, & Lowenkamp, 2010). Given that the Level of Service instruments are among the most widely used and researched instruments in the world (see Figure 10.1) and that the LSI-R is part of the family of Level of Service (LS) instruments, the LSI-R will serve as an illustration of third-generation assessment (it is also the precursor to fourth-generation assessment).

The Level of Service Inventory-Revised. The LSI-R is a theoretically based risk/needs assessment. The LSI-R samples 54 risk and needs (mostly criminogenic) items, each scored in a zero-one format and distributed across 10 subcomponents (e.g., Criminal History, Education/Employment, Companions, Substance Abuse, etc.). The research has ranged from examination of the psychometric properties of the LSI-R, such as its reliability, convergent validity, and factor structure, to the predictive validity of the instrument. The evidence on the predictive validity of the LSI-R has been summarized by Olver et al.

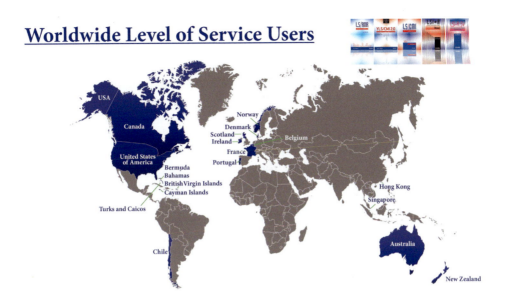

Figure 10.1

International Use of the Level of Service Instruments

(2014). The mean AUC for the prediction of general recidivism was 0.64; for violent recidivism, it was 0.63.

There have also been a number of meta-analytic comparisons of the LSI-R to other risk instruments including the SFS and the PCL-R. Although making such comparisons can be fraught with problems (see for example, Williams, Wormith, Bonta, & Sitarenios, 2017), the comparisons have shown the LSI-R to predict as well or better than the other instruments (Campbell, French, & Gendreau, 2009; Gendreau, Goggin, & Smith, 2002; Gendreau, Little, & Goggin, 1996). The most important application of the LSI-R, however, is informing the delivery of supervision and services to higher-risk justice-involved persons (risk principle) by identifying their criminogenic needs.

Criminogenic Needs and the Dynamic Validity of the LSI-R. Criminogenic needs are *dynamic* risk factors; according to the need principle in the RNR model, if we can reduce the criminogenic needs of a client then we can reduce the chances of future criminal behavior (Bonta, 2019b). Of course, increased criminogenic needs will also be associated with increased recidivism. A number of studies have demonstrated the dynamic nature of many of the Central Eight criminogenic needs. For example, changes in procriminal attitudes and associates, as well as employment, have been predictive of criminal behavior (Greiner, Law, & Brown, 2015; Serin, Lloyd, Helmus, Derkzen, & Luong, 2013).

To follow the need principle, the first step is to identify the criminogenic needs of the client in a reliable manner. The majority of the items that comprise the LSI-R are dynamic. Thus, we would expect that scores on the LSI-R would change with reassessments. The change could result from naturally occurring events (e.g., the client finds a job) or as the result of structured treatment (e.g., Community Reinforcement treatment for alcohol misuse). This information could prove useful for monitoring improvement or deterioration among clients if it could be shown that changes in LSI-R scores are related to recidivism.

The major results from the studies on the dynamic validity of the LSI-R are shown in Table 10.3. There are other studies that support the dynamic validity of the LSI-R, but the reporting of the results in logistic multivariate analysis does not allow the findings to be displayed in a two-by-two tabular form (e.g., Caudy et al., 2013). Therefore, these results are not shown in Table 10.3. The largest evaluations were conducted by Thomas Arnold (N = 1,064; Arnold, 2007) and Brenda Vose and her colleagues (N = 2,849; Vose, Smith, & Cullen,

TABLE 10.3 The Dynamic Validity of the LSI-R (% recidivated)

Study/Intake	Reassessment	
	Low risk	High risk
Andrews & Robinson (1984)		
Low Risk	4.2	28.6
High Risk	0.0	57.1
Arnold (2007)		
Low Risk	13.0	26.0
High Risk	32.0	54.0
Motiuk, Bonta, & Andrews (1990)		
Low Risk	0.0	33.3
High Risk	0.0	54.5
Raynor et al. (2000)		
Low Risk	26.2	54.8
High Risk	55.3	78.4
Raynor (2007)		
Low Risk	29.0	59.0
High Risk	54.0	76.0
Vose, Smith, & Cullen (2013)		
Low Risk	21.8	46.1
High Risk	22.9	32.6

Note: Vose, Smith, & Cullen (2013) reported five risk categories, and the middle (moderate risk) finding was evenly distributed to the low- and high-risk groupings.

2013). The remaining studies had smaller samples ranging from 55 (Motiuk, Bonta, & Andrews, 1990) to 203 (Raynor, 2007). The test–retest intervals were 8.6 months in Arnold's study and averaged one year in the other studies. Note that low-risk cases who became worse (had higher LSI-R scores on retest) showed higher recidivism rates, and high-risk cases who showed decreased scores demonstrated lower recidivism rates.

Summary of the LSI-R. The LSI-R has been expanded into another third-generation assessment instrument called the Level of Service/Risk, Need, Responsivity (LS/RNR; Andrews, Bonta, & Wormith, 2008). The LS/RNR is more theoretically aligned to the Central Eight risk/need factors compared to the LSI-R. The instrument also adds a number of specific risk/need factors (e.g., sexual assault, weapon use, homelessness, victimization experiences) as well as responsivity considerations (e.g., cultural and ethnic). Both instruments are products of a social learning perspective of criminal behavior. Particularly important to remember is that *changes* in LSI-R scores have predicted correctional outcomes.

Fourth-Generation Assessment: The Integration of Case Management with Risk/Needs

Having well-researched, evidence-based assessments and treatment interventions does not mean that they will be used in "the real world." The translation of knowledge to practice is a problem in the criminal justice system, just as it is in other fields (e.g., medicine). For example, even though the risk principle is widely known across the United States, a survey of 97 correctional programs in Ohio found only 20 percent adhered to the principle (Lowenkamp, Latessa, & Holsinger, 2006).

Third-generation risk/needs instruments are intended to assist staff in allocating supervision resources appropriately (risk principle) and targeting intervention (need principle). In a study of probation in the Canadian province of Manitoba, Bonta and his colleagues (Bonta, Rugge, Scott, Bourgon, & Yessine, 2008) reviewed the case management practices of 64 probation officers. Case files were read and probation officers submitted audio recordings of their sessions with probationers. There were a couple of important findings relevant to the present discussion. First, and just as Lowenkamp et al. (2006) found in their US study, probation officers showed poor adherence to the risk principle (e.g., medium-risk offenders were being seen as frequently as low-risk offenders). Second, the analysis of the recordings indicated that probation officers were not focusing on the criminogenic needs identified by the risk/needs assessment. The failure to act on the criminogenic needs has been replicated by Dutch (Bosker & Witteman, 2016), Canadian (Peterson-Badali, Skilling, & Haqanee, 2015) and American researchers (Viglione, Rudes, & Taxman, 2015).

The Manitoba probation study confirmed the fear that, although empirically based assessments were being *administered*, they were not being *used*.

A more structured mechanism was clearly needed to ensure that probation officers do not lose sight of the assessment when dealing with probationers.

Fourth-generation instruments emphasize the link between assessment and case management. This means more than adhering to the risk principle and targeting criminogenic needs. It also acknowledges the role of personal strengths in building a prosocial orientation, the assessment of special responsivity factors to maximize the benefits from treatment, and the structured monitoring of the case from the beginning of supervision to the end. Fourth-generation instruments include COMPAS (Brennan, Dieterich, & Ehret, 2009), the Service Planning Instrument (SPIn; Desmarais, Johnson, & Singh, 2016; Jones, Brown, Robinson, & Frey, 2015), and the most widely used fourth-generation instrument, the Level of Service/Case Management Inventory (LS/CMI; Andrews, Bonta, & Wormith, 2004). Because of the wealth of research and the instrument's well-developed theoretical base, the LS/CMI is used to illustrate the features of fourth-generation assessment.

The 10 original LSI-R subcomponents were reorganized to better reflect the Central Eight risk/need factors (see Figure 10.2). Section 1 of the LS/CMI provides the overall offender risk score. As this section is based on the items of the LSI-R, meta-analytic reviews have found scores on the LS/CMI to predict both general and violent recidivism (Campbell et al., 2009; Olver et al., 2014; Yang et al., 2010).

In addition to the core risk/needs assessment of Section 1, the LS/CMI measures specific risk and need factors (Section 2) and responsivity issues (Section 5). Section 2 recognizes the need to assess aspects of the person and the person's situation that may have criminogenic potential for that particular individual. For example, a sexual offender would be asked questions about the relationship to the victim, and a person involved in family violence would be queried about intimidating and stalking behavior. Table 10.4 presents an

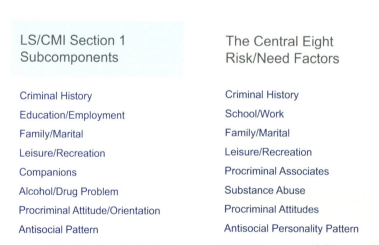

Figure 10.2

LS/CMI and the Central Eight Risk/Need Factors

TABLE 10.4 A Brief Sampling of the Level of Service/Case Management Inventory™ (LS/CMI™)

Section 1. General Risk/Need Factors

1.1   Criminal History
    1 Any prior youth dispositions or adult convictions
    4 Three or more present offenses
    5 Arrested or charged under age 16

1.2   Education/Employment
    9 Currently unemployed
    13 Less than regular grade 12 or equivalent
    17 Authority interactions

1.3   Family/Marital
    18 Dissatisfaction with marital or equivalent situation
    19 Nonrewarding, parental

1.4   Leisure/Recreation
    22 Absence of recent participation in an organized activity
    23 Could make better use of time

1.5   Companions
    25 Some criminal friends
    27 Few anticriminal friends

1.6   Alcohol/Drug Problem
    30 Alcohol problem, currently
    31 Drug problem, currently
    33 Marital/Family

1.7   Procriminal Attitude/Orientation
    36 Supportive of crime
    37 Unfavorable toward convention

1.8   Antisocial Pattern
    41 Early and diverse antisocial behavior
    42 Criminal attitude
    43 A pattern of generalized trouble (financial problems, unstable accommodations)

Section 2. Specific Risk/Need Factors

B1.   Personal Problems with Criminogenic Potential
    (2) Diagnosis of "psychopathy"
    (6) Anger management deficits
    (9) Poor social skills

B2.   History of Perpetration
    (2) Sexual assault, extrafamilial, child/adolescent—female victim
    (8) Physical assault (extrafamilial adult victim)
    (18) Gang participation

continued

TABLE 10.4 (*Continued*)

Section 5. Special Responsivity Considerations

1. Motivation as a barrier
2. Women, gender-specific
3. Low intelligence
4. Antisocial personality/psychopathy

Section 9. Case Management Plan

Program Targets and Intervention Plan		
Criminogenic Need	Goal	Intervention
1.		
2.		
3.		

Special Responsivity Considerations

Responsivity Issue	Proposed Approach to Address Issue
1.	
2.	
3.	

Section 10. Progress Record

Criminogenic Needs				
Date	Criminogenic Need	Improvement	Deterioration	No Change

overview of these sections (the LS/RNR also shares the same subcomponents with the LS/CMI except for Sections 9 and 10).

In Section 5, attention is given to responsivity considerations that may influence how staff will relate to their clients and supervise their cases. Thus, the LS/CMI covers the three major principles of effective intervention—risk, need, and responsivity. The assessment of responsivity factors is certainly not exhaustive in the LS/CMI, nor is it highly detailed. It covers only some of the major responsivity factors, and correctional staff are encouraged to explore other potential responsivity variables.

Finally, the most important feature of the LS/CMI is the integration of the assessment with case management. Referring back to Section 9 of Table 10.4, correctional staff must prioritize criminogenic needs, engage the person in setting concrete targets for change, and choose a means to reach these goals. Furthermore, each contact with the client (Section 10) requires a record of progress, or lack of progress, in reaching the goals. All of this information is in one booklet, ensuring that staff remain focused on attending to a client's risk and needs in a structured manner. In summary, fourth-generation assessment includes a comprehensive sampling of risk and needs, responsivity considerations, and the integration of this information with case management. The assessment of needs includes both criminogenic and noncriminogenic needs, as both types of needs influence the supervision plan. Figure 10.3 summarizes the four generations of risk assessment. Resource Note 10.1 gives a case example of a LS/CMI assessment.

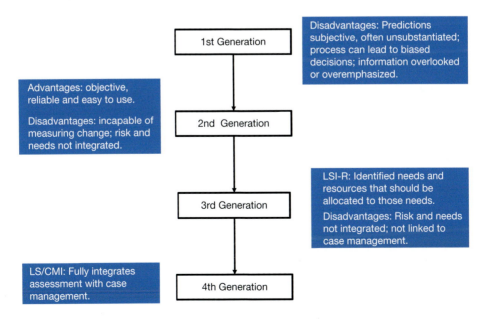

Figure 10.3

Four Generations of Risk Assessment

RESOURCE NOTE 10.1

An LS/CMI Assessment

The LS/CMI can be used for a variety of purposes. The LS/CMI can be administered to assist probation officers in developing a case plan for community supervision, help parole boards in making release decisions and assigning conditions for release, and enable prison classification officers to make an appropriate security classification and treatment plan for the inmate. Sometimes a probation officer may administer the LS/CMI as part of preparing a Pre-Sentence Report (PSR). A PSR may be requested by a judge to assist the court in a sentencing decision. Administering the LS/CMI may not only help the court but also the probation officer when it comes to supervising the case, as illustrated in the following case example.

In the following PSR report the **bolded** sections indicate information that is important for scoring the LS/CMI. The section in *italics* provides general comments on the report.

Pre-Sentence Report
Name: Frank Brown
Date of Birth: February 14, 1984
Age: 23 years old
Date: April 13, 2006

Reason for Assessment

Her Honor, Judge Belinda McCormick, requested a pre-sentence report on Mr. Brown, who is awaiting sentencing on May 15, 2022. The court is considering the appropriateness of a community disposition and recommendations for treatment.

Sources of Information

The *Level of Service/Case Management Inventory* (LS/CMI) was administered to determine the degree of risk that the client presents to the community and the client characteristics that contribute to such risk, some of which may be addressed through various kinds of active intervention or treatment. The LS/CMI does not encompass traditional principles of sentencing—most notably, offense severity—and therefore should not be used to address sentencing in the absence of these other considerations.

Mr. Brown was interviewed on April 10. I was unable to contact his common-law wife to corroborate some of Mr. Brown's information, but I was able to speak to his mother, Mrs. Edna Brown, and one of his sisters (Mrs. West). Other sources of information included a previous PSR (March 25, 2000) and probation case notes pertaining to his previous supervision.

At this point, the PSR describes in a narrative from Section 1 (General Risk/Need Factors) of the LS/CMI. Section 1 of the LS/CMI covers the Central Eight risk/need factors and yields an overall risk/need score for the prediction of reoffending and identifies the important criminogenic needs associated with the case.

continued

Criminal History

The scoring of criminal history information reflects the density of rewards associated with criminal behavior. A long and early onset history increases the likelihood of reoffending. In addition, this section of the LS/CMI taps into the individual's compliance with correctional supervision and seriousness of his or her offense pattern.

Mr. Brown was recently convicted of **three** property offenses (two counts of break and enter and one count of possession of stolen property). Mr. Brown completed a term of probation last year for a prior offense; he has **never been incarcerated**. Mr. Brown has **no** history as a juvenile delinquent. However, this is Mr. Brown's *second* set of convictions as an adult. Two years ago he received a sentence of one year of probation for possession of stolen property, which was **successfully completed** under my supervision.

Education/Employment

The LS/CMI's Section 2 (Specific Risk/ Need Factors) expands on the General Risk/Need Factors of Section 1 by including possible risk/need factors specific to certain kinds of offending (e.g., sexual offending, family violence). Reports based on the LS/CMI do not need to follow the order set out in the sections of the LS/CMI. In fact, if the report was written to exactly mirror the LS/CMI then it would be long and repetitive. During the course of an interview, the offender will give information that can be used to score different parts of the report. The reader can see in this section where such information is provided to inform different sections of the LS/CMI. The Education/Employment section is scored depending on whether the subject is a student or employed in the workforce. In the case of Mr. Brown, the scoring is based on the criminogenic need of employment and includes not only whether he is employed but also how rewarding employment is to Mr. Brown.

Mr. Brown **completed grade 12** and began working immediately in the automotive factory on the assembly line. Mr. Brown is trained to install windshields on cars and describes his work as "it's a job." He shows **very little enthusiasm for the work**, admitting that he is bored with the routine and would like to **find employment that is more challenging** (*Section 2.1, item "underachievement"*). Mr. Brown reported that he does **not get along with his foreman**, who he describes as narrow-minded and a "tyrant." His relationship with his **co-workers is satisfactory**. Mr. Brown eats lunch and spends coffee breaks with them. In sum, Mr. Brown presents as an individual who feels very unfulfilled in the workplace (*Once again, "underachievement" in Section 2.1*).

Family/Marital

In this section, the offender provides information that raises other client issues that although not criminogenic are relevant to supervising this offender. Mr. Brown's victimization by his partner and father could create obstacles to making positive changes in his life and present an emotional stress that needs to be addressed. Also highlighted in this section is the antisocial support provided by his wife and the possibility that Mr. Brown's sisters may be helpful in his supervision.

continued

The relationship between Mr. Brown and his common-law wife (Sherri) appears to be **problematic**. They have been living together for eight months and they have no children. Mr. Brown describes Sherri as a "bit wild." She would frequently leave the house unannounced and be absent for days. Mr. Brown suspects that she goes on drinking binges and **she has been arrested** a number of times. When at home, the couple drinks frequently, after which they often end up in an argument. Mr. Brown denies ever hitting his common-law wife. Quite the contrary, he reports that she has frequently struck him and often plays "mind games" with him by saying that she could go out with anyone she wants and that he is "nothing" (*Section 4, "victim of physical and emotional abuse"*). Mr. Brown becomes noticeably agitated when talking about his marital relationship and acknowledges that he does not know how to discuss these matters with his partner (*Section 2.1, "poor social skills"*). I was unable to confirm the above commentary from Sherri, but Mr. Brown's mother did agree with her son's description of his marital situation.

Mrs. Edna Brown reported that her son has had a difficult childhood. His father was an alcoholic and had been repeatedly abusive toward the children during his drinking. He took out his personal frustrations physically on Frank, as he was the only boy in the family (*Section 4, past physical abuse*). His **father died** in a car accident when Frank Brown was 16 years old. Mr. Brown only visits his mother at Christmas and on her birthday and acknowledges that he is **not able to discuss personal matters with his mother**.

There are two older sisters in the family living an hour away in Springfield. Nonetheless, Mr. Brown does manage to keep in touch with them on a regular basis on the phone and through e-mail. **Neither sister has had any difficulty with the law.** In my discussions with his married sister, Elizabeth West, it became apparent that both sisters are concerned about their brother and offer support in whatever way they can (*note, this may be a possible area of Strength*). She also noted that he often appears to be shy and withdrawn but becomes more relaxed and outgoing after a few drinks, suggesting that Mr. Brown uses alcohol as a disinhibiter.

Leisure/Recreation

This section shows both a positive side to Mr. Brown's leisure activities (i.e., his love of music) and the danger of too much unstructured time.

Mr. Brown is quite talented musically and he **devotes a considerable amount of time to practicing the guitar**, either on his own, or with a small group of fellow musicians. He and his colleagues, who Mr. Brown describes as older 'family' men, are asked to **play at various kinds of social events** about once a month, for which they are paid a modest fee. Mr. Brown finds this work **personally satisfying**, saying that he would love to make a career out of music.

He **does not have any other personal interests or hobbies**. A typical day involves coming home, eating his dinner, and watching television or playing his guitar while he drinks beer with his common-law wife. On weekends, he and his wife usually sleep until midday, do the grocery shopping, and then go out to the pub in the evening with friends.

continued

Companions

Companions are a major correlate of criminal behavior and the LS/CMI gives special attention to this risk/need factor. No other risk/need instrument gives this kind of attention to social support for crime. Also note that at the end of this section, information is provided that will permit scoring items from the Procriminal Attitude/Orientation subcomponent of Section 1.

None of Mr. Brown's friends from work, as far as he knows, has a criminal record. Although Mr. Brown enjoys their company, he hardly sees them outside of the work environment. He claims that his current friends are limited to a couple of his fellow musicians, who he describes as being **very straight**. However, Mr. Brown has now been introduced to his common-law wife's large circle of friends and he has settled in with her crowd quite comfortably. All of these people drink, and some of them *misuse drugs* and have been **involved in crime**. When asked what he thought of these people, he replied that they "are a lot of fun" and "as long as they don't hurt anyone, who cares if they get a little high or get involved in petty crime?"

Alcohol/Drug Problems

In the Alcohol/Drug Problems area it is not simply a matter of whether the person has a substance use problem but understanding how the problem contributes to criminal behavior. Thus, the interviewer collects information on how substance abuse interferes in the areas of work, family, and personal self-regulation. Notice again how Mr. Brown rationalizes his crimes by minimizing the harm to the victim. In addition, we see a responsivity issue when Mr. Brown indicates an unwillingness to participate in treatment.

Mr. Brown began to **drink regularly after his father's death**. He stopped drinking heavily after about a year and settled into work. Mr. Brown noticed that his drinking "picked up a little" after meeting his common-law wife. When I asked him to tell me how much he would drink on a daily basis, he estimated **5 or 6 beers during a weeknight and about 8 or 9 beers on the weekend**. The drinking would almost always be with his common-law wife, and they **often argued** about "stupid, little things." Mr. Brown's **mother reported that she has no interest in seeing her son** "until he breaks his father's habit" (referring to the alcoholism of Mr. Brown's father).

As best as I can ascertain, Mr. Brown does not drink at work, but he has **missed work** on a number of occasions because of a hangover and was **reprimanded** on two occasions by his supervisor. In addition, the **present offenses were initiated after drinking** with his friends. Mr. Brown remembers little of that night but that "**not much damage had been done**" and the owners "**recouped the stolen property anyway**." In our discussions about possibly participating in a treatment program for his alcohol use, Mr. Brown quickly dismisses the suggestion, saying that he has curtailed his consumption in the past and will do so in the future, making any such treatment a waste of government money (*Section 5, Responsivity, "motivation as a barrier"*).

continued

Mr. Brown asserts that he is **not currently using drugs** and has no interest in doing so. He acknowledges that he has tried marijuana on a few occasions with his friends, but that it just makes him sleepy.

Procriminal Attitude/Orientation

The assessment of procriminal attitudes is usually conducted by listening carefully throughout the interview for expressions of attitudes toward criminal behavior and convention (work, authority, etc.).

Mr. Brown demonstrated his support for antisocial behaviors on a number of occasions during our meeting. He **minimized** his present involvement with crime by blaming it on the alcohol. Furthermore, Mr. Brown sees no problem with associating with his present friends and **values their friendship**. On a more positive note, Mr. Brown considers **working as an important activity** and feels that everyone should work for a living, "including those on welfare." Although he does not particularly like his present work and supervisor, he has no plans to quit and he wants to remain an active member of the workforce.

Mr. Brown has been on probation supervision in the past and he always kept his appointments and **complied with the probation conditions**. In discussing his previous period of probation, it is clear that he had **established a positive working relationship with his probation officer**. Mr. Brown does, however, take exception to his current conviction. In spite of a finding of guilt, he thinks that the neighborhood shop owners should not have pressed charges because he was extremely **intoxicated**. When queried about the damage, he acknowledged responsibility and accepted the prospects of paying restitution, but added that he was certain the **businesses would have insurance**.

Antisocial Pattern

The Antisocial Pattern subcomponent assesses the general personality and behavioral patterns associated with criminal behavior. For the most part, Mr. Brown shows little of the instability often found among high-risk offenders with antisocial personality.

As an adult, Mr. Brown has had two run-ins with the law, both of which resulted in convictions. However, there is **no evidence of behavioral problems during his childhood** or delinquent behavior during his adolescence. He *does not have any history of perpetrating violent behavior*, either domestically or with others. Although somewhat self-centered, he **does not present as a particularly callous person**. Mr. Brown, on occasion, acts on impulse, particularly under the influence of alcohol.

There is **no history of mental health intervention** for Mr. Brown. Although currently anxious about his pending court disposition, there is **no evidence of depression** or suicidal ideation.

Mr. Brown **denied having any financial difficulties**. He has been renting an apartment and the car he owns has been completely paid for. Mr. Brown claims that he has no outstanding debts and is able to live within his means, but adds that he cannot afford many luxuries. Mr. Brown lives in a residential area of the city that is not noted for a high degree of criminal activity, and he has no intention of moving.

continued

Summary and Recommendations

Note in this section how the probation officer provides an estimate of Mr. Brown's risk to reoffend and outlines a plan that would allow the judge to consider a community placement as opposed to incarceration.

In reviewing Mr. Brown's personal history, the most noticeable change in his situation compared to his previous probation order is his return to drinking, precipitated by Mr. Brown's involvement with his common-law wife and her friends. The increased expression of attitudes and values supportive of criminal conduct may also reflect the influence of Mr. Brown's social circle.

When Mr. Brown was sentenced for his previous offense, he was assessed on the LS/CMI as falling into the low-risk/need category. Today, Mr. Brown's assessment places him in the moderate range for risk of reoffending. The increase in risk can be traced to his growing, but still limited, criminal history, his continued and more extensive alcohol use, his unstable marital situation, his increased exposure to and time spent with others who are involved in crime, and his growing dissatisfaction with his employment. Probationers within the medium-risk category have a 48 percent likelihood of reoffending within a two-year period. However, effective intervention may be expected to lower these probabilities to some extent.

The present assessment identifies a need for alcohol use counseling, in spite of the client's view that it is unnecessary, and a need to develop a more prosocial network of peers. Increasing ties to others who are not involved in criminal or drinking activity may lead to a more productive use of leisure time. His two older sisters have expressed positive sentiments toward their brother and can be helpful in providing encouragement to pursue prosocial activities (e.g. his interests in music).

In view of Mr. Brown's history of compliance while on probation, another probationary period with a condition to attend treatment may be advantageous in providing Mr. Brown the motivation and access to community resources to deal with his alcohol misuse. He already appears on the verge of severing ties with his common-law wife, which could assist in lowering his exposure to his current circle of antisocial associations, which in turn, may also contribute to reducing some of his procriminal attitudes. Furthermore, a community disposition would allow Mr. Brown to maintain employment and, with guidance from the supervisory probation officer, he may be able to build upon his workplace associations to expand his prosocial network.

J. Wordsmith,
Senior Probation Officer

The General Applicability of Theory-Based Offender Assessment

The GPCSL perspective holds that variations in behavior are explained by the fundamental principles of cognitive social learning theory. The behavior of individuals is under the control of rewards and costs within the personal, interpersonal, and immediate situations of action. Note the word "behavior" in the previous sentences without the qualifying adjective "criminal." This is purposeful. The general principles of learning (modeling, operant and classical conditioning, self-regulation) are applicable to all behaviors. Also, the Central Eight are the main risk/need factors in GPCSL. For a psychology of criminal conduct, this means that assessment and treatment strategies that are derived from a GPCSL perspective would have wide applicability to different populations (e.g., women, minorities, mentally disordered) and different types of criminal behavior (e.g., violent, sexual). The Level of Service instruments (LSI-R, LS/CMI, etc.) were developed from such a perspective. In this section we turn to the applicability of the Level of Service (LS) instruments across samples and criminal outcomes.

LS Risk Assessment across Different Populations

Within the criminal justice system there are youth and adults, there are males, females, and LGBTQs, there are the poor and the rich, and there are some who suffer from mental illness. We can classify all of them in many ways, and when we do so we will find variations in their criminal behavior. For example, men are more likely to engage in crime than women. However, does this mean that the risk factors differ substantially by group? To answer this question, we turn to the evidence of the predictive validity of the LS instruments with respect to age, gender, and race/ethnicity.

Age. The Youth Level of Service/Case Management Inventory (YLS/CMI; Hoge & Andrews, 2002, 2011) consists of 42 items organized around the Central Eight risk/need factors. There are also six parts to the instrument, which includes a general risk/need score based on the 42 items and a case management plan. Like the adult LS/CMI, the youth LS instrument is based upon theory and its relevance to youths (Hoge, 2021). Administration of the YLS/CMI is normally with youths between the ages of 12 and 17, although it has been used with youths as young as 10 years old.

Schwalbe (2007) examined the predictive validity of the YLS/CMI for general recidivism. Eleven tests of the instrument yielded a mean AUC of 0.64. This AUC was in the same range as other youth risk/needs assessment scales that were included in the review (e.g., PCL-R youth version). Schwalbe also undertook a calculation to estimate how many negative findings would be needed to overturn the positive predictive validity of the YLS/CMI. It would take 48 negative findings.

Eight derived from GPCSL. The LS instruments and other assessment tools developed on largely male, Caucasian samples have been particularly criticized for introducing bias into the risk/needs assessment of justice-involved minorities and women. Researchers have responded to the criticisms by attempting to cross-validate the instruments with minorities and women. Where differences are found, efforts are made to calibrate the instrument to fit the group under study. For example, Indigenous offenders score higher on risk than non-Indigenous offenders (Perley-Robertson, Maike Helmus, & Forth, 2019). In response Wilson and Gutierrez (2014) calibrated (adjusted) the risk groupings of the LS for Indigenous clients to meet a higher degree of fairness. Although calibration is one way of reducing bias (Berk & Elzarka, 2020), it may not be completely satisfactory (Ashford, Spivak, & Shepherd, 2022).

Primary studies continue to contribute to our understanding of the practical utility of a GPCSL perspective and the extent to which the LS instruments apply to ethnicity, race, and culture (Bhutta & Wormith, 2016; Chenane, Brennan, Steiner, & Ellison, 2015; Gordon, Kelty, & Julian, 2015; Hausam, Lehmann, & Dahle, 2018; Shepherd, Luebbers, Ogloff, Fullam, & Dolan, 2014; Zang & Liu, 2015). What all of this means is that the risk factors identified by GPCSL may be applicable to a wide range of justice-involved persons. This finding does not deflate the importance of gender, race, and ethnicity. It just reveals the extent to which offending reflects the Central Eight risk factors across samples.

LS Risk and Violence Outcomes

In the beginning of this chapter (predictive accuracy and the two-by-two table), we showed the difficulties in trying to predict low base rate behaviors. Compared to nonviolent offending, for which base rates often fall in the 40 to 60 percent range, violent offending is much lower (10 to 20 percent range), and certain forms of violence are lower still (e.g., sexual offending is in the neighborhood of 5 percent). Despite the difficulties in predicting low base rate behaviors, the seriousness of the harm caused to victims demands special attention to the prediction of violent behavior.

The general approach for dealing with the assessment of risk/needs for violent behavior is to develop specialized risk scales. Underlying this approach is the idea that those who commit violent acts are different enough from the run-of-the-mill justice-involved person that we need a unique set of predictors. Two risk instruments that are considered by many to be especially good at predicting violence are the PCL-R (Hare, 1991), discussed in Chapter 8, and the Violence Risk Appraisal Guide (VRAG; Harris, Rice, & Quinsey, 1993). The chapter poses the question: "Is an LS general risk/need assessment instrument, based on GPCSL, useful in the prediction of violent behavior?"

One way to answer this question is to compare some of the instruments specifically designed to predict violent recidivism with the LS instruments. There are three meta-analytic summaries that found the LSI-R to predict violent recidivism as well as the PCL-R and the VRAG (Campbell et al., 2009; Gendreau

TABLE 10.5 **The LSI-R and Violent Recidivism**

Study	k (N)	AUC
Campbell, French, & Gendreau (2009)		
LSI-R	19 (4,361)	.66
PCL-R	24 (4,757)	.65
VRAG	14 (2,082)	.68
Gendreau, Goggin, & Smith (2002)		
LSI-R	9 (2,777)	.67
PCL-R	7 (1,552)	.65
Yang, Wong, & Coid (2010)		
LSI-R	3 (355)	.67
PCL-R	16 (3,854)	.68
VRAG	17 (4,894)	.72

Notes: k = number of effect size, N = number of offenders.

et al., 2002; Yang et al., 2010). Table 10.5 summarizes these meta-analyses. None of the violence-specific risk scales (PCL-R and VRAG) predicted better than the general LSI-R (the confidence intervals overlapped among the scales).

In general, research with the LS suggests that a general, theory-based risk/needs assessment can predict violent behavior as well as the violence risk scales. One advantage that the LS has over the violence risk scales is that the LS measures the dynamic risk factors that are so important for the management of high-risk violent justice-involved persons. Most of the violence risk scales are composed of static items and have ignored dynamic risk factors (Douglas & Skeem, 2005). Can the prediction of violence be improved? Research on violence-specific risk scales continues, and progress is being made. In the LS/CMI, the introduction of an APP subcomponent and specific items that deal with violence is likely to bring improvements in predictive accuracy. For example, Lina Girard and Stephen Wormith (2004) found that a history of aggression together with the APP as measured by the LS/CMI yielded an AUC of 0.75 (Olver et al.'s [2014] meta-analysis found the average AUC for the LS instruments was 0.63 in the prediction of violent recidivism).

Obstacles to Using Empirically Based Risk/Needs Assessment

GPCSL strongly endorses risk/needs assessment for treatment purposes. As will be shown in the next chapter, treatment can reduce recidivism. In order to link assessment with treatment, at a minimum, third-generation instruments that measure criminogenic needs are required. However, there remain indications that many practitioners and correctional systems are not enjoying the full benefits of the research findings. There are many possible reasons for this state of affairs, and two deserve comment.

1. Reluctance to abandon clinical judgment. Given that we are now in an era of fourth-generation assessments, why then do some professionals still weigh their clinical judgment at least to the same degree, if not more, as actuarial assessment methods? For example, in Vrieze and Grove's (2009) survey of 491 clinical psychologists, almost all (98 percent) used clinical judgment and 31 percent used actuarial methods. Others have also found forensic practitioners using assessments to assess risk that are mostly inappropriate (McLaughlin & Kan, 2014; Neal & Grisso, 2014). The answer is complex and involves a number of factors. Resource Note 10.2 provides a listing of some of the possible "classification destruction techniques."

RESOURCE NOTE 10.2

Classification Destruction Techniques: Objections to Using Actuarial Risk/Needs Assessment

Objection	Reality
It is not "either/or"; I use both.	At the moment when a decision is made, if the two approaches do not agree, you have to use one or the other; you cannot use both.
The scale was developed on a different sample and does not apply to my sample.	There may be some slight statistical shrinkage on a new sample, but only when the sample is unique would this be an issue. Also, with the turnover of staff coming from different backgrounds, clinical predictions for the setting can also suffer. The relative advantage of actuarial prediction remains.
The research does not apply to me as the individual professional.	If there are more than 100 studies involving hundreds of professionals showing that they do not predict as well as actuarial instruments, then what makes you think you are so superior to others?
It is too expensive.	Possibly. But what of the time spent in team meetings, the cost of incarcerating someone needlessly or placing the public at risk by not identifying the dangerous offender?

continued

Objection	Reality
I want to change behavior, not just predict it.	If the goal is to change behavior, you need to know the probability of an outcome so you can judge whether your actions have an effect.
Predictions are based on group data: I deal with the unique individual.	Life is guided by probabilities. If the individual is similar to the reference group and there are no obvious differences, it would be foolish to ignore the data. If a doctor told you that surgery is successful in 90 percent of cases similar to yours, would you ignore it?
The important data is not measurable; people cannot be reduced to numbers.	Anything that is written can be coded. Further, rational and empirical does not mean being cold and unfeeling with clients.

Source: Adapted from Grove & Meehl, 1996

2. Adherence to second-generation risk assessment. Considering the fact that there are a number of well validated third- and fourth-generation risk assessment instruments, it is puzzling that there are many jurisdictions that use mostly second-generation, static risk assessment. Internationally, there are practitioners who still rely on professional judgment (Singh, Desmarais, et al., 2014). There are a number of explanations for this state of affairs. First, there is the argument that predictive efficiency trumps a comprehensive assessment. As noted earlier, some researchers have gone in the opposite direction and taken third- and fourth-generation instruments and distilled from them the items that predicted the best, with the result of a much shorter risk scale (Zhang, Roberts, & Farabee, 2014). Yes, the abbreviated risk scale may display the same effect size as the score on the whole instrument, but these short scales consist of mainly static items and miss the assessment of criminogenic needs.

Second, and related to the first, may be an underlying belief that justice-involved persons either cannot be rehabilitated or *do not deserve* to be rehabilitated. In the next chapter, we will see that the evidence clearly shows that rehabilitation works. Unfortunately, if one believes in only punishment for law-breakers, then there is not much that can be done in terms of rehabilitation. And finally, the use of brief, static risk scales may be due to financial constraints. After all, third- and fourth-generation instruments require more training, monitoring for integrity, and, in some cases, paying commercial fees.

Mixing Professional Judgment with Actuarial: Structured Professional Judgment

Structured clinical judgment (SCJ) guides the professional to consider certain factors that are scored but does combine these scores to a total score linked to a risk/needs category. This overall risk/needs classification decision is left to the professional. An example is the HCR-20 (Webster, Douglas, Eaves, & Hart, 1997). The HCR-20 is a 20-item instrument consisting of 10 Historical items (e.g., previous violence), five Clinical items (e.g., lack of insight), and five Risk management items (e.g., plans lack feasibility). Although each item is scored (0, 1, or 2) and the scores are added up for a total score, there is no instruction as to what score corresponds to low, moderate, or high risk. The professional makes the final judgment. In an international survey of 434 forensic experts, Neil and Grisso (2014) found the HCR-20 tied with the PCL-R in its use of assessments of risk for violence (35.6 percent of the experts reported using these instruments).

Although SCJ appears to be an improvement over unstructured clinical judgment, one meta-analysis on *sexual* offender assessment found its predictive accuracy to fall between first- and second-generation assessments (Hanson & Morton-Bourgon, 2009). Two meta-analyses have focused on the HCR-20 with general justice-involved persons. Campbell, French, and Gendreau (2009) found a mean AUC of 0.64 ($k = 11$, $N = 1{,}395$) in the prediction of violent recidivism, while Yang, Wong, and Coid (2010) found a large AUC of 0.75 ($k = 16$, $N = 4{,}161$). A recent meta-analysis of the HCR-R with women found an average AUC of 0.64 ($k = 5$) for general recidivism, and 0.68 ($k = 6$) for violent recidivism (Rossdale, Tully, & Egan, 2020). Systematic, non-meta-analytic reviews of the HCR-20 have reported average AUCs of 0.69 and 0.75 (Douglas & Shaffer, 2021).

The HCR-20 predicts as well as many of the actuarial instruments. So, how do we reconcile these findings to the fact that there is a level of clinical judgment (first-generation assessment) involved with the HCR-20? The answer may have much to do with the care taken in administering the HCR-20. Kevin Douglas and Catherine Shaffer (2021) describe the multiple steps in completing the HCR-20 that involve interviews, psychological testing, and gathering information from multiple sources by those with a high level of expertise. Such a level of professional commitment to the assessment process may be a huge factor in the predictive validity of the HCR-20 and other similar instruments (SAVRY: Borum, Bartel, & Forth, 2003; SVR-20: Boer, Hart, Kropp, & Webster, 1997).

Professional Override

Related to the preceding discussion is the use of a "professional override" to the actuarial risk score. A professional override is altering the risk level calculated by the instrument (e.g., the risk scale may score an individual as low risk but the assessor overrides the risk to medium risk because of the violent nature of the crime). Sometimes, policy may dictate an override (e.g., all murderers are classified as high risk for the first year of imprisonment before being reclassified to a lower level). Professionals often, and should, exercise discretion in making decisions—it is an important part of a fair and just system. In fact, the LS instruments have a section where overrides may be considered (professional override was also a principle in the original and the expanded RNR model).

The use of overrides must be used sparingly and must be justified. With the LS/CMI the recommendation is that overrides should not exceed 5 percent (Wormith & Bonta, 2018). However, overrides have sometimes exceeded this guideline, ranging from approximately 4 to 15 percent in the case of the LS/CMI (Frechette & Lussier, 2021; Guay & Parent, 2018; Orton, Hogan, & Wormith, 2021), almost 11 percent in the case of the risk/needs assessment used in the US federal system (Cohen, Lowenkamp, Bechtel, & Flores, 2020), and as high as 32.5 percent in a study of the YLS/CMI (Parent, Bilodeau, Laurier, & Guay, 2023). High rates with sexual offenders have also been reported (approximately 35 percent; Duwe & Rocque, 2018). Whether the override increases or decreases measured risk/needs level, and it usually increases risk/needs, predictive accuracy almost always *decreases*.

The excessive use of an override is not good correctional practice and tends to increase prediction error (Bonta & Wormith, 2018; Wormith, 2019). Does this mean that overrides should be abolished? Paul Meehl (1954) has provided an example demonstrating that a professional override can be valuable. His example is of a client who has attended a movie theatre every Saturday night for the past 10 years. It seems a safe bet to predict that next Saturday the client will go out to the movies. However, what would you predict if you were told that the client broke a leg Friday evening? Overrides should be used as an opportunity to improve our assessments by systematically monitoring the use of overrides. If patterns emerge, then they may be used to incorporate (or perhaps discover) a new principle of assessment. Some of this work is taking place but much more needs to be done (Schaefer & Williamson, 2018).

The Future of Offender Assessment

There has been considerable progress in the assessment of justice-involved persons, and changes continue at a rapid pace. The "professional judgment," first-generation approach to assessment is now hard to defend, but it is still used in some quarters. Evidence-based, second-generation assessments are widely accepted, but many of them focus on static risk factors and thus limit their usefulness for risk management.

The importance of the objective assessment of criminogenic needs reflected in third-generation assessment is demanded by GPCSL. Third-generation assessments will eventually be replaced by fourth-generation assessments. Evaluations of third- and fourth-generation assessments will be conducted with diverse samples and various outcomes, which will lead to new applications and improvements. This is already happening with the youth and adult versions of the LS/CMI and the LS/RNR.

Algorithms and Machine-Administered Risk/Needs Assessment

Second- to fourth-generation assessments are actuarial in nature and have led in recent years to *machine-based*, algorithmic assessments. That is, a computer gathers relevant information that is optimally combined to formulate an assessment of risk. On the face of it, this appears to be a good way of minimizing bias by removing the human assessor from the formulation of risk. Even if bias is found, it is a relatively simple matter to program a new algorithm to minimize bias (Berk & Elzarka, 2020). Computerized risk assessments have also found their way into the courts in the form of pretrial assessments (Desmarais, Zottola, Duhart Clarke, & Lowder, 2021).

COMPAS is a fourth-generation assessment (Northpointe, 2015; in 2017 Northpointe was rebranded to "equivant"). The assessor gathers information from the client and collaterals, inputs the information into a web-based program, and the software calculates risk/needs and a case management plan. There are other instruments that have web-based administration (e.g., LS/CMI; Ghasemi, Anavari, et al., 2021) but what has attracted attention to COMPAS is that the formulae for calculating risk/needs is not transparent due to software proprietary. Recall from the beginning of this chapter that clarity and transparency should be features of all assessments. This has made COMPAS vulnerable to criticisms of bias, especially racial bias. Critics of risk/needs assessment also argue that items such as employment and education level are proxies for minority status and, therefore, fundamentally unfair to certain segments of society (Starr, 2014; Ugwudike, 2022).

In 2016 Julia Angwin and her colleagues (Angwin, Larson, Mattu, & Kirchner, 2016) analyzed COMPAS data from a county in Florida and found that COMPAS overpredicted recidivism for Blacks. Using the same data, Dressel and Farid (2018) extended the findings by presenting 449 lay people with short narratives of the defendants that provided only age, sex, and criminal history. The participants were asked to judge their chances of reoffending within two years by classifying the defendants as low, medium, or high risk. The AUC for the non-experts was 0.71 and for COMPAS it was 0.70. In a second study, 400 new participants were given the same presentations but this time race was included. The AUCs when race was included were almost identical to when race was excluded. The authors concluded "that commercial software that is widely used to predict recidivism is no more accurate or fair than the predictions of people with little to no criminal justice expertise" (Dressel & Farid, 2018: p. 3).

The reports by Angwin et al. (2016) and Dressel and Farid (2018) received significant media attention. Their findings fly in the face of the general meta-analytic studies showing that actuarial outperforms professional judgment. As expected, the two aforementioned studies were vigorously challenged by researchers from Northpointe, the publisher of COMPAS (Dieterich, Mendoza, & Brennan, 2016), but also from researchers who have no commercial interest in COMPAS (Holsinger, Lowenkamp, et al., 2018; Lin, Jung, Goel, & Skeem, 2020; Skeem & Lowenkamp, 2020). Essentially, the problems with the analyses used to criticize COMPAS were that: (1) the vignettes presented were overly simplistic and unrepresentative of the real world, and (2) lay persons were given immediate feedback on accuracy and thereby improved their predictions over time. When more complex data without feedback was presented in the form of the LSI-R (Lin et al., 2020) and PCRA, an instrument used in U.S. Federal Probation (Skeem & Lowenkamp, 2020), the actuarial assessments outperformed lay judgment.

Ensuring that risk/needs instruments are bias-free is, and will continue to be, a goal of researchers, practitioners, and policymakers. Almost all of the risk/needs instruments of today have deleted items such as race, gender, and age (this was not true 30 years ago). Guidelines and recommendations for minimizing bias in the criminal justice system are presently available (e.g., Vincent & Viljoen, 2020) and should be followed.

Assessment of Strengths

Strengths are factors that decrease the influence of risk/needs factors or "protect" against risk. For example, a supportive prosocial family may mitigate the influence of procriminal peers. There is some debate as to whether strengths are simply the absence of risk factors or an independent construct from risk (see the editorial by Ttofi, Farrington, Piquero, & DeLisi, 2016). Terri Scott and Shelley Brown (2018) conducted a meta-analysis of 22 studies comparing risk with strength factors for justice-involved youth. Examples of the strength domains were prosocial peers, education/employment opportunities, and prosocial attitudes. Note that strengths in this study were the inverse of dynamic risk (procriminal peers, unemployment, and procriminal attitudes). Scott and Brown found non-involvement in substance misuse and having prosocial peers predicted an absence of recidivism for both males and females. However, for some of the other strengths (e.g., education/employment) the prediction of success varied by gender.

The RNR model and the LS instruments have sometimes been criticized for being overly risk focused. However, as we have seen the assessment of strengths is reflected in the RNR model (Principles 10 and 11a) and in the LS/CMI, LS/RNR, and YLS/CMI. Although the three instruments require the assessor to judge if a subcomponent may be a particular strength for the individual, strengths do not form a score.

There are other assessment instruments that do quantify strengths and it appears that strengths do add to the prediction of recidivism. Nathalie Jones and her colleagues (Jones, Brown, Robinson, & Frey, 2015) found high strength scores, as measured by the Service Planning Instrument (SPIn), mitigated recidivism among high-risk clients. Similar results were found among Indigenous and non-Indigenous adults under community supervision (Rieger, Drawbridge, & Robinson, 2023). However, in a large study involving over 50,000 youths and adults the risk/needs (high) by strengths interaction was not found (Brown, Robinson, Wanamaker, & Wagstaff, 2020). In addition to the predictive validity of strengths as measured by SPIn, dynamic validity has been demonstrated for predicting technical violations and new charges (Wanamaker & Brown, 2021, 2022). Future research with SPIn and other similar risk/needs instruments will certainly clarify the nature of strengths and its usefulness in assessment.

Assessment of Acute Risk/Needs

An exciting development is the assessment of "acute" dynamic risk factors (Hanson, 2009, 2014; Yesberg, Scanlan, Hanby, Serin, & Polaschek, 2015). Acute dynamic factors are risk/needs that can change in a very short period of time (e.g., intoxication, loss of a job, collapse of social support system). Being able to reliably identify acute factors has enormous practical utility. Imagine a probation/parole officer or a correctional officer being alerted to a crisis and intervening before an imminent criminal event. The assessment of acute risk factors goes beyond the more slowly changing Central Eight.

The Dynamic Risk Assessment of Offender Reentry (DRAOR; Serin, 2007; Serin, Chadwick, & Lloyd, 2019) stands out as an example of an assessment that tries to capture acute risk factors. Some of the items include sudden changes in negative mood and a newly presented opportunity to access a victim. Davies, Lloyd, and Polaschek (2022) examined the DRAOR subscale scores on 966 high-risk parolees from New Zealand. Because the sample was high-risk parolees they were assessed on a weekly basis (there were over 16,000 assessments). They found reassessments of acute risk factors to be a robust predictor of recidivism.

Trauma-Informed Risk/Need Assessment

Adverse Childhood Experiences (ACE) can have lasting effects on physical and psychological well-being (recall Chapter 7). ACE is also a predictor of adult criminality. However, ACE is not a criminogenic need. It may predict future criminal behavior, as does criminal history, but once an individual has experienced ACE it cannot be reversed. Criminogenic needs are dynamic and can be reversed (e.g., one can develop a drug dependency and one can overcome the addiction). This does not mean that ACE is to be ignored in the assessment and delivery of treatment. Rather, ACE can be considered as a specific responsivity factor. It is the personal-emotional *consequences* of ACE that are obstacles to successful treatment.

Before you can provide trauma-informed correctional treatment the assessor must: (1) determine if the person had experienced ACE, and (2) evaluate the range and severity of the consequences of ACE. Establishing the occurrence of ACE can be as simple as asking a few questions. It can range from a brief inquiry as part of a general risk/needs assessment to a detailed and comprehensive assessment. For example, in the LS/CMI there are a few questions asking about a history of physical and sexual abuse in childhood. The assessment can also be comprehensive by using questionnaires that cover in detail the three general categories of ACE (abuse, neglect, and household dysfunction).

Upon identifying childhood traumatic events, practitioners need to assess the post-traumatic *effects* of ACE. As examples, the levels of anxiety and interpersonal distrust may need to be evaluated and the extent to which substance misuse is used as a coping mechnism for unpleasant memories. These personal reactions to ACE, and many others, will greatly affect the development of a case management plan and how treatment is delivered. More will be said about trauma-informed care in the following treatment chapter. The responsivity principle is all about the *how* of treatment and requires trauma-informed assessment. Work has begun on introducing trauma into risk/needs assessment in a comphrensive manner and attention to the post-ACE well-being of the individual needs to continue (Bates-Maves & O'Sullivan, 2017).

Risk/Needs Communication

This chapter began by highlighting that the prediction of criminal behavior is central to the activities of criminal justice and crime prevention agencies. The decisions made based on risk/needs of the individual affect the provision of services and the lives of those who come in conflict with the law. With so many players involved, the communication of risk/needs in a useful manner is important to delivering the appropriate degree of supervision and treatment. Everyone must work from the same page.

Recently, there has been increased attention as to how the results from a risk/needs assessment are best communicated. For example, does one provide a specific score from a test along with the probability of reoffending or just a risk/needs level (e.g., moderate risk/needs)? Further complications arise when different instruments are used (Bourgon, Mugford, Hanson, & Coligado, 2018). Does a low-risk rating on the LS/CMI equate to low risk on SPIn? Some assessment tools have three risk/needs levels (e.g., LSI-R) and some have five levels (LS/CMI). Even the label of "high risk" can have different meanings to different people (Batastini, Hoeffner, et al., 2019).

The problem of making sense out of the results from multiple risk/needs instruments was addressed in a white paper sponsored by the Council of State Governments and the U.S. Bureau of Justice Assistance (Hanson, Bourgon, et al., 2017). Hanson et al. (2017) proposed a "common language" of risk/needs that is defined, in part, by the individual's criminogenic needs and predicted recidivism rates. The panel settled on five risk/needs levels. For example, in Level II the person has only one or two criminogenic needs and a predicted recidivism rate of 5 to 29 percent over two years. Note that labels such as "moderate-high risk" are not given, only numerical values. With each level there are also recommendations for the amount of treatment required and the need for custody.

There have been a number of tests of the five-level system with different risk/needs instruments. A study by Daryl Kroner and Bree Derrick (2022) compared the classification rates from the LSI-R and two newly created risk instruments using the five-level system. One of the new risk scales was created by selecting the best six predictors of recidivism from the correctional agency's database and the other scale was a selection of the seven most highly correlated items with the LSI-R. All three instruments predicted recidivism equally well (AUCs in the low 0.70s range). They found a 4 to 5 percent improvement in correct classification with the five-level system. This may not appear to be much of an improvement but when a correctional agency supervises cases in the thousands and hundreds of thousands the improvements are substantial in program efficiencies.

Further tests of the five-level system have been conducted with the DRAOR in New Zealand (Coulter, Lloyd, & Serin, 2022) and with risk assessments for sexual offenders (e.g., Hogan & Olver, 2021). In general, improvements in prediction and consistency have been noted. Although the five-level risk communication holds promise there are challenges. Researchers need to extend the findings to other groups (e.g., intimate partner violence) and outcomes (e.g., general violence; Olver, Mundt, et al., 2022). Thus far, the five-level system has been adopted by only a few jurisdictions worldwide (Kroner & Hanson, 2023).

Integrating Neuroscience into Risk/Needs Assessment

There is a considerable literature attesting to the importance of neurobiological factors for understanding criminal behavior (Chapter 4). There have been calls for introducing neurobiological factors into risk/needs assessment (Craig & Rettenberger, 2022), but many challenges are faced. Although neuropsychological tests are used in forensic assessments, they are used mostly in insanity defense hearings or to assess emotional injury rather than criminal risk (Archer, Wheeler, & Vauter, 2016). Incorporating neuropsychological testing into the far more frequent activity of assessing risk and needs in the justice system, at this point in time, would be extremely costly. Highly trained professionals would be needed to administer and interpret specialized tests. Perhaps computerized assessments may be developed that would be cost-effective and at that time we may have fifth-generation assessment protocols.

We leave this chapter with a reminder of some general guidelines for the use of offender assessment instruments (see Resource Note 10.3).

RESOURCE NOTE 10.3

Guidelines for Offender Assessment

1. *Use actuarial measures of risk*

2. *Risk assessments should demonstrate predictive validity*

There are many assessment instruments available for use, but sometimes the research on them is limited to psychometric properties such as internal reliability, face validity, inter-rater reliability, and so on. Practitioners must ask about the predictive validity of the instruments they use because it is this type of validity that has the greatest utility in a correctional context.

3. *The assessment instruments should be directly relevant to the business of corrections*

When dealing with those in conflict with the law, we have interest in two general classes of behaviors: (1) rule violation and (2) psychological instability. They are both important and sometimes interrelated (e.g., paranoid delusions and violent assaults), but not always (e.g., depression is unrelated to recidivism). What we need to be clear about is that emotional and psychological functioning is often minimally related to criminal behavior. Thus, assessment of psychological instability *for purposes of assessing risk for criminal behavior* is largely irrelevant. Test administrators should be aware of what the test does predict and understand that their assessments should be specific to the predicted outcome the situation demands.

4. *Use instruments derived from relevant theory*

The correlates derived from traditional criminological and psychopathological theories of crime have proved to be minor. The social learning perspectives have the strongest empirical support. In these theories criminal behavior is seen as a product of the interaction between cognitive-emotional-personality-biological factors and environmental reward–cost contingencies. Assessment instruments that are based on a general personality and cognitive social learning theory of criminal conduct offer robustness in their predictive accuracy and generalizability to a range of settings and samples.

5. *Assess criminogenic needs*

Criminogenic needs are the dynamic risk factors that are highly important for risk management. For correctional staff who are concerned about how to intervene and reduce the risk posed by their clients, knowledge of their criminogenic needs is vital. Assessing

continued

and reassessing criminogenic needs permits the evaluation of progress in treatment and changes in risk level during the course of normal supervision.

6. *Use general personality and cognitive tests for the assessment of responsivity*

The responsivity principle states that the style and mode of treatment must be matched to the cognitive, personality, and sociocultural characteristics of the individual. There are a number of classification instruments and general personality measures that have utility for the assessment of personal characteristics that could affect the individual's responsiveness to treatment. Test administrators must be cognizant that many personality and cognitive tests have very little evidence regarding their ability to predict criminal behavior. However, they are excellent tools for assessing responsivity.

7. *Use multi-method assessment*

No test measures a single domain perfectly, and each method has a weakness. An important way of dealing with the shortcomings associated with a specific assessment method is to use multiple, diverse methods. In this way, the weakness of one assessment method is compensated by the strength of another method.

8. *Use multi-domain sampling*

There are many factors or domains that contribute to criminal behavior (i.e., the Central Eight). Many of the tests used, however, measure relatively few domains. Therefore, assessments that incorporate multi-domain sampling should become a standard in risk/needs assessments.

9. *Exercise professional and ethical responsibility*

The creators of risk/needs instruments have an obligation to ensure the tests are fair and bias-free. What is done with the results from assessments can have serious consequences. Therefore, those who administer risk/needs assessments have a responsibility to be well trained and knowledgeable of the strengths and weaknesses of the tests they use, to apply the tests appropriately, and to communicate the results in a clear and constructive manner.

10. *Adhere to the least restrictive alternative*

Risk assessments should ensure that offenders are not deprived of liberty that is inconsistent with their risk level. It is not the job of risk assessment to increase punishment.

Source: Adapted from Bonta, 2002; Bucklen, Duwe, & Taxman, 2021

Worth Remembering

1. Criminal behavior is predictable.

    Predictions of criminal behavior exceed chance levels. However, these predictions are not perfect, and to expect perfection is unrealistic. Other fields (e.g., medicine) do not have perfect prediction, but their predictive accuracies are sufficient to have practical value. The same can be said for the criminal justice field.

2. Prediction is enhanced through knowledge of theory.

    The theory and research in PCC may be translated into valid, objective, and practical assessment instruments. The highlighting of the Central Eight and dynamic risk factors are desirable features to have in assessment.

3. The principles of risk, need, and responsivity can be reflected in assessment.

    The principles of effective intervention suggest who may profit from treatment services (the risk principle); what should be targeted (the need principle); and how treatment is delivered (the responsivity principle).

4. Fourth-generation assessments are integrated with case management plans.

    First-generation assessments are unstructured, clinical judgments of risk, and they perform poorly in the prediction of criminal behavior. Second-generation assessments predict well but mostly comprise static risk factors. Third-generation risk/needs instruments identify the criminogenic needs of offenders, while fourth-generation assessments (e.g., LS/CMI) guide the actual delivery of services targeting criminogenic needs.

5. Assessment based on GPCSL has wide applicability.

    The evidence suggests that the correlates of criminality are much the same across differing populations (e.g., gender). The evidence also suggests that many of the factors that predict general offending also predict violent offending.

Recommended Readings

The Grove, Zald, Lebow, Snitz, & Nelson (2000) and Ægisdóttier, White, et al. (2006) meta-analyses are perhaps the definitive reviews comparing first-generation, unstructured professional judgments with actuarial assessments. These reviews are not specific to criminal justice but speak to the broader issues of prediction.

For those interested in the wide applicability of theory and research-based risk/needs assessment see the chapter by Wormith and Bonta (2021) in Douglas and Otto's *Handbook of Violence Risk Assessment Tools*. This chapter includes applications not covered in the present chapter and reinforces the general position that a PCC can expand the uses of risk/needs assessment.

For the reader interested in Structured Clinical Judgment and the HCR-20, the chapter by Douglas and Shaffer (2021) is recommended. In fact, the entire edited book by Kevin Douglas and Randy Otto (2021) gives an excellent review of the major risk/needs assessment instruments.

Finally, for a summary of the four generations of risk assessment, the entry by James Bonta (2019c) in Robert Morgan's *The SAGE Encyclopedia of Criminal Psychology* is suggested.

 Visit the Instructor and Student Resource to access additional exercises, videos and study materials to support this chapter: psychologycriminalconduct.routledge.com

CHAPTER 11 Rehabilitation

The first objective of this chapter is to tell the "what works" story of rehabilitation in the criminal justice system. The chapter begins with an overview of the "nothing works" position, which launched the deterrence and "get tough" movement in criminal justice (to be described in more detail in Chapter 13). The second aspect of the story describes recognition of the value of human service in justice contexts (that is, the debate moved toward a "what works" position). Another objective of this chapter is to summarize the meta-analytic evidence in regard to the value of adhering to the Risk-Need-Responsivity (RNR) model. Finally, the chapter ends with a consideration of "what works" from the perspective of GPCSL. Much of the quantitative detail is located in Resource Note 11.1. Making "what works" actually work in the real world is presented in the next chapter of this book.

The How and Why of "Nothing Works"

The preamble to the "nothing works" idea starts with Kirby's (1954) review of the correctional treatment literature. Kirby (1954) classified "treatments" as follows: probation and parole, institution-based, capital punishment (sic), psychotherapy, and non-institutional. The non-psychotherapy classes of "treatment" may make some sense to administrators, bureaucrats, and policymakers, but they are of little direct relevance to the analysis of behavioral influence processes. At best, they are broad descriptions of the social context within which services are delivered, as opposed to descriptions of the content and processes of direct service. Kirby thereby set the stage for an early problem in the literature, namely, the failure to make a clear distinction between structural/setting variables and the clinical aspects of service (i.e., the behavior influence processes) that occur within that structure or setting.

Not surprisingly, Kirby (1954) found that the literature available in the early 1950s was methodologically weak. However, four studies of *direct* service (i.e., psychotherapy) included comparison conditions and objective measures of outcome. Three of the four of these better controlled studies yielded findings

DOI: 10.4324/9781003292128-14

favorable to counseling. Kirby's conclusion was astonishing: "Most treatment programs are based on hope and perhaps informed speculation rather than verified information" (p. 372).

Walter Bailey (1966) found 100 studies of correctional effectiveness; 22 of the studies approximated the experimental ideal. This was a considerable improvement on the state of the literature in the early 1950s. Sixty percent of the *better controlled* studies ($k = 22$) reported "marked improvement" or demonstrated statistically significant gains relative to the comparison conditions; 23 percent reported "harm" or "no change." Considering the total sample of 100 studies, approximately 50 studies reported "considerable improvement" in the treatment group.

Bailey's conclusions included a recognition that both the quality and quantity of studies had improved since the Kirby report. However, Bailey also stated that there had been no apparent progress in demonstrating the validity of correctional treatment. Lest the reader begin to think positively in the glow of a "hit rate" of 50 to 60 percent, Bailey reminded his readers that it was the authors of the studies who wrote the reports. This gratuitous comment has since been enshrined in Michael Gottfredson's (1979) list of "treatment destruction techniques," and it is echoed in our "knowledge destruction" anti-rehabilitation themes (see Technical Note 11.1 at psychologycriminalconduct. routledge.com).

Treatment of "knowledge destruction" proliferated in the 1970s. Charles Logan (1972) examined 100 studies and summarized their findings as follows: High Success ($k = 20$), Good Success (35), Fair Success (15), Failure (16), and Can't Say (14). The latter category included three studies in which the success varied with particular combinations of clients and treatment. Overall, 73 studies provided some evidence of success, 16 were clear failures, and 11 had unclassifiable outcomes.

Despite finding that almost three-quarters of the studies were successful, Logan's interpretation of the findings was negative. Logan found that not a single study was methodologically adequate. Thus, Logan was able to conclude:

> No research has been done to date that enables one to say that one treatment program is better than another or that enables us to examine a man and specify the treatment he needs. There is no evidence that probation is better than institutions, that institutions are better than probation, or that being given a parole is better than escaping... much of what is now being done about crime may be so wrong that the net effect of the actions is to increase rather than to decrease crime.
>
> (Logan, 1972: p. 381)

Now we come to the review conducted by Martinson (1974) and his colleagues (Lipton, Martinson, & Wilks, 1975) and "nothing works." Their summary of studies was a major accomplishment. Two hundred and thirty-one controlled studies were examined, carefully described, and tabulated.

Depending upon how the studies are classified, some 40 to 60 percent of the studies included reports of positive effects on at least some types of offenders. One hundred and thirty-eight studies included measures of recidivism. Furthermore, if studies of probation, parole, and imprisonment are removed as "treatments," 83 studies are left (with 48 percent showing a reduction in recidivism).

The conclusions drawn by Martinson and his colleagues took various forms both in the original review articles and in subsequent commentaries, but the dominant message was "nothing works" (Martinson himself never used the term, but it very quickly became the label for his analysis). The Martinson review also served to demonstrate *knowledge destruction*:

1. Studies that reached negative conclusions regarding the effectiveness of treatment were accepted almost without question.

2. Studies that were supportive of treatment were subjected to intense criticism of a pseudoscientific variety. These techniques included "stressing the criterion problem," "contaminating the treatment," and "discounting the underlying theory" (see below for definitions of these techniques).

3. What was almost never considered in these reviews was the possibility that the reasons provided for discounting the positive findings are the very factors that may be responsible for hiding or underestimating the effects of treatment.

    For example, unreliability in the measurement of outcome variables such as recidivism ("the criterion problem") should decrease, not increase, the chances of detecting the effects of treatment. Unreliability of measurement is a possible reason why effects are not found, and not a reason why effects are found.

    Similarly, errors in the conceptualization of crime and treatment should have the effect of preventing positive outcomes, not of promoting them. If the psychological model of crime is wrong ("discounting the underlying theory"), we would not expect to find any effects when service is guided by that model.

    A primary example of "contaminating the treatment" is to suggest that the positive effects of counseling reflect nothing but the "natural interpersonal skills" of the counselor. If the findings are that counseling is effective when it is offered by interpersonally skilled therapists, so be it. Such a finding begins to say something about the conditions under which counseling is effective. It is not a reason for discounting treatment.

Very soon after publication, Martinson was challenged (Adams, 1975; Palmer, 1975). Ted Palmer's paper was a particularly strong document because his descriptions of effective programs were often direct quotes from the descriptions provided by Martinson and his colleagues. What remains largely forgotten today is that Martinson had the courage to recant and admit that while some programs did not work, others clearly did provide positive evidence of effectiveness ("I have often said that treatment... is 'impotent'... the conclusion is not correct"; Martinson, 1979: p. 254). However, Martinson's turnabout on the effectiveness issue was too late. The damage was done. Mainstream criminologists and a conservative public seemed ready to promote the punishment of law-breakers.

The fact remained that positive and promising evidence resided in the research literature. Indeed, positive evidence was growing at a fast rate. Paul Gendreau and Robert Ross prompted many people to look again at the evidence (Gendreau & Ross, 1979; Ross & Gendreau, 1980). Their updated review was impressive: 95 experimental or quasi-experimental studies were published between 1973 and 1978; 86 percent of these reported positive outcomes. Not all of the 95 studies approximated the experimental ideal, but the evidence from studies published in the early 1970s was (like the earlier evidence) more supportive than unsupportive of correctional counseling.

Then, in 1990, Andrews, Bonta, and Hoge (1990) described the clinically relevant and psychologically informed principles of Risk, Need, and Responsivity. The RNR model provided a new lens to view the rehabilitation literature.

The Birth of "What Works"

By 1990, the number of reports published in English on controlled evaluations of community and correctional interventions with justice-involved persons was fast approaching 500. Now it was clear that, on average, "treatment" reduced recidivism to at least a mild degree. Even some "skeptical" scholars agreed with this fact (e.g., Lab & Whitehead, 1990). As many authors had been suggesting over the 1970s and 1980s (e.g., Andrews & Kiessling, 1980; Ross & Fabiano, 1985; Ross & Gendreau, 1980), some approaches to treatment were clearly better than others.

The early formulation of the RNR model in 1990 provided a psychologically informed explanation of why some treatments were more effective than others. These principles of effective treatment were hypothesized to apply regardless of the setting within which treatment was delivered (e.g., within probation services or prisons). Andrews, Zinger, and colleagues (1990) tested the principles of risk, need, and responsivity in a meta-analysis of 154 treatment comparisons, 30 of which were assigned to the criminal sanction set. Criminal sanctions involved variations in the type or severity of judicial processing. These included, for example, official processing versus police cautioning and probation versus closed custody.

Analysis of the 30 comparisons of criminal sanctions revealed that not a single positive correlation of 0.20 or greater was generated. Overall, the association between criminal sanctions and recidivism was minimal: −0.07. The fact that the effect size was negative indicates that more, as opposed to less, criminal justice processing was associated with slightly increased recidivism rates. In brief, if the type and severity of official punishment has any effect on recidivism, it appears to be that "less" is better than "more." The meta-analysis also confirmed what the earlier narrative reviews of the literature had uncovered. The mean effect of correctional treatment service ($r = 0.05$, $k = 124$) was clearly greater and more positive than that of criminal sanctioning without the delivery of treatment services ($r = -0.07$, $k = 30$). Moreover, differentiations within the treatment studies in adherence to the RNR principles were revealing and confirmatory.

The 124 tests of treatment services were assigned to the categories of "appropriate," "unspecified," or "inappropriate" treatment according to the principles of risk, need, and responsivity. Few studies, however, differentiated clients according to risk, and not many studies were clear on the criminogenic needs that were being targeted in treatment. Furthermore, many studies were quiet on the specifics of the style and mode of service employed. Thus, the major criterion governing assignment to "appropriate correctional treatment service" proved to be the simple designation of a program as "behavioral," and 70 percent (38/54) of the "appropriate" treatments were behavioral.

Additional treatments in the "appropriate" set were those clearly delivered to higher-risk cases, structured programs that were specific and appropriate regarding criminogenic need (e.g., targeting procriminal thinking), and a small set of treatments involving appropriate matching according to responsivity systems such as interpersonal maturity level.

Thirty-eight treatments were coded "inappropriate" because they employed deterrence methods (e.g., "Scared Straight") or nondirective client-centered/psychodynamic and non-behavioral approaches. Thirty-two comparisons entailed the delivery of some treatment service, but it was unclear whether that treatment was appropriate or inappropriate according to the clinical principles of effective service. These 32 comparisons were coded as "unspecified."

The average effect of *appropriate* treatment service ($r = 0.30$) was significantly greater than unspecified treatment ($r = 0.13$), inappropriate treatment ($r = -0.06$), and criminal processing without treatment ($r = -0.07$). Using the binomial effect size display explained in Chapter 2, an average correlation of 0.30 represents a recidivism rate of 65 percent in the comparison condition, compared to 35 percent in the appropriate treatment group. Even with the dimensions of risk and need ignored, behavioral and cognitive social learning treatment strategies had a substantially greater average effect on recidivism than did non-behavioral treatments (0.29, $k = 41$ versus 0.04, $k = 113$).

Differences emerged between programs delivered in custodial and residential facilities versus programs delivered in the community. There was a tendency for the effects of inappropriate service to be particularly negative in custody settings. The effects of appropriate, clinically relevant services showed positive effects in custodial/residential settings, but these services were even more effective when delivered in community settings (Principle 13 of the expanded RNR model). This finding, in combination with the mean negative effect of criminal sanctions, led Andrews and colleagues (Andrews, Zinger, et al., 1990) to conclude that they had initially underestimated the negative effect of custody. These research findings affirm a widely shared belief that custody is best viewed as the last resort.

Further Results from the Expanded Meta-Analysis

After the 1990 meta-analysis by Andrews, Zinger, et al., the databank was expanded to include 225 studies, yielding 374 tests of the effects of judicial and correctional interventions on recidivism (see Resource Note 11.1 for a more detailed summary). Slightly more than half of the studies (56 percent) were of youth. The overall mean effect of human service was 0.08 ($k = 374$). That level of effect is small, but clearly positive and utterly inconsistent with a blanket "nothing works" position. Using the binomial effect size display, an r of 0.08 reflects a difference of eight percentage points between the recidivism rates of the intervention and comparison groups: 46 percent reoffending in the intervention group compared with 54 percent reoffending in the comparison group.

RESOURCE NOTE 11.1

The Expanded Meta-Analysis of the Effects of Human Service in a Justice Context

The RNR model suggests that justice-involved persons may be differentiated according to their risk of reoffending; recognizes that the risk/need factors are personal, interpersonal, and tied to immediate situations in an array of behavioral settings such as home, work, school, and leisure; differentiates between major and minor risk factors; identifies the dynamic risk factors that may best be targeted if the objective is reduced reoffending; and—more than *any* alternative perspective—is very clear regarding some fundamental and very practical processes of behavioral influence and behavior change.

Thus, it is hypothesized that: (1) human service will have greater impact on reduced recidivism than will variation in retributive and/or restorative aspects of sanctioning, and (2) the positive impact of human service will increase with adherence to the principles of risk, need, and general responsivity. Further expected is that: (3) the positive impact of clinically appropriate human service will be enhanced when offered in community-based nonresidential settings (Principle 13 of RNR), (4) when staff make use of GPCSL-based practices that constitute the relationship and structuring principles (Principle 14), and (5) when programs are delivered with integrity (Principle 15). Indicators of integrity include the selection, training, and clinical supervision of staff and the structuring of programming through manuals and monitoring of service delivery. Finally, it is hypothesized that: (6) the crime reduction potential of clinically appropriate treatment will be evident across and within categories of methodological control variables.

continued

In the expanded set of 374 tests, the pattern of results first identified in 1990 remained. Inspection of Table 11.1.1 reveals that the mean effect size for criminal sanctions (−0.03) is lower than the mean effect size for human service (0.12) and in the negative direction (i.e., associated with increases in recidivism).

In the expanded meta-analysis, only the general responsivity principle was coded, and no attempt was made to code for specific responsivity. Thus, the single coding requirement for conformity with the responsivity principle is the use of behavioral, social learning, and/or cognitive-behavioral strategies. Adherence to the responsivity principle was associated with enhanced effect sizes. Table 11.1 also shows the significant contribution of adherence to the need principle and to the risk principle.

TABLE 11.1.1 Mean Effect Size by Adherence to Principles of Effective Correctional Treatment

Principle	Adherence to principle (k)	
	No	Yes
Human Service	.03 (101)	.12 (146)
Risk: Services to Higher-Risk Cases	.03 (96)	.10 (278)
Needs: # of Criminogenic Needs Targeted Exceed Noncriminogenic	−.01 (205)	.19 (169)
General Responsivity: Social Learning/Cognitive Behavioral Strategies	.04 (297)	.23 (77)
Full Adherence: Clinically Appropriate Treatment (adheres to all of the above)	.05 (314)	.28 (60)
Community-Based Full Adherence: Clinically Appropriate Treatment	.06 (219)	.35 (30)
Residential-Based Full Adherence: Clinically Appropriate Treatment	.002 (95)	.17 (30)

Clinically and psychologically appropriate treatment refers to adherence to risk-need-responsivity. The variable Appropriate Treatment is a composite of Any Service, Risk, Need, and General Responsivity. There are four levels of RNR adherence: "0" (criminal sanctions without human service or human service inconsistent with each of risk, need, and responsivity) and "1," "2," and "3," representing human service consistent with one, two, or three of the human service principles. The corresponding mean effect sizes were −0.20 ($k = 124$), 0.02 ($k = 106$), 0.18 ($k = 84$), and 0.28 ($k = 60$) for the four levels of RNR adherence.

Community Settings. The mean effect size increased with level of Appropriate Treatment both in community settings and institutional/residential settings (Principle 13). However, the positive effects of Appropriate Treatment were enhanced in community settings ($r = 0.35$, $k = 30$), while the negative effects of inappropriate service were augmented in custodial/residential settings ($r = −0.10$, $k = 25$).

Table 11.1.2 summarizes the mean effects found when personal and interpersonal domains are targeted appropriately and when they are targeted inappropriately. Personal targets such as self-control deficits and procriminal cognition yielded relatively large effect sizes, while the targeting of personal distress and fear of official punishment yielded weak effects on reduced reoffending.

continued

TABLE 11.1.2 **Mean Effect Sizes of Need Targeted (*k*)**

Need	Not targeted	Targeted
Criminogenic Needs		
Personal Targets:		
Procriminal Cognition and Skill Deficits	.04 (277)	.21 (97)
Interpersonal Targets:		
Family and Peers	.05 (392)	.22 (72)
School/Work	.06 (286)	.15 (88)
Substance Abuse	.08 (338)	.11 (36)
Noncriminogenic Needs		
Personal Targets:		
Personal distress, fear of punishment	.11 (203)	.04 (171)
Interpersonal Targets:		
e.g., Family process other than nurturance, supervision	.09 (329)	.01 (45)

GPCSL-based Staff Practice. Table 11.1.3 lists the basic elements of behavioral influence. They represent what should be part of the essential skills and qualities for those who work with justice-involved persons (i.e., Principle 14). As shown in the table, indicators of a high-quality relationship and structuring are associated with enhanced effect sizes.

TABLE 11.1.3 **Mean Effect Size by GPCSL-based Staff Skills (*k*)**

Staff skill	Skill present (*k*)	
	No	**Yes**
Relationship	.07 (361)	.34 (13)
Structuring	.06 (330)	.27 (44)
Effective Reinforcement	.07 (359)	.31 (15)
Effective Prosocial Modeling	.06 (337)	.28 (37)
Effective Disapproval	.08 (366)	.30 (8)
Structured Skill Learning	.06 (336)	.30 (38)
Problem-Solving	.06 (329)	.25 (45)
Advocacy/Brokerage	.08 (321)	.11 (53)
Effective Authority	.07 (359)	.26 (15)

Organizational and Validity Considerations. Effect size increased to at least a mild degree with all indicators of program integrity presented in Table 11.1.4 (Principle 15). Four variables were linked in a positive manner once controls for RNR Adherence were introduced. They were Community-Based Programs, Involved Evaluator, Non-Justice

continued

Ownership of the Program, and Referral to Program by Justice Officials. As presented in the main body of Technical Note 11.2 (psychologycriminalconduct.routledge.com), the strength of RNR adherence was evident even when offered under methodological conditions least favorable to large effect sizes. Overall, conditions that limit the magnitude of the mean effect size do not negate the evidence in favor of clinically relevant and psychologically informed human service in a variety of justice contexts.

TABLE 11.1.4 Mean Effects by Indicators of Integrity of Implementation and Service Delivery

Indicator	Indicator present (k)	
	No	Yes
Staff Selected for Relationship Skills	.07 (361)	.34 (13)
Staff Trained	.04 (206)	.13 (168)
Clinical Supervision of Staff	.06 (305)	.16 (69)
Printed/Taped Manuals	.05 (303)	.20 (71)
Specific Model Used	.03 (173)	.12 (201)
New/Fresh Program	.05 (250)	.13 (124)
Small Sample (N < 100)	.04 (340)	.15 (134)
Involved Evaluator	.04 (296)	.23 (78)

The mean r of 0.08 is an average, and the 95 percent confidence interval of 0.06 to 0.10 does *not* contain 0.00. In other words, correctional interventions do have an effect on recidivism. There is, however, a tremendous amount of variability around that mean. The poorest treatment outcome within all 374 estimates is in the area of −0.40, while the best single outcome is in the area of +0.80. Perhaps the really interesting question is, what are the sources of this variation?

The overall pattern of results favoring "clinically appropriate" human service continued in the expanded sample of studies (see Figure 11.1). With the coding of risk, need, and responsivity once again defining "appropriate" treatment, the mean correlation coefficients with reduced reoffending were as follows: Criminal Sanctions and Inappropriate Human Service (−0.02, $k = 124$); Human Service consistent with only one of risk, need, and responsivity (0.02, $k = 106$); Human Service consistent with two of the three principles (0.18, $k = 84$); and Appropriate Service (consistent with all three principles: 0.28, $k = 60$).

Breaking down the findings, and as expected from Principle 13 of the RNR model (i.e., community-based services are preferred) the impact of RNR is enhanced when delivered in a community setting (see Figure 11.2). Also

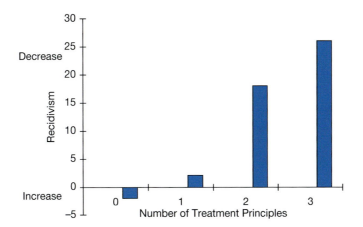

Figure 11.1

Mean Effect Size by Adherence to RNR

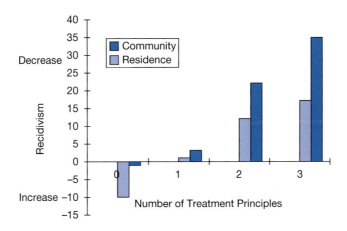

Figure 11.2

Adherence to RNR by Setting

noteworthy is that sanctions and inappropriate human service have a more detrimental effect when delivered in custodial/residential settings.

In the Andrews, Zinger, et al. (1990) report, the risk principle was assessed within those particular studies that allowed such an exploration. That is, within any particular study of a particular treatment program, if the effects of treatment were reported separately for lower- and higher-risk cases, then separate estimates were placed in the meta-analysis (the estimate for the higher-risk subgroup was placed in the appropriate treatment category and the estimate for the lower-risk group in the inappropriate treatment category). In the 1990 report there were clear differences, with much larger effects found in the higher-risk subsamples relative to the lower-risk samples. The expanded meta-analysis confirms the pattern. As displayed in Figure 11.3, programs that

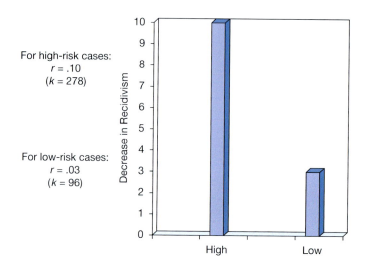

For high-risk cases:
$r = .10$
($k = 278$)

For low-risk cases:
$r = .03$
($k = 96$)

Figure 11.3

Adherence to the Risk Principle

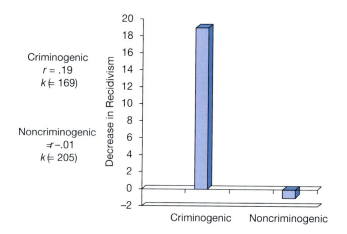

Criminogenic
$r = .19$
$k (= 169)$

Noncriminogenic
$= r - .01$
$k (= 205)$

Figure 11.4

Adherence to the Need Principle

targeted higher-risk offenders ($r = 0.10$, $k = 278$) showed a higher association with reduced recidivism compared to interventions targeting lower-risk offenders ($r = 0.03$, $k = 96$).

The need principle in the 1990 review was applied in a less-than-direct manner. In the expanded meta-analysis a more methodologically rigorous approach was adopted to evaluate the need principle. The dynamic risk factors supported by PCC were re-written in terms of more promising and less promising intermediate targets of change. Also counted was the number of promising targets represented in treatment programs as well as the number of less promising targets represented in treatment programs. The mean effect size for studies of programs that targeted a greater number of the more promising targets was 0.19 (k = 169), compared with a mean r of −0.01 (k = 205) for studies of programs that emphasized less promising targets (see Figure 11.4). The importance of the need principle should not be underestimated. Programs that placed a greater emphasis on less promising intermediate targets tended to increase reoffending rates. Not one program that targeted noncriminogenic needs predominately was associated with reduced recidivism.

The reviews described here show that the objective and quantitative findings of the existing literature on correctional effectiveness do not support a "nothing works" perspective. The "nothing works" perspective makes sense only if one limits one's view of the effects of treatment to that literature which deals with the effects of the type and/or severity of official processing and sanctioning on recidivism. In dramatic contrast, the research literature on the effects of treatment, offered under a variety of conditions of official processing, has revealed positive effects on average—and notably positive effects when the principles of risk, need, and responsivity have been applied.

Independent Meta-Analytic Summaries of the Effects of RNR Programming

The possibility of large reductions in recidivism resides in delivering appropriate treatment services to people in accordance with the RNR principles. Of course, the evidence provided comes from the authors of the RNR model, and if one wished to use the knowledge destruction technique of "question the motives and objectivity of scholars," then the relevance of RNR can be discounted. However, independent reviews of the treatment literature confirm the value of the RNR principles.

There are many meta-analyses of the effectiveness of correctional treatment. McGuire (2004) identified more than 40 meta-analytic studies and today the number is much higher. The vast majority of meta-analytic studies of correctional treatment tend to focus on particular programs or types of programs. Reviews of types of programs are often defined by the methods employed (e.g., cognitive-behavioral therapy; Lipsey, Landenberger, & Wilson, 2007; social skills training; van der Stouwe, Gubbels, et al., 2021), by intermediate targets (e.g., substance misuse; Bahr, Masters, & Taylor, 2012), and by who is served in treatment (e.g., youth; Koehler, Lösel, Akoensi, & Humphreys, 2013).

As the authors of the RNR model try to do, Mark Lipsey (2009) and Laceé Pappas and Amy Dent (2023) are also interested in a broader and more general understanding of the principles of effective correctional treatment. They refer to studies that collect and meta-analyze all the available research on the effects of intervention rather than limit their reviews to types of programs or types of offenders.

Their approach, however, was quite different: the reviews were atheoretical and heavily descriptive. The analyses were not associated with theories of crime or even with theoretical positions in regard to the processes of behavioral influence and behavior change. Basically, these two important meta-analyses worked with sets of potential moderators of effect size estimates, as described below:

Study Methodology

- Type of measure of recidivism (e.g., conviction, arrests, self-reported, follow-up period).

- Design issues (e.g., random assignment, matching, covariate adjustments).

Publication Bias

- Peer-reviewed journal article, book chapter, sample size, unpublished.

Characteristics of the Samples

- Mean age, gender mix, risk level, history of aggression.

Supervision and Control

- None, diverted from justice system, probation/parole, incarceration.

Setting

- Institutional, custody.

Type of Intervention

- Particular types within the following categories:
  — Surveillance (e.g., intensive supervision).
  — Deterrence (e.g., Scared Straight, specialized courts).
  — Restorative (e.g., restitution, mediation).
  — Counseling (e.g., individual; mentoring; family; group).
  — Skill-building (e.g., behavioral contracting, cognitive-behavioral, social skills training).

- Amount and quality of service (usually assessed by the program evaluator's involvement in the design and the delivery of the service program).

Lipsey's (2009) meta-analysis included 548 samples of juveniles (aged 12 to 21 years). The overall mean effect of human services was 0.06. Pappas and Dent (2023) summarized 48 meta-analyses and found an average effect size of 0.09 for treatment, close to that found in the expanded RNR meta-analysis for those under the age of 19 (0.10). However, both reviews also reported considerable variability in the findings. The following were some of the findings that differentiated less effective and more effective interventions with young offenders that support the RNR principles:

1. **RNR Principle 4, Introduce human service**: Lipsey—"Therapeutic" interventions were significantly more effective than interventions based on control or coercion; e.g., the mean effect size for counselling was 0.07 and −0.01 for deterrence; Pappas and Dent—effect sizes for therapeutic interventions varied from 0.10 to 0.23; deterrent programs such as shock incarceration were associated with *increased* recidivism.

2. **RNR Principle 5, Risk**: Lipsey—effectiveness increased with the risk level of youth; Pappas and Dent—effectiveness was diminished with the less serious cases.

3. **RNR Principle 7, General responsivity**: Lipsey—cognitive-behavioral programs were most effective with behavioral programs ranked second. Pappas and Dent—strangely, cognitive-behavioral interventions were modestly related to reduced recidivism (0.10). The authors coded studies as described but suspect that some studies did not actually use cognitive-behavioral principles.

4. **RNR Principle 13, Community-based**: Lipsey—effectiveness of counseling programs was reduced in samples of incarcerated youth and enhanced when delivered in the community; Pappas and Dent—surprisingly, the opposite was found. The mean effect was 0.13 for those in residential facilities compared to youth in the community ($r = 0.05$). The authors hypothesized that community programs may not be as well resourced as those in custodial settings although no direct evidence was provided.

5. **RNR Principle 14, Management**: Lipsey—effectiveness increased with the quality of implementation; Pappas and Dent—did not examine the quality of implementation, only the methodological quality of the evaluation.

The findings regarding the effectiveness of therapeutic approaches relative to deterrence and control are highly consistent with the RNR model (unfortunately, neither review tested the need principle). For the most part, the reviews also found that the findings were stable across categories of age, gender, and ethnicity. This is consistent with GPCSL's position regarding the general applicability of the theory and principles.

Other scholars have conducted reviews of the literature that have specifically been guided by the RNR model. An overview of these treatment reviews is presented in Table 11.1. In summary, clinically and psychologically appropriate treatment—as specified by the RNR model and GPCSL—outperforms alternative treatments. Now, the chapter closes with a discussion of "what works" and the linkage to GPCSL.

TABLE 11.1 Testing the RNR Model: Independent Meta-Analytic Reviews

Study	Description	Findings
Gutierrez & Bourgon (2012)	Drug treatment courts ($k = 25$)	No court adhered to all three principles (12 adhered to only one and one court to two principles); recidivism lowest for courts that adhered to at least one of the principles.
Gutierrez, Blais, & Bourgon (2016)	Domestic violence courts ($k = 21$)	Five courts adhering to at least one principle demonstrated lower recidivism.
Hanson et al. (2009)	Sex offender treatment studies ($k = 23$)	RNR treatments showed the largest decreases in sexual and general recidivism.
Koehler et al. (2013)	European studies of treatment programs for youth ($k = 25$)	Treatment works ($r = 0.08$); programs following the RNR principles ($k = 7$) had the highest mean effect ($r = 0.16$).
Lowenkamp, Latessa, & Holsinger (2006)	Testing the risk principle across 97 programs	Programs targeting higher risk cases showed the greatest reductions in recidivism ($r = 0.18$, $k = 58$).
Prendergast et al. (2013)	Treating drug users ($k = 243$)	Adherence to RNR ($k = 12$) associated with reduced crime ($r = 0.16$) but not drug use ($r = 0.06$, $k = 59$).

GPCSL and Intervention

The Central Eight risk/need factors are closely linked with the GPCSL model of criminal conduct. The mechanisms of reinforcement, punishment, antecedent control, and modeling are fundamental cognitive social learning processes (general responsivity). GPCSL also stresses GPCSL-based staff practices (Principle 14 of RNR), and two fundamental principles of interpersonal influence that are judged important are:

1. *The Relationship Principle*: Interpersonal influence is greatest in situations characterized by open, warm, enthusiastic, and nonblaming communication, and by collaboration, mutual respect, liking, and interest.

2. *The Structuring Principle*: The procriminal versus prosocial direction of interpersonal influence is determined by the procriminal/prosocial content of the messages communicated or by the procriminal/prosocial nature of the behaviors that are modeled, rehearsed, and subject to reinforcement and punishment. The structuring dimension reflects the use of effective authority practices, prosocial modeling, differential approval and disapproval, problem-solving, skill building, advocacy, the structuring aspects of motivational interviewing, and cognitive restructuring.

These two dimensions of interpersonal exchanges have a long history in the social psychology of interpersonal interaction, counseling theory, and the social psychology of criminal conduct (e.g., Sutherland's theory of differential association). The indicators of relationship and structuring are another way of describing general responsivity practices (Bourgon & Bonta, 2014). The indicators of a positive relationship establish the conditions favorable to modeling, to effective interpersonal reinforcement and/or effective disapproval, and to creating an attractive rather than aversive setting for intervention.

The first set of conditions (relationship), if positive, tends to promote learning and enhance interpersonal influence. The second set (structuring) determines what is learned or the direction of influence. In correctional counseling, the structuring dimension is responsible for movement or changes that are favorable or unfavorable to criminal behavior. From the expanded meta-analysis, the mean effect size for indicators of a positive relationship was 0.34 ($k = 13$), and the effective use of structuring displayed a mean effect size of 0.27 ($k = 44$).

Specific Responsivity and Trauma-Informed Treatment

Chapter 7 introduced Adverse Childhood Experiences (ACEs), which many justice-involved persons have suffered. Chapter 10 described ways in which the resulting traumas associated with ACEs can be reliably assessed. In preparing to close this chapter, a summary of trauma-informed treatment is in order.

ACEs are a predictor of adult criminality. In GPCSL, however, an ACE is not considered a criminogenic need that should be *directly* targeted in treatment. An ACE does not meet the basic definition of a criminogenic need as a dynamic risk factor. It may predict, as does criminal history, but once an individual has experienced an ACE it cannot be reversed. Criminogenic needs are dynamic and can change in two directions. For example, with the criminogenic need of substance misuse one can develop a problem and one can overcome the addiction. Yet when providing treatment ACEs cannot be ignored. Rather ACEs are considered as a specific responsivity factor because the personal-emotional effects of ACEs are obstacles to successful treatment.

Before one can provide trauma-informed correctional treatment, recognizing and assessing the presence of an ACE and its consequences is required. Some of the ways that this can be accomplished were described in Chapter 10. Once childhood traumatic events are properly identified, practitioners need to be on the lookout for the *effects* of ACEs. Are post-traumatic symptoms present? What are the levels of anxiety, interpersonal distrust, and emotional dysregulation for the individual? Is substance misuse a coping mechnism used by the client to deal with unpleasant memories? These personal reactions to ACEs, and many others, will greatly influence criminal trajectories, the development of a case management plan, and how treatment is delivered. Afterall, the responsivity principle is all about the *how* of treatment and specific responsivity delves into the details of the person's experiences. For example, Post Traumatic Stress Disorder symptoms may have to be addressed first, perhaps by a mental health specialist, before criminogenic needs are targetted in treatment.

A number of trauma-informed interventions have been developed and many are cognitive-behaviorally based (Zettler, 2021). These approaches attempt to enhance therapist–client collaboration by creating a non-confrontational environment of trust and safety. The relationship dimension of interpersonal influence is paramount in trauma-informed care. The emergence of trauma-informed treatment for *all* justice-involved persons is a relatively new area, although it has been present for decades in the treatment of women (Lehrer, 2021) and approximately 15 years for youth (Zettler, 2021). A meta-analysis of trauma-informed treatments for youth ($k = 30$) found significant increases in emotional well-being but no effect on delinquency (Olaghere, Wilson, & Kimbrell, 2021). However, another study reported that when the risk and need principles are applied in trauma-informed care, reductions in recidivism were found (Baglivio, Zettler, Craig, & Wolff, 2021). Integrating this area with the RNR model will hopefully improve the lives of many correctional clients.

Closing Comments

An overall model of programming suggests that the design and operation of effective programs are contingent upon a number of factors:

1. Selecting appropriate criminogenic needs, which, if changed, are associated with shifts in the chances of criminal behavior.

2. Offering services that are able to produce the desired changes in criminogenic needs (i.e., services along the relationship and structuring dimensions).

3. Building a program structure that will support effective process (for example, selecting and training staff in ways compatible with desired process and outcome).

4. Matching cases and programs to clients according to risk, need, and responsivity.

5. Conducting programs with due concern for justice, ethicality, and cost-effectiveness.

Paraphrasing Andrews and Kiessling (1980: pp. 462–463), effective rehabilitative efforts involve workers who are interpersonally warm, tolerant, and flexible, yet sensitive to conventional rules and procedures. These workers make use of the authority inherent in their position without engaging in interpersonal domination (i.e., they are "firm but fair"); they demonstrate in vivid ways their own prosocial attitudes, values, and beliefs; and they enthusiastically engage the client in the process of increasing rewards for noncriminal activity. The worker exposes and makes attractive the alternatives to procriminal attitudes, styles of thinking, and ways of acting. The worker does not depend upon the presumed benefits of a warm relationship with their clients and does not assume that they will self-discover these alternatives. The alternatives are demonstrated through words and actions, and explorations of the alternatives are encouraged through modeling, reinforcement, and specific guidance.

Worth Remembering

1. From "nothing works" to "what works" is an astonishing story at the nexus of ideology, professional identity, science, and public policy.

   Literally, the evidence did not matter for many years. Now, evidence does matter and evidence-based practice is an ideal in many justice, correctional, forensic, and community prevention agencies.

2. The positive effects of adherence to RNR are very robust across different types of programs, persons, settings, and methodological conditions.

   The effectiveness of treatment has been attributed to a host of variables outside the RNR principles. However, even after accounting for these factors, the RNR principles continue to offer the major explanation for program effectiveness.

3. Specific responsivity recognizes the importance of trauma-informed rehabilitation in facilitating humane and effective interventions.

Recommended Readings

Francis Cullen's (2012) review of three textbooks on rehabilitation is important for two reasons. First, it provides a personal and immensely readable account of the "nothing works" and the "what works" eras. One of the books reviewed is generally supportive of the RNR model (*Rehabilitation, Crime and Justice*, by Raynor and Robinson). The other two books offer alternatives to RNR (*What Else Works? Creative Work with Offenders*, edited by Brayford, Cowe, and Deering, 2011; *How Offenders Transform Their Lives*, edited by Veysey, Christian, and Martinez, 2009). These later books advocate different approaches to rehabilitation—the Good Lives Model by the former and Desistance by the latter (more will be said about these two models in the last chapter). Thus, the reader of these scholarly works is exposed to both the advantages and disadvantages of RNR. The second reason for reading Cullen's essay is his cautionary analysis of the alternatives to RNR. Whether the reader agrees or not with Cullen's conclusion that "my money remains with the Canadians" (p. 109), it remains an article worth reading.

This chapter gave an accounting of the "nothing works" to "what works." For another perspective of this story, Francis Cullen's (2013) chapter in the *Crime and Justice* series is highly recommended. Not only does Cullen share a very personal perspective, but he also outlines what needs to be done over the coming years to entrench rehabilitation in the criminal justice system and criminology itself.

 Visit the Instructor and Student Resource to access additional exercises, videos and study materials to support this chapter: psychologycriminalconduct.routledge.com

CHAPTER 12 Creating and Maintaining RNR Adherence: A Real-World Challenge

This chapter describes fundamental interpersonal influence processes and the challenges of applying evidence-informed RNR into "real-world" settings. Notice that the term "evidence-informed" is used rather than "evidence-based." Until a newly developed treatment program is formally evaluated and shown to reduce recidivism, the program can only say that it was informed by the existing research. This chapter deals with the classic issue of bridging the gap between research and practice. What is meant by "real world"? In Lipsey's (1999: p. 620) review of 400 juvenile treatment studies, a real-world program was one that was "initiated and supervised by personnel *other* than the researcher and implemented in *ordinary* youth service or juvenile justice settings" (italics added). In the expanded treatment meta-analysis, real-world programs fell into two categories: (1) mixed (evaluator involved *or* more than 100 cases), and (2) real world/routine (more than 100 cases and evaluator not involved). In contrast to real-world programs are demonstration projects. Demonstration projects have fewer than 100 cases and the evaluator(s) have responsibility for the design and delivery of the service.

Table 12.1 summarizes the effectiveness of treatment as a function of demonstration, mixed, and real-world programming. Inspection of Table 12.1 reveals that RNR adherence was associated with recidivism reduction in the case of each of the three types of programs. With full adherence, an *r* of 0.15 for real-world programs is modest compared to the comparable mean effects reported for demonstration projects (0.34). Yet a mean effect of 0.15 looks very good compared to the increased crime associated with real-world programs that show no adherence to RNR (−0.02). Treatment can work in real-world conditions. This is a conclusion also made by others. Lipsey's (1999) analysis of 196 "practical rehabilitative programs" led him to write that "rehabilitative programs of a practical 'real world' sort clearly can be effective" (p. 641).

Petrosino and Soydan (2005) reviewed 12 meta-analyses that explored the effects of program developer involvement in evaluations. Eleven of the 12 meta-analyses reported a positive correlation between involvement and effect size.

DOI: 10.4324/9781003292128-15

TABLE 12.1 **Effect Size by Level of RNR Adherence and by Demonstration, Mixed, and Real-World Programming (*k*)**

Program type	Level of adherence with the RNR			
	0 (None)	1	2	3 (Full)
Demonstration (47)	.01 (1)	.07 (7)	.31 (16)	.34 (23)
Mixed (118)	−.03 (30)	−.02 (28)	.20 (34)	.24 (26)
Real-world (209)	−.02 (93)	.04 (71)	.09 (34)	.15 (11)

Additionally, they conducted their own quantitative review of 300 randomized experimental evaluations. Averaged across 24 tests in which the evaluator was the program developer or creator, the rate of successful correctional outcomes was 61.8 percent in the experimental group, compared to a success rate of 38.3 percent for the control group. This translates to an *r* of 0.25.

In the general psychotherapy literature, it is well-established that when the author of a study is both the developer and evaluator of the treatment more positive results are found (Dragioti, Dimoliatis, Fountoulakis, & Evangelou, 2015). The larger effect size in treatment studies when the evaluator is involved is generally referred to as the allegiance effect (Boccaccini, Marcus, & Murrie, 2017). Some have interpreted the finding that effect sizes are larger when a researcher is involved as evidence of an artificial inflation of the effectiveness of treatment. Because many "evaluator-involved" studies are one-time, demonstration studies with extensive training and supervision of staff, the demonstration projects do not accurately represent what is really "out there." Programs may be efficacious in small-scale, tightly controlled demonstration projects but less effective in routine ("regular" or "real-world") programming.

As the reader has probably surmised, the issues are with quality control and the integrity of services. Although the illustration provided concerns treatment, it is also relevant to risk/need assessment. If staff are poorly trained and monitored in the administration of risk/need instruments, then errors in classification and prediction increase. Evaluator involvement is important, but why?

There are two obvious interpretations. The "cynical" interpretation is that involved researchers make decisions or take actions that improperly (if sometimes unknowingly) bias the findings in the direction favorable to the effectiveness of the program under investigation. This interpretation is often used to portray expert witnesses in court cases who are given financial incentives for adopting a certain position. The second, "high-fidelity" interpretation is that involved researchers take steps to enhance the integrity of service delivery in legitimate ways.

There is a third and fourth interpretation. Third, it is quite possible that evaluators who are involved with the programs they are evaluating are simply more knowledgeable of "what works." In the very direct words of Petrosino and Soydan (2005: p. 445): "involved researchers may be designing and testing 'smarter interventions.' They may know the clients, correctional workers, and effective correctional programming much more so than external evaluators." A fourth interpretation is that the positive effects of involved researchers reflect some combination of the "bias," "high-fidelity," and "smart" interpretations.

The remainder of this chapter reviews the implementation science on the two major RNR applications: assessment and rehabilitation. Implementation science refers to the systematic study of how new practices can be transformed into everyday practice (Stirman & Beidas, 2020). Taking an innovation into the real world must be done "with fidelity" and this requires proper staff training, supervision, and monitoring (Andrews & Dowden, 2005). The discussion on assessment is relatively brief because the solution to good assessment is straightforward (staff training and monitoring). The discussion on treatment is more complex and requires a more careful review.

Fidelity in Risk/Need Assessment

There is good, solid evidence for the predictive validity of many risk/needs assessment instruments. However, even when we examine such well-validated instruments as the Level of Service (LS) instruments described in Chapter 10, there is considerable variability in the predictive validity of the LS across studies. Sometimes the validity estimates are in the 0.40s and other times they are in the 0.20s or much lower. What explains this variation? There are many possible reasons for this state of affairs, and only four are presented here.

1. *Resistance to accepting new, but superior, assessment models.* Although actuarial risk/needs assessments are almost the standard across prison and probation systems (Bonta & Wormith, 2018; Kemshall, 2019), clinical judgment and reliance on assessments of psychopathology remain relatively popular among individual practitioners. In a survey of 102 forensic specialists 12.8 percent of respondents reported using projective tests sometimes or frequently to assess nonsexual violence risk (McLaughlin & Kan, 2014). Archer, Wheeler, and Vauter's (2016) review of the literature found the MMPI (a general measure of psychopathology), used by approximately two-thirds of forensic psychologists in their evaluations. Turning to corrections, Oleson and his colleagues (Oleson, VanBenschoten, Robinson, Lowenkamp, & Holsinger, 2012) surveyed 1,040 probation officers and found 48 percent of them ranked mental health as a top three "criminogenic" need. These findings suggest that some of the behavior of professionals is indeed difficult to change, and this resistance is justified by "classification destruction techniques" described in Resource Note 10.2.

2. *The allegiance effect.* The allegiance effect was introduced at the beginning of this chapter, and it has been debated in the general psychology assessment literature as well as the correctional literature. Usually, the skeptical interpretation is taken—the high predictive validity of an instrument found by the evaluators is because of bias since they are also the authors of the instrument.

   Of course, another interpretation is that the authors really care about the instrument and want to make sure it is administered correctly, and because they know the instrument better than anyone else, they are "smarter" about implementation. Andrews and his colleagues (Andrews, Bonta, et al. 2011) examined the reasons why predictive validity of the LS varied so widely. The major sources of variability examined were country, gender, length of follow-up, and author allegiance. They found, after introducing controls for country, that the predictive validity of the LS improved with length of follow-up and author allegiance. Further examination of the data led Andrews et al. to conclude that author allegiance brings "integrity... to the administration of their own instruments... by maximizing measurement precision" (p. 426). At a very minimum, authors of risk/needs instruments should be fully transparent and disclose their potential conflict of interest. All journals require this but in one review of 25 studies none of the authors did so (Singh, Grann, & Fazel, 2013).

3. *Organizational inattention to the integrity of assessment.* Until recently, there have been few studies examining whether the assessment instruments are used as they were designed to be used. That is, do classification and probation officers use the information to improve adherence to the RNR model? Although there are reports that officers who administer risk/needs assessments tend to follow the risk and need principles better (e.g., Miller & Palmer, 2020) this may be more the exception than the rule. In a review of 73 studies, Jodi Viljoen, Dana Cochrane, and Melissa Jonnson (2018) found that adherence to the risk principle was described as "moderate" and the need principle was "limited." These findings suggest that correctional agencies need to pay close attention to how assessments actually influence correctional responses.

Staff buy-in and training are probably the two most important things an agency can do to maximize success with a new offender assessment instrument (Gleicher, 2020; Viljoen & Vincent, 2020). For example, according to Haas and DeTardo-Bora (2009), when 128 parole officers, counselors, and case managers were surveyed about their views of the newly introduced LSI-R classification system, only 32 percent thought that it was a good idea for the agency. Although most staff dutifully complete the risk/need assessments, nearly 85 percent in one survey (Miller & Maloney, 2013), those that do not will produce assessments with poor predictive accuracy (Flores, Lowenkamp, Holsinger, & Latessa, 2006).

Failure to devote sufficient resources to training can result in a number of problems. Staff are often reluctant to change what they have done for years and adopt a new assessment procedure (Lowenkamp, Latessa, & Holsinger, 2004). Second, even after careful training, steps must be taken to ensure that levels of competency are maintained. For example, soon after the introduction of the LSI-R in the state of Colorado, a review of LSI-R records found that 13 percent of 336 files had errors (Bonta, Bogue, Crowley, & Motiuk, 2001). Many of the errors were simple addition mistakes, but others dealt with misunderstandings of how some of the items were to be scored. To the credit of Colorado's correctional system, the administration of risk/needs assessments was monitored and steps taken to improve the assessment process. Many jurisdictions fail to monitor and correct such an important process.

When staff are well trained and administer the assessments with integrity, the pay-offs can be significant. For example, Luong and Wormith (2011) examined the assessment and case management practices for 192 young offenders in the Canadian province of Saskatchewan. First of all, they found that supervision levels and case management plans followed the risk and needs assessment. That is, higher-risk cases were seen more frequently, and intervention plans followed most of the criminogenic needs identified. More importantly, intervention targeting needs was significantly related to reduced recidivism ($r = 0.21$). Because of the importance of training and supervision, many developers of risk/needs tools have developed networks of test experts to ensure that the training of users is conducted to maximize fidelity to the assessment instrument (Wormith & Bonta, 2021).

4. *Methodological biases.* Evaluations of risk/needs instruments are not without errors. Designing and implementing the perfect study is impossible and for this reason many journals use a peer review process to weed out studies that use poor methodologies, analyses, and interpretations of the results. A case in point is a large meta-analytic review by Viljoen and her colleagues (Viljoen, Jonnson, Cochrane, Vargen, & Vincent 2019). They reviewed 22 studies on the impact of using risk/needs instruments on three criminal justice outcomes (recidivism, pretrial detention, and postconviction placements). Their preliminary analyses showed that the use of these assessment tools was associated with some positive outcomes (e.g., less restrictive placements). However, when Viljoen et al. applied a risk of bias scale that measured, for example how participants were selected and the inclusion of missing data, the positive effects disappeared.

Using risk/needs and other risk assessments in the real world has tremendous implications and offers many promises. Most obvious are that the results from assessments can impact individual liberties, the achievement of satisfying and productive lives, and the safety of communities. As reviewed, the implementation of risk/needs scales by correctional agencies is not without difficulties. However, researchers have become acutely aware of some of the barriers to quality implementation of risk/needs assessment and some have even proposed a "road map" for research to address this area (Vijoen & Vincent, 2020).

Fidelity in Correctional Treatment

There are a number of examples of "star" programs that have turned out to be failures. Star programs are treatment interventions that have a strong record of success (e.g., supported by meta-analytic reviews). It is instructive

TABLE 12.2 Failures in RNR Implementation

Study	Unexpected finding(s)	Why the failure?
Substance misuse treatment for drug-involved clients (Farabee et al., 2004)	Increased recidivism	High-risk clients denied the most intensive services (violation of the Risk principle)
Functional Family Therapy (FFT) and Multi-Systemic Therapy (MST) (Barnoski, 2004)	FFT had no effect; MST increased recidivism	Poorly skilled therapists; failure to implement with integrity; (violation of the principles of GPCSL-based Staff Practices and Management)
Cognitive skills programs in England and Wales (Raynor, 2008)	System-wide failure in reducing recidivism	Risk/need assessments not available on a routine basis; therapists poorly trained (violation of Risk, Need, Structured Assessments, GPCSL-based Staff Practices, and Management principles)
RNR-based cognitive-behavioral treatment (Borseth, Myer, & Makarios, 2021)	No difference in recidivism; higher for those referred to substance misuse treatment	Hours of treatment approximately same across risk groups and insufficient dosage (less than 100 hours); up to a third of clients referred to program for whom there was no identified need (violation of Risk and Need principles)
Cognitive-behavioral and substance misuse program in New York (Wilson & Davis, 2006)	Increased recidivism	Involuntary participation; no risk/need assessment; clients with no substance problem placed in program; poorly trained staff (violation of Respect for the Person, Risk, Need, Structured Assessments, GPCSL-based Staff Practices, and Management principles)

to examine some of these failures to understand what went wrong. Some examples are shown in Table 12.2. In every case, the failure can be traced to a breakdown in the program's adherence to RNR. The RNR model would ask a number of questions when faced with a treatment that should have succeeded but did not. What is the risk level of those receiving treatment and their criminogenic needs? Are the intensity of treatment and the intermediate targets of change matched to risk and criminogenic needs? Were the therapists/counselors trained and supervised with regard to relationship and structuring skills? All of these questions ask: To what extent is the treatment in adherence with the principles of RNR?

The brief case studies of program failure described in Table 12.2 strongly suggest that even programs that were designed with reference to "what works" are often not well implemented. If agencies are serious about crime prevention, then routine programming has to overcome a number of challenges.

Some Major Barriers to RNR Adherence

A major issue here is whether the empirically validated principles of RNR can be implemented in the real world with sufficient levels of adherence so that reduced reoffending is actually achieved. It may appear straightforward but, in fact, it requires major policy and organizational changes and significant efforts on the part of managers and staff for adherence to be accomplished.

Some of them are as follows:

1. *Staff Roles.* Many correctional agencies are viewed by their staff and managers as the administrators of punishment and officers of the court. With the addition of an expectation of rehabilitation, the role of correctional agencies and agents changes dramatically. Now they are being asked to see themselves as human service agencies, albeit in a justice context. This is a situation that may be unpalatable to staff or requires some convincing to balance the two roles (see Figure 12.1).

2. *Community Resources.* Agencies that do have mental health counselors on staff must bring their counseling staff to think in RNR terms. Yet many mental health counselors have never heard of "RNR" and do not even think of reduced reoffending as a valued objective, focusing instead on reducing anxiety, increasing self-esteem, and the like.

3. *Staff Training.* Even if the setting buys into RNR, it may not know how to do it. Staff have to learn about RNR assessment and how to use specific instruments. They have to learn how to build a service plan consistent with RNR. They have to learn how to deliver that service. They may have to acquire the necessary relationship and structuring skills. They need

Figure 12.1

Role of Community Supervision Officers: Punish or Rehabilitate?

Source: Courtesy San Bernadino County Probation

feedback and reinforcement on how well they are doing so that their good work can continue and improve.

4. *Inter-agency Cooperation*. Even if the agency and agents have it all worked out, the broader system may begin to interfere. A local judge may begin to sentence low-risk cases to the program, or to send cases without a substance use problem to a substance misuse treatment program, or to send psychopaths to a program built for moderate-risk cases. As a consequence, inappropriate cases are placed in a program because the available seats need to be filled.

5. *Management*. Staff considerations are very important if RNR programs are going to succeed. If relationship and structuring skills, to be discussed shortly, are crucial to quality programming, there are three key management functions. First, select staff on the basis of their possession of relationship and structuring skills. Second, provide preservice and in-service training in those skills. Thirdly, provide high-quality clinical supervision to the workers. Staff need to know how they are doing and receive reinforcement when they are doing well and immediate assistance when they are not performing at the highest levels.

It is also important for management to foster a positive and supportive organizational environment. Failure to do so will detrimentally affect staff attitudes toward evidence-based practice (Debus-Sherrill, Breno, & Taxman, 2023; Viglione & Blasko, 2018).

6. *The Difficult Client.* A major issue is providing services to higher-risk cases. Higher-risk cases are less likely to voluntarily enter programs and more likely to drop out (Brunner, Neumann, et al., 2019; Olver et al., 2011). Indeed, dropping out of treatment is a serious matter. In a recent meta-analysis of programs for substance use disorder, it was estimated that approximately 30 percent of clients will not complete treatment (Lappan, Brown, & Hendricks, 2020). In part, this is a specific responsivity factor. Careful attention to several elements is called for, including all of the following: remove barriers to participation, build on strengths, and be responsive to motivational issues. Respect for personal autonomy and being collaborative in program planning are very important. Just as clinicians and correctional workers need to know how they are doing (as in Number 5 above), high-risk clients may profit from information on the meaning of their risk, need, and strength scores and the consequences of program completion relative to the consequences of dropping out. For example, King and Heilbrun (2021) found that providing clients with feedback on their LS/CMI results increased their motivation to change.

7. *Clinical Supervision.* Some supervisors of direct service staff may not possess a deep understanding of the program for which they are responsible, and they may not possess or even be aware of the relationship and structuring skills that are basic to the high-quality selection, training, and clinical supervision of staff. In brief, clinical supervision of front-line staff is needed, something often lacking in many correctional agencies (Salisbury, Sundt, & Boppre, 2019).

8. *External Unexpected Events.* Sometimes something comes along and agencies and staff have to pivot in how they do things. The COVID-19 epidemic certainly had an enormous impact on corrections. On a general level, and not surprisingly given the restriction of social movement, there was a decrease in crime internationally (Nivette, Zahnow, et al., 2021). In order to control the spread of COVID-19 and maintain the safety of prisoners and staff, prisons transferred people into the community, placing added burden onto probation and parole to supervise releasees (Brennan, 2020; Hummer, 2020). Community supervision which relied heavily on face-to-face interactions now had to move to remote supervision. With it came a host of challenges: what to do with high-risk clients, how to recognize risk behavior (e.g., you can't smell alcohol on the person's breath), how do you build a therapeutic relationship? The list can go on and on.

Although there are clearly some problems with remote supervision (see Phillips, 2022), there are examples of probation and parole agencies being quite adept at responding to the challenges created by COVID-19. In a survey of over 1,000 probation and parole officers in the US, Schwalbe and Koetzle (2021) found that the number of contacts did not change compared to pre-pandemic. The number of contacts simply shifted from face-to-face to virtual. In fact, with video conferencing contacts increased. Perhaps more importantly from the perspective of this book, the content of discussions became more therapeutic (e.g., more behavioral and less confrontative).

Assessment of Programs and Agencies

Is there a systematic, objective way of examining the potential effectiveness of a program without going through the time and expense of a formal evaluation? Two approaches have been used to answer this question. The first is the accreditation of a program by experts in the area (Rex & Raynor, 2008). For example, a sexual offender treatment program may be reviewed by an expert panel that examines treatment manuals, interviews therapists, and perhaps even the clients. The experts then reach a consensus as to how well the program matches what the evidence says about treatment effectiveness. The accreditation process is similar to the structured clinical judgment approach in the assessment of offender risk.

A more structured, actuarial approach is the use of scorable "check lists." A number of these assessment program protocols have been developed. A good example, and one of the first to be developed, is the Correctional Program Assessment Inventory-2010 (CPAI-2010; Gendreau, Thériault, & Andrews, 2012). The CPAI-2010 includes a measure of adherence to the RNR model. The content is briefly reviewed in Table 12.3.

The CPAI-2010 exercise is an important learning experience for agencies. It asks them to consider what their program is about and why they do what they do, and asks them to link intermediate objectives to ultimate effects on criminal behavior. The CPAI-2010 is completed by certified evaluators who: (1) interview staff, managers, and clients, (2) review agency documents and case files, (3) complete observations of ongoing program activities and interactions, and (4) conduct systematic observation of staff relationship and structuring skills in their therapeutic interactions with clients (see Section G in Table 12.3).

The validity of the instrument has been demonstrated by directly visiting and examining programs in the field. Christopher Lowenkamp, Edward Latessa, and Paula Smith (2006) surveyed 38 community-based halfway house programs in Ohio with a shortened 62-item version of the CPAI-2010. The recidivism rate for residents in the programs—more than 3,000 of them—was compared to a group of matched parolees who did not participate in residential programming. Figure 12.2 displays the reduction in recidivism by CPAI categories (68 percent of the programs were in the unsatisfactory range; not one program scored in the highest category, "very satisfactory"). As shown, the higher the CPAI category, the lower the recidivism rate. The correlation between CPAI score and a new offense was 0.35. Similar findings from youth facilities have also been reported (Lowenkamp, Makarios, Latessa, Lemke, & Smith, 2010).

TABLE 12.3 Overview of the Correctional Program Assessment Inventory-2010 (CPAI-2010)

A. A 10-item subscale of program demographics that can be correlated to future research. This section is not considered for scoring.

B. Organizational Culture: a 9-item subscale to evaluate clarity of goals, ethical standards, organizational context, harmony, staff turnover, in service training, self-evaluation and agency outreach.

C. Program Implementation/Maintenance: a 10-item subscale to evaluate program design and implementation, value congruence with stakeholders, piloting, maintenance of staffing and credentials, qualifications of managers and staff members with specific attention to selection, training and clinical supervision.

D. Management/Staff Characteristics: an 18-item subscale to examine management and staff experience, training, skill levels, and attitudes and beliefs regarding treatment services.

E. Client Risk/Need Practices: a 13-item subscale to measure adherence to the principles of risk, need, and responsivity assessment.

F. Program Characteristics: a 25-item subscale to measure adherence to RNR principles with an emphasis on treatment targets, intervention strategies, and relapse prevention.

G. Core Correctional Practice: a 45-item subscale to evaluate observed elements of core correctional practice including relationship skills and the structuring skills of problem solving, modeling, reinforcement, and skill building (i.e., GPCSL-based Staff Practices in the RNR model).

H. Inter-Agency Communication: a 5-item subscale to examine brokerage, referral, advocacy, and coordination.

I. Evaluation: an 8-item subscale to assess in-program and post-program research and monitoring activity.

The creation and development of these program assessment tools offers a new way of examining and improving services to justice-involved persons. Some of these instruments are very brief (e.g., the four-item Standardized Program Evaluation Protocol; Howell & Lipsey, 2012), some are a modified CPAI (e.g., Correctional Program Checklist; Duriez, Sullivan, Latessa, & Brusman Lovins, 2018), some are specific to RNR adherence (the RNR Program Tool; Ramezani, Bhati, Murphy, Routh, & Taxman, 2022), and others are intended for specific contexts (e.g., Correctional Program Checklist-Drug Court; Blair, Sullivan, Lux, Thielo, & Gormsen, 2016). Whatever the form or purpose, some researchers and program administrators are taking treatment implementation fidelity issues seriously.

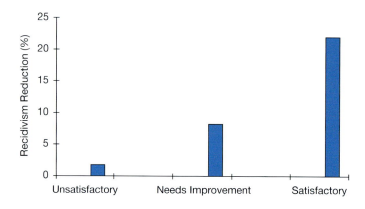

Figure 12.2

Reduction in Recidivism by CPAI Score

Although these findings give a sense of optimism in program development, a recent review by Farringer and her colleagues (Farringer, Duriez, Manchak, & Sullivan, 2021) is sobering. They reviewed the results from administering the Correctional Program Checklist (CPC) to 563 programs over a 14-year period. They found that RNR adherence, as measured by the CPC, improved from 2007 to 2012 and after that deteriorated to 2018 (the last year measured). Similarly, Jill Viglione (2019) found that after *eight* years of an agency adopting RNR practices and training staff the probation officers failed, by-and-large, to properly formulate case plans based on risk/needs assessment and refer clients to programming based on their needs. The problem of adopting evidence-based practice is not unique to the criminal justice system.

Finally, the challenges of implementing RNR into routine practice is reflected in a meta-analysis of 29 prison-based treatment programs that were evaluated experimentally (Beaudry, Yu, Perry, & Fazel, 2021). What is noteworthy is that the authors selected studies post-1990 when the RNR principles were first published. They could not identify one study that followed RNR. In medicine it has been estimated that it takes 17 years for new evidence-based practice to be widely adopted by doctors (Morris, Wooding, & Grant, 2011). Sustainability of a new initiative is a challenge for many professions.

The Components of Effective Correctional Supervision and Treatment

We are assuming that a correctional agency (and its management and staff) value the objective of reduced recidivism. In order to achieve this objective, the task of staff and managers is to increase prosocial "expressions" and decrease procriminal "expressions" of their clients. "Expressions" means attitudes, thoughts, and behaviors. The first step in altering the balance of prosocial and procriminal expressions is to ensure that managers and staff are able to recognize and distinguish between the two. In correctional agencies there are individual differences in the level of socialization among staff, and staff are sometimes inattentive to their own expressions of procriminal attitudes. For example, some staff may develop a cynicism regarding the criminal justice system that is readily reinforced by clients. Some staff may adopt "con talk" to show their clients how "down to earth" they can be and to gain their acceptance.

Procriminal expressions include procriminal attitudes and thoughts (recall Chapter 6). These include: (1) negative attitudes toward the law, courts, and police, (2) tolerance for rule violations in general and violations of the law in particular, (3) identification with criminal others, and (4) endorsement of exonerating mechanisms. Prosocial expressions include: (1) an emphasis on the negative consequences of law violations for the client, the victim, and the community at large, (2) rejection of, or placing more realistic limits on, "rationalizations" or "justifications" for law violations, and (3) expressions of the risks involved in associating with criminal others or in accepting their belief systems. Some specific criminal acts, such as sexual offenses, violent offenses, and intimate partner violence, have their own supporting cognitions and vocabulary to which workers must be sensitive.

Procriminal expression includes association with criminal others; prosocial expression is reduced association with criminal others and increased association with prosocial others. Procriminal expressions include continuing to seek out risky situations or circumstances (e.g., the same old bar scene) rather than avoiding them. The following examples of prosocial expressions are based on the links between self-management and problem-solving skills in relation to criminal behavior: (1) examining one's own conduct, making a judgment about how well the behavior corresponds to their prosocial attitudes and making self-evaluative comments—"good" or "bad"—depending upon how well the standards are being met, (2) thinking of the consequences before acting, and (3) weighing the merits of alternative ways of behaving in a given situation. Procriminal expressions in this area further include: (1) a lack of self-monitoring and self-evaluation, (2) evaluation against standards that are too severe, too lax, or frankly procriminal, (3) an insensitivity to or denial of significant problems, and/or (4) an inability to consider new ways of behaving in problem situations.

It is insufficient to describe the specifics of effective practice as adherence with the general responsivity principle of RNR. To simply say "employ behavioral and cognitive social learning procedures" does not provide sufficient guidance to program planners and managers. That is why the subset of Organizational Principles is part of the RNR model (Chapter 9). Principle 14 specifies two crucial sets of skills and competencies. The skill sets of relationship and structuring factors are based on GPCSL theory, but they are very practical. It is possible for correctional workers to recognize when the skills are being employed and when they are not. They are clear enough that with some training research staff can observe an interaction between a correctional worker and a client and "score" the interactions in terms of adherence with the principle of GPCSL-based staff practices. The practices provide guidance for the crucial managerial tasks of the selection of staff, the training of service delivery people, and the ongoing clinical supervision of those responsible for the delivery of services. This portion of the chapter is not more data but material intended to induce the look and feel of effective correctional counseling.

The Dimensions of Effective Correctional Counseling

1. Relationship

A major goal of correctional counseling is to promote prosocial thinking and behaviors in the clients. Workers who are successful in achieving this goal: (1) establish high-quality relationships with their clients, (2) demonstrate prosocial modeling, (3) reinforce the client's prosocial thoughts and behaviors, and (4) disapprove of the client's procriminal thoughts and behaviors, while at the same time demonstrating alternatives. Before the correctional worker can apply effective structuring skills (e.g., serve as a prosocial model and a source of reinforcement), a positive relationship must be established. Here are the elements of a positive relationship.

A high-quality interpersonal relationship creates a setting in which structuring skills can more easily take place. Important to such a relationship is an open, flexible, and enthusiastic style wherein people feel free to express their opinions, feelings, and experiences. Also needed are mutual liking, respect, and caring. The expression of disapproval is meaningful against a background of attentiveness, expressions of understanding ("real," not "phony"), mutual enjoyment of recreational activities, pleasant discussion, use of humor, and frequent contact.

Most workers in the criminal justice system are in a position of power and authority relative to the client. Ineffective use of authority relies on monitoring for compliance with the rules and initiating negative sanctions when violations are detected (i.e., an enforcement role). An effective and more helpful style of authority is a "firm but fair" approach that includes monitoring but also entails respectful guidance toward compliance (i.e., a helper role). Balancing the enforcement and helper roles is a challenge when working with justice-involved persons (Kennealy, Skeem, Manchak, & Eno Louden, 2012; Lovins, Cullen, Latessa, & Johnson, 2018; Trotter, 2013), but it is not insurmountable. Staff can meet the challenge by explaining to their clients that they have a professional obligation to their agency to address noncompliance and a responsibility to help their clients become more prosocial. They can also set goals collaboratively with their clients rather than impose goals. Through honest and mutually respectful discussion of roles and goals, relationship building is enhanced.

2. *Structuring*

Changing the balance between procriminal and prosocial expressions involves more than establishing a positive relationship with the client. If that was all that was needed, then nondirective, relationship-based counseling techniques or motivational interviewing would be sufficient. However, justice-involved persons need to learn new prosocial behaviors, and this depends upon the principles of learning discussed in Chapter 3. The key ingredients are as follows.

(a) Effective Model

1. Is respected and liked (i.e., is generally a source of rewards rather than only of costs or neutral events).

2. Demonstrates behavior in concrete and vivid ways.

3. Takes care to illustrate the behavior in some concrete detail when only a verbal description is being offered.

4. Rewards himself/herself for exhibiting the behavior and makes specific reference to the rewards if only a verbal illustration is offered.

5. Rewards the person for exhibiting the modeled behavior or some approximation of it.

6. Makes evident the general similarities between himself/herself and the other person (e.g., "I had a similar problem at your age").

7. Recognizes that the other person may have good reason to fear or distrust the modeled behavior and hence will model a "coping" as opposed to a "master" style (Staff: "I too was afraid to approach the teacher about my grades but, scared as I was, I went up and asked her about it," versus "I just walked up to her and…").

(b) Effective Reinforcement.
A high-quality relationship is a source of a variety of interpersonal rewards. Sometimes simple eye contact and statements that show the person is listening will be sufficient; at other times, there must be more emphatic expressions of support and agreement. Sometimes concrete events (such as a shared movie or shopping trip) will be the rewards.

High-level rewards in an interpersonal situation include the following elements:

1. Strong, emphatic, and immediate statements of approval, support, and agreement with regard to what the client has said or done.

2. Elaboration of the reasons why agreement and approval are being offered (i.e., exactly what it is you agree with or approve of).

3. Expression of support should be sufficiently intense to distinguish it from the background levels of support, concern, and interest that are normally offered.

With high-level verbal and gestural approval and with elaboration on the reasons for approval, there is an opportunity to demonstrate prosocial expressions while offering feedback. The helper's statement of approval may close with a gentle probe that encourages the client to explore further the issues involved in the prosocial expression.

(c) **Effective Disapproval.** Just as a high-quality relationship sets the occasion for effective modeling and rewards, it also establishes the conditions necessary for effective disapproval. Within the context of an open and warm relationship, disapproval may be delivered with less fear that the client will try to avoid or escape future contact with the staff member, and less chance of an aggressive response by the client. Within such a relationship, a simple reduction in the normal levels of expressed interest and concern may function as a cost. Finally, we have the "4-to-1" rule: give at least four positive supportive statements for every punishing one. Imagine if this rule was in the opposite direction. Would it favor a positive relationship between the worker and the client?

High-level disapproval in an interpersonal situation is characterized by:

1. Strong, emphatic, and immediate statements of disapproval with what the client has said or done (including the nonverbal: a frown, or even an increase in the physical distance between the worker and the client).

2. Elaboration of the reason why you disagree and disapprove.

3. Provide a prosocial alternative (i.e., simple disapproval may tell the client what *not* to do but does not tell the client what *to do*).

4. The levels of disapproval should be immediately reduced and approval introduced when the client begins to express or approximate prosocial behavior.

From the point of view of most criminal justice-involved persons, it would be silly to communicate a blind support for the justice system in all of its day-to-day operations, to accept the notion that there are no situations under which criminal activity is reasonable, or to state that "crime never pays." At the same time, staff who have direct contact with clients will be ineffective if they are explicitly unsupportive of the system, enamored with the positive aspects of criminal activity, or accepting of the rationalizations for law violations. The effective helper exposes the client to prosocial alternatives, is able to distinguish between specific negative instances within the criminal justice system and its general ideals (e.g., between a particularly obnoxious policeman and the role of the police), and can explore with clients the limits of the common justifications for criminal activity.

(d) Cognitive Restructuring. Modeling, reinforcement, and disapproval are essential to learn new behaviors. However, it is important that the client understands that there is a link between thinking and behavior. This is the essence of the "cognitive-behavioral" approach to correctional counseling (see Resource Note 12.1 for a more in-depth description of the approach). Once the client accepts the idea that "what I think" leads to "what I do," then real progress can be made. Accepting a cognitive-behavioral model of change has two important consequences. First, the responsibility and control of behavior resides in the client. No one but the client can control their thoughts. Others cannot control what you think and, therefore, how you behave. This is personal agency in action.

RESOURCE NOTE 12.1

Cognitive-Behavioral Therapy: An Overview

Cognitive-behavioral therapy is highly structured, hands-on, concrete, and practical. Behaviors are learned by watching respected models demonstrate the behaviors and through the systematic application of rewards and costs. Behaviors to be learned are broken down into small, manageable steps that are practiced, rehearsed, and role played. Cognitive-behavioral therapies match the learning style of the majority of the clients in the criminal justice system who learn through doing better rather than through didactic teaching. It is little wonder that cognitive-behavioral interventions are more effective with this clientele than other intervention techniques (see Figure RN 12.1-1).

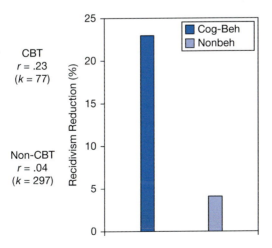

CBT
$r = .23$
$(k = 77)$

Non-CBT
$r = .04$
$(k = 297)$

Figure RN 12.1.1

Effectiveness of Cognitive Behavioral Treatment (CBT)

continued

The Difference Between Cognitive-Behavioral and General Behavioral Interventions

Many programs say that they use cognitive-behavioral programming, but on closer examination they are more "behavioral" with very little of the "cognitive" elements. General behavioral approaches are commonly found in skills training programs (e.g., job-related skills, assertiveness training, problem-solving skills). The analysis of behavior in behavioral interventions involves the identification of antecedents of behavior or "outside cues" and the external consequences of the behavior. Thus, changing the behavior requires changing the outside cues (e.g., avoiding friends who drink) or the external consequences of behavior (e.g., friends expressing disapproval for drinking). Cognitive-behavioral therapies place greater emphasis on antecedents to behavior that come from within the person ("inside cues") and consequences delivered by the self (i.e., personally mediated rewards and costs).

To illustrate the difference between the two approaches, a simple exercise is conducted as part of the training of probation officers in the Strategic Training Initiative in Community Supervision (see this chapter for more details on this project). The exercise starts with the trainer asking the participants to "stand up." Invariably, almost everyone does stand up (a few rascals remain seated). The trainer then asks each participant to explain to the group why they stood up or why they remained seated. The first explanation typically given is that "you told me to stand up." However, this explanation is insufficient given that some participants heard the same instruction but remained seated. With further discussion the group learns that many had a different thought running through their head that directly led to the behavior. A strictly behavioral explanation is all about the outside cues or antecedent stimuli and external consequences. A cognitive-behavioral explanation *requires* knowing the outside cues but also the inside cues or thought processes that directly led to the behavior and that follow the behavior.

Just as antecedents can be both external and internal, so are the consequences of behavior. The actor can deliver their own rewards or costs, and they may function independently from any external consequences. In the example of the "stand up" exercise (see Table RN 12.1-1), the person who stands up may say to himself or herself, "by standing up I showed the group leader that I can be counted on," thereby delivering an internal, personal reward. The group leader may also praise those who stood up and increase the density of rewards, but it may not be necessary to ensure future compliance to the request to stand up. On the other hand, all the praise in the world from the group leader may have little effect on the person who remained seated and who says, "I showed him that no one orders me around!" Using the example of the "stand up" exercise, the differences between a strictly behavioral and cognitive-behavioral understanding of behavior are outlined in Table RN 12.1-1.

continued

The Steps in Cognitive-Behavioral Treatment

The cognitive-behavioral approach to understanding behavior requires examining cognitive antecedents and consequences and then changing them. Procriminal attitudes, part of the Central Eight, are clearly cognitive antecedents to criminal behavior and a target for change. If you can replace procriminal thoughts with prosocial thoughts, then the likelihood of criminal behavior is diminished. When working with clients, this requires the following steps:

1. The client must understand and buy into the idea that his or her thinking directly leads to behavior. Many clients blame external events for their misbehavior and fail to see that there are intervening cognitions between the external events and their behavior. Therefore, they need to be taught that their inside cues (attitudes and cognitions) cause their behavior. Once they recognize this, then it also becomes apparent that only they can change their thoughts and control their behavior. The cognitive-behavioral model is self-empowering.

2. Teach the client how to identify personal thinking patterns related to the problem behaviors. Oftentimes, clients (and sometimes ourselves) do not recognize when rationalizations and excuses are made for antisocial behavior.

3. After the client understands the importance of cognitions in explaining behavior (steps 1 and 2), then teach the client to replace procriminal cognitions with alternative, prosocial cognitions. In the psychotherapy literature, this is referred to as *cognitive restructuring*.

The learning and maintenance of new behaviors is a gradual process that involves interpersonally mediated and nonmediated rewards and costs. In cognitive-behavioral interventions, personally mediated rewards and costs play a central role. The last step in cognitive-behavioral treatment is the following:

4. Facilitate the practice and generalization of the new cognitive and behavioral skills both in and outside of supervision sessions. This may involve modeling, role playing, graduated practice, and the assignment of "homework" (e.g., "try practicing this new thought the next time you get angry and tell me how it went at our next meeting"). At this point, not only is there abundant use of rewards from the therapist and others, but the client is also encouraged to deliver personally mediated rewards.

Cognitive-behavioral treatment is an effective approach to helping clients become more prosocial. It acknowledges the powerful influence of rewards and costs on behavior and pays particular attention to personal sources of antecedent and consequent control.

continued

The cognitive-behavioral approach also highlights the importance of personal agency in human behavior.

TABLE 12.1.1 "Stand Up" Exercise

Behavioral explanation			
Outside cue	**Inside cue**	**Behavior**	**Consequence**
"STAND UP"		*Stands up*	*Praise from trainer*

Cognitive explanation			
"STAND UP"	*I should do what I am told!*	*Stands up*	Outside consequence:
	She/He is the trainer!	*Stay seated*	*Praise from trainer*
	Ok sure!		Inside consequence:
	I don't take orders from anyone!		*"I can be counted on"*
			Outside consequence:
			Frown from trainer
			Inside consequence:
			"I showed him!"

Second, by recognizing the power of one's thoughts over one's actions, the client can take control of changing these thoughts. Instead of thinking, "it is OK to steal, the owner is insured," the client may say, "the owner worked hard to buy this and may not be insured." The reader can see how the two thoughts can lead to very different behaviors. For years, cognitive-behavioral psychologists have taught their clients how to replace problematic thoughts with less risky thoughts, a technique called "cognitive restructuring."

(e) **Skill Building.** The important skills to be taught include problem-solving and other aspects of self-management including cognitive restructuring. The elements of skill building are: (1) describe the components of the skill in detail, (2) model or demonstrate the skill components, (3) arrange for reinforced practice of the skill components through role playing with corrective feedback (i.e., rewards and disapproval), (4) extend learning opportunities through homework assignment, and (5) generally, provide opportunities to enhance the skill.

Although the focus has been on the justice-involved person, the dimensions of influence apply to all behavior. GPCSL is based on a *general* perspective of human behavior and specifies the personal and interpersonal mechanisms of learning. Effective therapists who deal with noncriminal behavior use the same intervention techniques just described. Even the layperson can benefit from these techniques when dealing with others within the contexts of family, friends, employment, and school. We now turn to the application of these principles in community correctional settings.

Training Correctional Staff to Apply the RNR Model

Recently, there have been a number of studies that examine the effectiveness of training staff to apply elements of the RNR model in their work with clients. The first such study was by Chris Trotter (1996) in Australia. Trotter (1996) provided a five-day training workshop to 12 probation officers. The training focused on prosocial modeling and problem-solving. The four-year recidivism rate for the 97 clients of the trained officers was 53.8 percent, and the rate for 273 clients of the 18 untrained officers was 64.0 percent. Since Trotter's initial study, there have been additional studies evaluating the results of training in RNR skills. Three training programs are particularly noteworthy because of the scale of implementation and their use of experimental designs for evaluation.

1. Strategic Training Initiative in Community Supervision (STICS)

In a meta-analysis of 15 studies yielding 26 effect size estimates, Bonta and his colleagues (Bonta, Rugge, Scott, Bourgon, & Yessine, 2008) found community supervision associated with only a 2 percent reduction in recidivism. Although some are cautiously optimistic that supervision in the community works (Smith, Heyes, et al., 2018), others are much more pessimistic. In a recent review of community supervision, the effectiveness of supervision was questioned, with a call of "extensive downsizing supervision or experimentation with its abolition" (p. 3.1; Lopoo, Schiraldi, & Ittner, 2023). However, the problem with the Lopoo et al.'s review is that the authors ignored the question of *why* supervision is not effective, especially in light of the treatment literature.

Returning to the Bonta et al. (2008) report, analyses of audio-recorded interviews between a sample of probation officers and their clients were also undertaken. The results showed that probation officers engaged in relatively few practices based on the RNR model (e.g., spent too much time on low-risk cases, did not target criminogenic needs sufficiently, made inadequate use of cognitive-behavioral techniques). Similar findings have been reported by other researchers. Without specific training, correctional officers do not maximize the potential benefits of RNR (Bonta, 2023; Labrecque, Schweitzer, & Smith, 2013).

The Bonta et al. (2008) findings set the stage for the STICS project. Work on the development of STICS by researchers at Public Safety Canada began in 2006, with the first study conducted between 2007 and 2010. The goal of the project was to deliver and evaluate the efficacy of training in intervention practices that are consistent with the RNR model. In designing STICS, the overall challenge was to translate the RNR model into specific, concrete actions that would be useful for probation officers, train the officers in their application, and evaluate the training's impact on the behavior of the officers and the clients they supervise.

Training Issues. Whether it is a treatment program for clients or a training program for probation officers, the issues are the same. The program must be guided by theory, be attentive to the general principles of risk-need-responsivity, and be concerned about the maintenance of skills.

The first task was to convey the message to probation officers that the antisocial behavior of their clients is under the control of the individual's cognitions and attitudes, with rewards and disapproval playing a role in the maintenance of behaviors. If probation officers accepted this GPCSL view then they would be more amenable to the idea that clients can learn prosocial behavior through the same processes that resulted in their criminal behavior.

The importance of having probation officers "buy in" to a theoretical view has been underestimated in many studies. The psychotherapy literature has long recognized the importance of an "explanation" for the problems of the patient and how these problems can be overcome (Wampold, 2015). Probation officers also need an explanation as to why they should change their behaviors and those of their clients and how they can do it. Therefore, the training program included didactic presentations of the research in support of GPCSL along with exercises to demonstrate the power of cognitive restructuring, prosocial modeling, reinforcement, and disapproval. Furthermore, probation officers were trained to teach their clients how cognitions control their behavior (for an example, see Resource Note 12.1), how rewards and costs influence future behaviors, and what they can do about it.

Figure 12.3 summarizes the modules of STICS training. As highlighted in Figure 12.3, the training placed considerable emphasis on recognizing expressions of procriminal attitudes in the clients, and how to use cognitive-behavioral techniques to replace these cognitions and attitudes with prosocial ones. Much of the first day of the three days of training was devoted to the issues just discussed.

Adherence to the responsivity principle was supported through exercises and practice on establishing rapport with the clients (relationship dimension) and teaching techniques such as cognitive restructuring, prosocial modeling, the effective use of rewards and disapproval, and various rehearsal strategies

Module	Description
1	Overview and Rationale
2	Risk Principle (medium to high)
3	Criminogenic Needs
4	**Procriminal Attitudes**
5	Responsivity—Building Rapport
6	**The Cognitive Behavioural Model**
7	**Cognitive Restructuring**
8	Prosocial Modeling and Reinforcement
9	Specific Intervention Techniques
10	Strategic Supervision

Figure 12.3

The STICS Training Modules

(structuring dimension). Probation officers supervise gender-diverse clients and often have clients from many different cultures and backgrounds. Therefore, training attended not only to gender issues but also to race and culture (i.e., specific responsivity).

The core of STICS training, and the most difficult task for the officers, occurred on the second day, when the focus was on the cognitive-behavioral model and cognitive restructuring. It was a challenge for probation officers because they themselves had to learn the basics of the cognitive-behavioral model and because it required them to teach cognitive restructuring skills to their clients (see Resource Note 12.2 for a description of the model and how it was taught). The emphasis was on making it concrete and understandable to the client (for example, "procriminal thoughts" were called "tapes," and "pro-social thoughts" were called "counters").

It was also important to provide probation officers with a structure to their individual session (typically lasting about 25 minutes). Most probation departments have policies that are relatively silent on what the probation officer should do when meeting a client for supervision. The only exception is to ensure that the client is complying with the conditions of probation. Probation officers were asked to structure each and every individual session into four components (Figure 12.4).

The first component was a brief "check-in" lasting no more than five minutes. The check-in involved spending time enhancing the working relationship with the client, checking for any new developments in the client's situation that may require immediate attention, and making sure that the probation conditions were being followed. The second component was a "review" of the last session, including the homework (see below). This review was designed to facilitate learning via discussions and/or rehearsal of previous material and linking one supervision session to the next. The third component was to actually conduct an intervention. This could be teaching the cognitive-behavioral model or doing a role play exercise (about 15 minutes). Lastly,

1. Check In
   - ⊙ Build relationship
   - ⊙ Assess for any crisis and compliance with conditions

2. Review
   - ⊙ Enhance collaboration and learning with repetition and feedback
   - ⊙ Community agency follow-up

3. Intervention
   - ⊙ Demonstrate cognitive-behavior link
   - ⊙ Use cognitive-behavioral techniques to teach new prosocial skills and attitudes

4. Homework
   - ⊙ Summarize what was learned and assign homework
   - ⊙ Connect to community resources

Figure 12.4

STICS Session Structure

"homework" (e.g., something as simple as trying a behavior and reporting on it at the next supervision session) was assigned that reinforced the learning of new concepts, skills, or prosocial cognitions.

In order to maintain and further develop staff skills, clinical supervision was provided to the probation officers after training. Probation officers met once a month in small groups to discuss their use of STICS concepts and skills. The trainers assigned specific exercises to be discussed at the monthly meetings. During the monthly meetings, the officers teleconferenced with the trainers and were given feedback on the exercises. In addition, approximately one year after the initial training, the probation officers attended a one-day STICS refresher workshop facilitated by one of the trainers.

RESOURCE NOTE 12.2

Strategic Training Initiative in Community Supervision (STICS)

The three-day STICS training program is based on GPCSL. Thus, the first module of a total of 10 modules (see Figure 12.3) was a 90-minute didactic overview of GPCSL and the importance of adhering to the risk-need-responsivity principles. It was important that probation officers "buy in" to a theoretical view if they were going to apply the skills learned in training. In STICS, the first goal was to change the behavior of the probation officer, and the second was to have probation officers use the skills taught to change the behavior of their clients. Thus, probation officers needed an explanation as to why they should change their behaviors and how they could help their clients change.

The next module, which was very brief, was an overview of the risk principle. In STICS probation officers are asked to work with medium- and high-risk clients. This structure ensures that minimal services are provided to low-risk probationers and more services directed to higher-risk clients (i.e., adherence to the risk principle).

The probation officers must use a validated risk/needs assessment instrument. This is important not only for assessing general risk but also for identifying the criminogenic needs to be targeted during supervision (e.g., procriminal attitudes, criminal associates, antisocial personality pattern). Module 3 was on criminogenic needs, but Module 4 (procriminal attitudes) begins the core of the STICS protocol. Probation officers are taught to quickly recognize expressions of procriminal attitudes in their clients and how to help the probationers also recognize when they express procriminal thoughts. After all, you cannot change something if you do not recognize it as a problem. The first four modules of the training represented most of the first day.

The responsivity modules have three components: (1) relationship building, (2) use of cognitive-behavioral techniques, and (3) attention to the particular learning style of the client. The power of rewards and costs in situations of interpersonal influence rests in the relationship. A probation officer's ability to influence a client through the delivery of a reward (e.g., words of praise, a smile) or a cost (e.g., words of disapproval, a frown) depends upon the client having some respect for and liking of the probation officer. To put it bluntly, if one does not care what the other thinks or feels, then one is free to act

continued

according to his or her wishes. Relationship-building skills such as expressing warmth and respect and providing constructive feedback are taught and practiced in Module 5.

Having prepared the probation officers to recognize the importance of criminogenic needs, especially procriminal attitudes, and the need to point this out to their clients within a respectful relationship, the next step was to exercise change in the appropriate direction. The structuring dimension of interpersonal influence began on the second day of STICS training with modules on the cognitive-behavioral model, cognitive restructuring, prosocial modeling, and the effective use of reinforcement and disapproval. The challenge for the probation officers is that they are being asked to provide structured learning for their clients—to be interventionists in the positive sense. Many probation officers are more comfortable with monitoring compliance to the probation conditions, advocating with social service agencies on their client's behalf, and being supportive when clients are faced with distress and interpersonal problems.

On days 2 and 3, probation officers are taught how to use cognitive-behavioral techniques with their clients one-on-one (for more detail, see Rugge & Bonta, 2014). What is critical in these modules is to teach the skills in a simple and concrete way so that the probation officers could, in turn, teach them to their clients.

Changing procriminal attitudes is done in two steps. First, a simple cognitive-behavioral model, called the "Behavior Sequence," is taught (see Figure RN 12.2-1). The Behavior

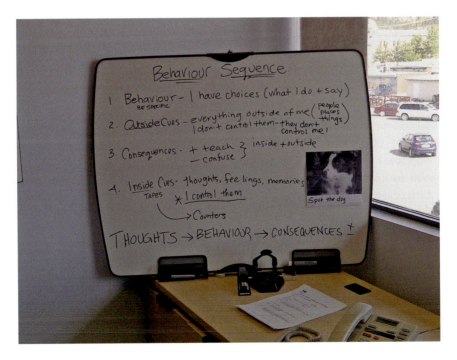

Figure RN 12.2.1

Probation Officer's Outline for Teaching the Behavior Sequence

Source: British Columbia Community Corrections

Sequence model examines behavior as a function of antecedent stimuli, consequences, and attitudes, with an emphasis on how attitudes, or internal cognitive cues, are the root causes of behavior. Also demonstrated are ways of teaching the Behavior Sequence model so that even a developmentally challenged client could understand how thoughts lead to behavior. Second, probation officers are taught how to teach cognitive restructuring to their clients. Cognitive restructuring is a technique for replacing procriminal thoughts with prosocial thoughts. The theme throughout the cognitive-behavioral modules is to keep it concrete and make it relevant to a wide range of clients (e.g., women, mentally disordered, racial minority).

The three-day STICS training is delivered in a structured format (a training manual is used) with classroom exercises and role plays. Repetition is the hallmark of skill mainten-ance. However, practice during a three-day training program is not sufficient to maintain new behaviors over a period of weeks or months. One feature of STICS is that it included ongoing clinical supervision. After training, probation officers met in small groups on a monthly basis to discuss their use of STICS skills, and they teleconferenced with the trainers. Homework related to the skills taught during training is assigned to the groups and discussed in the meetings. During teleconferences, participants are given feedback on their homework, and clinical supervision is provided.

The overall purpose of STICS is to demonstrate that the key ingredients of the RNR model can be successfully taught to probation officers and applied to their clients. The evaluations of STICS demonstrated that with training, probation officers can apply GPCSL-based practices in their supervision of offenders, and that this can result in reduced recidivism among their clients. Transferring "what works" into the real world is possible.

Evaluations of STICS. There are three key issues regarding the evaluations of STICS: (1) choosing the research design, (2) the assessment of change in the behavior of probation officers and their clients, and (3) maintaining participant motivation. Of particular importance is the effect of STICS training on the behavior of the probation officer, as it is the officer's behavior during supervision sessions that is hypothesized to influence change in the client's future criminal behavior.

1) The 2011 STICS Experiment

Following the development of the STICS training protocols an experi-mental evaluation was conducted with 80 volunteer probation officers from three Canadian provinces (Bonta, Bourgon, et al., 2011). The probation officers were randomly assigned to either a training or no-training condition. In order to enhance adherence with the risk principle, probation officers were asked to select only medium and high-risk clients for the project. Although a few low-risk probationers were recruited to the study, approximately 95 percent of the clients were medium- and high-risk offenders.

Evaluating the effects of the training consisted of measuring the behavior of probation officers and their clients through a combination of direct observation, self-report, and official records of criminal behavior. In order to examine the behavior of probation officers, the officers were asked to audio record their sessions with new clients at intake, after three months of supervision, and again after approximately six months of supervision. Teams of two trained raters assessed each audio-recorded session as to the content of discussions (e.g., discussions of criminogenic needs) as well as the quality of the specific skills of the officers (e.g., active listening skills and the use of cognitive restructuring interventions).

Maintaining participation in a research project is challenging. One aspect of project commitment and program integrity is managerial support (Rex & Hosking, 2013; see also Principle 15 of the RNR model in Chapter 9). Therefore, all of the managers of the front-line officers were required to attend the three days of training. A third trainer also led the managers through the exercises and role plays. The attendance of managers not only showed support to their staff during training but also yielded dividends when staff returned to the field to practice what was taught. The managers were more appreciative of the demands placed upon the officers by the research and often worked with staff to organize their workload to facilitate participation in the evaluation. Encouraging commitment for those officers who were assigned to the control condition was more of a challenge. Therefore, incentives to participate were introduced (e.g., the control group was promised the training if the results turned out to be favorable).

The probation officers submitted 295 post-training audio recordings on 143 clients. As hypothesized, the experimental group, compared to the control group, focused more on criminogenic needs and procriminal attitudes and demonstrated significantly better cognitive-behavioral skills. For example, the STICS-trained officers devoted on average 35 percent of their sessions to procriminal attitudes. Another example, scores on cognitive techniques were much higher among the experimental participants (the use of cognitive techniques was almost non-existent among the controls).

Overall, the STICS training improved the officers' RNR-based skills and improved the content of their discussions with clients. The results with respect to client recidivism were also positive. After a mean follow-up of two years, the recidivism rate for the trained probation officers' clients was 25 percent, compared to 39.5 percent for the untrained probation officers.

An important question asked in the 2011 STICS evaluation was whether the various clinical development activities (e.g., monthly meetings, refresher course) enhanced skill development and client outcome. The experimental group was sub-divided into a "high-support" subgroup and a "low-support" subgroup. The high-support group consisted of staff who attended monthly meetings and refresher courses more regularly and submitted audio recordings for clinical feedback (not just for research purposes). Taking advantage of the variety of clinical supports led to more relevant discussions with clients, better skills, and lower recidivism rates among their clients. It is noteworthy that even the low-support group did better than the control group.

Further analyses from the 2011 experiment have found that getting probation officers to understand and apply cognitive techniques with their clients may be critical to success (Bourgon & Gutierrez, 2012; Bourgon, Gutierrez, & Ashton, 2011). As a consequence, changes to the STICS training were made to give greater emphasis on these skills.

2) A Partial Replication (2019)

The second evaluation of STICS also involved a randomized experiment (Bonta, Rugge, Bourgon, & Wanamaker, 2019). Thirty-six volunteer probation officers from another Canadian province (i.e., they did not participate in the 2011 study) were randomly assigned to STICS training or probation-as-usual. Attrition reduced the samples to 15 probation officers in the experimental group and 12 in the control group. Nevertheless, 283 audio recordings were available for analysis. The research protocols were almost identical to the 2011 experiment.

The findings in this study failed to demonstrate the robust effects found in the 2011 evaluation. There were no differences between the trained and untrained officers with respect to the amount of time devoted to criminogenic needs except that the experimental probation officers showed a small but statistically significant increase in discussing procriminal attitudes. With respect to skills, the experimental officers scored higher on relationship and cognitive skills than the controls. However, the improvement on cognitive skills was small and was statistically significant only because no one in the control group demonstrated any cognitive techniques across the audio recordings.

Given the lackluster results regarding officer behavior it was unsurprising that there was no impact on client recidivism rates (51.9 percent for the clients of STICS officers vs. 48.8 percent for the controls; the CIs overlapped). The 2011 evaluation suggested that the use of cognitive techniques specifically may be an important ingredient for client change. Indeed, when statistical controls for age and risk were introduced, the recidivism rate for clients exposed to cognitive interventions was 43 percent compared to 54 percent for probationers not exposed to cognitive interventions (the differences were significant).

3) STICS Goes International: Sweden (2021)

In 2012 the Swedish probation service launched a small pilot of STICS with 36 probation officers. However, before the evaluation of the pilot was completed, Sweden moved forward with national implementation in 2014.

Louise Starfelt Sutton and her colleagues (Starfelt Sutton, Dynevall, et al., 2021) conducted a partial evaluation of the implementation in Sweden using case files ($N = 305$) and audio recordings ($N = 88$) collected in 2016. The aims of the study were to assess the extent to which probation officers adhered to the risk, need, and responsivity principles following training. The findings were as follows: (1) no differences were found in the number of face-to-face contacts between medium and high-risk clients, (2) small improvements in focusing on criminogenic needs were observed but with time officer behavior returned to baseline level, and (3) the use of cognitive-behavioral intervention techniques improved, although they were described as poor in quality.

Starfelt Sutton and her co-authors suggested that the weak findings may have been due to insufficient resources allocated to probation officers to properly learn RNR-based skills. A client recidivism analysis is planned but not yet reported.

4) A Province-Wide Implementation of STICS (2021)

The Canadian province of British Columbia (BC) was one of the provinces that participated in the original 2011 evaluation of STICS. Based on the results of that evaluation and estimates of future cost savings associated with the potential of reduced recidivism, the province decided to implement STICS (Bonta, Bourgon, Rugge, Gress, & Gutierrez, 2013). This large-scale implementation now involved *all* probation officers and not just volunteers. The evaluation of STICS implementation in BC differed from the Starfelt Sutton et al. (2021) report in two important ways. First, data was collected from across all years of implementation and not from one specific year. Second, the data was not limited to volunteer probation officers.

The implementation in BC began in September 2011 and continued to January 2015 (Bonta, Bourgon, Rugge, Pedneault, & Lee, 2021). The plan was to train over 350 probation officers over the course of three and a half years. In the province, there are two levels of probation officers. A more junior-level officer was responsible mainly for low-risk cases. The second level of officers focused on medium- to high-risk probationers. It was the latter group that received STICS training (i.e., in accordance with the risk principle).

Prior to attending STICS training, the probation officers were expected to submit a sample of audio recordings from supervision sessions. After training, another sample of audio recordings was submitted. The evaluation of training on officer behavior was conducted by comparing 201 pre-training recordings to 201 post-training recordings from the same staff member. The shifts in the discussion content areas were in the expected direction (Figure 12.5). The increase in the average proportion of a session devoted to procriminal attitudes was particularly large (from 0.02 prior to training to 0.18 after training).

The influence of training on skills was assessed by comparing scores on the pre- and post-training recordings. Skills improved in the hypothesized direction following training, with officers more likely to display cognitive-behavioral techniques (Figure 12.6). An important goal in STICS is to train staff to facilitate cognitive restructuring among their clients. This is a *cognitive* intervention (i.e., replacing procriminal attitudes with prosocial attitudes). Figure 12.6 also shows the results for cognitive skills separately from behavioral interventions

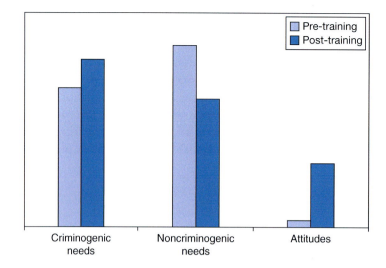

Figure 12.5

Pre- Post STICS Training in British Columbia: Discussion Content

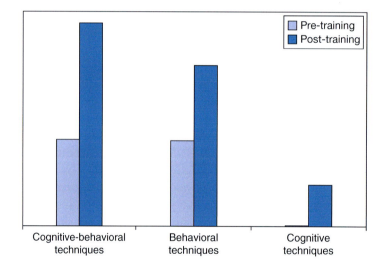

Figure 12.6

Pre- and Post STICS Training in British Columbia: Intervention Skills

(e.g., role playing, prosocial modeling). It is noteworthy that, without training, the use of cognitive interventions was almost non-existent.

Having found significant changes in staff behavior, the next step was to examine client recidivism. Recidivism outcome was based on 798 audio-recorded post-training clients that were compared to a random sample of 396 non-recorded clients supervised by the probation officers *prior* to STICS training. With such a large sample it was possible to also measure violent outcomes in a meaningful way (recall from Chapter 2 that violent behavior

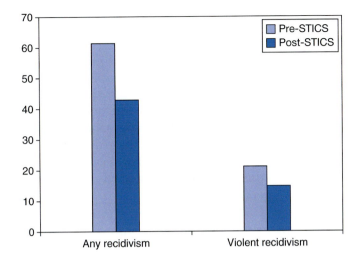

Figure 12.7

Pre- and Post-STICS Training in British Columbia: Recidivism

has a low base rate, making it difficult to predict). As displayed in Figure 12.7, probationers supervised by the STICS-trained probation officers had significantly lower two-year general and violent recidivism rates.

2. Staff Training Aimed at Reducing Re-arrest (STARR)

STARR consists of three and a half days of training on the relationship and structuring skills previously described, and STARR has considerable overlap with STICS. In fact, Christopher Lowenkamp, one of the co-developers of STARR, and Paula Smith, a co-developer of the EPICS training model (described next), visited the STICS development team in 2008. In the STARR experiment, 88 volunteer U.S. federal probation officers were randomly assigned to training or to routine supervision (Robinson, Lowenkamp, et al., 2012; Robinson, VanBenschoten, Alexander, & Lowenkamp, 2011). There was staff attrition for various reasons (e.g., job promotion), leaving a final sample of 41 officers in the experimental group and 26 in the control group (not everyone was randomly assigned; two districts refused the random assignment). The experimental probation officers supervised 295 medium- to high-risk clients, and the control officers supervised 218 clients.

Robinson and his colleagues used an evaluation methodology almost identical to the methods used in the STICS research. The participants were asked to submit audio recordings of their supervision sessions at the beginning of supervision, at three months, and again at six months. More than 700 audio recordings were submitted for analysis. Since the U.S. federal probation officers supervised two types of clients (pretrial and post-conviction), two definitions of recidivism were used. For the pretrial clients, recidivism was defined as a failure to appear in court, and for the other group, recidivism was defined as a new arrest within one year.

The analysis of the audio recordings showed that the experimental group was more likely to engage in role clarification, show the effective use of reinforcement and disapproval, and make more frequent use of the cognitive model. At one year, the clients of the trained officers also had a lower recidivism rate (26 percent) than the clients of the control officers (34 percent). The reduction in recidivism among the clients of the trained officers appeared to be concentrated among the moderate-risk offenders, as there was little difference in the recidivism of the high-risk clients of the trained staff (35 percent) and the control staff (37 percent).

In 2014, Lowenkamp, Holsinger, Robinson, and Alexander extended their follow-up of the STARR experiment to 24 months. The post-training experimental clients had a recidivism rate of 28 percent, and the control group's rate was 41 percent. However, the authors noted that this difference did not reach statistical significance. As described in Chapter 2, null hypothesis testing has been roundly criticized. The important finding is that the 13 percentage point difference is similar to that reported in 2011 (14.4 percent) and 2021 (18.4 percent) for STICS. Lowenkamp and his colleagues also found that for those officers trained in both STARR and motivational interviewing, recidivism was significantly lower for the high-risk clients.

Two more recent evaluations of STARR have been published. In the first study, Hicks, Holcomb, Alexander, and Clodfelter (2020) gathered federal supervision data over an 11-year period. Midway through the study STARR training was introduced. They found that clients of STARR-trained probation officers ($N = 541$), compared to a matched group of non-trained officers ($N = 3,364$), had fewer revocations for a new crime. However, no differences were found for revocations for drug use or other types of technical violations. The second study compared client outcomes for clients of STARR-trained staff and a matched group of clients from non-trained officers (there were 722 clients in both groups; Labrecque & Viglione, 2021). At one year, the clients of trained staff were slightly less likely to have a revocation, but there were no differences in re-arrest rates. Additional analysis found that the clients of coaches, a more highly trained group, had a lower re-arrest rate but this was also statistically nonsignificant.

STARR has been implemented across the U.S. federal probation service and approximately 5,000 staff have been trained. This includes front-line officers, coaches, and supervisors. At this point, an evaluation of this massive undertaking has not been conducted.

3. *Effective Practices in Community Supervision (EPICS)*

EPICS was developed by researchers at the University of Cincinnati (Smith, Schweitzer, Labrecque, & Latessa, 2012). The training curriculum is based on what is called Core Correctional Practice (CCP; Dowden & Andrews, 2004).

In earlier editions of this book, the term "CCP" was used, but in this edition, it is replaced by GPCSL-based Staff Practices in order to better reflect the theoretical basis of therapist skills. The EPICS curriculum is similar to STICS and STARR (e.g., same session structure, training on prosocial modeling and effective reinforcement, coaching sessions), and it has been delivered to at least 143 state correctional agencies, including one agency in Singapore and another in Canada (University of Cincinnati, 2020).

EPICS was first evaluated on a small sample of probation and parole officers (N = 10) who supervised both adults and youths (Smith et al., 2012). The trained officers demonstrated more of the skills taught in EPICS, compared to the control group. This study did not use random assignment, and recidivism data for the clients was not reported. A subsequent study with 44 probation and parole officers by Labrecque, Schweitzer, and Smith (2013) confirmed that EPICS training can change officer behavior, but again, recidivism data was not presented.

The one available study that examined recidivism outcomes was conducted by Latessa, Smith, Schweitzer, and Labrecque (2013). In the evaluation, 41 probation officers were randomly assigned to training or routine supervision. As expected, officer behavior changed with training and improved with coaching. Overall, the experimental probationers actually had *higher* arrest, incarceration, and technical violation rates than the control clients. However, when broken down by risk level, there was some evidence that the experimental high-risk offenders did better when they were supervised by "high-fidelity" officers (i.e., staff who actually used the skills taught).

A closing comment on the EPICS research is warranted. GPCSL postulates that replacing procriminal attitudes with prosocial attitudes will result in decreased criminal conduct. Labrecque and his colleagues (2013) tested this assumption by administering paper-and-pencil measures of procriminal attitudes to 238 probationers. Those probationers who were supervised by EPICS-trained officers had lower scores on most of the measures compared to clients of the untrained probation officers. However, the results were not statistically significant and further research is needed to explore mediating effect of attitudes on behavior.

Summary

In general, the research is promising—correctional systems can reduce recidivism through rehabilitation, and the RNR principles can guide those seeking to design, implement, and evaluate effective correctional interventions. However, there are considerable challenges in translating these principles into everyday practice, maintaining the integrity of such services, and ensuring adherence to the principles.

There are now a sufficient number of RNR-based training programs for probation and parole officers that two meta-analyses and a systematic review have been published. An early meta-analysis of 10 studies found an effect size of $r = 0.11$ (Chadwick, Dewolf, & Serin, 2015). A more recent meta-analysis of 25 studies by Ryan Labrecque, Jill Viglione, and Michael Caudy (2023) did not report the overall effect size for client outcomes (technical violation, re-arrest, reconviction). Rather, the analysis focused on methodological and training considerations. For example, among peer-reviewed studies, training was associated with reduced re-arrests ($r = 0.09$, $k = 4$) and reconvictions ($r = 0.09$, $k = 5$). Bonta's (2023) review was largely limited to evaluations of STICS, EPICS, and STARR. Depending on the study and outcome measure, the effect sizes ranged from nonsignificant (in the case of EPICS) to $r = 0.20$ (in a study of STICS).

Designing a program is one challenge, but implementing it into routine practice is another. For many jurisdictions it will require a dramatic over-haul of community supervision and the orientation of probation and parole officers. Time studies show that approximately 25 percent of an officer's time is spent in face-to-face meetings with clients (Bourgon, Rugge, Chadwick, & Bonta, 2018; Martin & Zettler, 2021). Training staff to deliver the service as intended, ensuring the integrity of service delivery, and maintaining staff skills and commitment are critical. The STICS, STARR, and EPICS projects ensured adherence to the RNR principles via the selection of high- and medium-risk clients based on validated risk/needs assessment instruments and structuring officer–client interactions. Monthly clinical supervision meetings and refresher workshops facilitated maintenance and improvement of skills. Audio recordings of officer–client sessions provided a means to assess fidelity by evaluating the behavior of the officers "behind closed doors." Some of the common issues faced by these RNR-based training programs and the way they were dealt with are summarized in Table 12.4.

Cost–Benefit Evaluations of Offender Treatment

Undoubtedly, the costs of crime to society are enormous. The "costs" can be measured in the value of goods lost, the salaries and associated costs of the criminal justice and social welfare systems, lost wages due to incarceration, and even such intangible costs such as "pain and suffering," which can be estimated from jury settlements. The 411 boys from the Cambridge Study in Delinquent Development cost *each* taxpayer in the United Kingdom $1,185 (Piquero, Jennings, & Farrington, 2013). In a study of more than 41,000 persons convicted in Australia, between the ages of 10 and 25 years, a small group of chronic offenders (4.8 percent) accounted for 41.1 percent of criminal justice and social costs (Allard, Stewart, et al., 2014). In a systematic review it was estimated that crime costs from $9 billion in Australia and up to $450 billion in the US (Wickramasekera, Wright, Elsey, Murray, & Tubef, 2015). The vari-ability in estimates is due to what is measured as a cost and what crimes are included (e.g., homicide and drug crimes are especially costly in the US). In a sophisticated analysis, Koegl and Farrington (2021) provided cost estimates

TABLE 12.4 **RNR-based Training for One-on-One Supervision: Challenges and Solutions**

Issue	Challenge	Solution
Theory of Criminal Behavior	To bring GPCSL theory to training	Ensure training model promotes an understanding of GPCSL with links to how it is incorporated into the practical aspects of supervision; ensure organizational policies align with RNR
Risk Principle	To ensure that services target higher-risk offenders	Train probation officers who supervise medium- and high-risk offenders
Need Principle	To ensure that treatment targets criminogenic needs	Use risk-need assessments; transfer information to supervision plans; target attitudes and cognitions
Responsivity Principle	To ensure that services are attentive to the learning styles of the clients	Training addresses: (a) relationship dimension, (b) structuring dimension, (c) relevance to the client, and (d) structure supervision
a) Relationship	To establish a therapeutic working alliance	Foster relationship building via skills and specific processes (e.g., collaborative goal setting, role clarification)
b) Structuring	To increase use of cognitive-behavioral techniques	Provide a cognitive-behavioral model, as well as the skills and strategies needed in supervision with medium- to high-risk clients
c) Relevance to Client	To ensure that key concepts and skills are used in a concrete and understandable fashion	Ensure concepts, skills, and materials are concrete, simple, and devoid of jargon; ensure flexibility to make them useful for all types of clients (e.g., gender, race)
d) Structuring Supervision	To structure the supervision session and the supervision period	Structure the individual session (check-in, review, intervention, homework) and the supervision period into steps (from assessment to using community resources)
Maintaining Skills	To provide professional development activities	Training programs can provide coaching, refresher sessions, and expert feedback on audio recordings
Maintaining and improving organizational performance	To support agency staff in GPCSL practices	Monitor staff practices; it does not need to be a comprehensive research study, but at a minimum measure what counts. Provide resources to allow staff to learn new practices and build internal capacity to maintain change over time

Source: Adapted from Bonta, 2023; Bourgon et al., 2010b

associated with risk factors among 379 young boys referred to a clinic for conduct disorder. The boys were followed through adolescence and into early adulthood and their criminal convictions recorded. The presence of the risk/need factor, procriminal attitudes, was estimated to cost over $920,000.

A final topic in this chapter, however, is to examine the cost–*benefit* of treatment. The simple question is: "How much does it cost to treat a justice-involved person, and how much money is saved through a reduction in recidivism?" For example, by successfully treating the person rather than incarcerating the person, we may avoid lost wages, welfare costs that may be needed to support the family of an incarcerated individual, and the "pain and suffering" of potential victims.

Studies that have directly applied cost–benefit analyses to controlled evaluations of treatment programs are few. This is somewhat surprising when one considers how the potential of saving money can spur organizations into adopting treatment on a large scale. However, this is changing, particularly in the United States. The Justice Reinvestment Initiative attempts to reduce correctional costs and then take the savings and apply them to evidence-informed strategies to reduce crime (Bureau of Justice Assistance, 2021). For example, Faye Taxman and her colleagues have also developed a tool to assess how well programs follow the RNR principles (Ramezani, Bhati, Murphy, Routh, & Taxman, 2022). In a simulation study, it was estimated that by expanding treatment programs for high-risk offenders in accordance with the RNR model, reincarceration could be reduced by about 6 percent (Taxman, Pattavina, & Caudy, 2014).

Elizabeth Drake (2018) conducted a meta-analysis of recidivism outcomes for four types of community supervision: (1) intensive supervision without treatment, (2) intensive supervision with treatment, (3) supervision by RNR-trained staff (e.g., STICS, EPICS), and (4) swift-and-certain supervision (a punishment-oriented approach to be discussed in the next chapter). Both supervision without treatment and swift-and-certain supervision failed to reduce recidivism. The two treatment-oriented supervision approaches were significantly successful in reducing recidivism. The average effect size for intensive supervision was $r = 0.10$ ($k = 17$) and for RNR supervision it was $r = 0.08$ ($k = 14$). Drake also estimated that the net benefits to a taxpayer exceeded $7,000. Swift-and-certain also had a net benefit (approximately $9,000) but it was largely due to individuals not being provided any treatment services being diverted from incarceration.

The following sampling of conclusions from different reports clearly demonstrates that rehabilitation programs have substantial cost benefits:

- "the present value of saving a high-risk youth is estimated to be $2.6 to $5.3 million at age 18" (Cohen & Piquero, 2009: p. 46)

- "the meta-analytic findings of RNR supervision... produced significant reductions in recidivism and positive net benefits to taxpayers and victims of crime of about US$7,000 per participant" (Drake, 2018: p. 56)

- "overall, every dollar spent on MST (Multisystemic Therapy) recovered $5.04 in savings" (Dopp, Borduin, Wagner, & Sawyer, 2014: p. 694)

- "the program produced… monetary savings of $9,493 to $17,404 per boy, on average. When this was compared to the cost of the program per boy of $4,641, the benefit-to-cost ratio ranged from 2.0 to 3.8" (Farrington & Koegl, 2015: p. 283)

This chapter suggests that effective treatments can be delivered in real-world settings. Appropriate treatments delivered with high levels of integrity can have significant impacts on recidivism and cost benefits. Our knowledge of the principles of effective treatment and the program integrity/implementation factors has been valuable for the delivery and monitoring of offender program systems. We know a great deal about the pitfalls in implementing treatment programs and a little bit about how to avoid at least some of them.

Worth Remembering

1. In the domains of both effective treatment and valid assessment, having an evaluator who was involved in the design of the treatment (or the construction of the assessment instruments) was associated with favorable conclusions. There are four interpretations to this effect. They are: "cynical" (experimenter bias); "smart" (programs or instruments); "fidelity" (treatment and/or assessment implemented with integrity); and "combination of the first three." Meta-analyses in the treatment domain support the combination interpretation.

2. Consideration of the involved evaluator effect has led to the distinction between short-term tightly controlled demonstration projects and routine programming (sometimes called "regular" programming or "real-world" programming). A huge challenge is to help make routine programming more like demonstration projects on the dimensions of "smart" and "fidelity." Demanding exquisitely clear reporting on methodological and operational aspects of research may additionally reduce "bias."

3. Three concrete ways of improving routine programming are: (1) RNR-based structured assessments of offenders, (2) RNR-based structured assessments of ongoing programming, with feedback on level of RNR adherence, and (3) RNR-based training and supervision of service providers (and their managers).

Recommended Readings

For those wishing to read an after-the-fact "autopsy" of failed programming, see Claire Goggin and Paul Gendreau's (2006) chapter "The Implementation and Maintenance of Quality Services in Offender Rehabilitation Programmes" in Clive Hollin and Emma Palmer's edited book, *Offending Behaviour Programmes: Development, Application and Controversies*. The other chapters in the book also provide commentaries on the range of issues surrounding implementation of best practices.

The paper by Christopher Lowenkamp, Edward Latessa, and Paula Smith (2006) in *Criminology and Public Policy*, "Does Correctional Quality Really Matter?", is the pioneer study on the prediction of which programs will be effective and which will not. In this article, the authors employed the CPAI to help identify the most effective programs.

For readers who wish to learn more about the techniques of cognitive-behavioral interventions, there is a "how-to" edited book by Raymond Tafrate and Damon Mitchell (2014) called *Forensic CBT: A Handbook for Clinical Practice*. Here the reader will not only find how the cognitive-behavioral model is taught in STICS but also its application to different behavioral problems (e.g., sexual aggression). A more recent practitioner's guide is also by Tafrate and Mitchell along with the late David Simourd, entitled *CBT with Justice-Involved Clients: Interventions for Antisocial and Self-Destructive Behaviors* (2018). This is a must read for those working with justice-involved clients. For another perspective on STICS, the reader is directed to the chapter by Bourgon, Chadwick, and Rugge (2020). Although it covers much of what is described in this chapter, it provides some additional interpretations of the research.

 Visit the Instructor and Student Resource to access additional exercises, videos and study materials to support this chapter: psychologycriminalconduct.routledge.com

CHAPTER 13 The Failed Experiment: Getting Tough on Crime

When one is hurt or wronged, a common response is to strike back. It occurs at both the individual and societal levels. Hurts are to be punished, but not unduly so. Fairness and justice must also apply. In almost all societies, punishment is a consequence of breaking the law, and the application of punishment is highly regulated. There are many purposes for punishment within the criminal justice system. They include retribution, denunciation of the act, and deterrence. This chapter touches upon these varying purposes, but the focus will be on the deterrent function of punishment.

Although most of this chapter deals with punishment, the reader is reminded that well-intentioned "treatment" can also cause harm. This has been recognized for a long time going back to at least Bailey's (1966) review, with almost one-quarter of the 100 reports classified as "harmful or no change" (p. 736). We have already seen, for example, that violating the risk principle by providing intensive treatment to low-risk clients is associated with increased recidivism. However, unanticipated harm is almost always the result with punishment-oriented interventions.

Criminal Justice Sanctions and Just Deserts

Laws define unacceptable behaviors and set the penalties for engaging in those behaviors. For the sake of simplicity, we will use the term "sanction" to refer to the official application of punishment for breaking the law (more generally, sanctions can also refer to the approval of behavior). Sanctioning criminal behavior follows three simple ideas. First, there is the moral imperative that wrongs do not go unpunished (retribution). Second, the sanction must be proportional to the crime ("just deserts"). That is, a punishment should not be overly harsh or too lenient. Finally, it is anticipated that sanctions will deter the individual (specific deterrence) and other members of society (general deterrence) from behaving illegally.

The world prison population in 2021 was approximately 11.5 million (it had fallen during the COVID-19 pandemic; Fair & Walmsley, 2021). Although the

DOI: 10.4324/9781003292128-16

number of people under correctional supervision has leveled off or decreased in the United States in the past few years, the country still holds the dubious distinction of having the highest prison population in the world. In 2021, the rate of incarceration in the United States was 629 per 100,000, easily outpacing many countries in the developed world. For example, the rate per 100,000 for Canada was 104; for England and Wales, 131; for France, 119; and for Australia, 167. The official figures may be questionable, but the rates for Russia (326) and China (119) do not match those of the United States. There were slightly more than 5.5 million persons under correctional supervision in 2020 in the United States (Kluckow & Zeng, 2022), the lowest number since 1996, with 1.7 million in jails and prisons. In 2022, 2,414 inmates were on death row, and 18 were executed (Death Penalty Information Center, 2022).

It is unclear when exactly the United States started "getting tough" on crime. Most scholars place the beginnings at some time in the 1970s (Cullen & Gilbert, 2013; Tonry, 2019). The social-political events of the time, the proclamation that "nothing works," and a revival of classical criminology were contributing factors to a shift to punishment to address crime. When Martinson (1974) declared treatment to be largely ineffective, he also suggested that deterrence may offer an alternative hope for dealing with crime (see Figure 13.1). Classical criminology saw individuals as rational beings who calculated the benefits and risks for certain behaviors. Therefore, if crime pays, then the costs for crime must increase. This utilitarian model also hypothesized that reducing the rewards for crime should also alter the probability of crime (see Table 13.1). Reducing criminal behavior can be achieved by shifting the rewards and costs for criminal *and* prosocial behavior. However, increasing punishment or the costs to crime (Cell B in Table 13.1) was the preferred choice in US criminal justice policy.

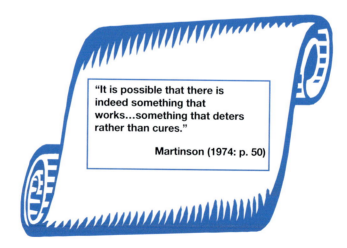

"It is possible that there is indeed something that works...something that deters rather than cures."

Martinson (1974: p. 50)

Figure 13.1

Martinson's Call for Deterrence

TABLE 13.1	**Decreasing the Chances of Crime**				
Behavior		**Rewards**		**Costs**	
Criminal	(A)	reduce	(B)	add	
Prosocial	(C)	add	(D)	reduce	

Note cell B = getting tough on crime

A report of the Committee for the Study of Incarceration authored by Andrew von Hirsch (1976) proved to be influential. The report questioned the effectiveness of rehabilitation and the ability to predict criminal behavior. Consequently, incarceration, except for rare situations, should have nothing to do with the potential danger a person might pose or the likelihood of rehabilitation. Parole and indeterminate sentences, which depend so much on rehabilitation, were unnecessary. Furthermore, punishment is morally justified because people who do wrong *deserve* to be punished. The purpose of sanctions is to give the person their "just deserts."

Sanctions that were tailored to fit the crime were supposed to result in a fair and just criminal justice system but also were presumed to deter criminal behavior. The United States went on a spree of adding sanctions and increasing the severity of sanctions. The state of Washington introduced a "three strikes and you're out" law in 1993, making life imprisonment mandatory for a third felony conviction. Three-strikes laws followed in California and at least 28 other states (Baumgartner, Daniely, et al., 2021). Discretion at the "back end" of the criminal justice system was also curtailed by the abolishment of parole boards and the introduction of "truth-in-sentencing" laws (Tonry, 2018).

The Effects of Imprisonment on Crime and the Community

The "get tough" approach to crime is reflected in laws with mandatory minimum penalties, longer prison sentences, and other efforts to make sanctions more unpleasant. Many jurisdictions had mandatory minimum penalties, but the penalties were limited either to very serious crimes, such as an intentional act of murder, or to a few specific crimes (e.g., brief periods of incarceration for impaired driving). What changed was that the list of offenses for which mandatory penalties were prescribed increased dramatically, and the penalties became more severe.

Three-strikes laws and truth-in-sentencing legislation are the most common examples of the "get tough" legislation. Three-strikes laws basically require a judge to give a life prison term after the third offense. Truth-in-sentencing laws require serving a minimum amount of a sentence (approximately 85 percent) before release on parole or some other form of conditional release. Both types of legislation are usually intended to target those who commit violent crimes and are based on the idea of selective incapacitation (i.e., selectively incapacitating the high-risk, high-frequency individuals).

Putting aside the difficulty in identifying the high-risk and the high-rate, the results from three-strikes laws have been disappointing. First of all, the laws do not always target the high-risk violent offender. Early examples come from California where approximately 20 percent of third-strike offenses were drug-related (Meehan, 2000) and 60 percent were for a nonviolent offense (Austin, Clark, Hardyman, & Henry, 1999). Second, the application of the law varies considerably across states, with little evidence that it deters crime. For example, Sundt and Boppre (2021) found that Oregon's "one strike and you're out" for sexual and violent crimes (this is not a typo, it is one strike) did not have any effect on crime rates in the state. To the credit of legislators listening to the data, California has since significantly scaled back its get-tough sentencing practices (called "The Public Safety Realignment Act"; Weisberg, 2019).

Four arguments are usually given to support get-tough legislation:

1. It takes bad people off the streets so they cannot commit crimes.

2. It restores faith in the criminal justice system.

3. It deters people from committing crime.

4. It is fair and just.

When examined in the light of the evidence, these arguments lose their persuasive appeal.

1. Incapacitation Effect: Taking the Bad Off the Streets

Without a doubt, if you remove someone from the community, then that person cannot commit a crime in the community. Therefore, so the argument goes, the more criminals that are imprisoned, the lower the crime rate. When crime rates decreased in the United States during the 1990s, many were quick to point to the increased policing and stiffer sentences as the reasons for the reduction in crime rates. To their thinking, that meant that the skyrocketing prison populations were well worth it. The real questions here are: (a) does imprisonment reduce criminal behavior in our communities? and (b) at what cost?

(a) Imprisonment and Crime Rates. Was increasing prison capacity partly responsible for decreased crime rates in the United States? The answer is a bit unclear, but it appears not. There are two reasons why imprisonment does not explain the decrease in crime rates. First, the increase in imprisonment began in the early 1970s, while the decrease in crime rates did not appear until

20 years later. Second, states that showed the highest increase in the rate of incarceration showed smaller decreases in crime than the states with below-average imprisonment rates (King, Mauer, & Young, 2005).

There may be a small incapacitation effect. The evidence is usually based upon the application of mathematical formulae, with certain assumptions about the rate at which people commit crimes; the probability of getting caught, convicted, and sent to jail; the average time spent in jail; and the average time left in the justice-involved person's "career" when returned to the community (see Piquero and Blumstein, 2007, for a review of some of the issues). As the reader may surmise, we have to make a number of educated guesses about the variables that go into the equation to estimate the number of crimes avoided through incarceration. Some investigators have reported significant increases in imprisonment would be required and this would produce only modest reductions in crime, with the associated costs exceeding the benefits (Wan, Moffatt, Jones, & Weatherburn, 2012).

(b) The Cost of Increasing Imprisonment. In 1987, Edwin Zedlewski claimed that the $25,000 of prison costs associated with one year in prison would avoid a whopping $430,000 in social costs. Almost as soon as Zedlewski's claim was published, his analysis and conclusions were challenged (Zimring & Hawkins, 1988). Rather, there is general agreement that the cost–benefit ratio is far smaller than what Zedlewski claimed. Bernard and Ritti (1991) estimated that if the incarceration rate was increased from two to six times for serious juvenile delinquents, the crime rate would decrease only by 6 percent.

One reason why the cost–benefit ratio has changed since Zedlewski's original analysis is that the profile of who is in prison has changed significantly. It used to be that imprisonment was reserved for the more serious law violator. The "war on drugs" changed all of that. Almost one-half of the prisoners (48 percent) in the U.S. federal system are there for drug crimes, and 42 percent are classified as low risk (Lowenkamp, Holsinger, & Cohen, 2015; Mears & Cochran, 2018). One of the lessons from the COVID-19 pandemic is that many low-risk prisoners can be released safely into the community (Hummer, 2020). In addition, incarcerating drug users does little to alter the "replacement effect." That is, as soon as you put a drug offender into prison, another takes his or her place on the street (King et al., 2005).

Beyond financial costs there are enormous social costs (Cohen & Farrington, 2021). It is not just the individual justice-involved persons who pay the price, but families and whole communities are destabilized at significant economic costs (Rodriguez & Turnavic, 2018). Not only has the "war on drugs" resulted in joblessness for those captured in the net and economic hardship for the families of those captured, but there is also the loss of basic rights in a democratic society. Although a few states are now reversing their stance on disenfranchisement, the numbers continue to grow. In 1976, there were 1.17 million people who had lost the right to vote, and in 2010 there were 5.85 million

(Uggen, Shannon, & Manza, 2012). Moreover, the rate of disenfranchisement was four times higher for African Americans.

Almost all inmates are eventually released, returning to the neighborhoods from which they came. The result is a high concentration of individuals who have few job prospects and loose ties to the community. This high concentration of ex-inmates in areas referred to as "million-dollar" blocks (because of the costs associated with incarcerating so many individuals) drives out small business and those law-abiding citizens who can afford to leave, thereby contributing to neighborhood decay (Clear, 2008; Harding, Morenoff, & Herbert, 2013). In Brooklyn alone, it is estimated that there were 35 of these "million-dollar" blocks (Gonnerman, 2004), and Chicago had 851 (Aspholm, 2022).

Another comment is needed before leaving the incapacitation effect. There is a need to consider if there are better and more cost-effective ways of reducing crime than through imprisonment. As seen in Chapter 12, treatment is a cost-effective alternative and there are others. For example, one can invest in million-dollar blocks and improve the social conditions of the community (Homel, 2014), or make wider use of diversion programs (Wilson & Hoge, 2014). There are many more ways of reducing our reliance on incapacitation, and these should be explored.

2. Restoring Faith in the Criminal Justice System

Political leaders argue that the consequences for law violation must be quick and severe in order to ensure law and order. Furthermore, they say, this is what the public expects and wants. Whether the public really wants a "get tough" approach depends upon how the question is posed. Public opinion surveys that ask very general questions (e.g., "Do you favor tougher sentences for criminals?") do find the majority of respondents agreeing to a "get tough" approach. The public thinks poorly of parole, that courts are too lenient, and that prisons are "country clubs." However, when the public is given *choices* or more factual and detailed information, a less punitive attitude emerges (Cullen, Jonson, & Mears, 2017).

A number of factors moderate what Cullen and his colleagues (2017) call the "mushy" "get tough" attitudes of the public. First, when questions are posed that provide alternatives to the most serious penalty (e.g., death penalty versus life in prison), it is the minority who endorses the harshest alternative. If more detail is given about the crime (e.g., the robbery did not cause physical harm) or about the law breaker (juvenile or mentally disordered), then the public is more understanding and tolerant. Nonetheless, "get tough" policies abound. It is understandable that the public cannot be informed on all facts related to public policy. However, it appears inexcusable that so many political leaders are neither well informed nor interested in educating their constituents. As Tonry (2004: p. 15) wrote, "Political courage is required… a vote to repeal, narrow, or weaken a three-strikes law can be portrayed as being soft on crime. This makes elected officials risk averse."

3. Deterrence

(a) Imprisonment as a Deterrent. There is little evidence that "get tough" interventions such as three-strikes and truth-in-sentencing laws deter crime. When we consider the general literature on the effect of imprisonment on recidivism, once again the evidence is elusive. Narrative and meta-analytic reviews of the literature agree that the severity or length of the sentence is unrelated to crime (e.g., Nagin, Cullen, & Jonson, 2009). In the most recent meta-analysis, Petrich and his colleagues (Petrich, Pratt, Jonson, & Cullen, 2021) found longer sentences were associated with an *increase* in the recidivism of those released from prison (see Resource Note 13.1). In other words, prisons may be criminogenic.

RESOURCE NOTE 13.1

The Effects of Prison Sentences on Recidivism

Imprisonment is expected to deter individuals from further crime. Incarceration curtails personal liberty and deprives one of the pleasures normally enjoyed in daily life. These are thought to be punishing enough that, when experienced, individuals would avoid the behavior that led to the punishment. If imprisonment does not deter, then perhaps the period of deprivation was simply not long enough to feel the full impact of punishment. Penal policy over the past decades has clearly followed this argument. However, does imprisonment and increasing the time spent in prison really reduce recidivistic crime?

Damon Petrich, Travis Pratt, Cheryl Jonson, and Francis Cullen (2021) tried to answer this question through a meta-analytic review of the prison literature. The studies selected fell mostly into two categories: (1) studies that compared community-based individuals (e.g., probationers) to inmates and (2) studies that compared prisoners serving longer sentences to inmates serving shorter sentences (e.g., inmates released on parole with inmates who were ineligible for parole). Petrich et al. also coded for a wide array of methodological and sample characteristics that permitted for a detailed moderator analysis.

Altogether, 116 studies from 15 countries representing more than 4.5 million individuals were identified for analyses. The 116 studies produced 981 effect sizes. A summary of the findings follows.

The overall average effect of custody and recidivism was $r = 0.08$ ($k = 981$). The way that recidivism was coded meant that custody was associated with an eight percentage point *higher* reoffending rate compared to community-based clients. An extensive moderator analysis showed that when study characteristics were considered the effects of a custodial sentence did not change. Sample size, study design, length of follow-up, measure of recidivism, publication type, and the application of statistical controls had no bearing on the overall results. Regardless of the type of analysis, imprisonment was not associated with any decreases in recidivism. In fact, the results were the contrary.

continued

Some penologists have suggested that prisons may be "schools for crime." Prisons bring people together where individuals are given opportunities to learn the techniques for crime and rationalizations for criminal behavior. Low-risk inmates may be particularly vulnerable to an "indoctrination" into criminal patterns of thinking and behaving. The high-risk, on the other hand, do not need to learn any new tricks of the trade or receive further encouragement for their procriminal ideas.

To be clear, the authors of the report were not saying that there should be no prisons. Our sense of justice requires imprisonment for serious violations against society. Society needs to encourage a respect for law and demonstrate that some acts will not be tolerated. There are also some who pose such an extremely high risk to reoffend violently that the only way to prevent harm is to incarcerate them. However, those requiring lengthy periods of confinement are a small proportion of the prisoner population. Advocates of imprisonment may argue that even if imprisonment does not deter, it at least takes offenders out of circulation and public safety is achieved. One area of research rarely considered is the antisocial behavior that goes on within prisons. Inmates and guards are assaulted, rapes occur, possessions are stolen, contraband is smuggled, and drugs are misused. Crime on the street may be simply shifted to a different environment hidden from the public view.

What explains the criminogenic effects of prison? A number of explanations have been forwarded, including the idea that prisons are "schools for crime" and that since there is so little treatment available in most prison systems, the way justice-involved persons enter prison is the way they leave it. In a meta-analysis by Marsh, Fox, and Sarmah (2009), a reduction in recidivism was only found when treatment was delivered. Another explanation relates back to the earlier discussion of the communities to which inmates return (the "million-dollar" blocks). Any potential deterrent effects may be counterbalanced by the criminogenic neighborhoods where the ex-offender resides (Liu, Visher, & Sun, 2021).

Before moving on to evaluations of noncustodial deterrents, it is worthwhile to examine the *general* deterrent value of the death penalty as it is the most severe form of punishment. The question posed here is whether the application of capital punishment will deter members of the general public from committing murder. There have been at least two meta-analytic reviews of the literature. The first review of 95 studies of executions found a small deterrent effect on homicides, but the effect was largely moderated by the study's methodology (Yang & Lester, 2008). The second review of 102 studies found the profession of the author to be the only variable related to a deterrent effect (Gerritzen & Kirchgässner, 2013). Economists who were the authors of the study tended to find the death penalty to work. At the very least, there is no convincing evidence that capital punishment deters crime.

(b) Deterrence and Intermediate Sanctions. *The Programs.* In the 1980s, because of the pressure of overcrowded prisons, alternatives to imprisonment were needed that were harsher than probation but not as severe or costly as prison. Alternative punishments were to give judges more choices in order to fit the crime properly to the punishment and achieve a "rational" sentencing system. The most well-known forms of intermediate sanctions are Intensive Supervision Programs (ISPs), shock incarceration (e.g., boot camps, Scared Straight), electronic monitoring, and more recently, Project HOPE.

Georgia was the first state to introduce an ISP (1982). The ISP in Georgia consisted of 25 probationers supervised by two officers—a probation officer who did the counseling and case management and a "surveillance" officer who checked curfews, conducted drug tests, and made unannounced home visits. Within a decade, almost every state had an ISP (Cullen, Wright, & Applegate, 1996). ISP programs were soon followed in the 1990s with aftercare programs for youth and young adults released from custody that included close supervision *and* treatment.

Shock incarceration programs expose offenders to the harshness of prison life with the hope that it will shock them away from a criminal lifestyle. The most popular form of shock incarceration is the military-style boot camp. Once again, Georgia holds the distinction of opening the first shock incarceration/ boot camp in the United States (1983). Georgia's program involved military-style drills and long hours of physical labor. There was no treatment. Although other boot camps had a counseling/treatment component, it was the drills, exercise, and labor that consumed eight or more hours of the day (Taxman, Smith, & Rudes, 2020). At the peak of their popularity in 2000, there were 95 boot camps for adults and 56 boot camps for juveniles (Armstrong, 2004). Boot camps were also established in Canada (briefly) and in the United Kingdom (Farrington, Hancock, Livingston, Painter, & Towl, 2000).

One variant of shock incarceration was New Jersey's Juvenile Awareness Project, more popularly known as "Scared Straight." Youths visited "lifers" in Rahway State Prison where the inmates described to their audience, in colorful detail, the horrors of prison life. This "shock confrontation" approach was intended to show the youths what would happen if they followed a life of crime. A television documentary popularized the program and led to similar projects in other parts of the United States, Canada, and Europe (Finckenauer, Gavin, Hovland, & Storvoll, 1999). Other forms of "awareness" programs (i.e., awareness of the personal costs of crime) have been instituted across school environments, especially in the area of substance misuse (Figure 13.2).

Electronic monitoring programs have an interesting origin. Judge Jack Love of New Mexico was reading a *Spider-Man* comic book in which the villain attached an electronic monitoring device to track Spider-Man. This allowed the criminal to carry out his crimes when Spider-Man was not around. Why not, thought Love, turn the tables and put electronic bracelets on the criminals so that the authorities would know their whereabouts? Thus was born electronic monitoring (EM) for justice-involved persons. Today, EM programs use GPS technology and can be found in all US states and throughout many parts of the world (Nellis, 2017). In 2015, it was estimated that there were more than

Figure 13.2

Teaching Awareness of the Consequences of Drug Misuse

Source: Wikipedia Commons

130,000 people under EM supervision in the United States alone, a 140 percent increase over 10 years (Pew Charitable Trusts, 2016).

One of the newest intermediate sanctions is Project HOPE (Honest Opportunity Probation with Enforcement). The project was developed by an Hawaiian judge called Steven Alm in 2004 (Alm, 2011). Judge Alm's view was that the frequent return of probationers to court for violations was because the violations were not followed with predictable and serious consequences. In order to remedy this problem, he introduced a program, with the cooperation of the police, probation, court prosecutors, and his fellow judges, where violations of the conditions of probation were met with a "swift and certain" punishment. Higher-risk probationers, as measured by the LSI-R, and sexual offenders from the Honolulu area of Hawaii were the target participants (the original name for the program began with "Hawaii" and later changed to "Honest" as the program's popularity grew). Upon entry into the program, the judge would give a "warning hearing" outlining the consequences for a violation of the conditions of probation. They were told that any violation would lead to an immediate arrest and placement in jail. This swift and certain punishment was hypothesized to deter further violations.

The Evidence. Leaving aside Project HOPE for now, none of these intermediate punishments have demonstrated reductions in recidivism. Furthermore, under certain conditions, these programs have made matters worse by increasing recidivism and correctional costs. A brief summary of the evaluation literature follows.

There have been a number of meta-analytic reviews on the effectiveness of ISP that found either no effect or a small reduction in recidivism depending on certain study characteristics (Farrington & Welsh, 2005; James, Stams, Asscher, De Roo, & van der Laan, 2013; Weaver & Campbell, 2015). A recent review examined the effectiveness of aftercare/reentry and IPS for youth. Aftercare/ reentry programs are for those released from custody who are supervised in the community and provided with services to enhance their chance of success. Jessica Bouchard and Jennifer Wong (2018) identified 10 aftercare and 15 ISP studies. The authors measured two types of outcomes: (1) charge/arrested, and (2) convicted. Of the 11 analyses conducted, only one demonstrated a significant effect and that was for aftercare when the outcome was a charge or re-arrest ($r = 0.05$).

A second meta-analysis by Elizabeth Drake (2018) also found ISP unrelated to recidivism ($r = 0.00$, $k = 14$). However, her meta-analysis also reported on ISP with RNR services and the cost benefits of different supervision strategies. First, ISP with RNR treatment was associated with a significant reduction in recidivism ($r = 0.08$, $k = 14$). Second, ISP without treatment yielded a net cost to taxpayers and crime victims of approximately $5,000, while ISP with RNR treatment showed a net benefit of $7,000 per participant. The meta-analytic findings of RNR supervision, where community supervision officers act directly as an "agent of change," also produced significant reductions in recidivism and positive net benefits to taxpayers and victims of crime of about US$7,000 per participant.

Evaluations of shock incarceration and boot camps have also found that treatment is required to reduce recidivism. Doris MacKenzie, Robert Brame, David McDowall, and Claire Souryal (1995) examined eight state boot camps. Although groups were not randomly assigned, statistical controls were introduced for factors that could have influenced recidivism. One-half of the programs evidenced lower re-arrest rates than the controls, but reductions in recidivism were with the boot camps that had a treatment component. Their conclusion: "military drill and ceremony, hard labor, physical training, and strict rules and discipline… in and of themselves do not reduce recidivism" (p. 351). More recent evaluations of boot camps have not altered this conclusion (Bergin, 2016; Meade & Steiner, 2010). Only when there is a treatment component do we find positive findings (Hoge, 2016).

The New Jersey Scared Straight program was first evaluated by James Finckenauer and his colleagues in the late 1970s. Forty-six juveniles who visited lifers in prison were compared to 35 control subjects. A six-month follow-up (Finckenauer, 1979) found that the youths who attended the Rahway program had *higher* re-arrest rates (41.3 percent) than the youths who were not exposed to the program (11.4 percent). Surprisingly, 19 of the 46 youths attending the program did not even have a prior criminal record (a violation of the risk principle).

Despite the contraindicative findings, Scared Straight programs continued to be adopted in other US jurisdictions and in the United Kingdom, Australia, and Norway. Evaluations of many of these programs have shown that none of them reduced recidivism. In a meta-analysis of nine randomized studies, Petrosino, Turpin-Petrosino, Hollis-Peel, and Lavenberg (2013) found that participation in Scared Straight, on average, actually was more harmful to juveniles than simple cautioning. A more recent meta-analysis of 13 studies found a nonsignificant $r = 0.05$ (van der Put, Boekhout, et al., 2021). Despite the lack of evidence, such programs remain popular, and as Jeff Maahs and Travis Pratt (2017) have pointed out, TV shows like *Beyond Scared Straight* are enormously entertaining.

Finally, there are the electronic monitoring (EM) programs (and included here are the more recent GPS systems used to track offenders). EM is supposed to be an "alternative" to imprisonment. Instead of a prison sentence, the person is given a community sentence and required to stay at home ("house arrest"). An electronic signaling device, usually attached to the ankle, permits monitoring of the individual's location. Leaving the home without permission would set off an alarm, and the authorities would seek the person's apprehension.

Research on EM has left us with four general conclusions. First, most EM programs do not offer an alternative to prison. The people in these programs are often low risk, who would have received a community-based sanction anyway. That is, EM programs appear to widen the correctional net, applying more rather than fewer controls (Nellis, 2017). Second, there is little convincing evidence that EM reduces recidivism. A meta-analysis by Belur et al. (Belur, Thornton, et al., 2020) reported mixed results that depended on a range of methodological factors. For example, when time to reoffend was used (i.e., how quickly someone recidivates), then EM showed a significant reduction in recidivism ($r = 0.09$, $k = 5$). However, when the measure was a binary yes/no then the effect size became nonsignificant ($r = 0.06$, $k = 14$). Third, and consistent with the findings reported earlier, it is the addition of a treatment component to EM that results in reduced recidivism (Bonta, Wallace-Capretta, & Rooney, 2000). And finally, at least with sexual offenders, EM is not cost-effective (Omori & Turner, 2015).

Returning to Project Hope, does a swift and certain punishment-oriented intervention work for high-risk probationers? There has been one randomized control evaluation completed by Hawken and Kleiman (2009). Probationers were randomly assigned to HOPE ($N = 330$) or routine probation ($N = 163$). At one year, the HOPE probationers had fewer new arrests compared to the probationers receiving the usual supervision (21 percent vs. 47 percent). Although a randomized experimental design was used, there were some problematic design flaws such as the failure to report on the actual risk level of the probationers (were they all high risk?) or exactly how the officers supervised their clients (did they follow RNR?). In addition, why would deterrence suddenly work so well now when it has not worked in other sanctions (Duriez, Cullen, & Manchak, 2014)?

Since the last edition of this book, research on HOPE has continued. A large well-designed randomized experiment was conducted across four sites in the

US (Lattimore, MacKenzie, et al., 2016). Over 1,500 individuals were randomly assigned to HOPE ($N = 743$) or probation-as-usual ($N = 761$). There were no differences in the recidivism rates for the two groups. A subsequent study of the sample found HOPE to cost more than probation-as-usual (Cowell, Barnosky, et al., 2018). So, in light of the evidence, will HOPE slowly fade away?

Cullen, Pratt, Turanovic, and Butler (2018) argue that this will not be the case. Once you have HOPE operating in 160 locations it is not only difficult to dismantle so many programs, but the advocates have been relentless in their support of HOPE. Advocates (Judge Alm, and researchers Angela Hawken and Mark Kleinman) write that HOPE, as practiced in the evaluations, did not truly follow the HOPE principles (Alm, 2016), criticize the external evaluations (Hawken, 2018; Kleiman, Kilmer, & Fisher, 2014), argue that even if it doesn't work it furthers the noble goal of therapeutic jurisprudence (Bartels, 2019), and repurpose HOPE with the goals of reducing substance misuse or increased personal accountability (Frailing, Rapp, & Taylor, 2023). According to Cullen and his colleagues (2018), HOPE is entering into a dangerous "post-factual world" where evidence no longer matters.

4. *The Unfulfilled Promise of Fairness*

Advocates of truth-in-sentencing have argued that the predictability of mandatory sentencing policy would reduce reliance on incarceration and bring fairness to the criminal justice system (the von Hirsch argument). Beginning in the 1970s judges would be required to operate within sentencing guidelines that matched the punishment to the crime and not the person. Thus, a similar act committed by different people would receive the same consequence. The guidelines are not all the same across 19 US jurisdictions that have them (Frase, 2019; Mitchell, 2017). Coupled with sentencing guidelines was the abolition of parole and the introduction of parole release guidelines. England and Wales also adopted sentencing guidelines in 2003 (Pina-Sánchez, Brunton-Smith, & Li, 2020). With respect to reducing imprisonment, the evidence is mixed, with some reporting no changes in the use of imprisonment while others have found increases (Frase, 2019). The variation in findings may be explained by differences in adherence to guidelines (in some jurisdictions prosecutors, judges, and corrections officials have found ways of sidestepping guidelines).

When it comes to achieving fairness, one does not have to search for long to find examples in which fairness was clearly not achieved. Austin and colleagues (Austin et al., 1999) presented a few "typical" cases from interviews with 100 three-strikes offenders. One person received 27 years for attempting to sell stolen property valued at $90; another received 25 years for reckless driving (a police car chase). Tonry (2021) adds the example of an individual who received a 20-year sentence for the theft of three pizzas.

Some may see these examples as nothing more than exceptions to the rule. Analyses of the racial composition of arrestees and prisoners suggest otherwise. With America's "war on drugs" and the police's targeting of drug crimes,

African Americans have been differentially affected (Kovera, 2019). General arrest rates are four times higher for African Americans than for whites, and the discrepancy widens for drug offenses (Donnelly, Wagner, et al., 2021). In 2017, 30 percent of the US prison population consisted of African Americans (Bronson, & Carson, 2019). Although legal factors are the best predictors of sentencing, a number of studies also report that racial factors often play a role in sentencing (Kovera, 2019; Painter-Davis, & Ulmer, 2020).

Racial bias has also been reported in death penalty sentencing. In 2020, there were 2,469 inmates on death row in the US; 41 percent were African American, 56 percent were Caucasian, and 15 percent were Hispanic (Snell, 2021). Note that in the general population, African Americans represent approximately 12 percent of the US population (Hispanics are approximately 18 percent of the population). These percentages have not changed significantly since at least 2005. Seventeen prisoners were executed that same year and six were African American (five were white, two were Hispanic, and the rest were undefined). Although early research found that African Americans convicted of homicide, especially if their victim was white, were more likely to receive the death penalty (Aguirre & Baker, 1990), recent research has found little evidence to support this view (Jennings, Richards, Smith, Bjerregaard, & Fogel, 2014; Ulmer, Kramer, & Zajac, 2020).

Finally, there has been considerable interest in the effects of mandatory sentencing policies and sentencing guidelines on women in conflict with the law. When sentencing guidelines are introduced, there were three possible options. First, sentences can be reduced for men to bring them more in line with the sentences women receive. Second, sentences for men and women can converge to some midpoint. Third, sentences can increase for women. Historically, women have enjoyed leniency from the courts. Sentencing guidelines, however, require that criminal acts are treated equally and render personal factors (e.g., gender) inconsequential. Some have found that the sentences for women increased under the guidelines (e.g., Frase, 2019). However, the effects are quite complicated. For example, women receive longer sentences if they are: (1) from the southern US states (Holland & Prohaska, 2021) and (2) from a political and religious conservative community (Kim, Wang, & Cheon, 2019)

Summary

It is astonishing that in spite of the negative findings, criminal justice sanctions still remain wildly popular. Legislators continually try to come up with harsher penalties, criminologists continue to conduct studies hoping to find that deterrence will work, and programs are made more demeaning.

A number of factors operate to keep punishment entrenched in criminal justice policy. First, people *believe* in the effectiveness of punishment (Lansford, Cappa, et al., 2017). Second, politicians and legislators, rightly or wrongly, think that being "tough on crime" is what the public wants. Third, rehabilitation is seen as being soft on crime and not effective. Finally, and borrowing from a point made by Finckenauer et al. (1999), the lack of awareness about the research facilitates program inertia. In some areas, this situation may be changing. For example, Francis Cullen and colleagues (Cullen, Blevins, Trager, & Gendreau, 2005) have found that the negative research on boot camps has diminished the appeal of this form of intermediate sanction. However, once a politically popular program is up and running, it takes a great deal of effort to alter its course.

The difficulty in discarding ineffective crime programs is a combination of the public panic about a perceived threat (with the media fueling the fear) and politicians' unquestioning promotions of the program in question. Griffin and Miller (2008) called the result "crime control theatre" (CCT). CCT describes interventions that *appear* to address crime but there is no evidence that they do (recall "correctional quackery" described in Chapter 2). Examples provided by DeVault, Miller, and Griffin (2016) are the "three-strikes" laws described in this chapter and sexual offender registration laws to be described in the next chapter.

The Psychology of Punishment

Why Doesn't Punishment Work?

The answer to the question posed above can be found in the hundreds of studies conducted by psychologists. We know a great deal about when punishment works (i.e., inhibits behavior) and when it does not work. This knowledge comes from both laboratory and applied studies with animals and humans that were conducted 40 and 50 years ago. Here, studies from the 1960s and 1970s are cited to underscore the point that knowledge of the effectiveness of punishment has been well known in the psychology community for a very long time. Yet criminologists and policymakers ignored this body of research as they developed "get tough" approaches for dealing with crime.

Punishment, or a cost, is defined as a consequence to a behavior that decreases the likelihood of the behavior from reoccurring (see also Chapter 3). There is no mention of pain or suffering in the definition. Any consequence to a behavior, painful or not, that reduces the probability of the behavior is a cost.

A cost can be additive or subtractive. Additive costs are what come to mind when most people think about punishment. Adding a painful stimulus (e.g., spanking a child, yelling at an employee, delivering an electric shock to a rat) is expected to inhibit or reduce the probability of behavior. However, *removing* a reward or something valued (i.e., a subtractive cost) can also decrease the probability of behavior re-occurring. Giving your partner "the cold shoulder" or sending a misbehaving child to their room ("time out") are examples of subtractive costs.

The literature on the effectiveness of punishment is rich and the types of punishments studied are varied. Many experiments use electric shock because of the high degree of control over its intensity and duration. However, there are studies using unpleasant odors, submerging a hand in freezing water, puffs of air to the eye, loud noises, removing money, placing children in a room away from rewards, forcibly repeating certain physical movements (overcorrection), and exposure to disgusting and unpleasant thoughts (Matson & Kazdin, 1981).

Conditions for Effective Punishment

Drawing on this literature, a brief summary of the important conditions for effective punishment, along with a commentary on the relevance of the research to the crime problem, follows.

Condition 1: Maximum Intensity. It is unclear whether the intensity of punishment is the most important factor in suppressing behavior, but it certainly ranks, along with immediacy, as one of the more important (Van Houten, 1983). At first blush, this last statement seems to say that if we simply "turn up the heat," then we can stop criminal behavior. However, it is not simply turning up the intensity dial. Studies suggest that we have to turn the dial to full in order to stop the targeted behavior completely.

In general, low levels of punishment do show an immediate suppression of behavior; however, the effects are temporary (Azrin, 1956). The behavior not only returns to its original levels, but it may even result in higher rates of responding. After all, the behavior must have been rewarded at some point for it to occur and, therefore, trying again and harder to gain reward should be expected. With the behavior returning at a higher rate, further increases in the intensity of punishment are needed to suppress behavior even for a short time. In addition, a low level of punishment intensity runs the risk of the subject learning to tolerate punishment (Solomon, 1964). In most Western countries and for justice-involved persons, sanctions are increased gradually. For example, the first-time offender who commits a minor nonviolent crime is likely to receive a minor sanction; only with return to the court for new crimes does the penalty increase.

Retributionists may propose to give law-breakers the maximum penalty right off the bat. Even when the maximum punishment as prescribed by law (barring the death penalty) is administered, the offending behavior continues for many. In a study of persons who had their driver's licenses suspended *for life*, only 17 percent gave up driving completely (Chang, Woo, & Tseng, 2006). The problem with a policy of maximum punishment for a crime is that it offends our sense of justice and fairness. Formalized systems of criminal justice try to follow a principle of proportionality (matching level of punishment to the severity of the crime). The option of maximum punishment is unacceptable to most.

Condition 2: Immediacy. The sooner a cost follows the behavior, the more likely that the behavior will be suppressed. Introducing a delay between the behavior and the cost can significantly alter the effectiveness of the punishment (Dinsmoor, 1998). Why is this? It is mainly because there are opportunities for the behavior to be reinforced prior to the delivery of punishment. One has to think of behavior as a chain of specific actions. The last action in the chain may be punished, and this may have some effect on the preceding responses, but the suppression effect diminishes the further the response is from the punishment.

To illustrate what could happen, consider someone who is caught breaking into a car (the behavior) and is arrested and placed in a police cell (the cost). What has the person learned? Perhaps what they have learned is that it is not worth opening a car door with a crowbar. However, the punishment is unlikely to affect the behaviors leading up to the crime (e.g., visiting criminal friends, smoking some drugs, and then going out for a little excitement). We can go one step further and imagine that the person is released on bail. What happens then? While waiting for trial and sentencing, the individual may still associate with criminal others, use drugs, and may even have occasion to commit undetected crimes. The opportunity for reinforcement of criminal behavior abounds.

Condition 3: Certainty. Avoidance theory explains how punishment "works" (Dinsmoor, 1955, 1998). Simply stated, punishment elicits an undesirable emotional response (fear, anxiety) and by *not* engaging in the behavior that produces punishment, the organism avoids the unpleasant emotion. Although behavior is inhibited because it avoids something unpleasant, the unpleasant feelings of anxiety and fear do not last forever. The physiological responses that we label as anxiety and fear (e.g., increased heart rate, sweating, etc.) dissipate. It is as though we forget how bad the punishment was; to be reminded, it is important that the undesirable behavior is punished every time it occurs.

Unlike rewards, with which infrequent or unpredictable reinforcement (referred to as variable ratio or interval schedules) lead to high-rate and stable behavior, allowing an undesirable behavior to go unpunished once in a while is counterproductive. People and animals *behave*; they rarely sit still. The criminal must be caught almost every time he or she commits a crime and not be allowed opportunities to engage in other unwanted behavior that may be rewarded.

Another factor that can influence perceived certainty of punishment is the peer group. Matthews and Agnew (2008) examined the interaction between perceived certainty of punishment and procriminal peer group among 1,625 high school students. Using self-reports of antisocial behavior and peer affiliation, they found that the perceived certainty of punishment (measured by a five-point scale of getting caught by the police) had no effect on criminal behavior for the students with delinquent peers. The authors hypothesized that procriminal peers may reduce the possibility of a deterrent effect by minimizing the chances of detection and reinforcing criminal behavior. Other moderators influencing the effects of perceived influence include age (Walters, 2018d) and procriminal thinking (Walters, 2020c).

Condition 4: No Escape or Reinforced Alternatives. When punished, an organism attempts to escape the situation. Escaping from an aversive situation can have two consequences: (1) the escape behavior is reinforced, or (2) the original behavior may continue because the organism now finds itself in a non-punishing situation (Van Houten, 1983). The behavioral outcome may be desirable (e.g., a boy leaves a group of children who are teasing him). Alternatively, the outcome could be undesirable (e.g., an inmate escapes from custody to rob again). Thus, a situation associated with punishment may serve as a cue to engage in escape behavior. To deal with such a situation, all routes to escape must be blocked to ensure that escape behavior is unrewarded.

The point was made earlier that people are always behaving and that behavior consists of a multitude of specific actions. Individuals have behavioral repertoires. For example, an individual may have the skills to read, cook an omelet, and paint murals. The activation of a certain set of behaviors depends upon whether the behavior is likely to be rewarded. It is unlikely that most people will read aloud a book to an empty classroom, cook a meal on an autobus, or paint a mural on the side of a stranger's house. The behaviors would not be rewarded in these situations. People choose behaviors that they think will be rewarded (i.e., signaled reward); if one behavior is not rewarded, then they choose another from their behavioral repertoire.

In any particular situation, an individual makes choices regarding what behavior to engage. A young man who is introduced to an attractive woman will choose from his behavioral repertoire the behavior that he thinks may gain her admiration. Should he smile, engage in polite conversation, or show her his tattoo of "Mom"? All of these behaviors may be in his repertoire, but they do not have equal chances of being met with success. In any given situation, behaviors form an ordering of their likelihood of being rewarded and punished. The most likely behavior in a specific situation is one that has the longest history of rewards and shortest history of costs in similar situations. The other behaviors follow according to their own individual reward/cost histories. The young man in our example may start with the behavior that was most successful for him in the past. However, if the behavior is met with a frown, then he resorts to another behavior that was perhaps not as successful in the past but may work this time. Thus, a punished response is not simply eliminated; it is displaced by another response (Dinsmoor, 1955).

Criminal behavior consists of many different acts, and high-risk, chronic justice-involved persons exhibit a variety of undesirable behaviors (e.g., dishonesty, physical aggression, thievery, etc.). Punishing one behavior (e.g., the dishonesty associated with fraud) leaves many other behaviors that could be used to achieve personal and illegitimate goals. Unless alternative pro-social behaviors are rewarded, criminal behavior, in one form or another, will continue.

Condition 5: The Density of Costs Must Outweigh the Density of Rewards. Any behavior has both rewards and costs associated with it (look back to Table 3.2 of Chapter 3). Going to work every day may produce a pay check and workplace friendship, but it also involves getting up in the morning, fighting rush-hour traffic, and coping with other irritants. Azrin, Holz, and Hake (1963) observed that behaviors with a significant history of rewards are more resistant to the effects of punishment than behaviors with a limited history of rewards. In the language of GPCSL, the greater the density of rewards associated with behavior in terms of intensity, immediacy, consistency, and variety, the greater the density of costs required to suppress behavior. High-risk individuals have high densities of rewards for criminal behavior and, thus, their behaviors are highly resistant to punishment.

Condition 6: The Effectiveness of Costs Interact with Person Variables. The effects of rewards and costs interact with a variety of person factors (e.g., biological, cognitive, state conditions). In other words, people respond differently to costs and even from one moment to another. A few days in jail may present very different costs for the individual who lives on the street versus the white-collar criminal. A verbal reprimand would have different effects depending upon whether an individual is intoxicated or not.

What does this say about the effectiveness of punishment? Gottfredson and Hirschi (1990) argued that the impulsiveness of many justice-involved persons would work against the threat of punishment. Indeed, those with high self-control are more deterred by punishment than those with low self-control (Fine & van Rooij, 2017). We must keep in mind, however, that there are many other person characteristics that come into play. For example, those with concrete thinking and oriented to the present situation are likely to have a childhood history of erratic and frequent punishment. This shapes a certain level of tolerance for punishment. Some may also have biological-temperamental traits that make them less responsive to punishment.

Inhibiting behavior requires judgments of the likelihood of certain outcomes (i.e., signaled costs). To the dismay of rational choice theories of crime, those who violate laws do not mimic computers. They do not always weigh the pros and cons of behavior carefully and accurately before making their choice. Studies show that they tend to underestimate the chances of being punished and overestimate the rewards of crime (Barnum, Nagin, & Pogarsky, 2021). Finally, when we consider some of the developmental experiences of many who come in conflict with the law—abuse and neglect—where is the logic that more of the same will suppress antisocial behavior? For costs to be effective, one of the necessary conditions is that they must be matched to the characteristics of the person. In the criminal justice system, a matching that depends on personal factors would violate the principles of fairness.

The Side Effects of Punishment

Even if we could replicate the conditions for effective punishment in the real world, we are still faced with what Skinner (1953: p. 190) referred to as the "unfortunate by-products of punishment." Punishment may suppress behavior, but it can also lead to unintended and undesirable behaviors (Newsom, Favell, & Rincover, 1983). Punishment is unpleasant either physically, emotionally, or psychologically. It is the avoidance of discomfort that explains why punishment suppresses behavior. An unpleasant consequence, however, may have the following "unfortunate by-products":

1. A painful consequence of sufficient intensity may interfere with other *desirable* behaviors. For example, a severe assault suffered by a woman at the hands of her partner may prevent her from socializing with friends, going to work, and enjoying recreational activities.

2. If intense punishment is coupled with a situation in which there is no escape, then there is the risk of developing "learned helplessness" (Seligman, 1975). This is a condition where a strategy for dealing with punishment is to do nothing. Learned helplessness has been used to explain depression (River, Borelli, Vazquez, & Smiley, 2018), poor coping with stress (Soral, Kofta, & Bukowski, M., 2021), and why battered women do not leave their partners (Heron, Eisma, & Browne, 2022).

3. When people are punished, they make attributions as to why they were punished. In the learned helplessness paradigm, the individual learns that he or she has no control over the environment. There are other attributions that can be triggered by punishment. One is to view procriminal behavior as inappropriate and that the punishment was deserved. This attribution, however, is dependent upon a commitment to prosocial values and respect for the law, a problematic area for many justice-involved persons.

    If punishment is seen as unfair and undeserving, then anger and hate toward the punisher or feelings of rejection may be elicited. These negative emotions may facilitate undesirable behaviors such as reflexive aggression toward the punisher or ignoring attempts at influence by the other (Church, 1963; McCord, 1997). It is now well-established that corporal punishment of children leads to a range of detrimental outcomes such as poor mental health, substance misuse, and delinquency (Gershoff, Goodman, et al., 2018; Gershoff, & Grogan-Kaylor, 2016; Joyner & Beaver, 2022). Children who judge the disciplining techniques of parents as harsh tend to avoid parental contact, which further interferes with socialization efforts. One is reminded of Patterson's coercion theory of family processes and of Adverse Childhood Experiences discussed in Chapter 7.

4. Vicarious learning is a very important process. Bandura and Walters (1963) demonstrated that children may imitate the aggressive practices displayed by their parents. Watching parents and other authority figures (e.g., teachers) use physical punishment that is rewarded may provide learning opportunities for young children. By watching such models, children learn that aggression is acceptable. Research with families shows that high levels

of aggressive behavior and harsh parenting are strong predictors of delinquency (Tanner-Smith, Wilson, & Lipsey, 2013b).

5. From meta-analytic reviews, sanctions or punishments are associated with a small increase in criminal behavior. Perhaps some of this increase in the undesirable behavior can be explained by the individual's tolerance for punishment, perception of the unfairness of punishment, and witnessing antisocial behavior. Another explanation of this increase in criminal behavior following punishment relates to the gambler's fallacy. The gambler's fallacy is the belief that a string of bad luck will be followed by good luck (Pogarsky & Piquero, 2003). For the law-breaker, it is saying, "Yes, I have been caught the last few times, but next time I will get away with it." Although this effect is highly related to decisions around the certainty of costs, studies with justice-involved persons within the gambler's fallacy model are rare (Pogarsky, Roche, & Pickett, 2018).

Summary of Punishment

A general policy of punishment is wrought with difficulties, and yet we are faced with a need to discourage inappropriate behaviors and express dissatisfaction with violation of law. Punishing to express disapproval of criminal behavior is one thing; punishing to deter is another matter. With respect to the latter, many jurisdictions have become tougher and meaner in their application of punishment in a futile attempt to deter (see Resource Note 13.2 for a discussion of how we can act so harshly toward others). Scholars have noted the conditions needed for punishment to suppress behavior (see Figure 13.3)—and they can only inhibit behavior—are virtually impossible to meet in the criminal justice system. Police cannot be everywhere, the courts cannot pass sentence quickly enough (Project HOPE as an exception?), and correctional officials have difficulties ensuring adequate supervision and monitoring.

Remember: Punishment inhibits—it does not teach new behavior
⇨ Vary punishers (few universal punishers)
⇨ Immediate
⇨ Appropriate intensity
⇨ Type of person it works best with:
    * nonimpulsive, future-oriented
    * average to above-average IQ
    * minimal punishment history
    * cautious, avoids/minimizes excitement

Figure 13.3

A Summary of Conditions for Punishment to Work

RESOURCE NOTE 13.2

Personal Rationalizations for "Get Tough" and Countering the Rationalizations

Around the world incarceration rates have been rising for more than a decade, and nowhere is it higher than in the United States. What is interesting is that it appears that subjecting nearly seven million citizens to some form of correctional control and depriving them of their liberty is insufficient to quench the thirst to punish. In some states, probationers are asked to pay to be supervised, leading many to further debt (Link, 2023), and inmates are subjected to "no frills" prisons that have no television or recreation, or have limited family visits (Gottschalk, 2011). In Maricopa County, Arizona, under Sheriff Joe Arpaio's administration, male inmates wore pink underwear and women marched in chain gangs. Other states introduced pink prison uniforms (see Figure RN 13.2-1). The list of humiliations seems endless. The question arises: "How can we, personally and as a member of society, live with our mean behavior toward our fellow man?" If we can understand the psychological mechanisms that avoid and alleviate any shame or guilt over such behavior, then we can exercise corrective actions.

The basic answer to what allows us to be mean-spirited at times is that we engage in cognitive techniques that justify the behavior and absolve personal responsibility. By this point in the text, the reader is familiar with many of these techniques. They are similar to Sykes and Matza's "techniques of neutralization" and what some psychologists label as "rationalizations" and "moral disengagement" (Bandura, 2015). Here, we call them "meanness justifications," and countering them requires invoking the research evidence. Some common justifications and their counters follow.

1. *Punishment deters.* Saying to oneself that "punishment deters," "it suppresses behavior," "I have seen punishment stop the behavior," and similar statements harken to an *Appeal to the Evidence*. The general counter to the notion that punishment deters is to point to the evidence that it does not work. There are three major sources of evidence. First, there are the psychology laboratory studies that show that punishment will suppress behavior but under highly controlled conditions that the real world does not meet. Second, there is the criminal justice sanctioning research that punishment does not reduce recidivism and may even increase recidivism. Third, there is the rehabilitation research demonstrating that human service reduces recidivism, especially if the RNR model is followed.

2. *Punishment is less expensive than rehabilitation.* One may accept the fact that punishment does not deter and that recidivism is reduced only with rehabilitation services, but the services of psychologists, psychiatrists, and other counseling professions cost too much. This justification is an *Appeal to the Wallet*. This can easily be countered with the now extensive evidence on the cost-effectiveness of rehabilitation programs. Many treatment programs have high financial benefits compared to punishment-oriented programs (Drake, 2018).

continued

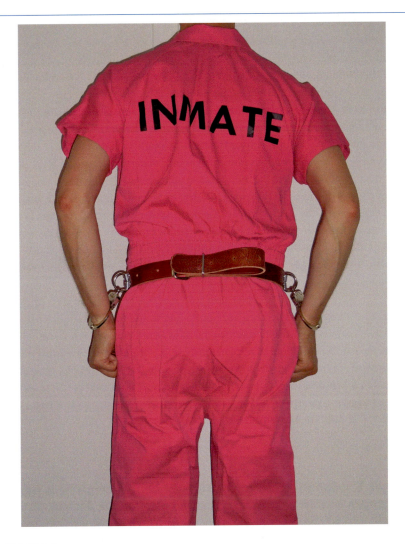

Figure RN 13.2.1

Wearing a Pink Prison Uniform

Source: Wikiwand.com

3. *People deserve to be punished for the harm they cause.* The "just deserts" argument is an *Appeal to Fairness.* No one can argue against fairness, but the methods used to achieve fairness (e.g., truth-in-sentencing, three-strikes, sentencing guidelines) have not resulted in fairness. One can counter this argument by: (1) citing outrageous anecdotes (e.g., a person receiving a 27-year sentence for stealing $90 worth of property), (2) noting it is an attack on democracy, with millions of Americans disenfranchised, (3) pointing out that the methods have resulted in bias against African Americans (e.g., an arrest rate four times higher than for whites) and women

continued

(e.g., under sentencing guidelines, there has been an increase in sentence length for women), and (4) referring to the negative consequences to family (e.g., one in 14 American children will have a parent in prison by the age of 14; Poehlmann-Tynan & Turney, 2021) and community (the million-dollar blocks). Is this fair?

4. *Revenge feels good*. In order to make it look like you are not mean, the statement "revenge feels good" is presented as an *Appeal to Victim Healing*. That is, the act of revenge helps the victim reach satisfaction through catharsis. This is referred to as the "comparative suffering hypothesis," wherein observing a similar level of suffering endured by the victim in the perpetrator will be satisfying. However, support for this hypothesis is weak (Gollwitzer, Meder, & Schmitt, 2011). Victim satisfaction is more likely when the justice-involved person understands that revenge is a justified response to his or her criminal behavior (Gollwitzer et al., 2011). This may explain some of the high victim satisfaction ratings found in restorative justice programs (Fulham, Blais, Rugge, & Schultheis, in press; Nascimento, Andrade, & de Castro Rodrigues, 2022).

The justifications for being mean are not limited to the four techniques listed. The list can be easily expanded by simply referring back to Sykes and Matza's techniques of neutralization. We can have *denial of responsibility* (e.g., "the jury decided the punishment, not me"), *denial of victim* (e.g., dehumanize the person; "he is a cold-blooded killer"), and even *appeal to a higher loyalty* (e.g., "God demands an eye for an eye"). The point is that we often engage in cognitive techniques meant to distance us from the harm caused to others, and we should be aware of them.

The great "get tough" experiment violates almost every RNR principle and especially the overarching principles of *Respect for the Person, Psychological Theory*, and the *Enhancement of Crime Prevention Services*. What many criminal justice policies fail to consider is that there are other ways of decreasing criminal behavior, and this is achieved by following Principle 4 of the RNR model, *Introduce Human Services*. Treatment is all about increasing the rewards associated with prosocial behavior to make the rewards associated with crime less attractive. A multi-pronged attack involving a shifting of the rewards and costs for both criminal and prosocial behavior rather than a one-sided attack would be more effective (recall Table 13.1). As we saw earlier, rehabilitation programs that teach and reward prosocial behaviors can achieve the desired effect.

An Alternative to Retribution: Restorative Justice

Not everyone has been pleased with the "get tough" movement. Victims were particularly dissatisfied with the criminal justice system for many reasons. They felt insignificant in the criminal justice process (i.e., reduced mainly to providing witness testimony) and ignored in the delivery of services (i.e., perpetrators of crime received treatment services while victims had to cope on their own).

The victim movement that began in the 1980s was influential in ensuring that law breakers received their just deserts. The dominant position among many victim advocacy groups was that the criminal justice system was too soft on justice-involved persons and that harsher penalties were needed to deliver justice for the harm suffered by victims. However, others saw things differently. In contrast to the just deserts perspective was the view that the hurts need to be healed. This healing process required a collaboration among wrongdoers, victims, and the community to correct the wrongs committed by offenders. The concepts of healing, collaboration, and making amends are central to *restorative justice.*

The first criminal justice- based, restorative justice program can be traced to a small town in Canada (Kitchener, Ontario). In 1974, a probation officer with strong ties to the Mennonite church asked a judge to delay the sentencing of two adolescents convicted of vandalism while he tried something different (Peachy, 1989). He proposed to the judge that he would take the teenagers to meet their victims and offer to make amends. The youths would benefit by understanding how their behavior affected the victims, and the victims would have the opportunity to say what they needed to make things right. From this trial grew what are called Victim–Offender Reconciliation Programs (VORPs).

Restorative justice programs such as VORP and Family Group Conferences (FGC; meetings of offender, victim, parents, and community members) have a number of characteristics. First of all, crime is seen as a violation of interpersonal relationships. Second, all who are harmed, the transgressor included, must take responsibility for "making right the wrong." This requires a dialogue between perpetrator and victim wherein they discuss how the crime has affected them, preferably through face-to-face meetings. The justice-involved person has the opportunity to make amends and offer an apology. The victim has the chance to tell the lawbreaker how he or she has been affected by the crime and what is needed to heal the pain. Perhaps the victim may even forgive the person, although this is not a necessary component. Finally, the two, sometimes with the support of community members, discuss how each of them can contribute to alleviating the harm created from the crime.

Accepting responsibility for the hurt and victim participation in resolving conflict are core to restorative justice. This said, however, there is controversy about how much victim involvement is required in order for a program to be called "restorative" (Strang & Braithwaite, 2017; Zehr & Mika, 2017). Programs such as VORP and FGC are unambiguous restorative justice practices. On the other hand, there are programs in which there is little, if any, direct contact between the victim and the perpetrator and agreements are brokered through an intermediary (Zehr & Mika, 2017). In these cases, the victim may agree to an offer of restitution (either financial or through community service) or to a written apology. Should court-ordered restitution or community service be considered "restorative" even though the victim provided no input? These are but two debatable illustrations of what could be considered restorative justice practices.

Restorative justice programs and practices exist in North America, Australia, New Zealand, Europe, and parts of Asia and Africa. Restorative justice principles are also exerting an influence on legislative policy and the criminal justice system. In New Zealand, the Children, Young Persons, and Their Families Act prevents the court from making a decision until an FGC is held. Finally, there have been various Truth and Reconciliation Commissions formed to deal with such issues as human rights abuses during a period of apartheid in South Africa (Villa-Vicencio, 1999) and in residential schools in Canada (Truth and Reconciliation Commission of Canada, 2015).

Restorative justice programs have proliferated, and although much of the research has been methodologically weak and largely descriptive of processes, there has been an increase in quasi-experimental and randomized experiments in recent years (Wilson, Olaghere, & Kimbrell, 2018; Weatherburn & Macadam, 2013). The difficulty in reaching definitive conclusions about the impact of restorative justice is two-fold. First, as noted earlier, there is little consensus over what constitutes a restorative justice intervention (Piggott & Wood, 2018). Second, what are the expected outcomes (e.g., victim satisfaction, reduced recidivism) and does achieving one outcome over another define success? For example, Robinson and Shapland (2008) do not agree that recidivism is an important outcome measure by which to judge the value of a restorative justice program. However, their opinion tends to be in the minority.

There have been at least five published meta-analyses/reviews. Achieving victim satisfaction has consistently been reported. In a meta-analysis of 13 studies, the average effect size for victim satisfaction was 0.19 (Latimer, Dowden, & Muise, 2005). A meta-analysis of 10 experimental studies of face-to-face victim–offender meetings found an average effect size was 0.16 (Strang, Sherman, Mayo-Wilson, Woods, & Ariel, 2013). A meta-analysis by Wilson, Olaghere, and Kimbrell (2018) found an effect size of 0.34 ($k = 7$) for victim satisfaction (this review focused on youth under the age of 18). The most recent meta-analytic review by Fulham and her colleagues (Fulham, Blais, Rugge, & Schultheis, in press) reported $r = 0.30$. Perpetrator satisfaction with the process is similar but slightly lower. Finally, Ana Nascimento and her colleagues (Nascimento, Andrade, & de Castro Rodrigues, 2022) reviewed 35 studies focused on the psychological impact on victims meeting the offender. Although they did not report effect size estimates, the range of positive outcomes is noteworthy. For example, 17 studies reported decreases in negative emotions and five studies found decreases in post-traumatic stress symptoms.

When it comes to recidivism, the findings are more modest. The findings are consistent with an average r around 0.07 (Andrews & Bonta, 2010a; Fulham et al., in press; Latimer et al., 2005; Strang et al., 2013). The two exceptions are that reported by Bradshaw and Roseborough ($r = 0.13$; 2005) and Wilson et al. ($r = 0.12$; 2018). Both reviews focused on youths. The average effect size of 0.07 found by most of the reviews is slightly smaller than providing any type of human service ($r = 0.10$) and much lower than RNR treatment ($r = 0.26$). However, restorative justice programs may have two advantages over criminal justice sanctions. First, there is some evidence that if treatment is added to a restorative justice context, the impact on recidivism is enhanced ($r = 0.25$; Bonta, Wallace-Capretta, Rooney, & McAnoy, 2002). Second, restorative justice programs are cost-effective (Strang et al., 2013; Weatherburn & Macadam, 2013).

Interpreting the results from evaluation studies is difficult because of the significant attrition rates found in many restorative justice programs. There are very few studies that exceed a victim–offender meeting rate of 50 percent (see Table 13.2 from Andrews & Bonta, 2010b). It is clear from the research that not all victims want to meet their perpetrator. Thus, the high levels of satisfaction could be due to a subject selection factor. Also, the majority of those who have committed nonviolent crimes (about 85 percent; Bonta, Jesseman, Rugge, & Cormier, 2006) with most programs typically exclude sexual offenders, domestic violence cases, and other serious crimes, although there are exceptions (Acker, 2006; Gang, Loff, Naylor, & Kirkman, 2021).

Theoretically, why should we expect restorative justice by itself to have an impact on criminal behavior? Besides possibly providing appropriate treatment to address criminogenic needs, there are a number of other possible mechanisms associated with restorative justice principles that may impact on reoffending. Understanding the impact of a crime on a victim may challenge a perpetrator's rationalizations for crime and increase empathy for the victim, thereby inhibiting harmful behavior. The forgiving, nonpunitive context of the victim–peretrator encounter may nourish a more prosocial attitude. When community members participate in a restorative justice process, they may act as an informal support system providing concrete assistance in acquiring prosocial behaviors. Evaluators of restorative justice programs are beginning to systematically examine the impact of restorative justice on these potential intermediary targets (Suzuki & Yuan, 2021).

Worth Remembering

1. "Getting tough" has failed miserably in achieving the goals of fairness, cost-effectiveness, and enhancing public safety. Mandatory sentences, three-strikes, and harsher sentences have affected minorities disproportionately and at enormous costs. The costs are measured not only in monetary terms but also in terms of social consequences. With respect to deterrence, "getting tough" does not explain the reduction in crime rates seen over the past decade, and it has had no impact on recidivism. Despite what politicians think the public wants, when given the complete picture, most public opinion surveys show people are open to less punitive interventions.

2. The psychology of punishment shows that punishment will only "work" under very specific conditions, conditions that the criminal justice system cannot duplicate. Laboratory studies of punishment clearly show that for punishment to be effective it must follow the behavior with certainty and immediacy and at the right intensity. Furthermore, punishment has many undesirable "side effects" that are counterproductive in the suppression of antisocial behavior.

3. Restorative justice, a more respectful and inclusive approach for dealing with those who hurt victims and the community, may offer a viable alternative to "get tough" approaches in reducing crime.

   There is a shift underway from an obsession with punishing the justice-involved persons to more humane approaches for dealing with them. The growing influence of restorative justice and renewed interest in treatment reflect a dissatisfaction with the adversarial and punitive orientation of the present justice system. How far the influence of restorative justice will reach remains to be seen. Rehabilitation, however, already has made tremendous inroads and holds a promising future.

Recommended Readings

Michael Tonry has been at the forefront in thinking about the "get tough" approach and its most vocal critic. His thoughts on the subject are summarized in the chapter entitled "Doing Justice in Sentencing" (2021). A companion piece suggested to the reader is Petrich, Pratt, Jonson, & Cullen's (2021) *Custodial Sanctions and Reoffending: A Meta-analytic Review*. The authors show that imprisonment has failed to reduce recidivism and may even be crime producing. Jeff Maahs and Travis Pratt (2017) explain the popularity of Scared Straight as portrayed in the media. The title alone, "I hate these little turds!", should grab your attention.

Those interested in the psychology of punishment should access Azrin and Holz's chapter in W. K. Honig's (1966) classic text, *Operant Behavior: Areas of Research and Application*. More recent reviews can be found in most general introductory psychology textbooks.

For a general introduction to restorative justice, see Dennis Sullivan and Larry Tifft's (2005) *Restorative Justice: Healing the Foundations of Our Everyday Lives*. For a more academic treatment and extensive review, see the edited readings in Strang and Braithwaite (2017).

 Visit the Instructor and Student Resource to access additional exercises, videos and study materials to support this chapter: psychologycriminalconduct.routledge.com

CHAPTER 14 Criminal Subtypes: Intimate Partner Violence, the Mentally Disordered, and Sexual Offenders

In this chapter, we look at different "types" of offenders. The word "type" is used with some hesitation because the word conveys the idea of a clearly defined category with little or no overlap. However, many justice-involved persons do not neatly fit into any one category. In fact, very few specialize in only one type of crime. Sexual offenders commit nonsexual crimes, and male batterers assault others who are unrelated to them. The versatility of criminal offenders is illustrated in a survey of more than 2,000 male inmates from Australian prisons. Makkai and Payne (2005) found only 26 percent of the prisoners reporting having committed just one offense type. The weight of the evidence does appear to support versatility rather than offense specialization (Mazerolle & McPhedran, 2018). However, many do show a preference for certain antisocial acts that allow us to make rough categorizations (although versatility within these categories is still evident). For example, in a review of 25 studies of untreated firesetters, they were five times more likely to set another fire during follow-up than non-firesetters (Sambrooks, Olver, Page, & Gannon, 2021). Moreover, approximately 60 percent of the firesetters committed other crimes.

Sometimes scholars begin with dissecting the criterion behavior, or the criminal act, and then develop theories to explain the offense. Thus, there are theories of white-collar crime, vandalism, and violence. Instead of emphasizing these "mini-theories," the position is taken that much can be learned from a more comprehensive theoretical base and that the correlates of general criminal behavior show remarkable similarities for specific forms of deviance. Three major subtypes of justice-involved persons are presented in this chapter: those who commit intimate partner violence, the mentally disordered, and persons committing sexual crimes. Other subtypes could have been selected but the three to be described have a literature that has been linked to the RNR model. There is an exploding interest in research with people who have committed

DOI: 10.4324/9781003292128-17

acts of terrorism but there is only one study applying the RNR model (Herzog-Evans, 2019). On the face of it, the three subtypes may appear to represent extreme groups with little in common. However, sometimes there are more similarities than there are differences.

Intimate Partner Violence

The most recent prevalence estimates of Intimate Partner Violence (IPV) are provided by Sardinha and her colleagues (Sardinha, Maheu-Giroux, Stöckl, Meyer, & García-Moreno, 2022). Using data from the World Health Organization 2018 survey, a literature review of 366 studies along with country consultations, Sardinha et al. (2022) found 27 percent of women from 161 countries to have suffered IPV. In addition, 13 percent experienced IPV within the past year. Lifetime prevalence of physical violence was 21 percent and for sexual violence it was 2 percent. In addition, it was estimated that with the COVID-19 lockdowns IPV violence increased approximately eight percentage points, with the largest spikes appearing within the first week of closures (Kourti, Stavridou, et al., 2023; Piquero, Jennings, Jemison, Kaukinen, & Knaul, 2021).

Certain segments are particularly affected by IPV. Among visible minorities, for example, 53.6 percent of 2,000 Latino women who were surveyed in 2008 reported being a victim of interpersonal violence over their lifetime (Cuevas, Sabina, & Milloshi, 2012) and four out of 10 Black women in America will have suffered IPV (St. Vil, Sabri, Nwokolo, Alexander, & Campbell, 2017). Other groups disproportionately represented are Indigenous populations (Lysova, Dim, & Dutton, 2019) and members of the LGBTQ community (Kim & Schmuhl, 2021).

In a review of 750 articles published between 2000 and 2010, Sarah Desmarais and her colleagues found, for women, a rate of violent victimization of 23.1 percent in the past year (Desmarais, Reeves, Nicholls, Telford, & Fiebert, 2012). However, men were also victims of intimate partner violence (19.3 percent). In criminal justice samples, the prevalence rates were much higher (31.1 percent for women). Only one study in the review included male offenders, but it was estimated based on other sources that the rate for men would be between 44 and 49 percent. For women, IPV is also the leading cause of homicide death in the world (Devries, Mak, et al., 2013). IPV is also evident among same-sex couples (Rollè, Giardina, Caldarera, Gerino, & Brustia, 2018) but because the majority of victims are women, our discussion will focus on male batterers.

Studying violence within intimate relationships is important for a number of reasons. First, it helps to uncover ways of decreasing victimization. The woman who is abused by her partner is not only at risk for her own personal safety (Keller & Wagner-Steh, 2005) but also for the safety of her children (Osofsky, 2003). Second, both the women and the children who witness the violence are more likely to experience emotional, psychological, and behavioral problems

(Vu, Jouriles, McDonald, & Rosenfield, 2016). A meta-analysis of 207 studies by Spencer and her colleagues (Spencer, Mallory, et al., 2019) found women to be at an increased risk for depression ($r = 0.28$, $k = 85$) and post-traumatic stress disorder ($r = 0.35$, $k = 53$).

Third, we need to know who are the high-risk abusers. Their accurate identification is needed to inform police and other social agents who are empowered to remove aggressors for the protection of other family members. Because the majority of women, for various reasons, find it difficult to leave abusive relationships (Rajah & Osborn, 2022), they are at risk for revictimization. Social service providers also require knowledge of effective interventions for male batterers. Even when a woman leaves an abusive partner, the violence may continue with another woman as the victim. A recent meta-analysis by Cordier, Chung, Wilkes-Gillan and Speyer (2021) is quite informative. The researchers reviewed 25 studies on the effectiveness of protection orders (i.e., court-imposed prohibitions for the abuser to avoid contact with the victim). Even with such restrictions IPV recidivism rates ranged from 28.2 percent for police reports of violence to 34.3 percent for victim-reported abuse.

Finally, understanding IPV is important for the primary prevention of future violence. There are now a number of reviews of the literature agreeing that children who experienced and witnessed family violence have an increased risk of growing up to be violent in both intimate and general interpersonal relationships (Theobald, Farrington, Coid, & Piquero, 2016; O'Leary, Tintle, & Bromet, 2014). Among justice-involved samples the prevalence of witnessing family violence is very high. A review of 62 studies found rates of 41 percent for boys and men and 48 percent for girls and women (Wanamaker, Brown, & Czerwinsky, 2022). Furthermore, childhood aggression may also be predictive of spousal violence. A persuasive study in this regard comes from the Concordia Longitudinal Risk Project (Temcheff, Serbin, et al., 2008). More than 1,700 inner-city children from Montreal, Canada, were followed over a 30-year span. The investigators found that aggressive behavior in childhood predicted self-reported partner violence in adulthood ($r = 0.14$).

In this section, and similarly in the subsequent sections, the following questions derived from a PCC are asked:

1. Do men who commit violence against their partners have risk factors similar to general justice-involved persons?

2. What are the effective interventions for those who assault their partners?

Risk Factors and IPV: How Different Are Men Who Batter from Regular Criminals?

How similar and how different IPV perpetrators are from general justice-involved persons can be approached in three ways. First, we can examine the criminal histories and criminal futures of men who abuse their partners. If the man convicted of assault has an extensive history of IPV and a reoffending pattern of IPV that excludes other violent acts then we may conclude specialization. However, if history and future consist of a variety of non-IPV crimes then we may conclude that the person is a generalist and not much different from non-IPV offenders. The evidence suggests the latter (Hilton, & Eke, 2016; Juarros-Basterretxea, Herrero, Fernández-Suárez, Pérez, & Rodríguez-Díaz, 2018; Verbruggen, Blokland, Robinson, & Maxwell, 2020) and it has been apparent since at least 2006 (Piquero, Brame, Fagan, & Moffitt, 2006).

1. Similarities in the Criminal Past and Futures for Male Batterers and General Offenders. In a large study, 4,261 medium- to high-risk IPV inmates were compared to 4,261 non-IPV inmates (Stewart & Power, 2014). The IPV sample committed a variety of offenses not limited to IPV. For example, 48.3 percent had a history of property offenses and 27.4 percent had prior drug offenses. The corresponding rates for the non-IPV group were 44.1 percent and 41.6 percent. What stood out was that the IPV inmates compared to the non-IPV were higher risk and had more criminogenic and noncriminogenic needs.

2. The Central Eight and Intimate Partner Abuse. Second, we can look at how well the Central Eight risk/need factors (Chapter 3) line up with the risk/need factors for men who abuse their partners. Recall that the Central Eight is derived from a *General* Personality and Cognitive Social Learning perspective of criminal behavior and note that the italics are purposely added. The hypothesis forwarded here is that the Central Eight would be just as relevant to IPV as it is with general justice-involved persons. Some minor adjustments may be required (e.g., "it is OK to steal" becomes "it is OK to hurt my partner") but the same general constructs apply. We begin with Criminal History.

(a) Criminal History. The average effect sizes from two meta-analyses ranged from $r = 0.08$ (Spencer & Stith, 2020) up to 0.49 depending on how prior history was measured (Spencer, Stith, & Cafferky, 2022). The smaller effect size reported by Spencer and Stith (2020) may be an outlier as it dealt solely with intimate partner homicide and was correlational (as was Spencer et al., 2022). A history of sexual violence, stalking, and controlling behavior is a common finding (e.g., Spencer & Stith, 2020) and they apply equally to Blacks and Whites ($r = 0.38$ and $r = 0.23$; Kelly, Spencer, Keilhotz, McAllister, & Stith, 2022).

(b) Procriminal Attitudes. Procriminal attitudes in studies of IPV focus on attitudes specific to supporting partner violence. The "distorted thinking about IPV" such as "it is her fault" or "the alcohol made me lose control" is at the core of IPV (Senkans, McEwan, & Ogloff, 2020). Many different ways of assessing attitudes have been conducted. For example, in Spencer and Stith's review it was "jealousy" (e.g., "my partner must give me all the attention and to no one else; $r = 0.25$). Jealousy and fear of infidelity is often viewed as a main driver in IPV. In a systematic review of 51 papers from 28 countries the authors concluded "we found that real or suspected infidelity and RJ (romantic jealousy) were strongly related to IPV" (Pichon, Treves-Kagan, et al., 2020: p. 17).

Attitudes are developed early, beginning with exposure to family violence as a child (Copp, Giordano, Longmore, & Manning, 2019). Pamela Pilkington and her colleagues (Pilkington, Noonan, May, Younan, & Holt, 2021) provide an informative meta-analysis. Their review was of maladaptive schemas. Schemas are mental representations of the self, one's relationship to others, and the world in general. A schema domain will include a number of specific attitudes. For example, the schema "Mistrust Abuse" can include the attitude that "my partner cannot be trusted" or that "I am the boss and should be obeyed". In Pilkington et al.'s meta-analysis, effect sizes found among five studies that measured the Mistrust Abuse schema ranged from $r = 0.22$ to 0.41. Attitudes supportive of IPV have a clear link to the behavior.

(c) Procriminal Associates. Friends that support one's behavior are a powerful risk/need factor in GPCSL. Associates can provide the reward/cost contingencies that influence behavior for good or for bad. Surprisingly, there has been little research on whether a male batterer associates with other male batterers. Perhaps men try to hide and keep the violence at home. However, we do know that deviant peer influence is an important factor in dating violence. Three meta-analytic reviews have reported effect sizes in the range of $r = 0.20$ to 0.25 (Garthe, Sullivan, & McDaniel, 2017; Hebert, Daspe, et al., 2019; Park & Kim, 2018). We have little reason not to believe that associates supportive of aggressive and violent behavior would not also apply to IPV.

(d) Antisocial Personality Pattern (APP). APP is a broad category and described in Table 3.1 as being "impulsive, adventurous, pleasure-seeking, generalized trouble (multiple victims, multiple settings), restlessly aggressive, callous disregard for others." Trying to assess the results from the research has some challenges because of the different descriptions of personality that are used and measured. A meta-analysis by Spencer and her colleagues (Spencer, Mallory, et al., 2019) reviewed 209 studies that assessed the relationship between mental health factors and IPV (both perpetration and victimization). The effect size was $r = 0.29$ for perpetrators of abuse who had a diagnosis of antisocial personality disorder.

In Spencer et al.'s (2022) meta-analysis of cross-sectional and correlational studies the effect sizes were: $r = 0.27$ for antisocial personality disorder, $r = 0.23$ for impulsivity, and $r = 0.32$ for anger. Birkley and Eckhardt (2015) further analyzed some of the key constructs in APP. The average effect size was $r = 0.28$ for hostility, $r = 0.24$ for anger, and $r = 0.32$ for studies that combined hostility with anger. Finally, Collison and Lynam (2021) examined the relationship of 10 personality disorders to IPV. Antisocial personality disorder displayed the highest effect size ($r = 0.35$).

(e) Family/Marital. Poor partner relationships represent an obvious criminogenic need. An early meta-analysis found a mean effect of $r = 0.27$ between dissatisfaction with the relationship and IPV (Stith, Green, Smith, & Ward, 2008). The research on this topic has also studied the specific behaviors within the partner relationship. For example, large effect sizes have been reported by Spencer and Stith (2020) for "controlling behaviors" ($r = 0.43$) and "threatened victim with a weapon" ($r = 0.48$).

(f) School/Work. Spencer et al. (2022) found a small but significant mean $r = 0.08$ for unemployment and $r = 0.15$ for lower education. In Spencer and Stith's (2020) meta-analysis, and remember that the outcome was femicide, the results for education and unemployment were $r = 0.14$ and $r = 0.19$ respectively.

(g) Substance Misuse. In a comprehensive meta-analysis, Cafferky, Mendez, Anderson, and Stith (2018) reviewed 285 studies specifically on substance misuse and IPV. The mean effect size for any substance use was $r = 0.23$. When the data was examined to see if alcohol use was more important than drug use there was no difference.

(h) Leisure/Recreation. There have been no studies reporting on this criminogenic need.

The summary of the Central Eight provides evidence that what is important with general criminal behavior is important with IPV. The one caution in interpretating the results is that all the meta-analyses are based on correlational studies. Longitudinal studies are notably absent. This leads us to a third way of answering the question of whether male batterers have some fundamental differences from the general offending population. We can look to see if risk/needs assessments do any better in predicting outcomes than general risk/needs instruments. One feature of these assessment instruments is that they are based on longitudinal research designs.

3. Actuarial Risk Scales for Intimate Partner Abuse. Murray Straus (1996) was perhaps the first to present an objective "checklist" for identifying high-risk male batterers. The checklist included items that we know are reliable predictors of criminal behavior (e.g., drug misuse, history of violence, rationalizations for abuse). However, the checklist was silent on social supports for the behavior and only indirectly tapped personality factors ("extreme dominance," "extreme jealousy"). Other experts in the area have presented similar lists based upon their reviews of the literature (Dutton & Kropp, 2000; Thompson, Saltzman, & Johnson, 2001). Today, such "lists" have been formalized into more structured and objective assessment instruments.

TABLE 14.1 Assessment of Intimate Partner Violence: Examples from the SARA and ODARA

SARA	ODARA
Past assault of family members	Prior violence against wife or children
Recent substance abuse/dependence	Substance abuse history
Past violation of no contact order	Failure on conditional release
Attitudes that support or condone wife assault	Assault on victim when pregnant
Use of weapons or credible threats	Threat to harm or kill
Recent psychotic and/or manic symptoms	Violence against others

Source: Adapted from Kropp et al., 1995 and Hilton et al., 2004

Two of the more widely used assessment instruments are the Spousal Assault Risk Assessment (SARA; Kropp, Hart, Webster, & Eaves, 1995) and the Ontario Domestic Assault Risk Assessment (ODARA; Hilton, Harris, et al., 2004). The SARA is a structured clinical judgment instrument consisting of 20 items covering five areas (criminal history, psychosocial adjustment, spousal assault history, current offense, and other considerations). The ODARA is a 13-item scale sampling historical and dynamic items (see Table 14.1 for a few illustrative items from the two scales). As with the SARA, there are a number of items of general criminal behavior (e.g., "has a prior nondomestic assault" and "offender is violent outside of the home"). Although many of the items overlap conceptually, there are some important differences (e.g., the SARA has items pertaining to a clinical diagnosis). One reason for the differences is the ODARA was originally designed to be administered by police officers, while the SARA is usually administered by trained clinical professionals.

In an early study of two samples of men (total of 589), with a follow-up of more than four years, scores on the ODARA predicted new assaults and the *severity* of new assaults. The AUC for the developmental sample was 0.77, and it was 0.72 for the cross-validation sample. However, a follow-up study of the ODARA found that the predictive validity estimates had significantly decreased (AUCs of 0.65 to 0.67 in two samples). This led the researchers to add the PCL-R to the ODARA, producing the Domestic Violence Risk Appraisal Guide (Hilton, Harris, Rice, Houghton, & Eke, 2008), but this only led to a small increase in AUC (from 0.70 to 0.71). However, with the addition of the PCL-R it is viewed as providing more nuanced information for higher-risk cases.

Research on both instruments has been extensive and generally supportive of their use (Hilton, Rice, Harris, Judd, & Quinsey, 2021; Kropp & Gibas, 2021; Radatz & Hilton, 2022). In a review of the AUC values for five IPV risk instruments, Jill Messing and Jonel Thaller (2013) found that the SARA and the ODARA had the highest AUCs among the five risk scales selected.

The ODARA predicted partner assault slightly better (AUC = 0.67, 95 percent CI = 0.665 to 0.668) than the SARA (AUC = 0.63, 95 percent CI = 0.627 to 0.629). A more recent review also reported AUCs in the range of 0.64 to 0.77 for the ODARA and 0.52 to 0.72 for the SARA (Graham, Sahay, Rizo, Messing, & Macy, 2021). One advantage of the ODARA over the SARA, as already noted, is that its administration does not typically require professional clinicians. With introductory training, front-line workers such as nurses and police officers can administer the ODARA in a reliable manner (Hilton et al., 2021; Jung & Himmen, 2022).

In the literature review by Nicholls and her colleagues (Nicholls, Pritchard, Reeves, & Hilterman, 2013) it was noted that relatively little research has been conducted comparing IPV-specific risk instruments to other risk instruments that have been shown to predict generally violent recidivism. For example, would the SARA or ODARA predict partner violence better than the VRAG or an LS instrument? GPCSL theory would suggest that there would be little difference in the predictive validities between IPV-specific instruments and the more general assessment tools. Nicholls and her colleagues examined the few studies that compared IPV-specific instruments with more general risk instruments. Unfortunately, given that there were few such comparisons, the reviewers were unable to reach a conclusion for the superiority of IPV-specific instruments over the more general assessment tools.

Zoe Hilton and Liam Ennis (2020), along with Louise Dixon and Nicola Graham-Kevan (2020), have also made strong cases for better integrating RNR into IPV assessment and the risk management of male batterers. They acknowledge that the IPV risk instruments do a satisfactory job in following the risk principle (i.e., differentiating lower-risk from higher-risk cases). However, the risk measures pay insufficient attention to criminogenic needs even though the Central Eight are relevant (recall our earlier discussion). In addition, responsivity factors need to be considered. For example, in one review the effect size between depression and IPV was $r = 0.15$ (Bacchus, Ranganathan, Watts, & Devries, 2018). As shown in Chapters 11 and 12, criminogenic needs and responsivity factors are crucial to effective intervention. Therefore, we now turn to treatment.

Treatment of Male Batterers

In 1984, Lawrence Sherman and Richard Berk conducted a study in which Minneapolis police officers who responded to calls of domestic disputes were randomly assigned to one of the following three conditions: (1) arrest the suspect, (2) remove the suspect from the home for eight hours, or (3) advise the suspect and victim to seek help. A six-month follow-up found a lower re-abuse rate for the arrest condition (13 percent, according to police data). The rate was 26 percent for the removal from the home condition and 18 percent for providing advice. Within a few years, states began passing mandatory arrest legislation in IPV incidents. Soon, 29 states had mandatory arrest laws

(Zelcer, 2014) and similar laws have been implemented in other countries (Yakeley, 2022).

Sherman and Berk's (1984) findings run counter to the rehabilitation literature, in which sanctions do not decrease recidivism but rather show small increases in recidivism. Could it be that "getting tough" for male batterers is the exception to the rule? The beauty of meta-analysis is that it reminds us that no one study can define or explain a phenomenon. In a recent meta-analysis of mandatory arrest policies, no deterrent effect was found ($r = 0.01$; Hoppe, Zhang, Hayes, & Bills, 2020). To make matters worse, Sherman and Harris (2015) followed up the 1,125 victims from one of the early replications of the Minneapolis experiment (Milwaukee, Wisconsin) and found approximately 25 years later that, for those whose partners were arrested, rather than warned, the women were more likely to die prematurely (perhaps the result of living in a stressful relationship?). Premature death was mostly due to cancer and heart disease. Homicide was rare (two for the arrested group and one for the warned group). The results were particularly salient for African Americans ($r = 0.40$).

As noted in Chapter 13, giving up on punishment does not come easily. Researchers searched for something in the mandatory arrest experiments to show that getting tough worked. For example, arrests "worked" for employed male batterers apparently because employed assaulters have a "stake in conformity" and, therefore, have much to lose by being arrested (Sherman, 2018). That is, mandatory arrests work for low-risk batterers but it is the high-risk who cause the most harm that really need to desist.

Male batterers may be arrested but not necessarily prosecuted. There are many reasons for this. For example, the victim may refuse to press charges (Belknap & Grant, 2018). Consequently, a number of jurisdictions introduced "no drop" prosecution policies. This has been problematic because it takes control away from the victim and risks re-traumatization when testifying in court (Durfee, 2021; Hamel, 2020). Evaluations of mandatory arrests and prosecution policies have reported a range of outcomes from slight to no decrease in recidivism, court backlogs, and victim dissatisfaction with the process (Johnson & Stylianou, 2022). There has also been interest in the severity of the sanction and its impact on IPV recidivism. A recent meta-analysis of 33 studies by Garner, Maxwell, and Lee (2021) evaluated the impact of three different types of sanctions on IPV. The three sanctions were prosecution (as opposed to a warning), conviction, and incarceration. Prosecution showed a small deterrent effect ($r = -0.05$, $k = 10$), receiving a conviction showed no effect ($r = 0.006$, $k = 26$), and receiving a custodial sentence actually increased future IPV ($r = +0.10$, $k = 21$).

At best, getting tough with male batterers may bring temporary relief and safety for the women, but it does not lead to long-term change in the perpetrator (Hoppe et al., 2020). Neither specialized probation supervision (Klein & Crowe, 2008) nor specialized courts that deal with IPV cases have demonstrated increased victim safety (Cissner, Labriola, & Rempel, 2015). This should not be surprising, given that criminal justice sanctions do not address the criminogenic needs of male batterers. Although mandatory arrest and similar policies remain widely used, many are recognizing that treatment must be part of the solution.

The earliest well-designed evaluation of a treatment intervention was by Donald Dutton (1986). Fifty men attending a four-month cognitive-behavioral program were compared to a matched group of 50 men who were not treated because their probation terminated before space was available in the program. Dutton found a re-abuse rate of 4 percent for the treated men and 16 percent for the untreated group at a six-month follow-up. At two and a half years, the treated group maintained the benefits of the treatment while the recidivism rate for the untreated group increased to 40 percent.

Since the early Dutton study, few subsequent evaluations of treatment programs have found such clear-cut results. Part of the problem has been that many evaluations have been hampered by weak methodologies (Eckhardt, Murphy, et al., 2013). For example, Thomas Akoensi and his colleagues (Akoensi, Koehler, Lösel, & Humphreys, 2013) complained that their review of European batterer programs were so plagued by design issues that they could reach no conclusion on the effectiveness of these programs (however, even randomized control trials have shown little effect; Mills, Barocas, & Ariel, 2013).

A number of reviews and meta-analyses of IPV treatment programs have reached differing conclusions. In an early meta-analysis, Julia Babcock, Charles Green, and Chet Robie (2004) reviewed 22 studies of treatment interventions. The overall result was that treatment was associated with a small reduction in re-abuse ($r = 0.09$). However, a meta-analysis of 19 articles (Arias, Arce, & Vilariño, 2013) reported no overall effect of treatment. One review of nine couples therapy interventions published between 2019 and 2021 found mixed results, with one study reporting increased IPV for high-risk couples (Stith, Topham, et al., 2022).

Reviews of the IPV treatment literature are not as informative as the reviews of the general rehabilitation literature. Often there is a lack of information as to what actually goes on in treatment. A treatment may be described as "cognitive-behavioral," but that only tells us how the treatment was delivered and not what was being treated. Substance misuse is often seen by clinicians as a major factor in IPV as it diminishes personal control. Thus, it is often targeted in treatment programs. Unfortunately, one meta-analysis of men who misuse alcohol or drugs found no differences between treated and untreated men on either substance use or IPV (Stephens-Lewis, Johnson, et al., 2021). The general rehabilitation literature with justice-involved persons is detailed enough to teach us the importance of focusing on criminogenic needs and adhering to the risk principle.

The outlook for the future, however, is promising. As described earlier there has been considerable progress in applying actuarial-based risk/needs assessments on a wide scale and introducing RNR principles (Hilton & Radatz, 2021). Regarding treatment, adopting RNR principles has been slow, with perhaps the first evaluation reported in 2014. In that evaluation Lynn Stewart and her colleagues (Stewart, Gabora, Kropp, & Lee, 2014) described a 25-session intervention for medium- to high-risk (assessed by the SARA) incarcerated batterers that focused on teaching prosocial communication skills and replacing violent attitudes toward women with prosocial attitudes. One hundred and fifty treated men were followed upon release and compared to an untreated group of releases. For the treatment group, IPV was significantly reduced ($r = 0.34$).

Áine Travers and her colleagues (Travers, McDonagh, Cunningham, Armour, & Hansen, 2021) reviewed eight studies of IPV interventions that could be categorized as to how closely the interventions followed the RNR principles. The overall effect size for treatment effectiveness was $r = 0.14$. When the results were analyzed with respect to the level of adherence to risk, need, and responsivity the results were as follows:

- No adherence: $r = -0.10$ ($N = 1$)

- Partial adherence: $r = 0.12$ ($N = 4$)

- Full adherence: $r = 0.34$ ($N = 3$)

Although the number of studies was low, the results were in the expected direction. Since Travers et al. (2021), another evaluation of an RNR-based intervention can be added with an effect size of $r = 0.39$ based on the women's report of controlling and aggressive behavior (Zarling & Russell, 2022). Others have now written that it is time to incorporate the RNR principles into program development (Radatz, Richards, et al., 2021; Richards, Gover, Branscum, Nystrom, & Claxton, 2022; Schafers, Olver, & Wormith, 2021).

In conclusion, the male batterer treatment literature tells us little about the needs targeted in treatment and the value of assigning men to the appropriate intensity of treatment based on risk (Graham-Kevan & Bates, 2020); Richards et al., 2022). The assessment and treatment of the perpetrators of IPV can benefit from the general offender literature.

The Mentally Disordered Offender (MDO)

When many people first hear the phrase "mentally disordered offender," images of senseless, grotesque, and extremely violent behavior flood the mind. These people are publicized daily in the news and entertainment media. To the average citizen, the prevalence of a mental illness among justice-involved persons appears high. Moreover, their behavior seems incomprehensible and almost always violent. Determining whether these views correspond to the facts is one of the purposes of this section.

Estimating the incidence of mental disorder among criminal offenders requires a clear definition of the "mentally disordered offender" (MDO). One definition involves the presence of serious psychological symptoms. When symptoms are examined in relationship to crime, one study found that psychosis *preceded* only 4 percent of crimes committed by 143 MDOs (Peterson, Skeem, Kennealy, Bray, & Zvonkovic, 2014). A widely accepted definition may still be off in the future. Part of the problem is that the two major social systems responsible for the MDO, the legal and the mental health systems, have differing interpretations of mental disorder. Furthermore, even within each system there is disagreement on the meaning of such terms as "insanity" and "mental illness."

Estimating the Prevalence of Mental Disorders

There have been a number of surveys on the prevalence of mental disorders among criminal populations, both country-specific and globally. Three important findings emerge from the research. First, hardly anyone escapes a diagnosis of a mental disorder. Fazel and Danesh (2002) summarized surveys conducted in 12 countries and found that, among men, 10 percent had a major depression, approximately 5 percent a major psychotic illness, and not unexpectedly, 65 percent had a personality disorder (the rates were slightly lower among women). In addition, these rates have not changed over time (Gottfried & Christopher, 2017).

Among youth the prevalence rates are similar. A summary of 30 studies revealed an average rate of 21 percent for depression, 6 percent for psychosis, and 62 percent for a personality disorder (Livanou, Furtado, Winsper, Silvester, & Singh, 2019). Second, the more serious mental illnesses (psychosis and major depression) are less frequent (5 to 6 percent). These rates are higher in prison settings and among certain subgroups. For example, Emily Edwards and her colleagues (Edwards, Greene, et al., 2022) found rates of 8.1 percent for psychosis, 25.6 percent for depression, and a PTSD rate of 23.9 percent for incarcerated veterans (the rate was 12.4 percent for non-veterans). Finally, the most frequent diagnosis was APD. In the general population, the estimate of the prevalence of APD is 3.6 percent (Grant, Hasin, et al., 2004), much lower than what is found in justice-involved samples. However, it is the most seriously mentally ill person that alarms the public and we now turn to examining whether or not it is justified.

Dangerousness Among the Noncriminal Seriously Mentally Ill

This section began with the comment that psychosis often elicits alarm and fear among the general public. Thus, it is instructive to examine briefly what we know about the relationship between psychosis and violent behavior. In general, psychiatric patients have higher arrest and conviction rates than nonpatients (Ballard & Teasdale, 2016; Hodgins, 2020). In a carefully controlled study, Bruce Link, Howard Andrews, and Francis Cullen (1992) compared various groups of mentally ill patients with a randomly selected sample of

TABLE 14.2 Criminal and Violent Behavior among Psychiatric and Nonpsychiatric Patients (%)

Group	Official		Self-reported		
	All arrests	Violent	Arrests	Weapon	Fighting
Patients	12.1	5.8	22.5	12.9	28.6
Nonpatients	6.7	1.0	9.9	2.7	15.1

Note: *Ns* vary for patients (93–173) and nonpatients (185–386).

Source: Adapted from Link et al., 1992

adults without any mental disorder. Table 14.2 summarizes the major criminal/violent behavior differences between the chronically disturbed patients and the nondisturbed adults. Whether the behavior was based upon official records or self-reports, the findings of the study were consistent. Chronically disturbed patients (having received treatment for at least one year) were more likely to be arrested and to have committed violent acts.

Mental illness is often viewed as a risk factor in combination with substance misuse (Baranyi, Fazel, Langerfeldt, & Mundt, 2022; Stompe, Ritter, & Schanda, 2018). However, an epidemiologic survey better situates the role of substance misuse in comparison to other risk factors for violence. Researchers under the direction of Eric Elbogen and Sally Johnson (2009) conducted structured mental health interviews with 34,653 persons between 2002 and 2003 and three years later asked them about their experiences during the prior three years (e.g., "Ever hit someone so hard that you injured them or they had to see a doctor?"). First of all, the base rate for violence was 0.03. Second, the rate for violence among those with a severe mental illness disorder (e.g., schizophrenia) was about *half* of the general base rate. Finally, Elbogen and Johnson identified the 10 best predictors of violence and rank ordered them. Mental illness came in at number nine ($r = 0.05$) but only when combined with substance misuse. Ahead of the list were the usual suspects: history of violence ($r = 0.29$), history of juvenile detention ($r = 0.19$), parental criminal history ($r = 0.14$), etc. Mental illness by itself pales in comparison to other risk factors for violence. Additional evidence for this last statement will be presented shortly but, for now, we will look at a thinking pattern that has stood out in the research: threat/control-override.

Threat/Control-Override Thoughts. In 1994, Link and Steuve proposed that "delusions of threat/control-override" (TCO) are closely linked to violence. That is, thoughts that people are trying to harm you or the delusional belief that others are in control of one's mind and, thereby, overriding self-control. This psychotic symptomatology then increases the likelihood of responding violently to these perceived threats. They found that TCO thoughts were associated with violence in both a patient and a nonpatient population. From a GPCSL perspective, cognitions supportive of antisocial behavior are important predictors of violence.

Link and Steuve's results were subsequently replicated in a large study of more than 10,000 adults. Swanson and his colleagues (Swanson, Borum, Swartz, & Monahan, 1996) examined three groups of respondents: (1) those with no major psychiatric disorder, (2) those with a major disorder, and (3) those with a major disorder combined with substance misuse. They also examined the presence of TCO symptoms and non-TCO symptoms (hallucinations, feelings of grandeur). Each respondent was asked about the commission of violent acts since the age of 18. A number of conclusions were drawn from their results (Table 14.3). First, TCO symptoms increased the likelihood of violence for those with a major mental disorder and non-disordered individuals. That is, if one thinks that someone is going to harm you then it doesn't matter if a mental illness is present or not. Second, substance misuse greatly increased the chances of violence. Third, psychotic and non-TCO symptoms were still presented as risk factors, although modest in comparison to substance misuse and TCO symptoms.

Although many studies have reported the TCO–violence relationship, not all have (Maria, Maria, Nikolaos, & Giorgos, 2017). Witt, van Dorn, and Fazel (2013) reviewed 110 studies of violence among mentally ill individuals (e.g., schizophrenia, bipolar disorder). In their review, TCO showed a nonsignificant relationship with violence ($r = 0.05$, $k = 5$). Significant predictors were what GPCSL would expect: impulsiveness, criminal history, treatment noncompliance, and substance misuse. These findings are contrary to two other meta-analyses.

The first, by Douglas, Guy, and Hart (2009), found a clinically meaningful relationship ($r = 0.18$, $k = 18$). The difference may be due to sample selection. Witt and her colleagues focused on individuals with a diagnosis of psychoses, while Douglas, Guy, and Hart had a stricter definition that no more than 5 percent of the sample was non-psychotic. Second, Jonathan Reinharth

---

TABLE 14.3 **Threat/Control-Override (TCO) Symptoms as a Risk Factor for Violence (Probability of self-reported violent acts since age 18)**

Symptom	Mental disorder present		
	No disorder	**No substance misuse**	**Substance misuse**
None	.17	.26	.70
Non-TCO	.27	.39	.75
TCO	.40	.63	.86

Source: Swanson et al., 1996

and his colleagues (Reinharth, Reynolds, Dill, & Serper, 2014) conducted a meta-analysis of cognitive predictors of violence among schizophrenics. The review examined a number of cognitive factors (e.g., attention, visual-spatial reasoning) but one specific cognition of relevance to the present discussion is what they called "hostile attribution bias", the "threat" in TCO. The average effect size was $r = 0.14$ ($k = 10$). For the most part, what predicts violence among psychiatric patients is similar to the risk factors for general offenders and procriminal thinking may be a mediator between a mental disorder and violent behavior (Walters, 2011b).

The discussion thus far has centered on the risk for violence among persons with a serious mental illness. In general, there is an increased risk for violence compared to the general population. Now we turn to the risk posed by justice-involved persons with a mental disorder.

Dangerousness and the Mentally Disordered Offender

The MDO has often been at the center of the debate surrounding dangerousness. Various criminal and civil commitment laws are used to confine MDOs for periods longer than the typical sentence given to non-MDOs for the same offense. The argument is that these individuals pose a risk for further violent behavior and that preventive confinement is needed until they are no longer "dangerous." One of the difficulties in making decisions about the individual's dangerousness is the lack of knowledge about the base rates of violent behavior for MDOs. Only a few studies provide such information.

One of the first studies was Henry Steadman and Joseph Cocozza's (1974) evaluation of the "Baxstrom patients." The story begins when inmate Johnnie Baxstrom took his case before the U.S. Supreme Court. Baxstrom was transferred from a prison to a hospital for the "criminally insane" because he was diagnosed as mentally disordered. Consequently, he was institutionalized beyond the end of his sentence. Baxstrom's lawyers argued that, without evidence of dangerousness, he must be released. The court agreed, and not only was Baxstrom transferred from the specialized hospital to a regular psychiatric hospital, but so too were 967 other individuals who had been housed in similar hospitals. Presumably, the most dangerous people in New York State were transferred to regular psychiatric facilities, and some were duly released at the completion of their sentence.

The Baxstrom patients were assessed as "dangerous mental patients"; thus, their transfer to a regular hospital and their eventual release provided an estimate of the base rate of violent behavior among this group of MDOs. Steadman and Cocozza (1974) traced 98 of those who were released over an average period of two and a half years. Twenty (20.4 percent) were re-arrested, 11 (11.2 percent) were reconvicted, and only two of them committed a violent offense (an assault and a robbery). Because patients released from psychiatric hospitals may be rehospitalized instead of arrested for a criminal offense, rehospitalizations were also examined (this would increase the base rate of the behavior). With the hospital and community information combined, the base rate of violent behavior was 14.3 percent. Steadman and Cocozza (1974: p. 152) concluded: "The Baxstrom patients were not very dangerous. Only 14 of 98 releases ever displayed behavior that could be classified as dangerous." In another similar study, Thornberry and Jacoby (1979) found that of 432 mentally disordered offenders released into the community, only 14.5 percent committed another violent offense (again, average follow-up period of two and a half years).

As in the previous section on IPV, we ask:

1. Do MDOs have risk factors similar to the general population of justice-involved persons?

2. What are the effective interventions for the mentally ill justice-involved person?

Risk Factors for MDOs. Two meta-analyses have been conducted on the relevance of the Central Eight risk/need factors to explain the behavior of MDOs. Bonta, Blais, and Wilson (2014) conducted a meta-analysis of 96 studies that evaluated predictors of general and violent recidivism. They asked whether factors considered important by psychopathological and clinical perspectives would predict recidivism and how these factors compared to predictors drawn from GPCSL. In this meta-analysis, there were hardly any studies measuring procriminal associates and leisure/recreation and, therefore, only six of the Central Eight risk/need factors were evaluated.

The second meta-analysis selected studies that were drawn from the community, namely, forensic outpatients or persons under probation supervision (Eisenberg, Van Horn, et al., 2019). Twenty-seven studies that were published in English, German, or Dutch were included in the meta-analysis. Unlike the Bonta et al. (2014) review, Eisenberg and her colleagues did not measure the predictive validities of severe mental illness. Instead, they evaluated more general "personal/psychological problems."

Table 14.4 presents the results for general and violent recidivism from both meta-analyses. There are two important findings. First, factors such as psychosis and other measures of serious psychological disturbance were poor predictors of recidivism. As displayed in Table 14.4, psychosis, schizophrenia, and mood disorder were all unrelated to general and violent recidivism (the confidence intervals included zero). Second, Eisenberg et al. (2017) essentially replicated the findings from Bonta et al. (2014), further strengthing our confidence in the relevance of the Central Eight to MDOs.

Another noteworthy finding from Bonta et al. (2014) not shown in Table 14.4 is the observation that studies that compared the recidivism of MDOs with non-disordered justice-involved persons showed that those with a mental illness were no more likely to reoffend with any offense ($r = 0.01$) or a violent offense ($r = -0.03$) than a non-disordered person. In conclusion, if the Central Eight risk/need factors are predictive of recidivism, then risk/

courts too, then why do we see reductions in recidivism? One reason may be reduced caseloads, permitting staff to give more attention to their clients. Another reason stems from consideration of specific responsivity. Psychotic symptoms and mental health concerns are minor predictors of criminality but they are obstacles to effective correctional treatment. It is nearly impossible to address criminogenic needs if the person suffers from delusions, distrusts the therapist, or is obsessed with suicidal thoughts.

A skilled therapist who can successfully diminish negative thoughts and feelings accomplishes two things. First, the client may be able to engage in prosocial activities such as obtaining and maintaining employment (a criminogenic need). In a sense, targeting mental health can have the unexpected benefit of removing the challenges the client faced prior to treatment. Second, a therapeutic alliance is established. The client is relieved from their psychological suffering with the help of the therapist and is now ready to tackle criminogenic needs. What the correctional helper needs to do is first address the immediate mental health issues (noncriminogenic) but not stop there. Long-term changes happen when criminogenic needs are successfully addressed.

The Sexual Offender

Along with the mentally disordered, sexual offenders elicit a great deal of public apprehension and fear. In 2021, there were 324,500 sexual assaults in the United States, which translates to 1.2 per 1,000 Americans over the age of 12 being sexually assaulted each year (Thompson & Tapp, 2022). The prevalence for child sexual abuse has been estimated at approximately 10 percent of the population (Perez-Fuentes, Olfson, et al., 2013) and among prison populations it is almost 34 percent (Dalsklev, Cunningham, Dempster, & Hanna, 2021). Keep in mind that these are officially recorded events and the numbers are estimated to be much higher for undetected sexual crimes (DeLisi, Caropreso, et al., 2016). The fact that these criminal acts involve victims who are, for the most part, women and children requires sustained attention from researchers, policymakers, and the general public.

How Unique Are Sexual Offenders?

Similar to the question posed for IPV, are sexual offenders so different from nonsexual offenders that a fundamentally different approach to theory, assessment, and treatment is required? For example, besides the offense, how do sexual offenders differ from others who violate the law in their behavioral histories, personalities, cognitions, and attitudes? Are their criminogenic needs limited to their sexual behavior, or are the criminogenic needs identified for the nonsexual criminal population (e.g., APP, substance misuse) just as relevant?

A commonly held view is that sexual offenders are "specialists." That is, their crimes are almost exclusively sexual in nature. If this is true, then treatment need only focus on factors directly associated with sexual behavior. For example, treatment should target sexual arousal, attitudes tolerant of sexual assault, inadequate intimate relationships, and so forth. These dynamic risk factors are important, but there is also evidence to suggest that *non*sexual criminogenic variables require attention.

First off, those who sexually offend are not homogenous. There are rapists, child molesters, Internet sexual offenders, and they are not all men (Wojcik & Fisher, 2019). Moreover, among sexual offenders, there is a significant amount of "crossover." A review of the literature found 19 percent of sexual offenders had both child and adult victims and 20 percent had extra- and intra-familial victims, with the rates *doubling* when self-report and polygraph measures were used (Scurich & Gongola, 2021). Even sexual sadists commit nonsexual crimes (DeLisi, Drury, et al., 2017).

Longitudinal studies also show that sexual offenders commit nonsexual crimes (Chouinard-Thivierge, Lussier, & Charette, 2023; Reale, McCuish, & Corrado, 2020). In a meta-analysis by Hanson and Morton-Bourgon (2009), the sexual recidivism rate was 11.5 percent, and the violent recidivism rate (including sexual and nonsexual violent crimes) was 19.5 percent. In an earlier meta-analysis, Hanson and Bussière (1998) reported a nonsexual, violent recidivism rate of 9.9 percent for child molesters and a rate of 22.1 percent for rapists.

These studies suggest that there are important similarities between sexual and nonsexual offenders. One example of the similarities is the role of procriminal supports. Many clinicians see sexual offenders as social isolates, awkward in social interactions, and introverted. This may be true for some, but not for all. There is the sexual abuse of children by women who are coerced by male partners (Brown & Kloess, 2020), the growth of organizations such as the North American Man/Boy Love Association (Renfro, 2020), and the use of the Internet for deviant sexual purposes or to overcome social isolation via chat rooms (Paquette, Fortin, & Perkins, 2020).

The importance of social or peer support for unwanted sex can be found in studies of "rape myth acceptance" (Trottier, Benbouriche, & Bonneville, 2021), date rape (St. George, 2022), sexual aggression among college students (Oberweis, Gorislavsky, & Cannon, 2022), and rape in the military (Mengeling, Booth, Turner, & Sadler, 2014). Studies specific to known sexual offenders are rare. In a study of convicted sexual offenders, Karl Hanson and Heather Scott (1996) asked 126 sexual offenders, 57 nonsexual justice-involved persons, and 119 citizen participants questions about their associations with others. Child molesters reported knowing other child molesters, and rapists reported knowing other rapists. The participants from the general population reported having no sexual offenders in their social networks. In another study by Underwood and his colleagues (Underwood, Patch, Cappelletty, & Wolfe, 1999), researchers asked 113 child molesters to report whether they had molested a child in the presence of another adult (they were not asked if the other adult was a convicted sexual offender). Thirty-eight percent reported that another adult was present during the commission of the offense.

This is not to say that sexual offenders are no different from those who commit nonsexual crimes. One consistent finding is that a sexual offender is more likely to recidivate with a sexual crime than a nonsexual offender (DeLisi, Bunga, Heirigs, Erickson, Hochstetler, 2019). Furthermore, some sexual offenders such as those who victimized both children and adults appear to be particularly more likely to reoffend violently with a nonsexual crime (Link & Lösel, 2021).

An important factor, both for adult and child victimization, is attitudes and cognitions (D'Urso, Petruccelli, Costantino, Zappulla, & Pace, 2019; D'Urso, Petruccelli, Grilli, & Pace, 2019). In a meta-analysis of 89 studies on risk factors for child sexual abuse, Daniel Whitaker and colleagues (Whitaker, Le, et al., 2008) found those who sexually abuse children differed significantly from non-abusers in terms of their attitudes. Those who abused children were more likely to minimize their responsibility (with an r of about 0.27) and were more tolerant of adult–child sex (with an r of about 0.25). In another meta-analysis, the average r between attitudes and sexual recidivism was considerably smaller at 0.11 (Helmus, Hanson, Babchishin, & Mann, 2013). However, the strength of the association varied on how attitudes were measured (e.g., self-report questionnaires yielded higher effect sizes compared to interviewer ratings).

With this general introduction, we now turn more directly to the questions of risk/needs assessment and treatment.

Risk Factors for Sexual Offending

The first point is that not all who sexually offend are equally likely to reoffend. Often, the public views anyone who commits a sexual offense as high risk. However, some individuals have a very low risk to reoffend sexually, while others pose a much higher risk. The simplest risk classification is to go by the offense type. For example, incest offenders have lower recidivism rates than nonfamilial child molesters (Hanson, Morton, & Harris, 2003). Nevertheless, we can do much better in risk differentiation than using the type of offense and victim.

A considerable amount of research has focused on deviant sexual fantasies (Rossegger, Bartels, Endrass, Borchard, & Singh, 2021). Such fantasies are often targeted in treatment (Allen, Katsikitis, Millear, & McKillop, 2020) and they play a role in theoretical models of sexual offending against adults and children (e.g., Dangerfield, Ildeniz, & Ó Ciardha, 2020). Although fantasies may predict sexual deviance (Hanson & Morton-Bourgon, 2005), their role in *causing* sexual offending is less clear. A study by Langevin, Lang, and Curnoe (1998) illustrates the point. A sexual fantasy scale was administered to 129 sexual offenders and 77 controls (22 nonoffenders and 50 nonsexual offenders). They found that the overall reported rate of deviant fantasies for the sexual offenders was relatively low (33.3 percent), although it was higher than for the controls (11 percent; probably an underestimate, as people tend to hide shameful behavior). Furthermore, more of the controls reported some type of fantasy (deviant or not) than did the sexual offenders (90.9 percent vs. 62.5 percent). The researchers interpreted the low rates of deviant fantasies and the finding that many of the sexual offenders reported normal sexual fantasies to mean that fantasies are unlikely to have etiological significance.

Sexual fantasies are an indicator of sexual preoccupation, which *is* a risk factor for sexual offending. Another indicator of sexual preoccupation is the use of pornography. Recognizing that there is some debate over what constitutes pornography and when its use becomes problematic, there are two perspectives on the role of pornography on sexual aggression. One view is that pornography may serve to stimulate deviant fantasies leading to acting out the fantasies. The other is that consuming pornography is sexually cathartic and leads to *less* sexual aggression.

Evidence for both positions can be found. In a survey of 146 persons incarcerated for committing a sexual offense, 41 percent admitted to using pornography at the time of the index offense (Saramago, Cardoso, & Leal, 2019). In another study of 561 sexual offenders, the researchers found that 19 percent used pornography at the time of their offense; the majority did not (Langevin & Curnoe, 2004). Among the child molesters, the rate was higher (55 percent) but consisted mainly of showing pornography to the victims rather than to arouse the perpatrator directly. On the other hand, using aggregate-level data, Ferguson and Hartley (2009) found an inverse relationship between pornography consumption and rape.

In summary, there is no clear consensus on the role of pornography and sexual offending (Mellor & Duff, 2019). Experts caution that the role of pornography will vary with each case, and the advice is that consideration must be given to risk level, type of sexual offender, and the nature of the pornography (Brandt, Prescott, & Wilson, 2013). For example, images of coercion and of children increase the risk of sexual aggression (Malamuth, 2018).

A new and emerging line of research related to the issue of pornography is the Internet sexual offender. The concern is that these individuals, especially pedophiles, are using the Internet to produce and distribute pornography and to lure victims. There have been a number of important meta-analytic reviews that inform the issue. The first is a review of the characteristics of Internet sexual offenders by Kelly Babchishin, Karl Hanson, and Chantal Hermann (2011). The question asked by the review is whether the Internet offender is unique and different from the typical contact sexual offender. Their review of 27 reports found that the Internet users (e.g., convicted of an online offense such as distributing child pornography), compared to offline sexual abusers, were more likely to be empathic toward their victims but also showed greater sexual deviance.

The next review addressed the question of how likely Internet sexual offenders are to commit a sexual offense offline (Seto, Hanson, & Babchishin, 2011). From their analysis of nine prospective studies, Seto et al. found that very few online offenders commit an officially detected sexual offense (4.6 percent). However, approximately half of them, where self-report data was available, admitted to a contact sexual offense. The third meta-analysis involved 30 samples on Internet child pornography users and found two important subgroups (Babchishin, Hanson, & VanZuylen, 2015). First, there were those who only viewed child pornography, and then were those who viewed Internet pornography *and* committed offenses against children. The latter were assessed as much higher risk to commit a contact offense.

Although not a meta-analysis, a systematic review of the literature expands on our understanding of the sexual offender who uses pornography online. Marie Henshaw, James Ogloff, and Jonathan Clough (2017) found that online child pornography offenders are different from contact child abusers in a number of ways. When online pornography users do act out, they tend to be specialists limiting their behavior to sexual offenses against children. Also, compared to contact offenders and except for their preoccupation with child pornography, they are more prosocial (e.g., more likely to be employed, higher education). The authors admit that the research on the topic is scanty but hypothesize that the online pornography user is sufficiently different from other sexual offenders that different assessment and treatment approaches may be warranted.

The literature on the risk factors of sexual recidivism has been summarized in a number of meta-analyses by Karl Hanson and his associates (Hanson & Bussière, 1998; Hanson & Morton-Bourgon, 2005; Whitaker et al., 2008). One of the practical applications that arises from meta-analytic reviews of risk factors is that it facilitates the development of evidence-based actuarial risk/needs scales. Hanson and Morton-Bourgon (2005) drew two important conclusions relevant to risk scales for sexual offenders. First, the individual risk factors showed only modest effect sizes, suggesting a need to combine the risk factors to increase predictive accuracy. Second, many risk factors (e.g., sexual preoccupations) were dynamic and could guide treatment because they represent potential criminogenic needs for offenders.

Hanson and his colleagues have been at the forefront of the development of actuarial risk scales for sexual offenders. Their early work focused on simple-to-use risk scales such as STATIC-99 (Hanson & Thornton, 2000), the updated STATIC-2002 (Hanson & Thornton, 2003), and the Rapid Risk Assessment for Sexual Offence Recidivism (RRASOR; Hanson, 1997). These scales have shown satisfactory predictive accuracy, with AUCs in the 0.70 range (Helmus, Hanson, Murrie, & Zabarauckas, 2021; Helmus, Kelley, et al., 2022), and have even been validated in South Korea (Lee, Hanson, & Yoon, 2022). Their disadvantage, however, is that they measure mainly static risk, and their predictive validity diminishes for treated sexual offenders (Olver & Wong, 2011). However, there has been a notable shift in attention to dynamic risk factors in the assessment of sexual offenders.

In a study of 997 sexual offenders under community supervision, participants were administered three types of risk scales—static, stable, and acute (Hanson, Harris, Scott, & Helmus, 2007; Hanson, Helmus, & Harris, 2015). Stable risk factors, assessed every six months, are dynamic risk factors that, although changeable, take longer to change (e.g., impulsivity, hostility toward women, deviant sexual interests). Acute risk factors, measured at each session, can change very quickly (e.g., intoxication, sudden access to a victim, collapse of social supports). Over an average follow-up of seven years, Hanson et al. (2007; Hanson et al., 2015) were able to validate two new dynamic risk scales for sex offenders, called STABLE-2007 and ACUTE-2007.

ACUTE-2007 requires a great deal of effort to administer regularly and within short time frames. However, STABLE-2007 is much more manageable and it is widely used. In a meta-analysis of 21 studies by Brankley, Babchishin, and Hanson (2021), STABLE-2007 significantly predicted sexual recidivism (AUC = 0.68) and it added predictive accuracy incrementally to STATIC-99. Today, STABLE-2007 is not the only dynamic assessment instrument used with sexual offenders and nor is STATIC-99 the only static risk assessment scale (see Rettenberger & Craig, 2020).

A recent meta-analysis examined the predictive validities of dynamic risk instruments used with men convicted of a sexual offense (Van den Berg, Smid, et al., 2018). Fifty-two studies were reviewed, with four important findings. First, the dynamic assessments do predict sexual recidivism ($r = 0.35$). Second, the instruments also predicted nonsexual violence but at a lower level of accuracy ($r = 0.22$). Third, the dynamic instruments improved prediction over and beyond static scales. And finally, changes in scores predicted sexual recidivism but not general or violent recidivism. Taking the findings together, dynamic sexual offender risk/needs assessments contribute to a meaningful prediction of sexual recidivism (i.e., needed to following the risk principle). In addition, these instruments can guide the selection of treatment goals and the monitoring of treatment in accordance with the need principle.

Before moving to treatment, a few comments on the application of RNR to the assessment of sexual offenders. In Chapter 10 we saw that the Level of Service (LS) instruments measure the Central Eight risk/needs factors. One of the main findings from the meta-analysis of the LS instruments by Olver et al. (2014) is that the LS not only predicts general and violent recidivism but it was also a significant predictor of sexual recidivism ($r = 0.11$). The effect size was smaller than that found for general ($r = 0.29$) and violent recidivism ($r = 0.23$). The review also reported the findings for the subcomponents of the LS (i.e., the Central Eight). Only three reached statistical significance: criminal history, family/marital, and leisure/recreation. These results suggest adding specific sexual risk instruments to assessment protocols.

The Treatment of Sexual Offenders

A recent estimate put the annual cost of incarcerating child sexual offenders in the US at $5.4 billion (Letourneau, Roberts, Malone, & Sun, 2023). We can only imagine the enormous cost if we include community supervision and sexual crimes against adults. From a victim's standpoint, Letourneau and her colleagues estimated the loss of future productivity, welfare costs, health care services, etc. (Letourneau, Brown, Fang, Hassan, & Mercy, 2018). For a female victim the average lifetime economic cost was also estimated to be $282,734 (for male victims there was insufficient data to calculate the equivalent cost). Considering the number of children abused each year in the US, the lifetime economic burden for society was pegged at $9.3 billion. As was argued in Chapters 12 and 13, we do have an alternative to punishment. Appropriate treatment interventions have been effective with a variety of justice-involved persons and they can also work with sexual offenders.

One approach to managing sexual recidivism involves decreasing deviant sexual arousal. High levels of the male hormone testosterone are assumed to be associated with high levels of sexual arousal and reducing testosterone levels has often been targeted in biologically based treatments. To many readers this makes sense but, surprisingly, the evidence suggests otherwise. A meta-analysis of seven studies found an overall nonsignificant effect size of $r = 0.002$ and the results did not change when broken down by rapists and child molesters (Wong & Gravel, 2018). Note, however, that the number of studies with reasonable evaluation methodologies (e.g., comparison group) was small. That said, sexual arousal can be controlled by a number of factors not dependent on testosterone. There have been efforts to reduce testosterone levels either through physical castration or through so-called "chemical castrations."

Physical castration presents serious ethical dilemmas as well as physical and psychological side effects. Even when a person voluntarily consents to the procedure there remains an undeniable element of coercion (i.e., consent in order for a more lenient punishment). As a result, physical castrations are not widely performed except in a few isolated jurisdictions (e.g., the Czech Republic, Germany, Texas; Voultsos, 2020). Instead, drugs that either block the release of the hormones (androgens) that stimulate testosterone secretion or compete with other hormones for the neurophysiological sites that release testosterone are used. Drugs such as cyproterone acetate (CPA, Androcur) and medroxyprogesterone (MPA, Provera) are commonly used medical treatments for sexual offenders. These drugs are typically administered to men who have sexually abused children and there is also a degree of coercion here, but not as consequential as the coercion associated with physical castration.

Reductions in arousal have followed with the administration of these drugs. A recent meta-analysis by Ian McPhail and Mark Olver (2020) found significant decreases in arousal to pornographic images of children as measured by phallometric testing. Many sexual offenders show reduced sexual recidivism rates while taking medication (Bradford, Federoff, & Gulati, 2013). However, taking these medications is not a guarantee against sexual offending. For example, 20 years after pharmacological treatment was given to 60 high-risk sex offenders in Denmark, 13.6 percent committed a new sexual offense (Colstrup, Larsen, et al., 2020). The treatment did help. Twenty-two participants discontinued their medication and they were seven times more likely to commit a new sexual offense compared to those who continued with the medical treatment. Although sexual arousal may decrease, the drugs may have little effect on other behavioral correlates of sexual behavior (e.g., deviant sexual thoughts and fantasies). In essence, medication may provide early and immediate stabilization of the problem behavior, but psychologically based intervention is still needed.

In 1989, Lita Furby, Mark Weinrott, and Lyn Blackshaw reviewed 42 treatment studies of sexual offenders. They concluded that "there is as yet no evidence that clinical treatment reduces rates of sex reoffenses" (p. 27). This review and their conclusion, like Martinson's, did not go unchallenged. A major criticism was that the review failed to describe what actually comprised treatment. It is possible that the failure of the treatment programs in Furby, Weinrott, and Blackshaw's (1989) review was the result of inappropriate treatments (i.e., non-RNR interventions).

Subsequent to Furby et al.'s (1989) report, there have been many reviews showing that the treatment of sexual offenders can work for adults (Bradford et al., 2013; Schmucker & Lösel, 2015; Tyler, Gannon, & Olver, 2021) and for juveniles ($r = 0.18$; Beek, Spruit, et al., 2018). However, in a meta-analysis by Schmucker and Lösel (2017) that invoked rigorous selection criteria for the inclusion of studies (officially recorded recidivism, appropriate control group), the overall effectiveness of these treatments was a modest $r = 0.09$.

A meta-analysis testing the RNR principles in sexual offender treatment has spurred an interest in exploring how a model of general justice-involved persons can be applied to sexual offenders. A meta-analysis by Hanson, Bourgon, Helmus, and Hodgson (2009) found support for the principles in the treatment of sexual offenders. A review of 23 studies showed that treated sexual offenders, compared to untreated sexual offenders, had lower general recidivism rates (31.8 percent vs. 48.3 percent) and sexual recidivism rates (10.9 percent vs. 19.2 percent). The weakest effects were with studies that did not adhere to any of the principles, and the effectiveness of the treatments increased with adherence to RNR. Adherence to all three principles was very infrequent ($k = 3$), but these treatments showed the largest decreases in recidivism (see Figure 14.1).

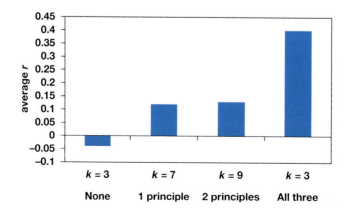

Figure 14.1

Effectiveness of Sexual Offender Treatment: Adherence to RNR

Hanson and his colleague (Hanson, 2014; Hanson & Yates, 2013) have observed that many of the risk factors associated with general criminal offenders overlap with those for sexual offenders. Consequently, the principles of effective rehabilitation should apply to sexual offenders. Certainly, the meta-analysis by Hanson et al. (2009) confirmed the relevance of RNR. However, there have been remarkably few investigations of RNR treatment and most deal with adherence to the risk principle (Abracen, Looman, Mailloux, Serin, & Malcolm, 2005; Lovins, Lowenkamp, & Latessa, 2009; Pederson & Miller 2022) or the responsivity principle (i.e., cognitive-behavioral therapy).

An exception to the above is an evaluation of two large prison-based treatment programs in Canada (Olver, Marshall, Marshall, & Nicholaichuk, 2020). One of the programs followed all three RNR principles and the other treatment, which had been established earlier, was less articulated with respect to RNR. An eight-year follow-up found a sexual recidivism rate of 4.2 percent for the RNR program. For the alternative treatment the rate was 10.7 percent and it was 20.2 percent for no treatment.

An innovative approach for helping men who have sexually offended desist from crime is Circles of Support and Accountability (COSA). COSA began in Canada but has spread internationally. Community volunteers surround the sexual offender ("core member") providing prosocial support (e.g., help in finding employment) and ensuring that the core member stays on course and does not deviate from the reintegration plan (accountability). An early evaluation with 44 sexual offenders found an 83 percent reduction in recidivism (Wilson, Cortoni, & McWhinnie, 2009).

Reviews of the literature have been cautiously optimistic (Clarke, Brown, & Völlm, 2017; Elliott & Zajac, 2015). Most studies showed reductions in recidivism but because of the small sample sizes failed to reach statistical significance. In addition, a few studies that measured psychosocial outcomes (e.g., improved family relations, securing employment) found positive effects. An interesting modification of COSA is the State of Minnesota's version. Instead of community volunteers forming the circles, volunteers are mostly college students who are selected and trained by the Department of Corrections.

In an experimental evaluation of the Minnesota COSA, 100 sexual offenders were randomly assigned to COSA or to a control group (Duwe, 2018). There was an 88 percent reduction in sexual recidivism (follow-up of approximately six years). Moreover, Duwe (2018) estimated a net economic benefit of nearly $41,000 per person. The question is: "If COSA is effective then how does it work?" From a GPCSL perspective there are many possibilities. As the research suggests, there are improvements in the criminogenic needs of employment and social relationships. Sexual offenders often find themselves socially isolated and circles help to reduce this isolation by rebuilding family and other pro-social relationships. Absolutely, more research with rigorous evaluation methodologies is needed to better understand the effectiveness of COSA and why.

Finally, there is evidence that sexual offenders' risk to reoffend diminishes over time. Drawing on an earlier report with a 20-year follow-up (Hanson,

Harris, Helmus, & Thornton, 2014), a 2018 study (Hanson, Harris, Letourneau, Helmus, & Thornton, 2018) reviewed the outcomes of 7,725 sexual offenders over a 25-year time span. With time, the sexual recidivism rates decreased. In the 2014 report, at five years, the recidivism rate for high-risk cases was 22 percent. For those high-risk offenders (measured by Static-99R) who stayed in the community for 10 years *without* committing an offense, the sexual recidivism rate was 4.2 percent. Each year without a sexual offense was associated with a 12 percent decrease in committing a new sexual crime. By the end of the 25-year follow-up, the rate approximated the probability of a nonsexual offender committing a sexual offense (about 1–2 percent).

Why was the decrease so dramatic with time? The decrease could not be fully explained by aging as the decrease was faster than would be expected with age. The authors speculated, and congruent with GPCSL, that the individuals who did not commit a sexual offense in the passing years learned and maintained prosocial behaviors. That is, the density of rewards for prosocial behaviors accumulated with each year, increasing the density of costs for deviant behavior. Whatever the reason is for desistance from sexual crimes, this landmark study puts into question policies such as placing individuals on sex offender registries for life.

Closing Comments

As noted earlier, there is considerable overlap in the risk/need factors for general justice-involved persons and sexual offenders. In fact, this is also true for MDOs and may be true for those involved in IPV. Table 14.5 shows the risk factors for MDOs, general, and sexual offenders based on meta-analytic reviews of the literature (there has been no meta-analysis of risk/need factors for IPV perpetrators based on longitudinal studies). Although it is difficult to directly compare the effect sizes drawn from the reviews that defined the Central Eight constructs differently, it is instructive that there are remarkable similarities. Note the consistency in the ordering of predictors across all three groups of offenders. For sexual offenders, as with MDOs and general justice-involved persons, criminal history was one of the best predictors, along with antisocial personality pattern and procriminal attitudes.

With respect to treatment, across all three subtypes, therapeutic interventions are effective in reducing the offensive behaviors. We are learning a great deal about what is required to maximize efforts to help justice-involved persons desist from crime. A meta-analysis by Theresa Gannon and her colleagues (Gannon, Olver, Mallion, & James, 2019) goes a long way in understanding the importance of the principles described in the expanded RNR model. Seventy studies of treatments for IPV, sexual offending, and general violence were reviewed. The first important take-away is that treatment decreases violent recidivism for all three types ($r = 0.12$). Second, the reductions are somewhat larger when Principle 15 (Management) is considered. When staff are provided

TABLE 14.5 **Predictors of Recidivism by Sample (*r*)**

Risk factor	General	MDO	Sexual
Procriminal Associates	.21	nr	nr
Antisocial Personality Pattern	.33	.21	.10
Procriminal Attitudes	.17	.19	.10
Criminal History	.29	.17	.15
Education/Employment	.22	.14	.10
Family/Marital	.13	.19	.05
Alcohol/Drugs	.20	.26	.06
Leisure/Recreation	.16	nr	.01

Source: General (Olver et al., 2014); MDO (Bonta et al., 2014); Sexual (Hanson & Bussière, 1998; Hanson & Morton-Bourgon, 2005, 2009). nr = not reported

with clinical supervision, outcomes improve ($r = 0.15$ for IPV; $r = 0.16$ for sexual offenders; and $r = 0.15$ for general violence). GPCSL seems relevant to many different individuals in conflict with the law.

Worth Remembering

1. There is more in common between male batterers and general justice-involved persons than there are differences.

   Contrary to some feminist theories, there are aspects of IPV that extend beyond patriarchal values. Male batterers appear very much like other criminals in their behavioral histories, personality, attitudes, and social support for intimate partner violence.

2. The risk factors for mentally disordered and sexual offenders are similar to the risk factors for general justice-involved persons.

   Meta-analytic findings indicate that the best predictors of criminal behavior among MDOs and sexual offenders are the same as those identified among the general population of those in conflict with the law (e.g., past criminal history and antisocial personality pattern). Thus, a general theory of criminal conduct can apply to a variety of groups committing criminal acts.

3. Knowledge of the varieties of criminal behavior can be forwarded by applying a psychology of criminal conduct (PCC) to the analysis. One of the themes in this text is that our knowledge of criminal behavior can be informed by applying PCC. The GPCSL approach to understanding criminal behavior does not rely on psychopathological models of behavior.

Understanding of the people discussed in this chapter—the IPV, MDOs, and sexual offenders—is enriched when we apply GPCSL theory.

Recommended Readings

In the area of intimate partner violence, there are a number of reviews of treatment interventions that were briefly described in this chapter. The reader may wish to examine more closely the reviews by Akoensi, Koehler, Lösel, & Humphreys (2013) for a European perspective, Arias, Arce, and Vilariño (2013) for a Spanish- and English-language review, and a largely North American review by Travers, McDonagh, Cunningham, Armour, and Hansen (2021).

Three meta-analytic review articles are highly recommended for those with an interest in the mentally disordered offender (Bonta, Blais, & Wilson, 2014; Eisenberg, Van Horn, et al., 2019) and the sexual offender (Hanson & Morton-Bourgon, 2009). All three reviews show the importance of considering the general literature for understanding the two groups of offenders. For the reader who would like a broad overview of the sexual offender research, there is the edited book *The Wiley Handbook of What Works with Sexual Offenders: Contemporary Perspectives in Theory, Assessment, Treatment, and Prevention* by Proulx, Cortoni, Craig, and Letourneau (2020). This book consists of 28 chapters covering different theoretical and research perspectives of criminal sexual behavior, from assessment to policy perspectives.

 Visit the Instructor and Student Resource to access additional exercises, videos and study materials to support this chapter: psychologycriminalconduct.routledge.com

PART 4 Summary and Conclusions

CHAPTER 15 A General Personality and Cognitive Social Learning Perspective of Criminal Conduct: Summary and Conclusions

This final chapter sets out what is known and where there are serious gaps in knowledge. The chapter will also contrast the RNR model with two competing perspectives on reducing criminal behavior: Desistance and the Good Lives Model. First, we look at the three types of understanding set for PCC: (1) an empirical understanding, (2) a theoretical understanding, and (3) an understanding of practical value. All in all, this chapter should provide a concise summary and evaluation of the key elements of PCC.

A distinct preference for general understandings is stated within each of the domains of research, theory, and applications. Important differences between girls and boys, women and men, the young and the older, and the rich and the poor are well established in the domains of risk, need, and general responsivity. Likewise, the differences among and within community corrections, halfway houses, jails, and prisons are so great that serious understandings of assessment and intervention must make some setting-specific accommodations. In addition to the obvious differences, there are a host of nuanced differences.

At the same time, similarities and differences are not simply assumed to exist or asserted to exist but are empirically explored. The empirical explorations strive to respect general theoretical positions along with gender-informed, racially informed, and/or other specific considerations. Likewise, theoretical considerations in regard to settings are open for investigation.

DOI: 10.4324/9781003292128-19

Empirical Understanding

The rational-empirical roots of the psychology of crime induce a healthy skepticism when summarizing research findings. They also feed a respect for evidence. The public has a right to hear what has been learned, and the people in positions to influence the revitalization of human service should know why they should support direct treatment services.

1. Incidence and Prevalence of Criminal Activity

(a) **Substantial Variation in the Criminal Behavior of Individuals.** People differ in their frequency of criminal activity and in the number, type, and variety of criminal acts in which they engage. In addition, while accounting for a disproportionate amount of the total criminal activity, the more criminally active persons tend not to be specialists. These findings are apparent across methods of measurement and particular types of offense, and they are found within the typical indicators of social location such as geography, age, race/ethnicity, gender, and social class.

(b) **Early and Late Starters.** The developmental criminologists have shown that there is considerable value in recognizing two major sets of justice-involved persons: the early starters, who tend to persist in their criminal activity, and late starters, who tend to desist. Of course, the "life-course-persistent" and the "adolescent-limited" typologies hide the fact that many within either group will show different patterns of being in and out of crime at different times.

(c) **Chronic and Serious Violent Offenders.** As dramatic as is the image of life-course-persistent delinquency, it is a small minority who are repeat violent offenders. In and around Phoenix, Arizona, only 1 percent of a cohort of 151,209 young persons was charged with two or more violent offenses over their youthful criminal career (Snyder, 1998).

(d) **Generality and Specificity.** In regard to criminal pathways, and not surprisingly in view of the well-established gender differences in the base rate of offending, males are overrepresented on the life-course-persistent pathway relative to females. However, the long-term consequences of being on the early and persistent pathway are characterized by gender similarities in terms of adult violence, poor health, poor mental health, and poor socioeconomic circumstances (Rivenbark, Odgers, et al., 2018).

2. The Correlates of Criminal Activity

A number of conclusions may be drawn in regard to the correlates of crime, and they are found in the Central Eight risk/need factors. The major risk/need factors may be conceptualized in other ways. For example, components of Antisocial Personality Pattern and Criminal History may be pulled together within the label "psychopathy," as Robert Hare has done with the PCL-R. Travis Hirschi's definition of "weak self-control" could incorporate the total of the Central Eight. Others, taking an atheoretical position, will let a statistical procedure determine what specific indicators within and across categories are selected to create an efficient prediction formula (e.g., the VRAG assessment and many of the second-generation instruments described in Chapter 10). Another approach would be to sum assessments across the Central Eight and call the resulting score an assessment of a general propensity for rule violations (as in the case of the LS/CMI General Risk/Need score).

3. *The Central Eight*

An abbreviated version of the Central Eight is outlined in Table 15.1 with a description of how the factors can serve as treatment targets. Note that addressing the risk/need factors involves building personal prosocial strengths, thereby reducing risk. Overall, the estimate for the predictive validity of the Central Eight, as measured by the LS/CMI subcomponents, is in the range of $r = 0.12$ to 0.31 (Olver et al., 2014). These predictive values are significant (the CI does not include zero) and greater than that achieved by risk/need factors in the minor set (such as lower-class origins and personal emotional distress). The Central Eight is also relevant to the prediction of violent recidivism with rs ranging from 0.09 to 0.23 (Olver et al., 2014).

4. *Wide Applicability*

The same sets of risk factors appear to be involved within categories of geography, class, age, gender, race, and ethnicity. Furthermore, the correlations with crime of these biological and social location variables are reduced, if not eliminated, when controls are introduced for the stronger of the personal and interpersonal risk factors. Remaining to be documented is whether the correlation between gender/ethnicity/race/class and crime that remains after controlling for the major personal and interpersonal factors is actually a result of the processing effects suggested by the social inequality versions of criminological theories.

The same risk factors apply across different types of criminal behavior, although crime-specific indicators of procriminal attitudes, associates, and behavioral history may be most useful when the focus is on violence or sexual offenses. For example, laboratory assessments of deviant sexual arousal may enhance predictive validity when working with pedophiles. Similarly, assessments of a history of violence will enhance the prediction of violent offenses.

TABLE 15.1 Central Eight Risk/Need Factors and Suggested Targets for Treatment

Criminal History. Early and continuing involvement in the number and variety of antisocial acts in a variety of settings.
Target goals: build up noncriminal alternative behavior in risky situations.

Antisocial Personality Pattern. Adventurous, pleasure-seeking, weak self-control, restlessly aggressive.
Target goals: build problem-solving skills, self-management skills, anger management, and coping skills.

Procriminal Attitudes. Attitudes, values, beliefs, and rationalizations supportive of crime and cognitive emotional states of anger, resentment, and defiance.
Target goals: reduce procriminal cognition, recognize risky thinking and feeling, build up alternative prosocial thinking and feeling, adopt a prosocial identity.

Procriminal Associates. Close association with criminal others and relative isolation from prosocial, immediate social support for crime.
Target goals: reduce association with criminal others, enhance association with prosocial others.

Family/Marital. Two key elements are nurturance/caring and monitoring/supervision.
Target goals: reduce conflict, build positive relationships, enhance monitoring and supervision.

School/Work. Low levels of performance and satisfactions in school and/or work.
Target goals: enhance performance, rewards, and satisfactions.

Leisure/Recreation. Low levels of involvement and satisfactions in prosocial leisure pursuits.
Target goals: enhance involvement, rewards, and satisfactions.

Substance Abuse. Misuse of alcohol and/or drugs.
Target goals: reduce substance misuse, reduce the personal and interpersonal supports for substance-oriented behavior, enhance alternatives to substance use.

Note: The minor risk/need factors include the following: personal/emotional distress, major mental disorder, physical health issues, fear of official punishment, physical conditioning, low IQ, social class of origin, and seriousness of current offense.

The Ability to Influence Crime

Meta-analyses of treatment programs that tap into GPCSL-based and empirically informed knowledge of risk/need factors will reduce reoffending to a significant degree. The reviews have drawn on two aspects of the GPCSL perspective on crime to provide clear guidance on effective correctional treatment. In brief, and first, assign service that is in adherence with the principles of *risk*, *need*, and general *responsivity* (RNR). Second, deliver treatment that adheres to RNR with integrity.

The evidence suggests that nonadherence with the principles of RNR has either no effect on crime or increases crime. Other variables and considerations do influence the overall level of crime reduction achieved through adherence to risk, need, and responsivity. The range of known variables is found in the full RNR model (refer back to Table 9.1). Notably important is the concept of criminogenic needs as intermediate targets of change in treatment programs. Prior to 1990, treatment was often directed at addressing noncriminogenic needs (e.g., self-esteem, anxiety). Only the criminogenic needs of substance misuse and uncontrolled anger received much attention. Even employment and academic programs focused on skill learning without teaching clients how to behave prosocially in the work and school environments. Today, service providers have a much larger view of what needs to be treated.

Table 15.2 illustrates some of the findings with reference to targeting the dynamic criminogenic needs of the Central Eight risk/need factors. The mean effect size associated with targeting the "central seven" is 0.20 (CI = 0.15–0.25). The mean effect size for targeting noncriminogenic needs is 0.05 (CI = −0.03–0.11). The latter mean value is not significantly different than zero and is significantly lower than the corresponding value for the targeting of criminogenic needs.

Table 15.3 presents a more comprehensive list of criminogenic and noncriminogenic needs. This table may provide service providers with a helpful list of targets for change and a list of targets that may actually run counter to reducing criminal conduct. Many programs try to target many needs of the clients. What we know is that the more criminogenic needs are targeted relative to noncriminogenic needs, the lower the recidivism rate. Programs that

TABLE 15.2 Mean Effect Size (*r*) by Targeting Criminogenic and Noncriminogenic Needs

Need area	*r*
Criminogenic Needs as Intermediate Targets of Change	
Procriminal Attitudes	.21
Procriminal Associates	.22
Antisocial Personality Pattern	.22
Family/Marital	.29
School/Work	.15
Substance Abuse	.11
Leisure/Recreation	.16
Noncriminogenic Needs as Intermediate Targets of Change	
Fear of Official Punishment	−.05
Personal Distress	.08
Physical Activity	.08
Conventional Ambition	.08

TABLE 15.3 **Criminoenic and Noncriminogenic Needs: A Listing**

Criminogenic Needs as Targets for Change

- Changing procriminal attitudes
- Reducing angry, hostile feelings
- Reducing procriminal associations
- Promoting familial affection/communication
- Promoting familial monitoring and supervision
- Promoting child protection (preventing neglect/abuse)
- Promoting identification/association with prosocial others
- Increasing self-control, self-management, and problem-solving skills
- Replacing the skills of lying, stealing, and aggression with prosocial alternatives
- Reducing substance use
- Shifting the density of the personal and interpersonal rewards and costs for criminal and prosocial activities in familial, academic, work, and recreational settings so that the noncriminal alternatives are favored
- Providing the mentally disordered offender with low-pressure, sheltered living arrangements
- Ensuring that the client is able to recognize risky thoughts and situations and has a concrete and well-rehearsed plan for dealing with them
- Confronting the personal and situational barriers to service (e.g., client motivation, restrictive criteria for entering programming)
- Changing other attributes of clients and their circumstances that, through individualized assessments of risk and need, have been linked to criminal conduct

Noncriminogenic Needs as Targets for Change

- Increasing self-esteem (without reductions in procriminal attitudes and associates)
- Focusing on vague emotional/personal complaints that have not been linked with criminal conduct
- Increasing the cohesiveness of procriminal groups
- Improving neighborhood-wide living conditions without targeting the criminogenic needs of higher-risk individuals and families
- Showing respect for procriminal attitudes on the grounds that the values of one culture are equally as valid as the values of another culture
- Increasing conventional ambition in the areas of school and work without concrete assistance in realizing these ambitions
- Attempting to turn the client into a "better person," when the standards for being a "better person" do not link with recidivism

---

predominantly target noncriminogenic needs are associated with increased crime. This is Principle 9 in the RNR model: *breadth*.

A Theoretical Understanding and Challenges to GPCSL

The General Personality and Cognitive Social Learning (GPCSL) perspective of criminal conduct embraces the richness of human experience. The pathways to crime are many, and social, cognitive, and personality factors pave the road. The application arm of GPCSL, the RNR model, has proven to be fruitful. Examples of RNR assessments and interventions have already been described and will be summarized further shortly. Although the RNR model has dominated the correctional psychology field, it is not the only paradigm of influence. Two particular alternatives/adjuncts to RNR that purport to address weaknesses and offer enhancements to RNR are the *Good Lives Model* and *Desistance*.

1. Good Lives Model (GLM)

Some scholars argue that RNR pays insufficient attention to motivation and personal agency and suggest that GLM offers an alternative. GLM differentiates itself from RNR by a focus on a strengths-based and restorative model of rehabilitation. GLM also is critical of the concept of criminogenic needs because it ignores more fundamental human needs and the pursuit of "basic goods" (Ward & Stewart, 2003). The basic goods are "friendship, enjoyable work, loving relationships, creative pursuits, sexual satisfaction, positive self-regard, and an intellectually challenging environment" (p. 142). Rather than following the RNR direction of reduce criminogenic needs and basic goods will follow, Ward and his colleagues have argued the reverse (Purvis & Ward, 2019; Ward, Mann, & Gannon, 2007; Ward, Yates, & Willis, 2012): achieve basic goods and criminogenic needs will be addressed. Attaining basic goods should be the primary goals for rehabilitation.

My colleagues and I have long argued that there is little added value of GLM over RNR (Andrews, Bonta, & Wormith, 2011; Bonta & Andrews, 2003; Wormith, Gendreau, & Bonta, 2012). GLM theorists minimize RNR's attention to strengths (i.e., Principle 10) and RNR's acceptance of the importance of motivation. Strengths and motivation *are* important in RNR. This has already been acknowledged with discussions of motivational interviewing and building collaborative working relationships in RNR-based training programs such as STICS.

What is most problematic with GLM is that it places the pursuit of personal fulfillment ahead of criminogenic needs. Noncriminogenic needs are important in human terms. However, there is no evidence that personal fulfillment and achieving basic goods without attention to criminogenic needs reduces criminal behavior. Although there is some evidence that GLM-based interventions improve motivation to engage in treatment (Netto, Carter, & Bonell, 2014), there are other approaches to enhancing motivation and building a therapeutic relationship with a therapist (Dickson & Willis, 2022). Furthermore, there is yet to be seen any quasi-experimental or experimental evidence that interventions based on GLM are effective in reducing recidivism (Mallion, Wood, & Mallion, 2020; Zeccola, Kelty, & Boer, 2021).

2. Desistance

Strictly speaking, desistance is ceasing criminal activity. However, criminology theorists describe desistance as the *process* by which a justice-involved person stops to engage in criminal behavior. Not all continue in crime throughout their lifetime. Why is it that some people stop or desist? Interest in desistance gained momentum with two important studies. The first was by Laub and Sampson (2003). They followed up, to the age of 70, the original sample of juvenile delinquents first identified by Glueck and Glueck in 1950. The basic findings from the study were that those who desisted from crime found meaningful work and a positive marital relationship (Laub & Sampson, 2011). Desistance theory explains the process of crime reduction as increasing ties to convention (i.e., social control theory, Chapter 3; Galli & Kroner, 2019).

Next, we have Shadd Maruna's (2001) Liverpool Desistance Study. Maruna matched a group of 30 ex-convicts who were crime-free for a year with 20 offenders still engaged in crime and illegal substance use. They were all interviewed, and their "narratives" or stories of how they changed (or did not change) were told. An important feature of Maruna's study was the emphasis on cognitive factors, in particular, changes in self-identity. He found that desisters had a "redemptive" narrative that emphasized personal responsibility and a motivation to do well. The persisters had a "condemnation" script and a sense of hopelessness and no choice over their criminal path.

The transition from condemnation to redemption is thought to be accelerated by life "turning points" such as marriage, parenthood, and reaching a milestone in age (Bersani & Doherty, 2018; Schinkel, 2019). Furthermore, turning points appear to apply equally to women and men (Rodermond, Kruttschnitt, Slotbloom, & Bijleveld, 2016). The concept of self-narratives has become increasingly important in criminology for drawing attention to self-cognitions and behavior (Maruna & Liem, 2021).

Does the desistance perspective add value to the RNR model? First of all, there is an underdeveloped theory as to why some desist from crime and others do not. The critical turning points that lead to desistance are major life events that lead to the adoption of a redemptive narrative. Family/marital and employment are certainly important criminogenic needs, but they are not the only ones. Aspects of desistance appear dependent upon seemingly random events such as gaining employment or finding a supportive, prosocial partner. In Maruna's interpretation of desistance, the closest to a theory we have is based on labeling theory, where the ex-offender adopts a prosocial identity (Maruna & LeBel, 2010). However, there is some evidence suggesting that people desist from crime *prior* to stable employment (Skardhamar & Savolainen, 2014) and marriage (Skardhamar, Savolainen, Aase, & Lyngstad, 2015). Thus, the direction of causality becomes a serious issue (Maruna & Liem, 2021). In contrast to desistance theory, GPCSL specifies the learning processes (operant and classical conditioning, and vicarious learning) and the personal and interpersonal contexts where behavior is learned.

Related to the issue of theory is practical application. Circling back to Chapter 1, much of the desistance literature describes *intra*-individual differences. That is, changes over time within the person. An objective of PCC is not only to understand variations in criminal conduct but also to inform practical means of influencing behavior. As noted in the preceding paragraph, desistance, or a reduction in recidivism in RNR language, depends on relatively unpredictable life events. Part of the redemptive narrative involves taking personal responsibility for behavior. As Fergus McNeill and his colleagues (McNeill, Farrall, Lightowler, & Maruna, 2012) write, "desisters manage to acquire a sense of 'agency'—of control over their lives" (p. 45). However, little is said about *how* desisters actually acquire this sense of agency. At least RNR says that to help people take control of their behavior and become prosocial, one should address the criminogenic needs of the offender using cognitive-behavioral interventions. In addition, advocates of desistance criticize RNR for ignoring strengths in the rehabilitation of offenders. As affirmed earlier, in the full RNR model, the notion of personal strengths is represented as a separate principle (Principle 10; see also Wormith & Truswell, 2022).

Finally, there is the question of evidence. Here desistance proponents become vague and evasive. The sub-heading "Whose Evidence?" in the article by McNeill et al. (2012) is telling. Reminiscent of "knowledge destruction" (described in Technical Note 11.1), the title itself prepares the reader for a questioning of the traditional scientific method. In the section, we are asked to listen to the "voices of ex-offenders and those who have supported them" (p. 50) because they are the real experts. Later, we learn that research is a "mechanistic conception" and that to really progress we need a dialogue between justice-involved persons and their families, academics, practitioners, and policymakers (the so-called "Discovering Desistance Project"). Perhaps out of this dialogue progress will be made, but given that RNR already has a proven track record, is it all necessary?

It is difficult to imagine any new or current perspective that would not recognize the importance of the Central Eight and the principles set out in the extended RNR model. There have been steps taken to better align GLM (Lutz, Zani, Fritz, Dudeck, & Franke, 2022; Wormith & Truswell, 2022) and desistance theory (Maruna & Mann, 2019; Polaschek, 2016) with RNR. As always, there is room for improvement. More research is needed on specific responsivity, especially with respect to race/ethnicity (Spiropoulos, Salisbury, & Van Voorhis, 2014; Stams, 2015) and personality (Van Voorhis, Spiropoulos, Ritchie, Seabrook, & Spruance, 2013). However, a GPCSL perspective works as well or better than any alternative. Cognitive research and service developments in the domains of both personally and interpersonally mediated control promise even more powerful prediction and clinical interventions.

An Understanding of Practical Value

1. Prediction Instruments

On the issue of practical prediction, there is no question that change has been revolutionary over the last 40 years. Unstructured clinical judgment does so poorly relative to structured assessment approaches that the ethicality of unstructured risk assessment is a serious professional issue. As reviewed in Chapter 10, several second-generation instruments do as well as third- and fourth-generation instruments in the *prediction* of reoffending. However, second-generation instruments that do not sample a variety of criminogenic needs cannot assist in the building of *treatment* plans that are in adherence with RNR. Nor can their predictive validity be improved through reassessments on static variables.

The great promise of fourth-generation instruments is that they will enhance adherence with risk, need, breadth, general responsivity, and specific responsivity. Recall that fourth-generation instruments follow the case management process from initial assessment, case management planning, service delivery, reassessment, and case closure. We are also now on the cusp of fifth-generation assessment tools. With research on the neurobiological correlates of crime, it is only a matter of time before these factors are integrated into the assessment process.

2. Effective Prevention and Treatment

The RNR principles were summarized in Table 9.1. A major issue is whether the empirically validated principles of the RNR model can be implemented in the real world with sufficient levels of adherence that reduced reoffending is actually achieved. It may appear straightforward but, in fact, it requires major policy and organizational changes and major efforts on the part of managers and staff for adherence to be accomplished.

The issue is so important that this text includes a separate chapter on the challenges faced by treatment in the real world. As outlined in Chapter 12, many agencies are struggling with the implementation of RNR. However, significant progress is being made, as demonstrated by the widespread adoption of risk/need instruments such as the Level of Service instruments and the training of staff in RNR-based supervision practices (e.g., STICS, STARR, EPICS). It is important that these and other initiatives continue. Otherwise, we risk returning to another "nothing works" era that exposes communities to more crime, negates human agency, and destroys hope.

(a) Specific Responsivity

The principle of specific responsivity needs to be explored and expanded upon. At this point, only the broad strokes are painted. Table 15.4 summarizes current thinking on specific responsivity. The cognitive-interpersonal skill-level factor combines empathy, interpersonal maturity, self-regulation skills, and verbal intelligence. The treatment recommendation here is that styles of

---

TABLE 15.4 Principles of Specific Responsivity and Treatment Recommendations

---

Cognitive/Interpersonal Skill Level (empathy, interpersonal maturity, self-regulation skills, verbal intelligence)
Treatment Recommendation. Use styles and modes of service that are verbally and interpersonally demanding and depend upon self-regulation, and interpersonal sensitivity only with high-functioning persons.

Interpersonal Anxiety
Treatment Recommendation. Approach calmly and in a supportive manner. Avoid both confrontation and intense interpersonal exchanges.

Antisocial Personality Pattern (APP). The personality elements of APP suggest not only risk (intensive supervision and service), criminogenic needs (multiple) but also specific responsivity issues.
Treatment Recommendation. Provide high structure including monitoring and supervision and open communication among involved service staff; program novel and exciting opportunities; treatment should be readily accessible.

Weak Social Support for Change
Treatment Recommendation. Neutralize procriminal associates, structure active exposure to others who model and reinforce prosocial styles of thinking, feeling, and acting.

Gender
Treatment Recommendation. Provide gender-responsive services; ensure child support services; be attentive to past abuse and trauma.

Age
Treatment Recommendation. Provide developmentally appropriate services.

Race/Ethnicity/Culture
Treatment Recommendation. Provide services responsive to the particular race, ethnicity, and culture; be attentive to past trauma and the effects of colonization.

Mental Disorder
Treatment Recommendation. Address needs specific to the disorder (medication, counseling, hospitalization, aftercare) thereby enhancing responsiveness to criminogenic programming.

Poor Motivation
Treatment Recommendation. Match services according to stages of change; use motivational interviewing techniques; engage in collaborative goal setting.

Strengths
Treatment Recommendation. Build on the strengths of the person; engage prosocial supports to assist in building the person's strengths.

---

service that are verbally and interpersonally demanding and depend upon highly developed cognitive skills and interpersonal sensitivity be avoided with all justice-involved persons but the very high-functioning ones. If you are in doubt about this factor, then use structured cognitive social learning strategies. Avoid the chance of inadvertently increasing crime through low structuring. In the main, always adhere to the principle of general responsivity, but when working with high-functioning persons, one may reduce the structure and build on their exceptional strengths. The remainder of the specific responsivity factors are fairly straightforward.

(b) Gender and Motivation

Gender responsivity and motivational level are particularly interesting. A very lively literature has evolved in regard to women-specific treatment recommendations (see Table 15.5). Entered in the table are the promising

---

TABLE 15.5 Women-Specific Needs, Responsivity, and Treatment Recommendations

Needs Compatible with RNR

Decision-making: objective observation to establish facts; decisions on building healthy support systems; reflective emotional reactions.

Express and contain negative emotions appropriately.

Empowerment through skill building.

Substance misuse: enhance quality of relationships at home, school, work, leisure; understand substance use as maintaining relationships with a drug-abusing partner or managing pain of abuse.

Question unhealthy relationships: recognize unhealthy, illusory or unequal relationships with partners, friends and family.

Life plan development.

Needs Incompatible with RNR

Expansion and growth of self: knowledge of sources of self-esteem; knowledge of the effects of sexism and racism on sense of self; develop own sense of self; address roles of mother, wife, partner, daughter; understand poor self-image and history of trauma and abuse.

Relationships: explore roles in family of origin; societal views of motherhood; relationships with mother; relationship histories including possible violence.

Sexuality: explore sexuality, body image, sexual identity, sexual abuse; dealing with sexual dysfunction, shame, fear, and/or trauma.

Spirituality: introduce concepts of spirituality, prayer and meditation and how they relate to healing and recovery.

Disability-related issues.

Appearance and overall health and hygiene.

Responsivity Considerations (Mode, style, influence strategies, service practices)

Women-only groups and individual sessions with female helper.

Staff model healthy relationships.

Create a community with a sense of connection.

Emphasis on safety.

Emphasis on connecting: mutual respect.

Build on strengths.

Emphasis on raising and exploring issues.

Least restrictive environment.

intermediate areas of change suggested by those who work with women. Specific responsivity recommendations are also listed. Also noted in Table 15.5 are those factors that are compatible with RNR and those that are less so.

For purposes of clarity, in the expanded RNR model, the normative and specific responsivity principles are very important. Noncriminogenic needs may be set as intermediate targets for humanitarian and entitlement reasons in accordance with the normative principle. Additionally, collaborative treatment planning may establish the motivational value of targeting selected noncriminogenic needs for particular offenders.

Motivational interviewing (MI) is creating a level of excitement in the fields of addiction and corrections. MI was introduced in the discussion of substance misuse in Chapter 8. In Table 15.6, the spirit of MI is displayed while also drawing attention to how stages of change are differentially linked to MI interventions. The value of MI is significant, and MI techniques have been integrated in probation and parole officer training programs such as STICS, STARR, and EPICS. MI builds collaborative relationships and enhances offender motivation to change, preparing clients to learn new prosocial skills and cognitions.

TABLE 15.6 Specific Responsivity: Stages of Change and Motivational Interviewing

Stages of change	Motivational interviewing focus
Precontemplation	
Reluctance	Use reflective listening, summarizing, affirmation to explore situation.
Rebellion	Roll with resistance, do not argue; agree that change cannot be forced upon one.
Resignation	Instill hope, explore barriers, encourage small steps, build self-efficacy.
Rationalization	Empathy and reflective listening; encourage examination of advantages and disadvantages.
Contemplation	Accurate information on the risky behavior; advantages and disadvantages; summarize; increase self-efficacy.
Preparation: developing an acceptable plan	Listen, reflect, realistic plan.
Action: implementing the plan	Listen and affirm.
Maintenance: relapse	A "slip" is not failure. Return to earlier stages.

Note: Table provides a very brief summary of key ideas from Miller & Rollnick, 2002.

The Impact of a Psychology of Criminal Conduct

PCC has introduced an alternative view to our traditional criminological understandings of criminal conduct. It is a perspective firmly based on a psychology of human behavior. The practical application of PCC through the RNR model has influenced the assessment and treatment of justice-involved

TABLE 15.7 **International Applications of the RNR Model**

Adult Level of Service (LS) Assessment Used in Correctional/Forensic Systems

Australia	Denmark	Scotland
Belgium	France	Singapore
Bermuda	Hong Kong	Sweden
British Virgin Islands	Ireland	Trinidad
Canada	Jersey (UK)	United States
Cayman Islands	New Zealand	
Chile	Portugal	

Youth Level of Service (LS) Assessment Used in Correctional/Forensic Systems

Australia	Hong Kong	Trinidad
Canada	Ireland	United Kingdom
Cayman Islands	Singapore	United States
Denmark		

Research Studies of the LS Instruments

Australia	Germany	Portugal
Belgium	Hong Kong	Scotland
Canada	Italy	Singapore
China	Jersey (UK)	United Kingdom
France	Pakistan	United States

RNR-based Training

Canada (STICS)

Denmark (MOSAIC; translated as "Motivational Intervention in Community Supervision" and
  modeled after STICS)

France (STICS)

Sweden (STICS)

United States (EPICS, STARR)

persons far beyond Canada, where the model was first developed and adopted. Disseminating PCC has expanded with translations of the fifth edition of *The Psychology of Criminal Conduct* (French), and the sixth edition (Japanese, Taiwanese, and soon Spanish and Arabic). Table 15.7 gives the reader a glimpse of some of the applications of RNR around the world.

Conclusion and Final Comments

There now is a human science of criminal conduct. There are empirically defensible theories of criminal conduct that may be helpful in designing and delivering effective service. The literature is reasonably strong and supports vigorous pursuit of ethical, decent, humane, and cost-efficient approaches to prevention and rehabilitative programming for moderate and high-risk cases under a variety of conditions. The active and effective human service agency may contribute to a still more powerful knowledge base by building assessment, reassessment, RNR-based treatment, and research into the agency.

Since the sixth edition of this text, the evidence on the value of PCC and RNR-based understandings continues to grow. A major issue remains: how to make use of what works. The implementation issues remain huge, and one important aspect of implementation is who should own, run, and deliver human service programs in the justice and correctional context. It is dismaying to see low levels of RNR adherence in "real world" corrections. As obvious as RNR may appear for many readers, adherence is a problem in the field. However, there is hope. The widespread use of the LS instruments and others based on the Central Eight and the recent RNR-based training programs suggest that in a few years RNR will become mainstream in corrections. It is also hoped that health and social services that serve justice-involved persons will come to recognize the value of offering programs that build rewarding alternatives to crime for offenders.

In closing this chapter, in Resource Note 15.1 I offer a personal account of how PCC came to be. I also thank Paul Gendreau for providing some of the early background to the development of PCC and reviewing the Resource Note.

RESOURCE NOTE 15.1

A Personal Story of the Psychology of Criminal Conduct

The seeds of what Frank Cullen (2012) called the "Canadian's RNR paradigm" were planted in 1961. My friend, mentor, and colleague Paul Gendreau began an internship in Kingston penitentiary, a maximum-security prison, located in Kingston, Ontario. The prison was opened in 1835 and finally closed in 2013 (it is now a museum that is open for tours). The

continued

following year, Paul was joined by another young intern: Don Andrews (1941–2010). Both studied at Queen's University where they received their PhDs in experimental psychology (Paul in 1968 and Don in 1970).

In 1971, Don assumed the position of Chief Psychologist at Rideau Correctional Centre, a minimum-security prison outside of Ottawa. Within a year, Don left the prison to become an assistant professor at St. Patrick's College. The College later became part of Carleton University and Don remained with the Psychology Department until his retirement in 2006.

In 1965, Paul went to Trent University (Peterborough, Ontario) as an Assistant Professor in the Department of Psychology. When Don left for Carleton University, Paul became the new Chief Psychologist for Rideau Correctional Centre (1972). Eventually, he held the position of Chief Psychologist for the Eastern Region of the Ontario Correctional Services until 1986.

As an undergraduate student in Psychology at McMaster University in Hamilton, Ontario (1968–1972), I was exposed to the justice system. I did some volunteer work at a children's family mental clinic working with hard-to-manage children and their families and conducting some psychometric testing for the juvenile court.

Upon graduating with a BA in Psychology I pursued studies at the Institute of Child Studies at the University of Toronto. I thought that my future was in Child Psychology. After two years at the Institute, I applied to the PhD program at the University of Ottawa (initially in child clinical psychology but I quickly switched to adult clinical psychology). Prior to entering the doctoral program in 1975, all students were required to have at least a year of work experience. I was hired to work as a psychometrist at a training school for juvenile delinquents under the age of 12. In the 1970s, training schools were the last resort for families that could not manage their children ("unmanageable" was the term used by juvenile courts).

I also had a second requirement for my postgraduate work. Since the Institute of Child Study granted a diploma, I had to complete a research study that was the equivalent of a master's thesis. Capitalizing upon my contacts with juvenile court judges in the Hamilton area, I embarked on a research study of decision-making among juvenile court judges. I also needed an external reviewer for my final report.

My thesis supervisor at the University of Ottawa was Bob Watters and he guided me through my dissertation on teaching sign language as a memory aid for severely autistic children. Yes, you read right, my thesis was *not* in the corrections area. Now Bob was good friends with Don Andrews and Don became my external reviewer. That's how I first met Don Andrews. Bob and Don would meet monthly for lunch and I soon joined them.

In 1976, my course work was wrapping up and my required clinical internships were winding down. I was ready to find some part-time work. Don alerted me that the psychometrist at the Ottawa-Carleton Detention Centre (OCDC) was going to shortly leave his position there. That person was Steve Wormith (1946–2019). Steve was graduating with a PhD in experimental psychology from the University of Ottawa and had accepted a job as a psychologist at a penitentiary outside of Winnipeg, Manitoba. Although we were on the same campus, I did not know him at the time but we became friends and collaborators

continued

a number of years later. Don also told me to contact Paul Gendreau, the regional psychologist, if I was interested in the job. I drove out to Rideau Correctional Centre for an interview and Paul hired me to work part time at the maximum-security detention center in Ottawa.

When I graduated in 1979, I was made full time and gradually established the only Psychology Department in a detention center in Canada. Psychology departments were usually in prisons housing sentenced offenders, but OCDC was for people awaiting trial and newly sentenced. While at OCDC I started doing research on the Level of Service Inventory (LSI) with the support and encouragement of Paul Gendreau and many others. Don Andrews was already developing the instrument in probation, and I began administering the LSI to inmates and conducting validity studies.

During those years at OCDC (1976–1990) I was exposed to the leading advocates of the rehabilitation field: Paul Gendreau, Don Andrews, Bob Ross, and Steve Wormith. Steve returned to the Ottawa area to take over Paul's position as Chief Psychologist at Rideau Correctional Centre when Paul accepted an academic position at the University of New Brunswick in 1986. Over the years, we met regularly, exchanged ideas, and our conversations nourished my commitment to corrections. It is noteworthy that my colleagues were all psychologists. In general, psychologists believe that behavior is learned. So, when Martinson's review of the rehabilitation literature came along, igniting the "nothing works" movement, it made little sense to us. Are those who commit crimes really unable to learn new prosocial behaviors? My clinical training certainly reinforced the view that treatment can work. However, what kind of treatment works best?

In 1980, my thinking about criminal behavior took a major step when Don Andrews asked me to teach the evening course of "The Psychology of Criminal Behavior." Don taught the course during the day and the course became so popular at Carleton University that an evening section was added. There was no formal textbook for the course, just a compilation of reproduced journal articles and book chapters. As the years went by (I taught the evening course until 1993) we gradually replaced the readings with our own chapters. In 1994, the first edition of *The Psychology of Criminal Conduct* was published.

Paul Gendreau and Bob Ross wrote a number of narrative reviews in response to "nothing works," arguing that treatment can work. Those reviews were written in the late 1970s and the 1980s. Then in 1990, with Don Andrews and Bob Hoge we published our literature review of treatment programs, arguing that treatment was most effective when interventions followed the principles of Risk, Need, and Responsivity. Thus was born the RNR model of classification and rehabilitation. That same year, based on Ivan Zinger's honour's thesis we published along with Paul Gendreau and Frank Cullen our meta-analysis demonstrating the importance of RNR.

The year 1990 was also an important year for me from a career perspective. I left OCDC and took the position of Director of Corrections Research in a federal department that would become Public Safety Canada. I left clinical practice and assumed full-time research. Working in the federal government expanded my opportunities to engage with other partners to advance effective correctional practice both within Canada and

continued

internationally. The research unit developed into a very influential group. For example, in 1991 Karl Hanson joined the unit and developed a world-renowned program in sexual offender research (we also collaborated on a number of other nonsexual offender projects). We also had many students who became successful researchers and academics in their own right. Although I was now a researcher, I did not lose sight of my clinical roots. Together with my colleagues Tanya Rugge and Guy Bourgon, we developed and evaluated STICS. I participated in many of the trainings and lived vicariously through the challenges that probation officers faced when working with their clients.

I retired in 2015 from Public Safety Canada, but I have not ceased to try and contribute to the correctional psychology field. This book is evidence of that. When I reflect over the years, I find myself lucky to have known so many colleagues who have influenced me professionally. To this day, there are many who still exercise an enormous impact on my efforts to promote the psychology of criminal conduct.

Suggested Reading: See Tamara Kang's (in press) detailed history of the theoretical thinking and early research behind the creation of the RNR model.

Visit the Instructor and Student Resource to access additional exercises, videos and study materials to support this chapter: psychologycriminalconduct.routledge.com

REFERENCES

Abracen, J., Looman, J., Mailloux, D., Serin, R., & Malcolm, B. (2005). Clarification regarding Marshall and Yates's critique of "Dosage of treatment to sexual offenders: Are we overprescribing?" *International Journal of Offender Therapy and Comparative Criminology, 49*, 225–230.

Abrams, L. S., Jordan, S. P., & Montero, L. A. (2018). What is a juvenile? A cross-national comparison of youth justice systems. *Youth Justice, 18*, 111–130.

Acker, J. R. (2006). Hearing the victim's voice amidst the cry for capital punishment. In D. Sullivan & L. Tifft (Eds.), *Handbook of restorative justice* (pp. 246–260). New York, NY: Routledge.

Adams, S. (1975). Evaluation: A way out of the rhetoric. Paper presented at the Evaluation Research Conference, Seattle, Washington.

Ægisdóttier, S., White, M. J., Spengler, P. M., Maugherman, A. S., Anderson, L. A., Cook, R. S., … Rush, J. D. (2006). The meta-analysis of clinical judgment project: Fifty-six years of accumulated research on clinical versus statistical prediction. *Counseling Psychologist, 34*, 341–382.

Agnew, R. (1992). Foundation for a general strain theory of crime and delinquency. *Criminology, 30*, 47–87.

Agnew, R. (2001). *Juvenile delinquency: Causes and control*. Los Angeles: Roxbury.

Agnew, R. (2012). Reflection on "a revised strain theory of delinquency". *Social Forces, 91*, 33–38.

Agnew, R., & Brezina, T. (2019). General strain theory. In M. D. Krohn, N. Hendrix, G. Penly Hall, & A. J. Lizotte (Eds.), *Handbook on crime and deviance* (pp. 145–160). New York: Springer.

Aguirre, A., & Baker, D. V. (1990). Empirical research on racial discrimination in the imposition of the death penalty. *Criminal Justice Abstracts*, March.

Ahmadi, K., Sangdeh, J. K., Aminimanesh, S., Mollazamani, A., & Khanzade, M. (2013). The role of parental monitoring and affiliation with delinquent peers in adolescents' sexual risk taking: Toward an interactional model. *International Journal of High Risk Behaviors & Addiction, 2*, 22–27.

Ahonen, L., Jennings, W. G., Loeber, R., & Farrington, D. P. (2016). The relationship between developmental trajectories of girls' offending and police charges: From the Pittsburgh Girls Study. *Journal of Development and Life Course Criminology, 2*, 262–274.

Ajzen, I. (2011). The theory of planned behaviour: Reactions and reflections. *Psychology & Health, 26*, 1113–1127.

Ajzen, I. (2020). The theory of planned behavior: Frequently asked questions. *Human Behavior & Emerging Technologies, 2*, 314–324.

Ajzen, I., & Cote, N. G. (2008). Attitudes and the prediction of behavior. In C. D. Crano & R. Radmila (Eds.), *Attitudes and attitude change* (pp. 289–311). Mahwah, NJ: Lawrence Erlbaum Associates.

Ajzen, I., & Fishbein, M. (1980). *Understanding attitudes and predicting social behavior*. Englewood Cliffs, NJ: Prentice Hall.

Akers, R. L. (1991). Self-control as a general theory of crime. *Journal of Quantitative Criminology, 7*, 201–211.

Akers, R. L., & Jennings, W. G. (2016). Social learning theory. In A. R. Piquero (Ed.), *The handbook of criminological theory* (pp. 230–240). New York: John Wiley & Sons.

Akoensi, T. D., Koehler, J. A., Lösel, R., & Humphreys, D. K. (2013). Domestic violence perpetrator programs in Europe, Part II: A systematic review of the state of the evidence. *International Journal of Offender Therapy and Comparative Criminology, 57*, 1206–1225.

Alalehto, T. (2018). The origin of white collar criminality? Exploring a gene x environment interaction hypothesis. *International Journal of Criminology and Sociology, 7*, 196–205.

Alexander, J. F., & Barton, C. (1976). Behavioral systems therapy for families. In D. H. L. Olson (Ed.), *Treating relationships* (pp. 167–188). Lake Mills, IA: Graphic.

Alexander, J. F., & Parsons, B. V. (1973). Short-term behavioral intervention with delinquent families: Impact on family process and recidivism. *Journal of Abnormal Psychology, 81*, 219–225.

Allard, T., Stewart, A., Smith, C., Dennison, S., Chrzanowkis, A., & Thompson, C. (2014). The monetary cost of offender trajectories: Findings from Queensland (Australia). *Australian & New Zealand Journal of Criminology, 47*, 81–101.

Allen, A., Katsikitis, M., Millear, P., & McKillop, N. (2020). Psychological interventions for sexual fantasies and implications for sexual violence: A systematic review. *Aggression and Violent Behavior, 55*, 101465.

Alltucker, K. W., Bullis, M., Close, D., & Yovanoff, P. (2006). Different pathways to juvenile delinquency: Characteristics of early and late starters in a sample of previously incarcerated youth. *Journal of Child and Family Studies, 15*, 479–492.

Alm, S. S. (2011). Hope for your probationers. *The Judges Journal, 50*, 18–21.

Alm, S. S. (2016). HOPE probation: Fair sanctions, evidence-based principles, and therapeutic alliances. *Criminology & Public Policy, 15*, 1195–1214.

Alquist, J., & Baumeister, R. F. (2012). Self-control: Limited resources and extensive benefits. *Wiley Interdisciplinary Reviews: Cognitive Science, 3*, 419–423.

American Psychiatric Association. (2013). *Diagnostic and Statistical Manual of Mental Disorders—DSM 5*. Arlington, VA: The American Psychiatric Association.

American Psychological Association. (2020). *Publication manual of the American Psychological Association* (7th ed.). Washington, DC: Author.

American Psychological Association. (2021). *Inclusive language guidelines*. www.apa.org/about/apa/equity-diversity-inclusion/language-guidelines.pdf

Anderson, N. E., & Kiehl, K. A. (2012). The psychopath magnetized: Insights from brain imaging. *Trends in Cognitive Science, 16*, 52–60.

Andrews, D. A. (1980). Some experimental investigations of the principles of differential association through deliberate manipulations of the structure of service systems. *American Sociological Review, 45*, 448–462.

Andrews, D. A. (2006). Enhancing adherence to risk-need-responsivity: Making quality a matter of policy. *Criminology & Public Policy, 5*, 595–602.

Andrews, D. A., & Bonta, J. (1995). *The Level of Service Inventory–Revised*. Toronto, Canada: Multi-Health Systems.

Andrews, D. A., & Bonta, J. (2010a). *The psychology of criminal conduct* (5th ed.). New Providence, NJ: Lexus/Nexus.

Andrews, D. A., & Bonta, J. (2010b). Rehabilitating criminal justice policy and practice. *Psychology, Public Policy, & Law, 16*, 39–55.

Andrews, D. A., Bonta, J., & Hoge, R. D. (1990). Classification for effective rehabilitation: Rediscovering psychology. *Criminal Justice and Behavior, 17*, 19–52.

Andrews, D. A., Bonta, J., & Wormith, J. S. (2004). *The Level of Service/Case Management Inventory (LS/CMI): User's manual*. Toronto, Canada: Multi-Health Systems.

Andrews, D. A., Bonta, J., & Wormith, J. S. (2006). The recent past and near future of risk and/or need assessment. *Crime & Delinquency, 52*, 7–27.

Andrews, D. A., Bonta, J., & Wormith, J. S. (2008). *The Level of Service/Risk, Need, Responsivity (LS/RNR): User's manual*. Toronto, Canada: Multi-Health Systems.

Andrews, D. A., Bonta, J., & Wormith, J. S. (2010). The Level of Service (LS) assessment of adults and older adolescents. In R. K. Otto & K. Douglas (Eds.), *Handbook of violence risk assessment tools* (pp. 199–225). New York, NY: Routledge.

Andrews, D. A., Bonta, J., & Wormith, J. S. (2011). The risk-need-responsivity (RNR) model: Does adding the good lives model contribute to effective crime prevention? *Criminal Justice and Behavior, 38*, 735–755.

Andrews, D. A., Bonta, J., Wormith, J. S., Guzzo, L., Brews, A., Rettinger, J., & Rowe, R. (2011). Sources of variability in estimates of predictive validity: A specification with Level of Service general risk and need. *Criminal Justice and Behavior, 38,* 413–432.

Andrews, D. A., & Dowden, C. (2005). Managing correctional treatment for reduced recidivism: A meta-analytic review of programme integrity. *Law and Criminological Psychology, 10,* 173–187.

Andrews, D. A., & Dowden, C. (2006). Risk principle of case classification in correctional treatment. *International Journal of Offender Therapy and Comparative Criminology, 50,* 88–100.

Andrews, D. A., Dowden, C., & Rettinger, J. L. (2001). Special populations within Canada. In J. A. Winterdyck (Ed.), *Corrections in Canada: Social reactions to crime* (pp. 170–212). Toronto, Canada: Prentice Hall.

Andrews, D. A., Guzzo, L., Raynor, P., Rowe, R. C., Rettinger, L. J., Brews, A., & Wormith, J. S. (2012). Are the major risk/need factors predictive of both female and male reoffending? A test with the eight domains of the Level of Service/Case Management Inventory. *International Journal of Offender Therapy and Comparative Criminology, 56,* 113–133.

Andrews, D. A., & Kiessling, J. J. (1980). Program structure and effective correctional practices: A summary of the CaVIC research. In R. R. Ross & P. Gendreau (Eds.), *Effective correctional treatment* (pp. 439–463). Toronto, Canada: Butterworth.

Andrews, D. A., & Robinson, D. (1984). *The Level of Supervision Inventory: Second report.* Report to Research Services (Toronto) of the Ontario Ministry of Correctional Services.

Andrews, D. A., & Wormith, J. S. (1984). Criminal sentiments and criminal behaviour. *Programs Branch User Report.* Ottawa, Canada: Solicitor General Canada.

Andrews, D. A., Zinger, I., Hoge, R. D., Bonta, J., Gendreau, P., & Cullen, F. T. (1990). Does correctional treatment work? A psychologically informed meta-analysis. *Criminology, 28,* 369–404.

Ang, R. P., Huan, V. S., Chan, W. T., Cheong, S. A., & Leaw, J. N. (2015). The role of delinquency, proactive aggression, psychopathy and behavioral school engagement in reported youth gang membership. *Journal of Adolescence, 4,* 148–156.

Angwin, J., Larson, J., Mattu, S., & Kirchner, L. (2016, May 23). Machine bias: There's software used across the country to predict future criminals, and it's biased against blacks. *Propublica.* www.propublica.org/article/machine-bias-risk-assessments-in-criminal-sentencing

Ansel, L. L., Barry, C. T., Gillen, C. T. A., & Herrington, L. L. (2015). An analysis of four self-report measures of adolescent callous-unemotional traits: Exploring unique prediction of delinquency, aggression, and conduct problems. *Journal of Psychopathological Behavior Assessment, 37,* 207–216.

Apel, R., Bushway, S. D., Paternoster, R., Brame, R., & Sweeten, G. (2008). Using state child labor laws to identify the causal effect of youth employment on deviant behavior and academic achievement. *Journal of Quantitative Criminology, 24,* 337–362.

Archer, J. (2013). Can evolutionary principles explain patterns of family violence? *Psychological Bulletin, 139,* 403–440.

Archer, M., Harwood, H., Stevelink, S., Rafferty, L., & Greenberg, N. (2020). Community reinforcement and family training and rates of treatment entry: A systematic review. *Addictions, 115,* 1024–1037.

Archer, R. P., Wheeler, E. M. A., & Vauter, R. A. (2016). Empirically supported forensic assessment. *Clinical Psychology: Science and Practice, 23,* 348–364.

Arias, E., Arce, R., & Vilariño, Y. M. (2013). Batterer intervention programmes: A meta-analytic review of effectiveness. *Psychosocial Intervention, 22,* 153–160.

Armour, J. A., Joussemet, M., Kurdi, V., Tessier, J., Boivin, M., & Tremblay, R. E. (2018). How toddlers' irritability and fearfulness relate to parenting: A longitudinal study conducted among Quebec families. *Infant and Child Development, 27,* e2062.

Armour, S., & Haynie, D. L. (2007). Adolescent sexual debut and later delinquency. *Journal of Youth and Adolescence, 36,* 141–152.

Armstrong, G. S. (2004). Boot camps as a correctional option. In D. L. MacKenzie & G. S. Armstrong (Eds.), *Correctional boot camps: Military basic training or a model for corrections?* (pp. 7–15). Thousand Oaks, CA: SAGE.

Arnold, T. (2007). *Dynamic changes in the Level of Service Inventory-Revised (LSI-R) scores and the effects on prediction accuracy.* Unpublished master's dissertation, St. Cloud University, St. Cloud, MN.

Ashford, L. J., Spivak, B. L., & Shepherd, S. M. (2022). Racial fairness in violence risk instruments: A review of the literature. *Psychology, Crime & Law, 46,* 911–941.

Aslan, L. (2018). Doing time on a TC: How effective are drug-free therapeutic communities in prison? A review of the literature. *Therapeutic Communities, 39,* 26–34.

Aspholm, R. R. (2022). Deaths of despair: Gang violence after the crack crisis. *Critical Criminology, 30,* 49–69.

Austin, J., Clark, J., Hardyman, P., & Henry, A. D. (1999). The impact of "Three strikes and you're out". *Punishment and Society, 1,* 131–162.

Auty, K. M., Farrington, D. P., & Coid, J. W. (2015). Intergenerational transmission of psychopathy and mediation via psychosocial risk factors. *The British Journal of Psychiatry, 206,* 26–31.

Auty, K. M., Farrington, D. P., & Coid, J. W. (2017). The intergenerational transmission of criminal offending: Exploring gender-specific mechanisms. *British Journal of Criminology, 57,* 215–237.

Azrin, N. H. (1956). Some effects of two intermittent schedules of immediate and non-immediate punishment. *Journal of Psychology, 42,* 3–21.

Azrin, N. H., & Holz, W. C. (1966). Punishment. In W. K. Honig (Ed.), *Operant behavior: Areas of research and application* (pp. 380–447). New York, NY: Appleton-Century-Crofts.

Azrin, N. H., Holz, W. C., & Hake, D. (1963). Fixed-ratio punishment. *Journal of the Experimental Analysis of Behavior, 6,* 141–148.

Azrin, N. H., Sisson, R. W., Meyers, R., & Godley, M. (1982). Alcoholism treatment by disulfiram and community reinforcement therapy. *Journal of Behavior Therapy and Experimental Psychiatry, 13,* 105–112.

Babchishin, K. M., Hanson, R. K., & Hermann, C. A. (2011). The characteristics of online sex offenders: A meta-analysis. *Sexual Abuse: A Journal of Research and Treatment, 23,* 92–123.

Babchishin, K. M., Hanson, R. K., & VanZuylen, H. (2015). Online child pornography offenders are different: A meta-analysis of the characteristics of online and offline sex offenders against children. *Archives of Sexual Behavior, 44,* 45–66.

Babcock, C. R. (2015). Nature-nurture controversy, history of. In J. D. Wright, *International encyclopedia of the social and behavioral sciences* (pp. 340–344). Oxford, England: Elsevier.

Babcock, J. C., Green, C. E., & Robie, C. (2004). Does batterers' treatment work? A meta-analytic review of domestic violence treatment. *Clinical Psychology Review, 23,* 1023–1053.

Babiak, P., & Hare, R. D. (2006). *Snakes in suits: When psychopaths go to work.* New York, NY: Regan Books.

Bacchus, L. J., Ranganathan, M., Watts, C., & Devries, K. (2018). Recent intimate partner violence against women and health: A systematic review and meta-analysis of cohort studies. *BMJ Open, 8,* e019995.

Baglivio, M. T., Wolff, K. T., Piquero, A. R., & Epps, N. (2015). The relationship between Adverse Childhood Experiences (ACE) and juvenile offending trajectories in a juvenile offender sample. *Journal of Criminal Justice, 43,* 229–241.

Baglivio, M. T., Zettler, H., Craig, J. M., & Wolff, K. T. (2021). Evaluating RNR-based targeted treatment and intervention dosage in the context of traumatic exposure. *Youth Violence and Juvenile Violence, 19,* 251–276.

Bahr, S. J., Masters, A. L., & Taylor, B. M. (2012). What works in substance abuse treatment programs for offenders? *The Prison Journal, 92,* 155–174.

Bailey, W. C. (1966). Correctional outcome: An evaluation of 100 reports. *Journal of Criminal Law, Criminology and Police Science, 57,* 153–160.

Baldry, A. C., Farrington, D. P., & Sorrentino, A. (2017). School bullying and cyberbullying among boys and girls: Roles and overlap. *Journal of Aggression, Maltreatment & Trauma, 26,* 937–951.

Ball, R. A. (1973). Ball's neutralization scale. In W. C. Reckless (Ed.), *American criminology: New directions* (pp. 26–36). New York, NY: Appleton-Century-Crofts.

Ballard, E., & Teasdale, B. (2016). Reconsidering the criminalization debate: An examination of the predictors of arrest among people with major mental disorders. *Criminal Justice Policy Review, 27,* 22–45.

Bandura, A. (1969). *Principles of behavior modification.* New York: Holt, Rinehart, & Winston.

Bandura, A. (1977). Self-efficacy: Toward a unifying theory of behavioral change. *Psychological Review, 84,* 191–215.

Bandura, A. (1986). *Social foundations of thought and action: A social cognitive theory.* Englewood Cliffs, NJ: Prentice Hall.

Bandura, A. (1989). Human agency in social cognitive theory. *American Psychologist, 44,* 1175–1184.

Bandura, A. (2002). Selective moral disengagement in the exercise of moral agency. *Journal of Moral Education, 312,* 109–119.

Bandura, A. (2015). *Moral disengagement: How people do harm and live with themselves.* Hamilton, NJ: Worth Publishers.

Bandura, A., Barbaranelli, C., Caprara, G. V., & Pastorelli, C. (1996). Mechanisms of moral disengagement in the exercise of moral agency. *Journal of Personality and Social Psychology, 71,* 364–374.

Bandura, A., Caprara, G. V., Barbaranelli, C., Regalia, C., & Scabini, E. (2011). Impact of family efficacy beliefs on quality of family functioning and satisfaction with family life. *Applied Psychology: An International Review, 60,* 421–448.

Bandura, A., & Walters, R. H. (1963). *Social learning and personality development.* New York: Holt, Rinehart, & Winston.

Banse, R., Koppehele-Gossel, J., Kistmaker, L. M., Werner, V. A., & Schmidt, A. F. (2013). Pro-criminal attitudes, intervention, and recidivism. *Aggression and Violent Behavior, 18,* 673–685.

Baranyi, G., Di Marco, M. H., Russ, T. C., Dibben, C., & Pearce, J. (2021). The impact of neighbourhood crime on mental health: A systematic review and meta-analysis. *Social Science & Medicine, 282,* Article 114106.

Baranyi, G., Fazel, S., Langerfeldt, S. D., & Mundt, A. P. (2022). The prevalence of comorbid serious mental illnesses and substance use disorders in prison populations: A systematic review and meta-analysis. *The Lancet Public Health, 7*(6), e557–e568.

Barnes, J. C., Beaver, K. M., & Boutwell, B. B. (2011). Examining the genetic underpinnings to Moffitt's developmental taxonomy: A behavioral genetic analysis. *Criminology, 49,* 923–954.

Barnes, J. C., Boutwell, B. B., Beaver, K. M., Gibson, C. L., & Wright, J. P. (2014). On the consequences of ignoring genetic influences in criminological research. *Journal of Criminal Justice, 42,* 471–482.

Barnes, J. C., Liu, H., Motz, R. T., Tanksley, P., Kail, R. M., Beckley, A. L., … Wertz, J. (2019). The propensity for aggressive behavior and lifetime incarceration risk: A test for gene-environment interaction (G x E) using whole genome data. *Aggression and Violent Behavior, 49, 101307,* 1–11.

Barnes, J. C., Wright, J. P., Boutwell, B. B., Schwartz, J. A., Connolly, E. J., Nedelec, J. L., & Beaver, K. M., (2014). Demonstrating the validity of twin research in criminology. *Criminology, 52,* 588–626.

Barnoski, R. (2004). *Outcome evaluation of Washington state's research-based programs for juvenile offenders.* Olympia, WA: Washington State Institute for Public Policy.

Barnum, T. C., Nagin, D. S., & Pogarsky, G. (2021). Sanction risk perceptions, coherence, and deterrence. *Criminology, 59,* 195–223.

Bartels, L. (2019). HOPE-ful bottles: Examining the potential for Hawaii's opportunity proba-tion with enforcement (HOPE) to help mainstream therapeutic jurisprudence. *International Journal of Law and Psychiatry, 63,* 26–34.

Barton, C., & Alexander, J. F. (1980). Functional family therapy. In A. S. Gurnam & D. P. Kniskern (Eds.), *Handbook of family therapy* (pp. 403–443). New York, NY: Brunner/Mazel.

Batastini, A. B., Hoeffner, C. E., Vitacco, M. J., Morgan, R. D., Coaker, L. C., & Lester, M. E. (2019). Does the format of the message affect what is heard? A two-part study on the communica-tion of violence risk assessment data. *Journal of Forensic Psychology Research and Practice, 19,* 44–71.

Bates-Maves, J. K., & O'Sullivan, D. (2017). Trauma-informed risk assessment in correctional settings. *International Journal of Criminology, 6,* 93–102.

Baumeister, R. F., Heatherton, T. F., & Tice, D. M. (1994). Losing control: How and why people fail at self-regulation. San Diego, CA: Academic Press.

Baumeister, R. F., Tice, D. M., & Vohs, K. D. (2018). The strength model of self-regulation: Conclusions from the second decade of willpower research. *Perspectives on Psychological Science, 13,* 141–145.

Baumgartner, F., Daniely, T., Huang, K., Johnson, S., Love, A., May, L., … Washington, K. (2021). Throwing away the key: The unintended consequences of "tough-on-crime" laws. *Perspectives on Politics, 19,* 1233–1246.

Beaudry, G., Yu, R., Perry, A. E., & Fazel, S. (2021). Effectiveness of psychological interventions in prison to reduce recidivism: A systematic review and meta-analysis of randomised con-trolled trials. *The Lancet Psychiatry, 8,* 759–773.

Beaver, K. M., Shutt, J. E., Boutwell, B. B., Ratchford, M., Roberts, K., & Barnes, J. C. (2009). Genetic and environmental influences on levels of self-control and delinquent peer affili-ation. *Criminal Justice and Behavior, 36,* 41–60.

Beaver, K. M., Wright, J. P., & Walsh, A. (2008). A gene-based evolutionary explanation for the association between criminal involvement and number of sex partners. *Biodemography and Social Biology, 54,* 47–55.

Bechtel, K., Lowenkamp, C. T., & Latessa, E. J. (2007). Assessing the risk of re-offending for juvenile offenders using the Youth Level of Service/Case Management Inventory. *Journal of Offender Rehabilitation, 45,* 85–108.

Becker, H. S. (1963). *Outsiders: Studies in the sociology of deviance.* New York, NY: Free Press.

Beek, E., Spruit, A., Kuiper, C. H., van der Rijken, R. E., Hendriks, J., & Stams, G. J. J. (2018). Treatment effect on recidivism for juveniles who have sexually offended: A multilevel meta-analysis. *Journal of Abnormal Child Psychology, 46,* 543–556.

Belisle, L., Keen, J. P., Trejbalová, T., Kelly, B., & Salisbury, E. J. (2022). Advances in female risk assessment. In S. L. Brown & L. Gelsthorpe (Eds.), *The Wiley handbook on what works with girls and women in conflict with the law: A critical review of theory, practice, and policy.* New York: John Wiley & Sons.

Belknap, J., & Grant, D. (2018). Fifty years after the 1967 Crime Commission Report: how nonpolicing domestic violence research and policies have changed and expanded. *Criminology & Public Policy, 17,* 467–481.

Belur, J., Thornton, A., Tompson, L., Manning, M., Sidebottom, A., & Bowers, K. (2020). A sys-tematic review of the effectiveness of the electronic monitoring of offenders. *Journal of Criminal Justice, 68,* 101686.

Bennett, T., Holloway, K., & Farrington, D. P. (2008). The statistical association between drug misuse and crime: A meta-analysis. *Aggression and Violent Behavior, 13,* 107–118.

Benning, S. D., Venables, N. C., & Hall, J. R. (2018). Successful psychopathy. In C. J. Patrick (Ed.), *Handbook of psychopathy* 2nd ed. (pp. 585–608). New York, NY: Guilford.

Berg, M. T., & Huebner, B. M. (2011). Reentry and the ties that bind: An examination of social ties, employment, and recidivism. *Justice Quarterly, 28,* 382–410.

Bergin, T. (2016). *The evidence enigma: Correctional boot camps and other failures in evidence-based policymaking.* New York: Routledge.

Berglund, A., Stochholm. K., & Gravholt, C. H. (2020). Morbidity in 47,XYY syndrome: A nation-wide epidemiological study of hospital diagnoses and medication use. *Genetics in Medicine, 22*, 1542–1551.

Bergstrøm, H., Larmour, S. R., & Farrington, D. P. (2018). The usefulness of psychopathy in explaining and predicting violence: Discussing the utility of competing perspective. *Aggression and Violent Behavior, 42*, 84–95.

Berk, R., & Elzarka, A. A. (2020). Almost politically acceptable criminal justice risk assessment. *Criminology & Public Policy, 19*, 1231–1257.

Bernard, T. J., & Ritti, R. R. (1991). The Philadelphia birth cohort and selective incapacitation. *Journal of Research in Crime and Delinquency, 28*, 33–54.

Berryessa, C. M., & Wohlstetter, B. (2019). The psychopathic "label" and effects on punishment outcomes: A meta-analysis. *Law and Human Behavior, 43*, 9–25.

Bersani, B. E., & Doherty, E. E. (2018). Desistance from offending in the twenty-first century. *Annual Review of Criminology, 1*, 311–334.

Besemer, S., Ahmad, S. I., Hinshaw, S. P., & Farrington, D. P. (2017). A systematic review and meta-analysis of the intergenerational transmission of criminal behavior. *Aggression and Violent Behavior, 37*, 161–178.

Besemer, S., Farrington, D. P., & Bijleveld, C. C. J. H. (2013). Official bias in intergenerational transmission of criminal behavior. *British Journal of Criminology, 53*, 438–455.

Bewley, M. T., & Morgan, R. D. (2011). A national survey of mental health services available to offenders with mental illness: Who is doing what? *Law and Human Behavior, 35*, 351–363.

Bhutta, M. H., & Wormith, J. S. (2016). An examination of a risk/needs assessment instrument and its relation to religiosity and recidivism among probationers in a Muslim culture. *Criminal Justice and Behavior, 43*, 204–229.

Birkley, E. L., & Eckhardt, C. I. (2015). Anger, hostility, internalizing negative emotions, and intimate partner violence perpetration: A meta-analytic review. *Clinical Psychology Review, 37*, 40–56.

Blackburn, R. (1993). Clinical programs with psychopaths. In K. Howells & C. R. Hollin (Eds.), *Clinical approaches to the mentally disordered offender* (pp. 179–208). West Sussex, England: John Wiley and Sons.

Blackburn, R. (2006). Other theoretical models of psychopathy. In C. J. Patrick (Ed.), *Handbook of psychopathy* (pp. 35–57). New York, NY: Guilford.

Blair, L., Sullivan, C. C., Lux, J., Thielo, A. J., & Gormsen, L. (2016). Measuring drug court adherence to the what works literature: The creation of the evidence-based Correctional Program Checklist-Drug Court. *International Journal of Offender Therapy and Comparative Criminology, 60*, 165–188.

Blais, J. (2015). Preventative detention decisions: Reliance on expert assessments and evidence of partisan allegiance within the Canadian context. *Behavioral Sciences and the Law, 33*, 74–91.

Blasko, B. L., Viglione, J., Toronjo, H., & Taxman, F. S. (2019). Probation officer–probation agency fit: Understanding disparities in the use of motivational interviewing techniques. *Corrections, 4*, 39–57.

Blokland, A. A. J., & Nieuwbeerta, P. (2007). Selectively incapacitating frequent offenders: Costs and benefits of various penal scenarios. *Journal of Quantitative Criminology, 23*, 327–353.

Boccaccini, M. T., Marcus, D., & Murrie, D. C. (2017). Allegiance effects in clinical psychology and practice. In S. O. Lilienfeld & I. D. Waldman (Eds.), *Psychological science under scrutiny: Recent challenges and proposed solutions* (pp. 323–339). New York: John Wiley and Sons.

Boccio, C. M., & Beaver, K. M. (2018). Psychopathic personality traits and the successful criminal. *International Journal of Offender Therapy and Comparative Criminology, 62*, 4834–4853.

Boccio, C. M., & Beaver, K. M. (2019). The influence of family structure on delinquent behavior. *Youth Violence and Juvenile Justice, 17*, 88–106.

Bodkin, C., Pivnik, L., Bondy, S. J., Ziegler, C., Martin, R. E., Jerrigan, C., & Kouyoumdjian, F. (2019). History of childhood abuse in populations incarcerated in Canada: A systematic review and meta-analysis. *American Journal of Public Health, 109,* e1–e11.

Boer, D. P., Hart, S. D., Kropp, P. R., & Webster, C. D. (1997). *Manual for the Sexual Violence Risk-SVR 20: Professional guidelines for assessing risk of sexual violence.* Vancouver, BC, Canada: Institute on Family Violence and Mental Health, Law, and Policy, Simon Fraser University.

Bogue, B. M., Pampel, F., & Pasini-Hill, D. (2013). Progress toward motivational interviewing proficiency in corrections: Results of a Colorado staff development program. *Justice Research and Policy, 15,* 37–66.

Bolaños, A. D., Mitchell, S. M., Morgan, R. D., & Grabowski, K. E. (2020). A comparison of criminogenic risk factors and psychiatric symptomatology between psychiatric inpatients with and without criminal justice involvement. *Law and Human Behavior, 44,* 336.

Bonta, J. (1996). Risk-needs assessment and treatment. In A. T. Harland (Ed.), *Choosing correctional options that work: Defining the demand and evaluating the supply* (pp. 18–32). Thousand Oaks, CA: Sage.

Bonta, J. (2002). Offender risk assessment: Guidelines for selection and use. *Criminal Justice and Behavior, 29,* 355–379.

Bonta, J. (2019a). Criminal risk assessment, generations of. In R. D. Morgan (Ed.), *The SAGE encyclopedia of criminal psychology* (pp. 288–290). Thousand Oaks, CA: Sage.

Bonta, J. (2019b). Criminogenic needs. In R. D. Morgan (Ed.), *The SAGE encyclopedia of criminal psychology* (pp. 324–328). Thousand Oaks, CA: Sage.

Bonta, J. (2019b). Criminogenic needs. In R. D. Morgan (Ed.), *The SAGE encyclopedia of criminal psychology* (pp. 324–328). Thousand Oaks, CA: Sage.

Bonta, J. (2019c). Criminogenic needs. In R. D. Morgan (Ed.), *The SAGE encyclopedia of criminal psychology* (pp. 288–290). Thousand Oaks, CA: Sage.

Bonta, J. (2023). Training community supervision officers in the risk-need-responsivity model of offender rehabilitation: A review and implications. *Journal of Offender Rehabilitation, 62,* 39–58.

Bonta, J., & Andrews, D. A. (2003). A commentary on Ward and Stewart's model of human needs. *Psychology, Crime, & Law, 9,* 215–218.

Bonta, J., & Andrews, D. A. (2007). *Risk-need-responsivity model for offender assessment and treatment (User Report 2007–06).* Ottawa, Canada: Public Safety Canada.

Bonta, J., Blais, J., & Wilson, H. A. (2014). A theoretically informed meta-analysis of the risk for general and violent recidivism for mentally disordered offenders. *Aggression and Violent Behavior, 19,* 278–287.

Bonta, J., Bogue, B., Crowley, M., & Motiuk, L. (2001). Implementing offender classification systems: Lessons learned. In G. A. Bernfeld, D. P. Farrington, & A. W. Leschied (Eds.), *Offender rehabilitation in practice: Implementing and evaluating effective programs* (pp. 227–245). Chichester, UK: Wiley.

Bonta, J., Bourgon, G., Rugge, T., Pedneault, C. I., & Lee, S. C. (2021). A system-wide implementation and evaluation of the Strategic Training Initiative in Community Supervision (STICS). *Journal of Criminal Justice, 74* (May/June), 1–12.

Bonta, J., Bourgon, G., Rugge, T., Gress, C., & Gutierrez, L. (2013). Taking the leap: From pilot project to wide-scale implementation of the Strategic Training Initiative in Community Supervision (STICS). *Justice Research and Policy, 15,* 17–35.

Bonta, J., Bourgon, G., Rugge, T., Scott, T. L., Yessine, A., Gutierrez, L., & Li, J. (2011). An experimental demonstration of training probation officers in evidence based community supervision. *Criminal Justice and Behavior, 38,* 1127–1148.

Bonta, J., Harris, A., Zinger, I., & Carriere, D. (1996). *The Crown Files Research Project: A study of dangerous offenders.* Ottawa: Solicitor General Canada.

Bonta, J., Harris, A., Zinger, I., & Carriere, D. (1998). The dangerous offender provisions: Are they targeting the right offenders? *Canadian Journal of Criminology, 40,* 377–400.

Bonta, J., Jesseman, R., Rugge, T., & Cormier, R. (2006). Restorative justice and recidivism: Promises made, promises kept? In D. Sullivan & L. Tifft (Eds.), *Handbook of restorative justice* (pp. 151–160). New York, NY: Routledge.

Bonta, J., Rugge, T., Bourgon, G., & Wanamaker, K. (2019). A conceptual replication of the Strategic Training Initiative in Community Supervision (STICS). *Journal of Experimental Criminology, 15,* 397–419.

Bonta, J., Rugge, T., Scott, T.-L., Bourgon, G., & Yessine, A. (2008). Exploring the black box of community supervision. *Journal of Offender Rehabilitation, 47,* 248–270.

Bonta, J., Wallace-Capretta, S., & Rooney, J. (2000). A quasi-experimental evaluation of an intensive rehabilitation supervision program. *Criminal Justice and Behavior, 27,* 312–329.

Bonta, J., Wallace-Capretta, S., Rooney, J., & McAnoy, K. (2002). An outcome evaluation of a restorative justice alternative to incarceration. *Contemporary Justice Review, 5,* 319–338.

Bonta, J., & Wormith, J. S. (2013). Applying the risk-needs-responsivity principles to offender assessment. In L. A. Craig, L. Dixon, & T. A. Gannon (Eds.), *What works in offender rehabilitation: An evidence based approach to assessment and treatment* (pp. 71–93). Chichester, West Sussex, UK: Wiley-Blackwell.

Bonta, J., & Wormith, J. S. (2018). Adult offender assessment and classification in custodial settings. In J. Wooldredge & P. Smith (Eds.), *Oxford handbook on prisons and imprisonment* (pp. 397–424). Oxford, UK: Oxford University Press.

Bootsman, F. (2019). Neurobiological intervention and prediction of treatment outcome in juvenile criminal justice. *Journal of Criminal Justice, 65,* 101554.

Borduin, C. M., & Dopp, A. R. (2015). Economic impact of multisystemic therapy with juvenile sexual offenders. *Journal of Family Psychology, 29,* 687.

Bornstein, M. C., Hahn, C.-H., Putnick, D. L., & Pearson, R. (2019). Stability of child temperament: Multiple moderation by child and mother characteristics. *British Journal of Developmental Psychology, 37,* 51–67.

Borseth, J. L., Myer, A. J., & Makarios, M. D. (2021). Superficial adherence to EBP: An example of low fidelity to the RNR model using a halfway house. *Corrections,* Online First.

Borum, R., Bartel, P., & Forth, A. (2003). *Manual for the structured assessment of violence risk in youth: Consultation version.* Tampa, FL: University of South Florida, Florida Mental Health Institute.

Bosker, J., & Witteman, C. (2016). Finding the right focus: Improving the link between risk/needs assessment and case management in probation. *Psychology, Public Policy, and Law, 22,* 221–233.

Botkins, J. R., McMahon, W. M., & Francis, L. P. (1999). *Genetics and criminality: The potential misuse of scientific information in court.* Washington, DC: American Psychological Association.

Bouchard, J., & Wong, J. S. (2018). Examining the effects of intensive supervision and aftercare programs for at-risk youth: A systematic review and meta-analysis. *International Journal of Offender Therapy and Comparative Criminology, 62*(6), 1509–1534.

Bouchard, J., & Wong, J. S. (2022). Seeing the forest and the trees: Examining the impact of aggregate measures of recidivism on meta-analytic conclusions of intervention effects. *Criminology & Criminal Justice,* Online First, May.

Bouchard, T. J. Jr., Lykken, D. T., McGue, M., Segal, N. L., & Tellegen, A. (1990). Sources of human psychological differences: The Minnesota Study of Twins Reared Apart. *Science, 250,* 223–228.

Bourgon, G., & Bonta, J. (2014). Reconsidering the responsivity principle: A way to move forward. *Federal Probation, 78,* 3–10.

Bourgon, G., Bonta, J., Rugge, T., & Gutierrez, L. (2010a). Technology transfer: The importance of ongoing clinical supervision in translating "what works" to everyday community supervision. In F. McNeill, P. Raynor, & C. Trotter (Eds.), *Offender supervision: New directions in theory, research and practice* (pp. 91–112). New York, NY: Willan Publishing.

Bourgon, G., Bonta, J., Rugge, T., Scott, T.-L., & Yessine, A. K. (2010b). The role of program design, implementation, and evaluation in evidence-based "Real World" community supervision. *Federal Probation, 74,* 2–15.

Bourgon, G., Chadwick, N., & Rugge, T. (2020). Beyond core correctional practice: Facilitating change through the Strategic Training Initiative in Community Supervision. In J. S. Wormith, L. A. Craig, & T. Hogue (Eds.), *What works in violence risk management: Theory, research, and practice* (pp. 505–525). New York: Wiley.

Bourgon, G., & Gutierrez, L. (2012). The general responsivity principle in community supervision: The importance of probation officers using cognitive intervention techniques and its influence on recidivism. *Journal of Crime and Justice, 35,* 149–166.

Bourgon, G., Gutierrez, L., & Ashton, J. (2011). The evolution of community supervision practice: The transformation from case manager to change agent. *Irish Probation Journal, 8,* 28–48.

Bourgon, G., Mugford, R., Hanson, R. K., & Coligado, M. (2018). Offender risk assessment practices vary across Canada. *Canadian Journal of Criminology and Criminal Justice, 60,* 167–205.

Bourgon, G., Rugge, T., Chadwick, N., & Bonta, J. (2018). The Living Laboratory studies: Providing insights into community supervision practices. *Federal Probation, 82,* 3–12.

Boutwell, B. B., Barnes, J. C., Beaver, K. M., Haynes, R. D., Nedelec, J. L., & Gibson, C. L. (2015). A unified crime theory: The evolutionary taxonomy. *Aggression and Violent Behavior, 25,* Part B, 343–353.

Boutwell, B. B., & Beaver, K. M. (2010). The intergenerational transmission of low self-control. *Journal of Research in Crime and Delinquency, 47,* 174–209.

Boutwell, B. B., Beaver, K. M., & Barnes, J. C. (2012). More alike than different: Assortative mating and antisocial propensity in adulthood. *Criminal Justice and Behavior, 39,* 1240–1254.

Bowen, S., Witkiewitz, K., Clifasefi, S. L., Grow, J., Chawla, N., Hsu, S. H., … Larimer, M. E. (2014). Relative efficacy of mindfulness-based relapse prevention, standard relapse prevention, and treatment as usual for substance use disorders: A randomized clinical trial. *JAMA Psychiatry, 71,* 547–556.

Bowlby, J. (1971). *Attachment and loss, Vol. 1: Attachment.* Harmondsworth, England: Penguin Books.

Bowlby, J. (1988). *A secure base: Clinical implications of attachment theory.* London, England: Routledge & Kegan Paul.

Boxer, P., Docherty, M., Ostermann, M., Kubik, J., & Veysey, B. (2017). Effectiveness of Multisystemic Therapy with gang-involved youth offenders: One year follow-up analysis of recidivism outcomes. *Children and Youth Service Review, 73,* 107–112.

Bozick, R., Steele, J., Davis, L., & Turner, S. (2018). Does providing inmates with education improve post-release outcomes? A meta-analysis of correctional education programs in the United States. *Journal of Experimental Criminology, 14,* 389–428.

Bradford, J. M. W., Fedoroff, P., & Gulati, S. (2013). Can sexual offenders be treated? *International Journal of Law and Psychiatry, 36,* 235–240.

Bradshaw, W., & Roseborough, D. (2005). Restorative justice dialogue: The impact of mediation and conferencing on juvenile recidivism. *Federal Probation, 69,* 15–21.

Braga, A. A., Brunson, R. K., & Drakulich, K. M. (2019). Race, place, and effective policing. *Annual Review of Sociology, 45,* 535–555.

Brandt, A. L. (2012). Treatment of persons with mental illness in the criminal justice system: A literature review. *Journal of Offender Rehabilitation, 51,* 541–558.

Brandt, J., Prescott, D. S., & Wilson, R. J. (2013). Pornography and contact offending. *Newsletter of the Association for the Treatment of Sexual Abusers, 25* (Winter).

Brankley, A. E., Babchishin, K. M., & Hanson, R. K. (2021). STABLE-2007 demonstrates predictive and incremental validity in assessing risk-relevant propensities for sexual offending: A meta-analysis. *Sexual Abuse, 33,* 34–62.

Brayford, J., Cowe, F., & Deering, J. (Eds.) (2011). *What else works? Creative work with offenders.* New York, NY: Routledge (Willan).

Brazil, K., & Forth, A. (2016). Psychopathy Checklist: Youth Version (PCL: YV). In V. Zeigler-Hill & T. K. Shackelford (Eds.), *Encyclopedia of personality and individual differences* (pp. 1–5). Zurich: Springer International.

Brennan, P. K. (2020). Responses taken to mitigate COVID-19 in prisons in England and Wales. *Victims & Offenders, 15*, 1215–1233.

Brennan, T., Dieterich, W., & Ehret, B. (2009). Evaluating the predictive validity of the COMPAS Risk and Needs Assessment System. *Criminal Justice and Behavior, 36*, 21–40.

Bronson, J., & Carson, E. A. (2019). *Prisoners in 2017*. Washington, DC: Bureau of Justice Statistics.

Brown, K. M., & Kloess, J. A. (2020). The motivations of female child sexual offenders: A systematic review of the literature. *Aggression and Violent Behavior, 50*, 101361.

Brown, S. L., Robinson, D., Wanamaker, K. A., & Wagstaff, M. (2020). Strengths matter: Evidence from five separate cohorts of justice-involved youth and adults across North America. *Criminal Justice and Behavior, 47*, 1428–1447.

Brown, S. L., St. Amand, M. D., & Zamble, E. (2009). The dynamic prediction of criminal recidivism: A three-wave prospective study. *Law and Human Behavior, 33*, 25–45.

Brunner, F., Neumann, I., Yoon, D., Rettenberger, M., Stück, E., & Briken, P. (2019). Determinants of dropout from correctional offender treatment. *Frontiers in Psychiatry, 10*, Article 142.

Bucklen, K. B., Duwe, G., & Taxman, F. S. (2021, July). *Guidelines for post-sentencing risk assessment*. Washington, DC: National Institute of Justice.

Buehler, R. E., Patterson, G. R., & Furniss, J. M. (1966). The reinforcement of behavior in institutional settings. *Behavioral Research and Therapy, 4*, 157–167.

Bureau of Justice Assistance. (2021). *The justice reinvestment initiative: A guide for states*. Washington: U.S. Department of Justice.

Burgess, E. W. (1928). Factors determining success or failure on parole. In A. A. Bruce, A. J. Harno, E. W. Burgess, & J. Landesco (Eds.), *The workings of the indeterminate-sentence law and the parole system in Illinois* (pp. 221–234). Springfield, IL: State Board of Parole.

Burgess, R. L., & Akers, R. L. (1966). A differential association-reinforcement theory of criminal behavior. *Social Problems, 14*, 128–147.

Burt, C. A., & Simons, R. L. (2014). Pulling back the curtain on heritability studies: Biosocial criminology in the postgenomic era. *Criminology, 52*, 223–262.

Burt, C. H. (2020). Self-control and crime: Beyond Gottfredson and Hirschi's theory. *Annual Review of Criminology, 3*, 43–73.

Bushman, B. J., Baumeister, R. F., Thomaes, S., Ryu, E., Begeer, S., & West, S. G. (2009). Looking again, and harder, for a link between low self-esteem and aggression. *Journal of Personality, 77*, 427–446.

Buss, D. M. (2009). The multiple adaptive problems solved by human aggression. *Behavioral and Brain Sciences, 32*, 271–272.

Buss, D. M., & Schmitt, D. P. (2019). Mate preferences and their behavioral manifestations. *Annual Review of Psychology, 70*, 77–110.

Button, T. M. M., Scourfield, J., Martin, N., Purcell, S., & McGuffin, P. (2005). Family dysfunction interacts with genes in the causation of antisocial symptoms. *Behavior Genetics, 35*, 115–120.

Byrd, A. L., & Manuk, S. B. (2014). MAOA, childhood maltreatment and antisocial behavior: Meta-analysis of a gene-environment interaction. *Biological Psychiatry, 75*, 1–19.

Byrne, J. M. (2020). The effectiveness of prison programming: A review of the research literature examining the impact of federal, state, and local inmate programming on post-release recidivism. *Federal Probation, 84*, 3–20.

Cafferky, B. M., Mendez, M., Anderson, J. R., & Stith, S. M. (2018). Substance use and intimate partner violence: A meta-analytic review. *Psychology of Violence, 8*, 110–131.

Cale, E. M. (2006). A quantitative review of the relations between the 'Big 3' higher order personality dimensions and antisocial behavior. *Journal of Research in Personality, 40*, 250–284.

Campbell, D. T., & Stanley, J. C. (1963). *Experimental and quasi-experimental designs for research*. Chicago: Rand McNally.

Campbell, M. A., Canales, D. D., Wei, R., Totten, A. E., Macaulay, W. A. C., & Wershler, J. L. (2015). Multidimensional evaluation of a mental health court: Adherence to the risk-need-responsivity model. *Law and Human Behavior, 39*, 489–502.

Campbell, M. A., French. S., & Gendreau, P. (2009). The prediction of violence in adult offenders: A meta-analytic comparison of instruments and methods of assessment. *Criminal Justice and Behavior, 36*, 567–590.

Canales, D. D., Campbell, M. A., Wei, R., & Totten, A. E. (2014). Prediction of general and violent recidivism among mentally disordered adult offenders: Test of the Level of Service/Risk-Need-Responsivity (LS/RNR) instrument. *Criminal Justice and Behavior, 41*, 971–991.

Cardinale, E. M., & Marsh, A. A. (2020). The reliability and validity of the Inventory of Callous Unemotional Traits: A meta-analytic review. *Assessment, 27*, 57–71.

Carey, G., & Goldman, D. (1997). The genetics of antisocial behavior. In D. M. Stuff, J. Breiling, & J. D. Maser (Eds.), *Handbook of antisocial behavior* (pp. 243–254). New York, NY: Wiley.

Carlisi, C. O., Moffitt, T. E., Knodt, A. R., Harrington, H., Ireland, D., Melzer, T. R., ... Viding, E. (2020). Associations between life-course-persistent antisocial behaviour and brain structure in a population-representative longitudinal birth cohort. *The Lancet Psychiatry, 7*, 245–253.

Carlson, J. S., Yohannan, J., Darr, C. L., Turley, M. R., Larez, N. A., & Perfect, M. M. (2020). Prevalence of adverse childhood experiences in school-aged youth: A systematic review (1990–2015). *International Journal of School & Educational Psychology, 8*, Supplemental Issue.

Carr, A. (2019). Family therapy and systemic interventions for child-focused problems: The current evidence base. *Journal of Family Therapy, 41*, 153–213.

Carr, W. A., Baker, A. N., & Cassidy, J. J. (2021). Diagnostic moderators of the risk-recidivism relationship for offenders with mental illness. *International Journal of Offender Therapy and Comparative Criminology, 65*, 1756–1774.

Caspi, A., Moffitt, T. E., Morgan, J., Rutter, M., Taylor, A., Arsenault, L., ... Polo-Tomas, M. (2004). Maternal expressed emotion predicts children's antisocial behavior problems: Using monozygotic-twin differences to identify environmental effects on behavioral development. *Developmental Psychology, 40*, 149–161.

Caspi, A., Moffitt, T. E., Silva, P. A., Stouthamer-Loeber, M., Krueger, R. F., & Schmutte, P. S. (1994). Are some people crime-prone? Replications of the personality-crime relationship across countries, genders, races, and methods. *Criminology, 32*, 163–195.

Caudy, M. S., Durso, J. M., & Taxman, F. S. (2013). How well do dynamic needs predict recidivism? Implications for risk assessment and risk reduction. *Journal of Criminal Justice, 41*, 458–466.

Cavicchioli, M., Movalli, M., & Maffei, C. (2018). The clinical efficacy of mindfulness-based treatments for alcohol and drugs use disorders: A meta-analytic review of randomized and nonrandomized controlled trials. *European Addiction Research, 24*, 137–162.

Chadwick, N., Dewolf, A., & Serin, R. (2015). Effectively training community supervision officers: A meta-analytic review of the impact on offender outcome. *Criminal Justice and Behavior, 42*, 977–989.

Chang, H.-L., Woo, H. T., & Tseng, C.-H. (2006). Is rigorous punishment effective? A case study of lifetime license revocation in Taiwan. *Accident Analysis and Prevention, 38*, 269–276.

Chenane, J. L., Brennan, P. K., Steiner, B., & Ellison, J. M. (2015). Racial and ethnic differences in the predictive validity of the Level of Service Inventory-Revised among prison inmates. *Criminal Justice and Behavior, 42*, 286–303.

Cheng, J., O'Connell, M. E., & Wormith, J. S. (2019). Bridging neuropsychology and forensic psychology: Executive function overlaps with the central eight risk and need factors. *International Journal of Offender Therapy and Comparative Criminology, 63*, 558–573.

Chess, S., & Thomas, A. (1984). *Origins and evolution of behavior disorders: From infancy to early adult life*. New York, NY: Brunner/Mazel.

Chess, S., & Thomas, A. (1990). The New York Longitudinal Study (NYLS): The young adult periods. *Canadian Journal of Psychiatry, 35*, 557–561.

Chouinard-Thivierge, S., Lussier, P., & Charette, Y. (2023). The adult offending outcomes of adolescents who have perpetrated a sex offense: Is sexual offending in adolescence indicative of things to come? *Youth Violence and Juvenile Justice, 21*, 3–26.

Choy, O., & Raine, A. (2018). Omega-3 supplementation as a dietary intervention to reduce aggressive and antisocial behavior. *Current Psychiatry Reports, 20*, 32–36.

Christiansen, K.O. (1977). A preliminary study of criminality among twins. In S. A. Mednick & K.O. Christiansen (Eds.), *Biosocial basis of criminal behavior* (pp. 89–108). New York, NY: Gardner Press.

Church, R. M. (1963). The varied effects of punishment on behavior. *Psychological Review, 70,* 369–402.

Cissner, A. B., Labriola, M., & Rempel, M. (2015). Domestic violence courts: A multisite test of whether and how they change offender outcomes. *Violence Against Women, 21,* 1102–1122.

Clarke, A. Y., Cullen, A. E., Walwyn, R., & Fahy, T. (2010). A quasi-experimental pilot study of the Reasoning and Rehabilitation programme with mentally disordered offenders. *The Journal of Forensic Psychiatry & Psychology, 21,* 490–500.

Clarke, M., Brown, S., & Völlm, B. (2017). Circles of support and accountability for sex offenders: A systematic review of outcomes. *Sexual Abuse, 29,* 446–478.

Clarke, M. C., Peterson-Badali, M., & Skilling, T. A. (2017). The relationship between changes in dynamic risk factors and the predictive validity of risk assessments among youth offenders. *Criminal Justice and Behavior, 44,* 1340–1355.

Clear, T. (2008). The effects of high imprisonment rates on communities. In M. Tonry (Ed.), *Crime and justice: A review of research,* Vol. *37* (pp. 97–132). Chicago, IL: Chicago University Press.

Cleckley, H. (1941). *The mask of sanity: An attempt to reinterpret the so-called psychopathic personality.* St. Louis, MI: Mosby.

Cleckley, H. (1982). *The mask of sanity* (4th ed.). St. Louis, MI: Mosby.

Cloward, R. A., & Ohlin, L. E. (1960). *Delinquency and opportunity: A theory of delinquent gangs.* New York: Free Press.

Cobbina, J. E., Huebner, B. M., & Berg, M. T. (2012). Men, women, and postrelease offending: An examination of the nature of the link between relational tires and recidivism. *Crime & Delinquency, 58,* 331–361.

Cofnas, N. (2016). Science is not always "self-correcting": Fact-value conflation and the study of intelligence. *Foundations of Science, 21,* 477–492.

Cohen, A. K. (1955). *Delinquent boys: The culture of the gang.* Glencoe, IL: Free Press.

Cohen, J. (1994). The earth is round ($p < .05$). *American Psychologist, 49,* 997–1003.

Cohen, M. A., & Farrington, D. P. (2021). Appropriate measurement and use of "Costs of Crime" in policy analysis: Benefit-cost analysis of criminal justice policies has come of age. *Journal of Policy Analysis and Management, 40,* 284–306.

Cohen, M. A., & Piquero, A. R. (2009). New evidence on the monetary value of saving a high risk youth. *Journal of Quantitative Criminology, 25,* 25–49.

Cohen, T. H., Lowenkamp, C. T., Bechtel, K., & Flores, A. W. (2020). Risk assessment overrides: Shuffling the risk deck without any improvements in prediction. *Criminal Justice and Behavior, 47,* 1609–1629.

Coid, J., & Ullrich, S. (2010). Antisocial personality disorder is on a continuum with psychopathy. *Comprehensive Psychiatry, 51,* 426–433.

Coid, J. W., Ullrich, S., Kallis, C., Keers, R., Barker, D., Cowden, F., & Stamps, R. (2013). The relationship between delusions and violence: Findings from the East London First Episode Psychosis Study. *JAMA Psychiatry, 70,* 465–471.

Coid, J., Yang, M., Ullrich, S., Zhang, T., Roberts, A., Roberts, C., … Farrington, D. (2007). Predicting and understanding risk of re-offending: The prisoner cohort study. *Research Summary.* London, England: Ministry of Justice.

Colins, O. F., Bijttebier, P., Broekaert, E., & Andershed, H. (2014). Psychopathic-like traits among detained adolescents: Reliability and validity of the Antisocial Process Screening Device and the Youth Psychopathic Traits Inventory. *Assessment, 2,* 195–209.

Collison, K. L., & Lynam, D. R. (2021). Personality disorders as predictors of intimate partner violence: A meta-analysis. *Clinical Psychology Review, 88,* 102047.

Colstrup, H., Larsen, E. D., Mollerup, S., Tarp, H., Soelberg, J., & Rosthøj, S. (2020). Long-term follow-up of 60 incarcerated male sexual offenders pharmacologically castrated with a combination of GnRH agonist and cyproterone acetate. *The Journal of Forensic Psychiatry & Psychology, 31,* 241–254.

Cooke, D. J., Hart, S. D., Logan, C., & Michie, C. (2004). Comprehensive assessment of psychopathic personality–Institutional Rating Scale (CAPP-IRS). Unpublished manuscript.

Cooke, D. J., Hart, S. D., Logan, C., & Michie, C. (2012). Explicating the construct of psychopathy: Development and validation of a conceptual model, the Comprehensive Assessment of Psychopathic Personality (CAPP). *International Journal of Forensic Mental Health, 11*, 242–252.

Cookston, J. T. (1999). Parental supervision and family structure: Effects on adolescent problem behaviors. *Journal of Divorce and Remarriage, 32*, 107–122.

Cooper, H. L. (2015). War on drugs policing and police brutality. *Substance Use & Misuse, 50*, 1188–1194.

Copas, J., & Marshall, P. (1998). The offender reconviction scale: A statistical reconviction score for use by probation officers. *Journal of the Royal Statistical Society, 47*, 159–171.

Copp, J. E., Giordano, P. C., Longmore, M. A., & Manning, W. D. (2019). The development of attitudes toward intimate partner violence: An examination of key correlates among a sample of young adults. *Journal of Interpersonal Violence, 34*, 1357–1387.

Cordier, R., Chung, D., Wilkes-Gillan, S., & Speyer, R. (2021). The effectiveness of protection orders in reducing recidivism in domestic violence: A systematic review and meta-analysis. *Trauma, Violence, & Abuse, 22*, 804–828.

Cornet, L. J. M., de Koegel, C. H., Nijman, H. L. I., Raine, A., & van der Laan, P. H. (2014a). Neurobiological factors as predictors of cognitive-behavioral therapy outcome in individuals with antisocial behavior: A review of the literature. *International Journal of Offender Therapy and Comparative Criminology, 58*, 1279–1296.

Cornet, L. J. M., de Koegel, C. H., Nijman, H. L. I., Raine, A., & van der Laan, P. H. (2014b). Neurobiological changes after intervention in individuals with antisocial behavior: A literature review. *Criminal Behaviour and Mental Health, 25*, 10–27.

Costa, P. T., Jr., & McCrae, R. R. (1992). *Revised NEO Personality Inventory (NEO-PI-R) and NEO Five-Factor Inventory (NEO-FFI) Professional Manual.* Odessa, FL: Psychological Assessment Resources.

Costa, P. T., & McCrae, R. R. (2010). Bridging the gap with the five-factor model. *Personality Disorders: Theory, Research, and Treatment, 1*, 127–130.

Costa, P. T., McCrae, R. R., & Löckenhoff, C. E. (2019). Personality across the life span. *Annual Review of Psychology, 70*, 423–448.

Coulter, D. J., Lloyd, C. D., & Serin, R. C. (2022). Combining static and dynamic recidivism risk information into the Five-Level risk and needs system: A New Zealand example. *Criminal Justice and Behavior, 49*, 77–97.

Cowell, A. J., Barnosky, A., Lattimore, P. K., Cartwright, J. K., & DeMichele, M. (2018). Economic evaluation of the HOPE demonstration field experiment. *Criminology & Public Policy, 17*, 875–899.

Craig, J. M., Malvaso, C., & Farrington, D. P. (2021). All in the family? Exploring the intergenerational transmission of exposure to adverse childhood experiences and their effect on offending behavior. *Youth Violence and Juvenile Justice, 19*, 292–307.

Craig, J. M., & Zettler, H. R. (2021). Are the effects of adverse childhood experiences on violence offense-specific? *Youth Violence and Juvenile Justice, 19*, 27–44.

Craig, L. A., & Rettenberger, M. (2022). Towards an integration of risk assessment, case formulation, and forensic neuroscience. In K. Uzieblo, W. J. Smid, & K. McCartan (Eds.), *Challenges in the management of people convicted of a sexual offence. Palgrave studies in risk, crime and society.* New York: Palgrave Macmillan.

Cross, A. B., Gottfredson, D. C., Wilson, D. M., Gaskin, M., & Connell, N. (2009). The impact of after-school programs on the routine activities of middle-school students: Results from a randomized, controlled trial. *Criminology & Public Policy, 6*, 391–412.

Crouch, E., Probst, J. C., Radcliff, E., Bennett, K. J., & Hunt McKinney, S. (2019). Prevalence of adverse childhood experiences (ACEs) among US children. *Child Abuse & Neglect, 92*, 209–218.

Cuevas, C. A., Sabina, C., & Milloshi, R. (2012). Interpersonal victimization among a national sample of Latino women. *Violence Against Women, 18*, 377–403.

Cullen, A. E., Clarke, A. Y., Kuipers, E., Hodgins, S., Dean, K., & Fahy, T. (2012). A multisite randomized trial of a cognitive skills program for male mentally disordered offenders: Violence and antisocial behavior outcome. *Journal of Consulting and Clinical Psychology, 80*, 1114–1120.

Cullen, F. T. (2012). Taking rehabilitation seriously: Creativity, science and the challenge of offender change. *Punishment & Society, 14*, 94–114.

Cullen, F. T. (2013). Rehabilitation: Beyond nothing works. In M. Tonry (Ed.), *Crime and justice, Vol. 42, Crime and justice in America 1975–2025* (pp. 299–376). Chicago, IL: University of Chicago Press.

Cullen, F. T., Blevins, K. R., Trager, J. S., & Gendreau, P. (2005). The rise and fall of boot camps: A case study in common-sense corrections. *Journal of Offender Rehabilitation, 40*, 53–70.

Cullen, F. T., Fisher, B. S., & Applegate, B. K. (2000). Public opinion about punishment and corrections. In M. Tonry (Ed.), *Crime and justice: A review of research*, Vol. *27* (pp. 1–79). Chicago, IL: University of Chicago Press.

Cullen, F. T., & Gilbert, K. E. (2013). *Reaffirming rehabilitation. 30th Anniversary edition.* Waltham, MA: Anderson.

Cullen, F. T., Jonson, C. L., & Mears, D. P. (2017). Reinventing community corrections. *Crime and Justice, 46*, 27–93.

Cullen, F. T., Pratt, T. C., Turanovic, J. J., & Butler, L. (2018). When bad news arrives: Project HOPE in a post-factual world. *Journal of Contemporary Criminal Justice, 34*, 13–34.

Cullen, F. T., & Wilcox, P. (Eds.) (2013). *The Oxford handbook of criminological theory*. NY: Oxford University Press.

Cullen, F. T., Wright, J. P., & Applegate, B. K. (1996). Control in the community: The limits of reform? In A. T. Harland (Ed.), *Choosing correctional options that work: Defining the demand and evaluating the supply* (pp. 69–116). Thousand Oaks, CA: Sage.

Cullen F. T., Wright, J. P., Gendreau, P., & Andrews, D. A. (2003). What correctional treatment can tell us about criminological theory: Implications. In R. L. Akers & G. F. Jenkins (Eds.), *Social learning theory and the explanation of crime: Advances in criminological theory*, Vol. *11* (pp. 339–362). New Brunswick, NJ: Transaction Press.

Cumming, G. (2014). The new statistics: Why and how. *Psychological Science, 25*, 7–29.

Currie, E. (1993). *Reckoning: Drugs, the cities, and the American future*. New York, NY: Hill and Wang.

Daisklev, M., Cunningham, T., Dempster, M., & Hanna, D. (2021). Childhood physical and sexual abuse as a predictor of reoffending: A systematic review. *Trauma, Violence, & Abuse, 22*, 605–618.

Dalgaard, O. S., & Kringlen, E. (1976). A Norwegian twin study of criminality. *British Journal of Criminology, 16*, 213–233.

Dalsklev, M., Cunningham, T., Dempster, M., & Hanna, D. (2021). Childhood physical and sexual abuse as a predictor of reoffending: A systematic review. *Trauma, Violence, & Abuse, 22*, 605–618.

Daly, K. (1992). Women's pathways to felony court: Feminist theories of lawbreaking and problems of representation. *Southern California Review of Law & Women's Studies, 2*, 11–52.

Daly, M. (1996). Evolutionary adaptationism: Another biological approach to criminal and antisocial behavior. In G. R. Bock & J. A. Goode (Eds.), *Genetics of criminal and antisocial behavior* (pp. 183–195). Wiley, Chichester (Ciba Foundation Symposium 194).

Dam, V. H., Hjordt, L. V., Da Cunha-Bang, S., Sestoft, D., Knudson, G. M., & Stenbaek, D. S. (2018). Five-factor personality is associated with aggression and mental distress in violent offenders. *European Neuropsychopharmacology, 28*, 535–536.

Dangerfield, B., Ildeniz, G., & Ó Ciardha, C. (2020). Theories that explain the sexual abuse of children. In J. Proulx, F. Cortoni, L. A. Craig, & E. J. Letourneau (Eds.), *The Wiley handbook of what works with sexual offenders: Contemporary perspectives in theory, assessment, treatment, and prevention* (pp. 23–37). New York: John Wiley & Sons.

Darmedru, C., Demily, C., & Franck, N. (2017). Cognitive remediation and social cognitive training for violence in schizophrenia: A systematic review. *Psychiatry Research, 251*, 266–274.

da Silva, D. R., Rijo, D., & Salekin, R. T. (2020). Psychopathic traits in children and youth: The state-of-the-art after 30 years of research. *Aggression and Violent Behavior, 55*, 101454.

Davies, S. T., Lloyd, C. D., & Polaschek, D. L. L. (2022). Does reassessment enhance the prediction of imminent criminal recidivism? Replicating Lloyd et al. (2020) with high-risk parolees. *Assessment, 29*, 962–980.

Davis, C., Bahr, S. J., & Ward, C. (2013). The process of offender reintegration: Perceptions of what helps prisoners reenter society. *Criminology & Criminal Justice, 13*, 446–469.

Dawkins, R. (1989). *The selfish gene.* New York, NY: Oxford University Press.

Death Penalty Information Center. (2022). Overview. https://deathpenaltyinfo.org/death-row/overview

Debowska, A., Boduszek, D., & Woodfield, R. (2018). The PCL-R family of psychopathy measures: Dimensionality and predictive utility of the PCL-R, PCL: SV, PCL: YV, SRP-III, and SRP-SF. In M. DeLisi (Ed.), *Routledge international handbook of psychopathy and crime* (pp. 225–240). New York: Routledge.

De Brito, S. A., Forth, A. E., Baskin-Sommers, A. R., Brazil, I. A., Kimonis, E. R., Pardini, D., ... Viding, E. (2021). Psychopathy primer. *Nature Reviews, 7*, 49.

De Buck, A., & Pauwells, L. J. R. (2019). Intention to shoplift: On the importance of dimensions of propensity in an integrated informal control/lifestyle model. *European Journal on Criminal Policy and Research, 25*, 297–315.

Debus-Sherrill, S., Breno, A., & Taxman, F. S. (2023). What makes or breaks evidence-based supervision? Staff and organizational predictors of evidence-based practice in probation. *International Journal of Offender Therapy and Comparative Criminology, 67*, 662–686.

Decker, S. H. (2007). Youth gangs and violent behavior. In D. J. Flannery, A. T. Vazsonyi, & I. D. Waldman (Eds.), *The Cambridge handbook of violent behavior and aggression* (pp. 388–402). Cambridge, England: Cambridge University Press.

Decker, S. H., Melde, C., & Pyrooz, D. C. (2013). What do we know about gangs and gang members and where do we go from here? *Justice Quarterly, 30*, 369–402.

De La Rue, L., & Espelage, D. L. (2014). Family and abuse characteristics of gang involved, pressured-to-join, and non-gang-involved girls. *Psychology of Violence, 4*, 253–265.

DeLisi, M., Bunga, R., Heirigs, M. H., Erickson, J. H., & Hochstetler, A. (2019). The past is prologue: Criminal specialization continuity in the delinquent career. *Youth Violence and Juvenile Justice, 17*, 335–353.

DeLisi, M., Caropreso, D. E., Drury, A. J., Piquero, M. J., Evans, J. L., Heinrichs, T., & Tahja, K. M. (2016). The dark figure of sexual offending: New evidence from federal sex offenders. *Journal of Criminal Psychology, 6*, 3–15.

DeLisi, M., Drury, M., & Elbert, M. J. (2019). The etiology of antisocial personality disorder; the differential role of adverse childhood experiences and childhood psychopathology. *Comprehensive Psychiatry, 92*, 1–6.

DeLisi, M., Drury, A., Elbert, M., Tahja, K., Caropreso, D., & Heinrichs, T. (2017). Sexual sadism and criminal versatility: Does sexual sadism spillover into nonsexual crimes? *Journal of Aggression, Conflict and Peace Research, 9*, 2–12.

DeLisi, M., Neppi, T. K., Lohman, B. J., Vaughn, M. G., & Shook, J. J. (2013). Early starters: Which type of criminal onset matters most for delinquent careers? *Journal of Criminal Justice, 41*, 12–17.

DeLisi, M., Spruill, J. O., Vaughn, M. G., & Trulson, C. R. (2014). Do gang members commit abnormal homicide? *American Journal of Criminal Justice, 39*, 125–138.

DeLisi, M., & Vaughn, M. G. (2014). Foundation for a temperament-based theory of antisocial behavior and criminal justice system involvement. *Journal of Criminal Justice, 42*, 10–25.

DeMatteo, D., Hart, S. D., Heilbrun, K., Boccaccini, M. T., Cunningham, M. D., Douglas, K. S., ... Reidy, T. (2020). Statement of concerned experts on the use of the Hare Psychopathy Checklist-Revised in capital sentencing to assess risk for institutional violence. *Psychology, Public Policy, and Law, 26*, 133–144.

Derefinko, K., & Lynam, D. R. (2013). Psychopathy from the perspective of the five-factor model of personality. In T. A. Widiger & P. T. Costa Jr. (Eds.), *Personality disorders and the five-factor model of personality* (pp. 103–117). Washington, DC: American Psychological Association.

Desmarais, S. L., Johnson, K. L., & Singh, J. P. (2016). Performance of recidivism risk assessment in U.S. correctional settings. *Psychological Services, 13*, 206–22.

Desmarais, S. L., Reeves, K. A., Nicholls, T. L., Telford, R. P., & Fiebert, M. S. (2012). Prevalence of physical violence in intimate relationships, Part 1: Rates of male and female victimization. *Partner Abuse, 3*, 140–169.

Desmarais, S. L., Zottola, S. A., Duhart Clarke, S. E., & Lowder, E. M. (2021). Predictive validity of pretrial risk assessments: A systematic review of the literature. *Criminal Justice and Behavior, 48*, 398–420.

DeVault, A., Miller, M. K., & Griffin, T. (2016). Crime control theater: Past, present, and future. *Psychology, Public Policy, and Law, 22*, 341–348.

Devries, K. M., Mak, J. Y. T., Garcia-Moreno, C., Petzold, M., Child, J. C., Bacchus, L. J., … Watts, C. H. (2013). The global prevalence of intimate partner violence against women. *Science, 340*, 1527–1528.

DeWall, C. N., Twenge, J. M., Gitter, S. A., & Baumeister, R. F. (2009). It's the thought that counts: The role of hostile cognition in shaping aggressive responses to social exclusion. *Journal of Personality and Social Psychology, 95*, 45–59.

Dezember, A., Stoltz, M., Marmolejo, L., Kanewske, L. C., Feingold, K. D., Wire, S., … Maupin, C. (2021). The lack of experimental research in criminology—evidence from *Criminology* and *Justice Quarterly*. *Journal of Experimental Criminology, 17*, 677–712.

Dickson, S. R., & Willis, G. M. (2022). The Good Lives Model: Next steps in research and practice. In C. M. Langton & J. R. Worling (Eds.), *Facilitating desistance from aggression and crime: Theory, research, and strength-based practice* (pp. 441–459). New York: John Wiley & Sons.

Dieterich, W., Mendoza, C., & Brennan, T. (2016). COMPAS risk scales: Demonstrating accuracy equity and predictive parity. Northpointe Inc. https://go.volarisgroup.com/rs/430-MBX-989/images/ProPublica_Commentary_Final_070616.pdf

Digman, J. M. (1990). Personality structure: Emergence of the five factor model. *Annual Review of Psychology, 41*, 417–440.

Dinsmoor, J. A. (1955). Punishment: II. An interpretation of empirical findings. *Psychological Review, 62*, 96–105.

Dinsmoor, J. A. (1998). Punishment. In W. O'Donohue (Ed.), *Learning and behavior therapy* (pp. 188–204). New York, NY: Allyn & Bacon.

Di Placido, C., Simon, T. L., Witte, T. D., Gu, D., & Wong, S. C. P. (2006). Treatment of gang members can reduce recidivism and institutional misconduct. *Law and Human Behavior, 30*, 93–114.

Dishion, T. J., & Snyder, J. J. (Eds.) (2016). *The Oxford handbook of coercive relationship dynamics*. New York: Oxford University Press.

Dixon, L., & Graham-Kevan, N. (2020). Assessing the risk and treatment needs of people who perpetrate intimate partner violence. In J. S. Wormith, L. A. Craig, & T. L. Hogue (Eds.), *The Wiley handbook of what works in violence risk management: Theory, research and practice* (pp. 297–314). New York: John Wiley & Sons.

Dodes, L., & Dodes, Z. (2014). *The sober truth: Debunking the bad science behind 12-step recovery programs and the rehab industry*. Boston, MA: Beacon Press.

Dollard, J., Miller, N. E., Doob, L. W., Mowrer, O. H., & Sears, R. R. (1939). *Frustration and aggression*. New Haven, CT: Yale University Press.

Domino, M. E., Gertner, A., Grabert, B., Cuddeback, G. S., Childers, T., & Morrissey, J. P. (2019). Do timely mental health services reduce re-incarceration among prison releasees with severe mental illness? *Health Services Research, 54*, 592–602.

Domjan, M. (2018). *The essentials of conditioning and learning* (4th ed.). Washington, DC: American Psychological Association.

Donnellan, M. B., Trzesniewski, K. H., Robins, R. W., Moffitt, T. E., & Caspi, A. (2005). Low self-esteem is related to aggression, antisocial behavior, and delinquency. *Psychological Science, 16*, 328–335.

Donnelly, E. A., Wagner, J., Stenger, M., Cortina, H. G., O'Connell, D. J., & Anderson, T. L. (2021). Opioids, race, and drug enforcement: Exploring local relationships between neighborhood context and Black–White opioid-related possession arrests. *Criminal Justice Policy Review, 32*, 219–244.

Dopp, A. R., Borduin, C. M., Wagner, D. V., & Sawyer, A. M. (2014). The economic impact of multisystemic therapy through midlife: A cost–benefit analysis with serious juvenile offenders and their siblings. *Journal of Consulting and Clinical Psychology, 82*, 694.

Dopp, A. R., Borduin, C. M., White, M. H. II, & Kuppens, S. (2017). Family-based treatments for serious juvenile offenders: A multilevel meta-analysis. *Journal of Consulting and Clinical Psychology, 85*, 335–354.

Douglas, K. S., Guy, L. S., & Hart, S. D. (2009). Psychosis as a risk factor for violence to others: A meta-analysis. *Psychological Bulletin, 136*, 679–706.

Douglas, K. S., & Otto, R. K. (Eds.) (2021). *Handbook of violence risk assessment.* New York: Routledge.

Douglas, K. S., & Shaffer, C. S. (2021). The science of and practice with the HCR-20 V3 (Historical-Clinical-Risk Management-20, Version 3). In K. S. Douglas & R. K. Otto (Eds.), *Handbook of violence risk assessment* (pp. 253–293). New York: Routledge.

Douglas, K. S., & Skeem, J. L. (2005). Violence risk assessment: Getting specific about being dynamic. *Psychology, Public Policy, and Law, 11*, 347–383.

Douglas, K. S., Vincent, G. M., & Edens, J. F. (2018). Risk for criminal recidivism: The role of psychopathy. In C. J. Patrick (Ed.), *Handbook of psychopathy* 2nd ed. (pp. 682–709). New York, NY: Guilford.

Dowden, C., & Andrews, D. A. (2004). The importance of staff practice in delivering effective correctional treatment: A meta-analytic review of core correctional practice. *International Journal of Offender Therapy and Comparative Criminology, 48*, 203–214.

Dowden, C., & Andrews, D. A. (2007). Using relapse prevention with offender populations: What works. In K. A. Witkiewitz & A. G. Marlatt (Eds.), *Therapist's guide to evidence-based relapse prevention* (pp. 339–352). Burlington, MA: Elsevier.

Dowden, C., & Brown, S. L. (2002). The role of substance abuse factors in predicting recidivism: A meta-analysis. *Psychology, Crime and Law, 8*, 243–264.

Doyle, M. F., Shakeshaft, A., Guthrie, J., Snijder, M., & Butler, T. (2019). A systematic review of evaluations of prison-based alcohol and other drug use behavioural treatment for men. *Australian and New Zealand Journal of Public Health, 43*, 120–130.

Dragioti, E., Dimoliatis, I., Fountoulakis, K. N., & Evangelou, E. (2015). A systematic appraisal of allegiance effect in randomized controlled trials of psychotherapy. *Annals of General Psychiatry, 14*, Article 25.

Drake, E. K. (2018). The monetary benefits and costs of community supervision. *Journal of Contemporary Criminal Justice, 34*, 47–68.

Drake, E. K., Aos, S., & Miller, M. G. (2009). Evidence-based public policy options to reduce crime and criminal justice costs: Implications in Washington State. *Victims and Offenders, 4*, 170–196.

Dressel, J., & Farid, H. (2018). The accuracy, fairness, and limits of predicting recidivism. *Science Advances, 4*, 1–5.

Drury, A. J., Elbert, M. J., & DeLisi, M. (2019). Childhood sexual abuse is significantly associated with subsequent sexual offending: New evidence among federal correctional clients. *Child Abuse & Neglect, 95*, 104035.

Dubow, E. F., Huesmann, R., Boxer, P., Smith, C., & Sedlar, A. E. (2018). Aggression and criminality over three generations. In V. I. Eichelsheim & S. G. A. van de Weijer (Eds.), *Intergenerational continuity of criminal and antisocial behaviour* (pp. 162–185). New York: Routledge.

Dugdale, R. L. (1877/1970). *The Jukes: A study of crime, pauperism, disease, and heredity.* New York, NY: Arno Press (originally published by G.P. Putnam).

Duke, A. A., Smith, K. M. Z., Oberleiter, L. M. S., Westphal, A., & McKee, S. A. (2018). Alcohol, drugs, and violence: A meta-meta-analysis. *Psychology of Violence, 8*, 238–249.

Dunaway, R. G., Cullen, F. T., Burton, V. S. Jr., & Evans, T. D. (2000). The myth of social class and crime revisited: An examination of class and adult criminality. *Criminology, 38*, 589–632.

Durfee, A. (2021). The use of structural intersectionality as a method to analyze how the domestic violence civil protective order process replicates inequality. *Violence Against Women, 27*, 639–665.

Duriez, S. A., Cullen, F. T., & Manchak, S. M. (2014). Is project HOPE creating a false sense of hope? A case study in correctional popularity. *Federal Probation, 78*, 57–70.

Duriez, S. A., Sullivan, S., Latessa, E. J., & Brusman Lovins, L. (2018). The evolution of correctional program assessment in the age of evidence-based practices. *Corrections, 3*, 119–136.

Durrett, C., & Trull, T. J. (2005). An evaluation of evaluative personality terms: A comparison of the big seven and five-factor model in predicting psychopathology. *Psychological Assessment, 17*, 359–368.

D'Urso, G., Petruccelli, I., Costantino, V., Zappulla, C., & Pace, U. (2019). The role of moral disengagement and cognitive distortions toward children among sex offenders. *Psychiatry, Psychology and Law, 26*, 414–422.

D'Urso, G., Petruccelli, I., Grilli, S., & Pace, U. (2019). Risk factors related to cognitive distortions toward women and moral disengagement: A study on sex offenders. *Sexuality & Culture, 23*, 544–557.

Dutra, L., Stathopoulou, G., Basden, S. L., Leyro, T. M., Powers, M. B., & Otto, M. W. (2008). A meta-analytic review of psychosocial interventions for substance use disorders. *American Journal of Psychiatry, 165*, 179–187.

Dutton, D. G. (1986). The outcome of court-mandated treatment for wife-assault: A quasi-experimental evaluation. *Violence and Victims, 1*, 163–175.

Dutton, D. G., & Kropp, P. R. (2000). A review of domestic violence risk instruments. *Trauma, Violence, and Abuse, 1*, 171–181.

Duwe, G. (2015). An outcome evaluation of a prison work release program: Estimating its effects on recidivism, employment, and cost avoidance. *Criminal Justice Policy Review, 26*, 531–554.

Duwe, G. (2018). Can circles of support and accountability (CoSA) significantly reduce sexual recidivism? Results from a randomized controlled trial in Minnesota. *Journal of Experimental Criminology, 14*, 463–484.

Duwe, G., & Rocque, M. (2018). The home-field advantage and the perils of professional judgment: Evaluating the performance of the Static-99R and the MnSOST-3 in predicting sexual recidivism. *Law and Human Behavior, 42*, 269–279.

Eamon, M. K., & Mulder, C. (2005). Predicting antisocial behavior among Latino young adolescents: An ecological systems analysis. *American Journal of Orthopsychiatry, 75*, 117–127.

Earp, B. D., Lewis, J., & Hart, C. L. (2021). Racial justice requires ending the war on drugs. *The American Journal of Bioethics, 21*, 4–19.

Eckhardt, C. I., Murphy, C. M., Whitaker, D. J., Sprunger, J., Dykstra, R., & Woodard, K. (2013). The effectiveness of intervention programs for perpetrators and victims of intimate partner violence. *Partner Abuse, 4*, 196–231.

Edens, J. F., & Campbell, J. S. (2007). Identifying youth at risk for institutional misconduct: A meta-analytic investigation of the Psychopathy Checklist measures. *Psychological Services, 4*, 13–27.

Edens, J. F., Marcus, D. K., Lilienfeld, S. O., & Poythress Jr., N. G. (2006). Psychopathic, not psychopath: Taxometric evidence for the dimensional structure of psychopathy. *Journal of Abnormal Psychology, 115*, 131–144.

Edens, J. F., Marcus, D. K., & Vaughn, M. G. (2011). Exploring the taxometric status of psychopathy among youthful offenders: Is there a juvenile psychopath taxon? *Law and Human Behavior, 35*, 13–24.

Edlund, J. E., Cuccolo, K., Irgens, M. S., Wagge, J. R., & Zlokovich, M. S. (2022). Saving science through replication. *Perspectives on Psychological Science, 17,* 216–225.

Edwards, E. R., Greene, A. L., Epshteyn, G., Gromatsky, M., Kinney, A. R., & Holliday, R. (2022). Mental health of incarcerated veterans and civilians: Latent class analysis of the 2016 Survey of Prison Inmates. *Criminal Justice and Behavior, 49,* 1800–1821.

Egley, A., Jr., Howell, J. C., & Harris, M. (2014). *Highlights of the 2012 National Youth Gang survey.* Washington, DC: Office of Juvenile Justice and Delinquency Prevention.

Eichelsheim, V. I., & van de Weijer, S. G. A. (Eds.) (2018). *Intergenerational continuity of criminal and antisocial behaviour.* New York: Routledge.

Eisenberg, M. J., Van Horn, J. E., Dekker, J. M., Assink, M., Van Der Put, C. E., Hendriks, J., & Stams, C. J. J. M. (2019). Static and dynamic predictors of general and violent criminal offense recidivism in the forensic outpatient population. *Criminal Justice and Behavior, 46,* 732–750.

Elbogen, E. B., & Johnson, S. C. (2009). The intricate link between violence and mental disorder: Results from the National Epidemiologic Survey on Alcohol and Related Conditions. *Archives of General Psychiatry, 66,* 152–161.

Elliott, I. A., & Zajac, G. (2015). The implementation of circles of support and accountability in the United States. *Aggression and Violent Behavior, 25,* 113–123.

Ellis, L. (2000). *Criminology: A global perspective: Supplemental tables and references.* Minot, ND: Pyramid Press.

Ellis, L. (2005). A theory explaining biological correlates of criminality. *European Journal of Criminology, 2*(3), 287–315.

Ellis, L., & Walsh, A. (1997). Gene-based evolutionary theories in criminology. *Criminology, 35,* 229–276.

Else-Quest, N. M., Hyde, J. S., Hill, H., Goldsmith, H., & Van Hulle, C. A. (2006). Gender differences in temperament: A meta-analysis. *Psychological Bulletin, 132,* 33–72.

Eme, R. (2020). Life course persistent antisocial behavior silver anniversary. *Aggression and Violent Behavior, 50,* 101344.

Eno Louden, J., Skeem, J. L., Camp, J., Vidal, S., & Peterson, J. (2012). Supervision practices in specialty mental health probation: What happens in officer-probationer meetings? *Law and Human Behavior, 36,* 109–119.

Esbensen, F.-A. (2004). *Evaluating G.R.E.A.T.: A school-based gang prevention program.* Washington, DC: National Institute of Justice.

Esbensen, F.-A., Matsuda, K. N., Taylor, T. J., & Peterson, D. (2011). Multimethod strategy for assessing program fidelity: The national evaluation of the revised G.R.E.A.T. program. *Evaluation Review, 35,* 14–39.

Esbensen, F.-A., & Osgood, D. W. (1999). Gang Resistance Education and Training (GREAT): Results from a national evaluation. *Journal of Research in Crime and Delinquency, 36,* 194–225.

Esbensen, F.-A., Osgood, D. W., Peterson, D., Taylor, T. J., & Carson, D. C. (2013). Short- and long-term outcome results from a multisite evaluation of the G.R.E.A.T. program. *Criminology & Public Policy, 12,* 375–411.

Esbensen, F.-A., Peterson, D., Taylor, T. J., Freng, A., Osgood, D. W., Carson, D. C., & Matsuda, K. N. (2011). Evaluation and evolution of the Gang Resistance Education and Training (G.R.E.A.T.) program. *Journal of School Violence, 10,* 53–70.

Esbensen, F.-A., Peterson, D., Taylor, T. J., & Osgood, D. W. (2012). Results from a multi-site evaluation of the G.R.E.A.T. program. *Justice Quarterly, 29,* 125–151.

Esbensen, F.-A., Winfree, L. T., He, N., & Taylor, T. J. (2001). Youth gangs and definitional issues: When is a gang a gang, and why does it matter? *Crime & Delinquency, 47,* 105–130.

Eysenck, H. J. (1964). *Crime and personality.* London: Routledge and Kegan Paul.

Eysenck, H. J. (1977). *Crime and personality* 2nd ed. London, England: Routledge and Kegan Paul.

Eysenck, H. J. (1998). Personality and crime. In T. Millon, E. Simonsen, M. Birket-Smith, & R. D. Davis (Eds.), *Psychopathy: Antisocial, criminal, and violent behavior* (pp. 40–49). New York, NY: Guilford.

Eysenck, H. J., & Gudjonsson, G. H. (1989). *Causes and cures of criminality*. New York, NY: Plenum.

Falk, Ö., Wallinius, M., Lundström, S., Frisell, T., Ankarsäter, H., Kerekes, N. (2014). The 1% of the population accountable for 63% of all violent crime convictions. *Social Psychiatry and Psychiatric Epidemiology, 49*, 559–571.

Falkenbach, D. M., Reinhard, E. E., & Zappala, M. (2021). Identifying psychopathy subtypes using a broader model of personality: An investigation of the Five Factor Model using model-based cluster analysis. *Journal of Interpersonal Violence, 36*, 7161–7184.

Fanti, K. A., Kyranides, M. N., Petridou, M., Demetriou, C. A., & Georgiou, G. (2018). Neurophysiological markers associated with heterogeneity in conduct problems, callous unemotional traits, and anxiety: Comparing children to young adults. *Developmental Psychology, 54*, 1634–1649.

Fair, H., & Walmsley, R. (2021). *World prison population list* 13th ed. London: Institute for Crime & Justice Policy Research.

Farabee, D., Hser, Y.-I., Anglin, M. D., & Huang, D. (2004). Recidivism among an early cohort of California's Proposition 36 offenders. *Criminology & Public Policy, 3*, 563–584.

Farahmand, P., Arshed, A., & Bradley, M. V. (2020). Systemic racism and substance use disorders. *Psychiatric Annals, 50*, 494–498.

Farringer, A. J., Duriez, S. A., Manchak, S. M., & Sullivan, C. C. (2021) Adherence to "What Works": Examining trends across 14 years of Correctional Program Assessment. *Corrections, 6*, 269–287.

Farrington, D. P. (2007). Childhood risk factors and risk-focused prevention. *The Oxford handbook of criminology, 4*, 602–640.

Farrington, D. P. (2013). Longitudinal and experimental research in criminology. In M. Tonry (Ed.), *Crime and justice: A review of research*, Vol. *42* (pp. 453–528). Chicago, IL: University of Chicago Press.

Farrington, D. P. (2019). The duration of criminal careers: How many offenders do not desist up to age 61? *Journal of Developmental and Life-Course Criminology, 5*, 4–21.

Farrington, D. P. (2021). New findings in the Cambridge study in delinquent development. In J. C. Barnes & D. R. Forde (Eds.), *The encyclopedia of research methods in criminology and criminal justice*, Vol. *1* (pp. 96–103). New York: John Wiley & Sons.

Farrington, D. P., Barnes, G. C., & Lambert, S. (1996). The concentration of offending in families. *Legal and Criminological Psychology, 1*, 47–63.

Farrington, D. P., Hancock, G., Livingston, M., Painter, K. A., & Towl, G. J. (2000). *Evaluation of intensive regimes for young offenders*. Research Findings No. 121. London, England: Home Office Research, Development and Statistics Directorate.

Farrington, D. P., Jolliffe, D., & Coid, J. W. (2021). Cohort profile: The Cambridge Study in Delinquent Development (CSDD). *Journal of Developmental and Life-Course Criminology, 7*, 278–291.

Farrington, D. P., Kazemian, L., & Piquero, A. R. (Eds.) (2019). *The Oxford handbook of developmental and life-course criminology*. New York: Oxford University Press.

Farrington, D. P., & Koegl, C. J. (2015). Monetary benefits and costs of the Stop Now and Plan program for boys aged 6–11, based on the prevention of later offending. *Journal of Quantitative Criminology, 31*, 263–287.

Farrington, D. P., & Loeber, R. (2013). Two approaches to developmental/life-course theorizing. In F. T. Cullen & P. Wilcox (Eds.), *The Oxford handbook of criminological theory* (pp. 227–252). Oxford, England: Oxford University Press.

Farrington, D. P., Lösel, F., Boruch, R. F., Gottfredson, D. C., Mazerolle, L., Sherman, L. W., & Weisburd, D. (2019). Advancing knowledge about replication in criminology. *Journal of Experimental Criminology, 15*, 373–396.

Farrington, D. P., Ttofi, M. M., Crago, R. V., & Coid, J. W. (2015). Intergenerational similarities in risk factors for offending. *Journal of Developmental and Life-Course Criminology, 1*, 48–62.

Farrington, D. P., & Welsh, B. C. (2005). Randomized experiments in criminology: What have we learned in the last two decades? *Journal of Experimental Criminology, 1*, 9–38.

Fass, T. L., Heilbrun, K., Dematteo, D., & Fretz, R. (2008). The LSI-R and the COMPAS: Validation data on two risk-needs tools. *Criminal Justice and Behavior, 35*, 1095–1108.

Fazel, S., Bains, P., & Doll, H. (2006). Substance abuse and dependence in prisoners: A systematic review. *Addiction, 101*, 181–191.

Fazel, S., & Danesh, J. (2002). Serious mental disorder in 23,000 prisoners: A systematic review of 62 surveys. *Lancet, 359*, 545–550.

Fazel, S., Yoon, I. A., & Hayes, A. J. (2017). Substance use disorders in prisoners: An updated systematic review and meta-aggression analysis in recently incarcerated men and women. *Addiction, 112*, 1725–1739.

Feinberg, A. P. (2018). The key role of epigenetics in human disease prevention and mitigation. *The New England Journal of Medicine, 378*, 1323–1334.

Felitti, V. J., Anda, R. F., Nordenberg, D., Williamson, D. F., Spitz, A. M., Edwards, V., … Marks, J. S. (1998). Relationship of child abuse and household dysfunction to many of the leading causes of death in adults: The adverse childhood experiences (ACE) study. *American Journal of Preventative Medicine, 14*, 245–258.

Felson, R. B., Burchfield, K. B., & Teasdale, B. (2007). The impact of alcohol on different types of violent incidents. *Criminal Justice and Behavior, 34*, 1057–1068.

Felson, R. B., & Staff, J. (2010). The effects of alcohol intoxication on violent versus other offending. *Criminal Justice and Behavior, 37*, 1343–1360.

Ferguson, C. J., & Hartley, R. D. (2009). The pleasure is momentary … the expense damnable? The influence of pornography on rape and sexual assault. *Aggression and Violent Behavior, 14*, 323–329.

Ferguson, L. M., & Wormith, J. S. (2012). A meta-analysis of moral reconation therapy. *International Journal of Offender Therapy and Comparative Criminology, 57*, 1076–1106.

Ferri, M., Amato, L., & Davoli, M. (2009). Alcoholics Anonymous and other 12-step programmes for alcohol dependence (review). *The Cochrane Library*, Issue 3.

Fields, R. D. (2005). Myelination: An overlooked mechanism of synaptic plasticity? *The Neuroscientist, 11*, 528–531.

Finckenauer, J. O. (1979). *Juvenile awareness project: Evaluation report no. 2*. Newark, NJ: School of Criminal Justice, Rutgers University.

Finckenauer, J. O., Gavin, P. W., Hovland, A., & Storvoll, E. (1999). *Scared straight: The panacea phenomenon revisited*. Prospect Heights, IL: Waveland.

Fine, A., & Van Rooij, B. (2017). For whom does deterrence affect behavior? Identifying key individual differences. *Law and Human Behavior, 41*, 354.

Fitton, L., Yu, R., & Fazel, S. (2020). Childhood maltreatment and violent outcomes: A systematic review and meta-analysis of prospective studies. *Trauma, Violence, & Abuse, 21*, 754–768.

Flood, M. (2011). Involving men in efforts to end violence against women. *Men and Masculinities, 14*, 358–377.

Flores, A. W., Lowenkamp, C. T., Holsinger, A. M., & Latessa, E. J. (2006). Predicting outcome with the Level of Service Inventory–Revised: The importance of implementation integrity. *Journal of Criminal Justice, 34*, 523–529.

Folk, J. B., Kemp, K., Yurasek, A., Barr-Walker, J., & Tolou-Shams, M. (2021). Adverse childhood experiences among justice-involved youth: Data-driven recommendations for action using the sequential intercept model. *American Psychologist, 76*, 268–283.

Fonagy, P., Target, M., Steele, M., Steele, H., Leigh, T., Levinson, A., & Kennedy, R. (1997). Morality, disruptive behavior, borderline personality disorder, crime, and their relationships to security attachment. In L. Atkinson & K. J. Zucker (Eds.), *Attachment and Psychopathology* (pp. 223–274). New York, NY: Guilford.

Fontaine, N., Carbonneau, R., Barker, E. D., Vitaro, F., Hébert, M., Côté, S. M., … Tremblay, R. E. (2008). Girls' hyperactivity and physical aggression during childhood and adjustment problems in early adulthood. *Archives of General Psychiatry, 65*, 320–328.

Forgatch, M. S., & Rodriquez, M. M. D. (2016). Interrupting coercion: The iterative loops among theory, science, and practice. In T. J. Dishion & J. J. Snyder (Eds.), *The Oxford handbook of coercive relationship dynamics* (pp. 194–241). New York: Oxford University Press.

Forth, A. E., Hart, S. D., & Hare, R. D. (1990). Assessment of psychopathy in male young offenders. *Psychological Assessment: A Journal of Consulting and Clinical Psychology, 2,* 342–344.

Forth, A. E., Kosson, D. S., & Hare, R. D. (2003). *Hare Psychopathy Checklist: Youth version (PCL:YV).* Toronto, Canada: Multi-Health Systems.

Fosco, W. D., Hawk Jr., L. W., Colder, C. R., Meisel, S. N., & Lengua, L. J. (2019). The development of inhibitory control in adolescence and prospective relations with delinquency. *Journal of Adolescence, 76,* 37–47.

Fowler, E., & Kurlychek, M. C. (2018). Drawing the line: Empirical recidivism results from a natural experiment raising the age of criminal responsibility. *Youth Violence and Juvenile Justice, 16,* 263–278.

Fox, B., & DeLisi, M. (2019). Psychopathic killers: A meta-analytic review of the psychopathy-homicide nexus. *Aggression and Violent Behavior, 44,* 67–69.

Fox, B. H., Perez, N., Cass, E., Baglivio, M. T., & Epps, N. (2015). Trauma changes everything: Examining the relationship between adverse childhood experiences and serious, violent and chronic juvenile offenders. *Child Abuse & Neglect, 46,* 163–173.

Fox, C., Harrison, J., Hothersall, G., Smith, A., & Webster, R. (2022). A rapid evidence assessment of the impact of probation caseloads on reducing recidivism and other probation outcomes. *Probation Journal, 69,* 138–158.

Frailing, K., Rapp, V., & Taylor, R. (2023). Swift and Certain probation as a HOPE-like model: Progress toward goals and lingering challenges. *Corrections, 8,* 1–16.

Frase, R. S. (2019). Forty years of American sentencing guidelines: What have we learned? *Crime and Justice, 48,* 79–135.

Frechette, J., & Lussier, P. (2021). Betting against the odds: The mysterious case of the clinical override in risk assessment of adult convicted offenders. *International Journal of Offender Therapy and Comparative Criminology,* Online First, October.

Frick, P. J., Barry, C. T., & Bodin, D. S. (2000). Applying the concept of psychopathy to children: Implications for the assessment of antisocial youth. In C. B. Gacono (Ed.), *The clinical and forensic assessment of psychopathy: A practitioner's guide* (pp. 3–24). Mahwah, NJ: Lawrence Erlbaum Associates.

Frick, P. J., & Hare, R. D. (2001). *Antisocial Process Screening Device.* Toronto, Canada: Multi-Health Systems.

Frick, P. J., O'Brien, B. S., Wootton, J. M., & McBurnett, K. (1994). Psychopathy and conduct problems in children. *Journal of Abnormal Psychology, 103,* 700–707.

Friese, M., Frankenbach, J., Job, V., & Loschelder, D. D. (2017). Does self-control training improve self-control? A meta-analysis. *Perspectives on Psychological Science, 12,* 1077–1099.

Friese, M., Loschelder, D. D., Gieseler, K., Frankenbach, J., & Inzlicht, M. (2019). Is ego depletion real? An analysis of arguments. *Personality and Social Psychology Review, 23,* 107–131.

Frisell, T., Pawitan, Y., Långström, & Lichtenstein, P. (2012). Heritability, assortative mating and gender differences in violent crime: Results from a total population sample using twin, adoption, and sibling models. *Behavior Genetics, 42,* 3–18.

Frize, M. C., Griffith, J., Durham, R., & Ranson, C. (2020). An evidence-based model of treatment for people with cognitive disability who have committed sexually abusive behavior. In J. Proulx, F. Cortoni, L. A. Craig, & E. J. Letourneau (Eds.), *The Wiley handbook of what works with sexual offenders: Contemporary perspectives in theory, assessment, treatment, and prevention.* NY: John Wiley & Sons.

Frost, H., Campbell, P., Maxwell, M., O'Carroll, R. E., Dombrowski, S. U., Williams, B., … Pollock, A. (2018) Effectiveness of Motivational Interviewing on adult behaviour change in health and social care settings: A systematic review of reviews. Plos One, *13*(10).

Fulham, L., Blais, J., Rugge, T., & Schultheis, E. A. (in press). The effectiveness of restorative justice programs: A meta-analysis of recidivism and other relevant outcomes. *Criminology and Criminal Justice.*

Furby, L., Weinrott, M., & Blackshaw, L. (1989). Sex offender recidivism: A review. *Psychological Bulletin, 105,* 3–30.

Galli, P. M., & Kroner, D. G. (2019). Desistance. In R. D. Morgan (Ed.), The SAGE encyclopedia of criminal psychology (pp. 357–359). Thousand Oaks, CA: Sage.

Gallupe, G., McLevey, J., & Brown, S. (2019). Selection and influence: A meta-analysis of the association between peer and personal offending. *Journal of Quantitative Criminology, 35,* 313–335.

Gallupe, O., Nguyen, H., Bouchard, M., Schulenberg, J. L., Chenier, A., & Cook, K. D. (2016). An experimental test of deviant modeling. *Journal of Research in Crime and Delinquency, 53,* 482–505.

Gang, D., Loff, B., Naylor, B., & Kirkman, M. (2021). A call for evaluation of restorative justice programs. *Trauma, Violence, & Abuse, 22,* 186–190.

Gannon, T. A., Olver, M. E., Mallion, J. S., & James, M. (2019). Does specialized psychological treatment for offending reduce recidivism? A meta-analysis examining staff and program variables as predictors of treatment effectiveness. *Clinical Psychology Review, 73,* 101752.

Gao, Y., & Raine, A. (2010). Successful and unsuccessful psychopaths: A neurobiological model. *Behavioral Sciences and Law, 28,* 194–210.

Gard, A. M., Dotterer, H. L., & Hyde, L. W. (2019). Genetic influences on antisocial behavior: Recent advances and future directions. *Current Opinion in Psychology, 27,* 46–55.

Garner, J. H., Maxwell, C. D., & Lee, J. (2021). The specific deterrent effects of criminal sanctions for intimate partner violence: A meta-analysis. *Journal of Criminal Law & Criminology, 111,* 227–271.

Garthe, R. C., Sullivan, T. N., & McDaniel, M. A. (2017). A meta-analytic review of peer risk factors and adolescent dating violence. *Psychology of Violence, 7,* 45–57.

Gaskin, D. J., Roberts, E. T., Chan, K. S., McCleary, R., Buttorff, C., & Delarmente, B. A. (2019). No man is an island: The impact of neighborhood disadvantage on mortality. *International Journal of Environmental Research and Public Health, 16,* Article 1265.

Gaspar, M., Brown, L., Ramler, T., Scanlon, F., Gigax, G., Ridley, K., & Morgan, R. D. (2019). Therapeutic outcomes of changing lives and changing outcomes for male and female justice involved persons with mental illness. *Criminal Justice and Behavior, 46,* 1678–1699.

Gatner, D. T., Douglas, K. S., Almond, M. F., Hart, S. D., & Kropp, P. R. (2022). How much does that cost? Examining the economic costs of crime in North America attributable to people with psychopathic personality disorder. *Personality Disorders: Theory, Research, and Treatment.* Advance online publication.

Geerts, M., Steyaert, J., & Fryns, J. P. (2003). The XYY syndrome: A follow-up study on 38 boys. *Genetic Counseling, 14,* 267–279.

Gendreau, P., Goggin, C., & Smith, P. (2002). Is the PCL-R really the 'unparalleled' measure of offender risk? A lesson in knowledge cumulation. *Criminal Justice and Behavior, 29,* 397–426.

Gendreau, P., Little, T., & Goggin, C. (1996). A meta-analysis of the predictors of adult offender recidivism: What works! *Criminology, 34,* 575–607.

Gendreau, P., & Ross, R. R. (1979). Effective correctional treatment: Bibliotherapy for cynics. *Crime & Delinquency, 25,* 463–489.

Gendreau, P., & Ross, R. R. (1987). Revivication of rehabilitation: Evidence from the 1980s. *Justice Quarterly, 4,* 349–408.

Gendreau, P., & Smith, P. (2007). Influencing the "people who count": Some perspectives on the reporting of meta-analytic results for prediction and treatment outcomes with offenders. *Criminal Justice and Behavior, 34,* 1536–1559.

Gendreau, P., Smith, P., & Thériault, Y. L. (2009). Chaos theory and correctional treatment: Common sense, correctional quackery, and the law of fartcatchers. *Journal of Contemporary Criminal Justice, 25,* 384–393.

Gendreau, P., Thériault, Y., & Andrews, D. A. (2012). *The Correctional Program Assessment Inventory-2010* (CPAI-2010).

Geraghty, K. A., & Woodhams, J. (2015). The predictive validity of risk assessment tools for female offenders: A systematic review. *Aggression and Violent Behavior, 21,* 25–38.

Gerritzen, B. C., & Kirchgässner, G. (2013). Facts or ideology: What determines the results of econometric estimates of the deterrence effect of death penalty? *A meta-analysis. CESifo Working Paper: Empirical Theoretical Methods, No. 4159.* Leibnez Information Centre for Economics.

Gershoff, E. T., Goodman, G. S., Miller-Perrin, C. L., Holden, G. W., Jackson, Y., & Kazdin, A. E. (2018). The strength of the causal evidence against physical punishment of children and its implications for parents, psychologists, and policymakers. *American Psychologist, 73,* 626–638.

Gershoff, E. T., & Grogan-Kaylor, A. (2016). Spanking and child outcomes: Old controversies and new meta-analyses. *Journal of Family Psychology, 30,* 453–469.

Ghasemi, M., Anavari, D., Atapour, M., Wormith, J. S., Stockdale, K. C., & Spiteri, R. J. (2021). The application of machine learning to a general risk-need assessment instrument in the prediction of criminal recidivism. *Criminal Justice and Behavior, 48,* 518–538.

Giguère, G., Brouillette-Alarie, S., & Bourassa, C. (2023). A look at the difficulty and predictive validity of LS/CMI items with Rasch modeling. *Criminal Justice and Behavior, 50,* 118–138.

Gini, G., Pozzoli, T., & Hymel, S. (2014). Moral disengagement among children and youth: A meta-analytic review of links to aggressive behavior. *Aggressive Behavior, 40,* 56–68.

Girard, L., & Wormith, J. S. (2004). The predictive validity of the Level of Service Inventory—Ontario Revision on general and violent recidivism among various offender groups. *Criminal Justice and Behavior, 31,* 150–181.

Glaser, D. (1956). Criminality theories and behavioral images. *American Journal of Sociology, 61,* 433–444.

Glaser, D. (1974). Remedies for the key deficiency in criminal justice evaluation research. *Journal of Research in Crime and Delinquency, 10,* 144–154.

Glasman, L. R., & Albarracín, D. (2006). Forming attitudes that predict future behavior: A meta-analysis of the attitude-behavior relation. *Psychological Bulletin, 132,* 778–822.

Glaze, L. E., & Palla, S. (2005). Probation and parole in the United States, 2004. *Bureau of Justice Statistics Bulletin, November.* Washington, DC: U.S. Department of Justice.

Gleicher, L. (2020). Effective practices in community supervision model: Staff perceptions of the model and implementation. *European Journal of Probation, 12,* 157–181.

Glenn, A. L., Raine, A., Venables, P. H., & Mednick, S. A. (2007). Early temperamental and psychophysiological precursors of adult psychopathic personality. *Journal of Abnormal Psychology, 116,* 508–518.

Glueck, S., & Glueck, E. T. (1950). *Unraveling juvenile delinquency.* Cambridge, MA: Harvard University Press.

Goel, S., Shroff, R., Skeem, J., & Slobogin, C. (2021). The accuracy, equity, and jurisprudence of criminal risk assessment. In R. Vogel (Ed.), *Research handbook on big data law* (pp. 9–28). Northampton, MA: Edward Elgar Publishing.

Goggin, C., & Gendreau, P. (2006). The implementation and maintenance of quality services in offender rehabilitation programs. In C. R. Hollin & E. J. Palmer (Eds.), *Offending behaviour programs: Development, application, and controversies* (pp. 247–268). Chichester, England: Wiley.

Golden, C. J., Jackson, M. L., Peterson-Rohne, A., & Gontkovsky, S. T. (1996). Neuropsychological correlates of violence and aggression: A review of the clinical literature. *Aggression and Violent Behavior, 1,* 3–25.

Gollwitzer, M., Meder, M., & Schmitt, M. (2011). What gives victims satisfaction when they seek revenge? *European Journal of Social Psychology, 41,* 364–374.

Gomez Auyong, Z. E., Smith, S., & Ferguson, C. J. (2018). Girls in gangs: Exploring risk in a British youth context. *Crime & Delinquency, 64,* 1698–1717.

Gomis-Pomares, A., Villanueva, L., & Adrián, J. E. (2022). The prediction of youth recidivism in a Spanish Roma population by the Youth Level of Service/Case Management Inventory (YLS/CMI). *International Journal of Offender Therapy and Comparative Criminology, 66,* 791–806.

Gonnerman, J. (2004, November 9). *Million-dollar blocks.* The Village Voice. www.villagevoice. com/2004/11/09/million-dollar-blocks/

Goodley, G., Pearson, D., & Morris, P. (2022). Predictors of recidivism following release from custody: A meta-analysis. *Psychology, Crime & Law, 28,* 703–729.

Goodnight, J. A., D'Onofrio, B. M., Cherlin, A. J., Emery, R. E., Van Hulle, C. A., & Lahey, B. B. (2013). Effects of maternal relationship transitions on offspring antisocial behavior in childhood and adolescence: A cousin-comparison analysis. *Journal of Abnormal Child Psychology, 41,* 185–198.

Gordon, H., Kelty, S. F., & Julian, R. (2015). An evaluation of the Level of Service/Case Management Inventory in an Australian community corrections environment. *Psychiatry, Psychology, and Law, 22,* 247–258.

Gordon, R. A., Rowe, H. L., Pardini, D., Loeber, R., White, H. R., & Farrington, D. P. (2014). Serious delinquency and gang participation: Combining and specializing in drug selling, theft, and violence. *Journal of Research on Adolescence, 24,* 235–251.

Goring, C. (1913). *The English convict.* London, England: His Majesty's Stationery Office.

Gottfredson, D. C., Kearly, B., Thornberry, T. P., Slothower, M., Devlin, D., & Fader, J. J. (2018). Scaling-up evidence-based programs using a public funding stream: A randomized trial of Functional Family Therapy for court-involved youth. *Prevention Science, 19,* 939–953.

Gottfredson, M. R. (1979). Treatment destruction techniques. *Journal of Research in Crime & Delinquency, 16,* 39–54.

Gottfredson, M. R., & Hirschi, T. (1990). *A general theory of crime.* Stanford, CA: Stanford University Press.

Gottfredson, M., & Hirschi, T. (2020). *Modern control theory and the limits of criminal justice.* New York: Oxford University Press.

Gottfried, E. D., & Christopher, S. C. (2017). Mental disorders among criminal offenders: A review of the literature. *Journal of Correctional Health Care, 23,* 336–346.

Gottlieb, A., & Sugle, N. F. (2019). Marriage, cohabitation, and crime: Differentiating associations by partnership stage. *Justice Quarterly, 36,* 503–531.

Gottschalk, M. (2011). The past, present, and future of mass incarceration in the United States. *Criminology & Public Policy, 10,* 483–504.

Götz, M. J., Johnstone, E. C., & Ratcliffe, S. G. (1999). Criminality and antisocial behaviour in unselected men with sex chromosome abnormalities. *Psychological Medicine, 29,* 953–962.

Gower, M., Morgan, F., & Saunders, J. (2022). Aboriginality and violence: Gender and cultural differences on the Level of Service/Risk, Need, Responsivity (LS/RNR) and Violence Risk Scale (VRS). *Psychiatry, Psychology and Law,* Online First, March.

Graham, L. M., Sahay, K. M., Rizo, C. F., Messing, J. T., & Macy, R. J. (2021). The validity and reliability of available intimate partner homicide and reassault risk assessment tools: A systematic review. *Trauma, Violence, & Abuse, 22,* 18–40.

Graham-Kevan, N., & Bates, E. A. (2020). Intimate partner violence perpetrator programmes: Ideology or evidence-based practice? In J. S. Wormith, L. A. Craig, & T. L. Hogue (Eds.), *The Wiley handbook of what works in violence risk management: Theory, research and practice* (pp. 437–449). New York: John Wiley & Sons.

Granic, I., & Patterson, G. R. (2006). Toward a comprehensive model of antisocial development: A dynamic systems approach. *Psychological Review, 113,* 101.

Grann, M., & Långström, N. (2007). Actuarial assessment of violence risk: To weigh or not to weigh? *Criminal Justice and Behavior, 34,* 22–36.

Grant, S., Colaiaco, B., Motala, A., Shanman, R., Booth, M., Sorbero, M., & Hempel, S. (2017). Mindfulness-based relapse prevention for substance use disorders: A systematic review and meta-analysis. *Journal of Addiction Medicine, 11,* 386–396.

Grant, B. F., Hasin, D. S., Stinson, F. S., Dawson, D. A., Chou, S. P., Ruan, W. J., & Pickering, R. P. (2004). Prevalence, correlates, and disability of personality disorders in the United States: Results from the national epidemiologic survey on alcohol and related conditions. *Journal of Clinical Psychiatry, 65,* 948–958.

Greiner, L. E., Law, M., & Brown, S. L. (2015). Using dynamic factors to predict recidivism among women: A four-wave prospective study. *Criminal Justice and Behavior, 42*, 457–480.

Grieger, L., & Hosser, D. (2014). Which risk factors are really predictive? An analysis of Andrews and Bonta's "Central Eight" risk factors for recidivism in German youth correctional facility inmates. *Criminal Justice and Behavior, 41*, 613–634.

Griffin, K. W., Botvin, G. J., Scheier, L. M., Diaz, T., & Miller, N. (2000). Parenting practices as predictors of substance abuse, delinquency, and aggression among urban minority youth: Moderating effects of family structure and gender. *Psychology of Addictive Behaviors, 14*, 174–184.

Griffin, T., & Miller, M. K. (2008). Child abduction, AMBER alert, and crime control theater. *Criminal Justice Review, 33*, 159–176.

Groh, D. R., Jason, L. A., & Keys, C. B. (2008). Social network variables in Alcoholics Anonymous: A literature review. *Clinical Psychology Review, 28*, 430–450.

Grove, W. M., Eckert, E. D., Heston, L., Bouchard, T. J. Jr., Segal, N., & Lykken, D. T. (1990). Heritability of substance abuse and antisocial behavior: A study of monozygotic twins reared apart. *Biological Psychiatry, 27*, 1293–1304.

Grove, W. M., & Meehl, P. E. (1996). Comparative efficiency of informal (subjective, impressionistic) and formal (mechanical, algorithmic) prediction procedures: The clinical-statistical controversy. *Psychology, Public Policy, and Law, 2*, 293–323.

Grove, W. M., & Vrieze, S. J. (2013). The clinical versus mechanical prediction controversy. In K. F. Geisinger (Ed.), *APA handbook of testing and assessment in psychology: Volume 2. Testing and assessment in clinical and counseling psychology*. Washington, DC: American Psychological Association.

Grove, W. M., Zald, D. H., Lebow, B. S., Snitz, B. E., & Nelson, C. (2000). Clinical versus mechanical prediction: A meta-analysis. *Psychological Assessment, 12*, 19–30.

Guay, J.-P., Knight, R. A., Ruscio, J., & Hare, R. D. (2018). A taxometric investigation of psychopathy in women. *Psychiatry Research, 261*, 565–573.

Guay, J. P., & Parent, G. (2018). Broken legs, clinical overrides, and recidivism risk: An analysis of decisions to adjust risk levels with the LS/CMI. *Criminal Justice and Behavior, 45*, 82–100.

Guay, J.-P., Ruscio, J., & Knight, R. A. (2007). A taxometric analysis of the latent structure of psychopathy: Evidence for dimensionality. *Journal of Abnormal Psychology, 116*, 701–716.

Guo, G., Roettger, M. E., & Cai, T. (2008). The integration of genetic propensities into social-control models of delinquency and violence among male youths. *American Sociological Review, 73*, 543–598.

Gutierrez, L., Blais, J., & Bourgon, G. (2016). Do domestic violence courts work? A meta-analytic review examining treatment and study quality. *Justice Research and Policy, 17*, 75–99.

Gutierrez, L., & Bourgon, G. (2012). Drug treatment courts: A quantitative review of study and treatment quality. *Justice Research and Policy, 14*, 47–77.

Gutierrez, L., Wilson, H. A., Rugge, T., & Bonta, J. (2013). The prediction of recidivism with Aboriginal offenders: A theoretically informed meta-analysis. *Canadian Journal of Criminology and Criminal Justice, 55*, 55–99.

Haas, S. M., & DeTardo-Bora, K. A. (2009). Inmate reentry and the utility of the LSI-R in case planning. *Corrections Compendium*, Spring, 11–16, 49–54.

Hamel, J. M. (2020). Perpetrator or victim? A review of the complexities of domestic violence cases. *Journal of Aggression, Conflict and Peace Research, 12*, 55–62.

Hanley, D. (2006). Appropriate services: Examining the case classification principle. *Journal of Offender Rehabilitation, 42*, 1–22.

Hannah-Moffat, K. (2009). Gridlock or mutability: Reconsidering 'gender' and risk assessment. *Criminology & Public Policy, 8*, 209–219.

Hanson, R. K. (1997). *The development of a brief actuarial risk scale for sexual offense recidivism*. Ottawa, Canada: Solicitor General Canada.

Hanson, R. K. (2009). The psychological assessment of risk for crime and violence. *Canadian Psychology, 50*, 172–182.

Hanson, R. K. (2014). Treating sexual offenders: How did we get here and where are we headed? *Journal of Sexual Aggression, 20,* 3–8.

Hanson, R. K. (2022). *Prediction statistics for psychological assessment.* Washington, DC: American Psychological Association.

Hanson, R. K., Bourgon, G., Helmus, L., & Hodgson, S. (2009). The principles of effective correctional treatment also apply to sexual offenders: A meta-analysis. *Criminal Justice and Behavior, 36,* 865–891.

Hanson, R. K., Bourgon, G., McGrath, R. J., Kroner, D. G., D'Amora, D. A., Thomas, S. S., & Tavarez, L. P. (2017). *A five-level risk and needs system: Maximizing assessment results in corrections through the development of a common language.* Washington: The Council of State Governments Justice Center.

Hanson, R. K., & Bussière, M. T. (1998). Predicting relapse: A meta-analysis of sexual offender recidivism studies. *Journal of Consulting and Clinical Psychology, 66,* 348–362.

Hanson, R. K., Harris, A. J. R., Helmus, L., & Thornton, D. (2014). High-risk sex offenders many not be high risk forever. *Journal of Interpersonal Violence, 29,* 2792–2813.

Hanson, R. K., Harris, A. J., Letourneau, E., Helmus, L. M., & Thornton, D. (2018). Reductions in risk based on time offense-free in the community: Once a sexual offender, not always a sexual offender. *Psychology, Public Policy, and Law, 24,* 48–63.

Hanson, R. K., Harris, A. J. R., Scott, T.-L., & Helmus, L. (2007). *Assessing the risk of sexual offenders on community supervision: The Dynamic Supervision Project (User Report 2007–05).* Ottawa, Canada: Public Safety Canada.

Hanson, R. K., Helmus, L., & Harris, A. J. R. (2015). Assessing the risk and needs of supervised sexual offenders: A prospective study using STABLE-2007, Static-99R and Static-2002R. *Criminal Justice and Behavior.*

Hanson, R. K., Morton, K. E., & Harris, A. J. R. (2003). Sexual offender recidivism risk: What we know and what we need to know. *Annals of the New York Academy of Sciences, 989,* 154–166.

Hanson, R. K., & Morton-Bourgon, K. (2005). The characteristics of persistent sexual offenders: A meta-analysis of recidivism studies. *Journal of Consulting and Clinical Psychology, 73,* 1154–1163.

Hanson, R. K., & Morton-Bourgon, K. (2009). The accuracy of recidivism risk for sexual offenders: A meta-analysis of 118 prediction studies. *Psychological Assessment, 21,* 1–21.

Hanson, R. K., & Scott, H. (1996). Social networks of sexual offenders. *Psychology, Crime and Law, 2,* 249–258.

Hanson, R. K., & Thornton, D. (2000). Improving risk assessments for sex offenders: A comparison of three actuarial scales. *Law and Human Behavior, 24,* 119–136.

Hanson, R. K., & Thornton, D. (2003). *Notes on the Development of Static-2002 (User Report 2003–01).* Ottawa, Canada: Public Safety Canada.

Hanson, R. K., & Yates, P. M. (2013). Psychological treatment of sex offenders. *Current Psychiatry Reports, 15,* 348.

Harden, K. P. (2014). A sex-positive framework for research on adolescent sexuality. *Perspectives on Psychological Science, 9,* 455–469.

Harden, K. P., Mendle, J., Hill, J. E., Turkheimer, E., & Emery, R. E. (2008). Rethinking timing of first sex and delinquency. *Journal of Youth Adolescence, 37,* 373–385.

Harden, K. P., Quinn, P. D., & Tucker-Drob, E. M. (2012). Genetically influenced change in sensation seeking drives the rise of delinquent behavior during adolescence. *Developmental Science, 15,* 150–163.

Harding, D. J., Morenoff, J. D., & Herbert, C. W. (2013). Home is hard to find: Neighborhoods, institutions, and the residential trajectories of returning prisoners. *Annals of the American Academy of Political Science, 64,* 214–236.

Hare, R. D. (1991). *The Hare Psychopathy Checklist–Revised.* Toronto, Canada: Multi-Health Systems.

Hare, R. D. (1993). *Without conscience: The disturbing world of the psychopaths among us.* New York, NY: Pocket Books.

Hare, R. D. (1996). Psychopathy: A clinical construct whose time has come. *Criminal Justice and Behavior, 23,* 25–54.

Hare, R. D. (1998). Psychopaths and their nature: Implications for the mental health and criminal justice systems. In T. Millon, E. Simonsen, M. Birket-Smith, & R. D. Davis (Eds.), *Psychopathy: Antisocial, criminal, and violent behavior* (pp. 188–212). New York, NY: Guilford.

Hare, R. D. (2003). *The Hare Psychopathy Checklist-Revised* 2nd ed. Toronto, Canada: Multi-Health Systems.

Hare, R. D. (2016). Psychopathy, the PCL-R, and criminal justice: Some new findings and current issues. *Canadian Psychology, 57,* 21–34.

Hare, R. D., Harpur, T. J., Hakstian, A. R., Forth, A. D., & Hart, S. D. (1990). The revised Psychopathy Checklist: Reliability and factor structure. *Psychological Assessment: A Journal of Consulting and Clinical Psychology, 2,* 338–341.

Hare, R. D., & Neumann, C. S. (2006). The PCL-R assessment of psychopathy: Development, structural properties, and new directions. In C. J. Patrick (Ed.), *Handbook of psychopathy* (pp. 58–88). New York, NY: Guilford.

Hare, R. D., & Neumann, C. S. (2010). The role of antisociality in the psychopathy construct: Comment on Skeem and Cooke (2010). *Psychological Assessment, 22,* 446–454.

Hare, R. D., Olver, M. E., Stockdale, K. C., Neumann, C. S., Mokros, A., Baskin-Sommers, A., … Yoon, D. (2020). The PCL-R and capital sentencing: A commentary on "Death is Different" DeMatteo et al. (2020a). *Psychology, Public Policy, and Law, 26,* 519–522.

Harpur, T. J., Hare, R. D., & Hakstian, A. R. (1989). Two-factor conceptualization of psychopathy: Construct validity and assessment implications. *Psychological Assessment: A Journal of Consulting and Clinical Psychology, 1,* 6–17.

Harris, G. T., & Rice, M. E. (2006). Treatment of psychopathy: A review of empirical findings. In C. J. Patrick (Ed.), *Handbook of psychopathy* (pp. 555–572). New York, NY: Guilford.

Harris, G. T., Rice M. E., & Cormier, C. A. (1989). *Violent recidivism among psychopaths and non-psychopaths treated in a therapeutic community.* Research report from the Penetanguishene Mental Health Centre VI(1), April, Penetanguishene, Ontario.

Harris, G. T., Rice, M. E., &, Quinsey, V. L. (1993). Violent recidivism of mentally disordered offenders: The development of a statistical prediction instrument. *Criminal Justice and Behavior, 20,* 315–335.

Harris, G. T., Rice, M. E., Quinsey, V. L., & Cormier, C. A. (2015). *Violent offenders: Appraising and managing risk* 3rd ed. Washington, DC: American Psychological Association.

Harrison, J. L., O'Toole, S. K., Ammen, S., Ahlmeyer, S., Harrell, S. N., & Hernandez, J. L. (2020). Sexual offender treatment effectiveness within cognitive-behavioral programs: A meta-analytic investigation of general, sexual, and violent recidivism. *Psychiatry, Psychology and Law, 27,* 1–25.

Hartnett, D., Carr, A., Hamilton, E., & O'Reilly, G. (2017). The effectiveness of Functional Family Therapy for adolescent behavioral and substance misuse problems: A meta-analysis. *Family Process, 56,* 607–619.

Hartung, F. E. (1965). A vocabulary of motives for law violations. In F. E. Hartung (Ed.), *Crime, law and society* (pp. 62–83). Detroit, MI: Wayne State University Press.

Hausam, J., Lehmann, R. J. B., & Dahle, K.-P. (2018). Predicting offenders' institutional misconduct and recidivism: The utility of behavioral ratings by prison officers. *Frontiers in Psychiatry, 9,* Article 679.

Hawken, A. (2018). Economic implications of HOPE from the demonstration field experiment. *Criminology & Public Policy, 17,* 901–906.

Hawken, A., & Kleiman, M. (2009). *Managing drug involved probationers with swift and certain sanctions: Evaluating Hawaii's HOPE.* Washington, DC: National Institute of Justice, Office of Justice Programs. www.ncjrs.gov/pdffiles1/nij/grants/229023.pdf

Hawks, L., Wang, E. A., Howell, B., Woolhandler, S., Himmelstein, D. U., Bor, D., & McCormick, D. (2020). Health status and health care utilization of US adults under probation: 2015–2018. *American Journal of Public Health, 110,* 1411–1417.

Healy, S. R., Valente, J. Y., Caetano, S. C., Martins, S. S., & Sanchez, Z. M. (2020). Worldwide school-based psychosocial interventions and their effect on aggression among elementary school children: A systematic review 2010–2019. *Aggression and Violent Behavior, 55,* Article 101486.

Hebert, M., Daspe, M. È., Lapierre, A., Godbout, N., Blais, M., Fernet, M., & Lavoie, F. (2019). A meta-analysis of risk and protective factors for dating violence victimization: The role of family and peer interpersonal context. *Trauma, Violence, & Abuse, 20,* 574–590.

Hecht, L. K., Latzman, R. D., & Lilienfeld, S. O. (2018). The psychological treatment of psychopathy. In D. David, S. J. Lynn, & G. H. Montgomery (Eds.), *Evidence-based psychotherapy: The state of the science and practice* (pp. 271–298). New York: John Wiley & Sons.

Heller, S. B. (2014). Summer jobs reduce violence among disadvantaged youth. *Science, 346,* 1219–1223.

Helmond, P., Overbeek, G., Brugman, D., & Gibbs, J. C. (2015). A meta-analysis of cognitive distortions and externalizing problem behavior. *Criminal Justice and Behavior, 42,* 245–262.

Helmus, L., Hanson, R. K., Babchishin, K. M., & Mann, R. E. (2013). Attitudes supportive of sexual offending predict recidivism: A meta-analysis. *Trauma, Violence, & Abuse, 14,* 34–53.

Helmus, L. M., Hanson, R. K., Murrie, D. C., & Zabarauckas, C. L. (2021). Field validity of Static-99R and STABLE-2007 with 4,433 men serving sentences for sexual offences in British Columbia: New findings and meta-analysis. *Psychological Assessment, 33,* 581–595.

Helmus, L. M., Kelley, S. M., Frazier, A., Fernandez, Y. M., Lee, S. C., Rettenberger, M., & Boccaccini, M. T. (2022). Static-99R: Strengths, limitations, predictive accuracy meta-analysis, and legal admissibility review. *Psychology, Public Policy, and Law, 28,* 307–331.

Hemphill, J. F., Hare, R. D., & Wong, S. (1998). Psychopathy and recidivism: A review. *Legal and Criminological Psychology, 3,* 139–170.

Henggeler, S. W., Schoenwald, S. K., Borduin, C. M., Rowland, M. D., & Cunningham, P. B. (2009). *Multisystemic treatment of antisocial behavior in children and adolescents* 2nd ed. New York, NY: Guilford.

Henshaw, M., Ogloff, J. R., & Clough, J. A. (2017). Looking beyond the screen: A critical review of the literature on the online child pornography offender. *Sexual Abuse, 29,* 416–445.

Heron, R. L., Eisma, M., & Browne, K. (2022). Why do female domestic violence victims remain in or leave abusive relationships? A qualitative study. *Journal of Aggression, Maltreatment & Trauma, 31,* 677–694.

Herrenkohl, T. I., Fedina, L., Roberto, K. A., Raquet, K. L., Hu, R. X., Rousson, A. N., & Mason, W. A. (2022). Child maltreatment, youth violence, intimate partner violence, and elder mistreatment: A review and theoretical analysis of research on violence across the life course. *Trauma, Violence, & Abuse, 23,* 314–328.

Herzog-Evans, M. (2019). Developing and implementing an EBP program in the French context. In M. Herzog-Evans & M. Benbouriche (Eds.), *Evidence-based work with violent extremists: International implications of French terrorist attacks and responses* (pp. 271–288). London: The Rowan and Littlefield Publishing Group.

Hettema, J., Steele, J., & Miller, W. R. (2005). Motivational interviewing. *Annual Review of Clinical Psychology, 1,* 91–111.

Hiatt, K. D., & Newman, J. P. (2006). Understanding psychopathy: The cognitive side. In C. J. Patrick (Ed.), *Handbook of Psychopathy* (pp. 334–352). New York, NY: Guilford.

Hicks, W. D., Holcomb, J. E., Alexander, M. A., & Clodfelter, T. A. (2020). Drug testing and community supervision outcomes. *Criminal Justice and Behavior, 47,* 419–436.

Higginson, A., Benier, K., Shenderovich, Y., Bedford, L., Mazerolle, L., & Murray, J. (2018). Factors associated with youth gang membership in low- and middle- income countries: A systematic review. *Campbell Systematic Reviews, 11.*

Hilton, N. Z., & Eke, A. W. (2016). Non-specialization of criminal careers among intimate partner violence offenders. *Criminal Justice and Behavior, 43*(10), 1347–1363.

Hilton, N. Z., & Ennis, L. (2020). Intimate partner violence risk assessment and management: An RNR approach to threat assessment. In J. S. Wormith, L. A. Craig, & T. E. Hogue (Eds.), *The*

Wiley handbook of what works in violence risk management: Theory, research and practice (pp. 163–182). New York: John Wiley & Sons.

Hilton, Z. N., Harris, G. T., & Rice, M. E. (2015). The step-father effect in child abuse: Comparing discriminative parental solicitude and antisociality. *Psychology of Violence, 5,* 8–15.

Hilton, Z. N., Harris, G. T., Rice, M. E., Houghton, R. E., & Eke, A. W. (2008). An in-depth assessment for wife assault recidivism: The Ontario Domestic Violence Risk Appraisal Guide. *Law and Human Behavior, 32,* 150–163.

Hilton, Z. N., Harris, G. T., Rice, M. E., Lang, C., Cormier, C. A., & Lines, K. J. (2004). A brief actuarial assessment for the prediction of wife assault recidivism: The Ontario Domestic Assault Risk Assessment. *Psychological Assessment, 16,* 267–275.

Hilton, N. Z., & Radatz, D. L. (2021). Criminogenic needs and intimate partner violence: Association with recidivism and implications for treatment. *Psychological Services, 21,* 566–573.

Hilton, N. Z., Rice, M. E., Harris, G. T., Judd, B., & Quinsey, V. L. (2021). Actuarial guides for appraising the risk of violent reoffending among general offenders, sex offenders, and domestic assaulters. In K. S. Douglas & R. K, Otto (Eds.), *Handbook of violence risk assessment* 2nd ed. (pp. 131–155). New York: Routledge.

Hipwell, A. E., Pardini, D. A., Loeber, R., Sembower, M., Keenan, K., & Stouthamer-Loeber, M. (2007). Callous-unemotional behaviors in young girls: Shared and unique effects relative to conduct problems. *Journal of Clinical Child and Adolescent Psychiatry, 36,* 293–304.

Hirschi, T. (1969). *Causes of delinquency.* Berkeley, CA: University of California Press.

Hirschi, T. (2004). Self-control and crime. In R. F. Baumeister & K. D. Vohs (Eds.), *Handbook of self-regulation: Research, theory and applications* (pp. 537–552). New York, NY: Guilford.

Hobson, J., Shine, J., & Roberts, R. (2000). How do psychopaths behave in a prison therapeutic community? *Psychiatry, Crime and Law, 6,* 139–154.

Hodgins, S. (2020). Antisocial and aggressive behaviour amongst persons with schizophrenia: Evidence and propositions for prevention. In J. Proulx, F. Cortoni, L. A. Craig, & E. J. Letourneau (Eds.), *The Wiley handbook of what works with sexual offenders: Contemporary perspectives in theory, assessment, treatment, and prevention* (pp. 419–436). Hoboken, NJ: John Wiley & Sons.

Hoeben, E. M., Meldrum, R. C., Walker, D., & Young, J. T. N. (2016). The root of peer delinquency and unstructured socializing in explaining delinquency and substance use: A state-of-the-art review. *Journal of Criminal Justice, 47,* 108–122.

Hoeben, E. M., & Weerman, F. M. (2016). Why is involvement in unstructured socializing related to adolescent delinquency? *Criminology, 54,* 242–281.

Hoffman, P. B. (1994). Twenty years of operational use of a risk prediction instrument: The United States Parole Commission's Salient Factor Score. *Journal of Criminal Justice, 22,* 477–494.

Hofmann, M. J., Schneider, S., & Mokros, A. (2021). Fearless but anxious? A systematic review on the utility of fear and anxiety levels to classify subtypes of psychopathy. *Behavioral Sciences & the Law, 39,* 512–540.

Hogan, N. R., & Olver, M. E. (2021). Consistency and construct validity of the Five-Level System for risk communication using static and dynamic tools: An investigation using the Static-99R and VRS-SO. *Assessment,* Online First.

Hoge, R. D. (2016). Risk, need, and responsivity in juveniles. In K. Heilbrun, D. DeMatteo, & N. E. S. Goldstein (Eds.), *APA handbook of psychology and juvenile justice* (pp. 179–196). Washington: American Psychological Association.

Hoge, R. D. (2021). Youth Level of Service/Case Management Inventory. In R. K. Otto & K. S. Douglas (Eds.), *Handbook of violence risk assessment tools* 2nd ed. (pp. 191–205). New York, NY: Routledge.

Hoge, R. D., & Andrews, D. A. (2002). *Youth Level of Service/Case Management Inventory: User's manual.* Toronto, Canada: Multi-Health Systems.

Hoge, R. D., & Andrews, D. A. (2011). *Youth Level of Service/Case Management Inventory: User's manual. Version 2.0.* Toronto, Canada: Multi-Health Systems.

Holland, M. M., & Prohaska, A. (2021). Gender effects across place: A multilevel investigation of gender, race/ethnicity, and region in sentencing. *Race and Justice, 11*, 91–112.

Hollin, C. R. (2017). Learning theory. In A. Brisman, E. Carrabine, & N. South (Eds.), *The Routledge companion to criminological theory and concepts* (pp. 42–45). New York: Routledge.

Holloway, K., Bennett, T. H., & Farrington, D. P. (2008). *Effectiveness of treatment in reducing drug-related crime*. Stockholm, Sweden: National Council on Crime Prevention.

Holsinger, A. M., Lowenkamp, C. T., & Latessa, E. J. (2006). Exploring the validity of the Level of Service Inventory-Revised with Native American offenders. *Journal of Criminal Justice, 34*, 331–337.

Holsinger, A. M., Lowenkamp, C. T., Latessa, E. J., Serin, R., Cohen, T. H., Robinson, C. R., … Vanbenschoten, S. (2018). A rejoinder to Dressel and Farid: New study finds computer algorithm is more accurate than humans at predicting arrest and as good as a group of 20 lay experts. *Federal Probation, 82*, 50–55.

Homel, R. (2014). Justice reinvestment as a global phenomenon. *Victims and Offenders, 9*, 6–12.

Honegger, L. N. (2015). Does the evidence support the case for mental health courts? A review of the literature. *Law and Human Behavior, 39*, 478–488.

Honig, W. K. (1966). *Operant behavior: Areas of research and application*. East Norwalk, CT: Appleton-Century-Crofts.

Hooten, E. A. (1939). *Crime and the man*. Cambridge, MA: Harvard University Press.

Hoppe, S. J., Zhang, Y., Hayes, B. E., & Bills, M. A. (2020). Mandatory arrest for domestic violence and repeat offending: A meta-analysis. *Aggression and Violent Behavior, 53*, 101430.

Hostinar, C. E., & Miller, G. E. (2019). Protective factors for youth confronting economic hardship: Current challenges and future avenues in resilience research. *American Psychologist, 74*, 641–652.

Houser, K. A., Saum, C. A., & Hiller, M. L. (2019). Mental health, substance abuse, co-occurring disorders, and 3-year recidivism of felony parolees. *Criminal Justice and Behavior, 46*, 1237–1254.

Howard, M. V. A., & van Doorn, G. (2018). Within-treatment change in antisocial attitudes and reoffending in a large sample of custodial and community offenders. *Law and Human Behavior, 42*, 321–335.

Howell, J. C., & Lipsey, M. W. (2012). Research-based guidelines for juvenile justice programs. *Justice Research and Policy, 14*, 17–34.

Hsu, S. H., & Marlatt, G. A. (2011). Relapse prevention in substance use. In D. B. Cooper (Ed.), *Practice in mental health-substance use* (pp. 203–217). London, England: Radcliffe Publishing.

Hubbard, R. (2019). Will the ASA's efforts to improve statistical practice be successful? Some evidence to the contrary. *The American Statistician, 73*, S1, 31–35.

Huey, S. J., Jr., Lewine, G., & Rubenson, M. (2016). A brief review and meta-analysis of gang intervention trials in North America. In C. L. Maxson & F.-A. Esbenson (Eds.), *Gang transitions and transformations in an international context* (pp. 217–233). Switzerland: Springer.

Hummer, D. (2020). United States Bureau of Prisons' response to the COVID-19 pandemic. *Victims & Offenders, 15*, 1262–1276.

Hunt, M. (1997). *How science takes stock: The story of meta-analysis*. Washington DC: The Russell Sage Foundation.

Hunt, D. E., & Hardt, R. H. (1965). Developmental stage, delinquency, and differential treatment. *Journal of Research in Crime and Delinquency, 2*, 20–31.

Hunt, G. M., & Azrin, N. H. (1973). A community-reinforcement approach to alcoholism. *Behavior Research and Therapy, 11*, 91–104.

Hunter, J. E., & Schmidt, F. L. (1996). Cumulative research knowledge and social policy formulation: The critical role of meta-analysis. *Psychology, Public Policy, and Law, 2*, 324–347.

Hyde, J. S. (2005). The gender similarities hypothesis. *American Psychologist, 60*, 581–592.

Ike, N. (2000). Current thinking on XYY syndrome. *Psychiatric Annals, 30*, 91–95.

Irvin, J. E., Bowers, C. A., Dunn, M. E., & Wang, M. C. (1999). Efficacy of relapse prevention: A meta-analytic review. *Journal of Consulting and Clinical Psychology, 67*, 563–570.

Ito, T. A., Miller, N., & Pollock, V. E. (1996). Alcohol and aggression: A meta-analysis on the moderating effects of inhibitory cues, triggering events, and self-focused attention. *Psychological Bulletin, 120,* 60–82.

Jacobs, P. A., Brunton, P., Melville, H. M., Brittain, R. P., & McClermont, W. F. (1965). Aggressive behavior, mental subnormality and the XYY male. *Nature, 208,* 1351–1352.

Jacobsen, S. K., & Zaatut, A. (2022). Quantity or quality? Assessing the role of household structure and parent-child relationship in juvenile delinquency. *Deviant Behavior, 43,* 30–43.

Jaffe, S. R., Belsky, J., Harrington, H., Caspi, A., & Moffitt, T. E. (2006). When parents have a history of conduct disorder: How is the caregiving environment affected? *Journal of Abnormal Psychology, 115,* 309–319.

Jaffe, S. R., Moffitt, T. E., Caspi, A., & Taylor, A. (2003). Life with (or without) father: The benefits of living with two biological parents depend on the father's antisocial behavior. *Child Development, 74,* 109–126.

James, C., Stams, G. J. J. M., Asscher, J. J., De Roo, A. K., & van der Laan, P. H. (2013). Aftercare programs for reducing recidivism among juvenile and young adult offenders: A meta-analytic review. *Clinical Psychology Review, 33,* 263–274.

Jarvik, L. F., Klodin, V., & Matsuyama, S. S. (1973). Human aggression and the extra Y chromosome. *American Psychologist, 28,* 674–682.

Jean-Richard-dit-Bressel, P., Killcross, S., & McNally, G. P. (2018). Behavioral and neurobiological mechanisms of punishment: Implications for psychiatric disorders. *Neuropsychopharmacology, 43,* 1639–1650.

Jennings, W. G., Richards, T. N., Smith, M. D., Bjerregaard, B., & Fogel, S. J. (2014). A critical examination of the "White victim effect" and death penalty decision-making from a propensity score matching approach: The North Carolina experience. *Journal of Criminal Justice, 42,* 384–398.

Jessor, R., & Jessor, S. L. (1977). *Problem behavior and psychosocial development: A longitudinal study of youth.* New York, NY: Academic Press.

Johansson, A., Rötkönen, N., & Jern, P. (2021). Is the association between childhood maltreatment and aggressive behavior mediated by hostile attribution bias in women? A discordant twin and sibling study. *Aggressive Behavior, 47,* 28–37.

Johnson, L., & Stylianou, A. M. (2022). Coordinated community responses to domestic violence: A systematic review of the literature. *Trauma, Violence, & Abuse, 23,* 506–522.

Johnston, T. M., Brezina, T., & Crank, B. R. (2019). Agency, self-efficacy, and desistance from crime: An application of social cognitive theory. *Journal of Developmental and Life-Course Criminology, 5,* 60–85.

Jones, N. J., Brown, S. L, Robinson, D., & Frey, D. (2015). Incorporating strengths into quantitative assessments of criminal risk for adult offenders: The Service Planning Instrument. *Criminal Justice and Behavior, 42,* 321–338.

Joseph, J. J., & Rembert, D. A. (2022). Exploring psychopathy's relationship with youth gang membership in males and females. *Women & Criminal Justice, 32,* 537–555.

Jotangia, A., Rees-Jones, A., Gudjonsson, G. H., & Young, S. (2015). A multi-site controlled trial of the R&R2MHP cognitive skills program for mentally disordered female offenders. *International Journal of Offender Therapy and Comparative Criminology, 59,* 539–559.

Joyner, B., & Beaver, K. M. (2022). Unpacking the association between corporal punishment and criminal involvement. *Criminal Justice and Behavior, 49,* 1845–1863.

Juarez, T., & Howard, M. V. A. (2022). Self-reported change in antisocial attitudes and reoffending among a sample of 2,337 males convicted of violent offenses. *Criminal Justice and Behavior, 49,* 3–19.

Juarros-Basterretxea, J., Herrero, J., Fernández-Suárez, A., Pérez, B., & Rodríguez-Díaz, F. J. (2018). Are generalist batterers different from generally extra-family violent men? A study among imprisoned male violent offenders. *European Journal of Psychology Applied to Legal Context, 10,* 8–14.

Jung, S., & Himmen, M. K. (2022). A field study on the police use of the Ontario Domestic Assault Risk Assessment (ODARA). *Journal of Threat Assessment and Management, 9,* 204–217.

Junger, M., Greene, J., Schipper, R., Hesper, F., & Estourgie, V., & Junger, M. (2013). Parental criminality, family violence and intergenerational transmission of crime within a birth cohort. *European Journal of Criminal Policy Research, 19*, 117–133.

Kaeble, D. (2021). Probation and parole in the United States, 2020. U.S. Department of Justice, Bureau of Justice Statistics, December.

Kajonius, P. L., & Johnson, J. (2018). Sex differences in 30 facets of the five factor model of personality in the large public (*N* = 320,128). *Personality and Individual Differences, 129*, 126–130.

Kang, T. (in press). The lost scrolls of the correctional bible: Before the Risk-Need-Responsivity model. In P. Magaletta, M. Ternes, & M. Patry (Eds.), *The history and future of correctional psychology*. New York: Springer.

Kang, T., Tanner, J., & Wortley, S. (2018). Same routines, different effects: Gender, leisure, and young offending. *Justice Quarterly, 35*, 1030–1072.

Kapala-Sibley, D. C., Olino, T., Durbin, E., Dyson, M. W., & Klein, D. N. (2018). The stability of temperament from early childhood to early adolescence: A multi-method, multi-informant examination. *European Journal of Personality, 32*, 128–145.

Karberg, J. C., & James, D. J. (2005). *Substance dependence, abuse, and treatment of jail inmates, 2000*. Washington, DC: Bureau of Justice Statistics.

Katsiyannis, A., Whitford, D. K., Zhang, D., & Gage, N. A. (2018). Adult recidivism in United States: A meta-analysis 1994–2015. *Journal of Child and Family Studies, 27*, 686–696.

Kavish, N., & Boutwell, B. (2018). The unified crime theory and the social correlates of crime and violence: Problems and solutions. *Journal of Criminal Psychology, 8*, 287–301.

Keller, J., & Wagner-Steh, K. (2005). A Guttman scale for empirical prediction of level of domestic violence. *Journal of Forensic Psychology Practice, 5*, 37–48.

Kelley, S. E., Edens, J. F., Mowle, E. N., Penson, B. N., & Rulseh, A. (2019). Dangerous, depraved, and death-worthy: A meta-analysis of the correlates of perceived psychopathy in jury simulation studies. *Journal of Clinical Psychology, 75*, 627–643.

Kelly, J. F., Abry, A., Ferri, M., & Humphreys, K. (2020). Alcoholics Anonymous and 12-step facilitation treatments for alcohol use disorder: A distillation of a 2020 Cochrane Review for clinicians and policy makers. *Alcohol and Alcoholism, 55*, 641–651.

Kelly, J. F., Magill, M., & Stout, R. L. (2009). How do people recover from alcohol dependence? A systematic review of the research on mechanisms of behavior change in Alcoholics Anonymous. *Addiction Research & Theory, 17*, 236–259.

Kelly, L. C., Spencer, C. M., Keilhotz, B., McAllister, P., & Stith, S. M. (2022). Is separate the new equal? A meta-analytic review of correlates of intimate partner violence victimization for Black and White women in the United States. *Family Process, 61*, 1473–1488.

Kemshall, H. (2019). *Risk in probation practice*. London: Routledge.

Kennealy, P. J., Skeem, J. L., Manchak, S. M., & Eno Louden, J. (2012). Firm, fair, and caring officer-offender relationships protect against supervision failure. *Law and Human Behavior, 36*, 496–505.

Kennealy, P. J., Skeem, J. L., Walters, G. D., & Camp, J. (2010). Do core interpersonal and affective traits of the PCL-R psychopathy interact with antisocial behavior and disinhibition to predict violence? *Psychological Assessment, 22*, 569–580.

Kim, B., Wang, X., & Cheon, H. (2019). Examining the impact of ecological contexts on gender disparity in federal sentencing. *Justice Quarterly, 36*, 466–502.

Kim, C., & Schmuhl, M. (2021). Assessment of research on intimate partner violence (IPV) among sexual minorities in the United States. *Trauma, Violence, & Abuse, 22*, 766–776.

King, C. M., & Heilbrun, K. (2021). Effects of criminogenic risk-needs assessment feedback during prerelease correctional rehabilitation. *Criminal Justice and Behavior, 48*, 575–595.

King, R. S., Mauer, M., & Young, M. C. (2005). *Incarceration and crime: A complex relationship*. Washington, DC: The Sentencing Project.

Kingston, D. A., & Olver, M. E. (2018). Psychometric examination of treatment change among mentally disordered offenders: A risk-needs analysis. *Criminal Justice and Behavior, 45*, 153–172.

Kingston, D. A., Olver, M. E., McDonald, J., & Cameron, C. (2018). A eneraliza controlled trial of a cognitive skills programme for offenders with mental illness. *Criminal Behaviour and Mental Health, 28,* 369–382.

Kirby, B. C. (1954). Measuring effects of treatment of criminals and delinquents. *Sociology and Social Research, 38,* 368–374.

Kivetz, R., & Zheng, Y. (2006). Determinants of justification and self-control. *Journal of Experimental Psychology: General, 135,* 572–587.

Klag, S., O'Callaghan, F., & Creed, P. (2005). The use of legal coercion in the treatment of substance abusers: An overview and critical analysis of thirty years of research. *Substance Use & Misuse, 40,* 1777–1795.

Kleiman, M. A. R., Kilmer, B., & Fisher, D. T. (2014). Response to Stephanie A. Duriez, Francis T. Cullen, and Sarah M. Manchak: Theory and evidence on the swift-certain-fair approach to enforcing conditions of community supervision. *Federal Probation, 78,* 71–74.

Klein, A. R., & Crowe, A. (2008). Findings from an outcome examination of Rhode Island's Specialized Domestic Violence Probation Supervision Program: Do specialized supervision programs of batterers reduce reabuse? *Violence Against Women, 14,* 226–246.

Klein, N. C., Alexander, J. F., & Parsons, B. V. (1977). Impact of family systems intervention on recidivism and sibling delinquency: A model of primary prevention and program evaluation. *Journal of Consulting and Clinical Psychology, 3,* 469–474.

Kluckow, R., & Zeng, Z. (2022). *Correctional populations in the United States, 2020–Statistical tables.* Washington: Bureau of Justice Statistics.

Koegl, C. J., & Farrington, D. P. (2021). Estimating the monetary cost of risk factors for crime in boys using the EARL-20B. *Psychological Services, 18,* 441–453.

Koehler, J. A., Humphreys, D. K., Akoensi, T. D., Sáncehez de Ribera, O., & Lösel, F. (2014). A systematic review and meta-analysis on the effects of European drug treatment programs on reoffending. *Psychology, Crime, & Law, 20,* 584–602.

Koehler, J. A., Lösel, F., Akoensi, T. D., & Humphreys, D. K. (2013). A systematic review and meta-analysis of the effects of young offender treatment programs in Europe. *Journal of Experimental Criminology, 9,* 19–43.

Koetzle Shaffer, D. (2011). Looking inside the black box of drug courts: A meta-analytic review. *Justice Quarterly, 28,* 493–521.

Koh, L. L., Day, A., Klettke, B., Daffern, M., & Chu, C. M. (2020). The predictive validity of youth violence risk assessment tools: A systematic review. *Psychology, Crime & Law, 26,* 776–796.

Kohlberg, L. (1958). *The development of modes of moral thinking and choice in the years ten to sixteen.* Unpublished doctoral dissertation, University of Chicago, IL.

Kohlberg, L., & Candee, D. (1984). The relationship of moral judgment to moral action. In L. Kohlberg (Ed.), *Essays in moral development, Vol. 2: The psychology of moral development* (pp. 498–581). New York, NY: Harper & Row.

Kopala-Sibley, D. C., Olino, T., Durbin, E., Dyson, M. W., & Klein, D. N. (2018). The stability of temperament from early childhood to early adolescence: A multi-method, multi-informant examination. *European Journal of Personality, 32,* 128–145.

Korecki, J. R., Schwebel, F. J., Votaw, V. R., & Witkiewitz, K. (2020). Mindfulness-based programs for substance use disorders: A systematic review of manualized treatments. *Substance Abuse Treatment, Prevention, and Policy, 15,* Article 51.

Kourti, A., Stavridou, A., Panagouli, E., Psaltopoulou, T., Spiliopoulou, C., Tsolia, M., … Tsitsika, A. (2023). Domestic violence during the COVID-19 pandemic: A systematic review. *Trauma, Violence, & Abuse, 24,* 719–745.

Kovera, M. B. (2019). Racial disparities in the criminal justice system: Prevalence, causes, and a search for solutions. *Journal of Social Issues, 75*(4), 1139–1164.

Krahé, B. (2021). *The social psychology of aggression* 3rd ed. New York: Routledge.

Kraus, S. J. (1995). Attitudes and the prediction of behavior: A meta-analysis of the empirical literature. *Personality and Social Psychology Bulletin, 21,* 58–75.

Kreager, D. A., Matseuda, R. L., & Erosheva, E. A. (2010). Motherhood and criminal desistance in disadvantaged neighborhoods. *Criminology, 48,* 221–258.

Kreager, D. A, Schaefer, D. R., Davidson, K. M., Zajac, G., Haynie, D. L., & De Leon, G. (2019). Evaluating peer-influence processes in a prison-based therapeutic community: A dynamic network approach. *Drug and Alcohol Dependence, 203*, 3–18.

Krebs, P., Norcross, J. C., Nicholson, J. M., & Prochaska, J. O. (2018). Stages of change and psychotherapy outcomes: A review and meta-analysis. *Journal of Clinical Psychology, 74*, 1964–1979.

Kroese, J., Bernasco, W., Liefbroer, A. C., & Rouwendal, J. (2021). Growing up in single-parent families and the criminal involvement of adolescents: A systematic review. *Psychology, Crime & Law, 27*, 61–75.

Kroner, D. G., & Derrick, B. (2022). The Council of State Governments Justice Center approach to increasing risk-level consistency in the application of risk assessment instruments. *Assessment, 29*, 169–180.

Kroner, D. G., & Hanson, R. K. (2023). Measuring what matters: Standardized risk levels for criminal recidivism risk. In G. Liell, L. Jones, & M. Fisher (Eds.), *Challenging bias in forensic psychological assessment and testing—Theoretical and practical approaches to working with diverse populations* (pp. 95–110). New York: Routledge.

Kroner, D. G., & Yessine, A. K. (2013). Changing risk factors that impact recidivism: In search of mechanisms of change. *Law and Human Behavior, 37*, 321–336.

Kropp, P. R., & Gibas, A. (2021). The Spousal Assault Risk Assessment guide. In K. S. Douglas & R. K. Otto (Eds.), *Handbook of violence risk assessment* 2nd ed. (pp. 388–409). New York: Routledge.

Kropp, P. R., Hart, S. D., Webster, C. D., & Eaves, D. (1995). *Manual for the Spousal Assault Risk Assessment Guide*, 2nd ed. Vancouver: British Columbia Institute of Family Violence.

Krueger, R. F., Moffitt, T. E., Caspi, A., Bleske, A., & Silva, P. A. (1998). Assortative mating for antisocial behavior: Developmental and methodological implications. *Behavior Genetics, 28*, 173–186.

Kruger, D. J., & Fisher, M. L. (2005). Males identify and respond adaptively to mating strategies of other men. *Sexualities, Evolution, and Gender, 7*, 233–243.

Kruis, N. E., Seo, C., & Kim, B. (2020). Revisiting the empirical status of social learning theory and substance use: A systematic review and meta-analysis. *Substance Use & Misuse, 55*, 666–683.

Kruttschnitt, C. (2016). The politics, and place, of gender in research on crime. *Criminology, 54*, 8–29.

Kuhns, J. B., Exum, M. L., Clodfelter, T. A., & Bottia, M. C. (2014). The prevalence of alcohol-involved homicide offending: A meta-analytic review. *Homicide Studies, 18*, 251–270.

Lab, S. P., & Whitehead, J. T. (1990). From 'Nothing Works' to 'The Appropriate Works': The latest stop on the search for the secular grail. *Criminology, 28*, 405–417.

Labrecque, R. M., Schweitzer, M., & Smith, P. (2013). Probation and parole officer adherence to the core correctional practices: An evaluation of 755 offender-officer interactions. *Advancing Practice*, University of Cincinnati, 20–23.

Labrecque, R. M., Smith, P., Schweitzer, M., & Thompson, C. (2014). Targeting antisocial attitudes in community supervision using the EPICS model: An examination of change scores on the Criminal Sentiments Scale. *Federal Probation, 77*, 15–20.

Labrecque, R. M., & Viglione, J. (2021). The impact of community supervision officer training program on client outcomes: A propensity score modeling analysis by officer training dosage. *Criminal Justice and Behavior, 48*, 315–331.

Labrecque, R. M., Viglione, J., & Caudy, M. (2023). The impact of community supervision officer training programs on officer and client outcomes: A systematic review and meta-analysis. *Justice Quarterly, 40*, 587–611.

Lacourse, E., Nagin, D. S., Vitaro, F., Coté, S., Aresenault, L., & Tremblay, R. E. (2006). Prediction of early-onset deviant peer group affiliation: A 12-year longitudinal study. *Archives of General Psychiatry, 63*, 562–568.

Lai, V., Zeng, G., & Chu, C. M. (2016). Violent and nonviolent youth offenders: Preliminary evidence on group subtypes. *Youth Violence and Juvenile Justice, 14*, 313–329.

Lalumilère, M. L., Harris, G. T., Quinsey, V. L., & Rice, M. E. (2005). *The causes of rape*. Washington, DC: American Psychological Association.

Lambdin, C. (2012). Significance test as sorcery: Science is empirical—significance tests are not. *Theory & Psychology, 22,* 67–90.

Lamont, M. (2019). From 'having' to 'being': Self-worth and the current crisis of American society. *British Journal of Sociology, 70,* 660–707.

Lange, J. (1929). *Crime as destiny* (translated 1931). London, England: Unwin.

Langevin, R., & Curnoe, S. (2004). The use of pornography during the commission of sexual offenses. *International Journal of Offender Therapy and Comparative Criminology, 48,* 572–586.

Langevin, R., Lang, R. A., & Curnoe, S. (1998). The prevalence of sex offenders with deviant fantasies. *Journal of Interpersonal Violence, 13,* 315–327.

Lansford, J. E., Cappa, C., Putnick, D. L., Bornstein, M. H., Deater-Deckard, K., & Bradley, R. H. (2017). Change over time in parents' beliefs about and reported use of corporal punishment in eight countries with and without legal bans. *Child Abuse & Neglect, 71,* 44–55.

Lappan, S. N., Brown, A. W., & Hendricks, P. S. (2020). Dropout rates of in-person psychosocial substance use disorder treatments: A systematic review and meta-analysis. *Addiction, 115,* 201–217.

Larsen, R. R., Jalava, J., & Griffiths, S. (2020). Are Psychopathy Checklist (PCL) psychopaths dangerous, untreatable, and without conscience? A systematic review of the empirical evidence. *Psychology, Public Policy, and Law, 26,* 297–311.

Latessa, E. J., Cullen, F. T., & Gendreau, P. (2002). Beyond correctional quackery: Professionalism and the possibility of effective treatment. *Federal Probation, 66,* 43–49.

Latessa, E. J., Smith, P., Lemke, R., Makarios, M., & Lowenkamp, C. T. (2010). The creation and validation of the Ohio Risk Assessment system (ORAS). *Federal Probation, 74,* 16–22.

Latessa, E. J., Smith, P., Schweitzer, M., & Labrecque, R. M. (2013). *Evaluation of the effective practices in community supervision model (EPICS) in Ohio*. Available from author, University of Cincinnati.

Latimer, J., Dowden, C., & Muise, D. (2005). The effectiveness of restorative justice practices: A meta-analysis. *The Prison Journal, 85,* 127–144.

Lattimore, P. K., MacKenzie, D. L., Zajac, G., Dawes, D., Arsenault, E., & Tueller, S. (2016). Outcome findings from the HOPE demonstration field experiment: Is swift, certain, and fair an effective supervision strategy? *Criminology & Public Policy, 15,* 1103–1141.

Laub, J, H., & Sampson, R. J. (1991). The Sutherland-Glueck debate: On the sociology of criminological knowledge. *American Journal of Sociology, 96,* 1402–1440.

Laub, J. H., & Sampson, R. J. (2003). *Shared beginnings, divergent lives: Delinquent boys to age seventy*. Cambridge, MA: Harvard University Press.

Laub, J. H., & Sampson, R. J. (2011). Sheldon and Eleanor Glueck's unraveling juvenile delinquency study: The lives of 1,000 Boston men in the twentieth century. In F. T. Cullen, C. L. Jonson, A. J. Myer, & F. Adler (Eds.), *The origins of American criminology: Advances in criminological theory* (pp. 369–396). New Brunswick, NJ : Transaction.

Laub, J. H., & Vaillant, G. E. (2000). Delinquency and mortality: A 50-year follow-up study of 1,000 delinquent and nondelinquent boys. American Journal of Psychiatry, 157, 96–102.

Laukkanen, J., Ojansuu, U., Tolvanen, A., Alatupa, S., & Aunola, K. (2014). Child's difficult temperament and mothers' parenting style. *Journal of Child and Family Studies, 23,* 312–323.

Leary, M. R. (2005). Sociometer theory and the pursuit of relational value: Getting to the root of self-esteem. *European Review of social Psychology, 16,* 75–111.

Leary, M. R. (2021). Emotional reactions to threats to acceptance and belonging: A retrospective look at the big picture. *Australian Journal of Psychology, 73,* 4–11.

Leary, M. R., Twenge, J. M., & Quinlivan, E. (2006). Interpersonal rejection as a determinant of anger and aggression. *Personality and Social Psychology Review, 10,* 111–132.

Lee, S. C., Hanson, R. K., & Yoon, J. S. (2022). Predictive validity of Static-99R among 8,207 men convicted of sexual crimes in South Korea: A prospective field study. *Sexual Abuse*, Online First, November.

Lehrer, D. (2021). Trauma-informed care: The importance of understanding the incarcerated women. *Journal of Correctional Health, 27,* 121–126.

Leistico, A.-M., Salekin, R. T., DeCoster, J., & Rogers, R. (2008). A large-scale meta-analysis relating the Hare measures of psychopathy to antisocial conduct. *Law and Human Behavior, 32,* 28–45.

Leschied, A. W., Chiodo, D., Nowicki, E., & Rodger, S. (2008). Childhood predictors of adult criminality: A meta-analysis drawn from the prospective longitudinal literature. *Canadian Journal of Criminology and Criminal Justice, 50,* 435–467.

Leshem, R., & Weisburd, D. (2019). Epigenetics and hot spots of crime: Rethinking the relationship between genetics and criminal behavior. *Journal of Contemporary Criminal Justice, 35,* 186–204.

Letourneau, E. J., Brown, D. S., Fang, X., Hassan, A., & Mercy, J. A. (2018). The economic burden of child sexual abuse in the United States. *Child Abuse & Neglect, 79,* 413–422.

Letourneau, E. J., Roberts, T. W., Malone, L., & Sun, Y. (2023). No check we won't write: A report on the high cost of sex offender incarceration. *Sexual Abuse, 35,* 54–82.

Lewis, R. H., Connolly, E. J., Boisvert, D. L., & Boutwell, B. B. (2019). A behavioral genetic analysis of the cooccurrence between psychopathic personality traits and criminal behavior. *Journal of Contemporary Criminal Justice, 35,* 52–68.

Lickliter, R., & Honeycutt, H. (2003). Developmental dynamics: Toward a biologically plausible evolutionary psychology. *Psychological Bulletin, 129,* 819–835.

Lilienfeld, S. O., Watts, A. L., & Smith, S. F. (2015). Successful psychopathy: A scientific status report. *Current Directions in Psychological Science, 24,* 298–303.

Lilienfeld, S. O., Watts, A. L., Smith, S. F., Patrick, C. J., & Hare, R. D. (2018). Hervey Cleckley (1903–1984): Contributions to the study of psychopathy. *Personality Disorders: Theory, Research, and Treatment, 9,* 510–520.

Lilley, D. R. (2017). Did drug courts lead to increased arrest and punishment of minor drug offenses? *Justice Quarterly, 34,* 674–698.

Lilley, D. R., Stewart, M., & Tucker-Gail, K. (2020). Drug courts and net-widening in U.S. cities: A reanalysis using propensity score matching. *Criminal Justice Policy Review, 3,* 287–308.

Lin, Z., Jung, J., Goel, S., & Skeem, J. (2020). The limits of human predictions of recidivism. *Science Advances, 6,* 1–8.

Ling, S., & Raine, A. (2018). The neuroscience of psychopathy and forensic implications. *Psychology, Crime & Law, 24,* 296–312.

Ling, S., Raine, A., Yang, Y., Schug, R. A., Portnoy, J., & Ho, M.-H. R. (2019). Increased frontal lobe volume as a neural correlate of gray-collar offending. *Journal of Research in Crime and Delinquency, 56,* 303–336.

Ling, S., Umbach, R., & Raine, A. (2019). Biological explanations of criminal behavior. *Psychology, Crime & Law, 25,* 626–640.

Link, B. G., Andrews, H., & Cullen, F. T. (1992). The violent and illegal behavior of mental patients reconsidered. *American Sociological Review, 57,* 275–292.

Link, B., & Steuve, C. (1994). Psychotic symptoms and the violent/illegal behavior of mental patients compared to community controls. In J. Monahan & H. Steadman (Eds.), *Violence and mental disorder* (pp. 137–159). Chicago, IL: University of Chicago Press.

Link, E., & Lösel, F. (2021). "Mixed" sexual offending against both children and adults: An empirical comparison with individuals who exclusively offended against child or adult victims. *Criminal Justice and Behavior, 48,* 1616–1633.

Link, N. W. (2023). Paid your debt to society? Court-related financial obligations and community supervision during the first year after release from prison. *Corrections, 8,* 202–218.

Lipsey, M. W. (1999). Can rehabilitative programs reduce the recidivism of juvenile offenders? An inquiry into the effectiveness of practical programs. *Virginia Journal of Social Policy and the Law, 6,* 611–641.

Lipsey, M. W. (2009). The primary factors that characterize effective interventions with juvenile offenders: A meta-analytic overview. *Victims & Offenders, 4,* 124–147.

Lipsey, M. W., & Cullen, F. T. (2007). The effectiveness of correctional rehabilitation: A review of systematic reviews. *Annual Review of Law and Social Science, 3,* 297–320.

Lipsey, M. W., & Derzon, J. H. (1998). Predictors of violent or serious delinquency in adolescence and early adulthood: A synthesis of longitudinal research. In R. Loeber & D. P. Farrington (Eds.), *Serious and violent juvenile offenders: Risk factors and successful interventions* (pp. 86–105). Thousand Oaks, CA: Sage.

Lipsey, M. W., Landenberger, N. A., & Wilson, S. J. (2007). Effects of cognitive-behavioral programs for criminal offenders. *Campbell Systematic Reviews, 6.*

Lipsey, M. W., & Wilson, D. B. (1998). Effective intervention for serious juvenile offenders: A synthesis of research. In R. Loeber & D. P. Farrington (Eds.), *Serious and violent juvenile offenders: Risk factors and successful interventions* (pp. 313–345). Thousand Oaks, CA: SAGE.

Lipsey, M. W., Wilson, D. B., Cohen, M. A., & Derzon, J. H. (1997). Is there a causal relationship between alcohol use and violence? A synthesis of evidence. In M. Galanter (Ed.), *Recent developments in alcoholism, Vol. 13: Alcoholism and violence* (pp. 245–282). New York, NY: Plenum Press.

Lipton, D., Martinson, R., & Wilks, J. (1975). *The effectiveness of correctional treatment: A survey of treatment evaluation studies.* New York, NY: Praeger.

Litt, M. D., Kadden, R. M., Kabela-Cormier, E., & Petry, N. (2007). Changing network support for drinking: Initial findings from the network support project. *Journal of Consulting and Clinical Psychology, 75,* 542–555.

Litt, M. D., Kadden, R. M., Kabela-Cormier, E., & Petry, N. M. (2009). Changing network support for drinking: Network support project 2-year follow-up. *Journal of Consulting and Clinical Psychology, 77,* 229–242.

I, J. H., Pigott, T. D., Nielsen, K. H., Green, S. J., & Montgomery, O. L. K. (2021). Multisystemic Therapy® for social, emotional, and behavioural problems in youth age 10 to 17: An updated systematic review and meta-analysis. *Campbell Systematic Reviews, 17,* e1158.

Liu, H., Li, Y., & Guo, G. (2015). Gene by social-environment interaction for youth delinquency and violence: Thirty-nine aggression-related genes. *Social Forces, 93,* 881–903.

Liu, L., Visher, C. A., & Sun, D. (2021). Do released prisoners' perceptions of neighborhood condition affect reentry outcomes? *Criminal Justice Policy Review, 32,* 764–789.

Livanou, M., Furtado, V., Winsper, C., Silvester, A., & Singh, S. P. (2019). Prevalence of mental disorders and symptoms among incarcerated youth: A meta-analysis of 30 studies. *International Journal of Forensic Mental Health, 18,* 400–414.

Livingston, J. D., Chu, K., Milne, T., & Brink, J. (2015). Probationers mandated to receive forensic mental health services in Canada: Risks/needs, service delivery, and intermediate outcomes. *Psychology, Public Policy, and Law, 21,* 72–84.

Lockwood, S., Nally, J. M., Ho, T., & Knutson, K. (2012). The effect of correctional education on post-release employment and recidivism: A 5-year follow-up study in the state of Indiana. *Crime & Delinquency, 58,* 380–396.

Loeber, R., Byrd, A. L., & Farrington, D. P. (2015). Why developmental criminology is still coming of age: The influence of biological factors on within-individual change. In J. Morizot & L. Kazemian (Eds.), *The development of criminal and antisocial behavior* (pp. 65–73). New York: Springer.

Loeber, R., & Farrington, D. P. (2014). Age-crime curve. In G. J. N. Bruinsma & D. L. Weisburd (Eds.), *Encyclopedia of criminology and criminal justice.* New York, NY: Springer.

Loeber, R., Menting, B., Lynam, D. R., Moffitt, T. E., Stouthamer-Loeber, M., Stallings, R., … Pardini, D. (2012). Findings from the Pittsburgh Youth Study: Cognitive impulsivity and intelligence as predictors of the age-crime curve. *Child & Adolescent Psychiatry, 51,* 1136–1149.

Loeber, R., Pardini, D., Homish, D. L., Wei, E. H., Crawford, A. M., Farrington, D. P., … Rosenfeld, R. (2005). The prediction of violence and homicide in young men. *Journal of Consulting and Clinical Psychology, 73,* 1074.

Logan, C. H. (1972). Evaluation research in crime and delinquency: A reappraisal. *Journal of Criminal Law, Criminology and Police Science, 63,* 378–387.

Logan, M. W., & Link, N. W. (2019). Taking stock of drug courts: Do they work? *Victims & Offenders, 14*, 283–298.

Lombroso, C. (1895/2004). Criminal anthropology: Its origin and application. In D. M. Horton & K. E. Rich (Eds.), *The criminal anthropological writings of Cesare Lombroso published in the English language periodical literature during the late 19th and early 20th centuries* (pp. 63–82). Lewiston, NY: Edwin Mellen Press.

Lombroso, C., & Ferrero, W. (1895/1980). *The female offender*. Littleton, CO: Fred B. Rothman & Co.

Lopoo, E., Schiraldi, V., & Ittner, T. (2023). How little supervision can we have? *Annual Review of Criminology, 6*, 3.1–3.20.

Lösel, F. (2018). Evidence comes by replication, but needs differentiation: The reproducibility issue in science and its relevance to criminology. *Journal of Experimental Criminology, 14*, 257–278.

Lovins, B., Cullen, F. T., Latessa, E. J., & Jonson, C. L. (2018). Probation officer as a coach: Building a new professional identity. *Federal Probation, 82*, 13–19.

Lovins, B., Lowenkamp, C. T., & Latessa, E. J. (2009). Applying the risk principle to sex offenders: Can treatment make some offenders worse? *The Prison Journal, 89*, 344–357.

Lovins, B., Lowenkamp, C. T., Latessa, E. J., & Smith, P. (2007). Application of the risk principle to female offenders. *Journal of Contemporary Criminal Justice, 23*, 383–398.

Lowder, E. M., Morrison, M. M., Kroner, D. G., & Desmarais, S. L. (2019). Racial bias and LSI-R assessments in probation sentencing and outcomes. *Criminal Justice and Behavior, 46*, 210–233.

Lowder, E. M., Rade, C. B., & Desmarais, S. L. (2018). Effectiveness of mental health courts in reducing recidivism: A meta-analysis. *Psychiatric Services, 69*, 15–22.

Lowenkamp, C. T., Holsinger, A. M., & Cohen, T. H. (2015). PCRA revisited: Testing the validity of the federal Post Conviction Risk Assessment (PCRA). *Psychological Science, 12*, 149–157.

Lowenkamp, C. T., Holsinger, A., Robinson, C. R., & Alexander, M. (2014). Diminishing or durable effects of STARR? A research note on 24-month re-arrest rates. *Journal of Crime and Justice, 37*, 275–283.

Lowenkamp, C. T., Hubbar, D., Makarios, M. D., & Latessa, E. J. (2009). A quasi-experimental evaluation of Thinking for a Change: A "real world" application. *Criminal Justice and Behavior, 36*, 137–146.

Lowenkamp, C. T., Latessa E. J., & Holsinger, A. M. (2004). Empirical evidence on the importance of training and experience in using the Level of Service Inventory–Revised. *Topics in Community Corrections—2004*. Washington, DC: National Institute of Corrections.

Lowenkamp, C. T., Latessa, E. J., & Holsinger, A. M. (2006). The risk principle in action: What have we learned from 13,676 offenders and 97 correctional programs? *Crime & Delinquency, 52*, 77–93.

Lowenkamp, C. T., Latessa, E. J., & Smith, P. (2006). Does correctional program quality really matter? The impact of adhering to the principles of effective interventions. *Criminology & Public Policy, 5*, 575–594.

Lowenkamp, C. T., Makarios, M. D., Latessa, E. J., Lemke, R., & Smith, P. (2010). Community corrections facilities for juvenile offenders in Ohio: An examination of treatment integrity and recidivism. *Criminal Justice and Behavior, 37*, 695–708.

Luong, D., & Wormith, J. S. (2011). Applying risk/need assessment to probation practice and its impact on the recidivism of young offenders. *Criminal Justice and Behavior, 38*, 1177–1199.

Lutz, M., Zani, D., Fritz, M., Dudeck, M., & Franke, I. (2022). A review and comparative analysis of the risk-needs-responsivity, good lives, and recovery models in forensic psychiatric treatment. *Frontiers of Psychiatry, 13*, 988905.

Lynam, D. R. (1997). Pursuing the psychopath: Capturing the fledgling psychopath in the nomological net. *Journal of Abnormal Psychology, 106*, 425–438.

Lynam, D. R., & Derefinko, K. J. (2006). Psychopathy and personality. In C. J. Patrick (Ed.), *Handbook of psychopathy* (pp. 133–155). NY: Guildford.

Lysova, A., Dim, E. E., & Dutton, D. (2019). Prevalence and consequences of intimate partner violence in Canada as measured by the national victimization survey. *Partner Abuse, 10,* 199–221.

Maahs, J., & Pratt, T. C. (2017). "I hate these little turds!": Science, entertainment, and the enduring popularity of Scared Straight programs. *Deviant Behavior, 38,* 47–60.

MacKenzie, D. L., & Armstrong, G. S. (Eds.) (2004). *Correctional boot camps: Military basic training or a model for corrections?* Thousand Oaks, CA: Sage.

MacKenzie, D. L., Brame, R., McDowall, D., & Souryal, C. (1995). Boot camp prisons and recidivism in eight states. *Criminology, 33,* 327–357.

MacLeod, J. F., Grove, P. G., & Farrington, D. P. (2012). *Explaining criminal careers: Implications for justice policy.* Oxford, England: Oxford University Press.

Madill, A. (2015). Qualitative research is not a paradigm: Commentary on Jackson (2015) and Landrum and Garza (2015). *Qualitative Psychology, 2,* 214–220.

Magill, M., Ray, L., Kiluk, B., Hoadley, A., Bernstein, M., Tonigan, J. S., & Carroll, K. (2019). A meta-analysis of cognitive-behavioral therapy for alcohol or other drug use disorders: Treatment efficacy by contrast condition. *Journal of Consulting and Clinical Psychology, 87,* 1093–1105.

Magyar, M. S., Edens, J. F., Lilienfeld, S. O., Douglas, K. S., & Poythress Jr., N. G. (2011). Examining the relationship among substance abuse, negative emotionality and impulsivity across subtypes of antisocial and psychopathic substance abusers. *Journal of Criminal Justice, 39,* 232–237.

Maisel, N. C., Blodgett, J. C., Wilbourne, P. L., Humphreys, K., & Finney, J. W. (2013). Meta-analysis of naltrexone and acamprosate for treating alcohol use disorders: When are these medications most helpful? *Addiction, 108,* 275–293.

Makkai, T., & Payne, J. (2005). Illicit drug use and offending histories: A study of male incarcerated offenders in Australia. *Probation Journal, 52,* 153–168.

Malamuth, N. M. (2018). "Adding fuel to the fire"? Does exposure to non-consenting adult or to child pornography increase risk of sexual aggression? *Aggression and Violent Behavior, 41,* 74–89.

Mallion, J. S., Wood, J. L., & Mallion, A. (2020). Systematic review of 'Good Lives' assumptions and interventions. *Aggression and Violent Behavior, 55,* 101510.

Malouff, J. M., Rooke, S. E., & Schutte, N. S. (2008). The heritability of human behavior: Results of aggregating meta-analyses. *Current Psychology, 27,* 153–161.

Mannheim, H. (1965). *Comparative criminology.* Boston, MA: Houghton Mifflin.

Maria, N., Maria, P., Nikolaos, N., & Giorgos, A. (2017). Delusions and violent behavior: A short review of the recent literature. *Journal of Forensic Sciences and Criminal Investigation, 3,* 23–25.

Mariz, C., Cruz, O. S., & Moreira, D. (2022). The influence of environmental and genetic factors on the development of psychopathy: A systematic review. *Aggression and Violent Behavior, 62,* 101715.

Mark, V. H., & Ervin, F. R. (1970). *Violence and the brain.* Hagerstown, MD: Harper & Row.

Marlatt, A., & Gordon, J. (1980). Determinants of relapse: Implications for the maintenance of behavior change. In P. O. Davidson & S. M. Davidson (Eds.), *Behavioral medicine: Changing health lifestyles* (pp. 410–452). New York, NY: Bruner-Mazel.

Marlatt, G. A., & Witkiewitz, K. (2010). Update on harm-reduction policy and intervention research. *Annual Review of Clinical Psychology, 6,* 591–606.

Marsee, M. A., Frick, P. J., Barry, C. T., Kimonis, E. R., Centifanti, L. C., & Aucoin, K. J. (2014). Profiles of the forms and functions of self-reported aggression in three adolescent samples. *Development and Psychopathology, 26,* 705–720.

Marsh, K., Fox, C., & Sarmah, R. (2009). Is custody an effective sentencing option for the UK? Evidence from a meta-analysis of existing studies. *Probation Journal, 56,* 129–151.

Marshall, E. A., & Miller, H. A. (2019). Consistently inconsistent: A systematic review of the measurement of pornography use. *Aggression and Violent Behavior, 48,* 169–179.

Martin, K. D., & Zettler, H. R. (2021). An examination of officer tasks by officer-caseload type. *Criminal Justice Policy Review, 32,* 693–717.

Martin, M. S., Dorken, S. K., Wamboldt, A. D., & Wooten, S. E. (2012). Stopping the revolving door: A meta-analysis on the effectiveness of interventions for criminally involved individuals with major mental illness. *Law and Human Behavior, 36,* 1–12.

Martinson, R. (1974). What works?—Questions and answers about prison reform. *The Public Interest, 35,* 22–54. Reprinted in *Rehabilitation, Recidivism, and Research* (1976), *National Council on Crime and Delinquency.*

Martinson, R. (1979). New findings, new views: A note of caution regarding prison reform. *Hofstra Law Review, 7,* 243–258.

Maruna, R. K. Jr., & Fox, B. (2021). Belief in the code of the street and individual involvement in offending: A meta-analysis. *Youth Violence and Juvenile Justice, 19,* 227–247.

Maruna, S. (2001). *Making good: How ex-convicts reform and rebuild their lives.* Washington, DC: American Psychological Association.

Maruna, S., & Copes, H. (2005). What have we learned from five decades of neutralization research? *Crime and Justice, 32,* 221–320.

Maruna, S., & LeBel, T. P. (2010). The desistance paradigm in correctional practice: From programmes to lives. In F. McNeill, P. Raynor, & C. Trotter (Eds.), *Offender supervision: New directions in theory, research and practice* (pp. 65–87). Abingdon, England: Willan Publishing.

Maruna, S., & Liem, M. (2021). Where is this story going? A critical analysis of the emerging field of narrative criminology. *Annual Review of Criminology, 4,* 125–146.

Maruna, S., & Mann, R. (2019). *Reconciling "Desistance" and "What Works".* London, England: HM Inspectorate of Probation.

Matseuda, R. L., & Anderson, K. (1998). The dynamics of delinquent peers and delinquent behavior. *Criminology, 36,* 269–308.

Matson, J. L., & Kazdin, A. E. (1981). Punishment in behavior modification: Pragmatic, ethical, and legal issues. *Clinical Psychology Review, 1,* 197–210.

Matthews, B., & Minton, J. (2018). Rethinking one of criminology's "basic facts": The age-crime curve and the crime drop in Scotland. *European Journal of Criminology, 15,* 296–320.

Matthews, S. K., & Agnew, R. (2008). Extending deterrence theory: Do delinquent peers condition the relationship between perceptions of getting caught and offending? *Journal of Research in Crime and Delinquency, 45,* 91–118.

Matza, D. (1964). *Delinquency and drift* 2nd ed. New York, NY: Wiley.

Mayer, J. D. (2005). A tale of two visions: Can a new view of personality help integrate psychology? *American Psychologist, 60,* 294–307.

Mazerolle, P., & McPhedran, S. (2018). Specialization and versatility in offending. In D. P. Farrington, L. Kazemian, & A. R. Piquero (Eds.), *The Oxford handbook of developmental and life-course criminology* (pp. 49–69). New York: Oxford University Press.

McAllister, K., Mechanic, L. E., Amos, C., Aschard, H., Blair, I. A., Chatterjee, N., ... Witte, J. S. (2017). Current challenges and new opportunities for gene-environment interaction studies of complex diseases. *American Journal of Epidemiology, 186,* 753–761.

McCord, J. (1997). Discipline and the use of sanctions. *Aggression and Violent Behavior, 2,* 313–319.

McFarland, J., Cui, J., Rathbun, A., & Holmes, J. (2018). *Trends in high school dropout and completion rates in the United States 2018* (NCES 2019–117). Washington: US Department of Justice.

McGee, T. R., & Farrington, D. P. (2019). Developmental and life-course theories of crime. *Oxford research encyclopedia, criminology and criminal justice.* Oxford University Press.

McGee, T. R., Wickes, R., Corcoran, J., Bor, W., & Najman, J. (2011). Antisocial behavior: An examination of individual, family, and neighbourhood factors. *Trends & Issues in Crime and Criminal Justice, No. 410* (pp. 1–6). Australian Institute of Criminology.

McGue, M., Osler, M., & Christensen, K. (2010). Causal inference and observational research: The utility of twins. *Perspectives on Psychological Science, 5,* 546–556.

McGuire, J. (2004). *Understanding psychology and crime: Perspectives on theory and action.* Berkshire, UK: Open University Press.

McGuire, J., Evans, E., & Kane, E. (2021). What works in school-based interventions? A systematic review of evaluation research. In J. McGuire, E. Evans, & E. K. (Eds.), *Evidence-based policing and community crime prevention. Advances in preventing and treating violence and aggression* (pp. 161–227). Springer Nature Switzerland.

McLachlan, K., Gray, A. L., Roesch, R., Douglas, K. S., & Viljoen, J. L. (2018). An evaluation of the predictive validity of the SAVRY and YLS/CMI in justice-involved youth with fetal alcohol spectrum disorder. *Psychological Assessment, 30,* 1640–1651.

McLaughlin, J. L., & Kan, L. Y. (2014). Test usage in four common types of forensic mental health assessment. *Professional Psychology: Research and Practice, 45,* 128–135.

McIntosh, L. G., Janes, S., O'Rourke, S., & Thomson, L. D. (2021). Effectiveness of psychological and psychosocial interventions for forensic mental health inpatients: A meta-analysis. *Aggression and Violent Behavior, 58,* 101551.

McMurran, M. (2009). Motivational interviewing with offenders: A systematic review. *Legal and Criminological Psychology, 14,* 83–100.

McMurran, M. (2012). Individual-level interventions for alcohol-related violence: Expanding targets for inclusion in treatment programs. *Journal of Criminal Justice, 22,* 14–28.

McNeill, F., Farrall, S., Lightowler, C., & Maruna, S. (2012). Reexamining evidence-based practice in community corrections: Beyond "a confined view" of what works. *Justice Research and Policy, 14,* 35–60.

McPhail, I. V., & Olver, M. E. (2020). Interventions for pedohebephilic arousal in men convicted for sexual offenses against children: A meta-analytic review. *Criminal Justice and Behavior, 47,* 1319–1339.

Mead, N. L., Baumeister, R. F., Gino, F., Schweitzer, M. E., & Ariely, D. (2009). Too tired to tell the truth: Self-control resource depletion and dishonesty. *Journal of Experimental Social Psychology, 45,* 594–597.

Meade, B., & Steiner, B. (2010). The total effects of boot camps that house juveniles: A systematic review of the evidence. *Journal of Criminal Justice, 38,* 841–853.

Mears, D. P., & Cochran, J. C. (2018). Who goes to prison? In J. Wooldredge & P. Smith (Eds.), *Oxford handbook on prisons and imprisonment* (pp. 29–52). Oxford, UK: Oxford University Press.

Mednick, S. A. (1977). A bio-social theory of the learning of law-abiding behavior. In S. A. Mednick & K. O. Christiansen (Eds.), *Biosocial basis of criminal behavior* (pp. 1–8). New York, NY: Gardner.

Mednick, S. A., Gabrielli, W. F., & Hutchings, B. (1984). Genetic influences in criminal convictions: Evidence from an adoption cohort. *Science, 234,* 891–894.

Mednick, S. A., Gabrielli, W. F., & Hutchings, B. (1987). Genetic factors in the etiology of criminal behavior. In S. A. Mednick, T. E. Moffitt, & S. A. Stack (Eds.), *The causes of crime: New biological approaches* (pp. 74–91). Cambridge, England: Cambridge University Press.

Meehan, K. E. (2000). California's three-strikes law: The first six years. *Corrections Management Quarterly, 4,* 22–33.

Meehl, P. E. (1954). *Clinical versus statistical prediction: A theoretical analysis and a review of the evidence.* Minneapolis: University of Minnesota Press.

Meier, M. H., Slutske, W. S., Arndt, S., & Cadoret, R. J. (2008). Impulsive and callous traits are more strongly associated with delinquent behavior in higher risk neighborhoods among boys and girls. *Journal of Abnormal Psychology, 117,* 377–385.

Melde, C., & Esbensen, F.-A. (2013). Gangs and violence: Disentangling the impact of gang membership on the level and nature of offending. *Journal of Quantitative Criminology, 29,* 143–166.

Meldrum, R. C., Trucco, E. M., Cope, L. M., Zucker, R. A., & Heitzeg, M. M. (2018). Brain activity, low self-control, and delinquency: An fMRI study of at-risk adolescents. *Journal of Criminal Justice, 56,* 107–117.

Mellor, E., & Duff, S. (2019). The use of pornography and the relationship between pornography exposure and sexual offending in males: A systematic review. *Aggression and Violent Behavior, 46*, 116–126.

Mengeling, M. A., Booth, B. M., Turner, J. C., & Sadler, A. G. (2014). Reporting sexual assault in the military. *American Journal of Preventative Medicine, 47*, 17–25.

Mercer, N., Crocetti, E., Meeus, W., & Branje, S. (2018). An experimental investigation of the influence of deviant peers on own deviancy: A replication study. *Journal of Experimental Criminology, 14*, 429–438.

Merrin, G. J., Davis, J. P., Berry, D., & Espeiage, D. L. (2018). Developmental changes in deviant and violent behaviors from early to late adolescence: Associations with parental monitoring and peer deviance. *Psychology of Violence, 9*, 196–208.

Merton, R. K. (1938). Social structure and anomie. *American Sociological Review, 3*, 672–682.

Merton, R. K. (1957). *Social theory and social structure.* New York, NY: Free Press.

Messing, J. T., & Thaller, J. (2013). The average predictive validity of intimate partner violence risk assessment instruments. *Journal of Interpersonal Violence, 28*, 1537–1558.

Meyers, R. J., Roozen, H. G., & Smith, J. E. (2011). The community reinforcement approach: An update of the evidence. *Alcohol Research & Health, 33*, 380.

Mielke, M., & Farrington, D. P. (2021). School-based interventions to reduce suspension and arrest: A meta-analysis. *Aggression and Violent Behavior, 56*, Article 101518.

Mier, C., & Ladny, R. T. (2018). Does self-esteem negatively impact crime and delinquency? A meta-analytic review of 25 years of evidence. *Deviant Behavior, 39*, 1006–1022.

Miguel, P. M., Pereira, L. O., Silveira, P. P., & Meaney, M. J. (2019). Early environmental influences on the development of children's brain structure and function. *Developmental Medicine & Child Neurology, 61*, 1127–1133.

Miller, J., & Maloney, C. (2013), Practitioner compliance with risk/needs assessment tools: A theoretical and empirical assessment. *Criminal Justice and Behavior, 40*, 716–736.

Miller, J., & Palmer, K. (2020). Juvenile probation officer decision-making in a reforming state. *Criminal Justice and Behavior, 47*, 1136–1155.

Miller, J. D., & Lynam, D. R. (2001). Structural models of personality and their relation to antisocial behavior: A meta-analytic review. *Criminology, 39*, 765–792.

Miller, J. D., & Widiger, T. A. (2020). The Five-Factor Model of personality disorders. In C. W. Lejuez & K. L. Gratz (Eds.), *The Cambridge handbook of personality disorders* (pp. 145–160). New York: Cambridge University Press.

Miller, W. B. (1958). Lower class culture as a generating milieu of gang delinquency. *Journal of Social Issues, 14*, 5–19.

Miller, W. R., & Carroll, K. M. (2006). *Rethinking substance abuse: What the science shows, and what we should do about it.* New York, NY: Guilford.

Miller, W. R., & Rollnick, S. (2002). *Motivational interviewing: Preparing people for change.* New York, NY: Guilford.

Millon, T., & Davis, R. D. (1998). Ten subtypes of psychopathy. In T. Millon, E. Simonsen, M. Birket-Smith, & R. D. Davis (Eds.), *Psychopathy: Antisocial, criminal, and violent behavior* (pp. 161–170). NY: Guilford Press.

Mills, J. F., Kroner, D. G., & Hemmati, T. (2005). The Measures of Criminal Attitudes and Associates (MCAA): The prediction of general and violent recidivism. *Criminal Justice and Behavior, 31*(6), 717–733.

Mills, L. G., Barocas, B., & Ariel, B. (2013). The next generation of court-mandated domestic violence treatment: A comparison study of batterer intervention and restorative justice programs. *Journal of Experimental Criminology, 9*, 65–90.

Mischel, W. (1968). *Personality and assessment.* New York, NY: Wiley.

Mischel, W., & Shoda, Y. (2010). The situated person. In B. Mesquita, L. F. Barrett, & E. R. Smith (Eds.), *The mind in context* (pp. 149–173). New York, NY: Guilford Press.

Mitchell, K. L. (2017). State sentencing guidelines: A garden full of variety. *Federal Probation, 81*, 28–36.

Moffitt, T. E. (1990). The neuropsychology of juvenile delinquency. In M. Tonry & N. Morris (Eds.), *Crime and justice: A review of research*, Vol. *8* (pp. 99–169). Chicago, IL: University of Chicago Press.

Moffitt, T. E. (1993). 'Life-course-persistent' and 'adolescent-limited' antisocial behavior: A developmental taxonomy. *Psychological Review, 100*, 674–701.

Moffitt, T. E. (2003). Life-course-persistent and adolescence-limited antisocial behavior: A 10-year research review and a research agenda. In B. A. Lahey, T. E. Moffitt, & A. Caspi (Eds.), *Causes of conduct disorder and juvenile delinquency* (pp. 49–75). New York, NY: Guilford.

Moffitt, T. E. (2005). The new look of behavioral genetics in developmental psychopathology: Gene-environment interplay in antisocial behaviors. *Psychological Bulletin, 131*, 533–554.

Moffitt, T. E. (2006). A review of research on the taxonomy of life-course persistent versus adolescence-limited antisocial behavior. In F. T. Cullen, P. Wright, & K. R. Blevins (Eds.), *Taking stock: The status of criminological theory*. New Brunswick, NJ: Transaction.

Moffitt, T. E. (2018). Male antisocial behaviour in adolescence and beyond. *Nature Human Behavior, 2*, 177–186.

Moffitt, T. E., Arsenault, L., Belsky, D., Dickson, N., Hancox, R. J., Harrington, H., … Caspi, A. (2011). A gradient of childhood self-control predicts health, wealth, and public safety. *Proceedings of the National Academy of Sciences, 108*, 2693–2698.

Moffitt, T. E., Caspi, A., & Rutter, M. (2012). Measured gene-environment interactions in psychopathology. *Perspectives on Psychological Science, 1*, 5–27.

Moffitt, T. E., Lynam, D. R., & Silva, P. A. (1994). Neuropsychological tests predicting persistent male delinquency. *Criminology, 32*, 277–300.

Moffitt, T. E., Ross, S., & Raine, A. (2011). Crime and biology. In J. Q. Wilson & J. Petersilia (Eds.), *Crime and public policy* (pp. 53–86). Oxford: Oxford University Press.

Mokros, A., Hare, R. D., Neumann, C. S., Santtila, P., Habermeyer, E., & Nitschke, J. (2015). Variants of psychopathy in adult male offenders: A latent profile analysis. *Journal of Abnormal Psychology, 124*, 372–386.

Moore, A. A., Blair, J, R, Hettema, J. M., & Roberson-Nay, R. (2019). The genetic underpinnings of callous-unemotional traits: A systematic research review. *Neuroscience Biobehavioral Review, 100*, 85–97.

Moore, C. C., Hubbard, J., Morrow, M. T., Barhight, R. R., Lines, M. M., Sallee, M., & Hyde, C. T. (2018). The simultaneous assessment of and relations between children's sympathetic and parasympathetic psychophysiology and their reactive and proactive aggression. *Aggressive Behavior, 44*, 614–623.

Mora, V. J., & Decker, S. H. (2019). Street gangs. In R. D. Morgan (Ed.), *The Sage encyclopedia of criminal psychology* (pp. 1468–1471). Thousand Oaks, CA: Sage.

Moreira, D., Moreira, D. S., Oliveira, S., Ribeiro, P. H., Barbosa, F., Fávero, M., & Gomes, V. (2020). Relationship between adverse childhood experiences and psychopathy: A systematic review. *Aggression and Violent Behavior, 53*, 101452.

Morgan, R., Kroner, D., Mills, J. F., Bauer, R. L., & Serna, C. (2014). Treating justice involved persons with mental illness: Preliminary evaluation of a comprehensive treatment program. *Criminal Justice and Behavior, 41*, 902–916.

Morizot, J. (2015). The contribution of temperament and personality traits to criminal and antisocial behavior development and desistence. In J. Morizot & L. Kazemian (Eds.), *The development of criminal and antisocial behavior* (pp. 137–165). New York: Springer.

Morris, Z. S., Wooding, S., & Grant, J. (2011). The answer is 17 years, what is the question: Understanding time lags in translational research. *Journal of the Royal Society of Medicine, 104*, 510–520.

Motiuk, L. L., Bonta, J., & Andrews, D. A. (1990). *Dynamic predictive criterion validity in offender assessment*. Paper presented at the Canadian Psychological Association Annual Convention, Ottawa, Ontario, Canada, June.

Moule Jr., R. K., & Fox, B. (2021). Belief in the code of the street and individual involvement in offending: A meta-analysis. *Youth Violence and Juvenile Justice, 19*, 227–247.

Mullen, R., Arbiter, N., Plepler, C. R., & Bond, D. J. (2019). In-prison therapeutic communities in California. *Therapeutic Communities: The International Journal of Therapeutic Communities, 40*, 142–158.

Nafekh, M., & Motiuk, L. L. (2002). The Statistical Information on Recidivism–Revised 1 (SIR-R1) Report 126. Ottawa: Correctional Service of Canada.

Nagin, D. S., Cullen, F. T., & Jonson, C. L. (2009). Imprisonment and reoffending. In M. H. Tonry (Ed.), *Crime and Justice: A review of research*, Vol. *38* (pp. 115–200). Chicago, IL: University of Chicago Press.

Nascimento, A. M., Andrade, J., & de Castro Rodrigues, A. (2022). The psychological impact of restorative justice practices on victims of crimes—a systematic review. *Trauma, Violence, & Abuse*, Online First, April 22.

Navon, D., & Thomas, G. (2021). Screening before we know: Radical uncertainties in expanded prenatal genetics. *OBM Genetics, 5*, 1–12.

Neal, T. M. S., & Grisso, T. (2014). Assessment practices and expert judgment methods in forensic psychology and psychiatry: An international snapshot. *Criminal Justice and Behavior, 41*, 1406–1421.

Nellis, M. (2017). Electronic monitoring. In K. R. Kerley (Ed.), *The Encyclopedia of Corrections* (pp. 1–3). New York: John Wiley & Sons.

Netto, N. R., Carter, J. M., & Bonell, C. (2014). A systematic review of interventions that adopt the "Good Lives" approach to offender rehabilitation. *Journal of Offender Rehabilitation, 53*, 403–432.

Neumann, C. S., Schmitt, D. S., Carter, R., Embley, I., & Hare, R. D. (2012). Psychopathic traits in females and males across the globe. *Behavioral Sciences & the Law, 30*, 557–574.

Newcomb, M. D., & Loeb, T. B. (1999). Poor parenting as an adult problem behavior: General deviance, deviant attitudes, inadequate family support and bonding, or just bad parents? *Journal of Family Psychology, 13*, 175–193.

Newman, H. H., Freeman, F. N., & Holzinger, K. J. (1937). *Twins: A study of heredity and environment*. Chicago: University of Chicago Press.

Newsom, C., Favell, J. E., & Rincover, A. (1983). The side effects of punishment. In S. Axelrod & J. Apsche (Eds.), *The effects of punishment on human behavior* (pp. 285–316). New York, NY: Academic.

Newsome, J., & Cullen, F. T. (2017). The Risk-Need-Responsivity model revisited: Using biosocial criminology to enhance offender rehabilitation. *Criminal Justice and Behavior, 44*, 1030–1049.

Nicholls, T. L., Pritchard, M. M., Reeves, K. A., & Hilterman, E. (2013). Risk assessment in intimate partner violence: A systematic review of contemporary approaches. *Partner Abuse, 4*, 76–168.

Nikolašević, Ž, Dinić, B. M., Smederevac, S., Sadiković, S., Milovanović, I., Ignjatović, V. B., … Bosić, D. (2021). Common genetic basis of the five factor model facets and intelligence: A twin study. *Personality and Individual Differences, 175*, 110682.

Nivette, A. E., Zahnow, R., Aguilar, R., Ahven, A., Amram, S., Ariel, B., … Eisner, M. P. (2021). A global analysis of the impact of COVID-19 stay-at-home restrictions on crime. *Nature Human Behaviour, 5*, 868–877.

Northpointe. (2015). *Practitioner's guide to COMPAS core* (March 10).

Nuffield, J. (1982). *Parole decision-making in Canada*. Ottawa, Canada: Solicitor General of Canada.

Nunes, K. L., Hermann, C. A., Maimone, S., & Woods, M. (2015). Thinking clearly about violent cognitions: Attitudes may be distinct from other cognitions. *Journal of Interpersonal Violence, 30*, 1322–1347.

Oberweis, T., Gorislavsky, E., & Cannon, K. (2022). Campus climate surveys: Towards a unified approach to measuring campus rape and sexual assault. *Journal of Human Behavior in the Social Environment*, 1–15, Online First.

O'Connell, D., & Marcus, D. K. (2019). A meta-analysis of the association between psychopathy and sadism in forensic samples. *Aggression and Violent Behavior, 46,* 109–115.

Odgers, C. L., Caspi, A., Russell, M. A., Sampson, R. J., Arsenault, L., & Moffitt, T. E. (2012). Supportive parenting mediates widening neighborhood socioeconomic disparities in children's antisocial behavior from ages 5 to 12. *Developmental Psychopathology, 24,* 705–721.

O'Donnell, C. R., Lydgate, T., & Fo, W. S. O. (1971). The buddy system: Review and follow-up. *Child Behavior Therapy, 1,* 161–169.

Office of National Drug Control Policy. (2014). *2013 annual report arrestee drug abuse monitoring program II.* Washington, DC: Office of National Drug Control Policy.

Ogilvie, J. M., Stewart, A. L., Chan, R. C. K., & Shum, D. (2011). Neuropsychological measures of executive function and antisocial behavior: A meta-analysis. *Criminology, 49,* 1063–1107.

Ogloff, J. R. P. (2006). Psychopathy/antisocial personality disorder conundrum. *Australian and New Zealand Journal of Psychiatry, 40,* 519–528.

O'Hagan, H. R., Brown, S. L., Jones, N. J., & Skilling, T. A. (2019). The reliability and validity of the measure of criminal attitudes and associates and the Pride in Delinquency scale in a mixed sex sample of justice-involved youth. *Criminal Justice and Behavior, 46,* 751–769.

Olaghere, A., Wilson, D. B., & Kimbrell, C. S. (2021). Trauma-informed interventions for at-risk and justice-involved youth: A meta-analysis. *Criminal Justice and Behavior, 48,* 1261–1277.

O'Leary, K. D., Tintle, N., & Bromet, E. (2014). Risk factors of physical violence against partners in the U.S. *Psychology of Violence, 4,* 65–77.

Oleson, J. C. (2016). The new eugenics: Black hyper-incarceration and human abatement. *Social Sciences, 5,* 66.

Oleson, J. C., VanBenschoten, S., Robinson, C., Lowenkamp, C. T., & Holsinger, A. M. (2012). Actuarial and clinical assessment of criminogenic needs: Identifying supervision priorities among federal probation officers. *Journal of Crime and Justice, 35,* 239–248.

Olver, M. E., & Kingston, D. A. (2019). Discrimination and calibration properties of the Level of Service Inventory–Ontario Revision in a correctional mental health sample. *Criminal Justice and Behavior, 46,* 5–23.

Olver, M. E., Marshall, L. E., Marshall, W. L., & Nicholaichuk, T. P. (2020). A long-term outcome assessment of the effects on subsequent reoffense rates of a prison-based CBT/RNR sex offender treatment program with strength-based elements. *Sexual Abuse, 32,* 127–153.

Olver, M. E., Mundt, J. C., Hogan, N. R., Coupland, R. B. A., Eggert, J. E., Higgs, T., … Wong, S. C. P. (2022). Assessing dynamic violence risk: Common language risk levels and recidivism rates for the Violence Risk Scale. *Psychological Assessment, 34,* 528–545.

Olver, M. E. Neumann, C. S., Sewall, L. A., Lewis, K., Hare, R. D., & Wong, S. C. P. (2018). A comprehensive examination of the psychometric properties of the Hare Psychopathy Checklist-Revised in a Canadian multisite sample of indigenous and non-indigenous offenders. *Psychological Assessment, 30,* 779–792.

Olver, M. E., Neumann, C. S., Wong, S. C., & Hare, R. D. (2013). The structural and predictive properties of the Psychopathy Checklist-Revised in Canadian Aboriginal and non-Aboriginal offenders. *Psychological Assessment, 25,* 167–179.

Olver, M. E., Stockdale, K. C., & Wormith, J. S. (2009). Risk assessment with young offenders: A meta-analysis of three assessment measures. *Criminal Justice and Behavior, 36,* 329–353.

Olver, M. E., Stockdale, K. C., & Wormith, J. S. (2011). A meta-analysis of the predictors of offender treatment attrition and its relationship to recidivism. *Journal of Consulting and Clinical Psychology, 79,* 6–21.

Olver, M. E., Stockdale, K. C., & Wormith, J. S. (2014). Thirty years of research on the Level of Service scales: A meta-analytic examination of predictive accuracy and sources of variability. *Psychological Assessment, 26,* 156–176.

Olver, M. E., & Wong, S. C. P. (2011). A comparison of static and dynamic assessment of sexual offender risk and need in a treatment context. *Criminal Justice and Behavior, 38,* 113–126.

Omori, M. K., & Turner, S. F. (2015). Assessing the cost of electronically monitoring high-risk sex offenders. *Crime & Delinquency, 61,* 873–894.

Orton, L. C., Hogan, N. R., & Wormith, S. J. (2021). An examination of the professional override of the Level of Service Inventory-Ontario revision. *Criminal Justice and Behavior, 48,* 421–441.

Osofsky, J. (2003). Prevalence of children's exposure to domestic violence and child maltreatment: Implications for prevention and intervention. *Clinical Child and Family Psychology Review, 6,* 161–170.

Ostermann, M., & Herrschaft, B. A. (2013). Validating the Level of Service Inventory-Revised: A gendered perspective. *The Prison Journal, 93,* 291–312.

Ostermann, M., & Salerno, L. M. (2016). The validity of the Level of Service Inventory–Revised at the intersection of race and gender. *The Prison Journal, 96,* 554–575.

Otto, R. K., & Douglas, K. S. (Eds.) (2010). *Handbook of violence risk assessment.* New York, NY: Routledge.

Painter-Davis, N., & Ulmer, J. T. (2020). Discretion and disparity under sentencing guidelines revisited: The interrelationship between structured sentencing alternatives and guideline decision-making. *Journal of Research in Crime and Delinquency, 57,* 263–293.

Palmer, T. (1975). Martinson revisited. *Journal of Research in Crime and Delinquency, 12,* 133–152.

Pan, Y., Lin, X., Liu, J., Zhang, S., Zeng, X., Chen, F., & Wu, J. (2021). Prevalence of childhood sexual abuse among women using the Childhood Trauma Questionnaire: A worldwide meta-analysis. *Trauma, Violence, & Abuse, 22,* 1181–1191.

Pappas, L. N., & Dent, A. L. (2023). The 40-year debate: A meta-review on what works for juvenile offenders. *Journal of Experimental Criminology, 19,* 1–30.

Paquette, S., Fortin, F., & Perkins, D. (2020). Online sexual offenders: Typologies, assessment, treatment, and prevention. In J. Proulx, F. Cortoni, L. A. Craig, & E. J. Letourneau (Eds.), *The Wiley handbook of what works with sexual offenders: Contemporary perspectives in theory, assessment, treatment, and prevention* (pp. 311–326). Hoboken, NJ: John Wiley & Sons.

Parent, G., Bilodeau, M. P., Laurier, C., & Guay, J. P. (2023). Clinical overrides with the YLS/CMI: Predictive validity and associated factors. *Criminal Justice and Behavior, 50,* 101–117.

Parhar, K. K., Wormith, J. S., Derkzen, D. M., & Beauregard, A. M. (2008). Offender coercion in treatment: A meta-analysis of effectiveness. *Criminal Justice and Behavior, 35,* 1109–1135.

Parisi, A., Wilson, A. B., Villodas, M., Phillips, J., & Dohler, E. (2022). A systematic review of interventions targeting criminogenic risk factors among persons with serious mental illness. *Psychiatric Services, 73,* 897–909.

Park, S., & Kim, S. H. (2018). The power of family and community factors in predicting dating violence: A meta-analysis. *Aggression and Violent Behavior, 40,* 19–28.

Pashler, H., & Wagenmaker, E.-J. (2012). Editors' introduction to the special section on replicability in psychological science: A crisis of confidence? *Perspectives on Psychological Science, 7,* 528–530.

Paternoster, R., McGloin, J. M., Nguyen, H., & Thomas, K. J. (2013). The causal impact of exposure to deviant peers: An experimental investigation. *Journal of Research in Crime and Delinquency, 50,* 476–503.

Patterson, G. R. (1982). *Coercive family process.* Eugene, OR: Castalia.

Patterson, G. R. (2016). Coercion theory: The study of change. In T. J. Dishion & J. J. Snyder (Eds.), *The Oxford handbook of coercive relationship dynamics* (pp. 7–21). New York: Oxford University Press.

Patterson, G. R., & Yoerger, K. (1999). Intraindividual growth in covert antisocial behaviour: A necessary precursor to chronic juvenile and adult arrests? *Criminal Behaviour and Mental Health, 9,* 24–38.

Patrick, C. J. (Ed.) (2018). *Handbook of psychopathy.* New York: Guilford.

Patrick, C. J., Fowles, D. C., & Krueger, R. F. (2009). Triarchic conceptualization of psychopathy: Developmental origins of disinhibition. Boldness, and meanness. *Development and Psychopathology, 21,* 913–918.

Patrick, C. J., Perkins, E. R., & Joyner, K. (2019). Psychopathy, etiology of. In R. D. Morgan (Ed.), *The Sage encyclopedia of criminal psychology* (pp. 1181–1184). Thousand Oaks: Sage.

Payne, D. C., & Cornwell, B. (2007). Reconsidering peer influences on delinquency: Do less proximate contacts matter? *Journal of Quantitative Criminology, 23,* 127–149.

Peachy, D. E. (1989). The Kitchener experiment. In M. Wright & B. Galaway (Eds.), *Mediation and criminal justice: Victims, offenders and community* (pp. 14–26). Newbury Park, CA: Sage.

Pearce, S., & Pickard, H. (2012). How therapeutic communities work: Specific factors related to positive outcomes. *International Journal of Social Psychiatry, 59,* 636–645.

Pearson, F. S., Prendergast, M. L., Podus, D., Vazan, P., Greenwell, L., & Hamilton, Z. (2012). Meta-analysis of seven of NIDA's Principles of Drug Addiction Treatment. *Journal of Substance Abuse Treatment, 43,* 1–11.

Pederson, K. M., & Miller, H. A. (2022). Application of the risk principle in the supervision and treatment of individuals who have sexually offended: Does "oversupervision" matter? *Criminal Justice and Behavior, 49,* 350–370.

Pederson, S. D., Curley, E. J., & Collins, C. J. (2021). A systematic review of Motivational Interviewing to address substance use with justice-involved adults. *Substance Use & Misuse, 56,* 639–649.

Pemment, J. (2013). The neurobiology of antisocial personality disorder: The quest for rehabilitation and treatment. *Aggression and Violent Behavior, 18,* 79–82.

Perez-Fuentes, G., Olfson, M., Villegas, L., Morcillo, C., Wang, S., & Blanco, C. (2013). Prevalence and correlates of child sexual abuse: A national study. *Comprehensive Psychiatry, 54,* 16–27.

Perley-Robertson, B., Maaike Helmus, L., & Forth, A. (2019). Predictive accuracy of static risk factors for Canadian Indigenous offenders compared to non-Indigenous offenders: Implications for risk assessment scales. *Psychology, Crime & Law, 25,* 248–278.

Peters, J., Shackelford, T. K., & Buss, D. M. (2002). Understanding domestic violence against women: Using evolutionary psychology to extend the feminist functional analysis. *Violence and Victims, 17,* 255–264.

Peterson, J. K., Skeem, J., Kennealy, P., Bray, B., & Zvonkovic, A. (2014). How often and how consistently do symptoms directly precede criminal behavior among offenders with mental illness? *Law and Human Behavior, 38,* 439–449.

Peterson-Badali, M., Skilling, T., & Haqanee, Z. (2015). Examining implementation of risk assessment in case management for youth in the justice system. *Criminal Justice and Behavior, 42,* 304–320.

Petrich, D. M., Pratt, T. C., Jonson, C. L., & Cullen, F. T. (2021). Custodial sanctions and reoffending: A meta-analytic review. *Crime and Justice, 50,* 353–424.

Petrosino, A., Derzon, J., & Lavenberg, J. (2009). The role of family in crime and delinquency: Evidence from prior quantitative reviews. *Southwest Journal of Criminal Justice, 6,* 108–132.

Petrosino, A., & Soydan, H. (2005). The impact of program developers as evaluators on criminal recidivism: Results from meta-analyses of experimental and quasi-experimental research. *Journal of Experimental Criminology, 1,* 435–450.

Petrosino, A., Turpin-Petrosino, C., Hollis-Peel, M. E., & Lavenberg, J. G. (2013). 'Scared Straight' and other juvenile awareness programs for preventing juvenile delinquency. *Cochrane Database Systematic Reviews,* April 30. CD002796.

Pew Charitable Trusts (2016). Use of electronic offender tracking devices expands sharply (September). www.pewtrusts.org/-/media/assets/2016/10/

Phillips, J. (2022). The impact of the pandemic on probation: Lessons for the future. *Safer Communities, 21,* 112–122.

Pichon, M., Treves-Kagan, S., Stern, E., Kyegombe, N., Stöckl, H., & Buller, A. M. (2020). A mixed-methods systematic review: Infidelity, romantic jealousy and intimate partner violence against women. *International Journal of Environmental Research and Public Health, 17,* 5682.

Pichot, P. (1978). Psychopathic behavior: A historical overview. In R. D. Hare & D. Schalling (Eds.), *Psychopathic behavior* (pp. 55–70). New York, NY: Wiley.

Piggott, E., & Wood, W. (2018). Does restorative justice reduce recidivism? Assessing evidence and claims about restorative justice and reoffending. In T. Gavrielides (Ed.), *Routledge international handbook of restorative justice* (pp. 359–376). New York: Routledge.

Pilkington, P. D., Noonan, C., May, T., Younan, R., & Holt, R. A. (2021). Early maladaptive schemas and intimate partner violence victimization and perpetration: A systematic review and meta-analysis. *Clinical Psychology & Psychotherapy, 28*, 1030–1042.

Pina-Sánchez, J., Brunton-Smith, I., & Li, G. (2020). Mind the step: A more insightful and robust analysis of the sentencing process in England and Wales under the new sentencing guidelines. *Criminology & Criminal Justice, 20*, 268–301.

Piotrowska, P. J., Stride, C. B., Croft, C. B., & Rowe, R. (2015). Socioeconomic status and antisocial behaviour among children and adolescents: A systematic review and meta-analysis. *Clinical Psychology Review, 35*, 47–55.

Piquero, A. R., & Blumstein, A. (2007). Does incapacitation reduce crime? *Journal of Quantitative Criminology, 23*, 267–285.

Piquero, A. R., Brame, R., Fagan, J., & Moffitt, T. E. (2006). Assessing the offending activity of criminal domestic violence suspects: Offense specialization, escalation, and de-escalation evidence from the Spouse Assault Replication Program. *Public Health Reports, 121*, 409–418.

Piquero, A. R., Farrington, D. P., Shepherd, J. P., & Auty, K. (2014). Offending and early death in the Cambridge Study in Delinquent Development. *Justice Quarterly, 31*, 445–472.

Piquero, A. R., Farrington, D. P., Fontaine, N. M. G., Vincent, G., Coid, J., & Ulrich, S. (2012). Childhood risk, offending trajectories, and psychopathy at age 48 in the Cambridge Study in Delinquent Development. *Psychology, Public Policy, and Law, 18*, 577–598.

Piquero, A. R., Farrington, D. P., Nagin, D. S., & Moffitt, T. E. (2010). Trajectories of offending and their relation to life failure in middle age: Findings from the Cambridge Study in Delinquent Development. *Journal of Research in Crime and Delinquency, 47*, 151–173.

Piquero, A. R., Jennings, W. G., Diamond, B., Farrington, D. P., Tremblay, R. E., Welsh, B. C., & Reingle Gonzalez, J. M. (2016). A meta-analysis update on the effects of early family/parent training programs on antisocial behavior and delinquency. *Journal of Experimental Criminology, 16*, 229–248.

Piquero, A. R., Jennings, W. G., & Farrington, D. P. (2010). On the malleability of self-control: Theoretical and policy implications regarding a general theory of crime. *Justice Quarterly, 27*, 803–834.

Piquero, A. R., Jennings, W. G., & Farrington, D. P. (2013). The monetary costs of crime to middle adulthood: Findings from the Cambridge Study in Delinquent Development. *Journal of Research in Crime and Delinquency, 50*, 53–74.

Piquero, A. R., Jennings, W. G., Jemison, E., Kaukinen, C., & Knaul, F. M. (2021). Domestic violence during the COVID-19 pandemic: Evidence from a systematic review and meta-analysis. *Journal of Criminal Justice, 74*, 101806.

Piquero, A. R., Jennings, W. G., Schon, E., Kaukinen, C., & Knaul, F. M. (2021). Domestic violence during the COVID-19 pandemic—Evidence from a systematic review and meta-analysis. *Journal of Criminal Justice, 74*, 101806.

Piquero, N. L., Piquero, A. R., Narvey, N., Boutwell, B., & Farrington, D. P. (2021). Are there psychopaths in white-collar jobs? *Deviant Behavior, 42*, 979–992.

Plomin, R., DeFries, J. C., Knopik, V. S., & Neiderhiser, J. M. (2016). Top 10 replicated findings from behavioral genetics. *Perspectives on Psychological Science, 11*, 3–23.

Poehlmann-Tynan, J., & Turney, K. (2021). A developmental perspective on children with incarcerated parents. *Child Development Perspectives, 15*, 3–11.

Pogarsky, G. (2007). Deterrence and individual differences among convicted offenders. *Journal of Quantitative Criminology, 25*, 59–74.

Pogarsky, G., & Piquero, A. (2003). Can punishment encourage offending? Investigating the 'resetting' effect. *Journal of Research in Crime and Delinquency, 40*, 95–120.

Pogarsky, G., Roche, S. P., & Pickett, J. T. (2018). Offender decision-making in criminology: Contributions from behavioral economics. *Annual Review of Criminology, 1*, 379–400.

Polaschek, D. L. L. (2012). An appraisal of the risk-need-responsivity (RNR) model of offender rehabilitation and its application in correctional treatment. *Legal and Criminological Psychology, 17*, 1–17.

Polaschek, D. L. L. (2016). Desistance and dynamic risk factors belong together. *Psychology, Crime and Law, 22*, 171–189.

Polaschek, D. L. L., & Skeem, J. L. (2018). Treatment of adults and juveniles with psychopathy. In C. J. Patrick (Ed.), *Handbook of psychopathy* (pp. 710–731). New York: Guilford.

Polaschek, D. L. L., & Wong, S. C. P. (2020). Risk-reducing treatment in high-risk psychopathic and violent offenders. In J. S. Wormith, L. A. Craig, & T. E. Hogue (Eds.), *The Wiley handbook of what works in violence risk management: Theory, research and practice* (pp. 369–384). New York: John Wiley & Sons.

Polderman, T. J. C., Benyamin, B., de Leeuw, C. A., Sullivan, P. F., van Bochoven, A., Visscher, P. M., & Posthuma, D. (2015). Meta-analysis of the heritability of human traits based on fifty years of twin studies. *Nature Genetics, 47*, 702–709.

Porter, S. (1996). Without conscience or without active conscience? The etiology of psychopathy revisited. *Aggression and Violent Behavior, 1*, 179–189.

Porter, S., Woodworth, M. T., & Black, P. J. (2018). Psychopathy and aggression. In C. J. Patrick (Ed.), *Handbook of psychopathy* (pp. 611–634). New York: Guilford.

Poulton, R., Moffitt, T. E., & Silva, P. A. (2015). The Dunedin multidisciplinary health and development study: Overview of the first forty years, with an eye to the future. *Social Psychiatry and Psychiatric Epidemiology, 50*, 679–693.

Poythress, N. G., & Skeem, J. L. (2006). Disaggregation psychopathy: Where and how to look for subtypes. In C. J. Patrick (Ed.), *Handbook of psychopathy* (pp. 172–192). New York, NY: Guilford.

Pratt, T. C., Cullen, F. T., Sellers, C. S., Winfree, T. Jr., Madensen, T. D., Daigle, L. E., ... Gau, J. M. (2010). The empirical status of social learning theory: A meta-analysis. *Justice Quarterly, 27*, 765–802.

Pratt, T. C., & Turanovic, J. J. (2019). A criminological fly in the ointment: Specialty courts and the generality of deviance. *Victims & Offenders, 14*, 375–386.

Prendergast, M. L., Farabee, D., Cartier, J., & Henkin, S. (2006). Involuntary treatment within a prison setting: Impact on psychosocial change during treatment. In C. R. Bartol & A. M. Bartol (Eds.), *Current perspectives in forensic psychology and criminal justice* (pp. 231–238). Thousand Oaks, CA: Sage.

Prendergast, M. L., Pearson, F. S., Podus, D., Hamilton, Z. K., & Greenwell, L. (2013). The Andrews' principles of risk, needs, and responsivity as applied in drug treatment programs: Meta-analysis of crime and drug use outcomes. *Journal of Experimental Criminology, 9*, 275–300.

Prince, J., Lovatt, K., Stockdale, K. C., & Olver, M. E. (2021). Predictive properties of a general risk-need measure in diverse justice involved youth: A prospective field validity study. *Criminal Justice and Behavior, 48*, 1511–1535.

Prior, D., Farrow, K., Hughes, N., Kelly, G., Manders, G., White, S., & Wilkinson, B. (2011). *Maturity, young adults and criminal justice*. Birmingham, UK: University of Birmingham.

Prochaska, J. O., & DiClemente, C. C. (1982). Transtheoretical therapy: Toward a more integrative model of change. *Psychotherapy: Theory, Research & Practice, 19*, 276–288.

Proulx, J., Cortoni, F., Craig, L. A., & Letourneau, E. J. (Eds.) (2020). *The Wiley handbook of what works with sexual offenders: Contemporary perspectives in theory, assessment, treatment, and prevention*. New York: John Wiley & Sons.

Purvis, M., & Ward, T. (2019). Good lives model. In R. D. Morgan (Ed.), *The SAGE Encyclopedia of Criminal Psychology* (pp. 581–583). Thousand Oaks, CA: Sage.

Pusch, N., & Holtfreter, K. (2018). Gender and risk assessment in juvenile offenders: A meta-analysis. *Criminal Justice and Behavior, 45*, 56–81.

Pyrooz, D. C., Turanovic, J. J., Decker, S. H., & Wu, J. (2016). Taking stock of the relationship between gang membership and offending: A meta-analysis. *Criminal Justice and Behavior, 43*, 365–397.

Quay, H. C. (1965). Psychopathic personality as pathological stimulus-seeking. *American Journal of Psychiatry, 122*, 180–183.

Quinsey, V. L. (2002). Evolutionary theory and criminal behavior. *Legal and Criminological Psychology, 7*, 1–13.

Quinsey, V. L., Skilling, T. A., Lalumière, M. L., & Craig, W. M. (2004). *Juvenile delinquency: Understanding the origins of individual differences.* Washington, DC: American Psychological Association.

Radatz, D. L., & Hilton, Z. N. (2022). The Ontario Domestic Assault Risk Assessment: predicting violence among men with a police record of intimate partner violence in the United States. *Criminal Justice and Behavior, 49*, 371–388.

Radatz, D. L., Richards, T. N., Murphy, C. M., Nitsch, L. J., Green-Manning, A., Brokmeier, A. M., & Holliday, C. N. (2021). Integrating 'principles of effective intervention' into domestic violence intervention programs: New opportunities for change and collaboration. *American Journal of Criminal Justice, 46*, 609–625.

Rafter, N. (2008). Criminology's darkest hour: Biocriminology in Nazi Germany. *Australian and New Zealand Journal of Criminology, 41*, 287–306.

Rafter, N. (Ed.) (2009). *The origins of criminology: A reader.* London: Routledge Cavendish.

Raine, A. (2013). *The anatomy of violence: The biological roots of crime.* New York, NY: Pantheon.

Raine, A. (2018). Antisocial personality as a neurodevelopment disorder. *Annual Review of Clinical Psychology, 14*, 259–289.

Raine, A., Leung, C-C., Singh, M., & Kaur, J. (2020). Omega-3 supplementation in young offenders: A randomized, stratified, double-blind, placebo-controlled, parallel-group trial. *Journal of Experimental Criminology, 16*, 389–405.

Raine, A., Moffitt, T. E., Caspi, A., Loeber, R., Stouthamer-Loeber, M., & Lynam, D. (2005). Neurocognitive impairments in boys on the life-course-persistent antisocial path. *Journal of Abnormal Psychology, 114*, 38–49.

Raine, A., Portnoy, J., Liu, J., Mahoomed, T., & Hibbeln, J. R. (2015). Reduction in behavior problems with Omega-3 supplementation in children aged 8–16 years: A randomized, double-blind, placebo-controlled, stratified, parallel-group trial. *Journal of Child Psychology and Psychiatry, 56*, 509–520.

Rajah, V., & Osborn, M. (2022). Understanding women's resistance to intimate partner violence: A scoping review. *Trauma, Violence, & Abuse, 23*, 1373–1387.

Ramezani, N., Bhati, A., Murphy, A., Routh, D., & Taxman, F. S. (2022). Assessing the reliability and validity of the Risk-Need-Responsivity (RNR) program tool. *Health & Justice, 10*, 19.

Rankin, J. H., & Kern, R. (1994). Parental attachments and delinquency. *Criminology, 32*, 495–515.

Ray, J. V., & Frick, P. J. (2020). Assessing callous-unemotional traits using the total score from the Inventory of Callous-Unemotional Traits: A meta-analysis. *Journal of Clinical Child & Adolescent Psychology, 49*, 190–199.

Ray, J. V., Frick, P. J., Thornton, L. C., Wall Myers, T. D., Steinberg, L., & Cauffman, E. (2017). Callous-unemotional traits predict self-reported offending in adolescent boys: The mediating role of delinquent peers and the moderating role of parenting practices. *Developmental Psychology, 53*, 319–328.

Raynor, P. (2007). Risk and need assessment in British probation: The contribution of the LSI-R. *Psychology, Crime, and Law, 13*, 125–138.

Raynor, P. (2008). Community penalties and Home Office research: On the way back to "nothing works"? *Criminology & Criminal Justice, 8*, 73–87.

Raynor, P., Kynch, J., Roberts, C., & Merrington, S. (2000). *Risk and need assessment in probation services: An evaluation.* Home Office Research Study No. 211. London, England: Home Office.

Re, L., & Birkhoff, J. M. (2015). The 47,XYY syndrome, 50 years of certainties and doubts: A systematic review. *Aggression and Violent Behavior, 22*, 9–17.

Reale, K., McCuish, E., & Corrado, R. (2020). The impact of juvenile sex offending on the adult criminal career. *Sexual Abuse, 32*, 400–422.

Rebellon, C. J. (2002). Reconsidering the broken homes/delinquency relationship and exploring its mediating mechanism(s). *Criminology, 40,* 103–135.

Reckless, W. C. (1967). *The crime problem.* New York, NY: Appleton-Century-Crofts.

Reinharth, J., Reynolds, G., Dill, C., & Serper, M. (2014). Cognitive predictors of violence in schizophrenia: A meta-analytic review. *Schizophrenia Research: Cognition, 1,* 101–111.

Reisig, M. D., Holtfreter, K., & Morash, M. (2006). Assessing recidivism risk across female pathways to crime. *Justice Quarterly, 23,* 384–405.

Renfro, P. M. (2020). *Stranger danger: Family values, childhood, and the American Carceral State.* New York: Oxford University Press.

Rettenberger, M., & Craig, L. A. (2020). Risk assessment in individuals convicted of sexual offenses. In J. Proulx, F. Cortoni, L. A. Craig, & E. J. Letourneau (Eds.), *The Wiley handbook of what works with sexual offenders: Contemporary perspectives in theory, assessment, treatment, and prevention* (pp. 87–101). New York: John Wiley & Sons.

Rettinger, L. J., & Andrews, D. A. (2010). General risk and need, gender specificity, and the recidivism of female offenders. *Criminal Justice and Behavior, 37,* 20–46.

Rex, S., & Hosking, N. (2013). A collaborative approach to developing probation practice: Skills for effective engagement, development and supervision (SEEDS). *Probation Journal, 60,* 332–338.

Rex, S., & Raynor, P. (2008). Accreditation. In G. McIvor & P. Raynor (Eds.), *Development in social work with offenders* (pp. 113–127). London, England: Jessica Kingsley Publishers.

Rhee, S. H., & Waldman, I. D. (2002). Genetic and environmental influences on antisocial behavior: A meta-analysis of twin and adoption studies. *Psychological Bulletin, 128,* 490–529.

Rhee, S. H., & Waldman, I. D. (2007). Behavior genetics of criminality and aggression. In D. J. Flannery, A. T. Vazsonyi, & I. D. Waldman (Eds.), *The Cambridge handbook of violent behavior and aggression* (pp. 77–90). New York: Cambridge University Press.

Rhee, S. H., Woodward, K., Corley, R. P., du Pont, A., Friedman, N. P., Hewitt, J. K., ... Zahn-Waxler, C. (2021). The association between toddlerhood empathy deficits and antisocial personality disorder symptoms and psychopathy in adulthood. *Development and Psychopathology, 33,* 173–183.

Rhule-Louie, D. M., & McMahon, R. J. (2007). Problem behavior and romantic relationships: Assortative mating, behavior contagion, and desistance. *Clinical Child and Family Psychology Review, 10,* 53–100.

Rice, M. E., & Harris, G. T. (2005). Comparing effect sizes in follow-up studies: ROC Area, Cohen's d, and r. *Law and Human Behavior, 29,* 615–620.

Richards, T. N., Gover, A. R., Branscum, C., Nystrom, A., & Claxton, T. (2022). Assessing states' intimate partner violence offender treatment standards using a principles of effective intervention framework. *Journal of Interpersonal Violence, 37,* NP20288–NP20310.

Rieger, D. J., Drawbridge, D. C., & Robinson, D. (2023). Examining dynamic risk and strength profiles for Indigenous and non-Indigenous young adults. *Psychology, Crime & Law, 29,* 222–241.

Rivenbark, J. G., Odgers, C. L., Caspi, A., Harrington, H., Hogan, S., Houts, R. M., ... Moffitt, T. E. (2018). The high societal costs of childhood conduct problems: Evidence from administrative records up to age 38 in a longitudinal birth cohort. *Journal of Child Psychology and Psychiatry, 59,* 703–710.

River, L. M., Borelli, J. L., Vazquez, L. C., & Smiley, P. A. (2018). Learning helplessness in the family: Maternal agency and the intergenerational transmission of depressive symptoms. *Journal of Family Psychology, 32,* 1109.

Robinson, C. J., Lowenkamp, C. T., Holsinger, A. M., VanBenschoten, S., Alexander, M., & Oleson, J. C., (2012). A random study of staff training aimed at reducing re-arrest (STARR): Using core correctional practice in probation interactions. *Journal of Criminal Justice, 35,* 167–188.

Robinson, G., & Shapland, J. (2008). Reducing recidivism: A task for restorative justice? *British Journal of Criminology, 48,* 337–358.

Robinson, C. J., VanBenschoten, S., Alexander, M., & Lowenkamp, C. T. (2011). A random (almost) study of staff training aimed at reducing re-arrest (STARR): Reducing recidivism through intentional design. *Federal Probation, 75*, 95–101.

Rocque, M., Welsh, B. C., & Raine, A. (2012). Biosocial criminology and modern crime prevention. *Journal of Criminal Justice, 40*, 306–312.

Rodermond, E., Kruttschnitt, C., Slotboom, A. M., & Bijleveld, C. C. (2016). Female desistance: A review of the literature. *European Journal of Criminology, 13*, 3–28.

Rodriguez, N., & Turnavic, J. J. (2018). Impact of incarceration on families and communities. In J. Wooldredge & P. Smith (Eds.), *Oxford handbook on prisons and imprisonment* (pp. 189–207). Oxford, UK: Oxford University Press.

Rollè, L., Giardina, G., Caldarera, A. M., Gerino, E., & Brustia, P. (2018). When intimate partner violence meets same sex couples: A review of same sex intimate partner violence. *Frontiers in Psychology, 9*, 1506.

Roman, C. G., Stodolska, M., Yahner, J., & Shinew, K. (2013). Pathways to outdoor recreation, physical activity, and delinquency among urban Latino adolescents. *Annals of Behavioral Medicine, 45* (Supplement 1), S151–S161.

Romero-Martinez, A., Bressanutti, S., & Moya-Albiol, L. (2020). A systematic review of the effectiveness of non-invasive brain stimulation techniques to reduce violence proneness by interfering in anger and irritability. *Journal of Clinical Medicine, 9*, 882.

Romero-Martinez, A., González, M., Lila, M., Gracia, E., Marti-Bonmati, L., Alberich-Bayarri, Á., … Moya-Albiol, L. (2019). The brain resting-state functional connectivity underlying violence proneness: Is it a reliable marker for neurocriminology? A systematic review. *Behavioral Sciences, 9*, 11.

Roose, A., Bijttebier, P., Decoene, S., Claes, L., & Frick, P. J. (2010). Assessing the affective features of psychopathy in adolescence: A further validation of the Inventory of Callous and Unemotional Traits. *Assessment, 17*, 44–57.

Rosen, J. D. (2021). *The U.S. war on drugs at home and abroad.* Cham, Switzerland: Springer Nature.

Rosenfeld, B., & Penrod, S. (2011). *Research methods in forensic psychology.* Hoboken, NJ: Wiley.

Rosenthal, R. (1984). *Meta-analytic procedures for social research.* Beverly Hills, CA: Sage.

Rosenthal, R., & Rubin, D. B. (1979). A note on percent variance explained as a measure of the importance of effects. *Journal of Applied Social Psychology, 9*, 395–396.

Ross, R. R., & Gendreau, P. (Eds.) (1980). *Effective correctional treatment.* Toronto, Canada: Butterworth.

Ross, R. R., & Fabiano, E. A. (1985). *Time to think: A cognitive model of delinquency prevention and offender rehabilitation.* Johnson City, TN: Institute of Social Science and Arts.

Rossdale, S.-V., Tully, R. J, & Egan, V. (2020). The HCR-20 for predicting violence in adult females: A meta-analysis. *Journal of Forensic Psychology Research and Practice, 20*, 15–52.

Rossegger, A., Bartels, R., Endrass, J., Borchard, B., & Singh, J. (2021). High risk sexual fantasies and sexual offending: An overview of fundamentals and interventions. *Sexual Offending: Theory, Research, and Prevention, 16*, 1–16.

Rozeboom, W. W. (1960). The fallacy of the null-hypothesis significance test. *Psychological Bulletin, 57*, 416–428.

Rubenson, M., Galbraith, K., & Huey, S. J. Jr. (2020). Understanding adverse effects in gang-focused interventions: A critical review. In C. Melde & F. Weerman (Eds.), *Gangs in the era of internet and social media* (pp. 271–291). Springer Nature Switzerland.

Rugge, T., & Bonta, J. (2014). Training community corrections officers in cognitive-behavioral intervention strategies. In R. C. Tafrate & D. Mitchell (Eds.), *Forensic CBT: A handbook for clinical practice* (pp. 122–136). Chichester, UK: John Wiley & Sons.

Rushton, J. P. (1988). Race differences in behaviour: A review and evolutionary analysis. *Personality and Individual Differences, 9*, 1009–1024.

Rushton, J. P., & Jensen, A. R. (2005). Thirty years of research on race differences in cognitive ability. *Psychology, Public Policy, and Law, 11*, 235–294.

Rushton, J. P., & Jensen, A. R. (2006). The totality of evidence shows the race IQ gap still remains. *Psychological Science, 17*, 921–922.

Rushton, J. P., & Jensen, A. R. (2008). James Watson's most inconvenient truth: Race, realism and moralistic fallacy. *Medical Hypotheses, 71*, 629–640.

Ryan, J. P., & Testa, M. F. (2005). Child maltreatment and juvenile delinquency: Investigating the role of placement and placement instability. *Children and Youth Services Review, 27*, 227–249.

Saadatmand, Y., Toma, M., & Choquette, J. (2012). The war on drugs and crime rates. *Journal of Business & Economics Research, 10*, 285–290.

Salekin, R. T., Rogers, R., & Sewell, K. W. (1996). A review and meta-analysis of the Psychopathy Checklist and Psychopathy Checklist-Revised: Predictive validity of dangerousness. *Clinical Psychology: Science and Practice, 3*, 203–215.

Salisbury, E. J. (2013). Social learning and crime. In F. T. Cullen & P. Wilcox (Eds.), *The Oxford handbook of criminological theory* (pp. 115–130). NY: Oxford University Press.

Salisbury, E. J., Sundt, J., & Boppre, B. (2019). Mapping the implementation landscape: Assessing the systemic capacity of statewide community corrections agencies to deliver evidence-based practices. *Corrections, 4*, 19–38.

Sambrooks, K., Olver, M. E., Page, T. E., & Gannon, T. A. (2021). Firesetting reoffending: A meta-analysis. *Criminal Justice and Behavior, 48*, 1634–1651.

Samenow, S. E. (2014). *Inside the criminal mind (revised and updated)*. New York, NY: Broadway Books.

Sampson, R. J., & Laub, J. H. (1993). *Crime in the making: Pathways and turning points through life*. Cambridge, MA: Harvard University Press.

Sampson, R. J., Laub, J. H., & Wimer, C. (2006). Does marriage reduce crime? A counterfactual approach to within-individual causal effects. *Criminology, 44*, 465–504.

Sampson, R. J., & Raudenbush, S. W. (2001). Disorder in urban neighborhoods—Does it lead to crime? *Research in Brief*. Washington, DC: National Institute of Justice.

Sanchez-Roige, S., Gray, J. C., MacKillop, J., Chen, C.-H., & Palmer, A. A. (2018). The genetics of human personality. *Genes, Brain and Behavior, 17*, 1–13.

Sancho, M., De Gracia, M., Rodríguez, R. C., Mallorquí-Bagué, N., Sánchez-González, J., Trujols, J., … Menchón, J. M. (2018). Mindfulness-based interventions for the treatment of substance and behavioral addictions: A systematic review. *Frontiers in Psychiatry, 9*, Article 95.

Sandberg, A. A., Koepf, G. F., Ishihara, T., & Hauschka, T. S. (1961). An XYY human male. *Lancet, 278*, 488–489.

Sanz-Garcia, A., Gesteira, C., Sanz, J., & Garcia-Vera, M. P. (2021). Prevalence of psychopathy in the general adult population: A systematic review and meta-analysis. *Frontiers in Psychology, 12*, 661044.

Saramago, M. A., Cardoso, J., & Leal, I. (2019). Pornography use by sex offenders at the time of the index offense: Characterization and predictors. *Journal of Sex & Marital Therapy, 45*, 473–487.

Sardinha, L., Maheu-Giroux, M., Stöckl, H., Meyer, S. R., & García-Moreno, C. (2022). Global, regional, and national prevalence estimates of physical or sexual, or both, intimate partner violence against women in 2018. *The Lancet, 399*, 803–813.

Sarteschi, C. M., Vaughn, M. G., & Kim, K. (2011). Assessing the effectiveness of mental health courts: A quantitative review. *Journal of Criminal Justice, 39*, 12–20.

Saudino, K. J., & Ganiban, J. M. (Eds.) (2020). *Behavior genetics of temperament and personality*. New York: Springer.

Savage, J., Ellis, S. K., & Wozniak, K. H. (2019). The role of poverty and income in the differential etiology of violence: An empirical test. *Journal of Poverty, 23*, 384–403.

Scanlon, F., & Morgan, R. D. (2021). The active ingredients in a treatment for justice-involved persons with mental illness: The importance of addressing mental illness and criminal risk. *Psychological Services, 18*, 474.

Scanlan, J. M., Yesberg, J. A., Fortune, C.-A., & Polaschek, D. L. L. (2020). Predicting women's recidivism using the dynamic risk assessment for offender re-entry: Preliminary evidence of predictive validity with community-sentenced women using a "gender-neutral" risk measure. *Criminal Justice and Behavior, 47*, 251–270.

Scarpa, A., & Raine, A. (2007). Biosocial basis of violence. In D. J. Flannery, A. T. Vazsonyi, & I. D. Waldman (Eds.), *The Cambridge handbook of violent behavior and aggression* (pp. 151–169). Cambridge, England: Cambridge University Press.

Schaefer, L., & Williamson, H. (2018). Probation and parole officers' compliance with case management tools: Professional discretion and override. *International Journal of Offender Therapy and Comparative Criminology, 62*, 4565–4584.

Schafers, C., Olver, M. E., & Wormith, J. S. (2021). Dynamic appraisal of intimate partner violence risk and need: Results from an outpatient treatment program. *Criminal Justice and Behavior, 48*, 481–501.

Schinkel, M. (2019). Rethinking turning points: Trajectories of parenthood and desistance. *Journal of Developmental and Life-Course Criminology, 5*, 366–386.

Schlager, M. D., & Simourd, D. J. (2007). Validity of the Level of Service Inventory–Revised (LSI-R) among African American and Hispanic male offenders. *Criminal Justice and Behavior, 34*, 545–554.

Schmidt, S. L. (1996). Statistical significance testing and cumulative knowledge in psychology: Implications for training of researchers. *Psychological Methods, 1*, 115–129.

Schmucker, M., & Lösel, F. (2015). The effects of sexual offender treatment on recidivism: An international meta-analysis of sound quality evaluations. *Journal of Experimental Criminology, 11*, 597–630.

Schmucker, M., & Lösel, F. (2017). Sexual offender treatment for reducing recidivism among convicted sex offenders: A systematic review and meta-analysis. *Campbell Systematic Reviews, 13*, 1–75.

Schneider, B. H., Atkinson, L., & Tardif, C. (2001). Child-parent attachment and children's peer relations: A quantitative review. *Developmental Psychology, 37*, 86–100.

Schorr, M. T., Tietbohl-Santos, B., Mendes de Olveira, L., Terra, L., de Borba Telles, L. E., & Hauck, S. (2020). Association between different types of childhood trauma and parental bonding with antisocial traits in adulthood: A systematic review. *Child Abuse & Neglect, 107*, 104621.

Schuessler, K. F., & Cressey, D. R. (1950). Personality characteristics of criminals. *American Journal of Sociology, 55*, 476–484.

Schur, E. M. (1973). *Radical nonintervention: Rethinking the delinquency problem*. Englewood Cliffs, NJ: Prentice Hall.

Schwalbe, C. S. (2007). Risk assessment for juvenile justice: A meta-analysis. *Law and Human Behavior, 31*, 449–462.

Schwalbe, C. S. (2008). A meta-analysis of juvenile risk assessment instruments: Predictive validity by gender. *Criminal Justice and Behavior, 35*, 1367–1381.

Schwalbe, C. S., & Koetzle, D. (2021). What the covid-19 pandemic teaches about the essential practices of community corrections and supervision. *Criminal Justice and Behavior, 48*, 1300–1316.

Schwartz, C. E., Snidman, N., & Kagan, J. (1996). Early childhood temperament as a determinant of externalizing behavior in adolescence. *Development and Psychopathology, 8*, 527–537.

Scott, E. S., & Steinberg, L. (2008). *Rethinking juvenile justice*. Boston, MA: Harvard University Press.

Scott, T., & Brown, S. L. (2018). Risk, strengths, gender, and recidivism among justice-involved youth: A meta-analysis. *Journal of Consulting and Clinical Psychology, 86*, 931–945.

Scurich, N., & Gongola, J. (2021). Prevalence of polymorphism ("crossover") among sexual offenders. *Journal of Criminal Justice, 77*, 101853.

Sechrest, L., & Sidani, S. (1995). Quantitative and qualitative methods: Is there an alternative? *Evaluation and Program Planning, 18*, 77–87.

Segal, N. L., & Niculae, F. J. (2019). Fullerton virtual twin project: Overview and 2019 update. *Twin Research and Human Genetics, 22*, 731–734.

Sellbom, M., & Drislane, L. E. (2021). The classification of psychopathy. *Aggression and Violent Behavior, 59*, 101473.

Seligman, M. E. P. (1975). *Helplessness: On depression, development, and death*. San Francisco, CA: Freeman.

Senkans, S., McEwan, T. E., & Ogloff, J. R. (2020). Conceptualising intimate partner violence perpetrators' cognition as aggressive relational schemas. *Aggression and Violent Behavior, 55*, 101456.

Serin, R. C. (2007). *The Dynamic Risk Assessment for Offender Re-Entry (DRAOR)*. Unpublished user manual. Department of Psychology, Carleton University.

Serin, R. C., Chadwick, N., & Lloyd, C. D. (2019). Integrating dynamic risk assessment into community supervision practice. D. L. L. Polaschek, A. Day, & C. R. Hollin (Eds.), *The Wiley international handbook of correctional psychology* (pp. 725–743). New York: John Wiley & Sons.

Serin, R. C., Lloyd, C. D., Helmus, L., Derkzen, D. M., & Luong, D. (2013). Does intra-individual change predict offender recidivism? Searching for the Holy Grail in assessing offender change. *Aggression and Violent Behavior, 18*, 32–53.

Serin, R. C., Peters, R. D., & Barbaree, H. E. (1990). Predictors of psychopathy and release outcome in a criminal population. *Psychological Assessment: A Journal of Consulting and Clinical Psychology, 2*, 419–422.

Seto, M. C., Hanson, R. K., & Babchishin, K. M. (2011). Contact sexual offending by men with online sex offenses. *Sexual Abuse: A Journal of Research and Treatment, 23*, 124–145.

Sevigny, E. L., Fuleihan, B. K., & Ferdik, F. V. (2013). Do drug courts reduce the use of incarceration? A meta-analysis. *Journal of Criminal Justice, 41*, 416–425.

Sharma, S., Mustanski, B., Dick, D., Bolland, J., & Kertes, D. A. (2019). Protective factors buffer life stress and behavioral health outcomes among high-risk youth. *Journal of Abnormal Child Psychology, 47*, 1289–1301.

Shaw, C. (1930/1966). *The Jack-Roller: A delinquent boy's own story*. Chicago, IL: University of Chicago Press.

Shelden, R. G., Tracy, S. K., & Brown, W. B. (2012). *Youth gangs in American society* (4th ed). New York, NY: Wadsworth.

Sheldon, W. H. (1942). *The varieties of temperament: A psychology of constitutional differences*. New York, NY: Harper.

Shepherd, S. M., Adams, Y., McEntyre, E., & Walker, R. (2014). Violence risk assessment in Australian Aboriginal offender populations: A review of the literature. *Psychology, Public Policy, and Law, 20*, 281–293.

Shepherd, S. M., Luebbers, S., Ogloff, J. R. P., Fullam, R., & Dolan, M. (2014). The predictive validity of risk assessment approaches for young Australian offenders. *Psychiatry, Psychology, and Law, 21*, 801–817.

Sherman, L. W. (2018). Policing domestic violence 1967–2017. *Criminology & Public Policy, 17*, 453–465.

Sherman, L. W., & Berk, R. A. (1984). The specific deterrent effect of arrest for domestic assault. *American Sociological Review, 49*, 261–272.

Sherman, L. W., & Harris, H. M. (2015). Increased death rates of domestic violence victims from arresting vs. warning suspects in the Milwaukee Domestic Violence Experiment (MilDVE). *Journal of Experimental Criminology, 11*, 1–20.

Shields, I. W., & Simourd, D. J. (1991). Pride in Delinquency Scale. *Criminal Justice and Behavior, 18*, 180–194.

Shields, I. W., & Whitehall, G. C. (1994). Neutralizations and delinquency among teenagers. *Criminal Justice and Behavior, 21*, 223–235.

Shoda, Y., & Dinitz, W. (2006). Applying meta-theory to aceneralizabilitybility and precision in personality science. *Applied Psychology: An International Review, 55*, 439–452.

Shoda, Y., & Mischel, W. (2006). Applying meta-theory to achieve generalizability and precision in personality science. *Applied Psychology, 55*, 439–452.

Shortt, J. W., Capaldi, D. M., Dishion, T. J., Bank, L., & Owen, L. D. (2003). The role of adolescent friends, romantic partners, and siblings in the emergence of the adult antisocial lifestyle. *Journal of Family Psychology, 17*, 521–533.

Sillekens, S., & Notten, N. (2020). Parental divorce and externalizing problems behavior in adulthood. A study on lasting individual, family and peer risk factors for external problem behavior when experiencing parental divorce. *Deviant Behavior, 41*, 1–16.

Silver, E., Smith, W. R., & Banks, S. (2000). Constructing actuarial devices for predicting recidivism: A comparison of methods. *Criminal Justice and Behavior, 27*, 733–764.

Silvertsson, F., & Carlsson, C. (2015). Continuity, change, and contradictions: Risk and agency in criminal careers to age 59. *Criminal Justice and Behavior, 42*, 382–411.

Simourd, D. J., & Hoge, R. D. (2000). Criminal psychopathy: A risk-and-need perspective. *Criminal Justice and Behavior, 27*, 256–272.

Simourd, D. J., Olver, M. E., & Brandenburg, B. (2016). Changing criminal attitudes among incarcerated offenders: Initial examination of a structured treatment program. *International Journal of Offender Therapy and Comparative Criminology, 60*, 1425–1445.

Simourd, D. J., & Van De Ven, J. (1999). Assessment of criminal attitudes: Criterion-related validity of the Criminal Sentiments Scale-Modified and Pride in Delinquency Scale. *Criminal Justice and Behavior, 26*, 90–106.

Singh, J. P., Desmarais, S. L., Hurducas, C., Arbach-Lucioni, K., Condemarin, C., Dean, K., Doyle, M., ... Otto, R. K. (2014). International perspectives on the practical application of violence risk assessment: A global survey of 44 countries. *International Journal of Forensic Mental Health, 13*, 193–206.

Singh, J. P., Grann, M., & Fazel, S. (2013). Authorship bias in violence risk assessment? A systematic review and meta-analysis. *Plos One, 8*, e72484.

Simons, D. J. (2014). The value of direct replication. *Perspectives on Psychological Science, 9*, 76–80.

Simons, R. L., Simons, L. G., Chen, Y. F., Brody, G. H., & Lin, K. H. (2007). Identifying the psychological factors that mediate the association between parenting practices and delinquency. *Criminology, 45*, 481–517.

Skardhamar, T., & Savolainen, J. (2014). Changes in criminal offending around the time of job entry: A study of employment and desistance. *Criminology, 52*, 263–291.

Skardhamar, T., Savolainen, J., Aase, K. N., & Lyngstad, T. H. (2015). Does marriage reduce crime? *Crime and Justice, 44*, 385–446.

Skeem, J. L., & Cooke, D. J. (2010). Is criminal behavior a central component of psychopathy? Conceptual directions for resolving the debate. *Psychological Assessment, 22*, 433–445.

Skeem, J. L., Emke-Francis, P., & Eno Louden, J. (2006). Probation, mental health, and mandated treatment: A national survey. *Criminal Justice and Behavior, 33*, 158–184.

Skeem, J. L., Eno Louden, J., Manchak, S., Vidal, S., & Haddad, E. (2009). Social networks and social control of probationers with co-occurring mental and substance abuse problems. *Law and Human Behavior, 33*, 122–135.

Skeem, J., & Lowenkamp, C. (2020). Using algorithms to address trade-offs inherent in predicting recidivism. *Behavioral Sciences & the Law, 38*, 259–278.

Skeem, J. L., Manchak, S., & Montoya, L. (2017). Comparing public safety outcomes for traditional probation vs specialty mental health probation. *JAMA Psychiatry, 74*, 942–948.

Skeem, J. L., Manchak, S., & Peterson, J. K. (2011). Correctional policy for offenders with mental illness: Creating a new paradigm for recidivism reduction. *Law and Human Behavior, 35*, 110–126.

Skeem, J. L., Montoya, L., & Manchak, S. M. (2018). Comparing costs of traditional and specialty probation for people with serious mental illness. *Psychiatric Services, 69*, 896–902.

Skeem, J. L., Steadman, H. J., & Manchak, S. M. (2015). Applicability of the risk-need-responsivity model to persons with mental illness involved in the criminal justice system. *Psychiatric Services, 66*, 916–922.

Skilling, T. A., & Sorge, G. B. (2014). Measuring antisocial values and attitudes in justice-involved male youth: Evaluating the psychometric properties of the Pride in Delinquency Scale and Criminal Sentiments Scale-Modified. *Criminal Justice and Behavior, 41,* 992–1007.

Skinner, B. F. (1953). *Science and human behavior.* New York, NY: Macmillan.

Slavin-Stewart, C., Minhas, M., Turna, J., Brasch, J., Olagunju, A. T., Chaimowitz, G., & MacKillop, J. (2022). Pharmacological interventions for alcohol misuse in correctional settings: A systematic review. *Alcoholism: Clinical and Experimental Research, 46,* 13–24.

Sleep, C. E., Weiss, B., Lynam, D. R., & Miller, J. D. (2019). An examination of the triarchic model of psychopathy's nomological network: A meta-analytic review. *Clinical Psychology Review, 71,* 1–26.

Smederevac, S., Mitrović, D., Sadiković, Riemann, R., Bratko, D., Prinz, M., & Budimlija, Z. (2020). Hereditary and environmental factors of the Five-Factor Model traits: A cross-cultural study. *Personality and Individual Differences, 162,* 109995.

Smith, A. K., Fox, C., Harrison, J., Kiss, Z., & Bradbury, A. (2018). The effectiveness of probation supervision towards reducing reoffending: A rapid evidence assessment. *Probation Journal, 65,* 407–428.

Smith, A., Heyes, K., Fox, C., Harrison, J., Kiss, Z., & Bradbury, R. (2018). The effectiveness of probation supervision towards reducing reoffending: A rapid evidence assessment. *Probation Journal, 65,* 407–428.

Smith, J. D., Dishion, T. J., Shaw, D. S., Wilson, M. N., Winter, C. C., & Patterson, G. R. (2014). Coercive family processes and early-onset conduct problems from age 2 to school entry. *Developmental Psychopathology, 26,* 917–932.

Smith, P., Cullen, F. T., & Latessa, E. J. (2009). Can 14,373 women be wrong? A meta-analysis of the LSI-R and recidivism for female offenders. *Criminology & Public Policy, 8,* 183–208.

Smith, P., Schweitzer, M., Labrecque, R. M., & Latessa, E. J. (2012). Improving probation officers' supervision skills: An evaluation of the EPICS model. *Journal of Crime and Justice, 35,* 189–199.

Snell, T. L. (2021). *Capital punishment, 2020–Statistical tables.* Washington: Bureau of Justice Statistics.

Snyder, H. N. (1998). Serious, violent, and chronic juvenile offenders: An assessment of the extent of and trends in officially recognized serious criminal behavior in a delinquent population. In R. Loeber & D. P. Farrington (Eds.), *Serious & violent juvenile offenders: Risk factors and successful interventions* (pp. 428–444). Thousand Oaks, CA: Sage.

Sohn, J. S., Raine, A., & Lee, S. J. (2020). The utility of the Psychopathy Checklist-Revised (PCL-R) facet and item test scores in predicting violent recidivism. *Aggressive Behavior, 46,* 508–515.

Solomon, R. L. (1964). Punishment. *American Psychologist, 19,* 239–253.

Somers, J. M., Goldner, E. M., Waraich, P., & Hsu, L. (2004). Prevalence studies of substance-related disorders: A systematic review of the literature. *Canadian Journal of Psychiatry, 49,* 373–383.

Soral, W., Kofta, M., & Bukowski, M. (2021). Helplessness experience and intentional (un-) binding: Control deprivation disrupts the implicit sense of agency. *Journal of Experimental Psychology: General, 150,* 289–305.

Spencer, C., Mallory, A. B., Cafferky, B. M., Kimmes, J. G., Beck, A. R., & Stith, S. M. (2019). Mental health factors and intimate partner violence perpetration and victimization: A meta-analysis. *Psychology of Violence, 9,* 1–17.

Spencer, C. M., & Stith, S. M. (2020). Risk factors for male perpetration and female victimization of intimate partner homicide: A meta-analysis. *Trauma, Violence, & Abuse, 21,* 527–540.

Spencer, C. M., Stith, S. M., & Cafferky, B. (2022). What puts individuals at risk for physical intimate partner violence perpetration? A meta-analysis examining risk markers for men and women. *Trauma, Violence, & Abuse, 23,* 36–51.

Spiropoulos, G. V., Salisbury, E. J., & Van Voorhis, P. (2014). Moderators of correctional treatment success: An exploratory study of racial differences. *International Journal of Offender Therapy and Comparative Criminology, 58,* 835–860.

Spruit, A., Hoffenaar, P., van der Put, C., van Vught, E., & Stams, G. J. (2018). The effect of sport-based intervention to prevent juvenile delinquency in at-risk adolescents. *Child and Youth Services Review, 94,* 689–698.

Spruit, A., van Vught, E., van der Put, C., van der Stouwe, T., & Stams, G. J. (2016). Sports participation and juvenile delinquency: A meta-analytic review. *Journal of Youth and Adolescence, 45,* 655–671.

St. George, S. (2022). Perceptions of common rape: How rape myth acceptance, victim gender, and victim resistance affect victim and perpetrator blame attributions in party rape and date rape. *Violence Against Women, 28,* 3505–3529.

St. Vil, N. M., Sabri, B., Nwokolo, V., Alexander, K. A., & Campbell, J. C. (2017). A qualitative study of survival strategies used by low-income Black women who experience intimate partner violence. *Social Work, 62,* 63–71.

Stams, G. J. J. M. (2015). From criminogenic risk to rehabilitation: Is there a need for a culturally sensitive approach? *International Journal of Offender Therapy and Comparative Criminology, 59,* 1263–1266.

Stanley, T. D., Carter, E. C., & Doucouliagos, H. (2018). What meta-analyses reveal about the replicability of psychological research. *Psychological Bulletin, 144,* 1325–1346.

Starfelt Sutton, L. C., Dynevall, M., Wennerholm, J., Åhlén, S., Rugge, T., Bourgon, G., & Robertsson, C. (2021). Evaluation of the implementation of a risk-need-responsivity service in community supervision in Sweden. *Criminal Justice and Behavior, 48,* 617–636.

Starr, S. B. (2014). Evidence-based sentencing and the scientific rationalization of discrimination. *Stanford Law Review, 66,* 842–873.

Steadman, H. J., & Cocozza, J. J. (1974). *Careers of the criminally insane: Excessive social control of deviance.* Lexington, MA: Lexington Books.

Steele, J. L., Bozik, R., & Davis, L. M. (2016). Education for incarcerated juveniles: A meta-analysis. *Journal of Education for Students Placed at Risk, 21,* 65–89.

Stein, D. M., Homan, K. J., & DeBerard, S. (2015). The effectiveness of juvenile treatment drug courts: A meta-analytic review of literature. *Journal of Child & Adolescent Substance Abuse, 24,* 80–93.

Stephens-Lewis, D., Johnson, A., Huntley, A., Gilchrist, E., McMurran, M., Henderson, J., … Gilchrist, G. (2021). Interventions to reduce intimate partner violence perpetration by men who use substances: A systematic review and meta-analysis of efficacy. *Trauma, Violence, & Abuse, 22,* 1262–1278.

Sternberg, R. J. (2005). There are no public-policy implications: A Reply to Rushton and Jensen (2005). *Psychology, Public Policy, and Law, 11,* 295–301.

Stevens, A., Berto, D., Heckman, W., Kerschl, V., Oeuvray, K., van Ooyen, M., … Uchtenhagen, A. (2005). Quasi-compulsory treatment of drug dependent offenders: An international literature review. *Substance Use and Misuse, 40,* 269–283.

Stewart, L. A., Gabora, N., Kropp, P. R., & Lee, Z. (2014). Effectiveness of risk-needs-responsivity-based family violence programs with male offenders. *Journal of Family Violence, 29,* 151–164.

Stewart, L. A., & Power, J. (2014). Profile and programming needs of federal offenders with histories of intimate partner violence. *Journal of Interpersonal Violence, 29,* 2723–2747.

Stirman, S. W., & Beidas, R. S. (2020). Expanding the role of psychological science through implementation science: Introduction to the special issue. *American Psychologist, 75,* 1033–1037.

Stith, S. M., Green, N. M., Smith, D. B., & Ward, D. B. (2008). Marital satisfaction and marital discord as risk markers for intimate partner violence: A meta-analytic review. *Journal of Family Violence, 23,* 149–160.

Stith, S. M., Topham, G. L., Spencer, C., Jones, B., Coburn, K., Kelly, L., & Langston, Z. (2022). Using systemic interventions to reduce intimate partner violence or child maltreatment: A systematic review of publications between 2010 and 2019. *Journal of Marital and Family Therapy, 48,* 231–250.

Stochholm, K., Bojesen, A., Jensen, A. S., Juul, S., & Gravholt, C. H. (2012). Criminality in men with Klinefelter's syndrome and XYY syndrome: A cohort study. *BMJ Open, 2*, e000650.

Stockdale, K. C., Olver, M. E., & Wong, S. C. P. (2010). The Psychopathy Checklist: Youth Version and adolescent and adult recidivism: Considerations with respect to gender, ethnicity, and age. *Psychological Assessment, 22*, 768–781.

Stoltenborgh, M., van IJzendoorn, M. H., Euser, E. M., & Bakermans-Kranenburg, M. J. (2011). A global perspective on child sexual abuse: Meta-analysis of prevalence around the world. *Child Maltreatment, 16*, 79–101.

Stompe, T., Ritter, K., & Schanda, H. (2018). Patterns of substance abuse in offenders with schizophrenia—illness-related or criminal life-style? *Frontiers in Psychiatry, 9*, 233.

Stouthamer-Loeber, M., Loeber, R., Wei, E., Farrington, D. P., & Wikström, P. H. (2002). Risk and promotive effects in the explanation of persistent serious delinquency in boys. *Journal of Consulting and Clinical Psychology, 70*, 111–123.

Strang, H., & Braithwaite, J. (2017). *Restorative justice: Philosophy to practice.* New York: Routledge.

Strang, H., Sherman, L. W., Mayo-Wilson, E., Woods, D., & Ariel, B. (2013). *Restorative justice conferencing (RJC) using face-to-face meetings of offenders and victims: Effects on offender recidivism and victim satisfaction. A systematic review.* Campbell Systematic Reviews, 12.

Straus, M. A. (1996). Identifying offenders in criminal justice research on domestic assault. In E. S. Buzawa & C. G. Buzawa (Eds.), *Do arrests and restraining orders work?* (pp. 14–29). Thousand Oaks, CA: Sage.

Stroebe, W., & Strack, F. (2014). The alleged crisis and the illusion of exact replication. *Perspectives on Psychological Science, 9*, 59–71.

Substance Abuse and Mental Health Services Administration. (2021). *Key substance use and mental health indicators in the United States: Results from the 2020 National Survey on Drug Use and Health.* (HHS Publication No. PEP21–07–01–003, NSDUH Series H-56). Rockville, MD: Center for Behavioral Health Statistics and Quality, Substance Abuse and Mental Health Services Administration.

Sullivan, D., & Tifft, L. (2005). *Restorative justice: Healing the foundations of our everyday lives*, 2nd ed.. Monsey, NY: Willow Tree Press.

Sundt, J., & Boppre, B. (2021). Did Oregon's tough mandatory sentencing law "measure 11" improve public safety? New evidence about an old debate from a multiple-design, experimental strategy. *Justice Quarterly, 38*, 1363–1384.

Sutherland, E. H. (1939). *Principles of criminology*, 3rd ed. Philadelphia, PA: Lippincott.

Sutherland, E. H. (1947). *Principles of criminology*, 4th ed. Philadelphia, PA: Lippincott.

Sutherland, E. H., & Cressey, D. R. (1970). *Principles of criminology*, 6th ed. New York, NY: Lippincott.

Swanson, J. W., Borum, R., Swartz, M. S., & Monahan, J. (1996). Psychotic symptoms and the risk of violent behaviour in the community. *Criminal Behaviour and Mental Health, 6*, 309–329.

Swearer, S. M., & Hymel, S. (2015). Understanding the psychology of bullying: Moving toward a social-ecological diathesis-stress model. *American Psychologist, 70*, 344–353.

Sweeten, G., Bushway, S. D., & Paternoster, R. (2009). Does dropping out of school mean dropping into delinquency? *Criminology, 47*, 47–91.

Swogger, M. T., & Kosson, D. S. (2007). Identifying subtypes of criminal psychopaths: A replication and extension. *Criminal Justice and Behavior, 34*, 953–970.

Suzuki, M., & Yuan, X. (2021). How does restorative justice work? A qualitative metasynthesis. *Criminal Justice and Behavior, 48*, 1347–1365.

Sykes, G. M., & Matza, D. (1957). Techniques of neutralization: A theory of delinquency. *American Sociological Review, 22*, 664–670.

Tafrate, R. C., Hogan, T., & Mitchell, D. (2019). Integrating Motivational Interviewing with Risk-Need-Responsivity-based practice in community corrections: Collaboratively focusing on what matters most. In D. L. L. Polaschek, A. Day, & C. R. Hollin (Eds.), *The Wiley international handbook of correctional psychology* (pp. 603–621). NY: John Wiley & Sons.

Tafrate, R. C., & Mitchell, D. (Eds.) (2014). *Forensic CBT: A handbook for clinical Practice.* Chichester, UK: John Wiley & Sons.

Tafrate, R. C., Mitchell, D., & Simourd, D. J. (2018). *CBT with justice-involved clients: Interventions for antisocial and self-destructive behaviors.* New York: Guilford Publications.

Taheri, S. A., & Walsh, B. C. (2016). After-school programs for delinquency prevention: A systematic review and meta-analysis. *Youth Violence and Juvenile Justice, 14,* 272–290.

Tanner-Smith, E. E., Lipsey, M. W., & Wilson, D. B. (2016). Juvenile drug court effects on recidivism and drug use: A systematic review and meta-analysis. *Journal of Experimental Criminology, 12,* 477–513.

Tanner-Smith, E. E., Wilson, S. J., & Lipsey, M. W. (2013a). The comparative effectiveness of outpatient treatment for adolescent substance abuse: A meta-analysis. *Journal of Substance Abuse Treatment, 44,* 145–158.

Tanner-Smith, E., Wilson, S. J., & Lipsey, M. W. (2013b). Risk factors and crime. In F. T. Cullen & P. Wilcox (Eds.), *The Oxford handbook of criminological theory.* New York, NY: Oxford University Press.

Tasgin, S., & Aksu, G. (2015). Examination of youth gangs and interventions in three contexts: American, European, and Turkish experiences. *Journal of Social Science Studies, 2,* 282–296.

Taxman, F. S. (2008). No illusions: Offender and organizational change in Maryland's Proactive Community Supervision efforts. *Criminology & Public Policy, 7,* 275–302.

Taxman, F. S., Pattavina, A., & Caudy, M. (2014). Justice reinvestment in the United States: An empirical assessment of the potential impact of increased correctional programming on recidivism. *Victims & Offenders, 9,* 50–75.

Taxman, F. S., & Smith, L. (2021). Risk-Need-Responsivity (RNR) classification models: Still evolving. *Aggression and Violent Behavior, 59,* 101459.

Taxman, F. S., Smith, L., & Rudes, D. S. (2020). Putting a square into a circle: The story of boot camps—A tribute to Doris MacKenzie's work. In P. K. Lattimore, B. M. Huebner, & F. S. Taxman (Eds.), *Handbook on moving corrections and sentencing forward* (pp. 216–232). Routledge.

Temcheff, C., Serbin, L., Martin-Storey, A., Stack, D., Hodgins, S., Ledingham, J., & Schwartzman, A. (2008). Continuity and pathways from aggression in childhood to family violence in adulthood: A 30-year longitudinal study. *Journal of Family Violence, 23,* 231–242.

Templer, D. I., & Rushton, J. P. (2011). IQ, skin color, crime, HIV/AIDS, and income in 50 states. *Intelligence, 39,* 437–462.

Tennenbaum, D. J. (1977). Personality and criminality: A summary and implications of the literature. *Journal of Criminal Justice, 5,* 225–235.

Theobald, D., Farrington, D. P., Coid, J. W., & Piquero, A. R. (2016). A longitudinal analysis of the criminal careers of intimate partner violence offender subtypes: Results from a prospective survey of males. *Violence and Victims, 31,* 999–1020.

Thielo, A., Cullen, F. T., Burton, A. L., Moon, M. M., & Burton, Jr., V. S. (2019). Prisons or problem solving: Does the public support specialty courts? *Victims & Offenders, 14,* 267–282.

Thomas, A., Chess, S., Birch, H. G., Hertzig, M. E., & Korn, S. (1963). *Behavioral individuality in early childhood.* New York, NY: New York University Press.

Thompson, A., & Tapp, S. N. (2022). *Criminal victimization, 2021.* Washington: Bureau of Justice Statistics.

Thompson, M. P., Saltzman, L. E., & Johnson, H. (2001). Risk factors for physical injury among women assaulted by current or former spouses. *Violence Against Women, 7,* 886–899.

Thornberry, T. P., & Jacoby, J. E. (1979). *The criminally insane: A community follow-up of mentally ill offenders.* Chicago, IL: University of Chicago Press.

Thornberry, T. P., Krohn, M. D., Lizotte, A. J., Smith, C. A., & Tobin, K. (2003). *Gangs and delinquency in developmental perspective.* Cambridge, England: Cambridge University Press.

Thornberry, T. P., Smith, C. A., Rivera, C., Huizinga, D., & Stouthamer-Loeber, M. (1999). Family disruption and delinquency. *Juvenile Justice Bulletin.* Washington, DC: Office of Juvenile Justice and Delinquency Prevention, U.S. Department of Justice.

Thornhill, R., & Palmer, C. (2000). *A natural history of rape.* Cambridge: MIT.

Thornton, L. C., Frick, P. J., Ray, J. V., Wall Meyers, T. D., Steinberg, L., & Cauffman, E. (2019). Risky sex, drugs, sensation seeking, and callous unemotional traits in justice-involved male adolescents. *Journal of Clinical Child & Adolescent Psychology, 48,* 68–79.

Tittle, C. R., & Meier, R. F. (1991). Specifying the SES/delinquency relationship by social characteristics of contexts. *Journal of Research in Crime and Delinquency, 28,* 430–455.

Tittle, C. R., Villimez, W. J., & Smith, D. A. (1978). The myth of social class and criminality: An empirical assessment of the empirical evidence. *American Sociological Review, 43,* 643–656.

Tong, J. L. S., & Farrington, D. (2006). How effective is the 'Reasoning and Rehabilitation' programme in reducing reoffending? A meta-analysis of evaluations in four countries. *Psychology, Crime and Law, 12,* 3–24.

Tonigan, J. S., Toscova, R., & Miller, W. R. (1996). Meta-analysis of the literature on Alcoholics Anonymous: Sample and study characteristics, moderate findings. *Journal of Studies on Alcohol, 57,* 65–72.

Tonry, M. (2004). *Thinking about crime: Sense and sensibility in American penal culture.* New York, NY: Oxford University Press.

Tonry, M. (2018). The President's commission and sentencing, then and now. *Criminology & Public Policy, 17,* 341–354.

Tonry, M. (2019). Fifty years of American sentencing reform: Nine lessons. In M. Tonry (Ed.), *Crime and justice: A review of research,* Vol. *48* (pp. 1–34). Chicago: University of Chicago Press.

Tonry, M. (2021). Doing justice in sentencing. In M. Tonry (Ed.), *Crime and justice: A review of research,* Vol. *50* (pp. 1–12). Chicago: University of Chicago Press.

Tostlebe, J. J., & Pyrooz, D. C. (2022). Are gang members psychopaths? In P. B. Marques, M. Paulino, & L. Alho (Eds.), *Psychopathy and criminal behavior: Current trends and challenges* (pp. 311–331). New York: Academic Press.

Trafimow, D., & Marks, M. (2015). Editorial. *Basic and Applied Social Psychology, 37,* 1–2.

Travers, Á., McDonagh, T., Cunningham, T., Armour, C., & Hansen, M. (2021). The effectiveness of interventions to prevent recidivism in perpetrators of intimate partner violence: A systematic review and meta-analysis. *Clinical Psychology Review, 84,* 101974.

Trinidad, A., Vozmediano, L., & San-Juan, C. (2018). Environmental factors in juvenile delinquency: A systematic review of the situational perspectives' literature. *Crime Psychology Review, 4,* 45–71.

Trotter, C. (1996). The impact of different supervision practices in community corrections. *Australian and New Zealand Journal of Criminology, 29,* 1–18.

Trotter, C. (2006). *Working with involuntary clients: A guide to practice,* 2nd ed. Crows Nest, Australia: Allen & Unwin.

Trotter, C. (2013). Reducing recidivism through probation supervision: What we know and don't know through four decades of research. *Federal Probation, 77,* 43–48.

Trotter, C., & Evans, P. (2012). An analysis of supervision skills in youth probation. *Australian & New Zealand Journal of Criminology, 45,* 255–273.

Trottier, D., Benbouriche, M., & Bonneville, V. (2021). A meta-analysis on the association between rape myth acceptance and sexual coercion perpetration. *The Journal of Sex Research, 58,* 375–382.

Trull, T. J., & Widiger, T. A. (2013). Dimensional models of personality: The five-factor model and the DSM-5. *Dialogues in Clinical Neuropsychiatry, 15,* 135–146.

Truth and Reconciliation Commission of Canada. (2015). *Honouring the truth, reconciling the future.* Ottawa: ON. www.trc.ca

Ttofi, M. M., Farrington, D. P., Lösel, F., & Loeber, R. (2011). The predictive efficiency of school bullying versus later offending: A systematic/meta-analytic review of longitudinal studies. *Criminal Behaviour and Mental Health, 21,* 80–89.

Ttofi, M. M., Farrington, D. P., Piquero, A. R., & DeLisi, M. (2016). Protective factors against offending and violence: Results from prospective longitudinal studies. *Journal of Criminal Justice, 45,* 1–3.

Tuvblad, C., Bezdjam, S., Raine, A., & Baker, L. A. (2014). The heritability of psychopathic personality in 14- to 15-year old twins: A multirater, multimeasure approach. *Psychological Assessment, 26*, 704–716.

Tuvblad, C., Grann, M., & Lichtenstein, P. (2006). Heritability for adolescent antisocialbox behavior differs with socioeconomic status: Gene–environment interaction. *Journal of Child Psychology and Psychiatry, 47*, 734–743.

Tyler, N., Gannon, T. A., & Olver, M. E. (2021). Does treatment for sexual offending work? *Current Psychiatry Reports, 23*, 1–8.

Uggen, C., Shannon, S., & Manza, J. (2012). *State-level estimates of felon disenfranchisement in the United States, 2010*. Washington, DC: The Sentencing Project.

Ugwudike, P. (2022). Predictive algorithms in justice systems and the limits of tech-reformism. *International Journal for Crime, Justice and Social Democracy, 11*, 85–99.

Ullmann, L., & Krasner, L. (1976). *A psychological approach to abnormal behavior*, 2nd ed. Englewood Cliffs, NJ: Prentice Hall.

Ulmer, J. T., Kramer, J. H., & Zajac, G. (2020). The race of defendants and victims in Pennsylvania death penalty decisions: 2000–2010. *Justice Quarterly, 37*, 955–983.

Umbach, R., Berryessa, C. A., & Raine, A. (2015). Brain imaging research on psychopathy: Implications for punishment, prediction, and treatment in youth and adults. *Journal of Criminal Justice, 43*, 295–306.

Underwood, R. C., Patch, P. C., Cappelletty, G. G., & Wolfe, R. W. (1999). Do sexual offenders molest when other persons are present? A preliminary investigation. *Sexual Abuse: Journal of Research and Treatment, 11*, 243–247.

University of Cincinnati. (2020). EPICS implementation: 143 agencies. Cincinnati: University of Cincinnati Corrections Institute.

U.S. Department of Justice. (2022). *Drug Courts*. Washington, DC: Office of Justice Programs. www.ojp.gov/pdffiles1/nij/238527.pdf

Vachon, D. D., Lynam, D. R., Widiger, T. A., Miller, J. D., McCrae, R. R., & Costa, P. T. (2013). Basic traits predict the prevalence of personality disorder across the life span: The example of psychopathy. *Psychological Science, 24*, 698–705.

Valdebenito, S., Eisner, M., Farrington, D. P., Ttofi, M. M., & Sutherland, A. (2019). What can we do to reduce disciplinary school exclusion: A systematic review and meta-analysis. *Journal of Experimental CriminologyMcFarlandDavis, 15*, 253–287.

Valdez, A., Kaplan, C. D., & Codina, E. (2000). Psychopathy among Mexican American gang members: A comparative study. *International Journal of Offender Therapy and Comparative Criminology, 44*, 46–58.

Van Deinse, T. B., Cuddeback, G. S., Wilson, A. B., Edwards, D., & Lambert, M. (2021). Variation in criminogenic risks by mental health symptom severity: Implications for mental health services and research. *Psychiatric Quarterly, 92*, 73–84.

Van Deinse, T. B., Givens, A., Cowell, M., Ghezzi, M., Murray-Lichtman, A., & Cuddeback, G. S. (2022). A randomized trial of specialty mental health probation: Measuring implementation and effectiveness outcomes. *Administration and Policy in Mental Health and Mental Health Services Research, 49*, 415–428.

van den Berg, J. W., Smid, W., Schepers, K., Wever, E., van Beek, D., Janssen, E., & Gijs, L. (2018). The predictive properties of dynamic sex offender risk assessment instruments: A meta-analysis. *Psychological Assessment, 30*, 179–191.

van de Rakt, M., Nieuwbeerta, P., & De Graaf, N. D. (2008). The relationships between conviction trajectories of fathers and their sons and daughters. *British Journal of Criminology, 48*, 538–556.

van der Put, C. E., Boekhout van Solinge, N. F., Stams, G. J., Hoeve, M., & Assink, M. (2021). Effects of awareness programs on juvenile delinquency: A three-level meta-analysis. *International Journal of Offender Therapy and Comparative Criminology, 65*, 68–91.

van der Put, C. E., Stams, G. J. J. M., Hoeve, M., Deković, M., Spanjaard, H. J. M., Van der Laan, P. H., & Barnoski, R. P. (2012). Changes in the relative importance of dynamic risk factors for recidivism during adolescence. *International Journal of Offender Therapy and Comparative Criminology, 56,* 296–316.

van der Stouwe, T., Gubbels, J., Castenmiller, Y. L., van der Zouwen, M., Asscher, J. J., Hoeve, M., … Stams, G. J. J. M. (2021). The effectiveness of social skills training (SST) for juvenile delinquents: A meta-analysis. *Journal of Experimental Criminology, 17,* 369–396.

van de Weijer, S., & Bijlevid, C. (2018). The transfive study: Five generations of crime? In V. I. Eichelsheim & S. G. A. van de Weijer (Eds.), *Intergenerational continuity of criminal and antisocial behaviour* (pp. 96–112). New York: Routledge.

van de Weijer, S. G. A., & Boutwell, B. B. (2022). Examining mate similarity for chronic and nonchronic criminal behavior. *Journal of Developmental and Life-Course Criminology, 8,* 298–314.

van Dijk, M., Eichelsheim, V., Kleemans, E., Souddijn, M., & van de Weijer, S. (2022). Intergenerational continuity of crime among children of organized crime offenders in the Netherlands. *Crime, Law and Social Change, 77,* 207–227.

van Dijk, M., Eichelsheim, V., Kleemans, E., Souddijn, M., & van de Weijer, S. (2022). Intergenerational continuity of crime among children of organized crime offenders in the Netherlands. *Crime, Law and Social Change, 77,* 207–227.

Van Dijk, R., van der Valk, I. E., Deković, M., & Branje, S. (2020). A meta-analysis on interparental conflict, parenting, and child adjustment in divorced families: Examining mediation using meta-analytic structural equation models. *Clinical Psychology Review, 79,* 101861.

van Hazebroek, B. C. M., Blokland, A. A. J., Wermink, H. T., Keijser, H. T., Popma, A., & van Domburgh, L. (2019). Delinquent development among early-onset offenders: Identifying and characterizing trajectories based on frequency across types of offending. *Criminal Justice and Behavior, 46,* 1542–1565.

van Hazebroek, B. C. M., Wermink, H., Domburgh, L., de Keijser, J. W., Hoeve, M., & Popma, A. (2019). Biosocial studies of antisocial behavior: A systematic review of interactions between peri/prenatal complications, psychophysiological parameters, and social risk factors. *Aggression and Violent Behavior, 47,* 169–188.

Van Horn, S. A., Morgan, R. D., Brusman-Lovins, L., Littlefield, A. K., Hunter, J. T., Gigax, G., & Ridley, K. (2019). Changing lives and changing outcomes: "What works" in an intervention for justice-involved persons with mental illness. *Psychological Services, 16,* 693–700.

Van Houten, R. (1983). Punishment: From the animal laboratory to the applied setting. In S. Axelrod & J. Apsche (Eds.), *The effects of punishment on human behavior* (pp. 13–44). New York, NY: Academic Press.

Van Voorhis, P. (2009). An overview of offender classification systems. In P. Van Voorhis, M. Braswell, & D. Lester (Eds.), *Correctional counseling and rehabilitation,* 7th ed. (pp. 133–161). New Providence, NJ: LexisNexis Matthew Bender.

Van Voorhis, P., Spiropoulos, G., Ritchie, P. N., Seabrook, R., & Spruance, L. (2013). Identifying areas of specific responsivity in cognitive-behavioral outcomes. *Criminal Justice and Behavior, 40,* 1250–1279.

Van Voorhis, P., Wright, E. M., Salisbury, E., & Bauman, A. (2010). Women's risk factors and their contribution to existing risk/needs assessment: The current status of gender-responsive supplement. *Criminal Justice and Behavior, 37,* 261–288.

van Vugt, E., Gibbs, J., Stams, G. J., Bijleveld, C., Hendriks, J., & Van der Laan, P. H. (2011). Moral development and recidivism: A meta-analysis. *International Journal of Offender Therapy and Comparative Criminology, 55,* 1243–1250.

Vasilaki, E., Hosier, S. G., & Cox, W. M. (2006). The efficacy of motivational interviewing as a brief intervention for excessive drinking: A meta-analytic review. *Alcohol & Alcoholism, 41,* 328–335.

Vasiljevic, Z., Öjehagen, A., & Andersson, C. (2020). Incremental validity of ambulatory assessment of acute dynamic risk in predicting time to recidivism among prisoners on parole. *Psychology, Crime & Law, 26,* 614–630.

Vaske, J., Galyean, K., & Cullen, F. T. (2011). Toward a biosocial theory of offender rehabilitation: Why does cognitive-behavioral therapy work? *Journal of Criminal Justice, 39,* 90–102.

Vaughan, T. J., Ward, J. T., Bouffard, J., & Piquero, A. R. (2019). The general factor of self-control and cost consideration: A critical test of the general theory of crime. *Crime & Delinquency, 65,* 731–771.

Vazsonyi, A. T., Mikuša, J., & Kelley, E. L. (2017). It's time: A meta-analysis on the self-control-deviance link. *Journal of Criminal Justice, 48,* 48–63.

Verbruggen, J., Blokland, A., Robinson, A. L., & Maxwell, C. D. (2020). The relationship between criminal behaviour over the life-course and intimate partner violence perpetration in later life. *European Journal of Criminology, 17,* 784–805.

Veysey, B., Christian, J., & Martinez, J. (Eds.) (2009). *How offenders transform their lives.* New York, NY: Routledge (Willan).

Viding, E., Jones, A. P., Frick, P. J., Moffitt, T. E., & Plomin, R. (2008). Heritability of antisocial behavior at 9: Do callous-unemotional traits matter? *Developmental Science, 11,* 17–22.

Viding, E., & McCrory, E. J. (2018). Understanding the development of psychopathy: Progress and challenges. *Psychological Medicine, 48,* 566–577.

Vieira, T. A., Skilling, T. A., & Peterson-Badali, M. (2009). Matching court-ordered services with treatment needs: Predicting treatment success with youth offenders. *Criminal Justice and Behavior, 36,* 385–401.

Vigdal, M. I., Moltu, C., Bjornestad, J., & Selseng, L. B. (2022). Social recovery in substance use disorder: A metasynthesis of qualitative studies. *Drug and Alcohol Review, 41,* 974–987.

Viglione, J. (2019). The risk-need-responsivity model: How do probation officers implement the principles of effective intervention? *Criminal Justice & Behavior, 46,* 655–673.

Viglione, J., & Blasko, B. L. (2018). The differential impacts of probation staff attitudes on use of evidence-based practices. *Psychology, Public Policy, and Law, 24,* 449–458.

Viglione, J., Rudes, D. S., & Taxman, F. S. (2015). Misalignment in supervision: Implementing risk/needs assessment instruments in probation. *Criminal Justice and Behavior, 42,* 263–285.

Viljoen, J. L., Cochrane, D. M., & Jonnson, M. R. (2018). Do risk assessment tools help manage and reduce risk of violence and reoffending? A systematic review. *Law and Human Behavior, 42,* 181–214.

Viljoen, J. L., Jonnson, M. R., Cochrane, D. M., Vargen, L. M., & Vincent, G. M. (2019). Impact of risk assessment instruments on rates of pretrial detention, postconviction placements, and release: A systematic review and meta-analysis. *Law and Human Behavior, 43,* 397–420.

Viljoen, J. L., Rudes, D. S., & Taxman, F. S. (2015). Misalignment in supervision: Implementing risk/needs assessment instruments in probation. *Criminal Justice and Behavior, 42,* 263–285.

Viljoen, J. L., Shaffer, C. S., Gray, A. L., & Douglas, K. S. (2017). Are adolescent risk assessment tools sensitive to change? A framework and examination of the SAVRY and the YLS/CMI. *Law and Human Behavior, 42,* 244–257.

Viljoen, J. L., Vargen, L. M., Cochrane, D. M., Jonson, M. R., Goosens, I., & Monjazeb, S. (2021). Do structured risk assessments predict violent, any, and sexual offending better than unstructured judgment? An umbrella review. *Psychology, Public Policy, and Law, 27,* 79–97.

Viljoen, J. L., & Vincent, G. M. (2020). Risk assessments for violence and reoffending: Implementation and impact on risk management. *Clinical Psychology: Science and Practice.* Advance online publication.

Villa-Vicencio, C. (1999). A different kind of justice: The South African Truth and Reconciliation Commission. *Contemporary Justice Review, 1,* 407–428.

Vincent, G. M., & Viljoen, J. L. (2020). Racist algorithms or systemic problems? Risk assessments and racial disparities. *Criminal Justice and Behavior, 47,* 1576–1584.

Vitaro, F., Brendgen, M., & Arsenault, L. (2009). The discordant MZ-twin method: One step closer to the holy grail of causality. *International Journal of Behavioral Development, 33,* 376–382.

Volkert, J., Gablonski, T.-C., & Rabung, S. (2018). Prevalence of personality disorders in the general adult population in Western countries: Systematic review and meta-analysis. *British Journal of Psychiatry, 213,* 709–715.

Von Hirsch, A. (1976). *Doing justice: The choice of punishments.* New York, NY: Hill and Wang.

Vose, B., Smith, P., & Cullen, F. T. (2013). Predictive validity and the impact of change in total LSI-R score on recidivism. *Criminal Justice and Behavior, 40,* 1383–1396.

Voultsos, P. (2020). Offering surgical castration to detainee sex-offenders: The "unkindest cut". *Aristotle Biomedical Journal, 2,* 11–39.

Vreeland, A., Ebert, J. S., Kuhn, T. M., Gracey, K. A., Shaffer, A. M., Watson, K. H., … Compas, B. E. (2020). Predictors of placement disruptions in foster care. *Child Abuse and Neglect, 99,* 104283.

Vrieze, S. I., & Grove, W. M. (2009). Survey of the use of clinical and mechanical prediction methods in clinical psychology. *Professional Psychology: Research and Practice, 40,* 525–531.

Vu, N. L., Jouriles, E. N., McDonald, R., & Rosenfield, D. (2016). Children's exposure to intimate partner violence: A meta-analysis of longitudinal associations with child adjustment problems. *Clinical Psychology Review, 46,* 25–33.

Vukasović, T., & Bratko, D. (2015). Heritability of personality: A meta-analysis of behavior genetic studies. *Psychological Bulletin, 141,* 769–785.

Waldo, G. P., & Dinitz, S. (1967). Personality attributes of the criminal: An analysis of research studies, 1950–1965. *Journal of Research in Crime and Delinquency, 4,* 185–202.

Wallace, D. S., Paulson, R. M., Lord, C. G., & Bond, C. F. Jr. (2005). Which behaviors do attitudes predict? Meta-analyzing the effects of social pressure and perceived difficulty. *Review of General Psychology, 9,* 214–227.

Walsh, A. (2019). *Reinforcement sensitivity theory: A metatheory for biosocial criminology.* New York: Routledge.

Walsh, A., & Jorgensen, C. (2018). Evolutionary theory and criminology. In R. L. Hopcroft (Ed.), *The Oxford handbook of evolution, biology, and society* (pp. 517–542). New York: Oxford University Press.

Walsh, A., & Yun, I. (2014). Epigenetics and allostasis: Implications for criminology. *Criminal Justice Review, 39,* 411–431.

Walters, G. D. (1992). A meta-analysis of the gene-crime relationship. *Criminology, 30,* 595–613.

Walters, G. D. (1996). The Psychological Inventory of Criminal Thinking Styles: Part III. Predictive validity. *International Journal of Offender Therapy and Comparative Criminology, 40,* 105–112.

Walters, G. D. (2011a). Childhood temperament: Dimensions or types. *Personality and Individual Differences, 50,* 1166–1173.

Walters, G. D. (2011b). Criminal thinking as a mediator of the mental illness-prison violence relationship: A path analytic study and causal mediation analysis. *Psychological Services, 8,* 189–199.

Walters, G. D. (2012). Criminal thinking and recidivism: Meta-analytic evidence on the prevalence and incremental validity of the Psychological Inventory of Criminal Thinking Styles (PICTS). *Aggression and Violent Behavior, 17,* 272–278.

Walters, G. D. (2014a). Pathways to early delinquency: Exploring the individual and collective contributions of difficult temperament, low maternal involvement, and externalizing behavior. *Journal of Criminal Justice, 62,* 321–326.

Walters, G. D. (2014b). Crime and substance misuse in adjudicated delinquent youth: The worst of both worlds. *Law and Human Behavior, 38,* 139–150.

Walters, G. D. (2015a). Recidivism and the "worst of both worlds" hypothesis: Do substance misuse and crime interact or accumulate? *Criminal Justice and Behavior, 42,* 435–451.

Walters, G. D. (2015b). Criminal and substance involvement from adolescence to adulthood: Precursors, mediators, and long-term effects. *Justice Quarterly, 32,* 729–747.

Walters, G. D. (2016a). Predicting recidivism with the Criminal Sentiments Scale: A meta-analysis of a putative measure of criminal thought content. *Criminal Justice and Behavior, 43,* 1159–1172.

Walters, G. D. (2016b). Neighborhood context, youthful offending, and peer selection: Does it take a village to raise a nondelinquent? *Criminal Justice Review, 41,* 5–20.

Walters, G. D. (2016c). The parent-peer interface: Does inductive parenting reduce the criminogenic effect of delinquent peers? *Youth Violence and Juvenile Justice, 14,* 411–425.

Walters, G. D. (2016d). Age of crime/substance onset and crime/drug versatility as dimensions of the "worst of both worlds" effect. *Criminal Justice Policy Review, 27,* 668–683.

Walters, G. D. (2016e). Breaking the cycle demonstration project: Using a quasi-experimental analysis to test the "worst of both worlds" hypothesis and risk principle. *Journal of Experimental Criminology, 12,* 127–141.

Walters, G. D. (2017). The drug-crime connection in adolescent and adult respondents: Interaction versus addition. *Journal of Drug Issues, 47,* 205–216.

Walters, G. D. (2018a). Mediating the relationship between parental control/support and offspring delinquency: Self-efficacy for a conventional lifestyle versus self-efficacy for deviance. *Crime & Delinquency, 64,* 606–624.

Walters, G. D. (2018b). Unsupervised routine activities as a mediator of the parental knowledge–delinquency relationship. *Justice Quarterly, 35,* 871–894.

Walters, G. D. (2018c). Structured community activities and moral engagement as deterrents to youth violence: A mediation analysis. *American Journal of Criminal Justice, 43,* 294–312.

Walters, G. D. (2018d). Change in the perceived certainty of punishment as an inhibitor of post-juvenile offending in serious delinquents: Deterrence at the adult transition. *Crime & Delinquency, 64,* 1306–1325.

Walters, G. D. (2019). Gang influence: Mediating the gang-delinquency relationship with proactive criminal thinking. *Criminal Justice and Behavior, 46,* 1044–1062.

Walters, G. D. (2020a). Positive parents and negative peers: Assessing the nature and order of caregiver and friend effects in practicing early delinquency. *Youth Violence and Juvenile Justice, 18,* 96–114.

Walters, G. D. (2020b). Unraveling the bidirectional relationship between bullying victimization and perpetration: A test of mechanisms from opportunity and general strain theories. *Youth Violence and Juvenile Justice, 18,* 395–411.

Walters, G. D. (2020c). Criminal thinking as a moderator of the perceived certainty–offending relationship: Age variations. *Psychology, Crime & Law, 26,* 267–286.

Walters, G. D. (2021). School-age bullying victimization and perpetration: A meta-analysis of prospective studies and research. *Trauma, Violence & Abuse, 22,* 1129–1139.

Walters, G. D. (2022). Crime and social cognition: A meta-analytic review of the developmental roots of adult criminal thinking. *Journal of Experimental Criminology, 18,* 183–207.

Walters, G. D., & Cohen, T. H. (2016). Criminal thought process as a dynamic risk factor variable: Variable- and person-oriented approaches to recidivism prediction. *Law and Human Behavior, 40,* 411–419.

Walters, G. D., & Espelage, D. L. (2018a). From victim to victimizer: Hostility, anger, and depression as mediators of the bullying victimization-bullying perpetration association. *Journal of School Psychology, 68,* 73–83.

Walters, G. D., & Espelage, D. L. (2018b). Resurrecting the empathy-bullying relationship with a pro-bullying attitudes mediator: The Lazarus effect in mediation research. *Journal of Abnormal Child Psychology, 46,* 1229–1239.

Walters, G. D., & Espelage, D. L. (2019). Bullying perpetration and subsequent delinquency: A regression-based analysis of early adolescent schoolchildren. *Journal of Early Adolescence, 39,* 669–688.

Walters, G. D., & Espelage, D. L. (2020). Assessing the relationship between cyber and traditional forms of bullying and sexual harassment: Stepping stones or displacement. *Journal of Psychosocial Research on Cyberspace, 14,* Article 2.

Walters, G. D., & Magaletta, P. R. (2015). Comorbid antisocial and substance misuse proclivity and mental health service utilization by female inmates: Testing the worst of both worlds hypothesis with the PAI. *Psychological Services, 12,* 28–36.

Walters, G. D., Wilson, N. J., & Glover, A. J. J. (2011). Predicting recidivism with the Psychopathy Checklist: Are factor score composites really necessary? *Psychological Assessment, 23,* 552–557.

Walton, J. S. (2021). Fit in your genes: An introduction to genes and epigenetics for forensic practitioners. *The Journal of Forensic Practice, 23,* 189–200.

Wampold, B. E. (2015). How important are the common factors in psychotherapy? An update. *World Psychiatry, 14,* 270–277.

Wan, W.-Y., Moffatt, S., Jones, C., & Weatherburn, D. (2012). *The effect of arrest and imprisonment on crime. Crime and Justice Bulletin*, No. 158. Sydney, Australia: New South Wales Bureau of Crime Statistics and Research.

Wanamaker, K. A., & Brown, S. L. (2021). The relationship between patterns of change in dynamic risk and strength scores and reoffending for men on community supervision. *Criminal Justice and Behavior, 48*, 1208–1228.

Wanamaker, K. A., & Brown, S. L. (2022). Assessing dynamic risk and dynamic strength change patterns and the relationship to reoffending among women on community supervision. *Criminal Justice and Behavior, 49*, 37–57.

Wanamaker, K. A., Brown, S. L., & Czerwinsky, A. M. (2022). Abuse, neglect and witnessing violence during childhood within justice-involved samples: A meta-analysis of the prevalence and nature of gender differences and similarities. *Journal of Criminal Justice, 82*, 101990.

Ward, T. (2000). Sexual offenders' cognitive distortions as implicit theories. *Aggression and Violent Behavior, 5*, 491–507.

Ward, T., Mann, R. E., & Gannon, T. A. (2007). The good lives model of offender rehabilitation: Clinical implications. *Aggression and Violent Behavior, 12*, 87–107.

Ward, T., & Stewart, C. (2003). Criminogenic needs and human needs: A theoretical model. *Psychology, Crime, and Law, 9*, 125–143.

Ward, T., Yates, P., & Willis, G. M. (2012). The good lives model and the risk-need-responsivity model: A critical response to Andrews, Bonta, and Wormith (2011). *Criminal Justice and Behavior, 39*, 94–110.

Warr, M. (1998). Life-course transitions and desistance from crime. *Criminology, 36*, 183–216.

Washington State Institute for Public Policy. (2019). *Outpatient or non-intensive drug treatment in the community*. Available at: www.wsipp.wa.gov/BenefitCost/Program/194

Wasserman, D., & Wachbroit, R. (Eds.) (2001). *Genetics and criminal behavior*. New York, NY: Cambridge University Press.

Wasserstein, R. L., Schirm, A. L., & Lazar, N. A. (2019). Moving to a world beyond "p < 0.05". *The American Statistician, 73*, S1, 1–19.

Wattanaporn, K. A., & Holtfreter, K. (2014). The impact of feminist pathway research on gender-responsive policy and practice. *Feminist Criminology, 9*, 191–207.

Weatherburn, D., & Macadam, M. (2013). A review of restorative justice responses to offending. *Evidence Base, 1*, 1–20.

Weaver, R. D., & Campbell, D. (2015). Fresh start: A meta-analysis of aftercare programs for juvenile offenders. *Research on Social Work Practice, 25*, 201–212.

Webster, C. D., Douglas, K. S., Eaves, D., & Hart, S. D. (1997). *The HCR-20: Assessing risk for violence (Version 2)*. Burnaby, Canada: Simon Fraser University.

Weisberg, R. (2019). The wild west of sentencing reform: Lessons from California. In M. Tonry (Ed.), *Crime and justice: A review of research*, Vol. *48* (pp. 35–77). Chicago: University of Chicago Press.

Weisburd, D. (2010). Justifying the use of non-experimental methods and disqualifying the use of randomized controlled trials: Challenging folklore in evaluation research in crime and justice. *Journal of Experimental Criminology, 6*, 209–227.

Wells, J., & Walsh, A. (2019). Biosocial theories in criminology. *Oxford research encyclopedia of criminology and criminal justice*. NY: Oxford University Press.

Werb, D., Kamarulzaman, A., Meacham, M. C., Rafful, C., Fisher, B., Strathdee, S. A., & Wood, E. (2016). The effectiveness of compulsory drug treatment: A systematic review. *International Journal of Drug Policy, 28*, 1–9.

Werner, K. B., Few, L., & Buchotz, K. K. (2015). Epidemiology, comorbidity, and behavioral genetics of antisocial personality disorder and psychopathy. *Psychiatric Annals, 45*, 195–199.

Wessel, M. (2015). Castration of male sex offenders in the Nordic welfare state in the context of homosexuality and heteronormativity, 1930–1955. *Scandinavian Journal of History, 40*, 591–609.

West, D. J., & Farrington, D. P. (1977). *Who becomes delinquent?* London, England: Heinemann Educational Books.

Whitaker, D. J., Le, B., Hanson, R. K., Baker, C., Ryan, G., McMahon, P., ... Rice, D. D. (2008). Risk factors for the perpetration of child sexual abuse: A review and meta-analysis. *Child Abuse & Neglect, 32*, 529–548.

Whiteside, M. F., & Becker, B. J. (2000). Parental factors and the young child's postdivorce adjustment: A meta-analysis with implications for parenting arrangements. *Journal of Family Psychology, 14*, 5–26.

Wickramasekera, N., Wright, J., Elsey, H., Murray, J., & Tubef, S. (2015). Cost of crime: A systematic review. *Journal of Criminal Justice, 43*, 218–228.

Widiger, T. A., & Costa Jr., P. T. (Eds.) (2013). *Personality disorders and the five-factor model of personality* (pp. 103–117). Washington, DC: American Psychiatric Association.

Widom, C. S. (1977). A methodology for studying non-institutional psychopaths. *Journal of Consulting and Clinical Psychology, 45*, 674–683.

Widom, C. S., & Newman, J. P. (1985). Characteristics of non-institutional psychopaths. In D. P. Farrington & J. Gunn (Eds.), *Aggression and dangerousness* (pp. 57–80). New York, NY: Wiley.

Wildeman, C. (2020). The intergenerational transmission of criminal justice contact. *Annual Review of Criminology, 3*, 217–244.

Williams, I. L., & Mee-Lee, D. (2019). Inside the black box of traditional treatment programs: Clearing the air on the original literary teachings of Alcoholics Anonymous (AA). *Addiction Research & Theory, 27*, 412–419.

Williams, K. M., Wormith, J. S., Bonta, J., & Sitarenios, G. (2017). The use of meta-analysis to compare and select offender risk instruments: A commentary on Singh, Grann, and Fazel (2011). *International Journal of Forensic Mental Health, 16*, 1–15.

Willis, G. W. (2018a). Why call someone by what we don't want them to be? The ethics of labeling in forensic/correctional psychology. *Psychology, Crime & Law, 24*(7), 727–743.

Willis, G. M. (2018b). Promoting accurate and respectful language to describe individuals and groups. *Sexual Abuse, 30*(5), 480–483.

Wilson, D. B., MacKenzie, D. L., & Mitchell, F. N. (2005). Effects of correctional boot camps on offending. *Campbell Systematic Reviews, 1*, 1–45.

Wilson, D. B., Olaghere, A., & Kimbrell, C. S. (2018). *Effectiveness of restorative justice principles in juvenile justice: A meta-analysis.* Inter-university Consortium for Political and Social Research. Washington: U.S. Department of Office of Justice Programs.

Wilson, D. B., Olaghere, A., & Kimbrell, C. S. (2019). Implementing juvenile drug treatment courts: A meta-aggregation of process evaluations. *Journal of Research in Crime and Delinquency, 56*, 605–645.

Wilson, H. A., & Gutierrez, L. (2014). Does one size fit all? A meta-analysis examining the predictive ability of the Level of Service Inventory (LSI) with Aboriginal offenders. *Criminal Justice and Behavior, 41*, 196–216.

Wilson, H. A., & Hoge, R. D. (2014). The effect of youth diversion programs on recidivism: A meta-analytic review. *Criminal Justice and Behavior, 40*, 497–518.

Wilson, J. A., & Davis, R. C. (2006). Good intentions meet hard realities: An evaluation of the Project Greenlight Reentry Program. *Criminology & Public Policy, 5*, 303–338.

Wilson, R. J., Cortoni, F., & McWhinnie, A. J. (2009). Circles of support & accountability: A Canadian national replication of outcome findings. *Sexual Abuse, 21*, 412–430.

Wilson, S. J., & Lipsey, M. W. (2007). School-based interventions for aggressive and disruptive behavior. *American Journal of Preventative Medicine, 33*, S130–S143.

Winston, A. S. (2020). Scientific racism in North American psychology. *Oxford Research Encyclopedias, Psychology*. Published online May 29, 1–25.

Witkin, H. A., Mednick, S. A., Schulsinger, F., Bakkestrom, E., Christiansen, K. O., Goodenough, D. R., ... Stocking, M. (1976). Criminality in XYY and XXY men: The elevated crime rate of XYY males is not related to aggression. It may be related to low intelligence. *Science, 193*, 547–555.

Witt, K., van Dorn, R., & Fazel, S. (2013). Risk factors for violence in psychosis: Systematic review and meta-regression analysis of 110 studies. *Plos One, 8*(2), e55942.

Wojcik, M. L., & Fisher, B. S. (2019). Overview of adult sexual offender typologies. In W. O'Donohue & P. Schewe, P. (Eds.), *Handbook of sexual assault and sexual assault prevention* (pp. 241–256). Cham: Springer.

Wolff, K. T., Baglivio, M. T., Piquero, A. R., Vaughn, M. G., & DeLisi, M. (2016). The Triple Crown of antisocial behavior: Effortful control, negative emotionality, and community disadvantage. *Youth Violence and Juvenile Justice, 14*, 350–366.

Wong, J. S., & Gravel, J. (2018). Do sex offenders have higher levels of testosterone? Results from a meta-analysis. *Sexual Abuse, 30*, 147–168.

Wong, J. S., Gravel, J., Bouchard, M., Descormiers, K., & Morselli, C. (2016). Promises kept? A meta-analysis of gang membership prevention programs. *Journal of Criminological Research, Policy and Practice, 2*, 134–167.

Wood, J. L. (2014). Understanding gang membership: The significance of group processes. *Group Processes and Intergroup Relations, 17*, 704–709.

Wood, P. R., Gove, W. R., Wilson, J. A., & Cochran, J. K. (1997). Nonsocial reinforcement and habitual criminal conduct: An extension of learning theory. *Criminology, 35*, 335–366.

Wooditch, A., Tang, L. L., & Taxman, F. S. (2014). Which criminogenic need changes are most important in promoting desistance from crime and substance use? *Criminal Justice and Behavior, 41*, 276–299.

Woodward, L. J., Fergusson, D. M., & Horwood, L. J. (2002). Deviant partner involvement and offending risk in early adulthood. *Journal of Child Psychology and Psychiatry, 43*, 177–190.

Wormith, J. S. (1984). Attitude and behavior change of correctional clientele: A three year follow-up. *Criminology, 22*, 595–618.

Wormith, J. S. (2019). Offender risk assessment: Use of the professional override. In R. D. Morgan (Ed.), *The SAGE encyclopedia of criminal psychology* (pp. 977–979). Thousand Oaks, CA: Sage.

Wormith, J. S., & Bonta, J. (2018). The Level of Service (LS) instruments. In J. P. Singh, D. G. Kroner, J. S. Wormith, S. L. Desmarais, & Z. Hamilton (Eds.), *Recidivism risk assessment: A handbook for practitioners* (pp. 117–145). New York: Wiley and Sons.

Wormith, S. J., & Bonta, J. (2021). Risk/Need assessment for adults and older adolescents: The Level of Service (LS) instruments. In R. K. Otto & K. Douglas (Eds.), *Handbook of violence risk assessment tools* 2nd ed. (pp. 159–190). New York, NY: Routledge.

Wormith, J. S., Gendreau, P., & Bonta, J. (2012). Deferring to clarity, parsimony, and evidence in reply to Ward, Yates, and Willis. *Criminal Justice and Behavior, 39*, 111–120.

Wormith, J. S., Hogg, S. M., & Guzzo, L. (2015). The predictive validity of the LS/CMI with Aboriginal offenders in Canada. *Criminal Justice and Behavior, 42*, 481–508.

Wormith, J. S., & Truswell, K. E. (2022). Strengths in the Risk-Need-Responsivity model of offender assessment and rehabilitation. In C. M. Langton & J. R. Worling (Eds.), *Facilitating desistance from aggression and crime: Theory, research, and strength-based practice* (pp. 136–164). New York: John Wiley & Sons.

Wormith, J. S., & Zidenberg, A. M. (2018). The historical roots, current status, and future applications of the Risk-Need-Responsivity model (RNR). In E. L. Jeglic & C. Calkins (Eds.), *New frontiers in offender treatment* (pp. 11–41). Springer Nature Switzerland AG.

Wright, B. R. E., Caspi, A., Moffitt, T. E., & Silva, P. A. (2001). The effects of social ties on crime vary by criminal propensity: A life-course model of interdependence. *Criminology, 39*, 321–352.

Wright, E. M., Van Voorhis, P., Salisbury, E. J., & Bauman, A. (2012). Gender-responsive lessons learned and policy implications for women in prison. *Criminal Justice and Behavior, 39*, 1612–1632.

Wright, J. P., & Cullen, F. T. (2004). Employment, peers, and life-course transitions. *Justice Quarterly, 21*, 183–205.

Wright, J. P., & Cullen, F. T. (2012). The future of biosocial criminology: Beyond scholars' professional ideology. *Journal of Contemporary Criminal Justice, 28*, 237–253.

Wright, J. P., Cullen, F. T., & Williams, N. (1997). Working while in school and delinquent involvement: Implications for social policy. *Crime & Delinquency, 43*, 203–221.

Wright, J. P., Cullen, F. T., & Williams, N. (2002). The embeddedness of adolescent employment and participation in delinquency: A life course perspective. *Western Criminology Review, 4*, 1–19.

Wright, J. P., Tibbets, S. G., & Daigle, L. E. (2014). *Criminals in the making: Criminality across the life course,* 2nd ed. Thousand Oaks, CA: Sage.

Wright, R. A., & Miller, M. J. (1998). Taboo until today? The coverage of biological arguments in criminology textbooks, 1961 to 1970 and 1987 to 1996. *Journal of Criminal Justice, 26*, 1–19.

Yakeley, J. (2022). Treatment for perpetrators of intimate partner violence: What is the evidence? *Journal of Clinical Psychology, 78*, 5–14.

Yang, B., & Lester, D. (2008). The deterrent effect of executions: A meta-analysis thirty years after Ehrlich. *Journal of Criminal Justice, 36*, 453–460.

Yang, M., Wong, S. C. P., & Coid, J. (2010). The efficacy of violence prediction: A meta-analytic comparison of nine risk assessment tools. *Psychological Bulletin, 136*, 740–767.

Yang, Y., & Raine, A. (2009). Prefrontal structural and functional brain imaging findings in antisocial, violent, and psychopathic individuals: A meta-analysis. *Psychiatry Research: Neuroimaging, 174*, 81–88.

Yazgan, I., Hanson, J. L., Bates, J. E., Lansford, J. E., Pettit, G. S., & Dodge, K. A. (2021). Cumulative early childhood adversity and later antisocial behavior: The mediating role of passive avoidance. *Development and Psychopathology, 33*, 340–350.

Yesberg, J. A., Scanlan, J. M., Hanby, L. J., Serin, R. C., & Polaschek, D. L. L. (2015). Predicting women's recidivism: Validating a dynamic community-based "gender neutral" tool. *Probation Journal, 62*, 33–48.

Yessine, A. K., & Bonta, J. (2008). *Pathways to serious offending. (User Report 2008–01).* Ottawa, Canada: Public Safety Canada.

Yessine, A. K., & Bonta, J. (2009). The offending trajectories of youthful Aboriginal offenders. *Canadian Journal of Criminology and Criminal Justice, 51*, 435–472.

Yip, V. C.-Y., Gudjonsson, G. H., Perkins, D., Doidge, A., Hopkin, G., & Young, S. (2013). A non-randomized controlled trial of the R&R2MHP cognitive skills program in high risk male offenders with severe mental illness. *BMC Psychiatry, 13*–267.

Yoon, I. A., Slade, K., & Fazel, S. (2017). Outcomes of psychological therapies for prisoners with mental health problems: A systematic review and meta-analysis. *Journal of Consulting and Clinical Psychology, 85*, 783–802.

Young, S. J., & Ross, R. R. (2007). *R&R2 for youths and adults with mental health problems: A prosocial competence training program.* Ottawa, Canada: Cognitive Centre of Canada.

Yukhnenko, D., Blackwood, N., & Fazel, S. (2019). Risk factors for recidivism in individuals receiving community sentences: A systematic review and meta-analysis. *CNS Spectrum, 25*, 252–263.

Zane, S. N., Welsh, B. C., & Mears, D. P. (2016). Juvenile transfer and the specific deterrence hypothesis: Systematic review and meta-analysis. *Criminology & Public Policy, 15*, 901–925.

Zane, S. N., Welsh, B. C., & Zimmerman, G. M. (2019). Criminal offending and mortality over the full life-course: A 70-year follow-up of the Cambridge-Sommerville youth study. *Journal of Quantitative Criminology, 35*, 691–713.

Zang, J., & Liu, N. (2015). Reliability and validity of the Chinese version of the LSI-R with probationers. *International Journal of Offender Therapy and Comparative Criminology, 59*, 1474–1486.

Zara, G., & Farrington, D. P. (2016). *Criminal recidivism: Explanation, prediction, and prevention.* New York, NY: Routledge.

Zarling, A., & Russell, D. (2022). A randomized clinical trial of acceptance and commitment therapy and the Duluth Model classes for men court-mandated to a domestic violence program. *Journal of Consulting and Clinical Psychology, 90*, 326–338.

Zeccola, J., Kelty, S. F., & Boer, D. (2021). Does the good lives model work? A systematic review of the recidivism evidence. *The Journal of Forensic Practice, 23*, 285–300.

Zedlewski, E. W. (1987). *Making confinement decisions. Research in Brief.* Washington, DC: National Institute of Justice.

Zehr, H., & Mika, H. (2017). Fundamental concepts of restorative justice. In H. Strang & J. Braithwaite (Eds.), *Restorative justice* (pp. 73–81). New York: Routledge.

Zelcer, A. M. (2014). Battling domestic violence: Replacing mandatory arrest laws with a trifecta of preferential arrest, officer education, and batterer treatment programs. *American Criminal Law Review, 51*, 5410–5561.

Zell, E., Krizan, Z., & Teeter, S. R. (2015). Evaluating gender similarities and differences using meta-synthesis. *American Psychologist, 70*, 10–20.

Zettler, H. R. (2021). Much to do about trauma: A systematic review of existing trauma-informed treatments on youth violence and recidivism. *Youth Violence and Juvenile Justice, 19*, 113–134.

Zhang, S. X., Roberts, R. E. L., & Farabee, D. (2014). An analysis of prisoner reentry and parole risk using COMPAS and traditional criminal history measures. *Crime & Delinquency, 60*, 167–192.

Zimring, F. E., & Hawkins, G. (1988). The new mathematics of imprisonment. *Crime & Delinquency, 34*, 425–436.

INDEX OF SELECTED ACRONYMS

PICTS	Psychological Inventory of Criminal Thinking Styles
R&R	Reasoning and Rehabilitation
R&R2M	Reasoning & Rehabilitation for Mentally Disordered Offenders
RNR	Risk-Need-Responsivity
ROC	Receiver Operating Characteristic
RP	relapse prevention
RRASOR	Rapid Risk Assessment for Sexual Offence Recidivism
SARA	Spousal Assault Risk Assessment
SAVRY	Structured Assessment of Violence Risk in Youth
SCJ	structured clinical judgment
SES	socioeconomic status
SFS	Salient Factor Score
SIR	Statistical Information on Recidivism
SMHP	specialty mental health probation
STARR	Staff Training Aimed at Reducing Re-arrest
STICS	Strategic Training Initiative in Community Supervision
TC	therapeutic communities
TCO	threat/control-override
VORP	Victim–Offender Reconciliation Program
VRAG	Violence Risk Appraisal Guide
YLS/CMI	Youth Level of Service/Case Management Inventory

SUBJECT INDEX

Note: Figures are shown in *italics* and tables in **bold type**. To save space, the acronyms "ACE" (Adverse Childhood Experiences), "GPCSL" (General Personality and Cognitive Social Learning), "LSI-R" (Level of Service Inventory-Revised), "MDO" (mentally disordered offender), "PCC" (psychology of criminal conduct) and "RNR" (Risk-Need-Responsivity) are used throughout the subject index in place of the full terms.

NAME INDEX